CANADA

FODOR'S TRAVEL GUIDES

are compiled, researched, and edited by an international team of travel writers, field correspondents, and editors. The series, which now almost covers the globe, was founded by Eugene Fodor in 1936.

OFFICES
New York & London

FODOR'S CANADA:
Area Editors: John Learney, Susan Learney, Roger Newman, Valerie Ross, Ralph Surette, Colleen Thompson, Kenneth Winchester, David Wishart
Contributing Editors: Nicholas Acocella, Roy Bongartz, Stephen Collier, Paul DiBlasi, Alan Freeman, Jack Herrmann, Barbara Lewis, Catherine Rodd, Bobbi St. Claire
Editor: Lisa A. Checchi
Editorial Associate: Mary Beth Brewer
Drawings: Brian Deines, Claude Detillieux
Cartography: Dyno Lowenstein
               BURMAR

FODOR'S®
CANADA
1985

HODDER AND STOUGHTON
LONDON SYDNEY AUCKLAND

All the following Guides are current (most of them also in
the Hodder and Stoughton British edition).

FODOR'S COUNTRY AND AREA TITLES:

AUSTRALIA, NEW
  ZEALAND AND
  SOUTH PACIFIC
AUSTRIA
BELGIUM AND
  LUXEMBOURG
BERMUDA
BRAZIL
CANADA
CANADA'S MARITIME
  PROVINCES
CARIBBEAN AND
  BAHAMAS
CENTRAL AMERICA
EASTERN EUROPE
EGYPT
EUROPE
FRANCE
GERMANY
GREAT BRITAIN
GREECE
HOLLAND
INDIA, NEPAL, AND
  SRI LANKA
IRELAND
ISRAEL
ITALY
JAPAN
JORDAN AND HOLY
  LAND
KOREA
MEXICO
NORTH AFRICA
PEOPLE'S REPUBLIC
  OF CHINA
PORTUGAL
SCANDINAVIA
SCOTLAND

SOUTH AMERICA
SOUTHEAST ASIA
SOVIET UNION
SPAIN
SWITZERLAND
TURKEY
YUGOSLAVIA

CITY GUIDES:

AMSTERDAM
BEIJING,
  GUANGZHOU,
  SHANGHAI
BOSTON
CHICAGO
DALLAS AND FORT
  WORTH
GREATER MIAMI
HONG KONG
HOUSTON
LISBON
LONDON
LOS ANGELES
MADRID
MEXICO CITY AND
  ACAPULCO
MUNICH
NEW ORLEANS
NEW YORK CITY
PARIS
ROME
SAN DIEGO
SAN FRANCISCO
STOCKHOLM,
  COPENHAGEN,
  OSLO, HELSINKI,
  AND REYKJAVIK
TOKYO
TORONTO
VIENNA
WASHINGTON, D.C.

FODOR'S BUDGET SERIES:

BUDGET BRITAIN
BUDGET CANADA
BUDGET CARIBBEAN
BUDGET EUROPE
BUDGET FRANCE
BUDGET GERMANY
BUDGET HAWAII
BUDGET ITALY
BUDGET JAPAN
BUDGET LONDON
BUDGET MEXICO
BUDGET
  SCANDINAVIA
BUDGET SPAIN
BUDGET TRAVEL IN
  AMERICA

USA GUIDES:

ALASKA
CALIFORNIA
CAPE COD
COLORADO
FAR WEST
FLORIDA
HAWAII
NEW ENGLAND
PACIFIC NORTH COAST
PENNSYLVANIA
SOUTH
TEXAS
USA (in one volume)

GOOD TIME TRAVEL GUIDES:

ACAPULCO
MONTREAL
OAHU
SAN FRANCISCO

CONTENTS

WESTERN CANADA

NORTHERN CANADA

SUPPLEMENTS

FOREWORD

Canada offers a vast vacationland ranging from the elegant sophistication of big city life to the physical challenge of wilderness exploration—and all shades of possibilities in between.

Canadians are proud of their country and the editors of and contributors to *Fodor's Canada* reflect that pride. We have tried to provide a backdrop to the Canadian scene by describing the people of Canada, their government, land, and culture. Then, in an attempt to sort out some of the myriad choices Canada offers its visitors, we explore the country province by province. Each province has a fascinating story of its own, and we take you on a tour of some of each area's most interesting places. We have concentrated on giving you the broadest range of things to see and do in each province, and selections that we believe are safe, solid, and of good value to you. In addition, we have tried to offer a range of choices, so that you can decide what best suits your taste and pocketbook.

Chapters on Canada's Northwest Territories and the Yukon cover major points of interest but the accent here is on the wilderness, for the more adventurous.

The selections and comments in *Fodor's Canada* are based on the editors' and contributors' personal experiences. We feel that our first responsibility is to inform and protect you, the reader. Errors are bound to creep into any travel guide, however. We go to press in mid-summer and much change can and will occur in Canada even while we are on press and during the succeeding twelve months or so that this edition is on sale. We cannot, therefore, be responsible for the sudden closing of a restaurant, a change in museum's days or hours, a shift of chefs (for the worse), price changes, and so forth. We are always grateful to readers who write to us with their experiences and suggestions for improving our guides. It is impossible to be totally accurate with information given the speed at which the modern world changes, especially in the field of travel. Your letters will help us get nearer to complete accuracy. Please write:

In the U.S.: **Fodor's Travel Guides,** 2 Park Avenue, New York, New York 10016.

In Europe: **Fodor's Travel Guides,** 9-10 Market Place, London W1N 7AG, England.

FACTS AT YOUR FINGERTIPS

 PLANNING YOUR TRIP. Once you have decided to take a trip, it's time to get down to the details of making hotel and airline reservations and other arrangements. Consider using a travel agent to help you with trip planning and arrangements. (See travel agents section in this chapter.)

"Package tours" can be great money-savers, since they usually cover a variety of sightseeing stops, recommend selected restaurants, include tour guides, and offer the opportunity to meet other people in the group—for an all-inclusive rate. Tours of the fly/drive variety also are quite popular, since they offer a "do-it-yourself" opportunity.

If you plan to travel by car and you don't belong to an auto club, now is the time to join one. They can be very helpful about routings and providing emergency service on the road. If you plan the route yourself, make certain the map you purchase or get from your local service station is dated for the current year. The provincial tourist offices can be helpful here. Local chambers of commerce are also good sources of information.

Plan to board your pets, discontinue newspaper and milk deliveries, and tell your local police and fire departments when you'll be leaving and when you expect to return. Ask a kindly neighbor to keep an eye on your house or apartment, and take in your mail, or have it held temporarily at the post office. Consider having your telephone temporarily disconnected if you plan to be away more than a few weeks. Look into the purchase of trip insurance (including baggage), and make certain your auto, fire, and other policies are up-to-date. Convert the greater portion of your trip money into traveler's checks. Arrange to have your lawn mowed at the usual times, and leave your itinerary (insofar as possible) with that kindly neighbor or with a relative. Also leave your car licence number and a key to your home.

 WHAT WILL IT COST? Canada is one of the more expensive countries in the world for travelers, although the recent proliferation of budget accommodations such as hostels and campgrounds has made it possible to travel on an economy budget. Costs will vary from region to region. (The cities are generally more expensive than the countryside.) But the rise of the hotel, motel, and restaurant chains has leveled these differences somewhat.

Note: All prices quoted in this guide are in Canadian dollars unless otherwise noted.

The downtown areas of most cities have older hotels, formerly elegant, that have had to lower their prices to meet the competition on the outskirts. Often, however, they are quite adequate and may compare favorably with European, if not American, standards.

The prices in the table reflect average figures for the entire country. Adjustments may be neccessary from province to province and from urban to rural locations.

Every province except Alberta, the Yukon Territory, and the Northwest Territories imposes a sales tax of anywhere between 4 and 11 percent on consumer goods, restaurant meals, and sometimes lodgings. A pleasant surprise, however, was the provincial government of Ontario's lifting of the 7 percent hotel room tax.

1

Typical Daily Budget for Two People

Room at a moderate hotel or motel	$50.00
Light breakfast for two at hotel or motel (incl. tip)	7.00
Lunch for two at an inexpensive restaurant (incl. tip)	10.00
Dinner for two at a moderate restaurant (incl. tip)	30.00
One sightseeing bus tour (two fares)	6.00
One cocktail apiece for two persons	7.00
Admission for two to one museum or historic site	4.00
	$114.00

In planning your budget don't forget to allow a realistic amount for recreation and entertainment expenses such as the rental of sports equipment, entrance fees to amusement parks, museums, galleries and historical sites; and tickets to movies, concerts, plays, and exhibitions. You'll also need to include souvenirs, extra camera film, and perhaps incidental medical fees that might not be covered by your insurance. Tipping will be another big extra; in some situations this can increase your costs by as much as 15–20 percent.

Picnicking is an excellent way to cut food costs. Most major scenic highways have well-maintained picnic and rest areas equipped with tables, benches, and trashcans, and often fireplaces, running water, and toilets.

SENIOR CITIZEN AND STUDENT DISCOUNTS. Many attractions throughout Canada—and many hotels, motels, and restaurants—offer discounts to senior citizens and students. In most cases, showing a driver's license, passport, or some other proof of age will suffice—"senior" generally being defined as 65 or over. Museums, movie theaters, and even some stores will often post special senior-citizen rates. Some airlines give seniors a 10% discount on air travel. Those places offering student discounts are generally more stringent in their proof requirements—a high school or college ID, international student travel card, or evidence of age may be requested. Persons under 22 get a discount of up to 25% on air travel on a standby basis.

FACTS AND FIGURES. The country of Canada, the second largest in the world, covers 3,851809 square miles. It is broken down into ten provinces plus the Yukon Territory and the Northwest Territories. The total population is approximately 24,341,181.

Note: References to Canadian areas are often defined as follows:

The Atlantic Provinces are Newfoundland, Nova Scotia, New Brunswick, and Prince Edward Island. Nova Scotia, New Brunswick and Prince Edward Island are often referred to as the *Maritime Provinces.*

The Central Provinces are Québec and Ontario.

The Prairie Provinces are Manitoba, Saskatchewan, and Alberta.

The Western Province is British Columbia.

The Northern Territories are the Yukon and Northwest Territories.

TOURIST INFORMATION. The Canadian Government Office of Tourism is a well-staffed and efficient office prepared to handle any kind of travel query. If they don't have the information on hand, they'll refer you to the provincial or local tourism office that does. For specific information on accommodations, provincial events, recommended driving tours and points of interest, contact the individual provincial tourism offices.

National: Canadian Government Office of Tourism, Department of DRIE, 235 Queen St., Ottawa, Ont. K1A 0H6; 613–966–4610.

British Columbia: Tourism British Columbia, 1117 Wharf St., Victoria, B.C. V8W 2Z2; 604–387–1642.

Alberta: Travel Alberta, Box 2500, Edmonton, Alberta T5J 0H4; 403–427–4321.

Saskatchewan: Tourism Saskatchewan, Bank of Montreal Bldg., 2103 11th Ave., Regina, Sask. S4P 3V7; 306–565–2300.

Manitoba: Travel Manitoba, 7th Floor, 155 Carlton St., Winnipeg, Manitoba R3C 3H8; 204–944–3777.

Ontario: Ontario Travel, 77 Bloor St. W., 9th Floor, Toronto, Ont. M7A 2R9; 416–965–4008.

Québec: Tourism Quebec, P.O. Box 20000, Quebec City, Quebec G1K 7X2; toll-free 800–361–6490 (from Canada), 800–443–7000 (From U.S.).

Nova Scotia: Tourism Bureau, Box 130, Halifax, Nova Scotia B3J 2M7; 902–424–5000.

New Brunswick: Tourism New Brunswick, Box 12345, Fredericton, New Brunswick E3B 5C3; toll-free 800–561–0123 (U.S. and Canada).

Prince Edward Island: Visitor Services Division, Box 940, Charlottetown, P.E.I., C1A 7M5; 902–892–2457.

Newfoundland: Tourism Branch, Dept. of Development, Box 2016, St. John's, Newfoundland A1C 5R8; 709–737–2830.

Yukon: Yukon Department of Tourism and Information, P.O. Box 2703, Whitehorse, Yukon, Y1A 2C6; 403–667–5340.

Northwest Territories: Travel Arctic, Government of N.W.T., Dept. of Economic Devel. and Tourism, Yellowknife, N.W.T. X1A 2L9; 403–873–2611.

In addition, Parks Canada, Department of the Environment, Ottawa, Ontario K1A 1G2, 613–997–2800, handles information on national parks and national historic sites throughout Canada.

WHERE TO GO. Almost anywhere you point your finger on a map of Canada will provide the raw materials for an interesting tour. Here are some suggestions to help you narrow your choices and map out a tour.

Newfoundland. The route from Argentia to St. John's in Newfoundland offers bird sanctuaries at Cape St. Mary's and Witless Bay, the headquarters of pirate Peter Easton at Harbour Grace, and St. John's, the oldest city founded by Europeans on the North American Continent.

For the more rugged side of Newfoundland there is the route from Channel Port-aux-Basques at the end of the ferry from North Sydney, Nova Scotia, to St. John's. Along the way there are Deer Lake, Gros Morne National Park and Terra Nova National Park. The first park is an undeveloped wilderness and the second has interesting wildlife and rugged, forested highlands.

Prince Edward Island. Prince Edward Island is small enough to be taken in on one tour. The Blue Heron Drive will take you through Charlottetown, where Canada's independence was charted at a Confederation Conference in 1864, to Prince Edward Island National Park, with its water sports, nature trails and miles of beaches and bright sand dunes.

Nova Scotia. Nova Scotia offers a number of possibilities. West from Truro, a center of Scottish culture, there are the miner's museum of Springhill, the ruins of Fort Lawrence in Amherst, and (back to the east again) Pictou and the ferry to Prince Edward Island. To the northeast there are the antique steam engines of New Glasgow, the Gaelic-speaking community in Antigonish, the eighteenth-century Fortress Louisbourg, Sydney, and the historic Cabot Trail. To the southwest there is the boat Building community in Lunenburg, the Citadel at Halifax, Captain Kidd's alleged buried treasure at Oak Island, the 40-foot tides of Windsor, and a recreation of the first Canadian settlement at Port Royal National Historic Park. In addition, there is the famous Lighthouse Route, 227 miles of rugged seacoast from Yarmouth to Halifax with pirate coves on one side of the road and scenic farms on the other.

New Brunswick. In northern New Brunswick you can take in the Acadian villages of Edmundston, St. Leonard, and Caraquet with its French-speaking population and its fine seafood. Grand Falls, with a 120-foot cataract, is also in the area. Clustered in the southern part of the province are the cities of St. John, Fredericton, and Moncton with the fascinating Bay of Fundy coastline.

Québec. Québec Province offers travelers everything from cities with an Old World flavor to raw wilderness. The Public Relations Department of the City of Montréal offers an excellent booklet that describes a 2.2-mile walk through the historic quarter of the city. It is worth the half day.

A tour of the Laurentian playground to the north of Montréal combines the unique food, culture, and language of La Belle Province with some of the most exciting canoe, camping, and skiing country in the world. A trip along the south shore of the St. Lawrence will take you through the old seignieuries, manor houses, and churches of Varennes, Sorel, Ste. Hyacinthe, and Longueuil. The Richelieu Valley is scenic farm country with markets and fairs in Valleyfield, Drummondville, and Sherbrooke. But for old French Canada you have to take the Chemin du Roy from Montréal to Trois Rivières to Québec City and then go up Route 54 to Chicoutimi, on to Rivière du Loup, and back down to Ste. Anne de Beaupré. Starting with the only walled city in North America north of Mexico City and ending at the most famous shrine on the continent, this tour is designed to bring the traveler back into 18th-century Canada. Finally, there is the Gaspé Peninsula at the mouth of the St. Lawrence River. Heading out onto the peninsula from Rivière du Loup you will pass fishing and farming villages, covered bridges, Forillon National Park (with its 22 species of whales), and shrines and missions.

Québec has been packaged in hundreds of forms, from a day tour to trips of a few weeks. The Québec Tourist Information Office can provide more information about these tours and the companies that run them, but it is safe to assume that you will pay at least $50 per person per day if you choose to travel that way.

Ontario. There are perhaps more ways to see Ontario than there are to see Québec. There are horseback tours, canoe tours, camping tours, fly/drive tours, tulip festival tours, and even houseboat tours. We'll stick here with tours by region, but there is no end to the ways you can see Ontario. There is a northern route through the Lake of the Woods country. There is the Lake Superior region including Sault Ste. Marie. There is northeastern Ontario with its fishing, camping, and canoeing. Stratford with its Shakespeare Festival is in the middle of the most English part of the world between Liverpool and Victoria. And the famous parks and gardens around Niagara Falls and the Niagara Peninsula are always a popular favorite.

Toronto and its environs offer a number of possibilities for well-planned tours. Another manageable trip would include Ottawa and the Ottawa Valley, which Champlain explored in the seventeenth century. Ottawa, Canada's capital, is a city that revels in pomp and pageantry, and has more museums and monuments than any other Canadian city. Upper Canada on the Heritage Highway includes the St. Lawrence Islands National Park and Upper Canada Village (a re-created Canadian village of about 1850). And these hardly cover the province's points of interest. Once again, write to the provincial tourist office for a list of tours and tour companies, if you want a package. If not, buy a map and plan your own.

Manitoba. Northern Manitoba is large. But if you are up to a 600-mile drive from Prince Albert to The Pas to Churchill to Flin Flon and back again, you can catch the flavor of the frontier. If cities are more to your liking, try a walking tour of Winnipeg—along with short drives to the Icelandic village of Gimli and to Hecla Provincial Park.

Saskatchewan. There are a handful of ways to divide up Saskatchewan. In the north-central part of the province there is the area around Prince Albert and Prince Albert National Park that goes as far south as Saskatoon. Further south, in the triangle formed by Saskatoon, Swift Current, and Regina, you have Indian Country with impressive re-enactments of the Old West (i.e., Sitting Bull's escape after Little Big Horn) in Swift Current and Moose Jaw. Regina, the home of the Mounted Police, is the starting point for a trip through three provincial parks.

Alberta. In Alberta you can plan a trip to see dinosaur remains in the south-central badlands and at Dinosaur Provincial Park in the southeastern part of the province. Calgary and the area to the south have a western atmosphere celebrated each July during Stampede Week, the rich farmland of Lethbridge, and Waterton Lakes National Park. Edmonton was the starting point of the long road to the Klondike at the turn of the century, and its reminders of that period are worth a trip, especially if you include Elk Island National Park just outside the city. And finally there is the string of mountain parks: Willmore Wilderness Park, Jasper National Park, and Banff National Park—all full of sparkling lakes, streams, mountains, canyons, and forests.

British Columbia. British Columbia is more than Vancouver and Victoria. In the northern part of British Columbia there is wilderness, the fishing center of Prince Rupert, the model city of Kitimat, and the mining town of Prince George. Glacier National Park and its environs are a possibility for a compact trip. Vancouver and the Fraser Valley combine the sophistication of a large city with rural western life. Or you can combine Vancouver with Victoria (and the rest of Vancouver Island) to get two sophisticated cities and the Sunshine Coast.

Yukon Territory. If you don't mind driving and roughing it, you can take in almost all of the accessible parts of the Yukon Territory in one swing. Start at Watson Lake on the British Columbia border and drive 270 miles up the Alaska Highway to Whitehorse, a gold rush center 70 to 80 years ago and the capital of the Yukon today. Then it is a little less than 100 miles, a short drive (in these parts), to Haines Junction. From there it is 190 miles, almost half of it along the edge of Kluane National Park, to the Alaskan border and another 100 miles to Tetlin Junction, Alaska, where you can turn north toward the City of Gold, Dawson, on the Klondike River, about 180 miles away. (In Dawson

City you will find the only legal gambling casino in Canada, an establishment with the remarkable name of Diamond Tooth Gerties.) About 22 miles more will bring you to Carmacks, a picturesque mining town, another 110 miles will take you back to Whitehorse.

Northwest Territories. The Northwest Territories are too large for a single trip. The one tour suggested for the newcomer to this vast and rugged world is confined to the southern region where summer temperatures are comfortable (and you *should* travel here in the summer). Going from Forth Smith, the old Hudson's Bay Company trading post, to Hay River, to Yellowknife will bring you past Wood Buffalo National Park—the world's largest national park—and Indian reservations, past waterfalls, onto the shores of Great Slave Lake, and into Eskimo artifact museums. It also just might whet the appetite for more of the North.

A number of organizations offer tours for your convenience. Among them are *Pacific Western Airlines,* Vancouver, B.C.; *Nortour,* Montreal, Quebec; *Horizon Holidays,* Toronto, Ont.; *Goliger's Tours,* Toronto, Ont.; *Atlas Tours,* Whitehorse, Yukon; *Holidays by Majestic,* Edmonton, Alberta; *DeWest Tours, Ltd,* Vancouver, B.C.; *Society Expeditions,* Seattle, Wash.; *Special Odysseys,* Medina, Wash. See your travel agent for details.

WHEN TO GO. There is no *one* time to go to Canada. The country is too big and too diverse for anything as specific as that.

When you prefer to go will depend on what you like in the way of weather, sports, sightseeing, cultural events, and local color. Be sure to consult the section on *Seasonal Events,* because Canada's pageants, and fairs and festivals of every kind, from the cultural to the agricultural, should be an important part of your planning and enjoyment of this vast and varied country.

While it is impossible to generalize about the best seasons, the area along the border with the United States is most pleasant during May and June or September and October. While the summer heat can make travel in the temperate region uncomfortable, it is, however, an absolutely essential requirement for travel in the North—at least for those who prefer mosquitoes and other insects to the bitter cold. The summer months are also comfortable in the Rockies. And beautiful British Columbia is, of course, a delight year round.

Winter, though all but intolerable in the North, brings a tolerable dry cold to the Prairies. Autumn is most beautiful in the forests of the Atlantic Provinces and the West. And spring, even though it is the most beautiful time for the orchards, suffers in appeal because of the melting snow—especially during April.

Seasonal Temperature Ranges in Canada

Area	*Summer*	*Winter*
Maritimes	low 70s (23°C)	mid 20s (-5°C)
Ontario and Québec	high 70s (25°C)	0°-10° (-15°C)
The Prairies	high 70s (25°C)	0° (-18°C)
British Columbia	mid 70s (24°C)	32° (0°C)
The North	mid 60s (15°C)	-25° (-32°C)

SEASONAL EVENTS. In deciding when you will go and in determining your itinerary, you may want to take into account the various seasonal festivals and events that take place in Canada. The list below is by no means all-inclusive; it merely describes some of the more popular events. For exact dates and for more information write to the relevant provincial tourist office.

Newfoundland: *May:* Opening of the salmon fishing season. *June:* Opening of rainbow trout fishing season. *July:* Summer arts festival in St. John's; Newfoundland Amateur Golf Championship at St. John's Bally Hally Golf Club; Canada's Day Pageant in St. John's. *August:* St. John's Annual Regatta. *September:* Newfoundland Golf Association Match Play Championship at the Bally Hally Golf Club in St. John's; Opening of hunting season. *September and October:* A variety of agricultural fairs and exhibitions throughout the province.

Prince Edward Island: *July:* The Potato Blossom Festival in O'Leary. *August:* Highland Games in Eldon; Old Home Week in Charlottetown; The Harvest Festival in Kensington; The Acadian Festival in Abrams Village.

Nova Scotia: *June:* Blessing of the Fleet in Meteghan; Apple Blossom Festival in Annapolis Valley. *July:* Gathering of the Clans in Prigwash; Highland Games in Sydney; The Lobster Carnival in Pictou; The Annual Jamboree in Bras d'Or; Old Times Fiddling Contest in Dartmouth; Highland Games in Antigonish; Cape Breton Highlanders' Reunion in Glace Bay; Annual Piping Festival in Dartmouth; Sportsman's Meet in Stillwater; Acadian Day Festival in L'Ardoise. *August:* South Coast Exhibition in Bridgewater; Highland Summer Festival in Inverness. *September:* Blueberry Harvest Festival in Amherst; Fisheries Exhibition in Lunenburg.

New Brunswick: *May:* Maple Festival in Elgin. *June:* Pioneer Days in Oromocto; Potato Festivals in Grand Falls and Hartland. *July:* Loyalist Days in St. John. *August:* Frontier Festivals in Chatham and Fredericton; Acadian Festivals in Cocagne and Caraquet. *September:* Lumberman's Festival in Edmundston.

Québec: *January:* International Bonspiel in Québec; National Skating Championship in Québec. *February:* Winter Carnival in Québec. *April:* Maple festivals throughout the province. *May:* Festival des Cantons in Sherbrooke. *June:* Québec City's 300th Anniversary and Tall Ships Festival (throughout summer); Man and His World Exhibition in Montréal (through September); St. Jean Baptiste Day Celebrations. *July:* Raftsman's Festival in Hull; Summer Festival in Québec; International Regatta in Valleyfield; Summer Festival in Rivière du Loup. *August:* National Folklore Festival in Chicoutimi; Kayak Canoe Races in Chicoutimi. *September:* Expo Québec in Québec City; Western Festival in St. Tite. *October:* Hunting Festival in St. Michel des Saints; Salon du Sport in Montréal; Snow Goose Festival in Montmagny. *December:* Salon des Métiers d'Art in Montréal; Salon des Artisans in Québec.

Ontario: *March:* Winter Fun Carnival in North Bay. *April:* the Guelph Festival in Guelph; Maple Syrup Festival in Elmira. *May:* Canadian Tulip Festival in Ottawa; Blossom Festival in Niagara Falls; Folk Arts Festival in St. Catherines. *June:* Shakespeare Festival in Stratford (through October); Metro Caravan ethnic fair in Toronto; Queen's Plate thoroughbred horse race in Toronto; Changing of the Guard at Ottawa's Parliament Buildings (through

September). *July:* Fun in the Sun in Fort Frances; Highland Games in Cobourg; Highland Games in Brantford; Royal Canadian Henley Regatta in St. Catherines; Horse Show in St. Catherines. *August:* Miner's Festival in Cobalt; Bancroft Jamboree in Bancroft; Glengarry Highland Games in Maxville; Wikwemikong Indian Pow-Wow on Manitoulin Island; Six Nations Indian Pageant in Brantford; Highland Games in Fergus; Canadian National Exhibition in Toronto. *September:* Western Fair in London; Grape and Wine Festival in St. Catherines; Pioneer Festival in Toronto. *October:* Oktoberfest in Kitchener–Waterloo; Pioneer Day (Mennonite) Celebration in Jordan. *November:* Royal Winter Fair and Horse Show in Toronto.

Manitoba: *February:* Trappers' Festival in The Pas. *April:* Royal Manitoba Winter Fair in Brandon. *June:* Provincial Exhibition in Brandon; Nickel Days in Thompson; Red River Exhibition, Winnipeg. *July:* Trout Festival in Flin Flon; Winnipeg Folk Festival; Manitoba Stampede in Morris; Threshermen's Reunion in Austin; Northwest Roundup and Agricultural Fair in Swan River; National Ukrainian Festival in Dauphin. *August:* Pioneer Days in Steinbach; Opasquia Indian Days in The Pas; Icelandic Festival in Gimli; Corn and Apple Festival in Morden. *October:* Turkey Shoot in Winnipeg.

Saskatchewan: *March:* Winter Festival in Meadow Lake. *April:* Sportsman Show in Saskatoon. *May:* Ukrainian Folk Heritage in Saskatoon; Big Muddy Rodeo in Bengorigh; *June:* Antique Car and Gun Show in Weyburn; Ethnic Festival in Yorkton; Frontier Days in Swift Current; Pike Festival in Nipawin. *July:* Reunion Days in Indian Head; Rodeo in Wood Mountain; Saskatchewan Stampede in Yorkton; Exhibition in North Battleford; Buffalo Days in Regina. *August:* Silver Spur Galaxy Horse Show in Lloydminster; Threshing Bee and Hobby Show in Maple Creek. *September:* Threshermen's Reunion in Frobisher. *October:* Western Canadian Amateurs Championship Fiddling Contest in Swift Current; Annual Goose Festival in Kindersley; Rodeo in Cutknife. *November:* Annual Carnival in Climax; Fall Carnival in Frontier; Annual Turkey Shoot in Kindersley; Western Canadian Agribition in Regina; Annual Winter Festival in Spalding; International Short Film and Video Festival, Yorkton.

Alberta: *May:* International Horse Show in Calgary; Rodeo in Taber; Pioneer Days in Hanna. *June:* Big Horn Rodeo in Hinton; Agricultural Fair and Stampede in Rocky Mt. Horse; Rodeo Week in St. Albert; Stampede in Wainwright; Little Britches Rodeo in Didsbury. *July:* Stampede in Calgary; Midnight Days in Fort Macleod; Klondike Days in Edmonton. *August:* Lac Cardinal Stampede in Grimshaw; Festival of the Arts in Banff; Indian Days in Banff. *September:* Rifleman's Rodeo in Panoka; Blueberry Festival in Fort McMurray.

British Columbia: *May:* Victorian Days in Victoria; Fraser River Canoe Marathon in New Westminster; Camel Jockey Racing in Chilliwack; Oyster Festival in Denman Island. *June:* Stampede on Williams Lake; B.C. Salmon Derby in Howe Sound. *July:* Nelson's Curling Bonspiel in Nelson; Logger's Sports in Sooke; Sea Festival in Vancouver. *August:* Peach Festival in Penticton; Loggers' Sports Day in Squamish; Vancouver Island Exhibition in Nanaimo; Salmon Day in Vancouver; Pacific National Exhibition in Vancouver. *September:* Big Dam Canoe Race in Hudson's Hope; Gold Panning Taylor Day Festivities in Taylor; Rodeo in Lillooet. *October:* Oktoberfest in Vancouver.

Northwest Territories: *March:* International Airling Bonspiel at Inuvik. *April:* Toonik Tyme in Frobisher Bay. *June:* Pine Days in Pine Point. *July:* Arctic Fly-in in Inuvik.

Yukon Territory: *February:* Sourdough Rendezvous in Whitehorse. *March:* Winter Carnival in Mayo; Spring Carnival in Dawson City. *August:* Discovery Day in Dawson City.

It is almost impossible to find any generalizations to cover such variety and ingenuity. Every region, every season, every occasion, every product, every activity is likely to have its own festival somewhere in this country. Almost the only thing you can do is decide when you can travel, where you want to go, and then begin to check into what will be going on there at that time. In addition to the events listed in this book, the various tourist offices and local chambers of commerce are gold mines of fascinating information.

TRAVEL AGENTS. The critical issues in choosing a travel agent are how knowledgeable that person is about travel and how reliable his or her bookings are, regardless of whether you are looking for a package tour or planning to go it independently. The cost will be substantially the same whether you go to a major tour operator such as *Maupintour, American Express, Thos. Cook & Son* and *Olson's* or to the small agency around the corner.

The importance of a travel agent is not merely for the making of reservations, however. A good travel agent booking a flight for a customer will know what general discounts are in effect based on how long your stay will be, how far in advance you are able to make your reservations, whether you are making a simple round trip or adding extra stops and other factors. He or she will also likely be able to suggest suitable accommodations or packages that offer the kind of services you want.

In the case of package tours, you want to be sure that the tour operator can deliver the package being offered. Here again, a travel agent can be helpful. Certainly the organizations named above have established their reputations based on reliability—the inevitable occasional foul-up notwithstanding.

Not all U.S. travel agents are licensed, as the laws vary from state to state, but membership in the American Society of Travel Agents (ASTA) is a safeguard. Similarly, U.K. agents belong to the Association of British Travel Agents (ABTA). Members prominently display ASTA or ABTA shields.

Make travel arrangements carefully. To avoid being victimized by fly-by-night operators who might claim better bargains, look for the ASTA member shield—the hallmark of dependable travel service. You'll find the shield on entrance doors, windows, and all office forms of the member agency you select.

ASTA membership indicates that the agent has been in business for a minimum of three consecutive years and is officially approved by the Society to sell tickets on behalf of airlines and cruise ships. ASTA agents also will arrange bookings for trains, buses, or car rentals. For further information write ASTA, 4400 MacArthur Blvd.; N.W., Washington, D.C. 20007, or call 202–965–7520.

HOW TO GET THERE. By commercial airline. Almost all of the international airlines have service into and out of Montréal and/or Toronto. You can fly to Canada from the major European capitals and from Central America, the Caribbean, and the Middle East on *Air France, Alitalia, Aeromex-*

ico, British Airways, El Al, KLM, Lufthansa, Sabena, Scandinavian Airlines, Air Maroc, and *Swissair.* Also, *Air Canada* has service to several European capitals.

The major international airport on the West Coast is at Vancouver International, which has regular arrivals from many parts of the world.

Flying to Canada from the United States is a very simple matter. New York is connected with Toronto, Montréal, Québec, Ottawa, Halifax and other eastern cities. There are flights from Chicago to Winnepeg, Calgary, Toronto, Ottawa, and Montréal; and from Boston to Halifax, Yarmouth, St. John, Montréal, Toronto, and other cities. There are also direct links from Cleveland, Buffalo, Detroit, Pittsburgh, Miami, Tampa, Dallas, Houston, and Hartford to various points in eastern Canada.

On the West Coast you can fly from San Francisco and Los Angeles to Calgary, Edmonton, Vancouver, Toronto, and Montréal.

In between there are flights on regional airlines to Winnipeg from Minneapolis, Minnesota, and Fargo and Grand Forks, North Dakota; to Lethbridge, Alberta, from Great Falls, Montana.

Before booking a flight be sure to consult your travel agent to see if you are eligible for any of the economy, youth, or tour fares. (See the *Canada by Air* section.)

By private plane. Access to Canada by private airplane is relatively easy. All you need are a certificate of aircraft registration, an aeronautic certificate, a log book, and a valid pilot's licence. Landing fees are moderate, but remember that the usual customs provisions are in effect whether you arrive by private plane or by some other, more mundane method. Visiting pilots should obtain a booklet, *Air Tourist Information—Air Canada,* from Transport Canada, AISP/A, Ottawa, Ont. K1A 0N8; 613–995–0197. Aeronautical charts are supplied by the Canada Map Office, 615 Booth St., Ottawa, Ont. K1A 0E9; 613–998–9900.

There are also a number of charter companies which will take you anywhere in Canada that has an airstrip or will make available a bush plane for travel in the North.

For details write to the appropriate provincial tourist office.

By car. Arriving in Canada by car offers you the most flexibility of any form of travel because it allows you to enter at your own convenience and to stop wherever, whenever, and however long you wish. (See *Canada by Car* section.)

You may bring your automobile into Canada free of duty for your own personal use for up to six months.

The U.S. Interstate Highway System leads directly into Canada at twelve points: US 95 from Maine to New Brunswick; US 91 and US 89 from Vermont to Québec; US 87 from New York to Québec; US 81 and a spur off US 90 from New York to Ontario; US 94, US 96, and US 75 from Michigan to Ontario; US 29 from North Dakota to Manitoba; US 15 from Montana to Alberta; and US 5 from Washington State to British Columbia.

Most of these connections and many of the less important ones, via national highways and state roads, hook up with a Trans-Canada Highway within a few miles.

The only route from Alaska into Canada is the Alaska Highway.

By bus. The only bus company that makes long-distance runs from the United States to Canada is *Greyhound,* but its network of routes can get you from almost any point in the United States to any point in Canada. Inquire for information at your local Greyhound office. Sample fares run about $90 round-trip from New York to Montréal, and about $178 round-trip from San Francisco to Vancouver.

By rail. There are only three direct *Amtrak* connections with Canada: New York to Montréal, Buffalo to Toronto, and Chicago to Toronto. The one way coach fares from New York to Montréal run about $61; New York to Toronto with a change of trains at Buffalo runs about $72; Chicago to Toronto $68. A variety of excursion fares are available for round-trip fares so inquire first from Amtrak or your travel agent.

In addition to the three Amtrak direct routes, there are connecting services from many major cities along the U.S.-Canadian border. For information call or write to your nearest Amtrak office.

By yacht. Many Canadian cities allow entry by sea on private yachts and boats. Local marine authorities can advise you about the necessary documentation and procedure.

HINTS TO HANDICAPPED TRAVELERS. One of the newest and largest groups to enter the travel scene is the handicapped. There are millions of people who are physically able to travel and who do so enthusiastically when they know they will be able to move about with safety and comfort. A growing number of travel agents specialize in this market. Generally, their tours parallel those of the non-handicapped traveler but at a more leisurely pace, with everything checked out in advance to eliminate inconvenience. Important sources of information in this field are: The Travel Information Center, Moss Rehabilitation Hospital, 12th St. and Tabor Road, Philadelphia, PA 19141; *Easter Seal Society,* Director of Education and Information Service, 2023 Ogden Ave., Chicago, IL. 60612. International Air Transport Association, 2000 Teel St., Montreal, Quebec H3A 2R4 publishes a free pamphlet, *Incapacitated Passengers Air Travel Guide.* Other publications giving valuable information about facilities for the handicapped are: *TravelAbility,* by Lois Reamy, published by Macmillian; *Access to the World,* by Louisa Weiss, published by Facts on File, 460 Park Avenue South, New York, N.Y. 10016; the annually revised guide *The Wheelchair Traveler,* by Douglass R. Annand, Ball Hill Road, Milford, NH 03055; and A *Guide for the Disadvantaged,* published by Transport Canada, Tower C, 21st Floor, Place de Ville, Ottawa, Ontario, K1A 0N5, 613–996–5861, published by Transport Canada.

METRIC CONVERSION

Converting Metric to U.S. Measurements

Multiply:	by:	to find:
Length		
millimeters (mm)	.039	inches (in)
meters (m)	3.28	feet (ft)
meters	1.09	yards (yd)
kilometers (km)	.62	miles (mi)
Area		
hectare (ha)	2.47	acres
Capacity		
liters (L)	1.06	quarts (qt)
liters	.26	gallons (gal)
liters	2.11	pints (pt)
Weight		
gram (g)	.04	ounce (oz)

| kilogram (kg) | 2.20 | pounds (lb) |
| metric ton (MT) | .98 | tons (t) |

Power

| kilowatt (kw) | 1.34 | horsepower (hp) |

Temperature

| degrees Celsius | 9/5 (then add 32) | degrees Fahrenheit |

Converting U.S. to Metric Measurements

Multiply:	by:	to find:

Length

inches (in)	25.40	millimeters (mm)
feet (ft)	.30	meters (m)
yards (yd)	.91	meters
miles (mi)	1.61	kilometers (km)

Area

| acres | .40 | hectares (ha) |

Capacity

pints (pt)	.47	liters (L)
quarts (qt)	.95	liters
gallons (gal)	3.79	liters

Weight

ounces (oz)	28.35	grams (g)
pounds (lb)	.45	kilograms (kg)
tons (t)	1.11	metric tons (MT)

Power

| horsepower (hp) | .75 | kilowatts |

Temperature

| degrees Fahrenheit | 5/9 (after subtracting 32) | degrees Celsius |

 WHAT TO TAKE. First of all, don't try to pack at the last moment. Instead, begin in advance and make a list of things each member of the family will need; then check off the items as you pack them. You'll find it saves time and reduces confusion.

If you wear prescription glasses or contact lenses always take an extra pair or set; at the very least have a copy of your prescription. This is true of prescription sunglasses, too. A travel iron often comes in handy. Transparent plastic bags (large and small) are useful for wet bathing suits, socks, shoes, spillable cosmetics, and other easily damaged items. Plenty of photo film, suntan lotion, insect repellent, toothpaste, soap, and so forth, if purchased before you go, will help reduce those nuisance stops to pick up things you forgot. Binoculars, a compass, and a magnifying glass for reading those fine-print maps are all handy items which won't take up much space.

All members of the family should have a sturdy pair of shoes with nonslip soles. Keep them handy in the back of the car. You never know when you may want to stop and clamber along a rocky trail to fully enjoy the Canadian terrain.

Carry raingear in a separate bag in the back of the car (so no one will have to get out and hunt for it in the middle of a downpour).

If you're stopping en route, you'll find it's convenient to pack separately those few things you'll need for just an overnight stay. It saves unloading the entire car, only to reload it the next morning.

Apart from these general considerations, when you assemble your traveling wardrobe you need to take into account the temperature and weather of the region you're visiting. Light, loose-fitting clothing is best for hot areas. For the cold and snow, you'll want a very warm coat, gloves, hat, scarf or muffler, and even boots. In the North you can't have too much warm clothing, although you may not want to wear it all at once if you plan to engage in strenuous physical activity. Synthetic fabrics won't keep you warm in the North. A slicker or an umbrella is a must.

Finally, be wise about packing. Regardless of how or where you plan to travel, it is more convenient to travel light.

 TRAVELING WITH CHILDREN. Minor medical problems can easily be handled with a good first-aid kit. Include the standard contents as recommended by the Red Cross, any special prescriptions required, spare glasses, a cough syrup, a stomachache remedy, a laxative, children's aspirin, an ophthalmic ointment, and antidiarrheal tablets (they travel more safely than liquid). One of the greatest triumphs of medical science, as far as traveling with children is concerned, is the individually packaged gauze pad pretreated with antiseptic and a mild local anesthetic. These are ideal for cleaning up scrapes and scratches. A tube of zinc oxide is a versatile aid for sun- and windburn, diaper rash, and minor abrasions. The dosage and directions for all medicines should be checked with your physician before departure. Pack the kit in a small shoulder bag so it can be kept handy.

Packing for children requires a little extra effort. Clothing should be simple, comfortable, and as versatile as possible. Wash-and-wear and stain-resistant fabrics will make life easier for mother. One of the handiest items is a box of small premoistened towelettes for impromptu clean-ups of hands and face. If a child is not yet a secure walker, it is a good idea to pack him too—in one of the back carriers that allow parents to carry the child while keeping their own hands free.

In your sightseeing, try to include something of interest to children. Public parks, zoos, aquariums, and amusement parks are perfect child-pleasers and often have special attractions for the kids. Canada is particularly rich in zoos. There are four in Québec (Charlesbourg, Granby, St. Felicien, and Montréal), three in Ontario (two in Toronto and one in Thunder Bay), two in Saskatchewan (Saskatoon and Moose Jaw), two in Alberta (Calgary and Edmonton), and one each in Manitoba (Winnipeg) and British Columbia (Vancouver). Beaches, circuses, and forts also make big hits with tiny tourists.

 MONEY. The Canadian dollar, like the U.S. dollar, is divided into 100 cents, and coins and bills exist in the same denominations as in the U.S.—i.e., 1¢, 5¢, 10¢, etc.; $1, $2, $5, $10, etc.

Actual exchange rates fluctuate from day to day but the Canadian dollar is usually worth about 83 U.S. cents and about 49 British pence. In order to get the most for your money, convert it before you leave home. Waiting until you get to Canada can create problems. The banks, which are generally open only from 10 A.M. to 3 P.M. Monday through Friday, are sometimes not prepared to exchange foreign currency, and, even if you find one that will, it is not always convenient to go to a bank. Furthermore, hotels, stores, and restaurants may offer something less than the best rate. The best policy is to find the nearest Deak-Perera foreign exchange office. There are Deak bureaus in Vancouver (617 Granville); Toronto (10 King St. E. and 55 Bloor St. W.); and Montréal (1155 Sherbrooke St. W.).

There are no restrictions on the amount of money you may bring into or take out of Canada. Both Canadians and foreign visitors may convert money from Canadian tender to another currency or from a foreign currency to Canadian dollars as often as they want, in amounts as great as they want, either inside or outside Canada.

CREDIT CARDS. The main types of credit and bank cards widely accepted in Canada are *American Express, Carte Blanche, Diners Club, Visa* (formerly *BankAmericard* in the U.S. and *Chargex* in Canada) and *MasterCard*. If you don't already have a card, inquire locally to see where they are available in your area.

These cards have several advantages. Obviously they spare you the nuisance and risk of carrying large amounts of cash, or even traveler's checks, which are sometimes difficult to cash without full identification. They can be used to draw extra funds in case of emergencies, or to take advantage of sales and special opportunities. They can eliminate losses from unfavorable rates of exchange and commissions in hotels, restaurants and resorts, or from the need to change large sums to pay small bills. For people traveling on expense accounts, or seeking tax deductions for business and professional expenses, they provide the required records. They can make it easier to return unwanted merchandise to stores, because the store simply makes out a credit slip to your card's account.

Despite these conveniences, there are various special restrictions and charges that apply in particular cases and these can raise the final cost of an item to considerably more than what you expected or what the introductory brochure led you to expect.

TRAVELER'S CHECKS. These are the best way to safeguard travel funds. They are sold in various banks and financial companies in terms of American and Canadian dollars and, with proper identification, are as readily accepted as cash. *American Express* has offices throughout the U.S. and Canada; also widely accepted in Canada are *Thomas Cook* traveler's checks, represented by Canada Permanent Trust Company and Toronto Dominion Bank. *Deak-Perera Company* also issues traveler's checks in Canadian funds, although these may be harder to cash outside banks or major hotels.

 ENTERING CANADA. Customs regulations between the United States and Canada are among the most liberal in the world. Passing from one country to the other is usually a simple matter of presenting some valid and acceptable form of identification and answering a few simple questions about where you were born, where you live, why you are visiting Canada, and how long you will stay.

The identification need not be a passport, although this is certainly acceptable. You can also use a driver's licence, birth certificate, draft card, Social Security card, certificate of naturalization, or resident alien ("green") card.

Entry procedure for citizens of Great Britain, Australia, and New Zealand is similarly simple.

Canada allows British and American guests to bring their cars (for less than 6 months), boats or canoes, rifles and shotguns (but not handguns or automatic weapons) and 200 rounds of ammunition, cameras, radios, sports equipment, and typewriters into the country without paying any duty. Sometimes they will require a deposit for trailers and household equipment, but these are refundable when you cross back over the border. (This is to guarantee that you do not sell these items in Canada for a profit.) Needless to say, you may bring clothing, personal items, and any professional tools or equipment you need (if you work in Canada) without charge or restriction. It is also a good idea to carry your medical insurance and insurance for boats, vehicles, and personal luggage.

Some items are restricted, however. You need the contract for a rented car. And, if you are going to return home and leave behind a car you rented in the States, you have to fill out an E29B customs form. Tobacco is limited. Dogs, for hunting or pets, are duty-free, but you must bring a certificate from a veterinary inspector to prove that the dog has no communicable diseases. (Cats may enter without restriction.) All plants must be examined at the customs station to preclude the entry of destructive insects. Most important, Canadian officials are diligent in pursuing smugglers of narcotics and other illegal items.

 TIME ZONES. Canada spans six time zones, but only 4½ hours separate Newfoundland from the Yukon. This is because there is only ½ hour difference between Newfoundland Standard Time and Atlantic Standard Time. From East to West the six zones include the following regions of Canada:

Newfoundland Standard Time: Newfoundland, Labrador, and parts of Baffin Island.

Atlantic Standard Time: The Maritime Provinces, Gaspé Peninsula, Anicosti Island, Québec Province east of Comeau Bay, most of Baffin Island and Melville Peninsula.

Eastern Standard Time: Québec Province west of Comeau Bay and all of Ontario east of 90° longitude.

Central Standard Time: Ontario west of 90° longitude, Manitoba, and the Keewatin district of Saskatchewan in the southeastern part of the province.

Mountain Standard Time: The rest of Saskatchewan, Alberta, those portions of the Northwest Territories directly to the north of Saskatchewan and Alberta, and the northeastern corner of British Columbia.

Pacific Standard Time: The rest of British Columbia.

When the noon gun booms out in Vancouver's Stanley Park, it is: 1 P.M. in Calgary and Edmonton; 2 P.M. in Winnipeg; 3 P.M. in Toronto, Ottawa, and Montréal; 4 P.M. in Halifax, Charlottetown, and St. John, N.B.; and 4:30 P.M. in Newfoundland.

Outside of Québec Province, Daylight Saving Time is largely a matter of local option. Most of Québec observes DST and so do Halifax, St. John, Winnipeg, and Regina. But elsewhere it is up to municipalities, an option many communities exercise one year and ignore the next. The only certain way of telling whether DST is in effect is by inquiring—in advance, if you are curious; when you get there, if you can handle the mystery. And, oh yes, if you have trouble remembering when DST is (optionally) in effect, it is from the last Sunday in April to the last Saturday in October. And the clocks are turned *ahead* one hour!

CANADA BY CAR. Canada's most important road, the Trans-Canada Hwy. (Hwy. 40), traverses just under 5,000 miles from Victoria, British Columbia, to St. John's, Newfoundland.

Most of the Trans-Canada Hwy., as far east as Sydney, Nova Scotia, was constructed by 1962 after 12 years of widening old roads and building new stretches so that a single highway, now marked by signs with a white maple leaf on a green field, would cross the country from coast to coast. The finished product runs from Victoria through Kamloops, Calgary, Regina, Winnipeg, Montréal, Québec, Fredericton, and Halifax to Sydney. Ferries connect the highway with Prince Edward Island and Newfoundland extensions.

The second longest Canadian road, the Yellowhead Hwy. (Hwy. 16), follows the old Indian route from the Pacific Coast and over the Rockies to the Prairie. It begins in Prince Rupert, British Columbia, and runs through Jasper National Park, Edmonton, and Saskatoon to its junction with the Trans-Canada Hwy. at Portage la Prairie, just over 50 miles east of Winnipeg.

Dawson Creek, British Columbia, just over the Alberta border, is the beginning of the 1,523-mile Alaska Hwy. (Hwy. 1), two-thirds of which is in Canada and most of which is unpaved. The Alaska Hwy. goes through Fort St. John and Fort Nelson before crossing the northernmost Rockies, where it rises to over 4,000 feet above sea level. Then it enters the Yukon at Watson Lake, proceeding to the Alaska border via Whitehorse, Carnacks, and Dawson. The last stretch, in Alaska, terminates at Fairbanks.

These primary arteries, along with the complex of roads in southeastern Ontario, around Toronto, bear most of the traffic in Canada. Along with connecting routes—such as the one between Calgary and Edmonton—they will take you anywhere you want to go in the populated areas.

North of the population centers roads become fewer and less developed. The unpaved Mackenzie Highway runs north from central Alberta to Yellowknife, Northwest Territories, but there are few other roads that far north.

Speed limits vary from province to province, but they are usually within the 50–60 mph (90–100 kilometers per hour) range outside the cities. The price of gasoline varies more than the speed limit. And Canada is much farther along in adopting the metric system than the United States. Distances are shown in kilometers, and liquids, including gasoline, are usually sold in liters. (There are 3.78 liters in a U.S. gallon.)(Comprehending the cost of gas in liters may be confusing but no less so than understanding your purchases in terms of the old Imperial gallon—the equivalent of 1.2 U.S. gallons or 4.5 liters—which, to confuse the traveler even further, is still in use in many places.)

The price of gasoline ranges from 40¢ to 52¢ per liter. Ontario prices are the norm, dropping slightly in Québec, Manitoba, Saskatchewan, and British Columbia but rising slightly in the Atlantic provinces, the Yukon and the Northwest Territories. The only "bargain" is in Alberta, where the absence of a provincial tax drops the cost considerably. Regular gas is a few cents less in all provinces, unleaded premium a few cents more. And, needless to say, prices could jump higher at any time.

If you drive your own car into Canada from the United States, you should get a Canadian Non-Resident Inter-Province Motor Vehicle Insurance Liability Card, which is available from insurance companies in the States. The best source of information and advice about automobile insurance is *The Insurance Bureau of Canada,* 181 University Ave., Toronto, Ont. M5H 3M7; (416) 362–2031. Your U.S. driver's license is valid throughout Canada. Drivers from other countries are urged to obtain an International Driver's License before they come to Canada. These are available through various motor clubs in your native country.

Québec is the only province with toll roads (25 cents to 50 cents per gate on the Laurentian and Eastern Townships auto routes). In a number of places you will have to take a ferry to get where you are going by car.

Obviously you can't take your car from the mainland to Newfoundland or Prince Edward Island without a ferry. But ferry travel has become a popular form of recreational travel on both coasts and even on the Great Lakes. The Canadian Government Travel Bureau in Ottawa publishes an invaluable booklet, *Ferries, Bridges, Cruises,* which lists all rates, departure and arrival times, and restrictions (if any).

If you are a member of AAA, you can dial 1–800–336–HELP for emergency road service in Canada.

Car Rentals. If you come to Canada by air or rail and want to rent a car, you can deal through *Hertz, Avis,* and *Budget Rent-A-Car,* whose rates are comparable to those in the States. They all have stations at major airports and you can reserve your car before you leave home.

However, if you are looking for a bargain or a recreational vehicle, ask the Canadian Government Travel Bureau for advice or try: *Tilden Rent-A-Car,* 1485 Stanley St., Montréal, Québec H3A 1P6, (514) 842–9445 in Canada.

If you are planning a round-trip drive out of and back to Whitehorse, try one of these companies in Whitehorse, *Tilden Rent-A-Car Service,* 2089 2nd Ave; *Whitehorse, Yukon, 403–668–2521; Ford Motors U-Drive* (Hertz), 4178 4th Ave., 403–667–2505; *Yukon Travel Agency,* 212 Main St.

 CANADA BY AIR. *Air Canada,* the state-owned airline, operates in every province. Aside from *Air Canada,* the major domestic carriers are *CP Air, Eastern Provincial Airways, Norcanair, Nordair, Pacific Western Airlines, and Québecair.* There are regularly scheduled flights to every major city and to most smaller cities, including many in the Yukon and the Northwest Territories.

In addition to the regular flights in the North, there are also a number of charter airlines and fly-in airports. Check with the territorial tourist agencies for charter companies and with the District Controller of Air Services in the territorial (and provincial) capitals for the locations of air bases that allow private flights and for regulations.

Major international credit cards are generally accepted by airlines. Best to check ahead, though.

Be sure to identify all bags by firmly affixing your name to the outside and inside. The airlines will not accept them for checking otherwise. Name tags ensure a faster tracing of misdirected luggage. They also avoid the possibility of picking up someone else's bag.

Canada is a huge country. The airplane has shrunk it considerably and the flying time between coasts is tolerable. However, service to smaller cities is often only once or twice a day. Therefore, you may encounter long stopovers when trying to reach your destination.

Fly/Drive. As an alternative to waits in airports, you may want to consider a fly/drive package, which offers a different way to satisfy a deeper curiosity. Most airlines, in conjunction with car-rental companies, offer these combination opportunities to most parts of the country all year round.

All you have to do is decide where you want to go, and what you would like to see and do. Then visit your travel agent, who will have a large selection of fly/drive packages from which you can make a choice.

Fly/drive package rates and flexibilities vary considerably. Generally, they cover one or more cities plus the use of a rented car for a specified number of days.

Car usage also varies. For example, with some packages you can drive an unlimited number of miles free. With others you get a specified number of miles free, then must pay an additional charge per mile for the overage. Gas is generally not included, but insurance is.

Some packages offer plans for small groups and a choice of hotel accommodations. Some even offer motor homes, if you're interested in roughing it. Check into special children's rates as well.

Before booking, though, check with your agent about where to pick up the car (at airport or other station), and about the time it will take you to arrive at your hotel to meet your reservation. If you are not going to pick up the car at the airport, check ahead on airport limousines and bus and taxi service to your hotel.

Air fares are similar to those in the United States for similar distances (one way from Montréal to Vancouver costs around $422 economy and $591 first-class, plus tax). But there is a wealth of special excursion rates, youth fares, and family plans. Check with your travel agent before booking a flight.

For More Information. In Ontario: *Aeronautical Information Services,P/T,* Transport Canada, Place de Ville, Ottawa, Ont. K1A 0N8. **In British Columbia:** *CP Air,* One Grant McConachie Way, Vancouver International Airport, B.C. V7B 1V1. In Newfoundland: *Eastern Provincial Airways,* Box 5001, Gander, Nfld. A1V 1W9. **In Saskatchewan:** *Norcanair,* Hanger 2, Mobile 3, Saskatoon, Sask. S7M 5X4. **In Québec:** *Québecair,* Montréal International Airport, P.O. Box 490, Dorval, Que., H4Y 1B5; *Air Canada,* Place Air Canada, Montréal, Québec H2Z 1X5; *Nordair,* 1320 Graham Blvd., Town of Mount Royal, Quebec, H3P 3C8; *CP Air,* 1500 Atwater, Montreal, Quebec. **In Alberta:** *Pacific Western Airlines,* 700 2nd St., S.W., Calgary, Alberta T2P 2W2. **In Manitoba:** *Pacific Western Airlines,* 570 Fairy Rd., Winnipeg, Manitoba, R3H 0T7 204–632–2811.

 CANADA BY RAILROAD. Since CP and CN Rail have terminated all passenger service the only transcontinental railroad is *Via Rail Canada.* It takes about four days and five nights to cross Canada by train. The line also runs shorter routes between major eastern cities. In addition there are smaller lines which operate within individual provinces. Information is available from the lines listed below. Or you can check with your travel agent or with the provincial tourist agencies for these local lines.

There are no trains at all in the Northwest Territories, but *The White Pass and Yukon Railway* operates a narrow-gauge line along the gold-rush route from Whitehorse, Yukon, to Skagway, Alaska. Boat connections back to Vancouver or Prince Rupert are available in Skagway.

Both first-class and coach accommodations exist on most trains. Both classes allow access to dining cars, but sleepers are generally not available in coach except on some long-distance runs.

First-class passengers, however, can enjoy comfortable parlor cars, drawing rooms, bedrooms, and roomettes. Fares are reasonable. (Vancouver to Montréal costs about $220 coach, $320 for an upper berth, $360 for a lower berth, and

$380 for a roomette.) And a variety of round trip, advance purchase, youth, senior citizen, family and group rates reduce fares anywhere up to 50 percent.

Canrailpass offers flat-rate passes for 8, 15, 22, and 30 days that can result in substantial savings.

For More Information. In **Québec:** *Via Rail Canada,* Rail Travel Bureau, Central Station, Montréal, P.Q. H3C 3N3; *Cartier Railway,* Gaganon, Quebec, GOG 1K0; *Québec Central Railway,* 780 CP Rail Terrace, Sherbrooke, Quebec, J1H 1T8; *Québec North Shore and Labrador Railroad,* 100 Retty St., Sett-iles, Quebec; G4R 3E1. In **Ontario:** *Algoma Central Railway,* P.O. Box 7000, Saulte Ste. Marie, Ont. P6A 5P6; *Ontario Northland Railway,* 195 Regina St., North Bay, Ont. P1B 8L3. In **British Columbia:** *British Columbia Railway,* P.O. Box 8770, Vancouver, B.C., V6B 4X6. In **Alberta:** *Canadian Pacific Railway,* 10020–101A Ave., Fipps McKinnon Bldg., 6th Floor, Edmonton, Alberta, T5J 3G2. In **the Yukon:** *White Pass and Yukon Railway,* P.O. Box 4070, Whitehorse, Yukon, Y1A 3T1.

Also contact *Amtrak,* National Railroad Passenger Corp., 400 North Capitol Street, N.W., Washington, D.C. 20001.

 CANADA BY BUS. The long-distance bus system in Canada is important because it services towns without airports and rail lines. It reaches into almost every populated area of the country.

The **Atlantic Provinces** have the *St. John's Transportation Commission* and a number of smaller companies in Newfoundland, the *SMT System* in New Brunswick and Prince Edward Island, and *Acadian Lines* and the *Mackenzie Line* in Nova Scotia.

Québec has long-distance bus routes along both banks of the St. Lawrence, on the Gaspé, in the eastern townships, up into the Laurentians, and out to the northwestern part of the province.

Ontario is equally well served by *Colonial Coach Lines, Gray Coach Lines, Greyhound, Ontario Northland, Grey Goose Bus Lines,* and *Chatham Bus Lines.*

Greyhound, Grey Goose, Eagle, Beaver, Manitoba Motor Transit and *North Star Bus Line* leave **Manitoba.** *Greyhound, Saskatchewan Bus Company, Crossland Coachways, Beacon Bus Line, Leader-Climax Bus Line, Moose Mountain Bus Line,* and *Safe-T Motor Coach Line* all have routes in parts of **Saskatchewan.** *Greyhound, Coachways,* and *Cardinal Coach Lines* cover **Alberta.** And *Greyhound, Coachways, Vancouver Island Coach Lines, Pacific Coach Lines, Squamish Coach Lines, Misty Islands Transportation Co., Barkerville Stage Lines, Lillooet Coach Lines,* and *Cranbrook Golden Bus Lines* will take you where you want to go in **British Columbia.**

Greyhound ventures into selected areas in the **Northwest Territories.** And *Coachways* and *Northern Stages Ltd.* go into the **Yukon.** The *White Pass and Yukon Route* has regular service along the Alaska Hwy. And *Alaska Coachways* offers regular service to Fairbanks and Anchorage, Alaska, from the Canadian border.

Canada's two major carriers, *Voyageur* and *Greyhound,* offer several cost-cutting options. Greyhound's *Ameripass,* modeled after European rail passes, permits unlimited travel on any Greyhound line in North America, except Mexico, Alaska, and Vancouver Island. A 7-day pass costs about $225 (Canadian); 15 days, $296; 30 days, $415. For long-distance bus travel in Canada, another alternative is Voyageur's excursion discount plan. To qualify, you must leave any day except Friday and return within five days. The regular return rate between Toronto and Montréal, for example, drops about 25% if these conditions are met.

Addresses for bus lines: *Acadian Lines,* 6040 Almon St., Halifax, Nova Scotia B3K 5M1. *Gray Coach Lines,* Toronto Bus Terminal, 610 Bay St., Toronto, Ontario M5G 1M5. *Greyhound Lines of Canada Ltd.,* 222 First Ave. S.W., Calgary, Alberta T2P 0A6. *Pacific Coach Lines,* 150 Dunsmuir Street, Vancouver, British Columbia V6B 1W9. *Saskatchewan Transportation Company,* Transportation Building, 2041 Hamilton St., Regina, Saskatchewan S4P 2E2. *Voyageur Colonial Ltd.,* 265 Catherine St., Ottawa, Ontario K1R 7S5.

ACCOMMODATIONS. Although there are many establishments available for the traveler across Canada, they vary substantially in accommodations. If you do not have reservations, it is wise to begin looking for a suitable place to stay early in the afternoon and not run the risk of having to settle for pot luck later in the day when most motorists have decided to settle in for the night. If you have reservations, you should advise the establishment in advance if you expect to arrive late, since, otherwise, some places will not hold reservations after a certain hour.

Reserve well in advance for hotels and motels in popular resort areas at peak seasons. Also, many cities, in any season, may be hosting conventions or special events at the time you arrive. Planning your trip early will either provide you with the accommodations you want or give you plenty of time to make alternative arrangements.

A number of hotels and motels have one-day laundry and dry-cleaning services, and many motels have coin laundries. If your hotel does not have these services or a barbershop or beauty salon, there will almost certainly be local establishments nearby. Just ask your hotel clerk.

Most motels, but not all, have telephones in the rooms. However, if you want to be sure of room service, you will be better off in a hotel.

Many motels, even some in central cities, have swimming pools.

You can assume free parking at motels, motor hotels, and country and resort hotels. But you will pay for parking at most city hotels, although certain establishments do have free parking.

Cribs for the children are almost always on hand—sometimes at no cost, but more frequently at a minimal charge. Cots to supplement the beds in your rooms will also involve a minimal charge. The better hotels and motels generally add a moderate charge for moving an extra single bed into your room.

Chains. In addition to the hundreds of excellent independent hotels and motels throughout the country, there are also many fine establishments in both categories that belong to chains. A major advantage of the chains is the ease with which you can make reservations—either one at a time en route, or all at once in advance. If you are staying at a member hotel or motel, the management will be delighted to secure you a booking at one of its affiliated hotels or motels for the coming evening—at no extra cost to you.

Categories: Hotels and motels in this guidebook are divided into five categories, arranged primarily by price but also taking into consideration the degree of comfort you can expect to enjoy. Failure to include certain establishments in our lists does not mean that they are not worthwhile, only that we lack the space to include every acceptable place.

Although the names of the various hotel and motel categories are standard, the prices listed under each category may vary from area to area. This variance reflects local price standards and takes into account regional differences in what is considered "moderate" or "expensive." In every case, however, the dollar ranges for each category are clearly stated before each listing of establishments.

Super deluxe: In addition to offering all of the amenities discussed in the deluxe category below, the super deluxe hotel has a special atmosphere of glamour, good taste, and dignity—and prices certainly will reflect this.

Deluxe: For a rough rule-of-thumb index, we suggest that the minimum facilities of a deluxe hotel must include bath and shower in all rooms, valet and laundry service, available suites, a well-appointed restaurant and bar (local law permitting), room service, television and telephone in every room, heat and air conditioning (if necessary), and a pleasing décor.

Expensive: All rooms should have bath or shower, valet and laundry service, restaurant and bar (local law permitting), limited room service, television and telephone in each room, heat and air conditioning (if necessary), and a pleasing décor.

Moderate: Each room should have an attached bath or shower. There usually will be a restaurant or coffeeshop. Television will be available. Telephones and heat and air conditioning (if necessary) will be provided in each room. The establishment will also have a relatively convenient location, clean and comfortable rooms, and public rooms. Motels in this category may not have attached bath or shower, may not have a restaurant or coffeeshop (though one is usually nearby), and may have no public rooms.

Inexpensive: Rooms in such establishments will have a nearby bath or shower and a telephone available. Clean rooms are the bare minimum.

HOSTELS. As students have known for years, hostels are comfortable, clean, inexpensive places to stay when traveling on a tight budget. But hostels are not just for young people. Adults—even families—are welcome at many of Canada's 60 hostels.

The Canadian Hostelling Association was established in 1933. It is a nonprofit organization whose aims are to help all, but especially young people, to a greater knowledge and appreciation of the countryside, particularly by providing accommodations for them while traveling.

A hostel offers simple overnight accommodation. It is open to everyone, and is a common meeting place for people from every nationality and background, particularly those interested in traveling off the beaten track. A hosteler may stay up to a maximum of three consecutive nights, though in some hostels this may be longer. In Canada, the cost of overnight accommodation ranges from $3 to $10 per person. Meals, where available, are extra. Many hostels have a kitchen and most provide blankets, pillows, cooking utensils, and cleaning equipment. Guests are often expected to help with hostel chores during their stay. Only those holding current membership cards are admitted to youth hostels. Canada generally has a fee differential for non-members. In addition, a CHA card represents membership in the international organization—valid in some 50 countries.

For information write the *Canadian Hostelling Association,* Place Vanier, Tower A, 333 River Rd., Ottawa, Ont. K1L 8H9.

FARM VACATIONS AND BED-AND-BREAKFAST ACCOMMODATIONS. Two interesting low-cost options are farm vacations and the increasingly popular bed-and-breakfast lodging available throughout Canada. For as little as $15 a day, Canadians will put you up and feed you in their own homes. In addition to saving money, you'll get a closer look at the land and its people. The big-city version of this type of accommodation is the guest house, common in Toronto, Montréal, and Québec. These are usually well-maintained private homes with rooms available on a daily or weekly basis. Most are listed in local phone books or newspapers. Standards of quality vary widely, so compare homes early in the day before making your choice. Private bathrooms are rare, and some proprietors lock up early, a practice that could put a damper on your plans for a night on the town.

An excellent source is John Thompson's *Country Bed and Breakfast Places in Canada,* which lists more than 160 places from Gertie Legge's "Hospitality Home" in Heart's Delight, Newfoundland, to Olga Maye's single room in Oliver, British Columbia.

Eight provinces have farm vacation associations, which distribute lists of guest farms, inspect facilities, and handle consumer complaints: **National:** Canadian Country Vacations Association, Hopewell Hill, N.B. E0A 1Z0; **Alberta:** Alberta Country Vacations, R.R. 1, Chauvin, Alberta T0B 0V0; **Saskatchewan:** Saskatchewan Farm Vacations Assoc, Box 214, Allan, Saskatchewan S0K 0C0; **Manitoba:** Manitoba Farm Vacations Assoc, Box 23, R.R. 2, Morris, Manitoba R0G 1K0; **Ontario:** Ontario Farm Vacations Assoc, R.R. 1, Bruce Mines, Ontario P0R 1C0; **Québec:** Agricotours, 525 ave. Viger, Montréal, Québec H2L 2P1; **New Brunswick;** New Brunswick Farm Vacations Assoc, R.R. 1, Harcourt, Kent County, New Brunswick E0A 1T0; **Nova Scotia:** Nova Scotia Farm and Country Vacations Assoc, Centreville, Kings County, Nova Scotia B0P 1J0; **Prince Edward Island:** P.E.I. Farm Vacations, R.R. 2, Winsloe, Prince Edward Island C0A 2H0.

DINING OUT. The general rule for metropolitan areas is to make reservations in advance whenever possible for midday and evening meals. In other areas the lack of reservations may not pose any problem for lunch, but remember that at dinnertime most travelers have settled in a particular place for the evening and will quickly fill up the nearby restaurants. If you prefer a motel, life is simpler if the motel has a restaurant, since their hours are more accommodating to early and late traffic. If it doesn't, try to stay at one located near a restaurant.

Although universal dress standards have become more casual, some restaurants, particularly the better ones and those in heavily populated areas, are relatively fussy about customers' dress, especially in the evening. If you have any doubt about acceptable dress at a particular restaurant, call ahead. But as a general rule, a neatly dressed customer—and in major metropolitan cities, a more conservatively dressed customer—usually will not experience any problems.

Restaurant chains serving fast foods have begun to spring up in Canada and will be instantly recognizable to the motoring public by their specific type of food if not by their outer signs. The popularity of these chains makes low prices and high-speed service possible. While the menu may be limited, the average lunch or dinner ranges from under $3 to about $5, and you can carry out the food or eat it on the premises.

Categories: Restaurants in this volume are divided into five price categories: super deluxe, deluxe, expensive, moderate, and inexpensive. As a general rule, restaurants in metropolitan areas tend to be higher-priced, although many restaurants that feature foreign cuisine are often surprisingly expensive. In Ontario particularly (and in Toronto especially), one finds almost every kind of ethnic restaurant: Chinese, French, Japanese, Spanish, Italian, Greek, Jewish, etc.

We should also point out that space limitations make it impossible to include every establishment worth sampling. We have, therefore, included those we consider the best within each price range.

As with hotels and motels, while the names of the various categories are standard in this volume, the prices listed under each category may vary from area to area. Again, this variance reflects local price standards.

Super Deluxe: This category will probably be pertinent to the large metropolitan areas. Super deluxe indicates comfort, excellent service, and a well-trained staff. More often than not, such restaurants will be overpriced and perhaps overrated, but for those who can afford to splurge, it may prove a delightful experience to dine at one. As in all the other categories, the price range does not include cocktails, wine, cover or table charges, tips, or extravagant house specialties.

Deluxe: Many a fine restaurant falls into this category. It will have its own well-deserved reputation for excellence, perhaps a house specialty or two for which it is famous, and an atmosphere of comfort and elegance, or a unique décor. It will have a good wine list (where the law permits), and an attentive staff.

Expensive: Restaurants in this category will have a general reputation for very good food. In addition to the expected dishes, it may offer one or two house specialties. There will be a wine list and cocktails (where the law permits). An adequate staff, air conditioning (where necessary), and an elegant décor.

Moderate: This category indicates a general reputation for good, wholesome food. Such restaurants will have clean kitchens, adequate staff, better-than-average service, and air conditioning (where necessary). They will also serve cocktails and/or beer where the law permits.

Inexpensive: This designation indicates the bargain place in town. It will be clean, if plain. It will have air conditioning (where necessary), tables (not a counter), a clean kitchen, and adequate service.

NIGHT LIFE. In the large cities of Montréal and Toronto the problem is never what to do in the evening but how to choose from among the hundreds of attractions available. Whatever form of entertainment you fancy, these cities inevitably offer something to suit your taste.

Theater thrives all over Canada, but especially in Toronto and Montréal. Dance is one of the most popular art forms and there are performances in every large city. The section on *Culture* lists some of the larger and more popular theaters, dance companies, opera houses, and concert halls in the major cities.

Nightclub and jazz entertainment are also popular in the cities. To find out what is going on in a city consult the local papers or entertainment brochures.

Outside the big cities, there is still a good deal of nighttime entertainment, especially in areas that cater to tourists. Most often, however, evening entertainment in smaller cities will be confined to weekends and the local hotels and larger motels. (Your desk clerk is probably the best source of information about what's going on.)

TIPPING. There is no law in Canada that says you must leave a tip for service. However the unwritten laws of custom make tipping necessary more often than not.

Tipping is a personal thing, your way of expressing appreciation of someone who has given you attentive, efficient, and personal service. Because standards of service in Canada are uneven, you should, when you get genuinely good service, reward it. And when you feel that the service you got was indifferent or surly, don't hesitate to recognize this by the size, or withholding, of your tip. Remember that in many places those who serve you are paid very little and depend on tips for part of their income. This is supposed to give them an incentive to serve you well. These days, the going rate on restaurant service is 15 percent on the amount *before* taxes. Tipping at counters is not universal, but many people leave at least 50¢, and 10 percent when it comes to anything over that. For bellboys, 50¢ per bag is usual. For one-night stays in most hotels and motels you leave nothing. If you stay longer, at the end of the stay leave the maid $1.00–$1.50 per day, or $5.00 per person per week for multiple occupancy. If you are staying in an American Plan hostelry (meals included), $2.00–$3.00 per person for the waitress or waiter is considered sufficient, and is left at the end of your stay. However, if you have been surrounded by an army of waiters, sommeliers, and stewards, add a few extra dollars and give the lump sum to the captain or *maître d'hôtel* when you leave, asking him to allocate it. Outside of Canada and the United States, it is customary for restaurants and nightclubs to add a percentage for service to your bill. In Canada this practice is permitted only with the consent of the customer. If a tip is added without your knowledge and consent, you can refuse to pay it.

For the many other services you may encounter in a hotel or resort, figure roughly as follows: doorman, 50¢ for taxi handling, $1.00 for help with baggage; bellhop, 50¢ per bag, more if you load him down with extras; parking attendant, $1.00; bartender, 15 percent; room service, $1.00; laundry or valet service, 15 percent; barbers, $1.00; Shoeshine attendants, 50¢; hairdressers, $2.00.

Transportation: Taxi and limousine drivers in Canadian cities expect 15 percent. Car-rental agencies, nothing. Bus porters are tipped 50¢ per bag, drivers nothing. On charter and package tours, conductors and drivers usually get $10.00 per day from the group, but be sure to ask if this has been already figured into the package cost. On short local sightseeing runs, the driver-guide may get 50¢–$1.00 per person, more if he has been especially helpful or informative. Redcaps, 50¢ per suitcase. Tipping at curbside check-in is unofficial, but same as above.

Railroads suggest you leave 10–15 percent per meal for dining-car waiters, but the steward who seats you is not tipped. Sleeping-car porters get about $2.00 per person per night. Baggage porters are tipped 50¢ per bag, depending on how heavy your luggage is.

 NATIONAL PARKS. There are 28 Canadian National Parks, divided among five regions. For complete information on facilities and accommodations write to the central office in Ottawa, the relevant regional office, or the headquarters of the park you wish to visit: *Parks Canada,* Department of the Environment, Ottawa, Ont. K1A 1G2.

Atlantic Region

Parks Canada—Atlantic Division, Upper Water St., Halifax, N.S. B3J 1S9; (902) 426–3457.

Cape Breton Highlands National Park (367 square miles) has skiing, swimming, salmon fishing, hiking trails, rocky coastline, forests, and a Scottish atmosphere. (Ingonish Beach, Cape Breton, N. S. B0C 1L0; 902—285–2270.)

Fundy National Park (almost 80 square miles) includes oddly formed sandstone cliffs punctuating lovely beaches. (P.O Box 40, Alma, N. B. E0A 1B0; 506–887–2000.)

Gros Morne National Park (750 square miles) contains the Long Range Mountains, lakes that look like fiords, a rugged coast, and heavy forests. (P.O. Box 130, Rocky Harbour, Bonne Bay, Nfld. A0K 4N0; 709—458–2417.)

Kejimkujik National Park (147 square miles) features rolling woodland and fishing lakes. (P.O. Box 36, Maitland Bridge, Annapolis County, N. S. B0T 1N0; 902–242–2770.)

Kouchibouguac National Park (87½ square miles) includes swimming, campgrounds and offshore sandbars in the bay. (Kent County, N. B. E0A 2A0; 506–876–2443.)

Prince Edward Island National Park (7 square miles) is a strip of Gulf of St. Lawrence coast 25 miles long, with the warmest beaches north of the Carolinas. (P.O. Box 487, Charlottetown, P.E.I. C1A 7L1; 902–566–7050.)

Terra Nova National Park (153 square miles) surrounds Bonavista Bay with its inlets, its boreal forest on the land side, and its enormous icebergs floating into the Bay to melt. (Glovertown, Nfld. A0G 2L0; 709–533–2801.)

Québec Region

Parks Canada—Québec Region, 3 Buade, P.O. Box 6060, Québec City, Québec G1R 4V7 (418) 694–4042.

Forillon National Park (92.8 square miles) on the tip of the Gaspé region is an incomplete park situated in a region of seascapes and preserved French Canadian villages. (P.O. Box 1220, Gaspé, P.Q. G0C 1R0; 418–368–5505.)

La Mauricie National Park (210 square miles) in the Laurentians is largely undeveloped and heavily wooded. (P. O. Box 758, Shawinigan, P.Q. G9N 6V9; 819–536–2638.)

Ontario Region

Parks Canada—Ontario Region, P.O. Box 1359, Cornwall. Ont. K6H 5V4; (613) 933–7951.

Georgian Bay Islands National Park (5.4 square miles on 40 islands) is characterized by rock formations created by glaciers and old forests. (Box 28, Honey Harbour, Ont. POE 1E0; 705–756–2415.)

Point Pelee National Park (6 square miles) sticking into Lake Erie contains a 14-mile-long beach and a sanctuary for 100 species of birds. RR # 1. (Leamington, Ont. N8H 3Z4; 519–326–3204.)

Pukaskwa National Park (725 square miles) attempts to preserve the wilderness of northern Ontario and its wildlife. (Box 550, Marathon, Ont. P0T 2E0; 806–229–0801.)

St. Lawrence Islands National Park (1.6 square miles) includes a tip of the mainland, 18 wooded islands, and 80 rocky inlets in excellent boating water. (P.O. Box 469, R.R. #3, Mallorytown Landing, Ont. K0E 1R0; 613–923–5261.)

Prairie Region

Parks Canada—Prairie Region, 391 York Ave., Winnipeg, Man. R3C 4B7; 204—949–4044.

Auyittuq National Park on Baffin Island (8,290 square miles) is in the planning stages and includes fiords along Cumberland Peninsula mountains, ice floes and glaciers, and polar bears, seals, and whales. (Pangnirtung, N.W.T., X0A 0R0 819—473–8962.)

Kluane National Park (8500 square miles) in southwestern Yukon is full of high mountains, glaciers, ice fields and lakes. Travel without a guide is discouraged. (Mile 1019, Alaska Highway, Haines Junction, Y. T. Y0B 1L0; 403—634–2251.)

Nahanni National Park (1840 square miles) lies around the South Nahanni River, which few travelers have ever navigated, with its canyons, Virginia Falls, and nearby hot springs. (Postal Bag 300, Fort Simpson, N.W.T. X0E 0N0; 403–695–3151.)

Prince Albert National Park (1496 square miles) surrounds Lake Waskesiu and its fauna and flora are representative of the Prairie Region. (P.O. Box 100, Waskesiu Lake, Sask. S0J 2Y0; 306–663–5322.)

Riding Mountain National Park (1150 square miles) sits on a plateau 1,500 feet above the countryside and has over 50 lakes. (Wasagaming, Man. R0J 2H0; 204–848–2811.)

Wood Buffalo National Park (17,300 square miles), the largest national park in the world, is larger than a number of countries and provides a haven for about 8,000 bisons and about 50 of the nearly extinct whooping cranes. (Fort Smith, N.W.T. X0E OP0; 403–872–2649.)

Western Region

Parks Canada—Western Region, P.O. Box 2989, Sta. M, Calgary, Alta. T2P 3H8; 403—231–4440.

Banff National Park (2564 square miles) is the oldest and best-known Canadian National Park. It runs through the Continental Divide and has snow-capped mountains, ski slopes, hot springs, deep valleys, glaciers and lakes. (Box 900, Banff, Alta. T0L 0C0; 403–762–3324.)

Elk Island National Park (75 square miles) is the home of a 600-head bison herd, aspen and spruce forests, and is surrounded by level farmland and numerous lakes. (Site 4, R.R. # 1, Fort Saskatchewan, Alta. T8L 2N7; 403–998–3781.)

Glacier National Park (521 square miles) is in the Selkirk Mountains and contains over 100 glaciers as well as hemlock and cedar forests and excellent fishing streams. (P.O. Box 350, Revelstoke, B. C. V0E 2S0; 604–837–5155.)

Jasper National Park (4200 square miles) takes in high peaks in the Rockies, large rivers, rapid streams, hot springs, ice fields, and ski slopes. (Box 10, Jasper, Alta. T0E 1E0; 403–852–6161.)

Kootenay National Park (543 square miles) is a narrow valley on the western slopes of the Rockies and includes colossal Sinclair Canyon and Radium Hot Springs. (P.O. Box 220, Radium Hot Springs, B. C. V0A 1M0; 604–347–9615.)

Mount Revelstoke National Park (100 square miles) on the rugged western slopes of the Selkirks is a mountaintop park with ski slopes and alpine meadows. (P.O. Box 350 Revelstoke, B. C. V0E 2S0; 604–837–5155.)

Pacific Rim National Park (250 square miles) on the western slope of Vancouver Island is most famous for sandy Long Beach and the sea lions living on rocky offshore islets. (P.O. Box 280, Ucluelet, B. C. V0R 3A0; 604–726–7721.)

Waterton Lakes National Park (203 square miles) adjoins Glacier National Park in Montana. It includes flat meadows and towering mountains in a striking contrast of prairie and alpine terrain. (Waterton Park, Alta. T0K 2M0; 403–859–2262.)

Yoho National Park (507 square miles)—"How Wonderful," in the local Indian language—has spectacular Yoho Glacier, Lake O'Hara, Takkakaw

Falls, and a famous pass through the Rockies following Kicking Horse River. (P.O. Box 99, Field, B. C. V0A 1G0; 604–343–6324.)

These by no means cover all the parks in Canada. The provinces have their own systems of parks. Information about them can be obtained from the pertinent provincial tourist office.

CAMPING. If you own a tent, trailer or recreational vehicle, camping may be the cheapest way to travel. There are more than 2,000 campgrounds in Canada, from simple roadside turn-offs with sweeping mountain vistas to fully equipped facilities with groomed sites, trailer hookups, recreational facilities, and vacation-village atmosphere. Many of the finest are in Canada's 28 national and more than 300 provincial parks. Here it is first-come, first-served, with nominal overnight fees. Commercial campgrounds offer more amenities, such as electrical and water hookups, showers, even game rooms and grocery stores, but usually charge more per night. Nevertheless, camp fees are a bargain compared to the cost of hotel or motel accommodation.

It pays to arrive early and to make your camping stops in areas that have a number of parks or privately owned campgrounds. If one is full, there is likely to be space in another. It pays also to check how long you can stay, and plan your travels accordingly. Provincial tourist offices publish lists of their area's private and public camping facilities. In addition, the AAA and its Canadian affiliate, the CAA (1775 Courtwood Crescent, Ottawa, Ont. K2C 3J2), publish a series of guidebooks to campgrounds in North America.

If all you need is a clear patch of ground to pitch a tent, then you can simply pull off the road on millions of square miles of Crown lands and simply set up camp.

For listings of private and public campgrounds, contact the tourist office of the province you plan to visit. Brochures and other information on national and provincial parks are also available from the National and Provincial Parks Association of Canada, 69 Sherbourne St., Box 313, Toronto, Ontario M5A 3X7.

SPORTS. Canadians are enthusiastic about all kinds of sports. We have discussed hunting, fishing, and canoeing elsewhere, but the range of sporting activities for both spectators and participants goes well beyond these three staples.

Participant Sports. Swimming is excellent all over the country, whether off the Atlantic coast of the Maritime Provinces, in the thousands of lakes all over the country, or on the Pacific coast of Vancouver Island.

Tennis too is popular throughout the country. There are dozens of golf courses in every province that welcome tourists. And there are about two dozen golf tournaments in Canada, the most important of which is the Canadian Open.

There is skiing wherever there are mountains, and there are helicopter skiing trips in Alberta and British Columbia.

Sailing is common on both coasts and rentals are available in many places. Nova Scotia offers a unique attraction for divers. There are about 3,000 wrecked ships off the coast of Nova Scotia, some of them containing treasure. The provincial Department of Tourism will provide details on the locations of wrecks and where to buy or rent equipment. If you're lucky, you could pay for your trip.

Canada also offers the full range of winter sports: ice skating, tobogganing, snowmobiling, dogsledding, etc. But skiing is probably the most popular winter sport. There are slopes in every province, but those in Québec, Alberta, and British Columbia are the best. The Rockies are also particularly good for climbing and hiking.

Horseback riding is popular all over Alberta.

For something completely unique you might even try curling, either as a spectator or a participant. Best described as lawn bowling on ice, curling has two teams, of four players each, who compete by sliding large stones toward a mark in the center of a circle or "house."

Spectator Sports. Professional organized team sports are widespread. The addition of Toronto and Vancouver franchises in the North American Soccer League has brought new attention to that sport. But baseball, football, and hockey deserve special mention.

Baseball, long a favorite, increased dramatically in popularity when the major leagues expanded into Montréal in 1969. In 1977 the opening of the Montréal Expos' new home at Olympic Stadium and the initial season of the new American League franchise, the Toronto Blue Jays, further stimulated Canadian interest in the game. There are also minor league teams in Vancouver, Edmonton, Calgary, Lethbridge, and Medicine Hat.

Canadian football differs from the game as it is played in the United States. It allows only three downs, employs a 110-yard field, and permits 12 players per team. British Columbia, Calgary, Edmonton, Hamilton, Montréal, Ottawa, Saskatchewan, Toronto, and Winnipeg all field teams in the professional Canadian Football League.

Hockey, however, is still the most popular sport in Canada. Montréal, Toronto, Vancouver, Edmonton, Québec and Winnipeg are represented in the National Hockey League. Hockey goes far beyond the major leagues in Canada, however. Moncton, N.B., and Nova Scotia have teams in the American League. And there are junior leagues (for the 16- to 20-year-olds) in Québec, Ontario, and Western Canada. Schools and clubs sponsor teams everywhere, and pick-up games are ubiquitous.

There are rodeos all over the Prairie Provinces, especially in Alberta.

There is thoroughbred racing in Ontario, Manitoba, Saskatchewan, Alberta, and British Columbia during the spring, summer, and fall. In Québec, Newfoundland, and the other Atlantic Provinces there are a number of harness racing tracks, especially on Prince Edward Island where it is the most popular spectator sport. There is also stock car racing in Manitoba, Saskatchewan, and on Prince Edward Island.

Colleges compete in basketball, football, soccer, swimming and diving, volleyball, wrestling, and hockey, among others. Baseball is extremely popular all over the country; lacrosse is played in Ontario, and rugby and cricket in British Columbia.

 CANOEING. Canada has thousands of miles of rivers and streams. While some of them are mild and gentle, many include rapids and falls. Some of them are great rivers in developed areas, but many more are fast streams running through wilderness. Your degree of expertise and experience will dictate where you will canoe. Beginners will look for waterways in more settled areas. The real pro will head north to the streams and rivers that flow into the Arctic Ocean. The Canadian Government Travel Office offers maps, information, and advice for those in either category. Provincial tourist offices and the federal Department of Northern Development and Indian Affairs can also be of assistance, especially in locating an outfitter to suit your needs.

The Humber and Lloyds-Exploits Rivers in **Newfoundland** are rugged and for experts only. The Kanairiktok River in Labrador is for novices, but Goose River in the same area is only for those familiar with line hauling and portage.

Canoeists on **Prince Edward Island** will have to bring their own gear and will find no river longer than 18 miles.

There are no outfitters in **Nova Scotia** either, but there are fine waters, especially in Kejimkujik National Park.

In **New Brunswick** there are four main canoeing rivers: the St. John, the St. Croix, the Miramichi, and the Restigouche. Each has a number of tributaries feeding into it. Other waterways in the province are used primarily for fishing and do not offer canoeists much of a challenge.

The provincial government of **Québec** has largely restricted canoeing to the confines of provincial and national parks, but this action has hardly limited the sport, since there are 8 major drainage basins flowing through the parks. Other river systems in Québec are off limits at certain times of the year because of pulp driving. It's best to inquire first from the provincial tourist office. A third group of waterways, near James Bay, is restricted by Hydro Québec, the power company.

Canoeing in **Ontario** is an industry. There are nine major drainage basins in northern Ontario and four in southern Ontario. There are dozens of outfitters and hundreds of miles of rivers and lakes, ranging in difficulty from the simplest to the most difficult.

The nine basic drainage basins in **Manitoba** all flow into or out of Lake Winnipeg, and all of them are well charted. The Hayes River and Seal River basins offer the longest trips (about 600 miles each), while others in the province are as short as 10 miles.

The **Saskatchewan** routes are concentrated into three major systems: the Saskatchewan River System, the Churchill River system, and the Lake Athabaska system. Each offers its own special pleasures, but the last of them includes 6 old fur trade canoe routes, which add an extra, romantic, dimension to canoeing there.

Alberta offers canoeists the most varied terrain in Canada. There are rugged mountains, flat plains, and Pre-Cambrian Shield terrain. The Bow River in Banff National Park is perhaps the most popular canoe route in the province.

British Columbia is almost as varied as Alberta. The range of routes is from the easiest novice streams to the treacherous whitewater Thompson River, where upendings are almost inevitable and where at least three canoes should travel together to assure rescues.

Three rivers in the **Yukon**—the Yukon, the Teslin, and the Stewart—can be tackled by those of intermediate skill. But the Big Salmon, the Klondike and others should not be attempted without considerable experience. All nonresidents must register with the Mounted Police in Whitehorse for their own protection.

Only the most experienced canoeists should try the rivers of the **Northwest Territories**—and even for them rivers like the Coppermine, the South Redstone, the South Nahanni, the Kazan, and the Dubawnt can be dangerous.

Two excellent sources for planning a canoe trip are: *Wild Rivers,* a booklet published by the Canadian government and available through Supplies and Services Canada, Printing and Publishing Office, 45 Sacre Coeur, Ottawa, Ont., K1A 0S9; specify which region you're interested in; 613–997–2560; and Nick Nickel's *Canoe Canada* (Van Nostrand-Reinhold).

FISHING. Each Canadian province offers something for the fisherman. Bag limits, seasons, and licensing regulations vary from province to province and the prospective angler should inquire at provincial tourist offices in advance.

Newfoundland offers cod, mackerel, salmon, and sea trout in the Atlantic and speckled trout and rainbow trout in the 30 percent of Newfoundland that is water. The booklet *Fishing in Newfoundland* is available from the *The Wildlife Division,* 810 Bldg., Plazaville, Suite 4750., St. John's, Nfld. A1C 5T7; 709—737 –2815.

The same species are available on **Prince Edward Island.** The deep-sea fishing—especially for tuna—is best in the eastern part of the province. The *Fish and Wildlife Branch,* P.O. Box 2000, Charlottetown, P.E.I. C1A 7N8, 902—892 –0311, is the primary source of information.

Nova Scotia has the most stringent freshwater restrictions in Canada, but the availability of Atlantic salmon, speckled trout, and striped bass make the trouble worthwhile. Nonresidents, for instance, are required to hire a guide for each three fishermen. Going for saltwater fish such as mackerel, cod, swordfish, and bluefin tuna is also popular—and almost as restricted. Inquire at *The Wildlife Division,* P.O. Box 516, Kentville, N.S. B4N 3X3, (902) 678–8921, for details.

The salmon, trout, and black bass in **New Brunswick** are abundant and fine. However, many of the streams and rivers are leased to private freeholders, either individuals or clubs. A daily licence is available for some waters. Inquire at the *Fish and Wildlife Branch,* 349 King St., P.O. Box 6000, Fredericton, N.B. E3B 5H1; (506) 453–2440.

The lakes of **Québec** hold trout, bass, pike, and landlocked salmon (called "ouananiche"). The tributaries of the St. Lawrence River teem with brook trout and landlocked salmon. Licenses can be exclusive, as in New Brunswick, or to individuals. And, although the season varies with the species and the location, you may fish for most species in most places from June 15 through Labor Day—provided you have a license. Further information is available from *The Department of Recreation, Fish, and Game,* Place de la Capitale, 150 St. Cyrille Blvd. E., 15th Fl., Québec, P.Q. G1R 4Y1; (418) 643–2266.

Just about every kind of North American freshwater game fish is available in some part of **Ontario.** Bass, perch, trout, walleye, salmon, muskies, pike, and whitefish in all their forms can be had either within a short drive of Ontario or deep in the wilderness. Unfortunately, the variety of regulations is almost as great as the variety of fish. Get full details from *The Wildlife Branch, Ministry of Natural Resources,* 99 Wellesley St. W., Room 3304, Whitney Block, Queen's Park, Toronto, Ont. M7A 1W3; (416) 965–4251.

Manitoba offers lake trout, brook trout, pike, grayling, walleye, Hudson Bay salmon, and smallmouth bass. It also offers a winter fishing season, but some areas require a guide. (You can even hunt whales, with a camera, out of Churchill.) *The Game and Fisheries Branch* of the Department of Mines and Natural Resources, P.O. Box 24, 1495 James St., Winnipeg, Man. R3H 0W9, (204) 786–9173, issues licenses and offers assistance.

The lakes and rivers of **Saskatchewan** hold lake trout, pike, grayling, perch, and walleye. The small streams contain trout, whitefish, and splake. The *Fisheries Branch,* 3211 Albert St., Regina, Sask. S4S 5W6, 306—565–2884, will provide details.

Alberta is a paradise for sportsfishermen with its trout in streams; pike, walleye, and perch in lakes; grayling, goldeye, and whitefish in rivers. Fishing is permitted in the mountain national parks, but regulations are different from those for waters outside the parks. The *Fish and Wildlife Branch,* 9945 108th

St., Edmonton, Alta. T5K 2C9, 403-427-0326, is the primary source of information.

The salmon fishing in **British Columbia** is unparalleled, even though only two of the five available species may be taken in nontidal waters. There are also plentiful char, grayling, whitefish, bass, perch, and nine varieties of trout in the streams and rivers. The *Fish and Wildlife Branch,* 780 Blanchard St., Victoria, B.C. V8V 1X5, 604—387-1628, will tell you everything you need to know about fees and regulations.

The **Yukon Territory** has a wide variety of trout, salmon, grayling, and pike even in waters right off the main roads, so fishermen don't have to go into the remote wilderness. For up-to-date information write: *Department of Renewable Resources,* P.O. Box 2703, Whitehorse, Yuk. Y1A 2C6; (403) 667-5221.

Commercial fishing dominates the **Northwest Territories,** especially at Great Slave Lake. But there are still sufficient amounts of game fish, most spectacularly the giant lake trout in Great Bear Lake. Information is available from *Department of Renewable Resources,* P.O. Box 1320, Yellowknife, N.W.T. X1A 2L9; (403) 873-7411.

HUNTING. Bag limits and firearms regulations vary widely from province to province. Handguns are not allowed anywhere, but nonresidents may take any other equipment they need into any province. Guides are required in many places and available almost everywhere. *Good Hunting in Canada,* a booklet offering information about restrictions, game, outfitters, firearms, and licences, is available from the Canadian Government Travel Bureau. Provincial offices listed in the section on fishing can also be helpful.

The following list gives some idea of the variety of game available.

Newfoundland: moose, caribou, bear, rabbit, snipe, wild goose, and duck.

Prince Edward Island: small game only.

Nova Scotia: moose, caribou, bear, wildcat, fox, raccoon, rabbit and hare, marten, beaver, mink, otter, weasel, muskrat, ruffed grouse, partridge, pheasants, duck, snipe, and woodcock.

New Brunswick: deer, rabbit, ruffed grouse, spruce, partridge, migratory game birds, bear, bobcat, fox, raccoon, skunk, porcupine, groundhog, and crow.

Québec: moose, deer, bear, caribou, wolf, small game, partridge, goose, ptarmigan, pheasant, grouse, and waterfowl. (A warning here. Much of Québec's best hunting areas are under lease, although many leaseholders permit individuals to come onto their preserves for a fee.)

Ontario: deer, moose, black bear, small game, grouse, and waterfowl.

Manitoba: deer, moose, bear, and caribou.

Saskatchewan: deer, elk, moose, caribou, deer, bear, and a variety of birds.

Alberta: moose, deer, caribou, bear, coyote, antelope, wapiti, mountain sheep and goat, elk, waterfowl, and pheasant and other birds.

British Columbia: mountain goat and sheep, black and grizzly bear, moose, wapiti, caribou, deer, wolf, cougar, and waterfowl. (The difficulty of reaching the north central part of British Columbia is amply rewarded by the abundance of game.)

Yukon Territory: moose, caribou, black and brown bear, mountain goat and sheep, grouse, ptarmigan, goose, and duck.

Northwest Territories: Large game is pretty much the only thing that makes a hunting trip here worthwhile. The Commissioner of the Territories distributes licenses.

Other Useful Addresses. In British Columbia: *B.C. Fish and Game Assoc.,* 780 Blanchard St., Victoria, B.C. V8V 1X5. **In Alberta:** *Alberta Fish and Game Assoc.,* 6024–103rd St., Edmonton, Alta. T6H 2H6. **In Manitoba:** *Winnipeg Game and Fish Assoc.,* 301–289½ Garry, Winnipeg, Man. **In Ontario:** *Ontario Federation of Anglers and Hunters,* Box 28, 169 Charlotte St., Peterborough, Ontario K9J 6Y5. **In Québec:** *Montréal Anglers and Hunters,* 319 St. Zoteque Est., Montréal, Qué. H2S 1L5.

 HOLIDAYS. National public holidays in Canada are: New Years Day (January 1); Good Friday (the Friday before Easter); Easter Monday (the Monday following Easter); Victoria Day (the Monday preceding May 25); Dominion Day (July 1); Labour Day (the first Monday in September); Thanksgiving Day (the second Monday in October); Remembrance Day (November 11); Christmas Day (December 25).

When a holiday falls on a Saturday or Sunday, it is observed on the following Monday. In recent years there has been a tendency to observe all holidays on the nearest Monday to the actual date. Remember, though, that many stores and resort attractions remain open on holidays even though banks, schools, and government offices may close. Remembrance Day, for instance, is almost exclusively a school and government holiday.

In addition to the national holidays there are also a number of provincial holidays.

Newfoundland: St. Patrick's Day, (March 17); St. George's Day (around April 23); Discovery Day (second to last Monday in June); Memorial Day (July 3); Orangemen's Day (July 12); and Boxing Day (December 26).

Nova Scotia: Sir John A. MacDonald's Birthday (January 11); Boxing Day (December 26).

New Brunswick: Boxing Day (December 26).

Prince Edward Island: Boxing Day (December 26).

Québec: Epiphany (January 6); Ash Wednesday (first day of Lent), Ascension Day (40 days after Easter), St. Jean Baptiste Day (June 24); All Saints' Day (November 1); and Immaculate Conception (December 8).

Ontario: Civic Holiday (first Monday in August); Boxing Day (December 26).

Manitoba: Civic Holiday (first Monday in August); Boxing Day (December 26).

Saskatchewan: Boxing Day (December 26).

Alberta: Boxing Day (December 26).

British Columbia: Boxing Day (December 26).

Yukon Territory: Discovery Day (third Monday in August).

Northwest Territories: Civic Holiday (first Monday in August); Boxing Day (December 26).

 BUSINESS HOURS. Opening times for stores, shops, and supermarkets are similar to those in the United States: 9 A.M. to 5 P.M., Monday through Saturday. Blue laws (enforced Sunday closings) are in effect in much of Canada, so don't expect to get much souvenir shopping done on Sunday. Retail stores are generally open on Thursday and Friday evenings; most shopping malls till 9 P.M. Traditionally, Canadian banks open only between 10 A.M. and 3 P.M., Monday through Friday. But the trend is toward extended hours and Saturday-morning openings. Drugstores and convenience shops in major cities are often open until 11 P.M.

DRINKING LAWS. Rules and regulations governing what kinds of alcoholic beverages may be sold, at what hours and to whom, vary from province to province.

In *Newfoundland* the legal drinking age is 19 and women are permitted in taverns and cocktail lounges.

On *Prince Edward Island* liquor stores are open six days a week for upwards of 12 hours a day. The legal drinking age is 18.

New Brunswick allows women in taverns, and you must be 19 to buy alcohol.

Nova Scotia allows women in all drinking establishments. The legal age to buy alcohol is 19.

In *Ontario* the drinking age is 19, but some communities are completely dry and others impose severe restrictions.

Québec does not allow women in taverns, and the few liquor stores close early. But cocktail lounges and cabarets stay open until 2 A.M. and 3 A.M., respectively, in Montréal. The legal drinking age is 18.

Mixed-company drinking is legal everywhere in *Manitoba* except in beer parlors. The legal drinking age is 18.

Mixed drinking is legal for anyone in *Saskatchewan* over the age of 19.

Alberta imposes no drinking restrictions on women, and the liquor prices are the lowest in Canada. The legal age is 18.

British Columbia allows mixed drinking for those over 19.

The Yukon permits drinking for anyone 19 and over.

In the *Northwest Territories* the legal drinking age is 19.

MAIL. Stamps can be purchased at any post office in Canada, often from your hotel desk, or from coin-operated vending machines located in transportation terminals, banks, and some shops (stationers and drugstores, for example). They cost the same from a machine as from the post office, but the machines only sell in 50¢ lots. Postal rates are listed in the table below. Post offices are usually open during business hours and sometimes on Saturdays.

Stamped mail can be posted in the letter drops at the post office, in the letter chutes of some hotels and office buildings, in the red mailboxes on many street corners. Or you may leave it with the hotel desk clerk, who will post it for you.

If you expect to receive mail while traveling, you can have it addressed to you in care of your hotel(s).

There is no separate air mail rate for letters or postcards posted in Canada for delivery within the country or to the United States. Mail for distant points is automatically airlifted. The following postal rates, in Canadian money, were in effect as of January 1982, but they are subject to change—usually up, not down—so check when you buy stamps to be sure.

Letters & Postcards

Within Canada	32¢ for the first ounce
To the United States	37¢ for the first ounce
Air Mail to all other countries	60¢ for the first ounce and for Mailgrams

TELEPHONE. Coin-operated telephones are available almost everywhere. To use the coin telephone, just follow the instructions on the phone box. Local calls usually cost 25¢ and can be dialed directly. If you don't reach your party, your money is refunded to you automatically when you hang up.

For long-distance calls, have plenty of coins available unless you are calling "collect." The operator may ask for enough change to cover the initial time period before she connects you. To place a call outside Canada, dial "0" and ask for the overseas operator. You can, however, dial any point in the United States from most places in Canada directly.

In hotels, your switchboard operator will either place your outside call for you, or tell you how to dial directly from your room. The telephone charges will be added to your hotel bill (although many times local calls are free), and you will pay for them when you check out.

TELEGRAPH. To send a telegram to a destination anywhere within Canada, ask for assistance at your hotel, or go to the nearest CNCP telegraph office. Overseas cablegrams can also be dispatched by CNCP.

LEAVING CANADA. U.S. Customs. American citizens and other residents of the U.S. who visit Canada for more than 48 hours and who have claimed no exemption during the previous 30 days are entitled to bring in duty free up to $400 (retail value) worth of foreign purchases. The items may be intended for personal use or as gifts for those back home. They all count, even if some are personal effects you have already worn.

All your purchases are to accompany you, and it is wise (and simpler when inspection time comes) to try to put everything, or as much as possible, into one suitcase or carryall.

Also try to keep your purchase receipts together and handy, in case you have to produce them.

Members of a family can pool their exemptions because each separate member, including all minors, is entitled to the $400 exemption.

Small gifts under $50 in value may be mailed home to friends duty-free, but not more than one package to any one address. Such packages cannot contain perfumes, tobacco, or liquor. The outside of such a package must be marked: "Unsolicited Gift, value under $50," followed by the contents of the package.

Packages mailed to yourself are subject to duty. Your best bet, again, is to carry everything with you. Further information will be provided by the nearest U.S. Customs office or by U.S. Customs Service, Washington, D.C. 20229.

Great Britain. You may bring into the U.K. the following goods duty-free: 200 cigarettes, or 100 cigarillos, or 50 cigars, or 250 grams tobacco; plus one liter of alcohol of more than 38.8% proof, or 2 liters of alcohol not more than 38.8% proof, or 2 liters of fortified or sparkling wine and 2 liters of still table wine; plus 50 grams of perfume and ¼ liter of toilet water; plus other goods to the value of £28.

THE CANADIAN SCENE

AN INTRODUCTION TO CANADA

By Way of Background

by
NICHOLAS ACOCELLA
and
CATHERINE RODD

Nicholas Acocella is a freelance writer and traveler with a special interest in Canada. Catherine Rodd is a Toronto-based freelance writer who has traveled extensively in Canada.

To many people Canada is the other half of the North American continent. The country's proximity to the more prominent and more populous United States has obscured both the differences between the two countries and the rich excitement and variety Canada holds for the traveler.

And yet, Canada, which covers more than half of the continent, is a diverse and fascinating land of spectacular mountains and level plains, near-deserts and glacial tundra, rich forests and fertile farmland, fishing villages and modern cities, sophisticated French-Canadians, and native Eskimos and Indians.

The Canadian Population

There are well over 24 million Canadians. They are among the most affluent and sophisticated people in the world. Largely for reasons of climate and geography, about 85 percent of them live within 200 miles of the United States border. One critic ruefully observed that the Canadian population is like one long clothesline strung across the 49th parallel.

Despite their proximity to the U.S., Canadians stalwartly maintain they have a very different approach to life from their American counterparts. Urban areas are still largely free of the violence and crime that have turned so many American cities into ghost towns after dark. U.S. visitors are often amazed to find that at night they can walk the streets of large cities such as Toronto, Montréal, and Vancouver quite safely. Peace, order, and good government are the principles which underly the Canadian constitution and spell out the essence of Canadian attitudes. (As in cities everywhere, however, it would be foolhardy to venture into deserted areas or take unknown shortcuts.) Main avenues are sometimes the most intriguing aspects of a city at night—suddenly, once the sedate business crowd has left, the streets become the parade ground for the ultra-chic and the bizarre.

Underpinning the sometimes outlandish manifestations of modern lifestyle is the Canadian passion for tradition and strong belief in the order of things. British visitors are amused to find that in some ways Canadians are more English than the English. For example, in Victoria high tea is a revered ritual at the stately Empress Hotel and the word "Royal" prefaces distinguished institutions such as research groups and ballet companies throughout the country.

Indeed, nowhere is the Canadian desire to maintain tradition more apparent than in Québec. Québec is Canada's only official French-speaking province in an otherwise English-speaking country; thus devotion to Québecois culture is intense and has ensured its survival. The narrow streets of old Québec City are reminiscent of those in France. Montréal, Canada's Paris, resounds with rich cosmopolitan flair. Since the election of the Parti Québecois government in 1976, French has become the official language of the province. Don't let this deter you from sampling the delightful atmosphere of Québec, for even the roughest attempts to speak French are appreciated and most store clerks and restaurant personnel will speak to you in English if the going gets rough.

Although Québec is the focus of French culture in Canada, there are also strong French populations in Ontario, New Brunswick (officially bilingual), and Manitoba. You will also find Francophones in Nova Scotia, Prince Edward Island, and Newfoundland.

French customs and culture were not always embraced in Canada— they had to be fought for. When the English conquered Québec in 1763 and assumed control of Canada, the French, who had settled the area long before the British came, were relegated to minority status. Resentment of their second-class citizenship festered for generations. Around the middle of the 20th century, French-Canadians began moving from their traditional bases in rural areas to the vibrant and opportunity-laden, English-speaking centers of Montréal and Québec. Their anger soon galvanized into a serious political movement to gain recognition of French achievements and contributions to the nation. In the early 1960's the word "separatist" was first heard. By the 1970's the notion of an independent Québec became the platform of the Parti Québecois which now governs the population. In May 1980 the Parti Québecois held their long-awaited referendum on sovereignty-association. The notion guaranteed an independent government with economic ties to the rest of Canada. The majority of Québecois voted against the referendum but the motion for separatism is still in the air.

Despite its conflicts, ethnic diversity is still a quality on which Canada prides itself and thereby denies the North American melting-pot theory. The dominant background is British, followed by French. Immigrants from Europe, Africa, Asia, and the West Indies also enrich the Canadian mosaic. Just as older Canadians cling to their past, these newer Canadians also retain many of their native customs. Like immigrants to the United States, new Canadians tend to settle in areas which already house people from their homeland. Thus cities have China-towns, little Italies, Portuguese and Greek areas, and so on. Unlike the United States, pride in ethnic origin is reinforced and encouraged as people call themselves Chinese-Canadians, Scottish-Canadians, Italian-Canadians, etc. Finally, despite their inaccessibility and small numbers, there are the Indian and Inuit communities, Canada's original inhabitants.

Native Canadians

The Native population is altogether unique. Their ancestors probably came from Asia, across the Bering Strait, many centuries ago. When the Europeans "discovered" America and began to explore it, there were just over 200,000 Indians in Canada, about one-third of whom lived in the North.

The early contacts with European hunters and trappers brought tribes into each other's lands in search of pelts and tempered somewhat the old nomadic life. As contact increased in frequency, some Indians were drawn to trade, but civilization's gifts to the native North Americans also included hunger, pestilence, and warfare. By the 1880's there were only half as many Indians in Canada as there had been four centuries earlier.

Today there are about 300,000 Indians. Over 70 percent of them live on reserves that range in size from a few acres to about 500 square miles. The Department of Indian Affairs and Northern Development supervises these reserves for the welfare of the Indians and administers a variety of educational, housing, business, and construction programs designed to bring the Indians into the mainstream of Canadian social and economic life.

The other 25 percent of the Indian population lives outside the reserves and within the Canadian society at large. Generally, they have integrated well into a pluralistic society and can be found in just about every walk of life, from the professional to the laboring classes.

The Inuit, almost all of whom live in the North, number fewer than 20,000, but they may be the most fascinating people in Canada. Once a coastal people who ranged quite far to the south along the Pacific Coast, they hunted walrus, seal, and whale, to provide all their needs—food, clothing, and lodging.

For decades virtually the only contact the Inuit had with Europeans was with whalers and traders who compromised somewhat the Stone Age nature of the quest for caribou and lake fish by introducing simple weapons and tools. Later, The Hudson's Bay Company institutionalized this trade.

It wasn't until the airplane made the Arctic reasonably accessible that the isolation of the Inuit diminished. The construction of communications installations and weather stations has transformed life in the North, shrinking somewhat the vast distances between the small settlements, reducing the sense of isolation, and bringing radio and telephone communications, and even television, to the people of the Arctic and Subarctic areas.

The Inuit adapted quickly to modern lifestyle. Whereas once hunting and fishing were virtually the only employment, today there are tentative efforts at small-scale urban living and at employment in the burgeoning petroleum and mining industries. Eskimo art was once an exotic and rare treat; today cooperatives market Inuit carvings of bone, stone, and ivory throughout the country. Once wards of the state, today the Inuit govern themselves and have three elected representatives on the territorial council.

The modernization of the Inuit created some concern for the fate of their indigenous culture and led to the formation of Inuit Tapirisat of Canada, a government-run association that protects the interests of the Inuit, studies land claims and land use, and offers legal assistance and cultural support.

Regionalism

Regionalism, as well as place of origin, has had an effect on the shaping of Canada's people. Canadians are, by and large, friendly people who enjoy meeting foreigners and treat them well. A certain defensiveness about the United States is not uncommon, but this feeling generally does not extend to individual Americans, with whom they feel a certain kinship.

The best way to meet Canadians is to take part in their activities. They are a very socially minded nation, and attendance at sports events or, if possible, local social and civic events will bring you into direct contact with Canadians at their best.

In the Atlantic Provinces people tend to be a bit more reserved and reticient than are the residents of Ontario, but a sincere interest in their rural and Celtic backgrounds will usually bring them out.

To make the acquaintance of the Québecois or old Acadians, a working knowledge of French is almost a necessity everywhere except in the large cities, and even in some urban quarters. The rural French-

Canadians offer the double barrier of langauge and inbred rural reserve, but a little French goes a long way with these basically friendly people.

In the West people are naturally outgoing. They live in the land of big skies and wide country and their collective personality has borrowed generously from the openness of their natural surroundings. This characteristic predisposes them to welcome all kinds of foreigners.

The people of British Columbia are equally open for different reasons. Like Californians, they live at the end of the open road, the place people came to. And the British in Victoria share the congenital politeness of their cousins in the mother country.

Northerners are an independent lot for the most part. They wait for strangers to prove themselves in the skills required for survival in the rough North. But anyone who demonstrates an ability to cope—or sometimes even an appreciation of that ability—will do fine.

Only the Indians and Eskimos who have remained in the old life are unapproachable. The more sophisticated of them are often very forthright and willing to discuss their ancient cultures.

Physical Features

Canada, the giant of the North American continent, is larger than every other country in the world except the Soviet Union. To state simply that Canada covers 3,851,809 square miles is a fact not easily comprehended. Perhaps it is more meaningful to point out that Montréal, Québec is as close to Paris, France, as it is to Dawson City in the Yukon. Or that Halifax, Nova Scotia is closer to Caracas, Venezuela, than it is to Calgary, Alberta.

Canada's ten provinces and two territories stretch over 4,000 miles from the capes of Newfoundland on the Atlantic to the Queen Charlotte Islands in the Pacific, and almost 3,000 miles from the temperate Great Lakes to Cape Columbia on Ellesmere Island, within 500 miles of the North Pole.

In between, the glaciers of the Ice Age have carved enormous valleys, and, when they melted, filled deep lakes that now cover about 7.6 percent of Canada with about 15 percent of the world's fresh water.

In other millennia volcanoes and earthquakes pushed vast mountain ranges up out of the earth. In still others, erosion and glaciation compressed and contorted older mountains.

These physical disruptions have left Canada with six distinguishabl' geographic regions, each with its own characteristic features and attractions.

The Atlantic Provinces. This Eastern Canadian region includes Newfoundland, and the Maritime Provinces of Prince Edward Island, Nova Scotia and New Brunswick. This area, along with southeastern Québec, is a less altitudinous extension of the Appalachian mountain range in the United States. This region alternates between rugged, wooded hills and rich, fertile valleys cut by numerous rivers.

The approximately 15 percent of Canada's more than 24 million people who live in this region make their living primarily by lumbering and farming in the interior and fishing along the coast.

The St. Lawrence Lowlands. The most productive region of Canada and the home of about 60 percent of its population, the St. Lawrence lowlands in Ontario and southern Québec is a rich area of farms and orchards as well as the industrial center of the country. The single most important geophysical feature of the area is the St. Lawrence River, which drains over 300,000 square miles on its way to the Atlantic Ocean. This river and the waterway that accompanies it supply the hydroelectric power and carry fossil fuel for the region's factories. But, more important, they provide a highway from the Atlantic Ocean to the heartland of the continent.

Above Québec City the St. Lawrence Valley gives way to the Laurentian Hills, which in turn fall off into a fertile valley stretching into Ontario. Prosperous dairy farms, fruit orchards, and tobacco plantations have replaced most of the elm, ash, walnut, and maple forests which the original French and English settlers found there, and make it the most prosperous region in Canada even though it is only 150 miles across at its widest point.

The Pre-Cambrian Shield. The largest of Canada's geographic regions is the Pre-Cambrian (or Canadian) Shield, which reaches out in a huge horseshoe around Hudson Bay, covering about 1.6 million square miles, or roughly half of the entire country.

This vast expanse sweeps southwestward from Labrador, across most of Québec and Ontario, up through eastern Manitoba and northern Saskatchewan and Alberta, then along the eastern end of the valley of the Mackenzie River, Canada's second great waterway, up to the Arctic Circle.

Sparsely populated and virtually unsuited for cultivation, except in the clay belt south of James Bay, this is a region of endless forests, mineral deposits, and rivers. These features make the Pre-Cambrian Shield extremely rugged—and extremely rich.

The numerous rivers flowing into Hudson Bay are sources of valuable hydroelectric power and an equally valuable means of transportation. Since there are few roads, these rivers—and the lakes between them—enable trappers to penetrate deep into the wilderness in pursuit of fur-bearing animals, as they have done for over 300 years. These water highways also make possible the area's timber industry. Thousands of acres of timber are cut each year and the logs are floated down the rivers and shipped by raft across the lakes to mills where they are processed into pulp and paper.

Another source of wealth in the area is mining. Some of the oldest rocks in the world are in the Pre-Cambrian substratum. And while the value of the rocks themselves is almost purely scientific, the gold, silver, nickel, iron, copper, platinum, radium, cobalt, and uranium that they contain is commercially valuable. Indeed, Canada is the world's largest supplier of nickel and silver, and ranks second in the production of gold and uranium.

Finally, the region is a sportsman's paradise. The hunting, fishing, and canoeing are spectacular even though (or perhaps because) the remoteness of the area and the nature of the terrain limit these activities to only the most hardy.

The Plains. The Interior Plains lie to the west and southwest of the Pre-Cambrian Shield. The southern portion of the Plains, the prairies, which stretch across southern Manitoba, Saskatchewan, and Alberta, is mostly flat and fertile. The elevation increases in three steps as you travel west, and even in the rolling foothills of the Rockies in western Alberta there is excellent farmland 3,000 feet above sea level.

The northern part of the Plains runs through Alberta and the Mackenzie River Valley for 2,635 miles, where the farmland is wooded all the way to the Arctic Circle.

The almost 1,000 miles of rich farmland between the Pre-Cambrian Shield and the Rocky Mountains are wheat and cattle country. The rich soil is accessible and productive, and even though the natural limitations of the area—a short growing season, minimal rainfall, and frequent early frost—make life precarious for the farmers, scientific methods and raw determination have made Canada the second largest exporter of grain in the world.

The rolling grassland of southwestern Saskatchewan and southern Alberta were once home to huge herds of bison. Today cattle graze on this part of the Plains and provide beef for eastern markets.

The Interior Plains also provide gold and coal. And near Calgary and to the north of Edmonton are Canada's most significant petroleum deposits.

The Canadian Cordillera. The Canadian Cordillera, the western region of Canada, is the northernmost extension of the great chain of mountains that forms a spine through the body of the Americas from the South American Andes to the Alaska Range.

The Canadian segment of this great chain of mountains runs in three parallel lines: the massive and rugged Canadian Rockies in western Alberta and eastern British Columbia; the Pelly, Selwyn, and Mackenzie Mountains in the Yukon and the western part of the Northwest Territories, along with the Cassiar Mountains in northern British Columbia and the Selkirk Mountains to the south; and the coastal range that extends the Cascades of Washington State all the way into Alaska. In the extreme south a narrow plain separates the coastal range from the submerged mountains whose peaks rise above the sea as the offshore archipelago of Vancouver and the Queen Charlotte Islands.

In between these mountains there are river basins flowing to the Pacific fertile plateaus of farmland and orchards; sizable deposits of minerals, especially copper ore; and gorges and moraines with few passes around them.

The highest point in Canada, Mount Logan (19,850 feet), is in the northern Rockies, in the Yukon. And scenic Banff National Park—with its hot springs, its 140-square-mile frozen lake at Columbia Icefield, and its abundant wildlife—is in the south, on the Alberta-British Columbia border.

Canada Cordillera varies from year-round snow on mountain peaks to the mildness of the coastal plain just below the tremendous Douglas fir trees on the western slopes of the coastal range. Once much larg..., like the central valley of Canada, most of this plain is now submerged, leaving only a small area in southwestern British Columbia, including the major Pacific port of Vancouver, the third-largest city in the country. Despite its small size, this plain is one of the most economically successful areas of Canada.

The Arctic North. The sixth geographic region of Canada is the Arctic North, which includes the northern part of the Yukon and Northwest Territories, three of the ten largest islands in the world (Baffin, Ellesmere, and Victoria), four other large islands (Banks, Devon, Melville, and Axel Heiberg), and numerous smaller islands.

This area, covered by ice the whole year, was virtually unknown until the advent of the airplane. It is still almost completely uninhabited and inaccessible. Its unquestioned mineral resources remain largely unexploited. Its location, however, makes possible an average of 20 hours of daylight in summer, and on June 21 near the delta of the Mackenzie River you can experience almost 24 consecutive hours of sunlight.

Government and Administration

Officially Canada is a monarchy ruled by Queen Elizabeth II, the titular head of state. Actually the British monarch has no power in the scheme of government and politics, and exercises even less influence over these matters in Canada than in England.

Canada's government is a curious mixture of the parliamentary system of Great Britain and the federal system of the United States. As such, it combines many of the best features of the two great traditions of Anglo-Saxon democracy: a composite executive from Great Britain and proportional representation from the United States.

Canada has been an independent country since 1867 when the government of Great Britain passed the British North America (BNA) Act by which the provinces of Upper and Lower Canada, Nova Scotia, and New Brunswick became the Dominion of Canada. (The other provinces joined later.) Up until 1982, the BNA served as the constitution for Canada and was amended a number of times with Britain's approval.

In 1931, Canada became a sovereign state, not a colony of Great Britain—but not a republic either. Britain was asked to retain control of Canada's central government until the provinces could agree on an amending procedure that would protect provincial rights. In 1982, through the efforts of Canadian Prime Minister Pierre Elliott Trudeau, a new constitution was approved by all provinces except Québec. The Constitution Act was signed in a ceremony by Queen Elizabeth II, thus formally ending Britain's nominal role in Canadian Government.

Although Canada now has its own constitution, it will remain a member of the British Commonwealth and will continue to share Britain's monarch. The monarch's role is confined to opening Parliament (with a speech written by the majority party) and awarding honors. And even these duties she exercises almost always through her representative, the Governor-General. This role, too, is largely ceremonial.

In addition to the Governor-General, the Queen is represented by ten Lieutenant-Governors, one in each province. They serve the same function in the provincial capitals that the Governor-General serves in Ottawa, the national capital.

However, the actual government of Canada is in the hands of the Prime Minister and his cabinet. The Prime Minister is the leader of the majority party in the national Parliament and is chosen by those members of the lower branch of the Parliament, the House of Commons, who belong to his party. If no party holds a majority of the seats, the Governor-General will call upon the leader of the party with a plurality of the seats to form either a coalition or a minority government.

The Prime Minister selects the members of his cabinet from his party colleagues—usually with an eye toward regional balance—and appoints them to head the various ministries—Foreign Affairs, Finance,

Defence, etc. As in England, each minister must be a member of one or the other houses of Parliament.

As the first among equal members of this collective executive, the Prime Minister leads his cabinet in introducing legislation. He may also ask the Governor-General to assemble or dissolve Parliament.

The Cabinet as a unit selects and appoints the members of the upper chamber, the Senate; ambassadors; superior, district, and county judges; territorial commissioners; and the lieutenant-governors. It is also responsible for maintaining a military establishment, declaring war and making peace, ratifying treaties, issuing currency, directing the economy, and administering the governmental departments.

The legislature is bicameral. The 104 members of the Senate are appointed by the government. Theoretically, the Senate has coequal power with the House of Commons, but, while it often reviews bills carefully and sometimes conducts its own investigations of national problems, it rarely rejects a bill passed by the lower chamber.

The House of Commons has 282 members elected by constituencies with roughly equal numbers of voters. Members are elected every five years, or sooner if the Prime Minister so decides. Three major parties compete in these elections: the Liberal Party, the Progressive Conservative Party, and the New Democratic Party.

The Canadian courts are independent of the political process, and judges serve for life. At the national level there is a Federal Court of Canada, dealing with admiralty, aeronautic and patent law, and a Supreme Court, which may review the decisions of provincial courts. (The Supreme Court has nine members, three of whom must be from Québec because of that province's adherence to Napoleonic Law.)

Most police functions reside with the municipalities or, where there are no municipalities or where they are too small, with the provinces. However, the historic and colorful Royal Canadian Mounted Police, a federal force, keeps the peace in the territories and enforces drug, smuggling, and immigration laws.

The Canadian military is a unified command of about 80,000 officers and enlisted personnel, both men and women. In 1968 the Royal Canadian Navy, the Canadian Army, and the Royal Canadian Air Force were brought together into the Canadian Armed Forces, for which there is a common support system, common training, and a common uniform.

Each of the provinces has a governmental structure parallel to that of the federal government, complete with provincial parliaments, cabinets, and premiers. These provincial governments bear the major responsibility for establishing municipalities, building highways, and legislating in the areas of health and education, but the federal cabinet has the power to undo any act passed by a provincial parliament within one year of its passage.

The Yukon Territory and the Northwest Territories are directly under the jurisdiction of the federal government in Ottawa, which appoints the resident commissioners. In recent years, however, the Territories have enjoyed an increasing degree of self-government.

Education is primarily a provincial affair, although there is a tendency toward uniformity—except in Québec, where the French educational system prevails. Public schools, which are free and compulsory up to the age of 15 or 16, according to province, are operated by municipalities or in small towns by the provinces. Parochial schools form a parallel system in some provinces. In Québec, for instance, there are Protestant separate schools, while Ontario has Catholic separate schools. In Newfoundland *all* the schools are run by religious organizations subsidized by the provincial government. Québec has the second-highest percentage of students under religious instruction. In addition to those in Protestant separate schools, about 10 percent of all students there attend schools run by Roman Catholic religious orders.

Higher education is also largely run by the provinces, although some smaller colleges are run by Roman Catholic groups. Subsidies reduce tuition at state schools to less than $1,000 per year. There are 57 colleges and universities in the country with enrollments of over 200, but only 25 of them have 5,000 or more full-time day students.

Final Notes

Canada is an enigmatic country. It is both foreign and familiar with a vast terrain as varied and adventurous as the people who populate it. It is steeped in history, yet it's modern and cosmopolitan. Canada is a land worth exploring intensively—even though it is unlikely that it can ever be known in its entirety.

THE ARTS IN CANADA

Film, Music, Theater, and Fine Arts

by
ROY BONGARTZ

Roy Bongartz, a travel writer with a special interest in the arts, is a frequent contributor to newspapers and magazines.

A real cultural explosion is taking place in Canada, traceable to the artistic ferment from dozens of different nationalities and traditions working at their arts in a new and vast land with apparently limitless horizons. The sheer volume of activity in every field has tripled or quadrupled in a mere 25 years thanks to the new spirit of experimentation brought mainly by young immigrants from Europe and the other continents. Besides this human artistic resource, the government stimulates the arts further in the many excellent support programs of the Canada Council, which provides financial aid with a minimum of interference. Comments Canadian historian George Woodcock: "The Canada Council is probably the best example of Canada's characteristic pluralism, by which the state provides the means for individual artists to follow their vocations in just the same way as, with subsidized railways and gifts of land, it provided the means for individual farmers to populate the prairies."

The Fine Arts

At the head of the burgeoning cultural expansion in Canada are the legions of painters, sculptors, and other visual adepts who have established three influential centers of creativity—Montréal, Toronto, and Vancouver—that are challenging the traditional pre-eminence of Paris and the moneyed foothold of New York in this field. They can be traced back to the Group of Seven, the first Canadians who in the 1920's reached out into their own landscape and people for visual inspiration instead of copying styles from other countries. Says Canadian critic George Woodcock: "The Group of Seven has a position in the history of Canadian art out of all proportion to the talents of any of its members because it liberated artists from their dependence on foreign masters and influences."

This preoccupation with Canadian subject matter for inspiration in all the arts has sometimes made objective criticism difficult because, as Robert Fulford, editor of the magazine *Saturday Night*, says, "It is a process which makes culture into an artificial historical event, a part of an unending quest for Canadian identity." Although it may be impossible to see anything specifically Canadian about much modern art, this Canadianness remains a concern of many artists who further divide their loyalties sometimes into regional trends, preferences, or schools of work. In sum Canada is experiencing a great bubbling of art production that is constantly taking turns into new fields of experimentation.

Nevertheless, two French-Canadian artists, Alfred Pellan and Paul-Emile Borduas, have, by their example, established a certain non-provincial outlook in Canada to counter the exclusively Canadian self-portrayal of the famous Seven. Studying in Paris in the forties, they absorbed brands of abstract expressionism that were truly international in outlook, returning home to Montréal with them to strongly influence many younger painters, including the now-famous Jacques de Tonnancour and Jean-Paul Riopelle. Although the New York art world today strongly influences Canadian art as it does the rest of the world, Montréal still gets considerable feeling from Paris, while Vancouver retains strong cultural connections with both Britain and the Orient.

The proliferation of art museums has been extremely rapid; where there were 18 only 25 years ago, today there are 86 art museums and galleries, drawing over 7,500,000 visitors a year. A new government program started a few years ago to "decentralize and democratize the museums" is moving collections and exhibits throughout the country so that every region may benefit from seeing them. Important centers are the *Montréal Museum of Fine Art* and, also in Montréal, the *Musée des Arts Contemporains* (at the Expo grounds); the *Art Gallery of Ontario,* in Toronto; the *McMichael Collection* in Kleinburg, Ontario; the *National Gallery of Canada,* in Ottawa; and outstanding museums in Vancouver, Calgary, Edmonton, Saskatoon, and Winnipeg. The

Atlantic provinces have also shared in the museum boom in expanded space and shows in Halifax, Saint John, and elsewhere.

An amazing Canadian innovation has been the *Art Bank,* established about 12 years ago to encourage Canadian art by the deceptively simple means of using a million dollars a year of government money to buy paintings, sculptures, prints, and photos which are then rented out to any government agency that wants them to embellish its buildings. Headquartered in Ottawa, the Bank occupies a vast warehouse where delegates from various agencies may browse and select what they like, depending on the resources their agencies can provide for the purpose. The program has been very successful and seems to exemplify the Canadian spirit of innovation in attempting in every way possible to bring art of all kinds to the people. Works are chosen by small juries made up of established artists, so there is no cold hand of bureaucracy at work in the selection. Rejected artists are invited to keep submitting work. "Nothing like this has ever been done in the world," says Geoffrey James, who helped found the Bank. "The juries are free to buy what they like, using their own taste to get good art. It's a government purchasing program controlled by artists themselves. I think every country should do it!"

Music

The worldwide cultural sources that enliven the Canadian scene are nowhere more evident than in music, composed and performed by creative professionals of every national origin as well as by Canadian natives. Symphony orchestras are the dominant influence across the country, but smaller instrumental groups, choral organizations, grand opera, and solo competitions in festivals also draw wide audiences.

Major orchestras are the *Toronto Symphony,* which has Britain's Andrew Davis as conductor, and the *Montréal Symphony,* under the baton of Charles Dutoit, five times winner of the coveted French Grand Prix du Disque and the man responsible for giving Montreal "the world's finest French symphony" (in the opinion of the pretigious music magazine *Gramophone).* Canadian symphonies make regional and national tours and fulfill a considerable number of foreign dates in Europe, Asia, and throughout the Americas.

Other important musical organizations include the *National Arts Centre Orchestra of Ottawa,* which emphasizes original Canadian works and commissions compositions regularly. Performances have included the premiere of *Turtle Rock,* by Montréal composer Galt McDermott, creator of the music for *Hair.* In Hamilton, Ontario, another work by McDermott opened a new $8 million performing arts center several years ago. Probably the most magnificent concert center in Canada is the *Grande Salle* of the *Place des Arts* in Montréal, home since 1963 of the *Montréal Symphony.* In the spring of 1982, Toronto's new *Roy Thomson Hall* opened to rave reviews.

Altogether Canada has some 30 symphonies. Those in smaller cities may play limited seasons, but most go from October to April. A particular Canadian success has been the *National Youth Orchestra,* with an upper age limit of 25. World-famous teachers accept 100 out of thousands of applicants across the country for instruction, rehearsals, and a performing tour of Canada each summer, and critics have occasionally rated it above some professional groups.

Most music by Canadian composers to have had an impact on the world scene has been in the modern idiom. Avant-garde composers include Serge Grant, Gilles Tremblay, Murray Schafer, Norma Beecroft, Robert Aitken, Bruce Mather, and John Hawkins. As with art and the dance, music generally crosses the language and cultural barriers that divide Canadians, although there are unique choral traditions in French-speaking Québec. A number of Canadian performers in music have won international fame, most notably operatic star Teresa Stratas, guitarist Liona Boyd, and the late pianist Glenn Gould. Says Canadian critic Ernest MacMillan: "The pity of it is that Canadians are still slow to recognize excellence in their own young musicians until other countries put upon them the stamp of approval. However, we are gradually learning to trust our own judgment and to accord due recognition to a number of fine artists born in this country."

Canadian choirs are world renowned. A specialty of certain smaller groups is a cappella singing. Elmer Isler's famous *Festival Singers* of Toronto, and the *Bach Choir* of Montréal, should not be missed by music lovers visiting Canada. Small chamber music groups appear frequently in every Canadian city, each with its own excellence; the repertoire of one Montréal group, the *Baroque Trio,* includes both baroque and contemporary pieces for flute, oboe, and harpsichord.

Perhaps because of the great distances separating their cities, Canadians love to get together, especially in summertime, at festivals of every kind. They have a particular passion for musical competitions that can go on day and night for a week or longer. There are every summer more than 200 of these festivals, and there is even one series, in smaller prairie communities, that is run in a "chain" all summer long so that performers may follow the musical contests from town to town. Originating in 1905 in Alberta with the encouragement of Canadian Governor-General Earl Grey, the festivals began sending competitors to an annual national competition to vie for the *Earl Grey Trophy.* The festivals make a delightful entertainment for visitors to Canada, who in summer never have to look far to find one. And the lavish mixing of music of all ethnic groups, including Canadian Indians and Eskimos, underscores the variety of the people and the land.

Finally, there are the enthusiastically received Canadian opera companies—notably the *Canadian,* of Toronto, which attracts guest artists from all over the world, and the companies of Vancouver, Edmonton, Montréal, Calgary, and Winnipeg. Although the *Opéra du Québec* has suspended productions because of money troubles, the others are surviving financially and thriving artistically.

Cinema

Canada produces over 5,000 full-length feature films and videotape programs every year, the work of some 300 independent companies ranging in size from small bands of freelance artists and technicians to Hollywood-style corporations. Film and television producers until recently lived and operated in separate worlds but now the lines that divide them are disappearing. A concrete result is the *Canadian Film and Television Association,* an organization whose members make up the mainstream of video and cinema enterprise in the country. It deals with labor and contract matters and relations with the government, which supplies funds for grants to many producers and will control the development of television and film in the future.

Out of the proliferation of film and video activity across Canada, much of it restricted to regional audiences, there were in 1980 twenty-five major film productions of some international stature, a few of them co-productions with France, Italy, and England, but shot in Canada with Canadian crews. Six of these are in the French language.

English-language films include *Murder by Decree,* starring Christopher Plummer; *Heartaches,* a love story starring Margot Kidder; *The Grey Fox,* a true story of turn-of-the century train robber Bill Miner, starring Richard Farnsworth and directed by Phillip Borsos; *Ticket to Heaven,* a look at life in religious cults starring Nick Mancuso; and *Quest for Fire* starring Rae Dawn Chong.

One of the better known films made in Canada recently is Peter Shaffer's screen version of his hit play *Equus,* starring Richard Burton, Peter Firth, Colin Blakely, and Joan Plowright and completed early in January 1977. It was made at *Toronto International Studios,* with exteriors shot in Georgetown, Ontario. Said Peter Firth: "It's remarkable how an English telephone box and a zebra crossing painted on a Canadian street can transform it into an English one." Playright Shaffer says: "The basic change is that instead of all the characters coming to the psychiatrist as they did on stage, the psychiatrist now goes to them, like a mental detective. I wanted to make it a real film, not just an adapted version of the play."

An international flavor spices much private-sector film making but the governmentally run National Film Board strives to capitalize on the beauties and immensities of Canada in a wide range of noncommercial productions. Created in 1939, the Board makes on the average 150 films in French and English every year, from short documentaries to two-hour features on subjects of national concern; currently the problems of the environment and energy resources provide much material. Twenty-seven film libraries across Canada provide film bookings at the rate of 400,000 annually to every kind of audience, including many to commercial movie houses. For two years in a row (1982 and 1983) NFB short films have won Oscars. Meanwhile, the Board continues to co-produce such major Canadian feature films as *The Wars,* based on Timothy Findley's award-winning novel. With healthy stimulation from foreign film companies and from its own government, the Canadian cinema, with severe growing pains to be sure, can be said to be booming.

Dance

Like other aspects of the cultural explosion in Canada, the dance—both traditional ballet and modern—has seen a meteoric rise in prominence and popularity. Where at one time there was but one major company, today there are three large ones and a couple of dozen others of thoroughly professional status that are drawing an ever-increasing audience. The year 1981–82 was the 30th birthday season for the excellent *National Ballet,* of Toronto, whose founding was given impetus by the older *Royal Winnipeg Ballet.* Remarks dance critic Lauretta Thistle: "Toronto could not bear the thought of the prairie city Winnipeg being the center of ballet in Canada."

That comment shows the high level of competitiveness in all the arts among the regional centers of Canada, each part of the country striving to prove its cultural creativity against the other parts. Alexander Grant, retired artistic director of the *National Ballet,* says, "Everybody seems to tell us what a miracle it all is: an internationally recognized classical ballet company here in Canada. Wow!" It was with the help of Rudolf Nureyev a few years ago that the company became a star on the world dance map: "It was a gamble which led to a deal of internal bickering," says Grant, "and an almost crippling deficit as the bill ran up on Nureyev's extravagantly sumptuous version of *The Sleeping Beauty.* Thankfully it paid off. The new exposure to audiences in Europe and New York gave the company the international status it desperately needed." Under new artistic director Eric Bruhn, once regarded as the world's leading *danseur noble,* the company is expanding its repertoire and basking in international acclaim.

The *Royal Winnipeg Ballet,* which was the inspirational force for all of Canada's classic ballet troupes, has fostered many regional ballet festivals around the country while increasing its own stature. The modern work called *The Green Table* originated in an anti-militarist conception produced on a German dance stage in the Hitler era. Among the many noted choreographers who have worked with the Winnipeg company is the Canadian Brian Macdonald, who gave it a dozen ballets, including the innovative *Ballet High,* set to rock music.

The third important group is *Les Grands Ballets Canadiens* of Montréal, born out of television choreography as practiced by a Swiss, Ludmilla Chiriaeff, who founded the company in 1958. One of its biggest hits was a ballet called *Tommy,* a creation of Fernand Nault set to rock opera music. Another work has been a Brian Macdonald ballet treatment of *Romeo and Juliet* in which dancers performed not to music but instead to readings of excerpts from the original Shakespeare. An all-Canadian ballet based on the *Song of Songs* is another recent success.

Among first-rate regional groups are the *Alberta Ballet Company* and the *Pacific Ballet Theatre.* Modern dance companies are also growing in number and in influence. The *Toronto Dance Theatre,* founded in 1968, is probably the leader. The two men and one woman who animate the company have a strong repertoire of 50 original dances, and have commissioned some 30 musical scores. They were all at one time students of Martha Graham, and have been accused of having created an imitation of the Graham troupe, but they reply, "We work not in the shadow of Martha Graham but in the light of her achievement."

The annual *Dance in Canada Conference* in Halifax, Nova Scotia, is a delightful get-together for dancers and for audiences as well, for it includes a *Canadian Dance Festival* that is an energetically staged potpourri of every kind of dance imaginable. Besides ballet and modern dance exponents from the major troupes there are ethnic dancers, a world champion Highland dancer, and even ballroom dancing competition winners. According to one professional, "It gave all concerned the contagious exhilaration of an Olympic event." There is excitement everywhere in the Canadian dance world, typified by the enthusiasm of the participants of this festival, where dancing goes on day and night like a marathon—there is no stopping them.

Theater

Where about 25 years ago the Canadian critic William Angus wrote that "except for a few large cities, theatre in Canada is a vast arid desert," today the country is enjoying a boom in professional theater of every kind—repertory companies, theater festivals, and experimental stages burgeoning in new surroundings that range from multimillion-dollar performing arts centers to makeshift spaces in warehouses or storefronts. It is a good time for the theater in Canada and at last Canadian playwrights dealing with Canadian life are having their works performed and their spirit and their ideas felt and discussed as a new part of a common culture.

Toronto is the center of the English-speaking theater and the third largest theater center in the world, while Montréal is the hub of the French-language stage (not dealt with here). But Canadian theater has become a wide-ranging community with individual actors and even entire troupes performing in widely separated centers in all the provinces.

A look at what is going on at present in theaters across the country gives an idea of the wealth and variety to be found. Year-round programs go on in scores of theaters. The *Bastion Theatre,* Victoria, put on Shakespeare and Chekhov among others in one recent season. The *Playhouse Theatre Centre,* Vancouver, has staged plays by Alan Mark and John Morel. The *Citadel Theatre* of Edmonton recently premiered *Duddy,* a $1 million musical adaptation of Mordecai Richler's novel. The 15th season of Theatre Calgary had George Bernard Shaw and Edward Moore plays. The *Manitoba Theatre Centre* in Winnipeg had a musical tribute to the works of French composer Jacques Brel and on its second stage Shakespeare and Sondheim plays. *Theatre London* had works by Ibsen and Edward Albee. All these are samples of full programs running from fall to late spring, and many centers have a second theater for new works that can be produced on a modest scale.

An English-speaking theater in Montréal, the *Centaur,* has a playwright in residence and two stages, and there are full seasons also at the *Neptune* in Halifax and the *National Arts Centre* in Ottawa. But the single metropolis with the most theatrical variety and innovation is Toronto, where one multicultural theater group reflects the incredibly rich ethnic fabric of Canada: in 1981 it put on 19 plays in 14 languages. But there remains a lingering prejudice in the minds of Canadian playgoers about the value of native works that is only slowly being dispelled. Says one Canadian playwright, Michael Cook: "There appears to be a basic inferiority at work in the Canadian psyche as it applies to art, to theatre in particular, an inferiority aggravated by the fear of the primitive, the abundance of dialect, and the excesses of the environment itself. Almost from the beginning, we began to turn our back upon it, did not see in its artifacts, as the Indian and Eskimo see, the Spirit of the land struggling for release."

But a new national pride in home-grown drama is developing among numerous theater centers such as the *St. Lawrence Centre Theatre,* the *O'Keefe Centre,* and the *Royal Alexandra Theatre,* all in Toronto. With this pride comes a greatly widening opportunity to explore all that the world has to offer in plays and other stage works. Theater buffs are particularly drawn beyond the better established houses named here to the "alternative" theaters of Toronto that seat between 100 and 300 persons. *The Bayview Playhouse* is the oldest of these, and specializes in rock musicals. Cabaret-style theater goes on in the *Theatre-in-the Dell,* which gives musical reviews. *Young Peoples Theatre* presents imaginative drama geared to children, including a punk version of Shakespeare's *Twelfth Night.* A converted warehouse holds *Toronto Workshop Productions,* with original Canadian plays all year except in the summer. A so-called "flexible" theater is *Theatre Passe Muraille,* described as "Canadian folk theatre and a grass roots collective," which presents excellent plays in both French and English. Other stages in Toronto include the *Tarragon,* the *Factory Theatre Lab,* the *Second City Fire Hall,* the *Toronto Free Theatre,* the *Adelaide Court,* and *Toronto Arts Productions;* all encourage original Canadian plays.

Summertime visitors to Canada swell the crowds at the numerous excellent regional theatrical festivals, the most famous being the *Stratford Shakespearean Festival,* founded in 1953. A *Shaw Festival* goes on at Niagara-on-the-Lake, Ontario, while Banff, in the Rockies, has the *Banff Festival of the Arts* in August. Original musicals are shown in the *Charlottetown Festival,* famous for the musical *Anne of Green Gables,* set here in Prince Edward Island. Newfoundland has the *St. John's Festival,* New Brunswick has summer plays at the *Playhouse* in Fredericton, while the national capital, Ottawa, includes a number of plays in its annual *Festival Canada* in July. Canadian theater in English is also encouraged in the *Festival Lennoxville* in Québec during July and August.

Manitoba has three theater festivals in summer, at Winnipeg, Gimli, and Neepawa, while the *Regina Little Theatre* has plays three days a week in summer. Victoria and Vancouver also have summer theater, and there are reconstructed old-time gaslight stages in the towns of Dawson and Whitehorse in the Yukon Territory. Wherever you go in Canada you will discover theater around you, much of it original, experimental, and exciting.

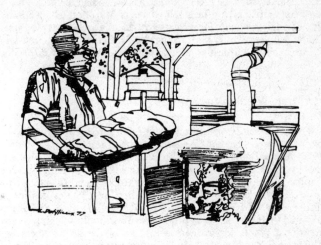

FOOD AND DRINK IN CANADA

Tradition and Innovation

by
BOBBI ST. CLAIRE

Bobbi St. Claire, a Western Canadian married to an Eastern Canadian, frequently visits family on both sides of the country. She also enjoys a close relationship with her Eskimo relatives along the Arctic coastline.

"The discovery of a new dish does more for the happiness of mankind than the discovery of a star," was the judgment of Anthelme Brillat-Savarin (1755–1826), French politician and gastronomer. Did he, perhaps, have Canadian cookery in mind? The end product of centuries of discovery, development, and adaptation by early European colonists and more recent settlers, Canadian cuisine now ranks among the world's finest in many areas of the country.

Here, multi-cultural influences give us clues to the diversity and originality of Canadian cooking. Unknown foods, introduced by Indian tribes to newcomers from the British Isles, France, the Netherlands, and Germany included venison, bison, pinchberries, blueberries, saskatoons, wild rice, and corn—all in plentiful supply at the time, and prepared in various ways by the original inhabitants of the New World.

Along the way, European settlers developed new foods as, for example, Ontario cheese, processed commercially in 1864 at the first cheese factory built in Oxford County. Export production of maple syrup and other maple products, incorporating a basic Indian technique for boiling maple sap, has put the small village of Mapleton, Nova Scotia, on the international map. Québec also produces a special maple sugar—a family industry dating back to the 1600's. Prairie honey, well known for its quality, uniformity, and color, is another Canadian product.

A Prize-Winning Cuisine

The combination of certain indigenous products, native cooking methods, necessity, and imagination have created a cuisine that, in 1976, resulted in a prize-winning effort in the World Culinary Olympics in Frankfort, Germany. Competing with chefs from 21 countries, Canada placed second overall in the eight-day round-the-clock contest (Switzerland placed first; France and the United States tied for third place), and took 30 gold medals. To qualify for an award, each dish was required to sell at least 100 portions to visitors to the Olympics, earning additional points for greater sales. One of the 26 members of the Canadian Federation of Chefs de Cuisine commented at the time: "Our roast prime rib of Alberta beef and Arctic char sold a record 246 servings. Our stuffed lamb from British Columbia and breast of duckling also did very well." Mouthwatering news for travelers!

Quality Beef

Canadians, who produce a great deal of the world's best beef, consume less of it in proportion to their population than other major meat-producing countries (New Zealand, Argentina, and the United States). They eat more poultry, however, than any of these countries except the United States. Pork, lamb, and veal also make up a substantial part of a Canadian's meat diet.

Despite an abundance of freshwater lakes and rivers yielding white fish, walleye, smelts, lake trout, and many other fish, as well as oceans bordering on the east, west, and the north providing salmon, cod, halibut, herring, haddock, and shellfish, Canadians consume relatively little fish. With the demand for Atlantic and Pacific salmon and Canada's incomparable lobster from the cool Atlantic coastal waters—a demand that far exceeds the supply—commercial fishing for export is a leading industry.

The growing season in Canada is short, but a wide variety of carrots, beets, parsnips, turnips, onions, and potatoes are stored for winter use. Cereal grains, used in the production of world-famous breads, are grown on the prairies. Canada also exports a sizable crop of seed potatoes as well as a portion of the annual apple crop from the Atlantic provinces, Ontario, and British Columbia.

Canada's Culinary Tradition

Canadian cuisine developed from very simple traditions and practices. For example, the early European settlers, enjoying the plentiful fish from Canada's streams, lakes, and ocean waters, were quick to develop chowder—the now-traditional way of cooking fruit of the sea. The word "chowder" comes from the French *chaudière,* which means soup kettle. One can only speculate if the introduction of potatoes to the New World by Sir Walter Raleigh in the late 1500's influenced the recipe for "chaudière" when the French arrived. Today, potatoes, grown in almost every province, are daily fare for Canadians. Some provinces, including the Atlantic provinces as well as British Columbia and Ontario, also grow them for export.

In 1634, the Jesuits began using an Indian method of milling corn—mixing it with a little wheat in bark or wooden mortars. For fine cooking, however, flour was still imported as the local variety was too coarse.

Blueberries, unknown in the Old World, were discovered about the same time when the Jesuits observed the Indians mixing these strange berries—as well as other wild fruits—into their cornbread batter. The priests adopted the custom, added a few refinements, and *voilà!* the first "upside down" cake was created. Somewhat earlier (1608), Champlain planted the first grapevine in Québec; a bit later (1639), cultivated apples were noted in the Georgian Bay district of Ontario, also the result of Jesuit planting. The year 1646, however, marks the true beginning of a distinctly Canadian cuisine. Credit goes to the Ursuline nuns of Québec who began adapting French methods of cooking to the local produce.

Wild fruits—strawberries, blueberries, blackberries, cranberries, pembina berries, and plums—were always a staple of the native Canadian diet, though largely untouched by the colonials until about 1688. By 1699, the colonials had also begun to experiment with dried corn, fiddleheads (fern fronds—see the section on the *Eastern Coastal Region*), wild mint, wild savory, and wild parsley. In New Brunswick, where fiddleheads are still picked, they are sold throughout the country and have become a well-known restaurant specialty.

Pork, lamb, and veal were in common use from earliest times. Roasts and steaks appeared on the table only when the British colonists arrived. The French used beef only for stew and soup. In Western Canada, bison was the staple meat, supplemented by small game and wild fowl. The Indians had eaten bison meat for a long, long time and settlers soon learned to use it in their recipes.

Canada's Seven Food Regions

This survey of Canadian cuisine divides the country into seven regions, each with a unique food history. Various dishes have become well known locally; some are world-famous.

Western Coastal Region

The cuisine of British Columbia, the single province in this region, is enhanced by Enlgish traditions. Along its rugged coastline, the Pacific Ocean yields a great variety of seafood—King crab (a popular restaurant dish), oysters, shrimp, and other shellfish—as well as cod, haddock, and five varieties of salmon (coho, chinook, chum, sockeye, and pink) which are smoked, pan-fried, breaded, baked, canned, barbecued—and well complemented by local vegetables.

British Columbia grows a variety of fruit that is marketed elsewhere in Canada and also shipped throughout the world. Be sure to enjoy fresh fruits and sparkling wines if you travel through the Okanagan Valley—one of the great fruit-growing areas of North America. Here, apples and peaches are in great demand year-round. And, throughout the summer months, there are luscious crops of pears, plums, apricots, strawberries, raspberries, and blackberries as well as the famous Bing cherries and loganberries, specialties of this province. A cross between raspberries and blackberries, the loganberry developed on Vancouver Island makes loganberry pie a favorite dish of British Columbians. Zucca melons are also a unique product in this area.

Many of these fruits are also used to make native wines—loganberry wine, blackberry cordial, strawberry wine, and apple cider.

Saltspring lamb, raised here on the salty marshes of Saltspring Island, is a traditional English roast, served with mint sauce.

Vegetables are plentiful in British Columbia and there are large market gardening enterprises throughout the province. Tomatoes, an excellent crop, are often served fresh, sliced with a pinch of powdered thyme or dillweed, or baked with onions and spices, cheese, and bread crumbs.

Victoria creams, a famous chocolate delicacy derived from an arcane recipe dating back to 1885, are exported worldwide from British Columbia.

The Prairies

Each of the three provinces in this region—Alberta, Saskatchewan, and Manitoba—has unique ways of preparing foods common to all of them. The rolling plains and foothills of Alberta are ideal pasture land for cattle, and western beef is world famous. Albertans think no food in the world equals thick, rare, tender beef steaks. Beef is cooked in many ways—barbecued, braised, grilled, minced, and skewered (kebabs)—with different complements such as onions, mushrooms, green peppers, rice, sauces, and beans.

"Dinner on the hoof" has been a part of the Westerner's diet since the Indians and bison lived here. Bison no longer "blacken the prairie" but, occasionally, bison meat is served in households when local bison herds are thinned and the meat is made available through supermarkets. As "gamey meals" become more popular, restaurants across Canada are serving the prairie fare.

Two unusual beef dishes have been produced in Alberta—*Chuck Wagon Stew* and *beef mincemeat.* Chuck Wagon Stew, named for the covered wagon used to take dinner to the cowhands on the range, is a combination of chopped steak, garden vegetables, and biscuits, cooked in a rich gravy. Beef mincemeat, which combines chopped meat, fruits and spices, is used in pies and tarts. In many homes, it is a traditional Christmas season dish, served with whipped cream, ice cream, or rum sauce.

Albertans use wild berries, nuts, and flowers in making desserts, wine, honey, and catsup. Yes—catsup—from "Alberta Oranges," commonly called rose hips. Alberta is also famous for the excellent honey made from its alfalfa and clover nectar and many indigenous recipes call for honey as a sweetener. Honey and toast or biscuits, or cereal with honey are popular breakfast foods.

The sugar beet is as important to Alberta as the maple tree is to Québec. In the southern part of the province, a large area of land is irrigated for sugar beet production. Local manufacturing plants process the beets which provide Albertans with white granulated sugar. The remainder is marketed in other provinces or exported.

Saskatchewan brings to mind high-quality grain for bread and wonderful freshwater fish. Whitefish and walleye are marketed commercially by Indian cooperatives, and lake trout, although not for sale, can be caught. Wild rice found in the marshy land of northern Saskatchewan is harvested for commercial sale by the Indians. Following the customs of their ancestors, they bend the rice stalks into their canoes and flail the stems with a paddlelike stick. This rice is an excellent accompaniment to the wild fowl abundant in this province—partridge, prairie chicken, wild duck, and goose—all fit for a gourmet's repast. Saskatchewan, which lies beneath two major North American migration channels, permits hunting every fall.

Saskatoons, berries which resemble small blueberries with crowns, are used for jams and jellies and a variety of desserts—saskatoon pie with fresh country cream is a delicious end to a meal. Other wild berries, such as pinchberries and cranberries, make tart, tangy jelly—excellent with the wild fowl meals of Saskatchewan.

Manitoba features Winnipeg goldeye—a delicate fish (average weight is three-quarters of a pound) that is smoked over oak logs and then dyed a deep coral. Served with champagne, Winnipeg goldeye makes an elegant breakfast. According to local history, Robert Firth, a young Englishman, arrived in Canada in the early 1890's to operate his new store in Winnipeg. Finding it necessary to supplement his income by fishing, he constructed a makeshift smokehouse from a barrel to cure his catches. Through a miscalculation, one batch of fish became considerably more than half cooked instead of merely smoked! But it had a fine taste and so the processing of Winnipeg goldeye became a tradition of the region.

Covered with lakes and marshes, Manitoba has an abundance of wild rice as well as wild fowl and many kinds of fish. Caviar and Selkirk whitefish are commonly served throughout the province.

The prairie area cannot be left without mentioning the food heritage brought by the many European immigrants who flooded west to these level lands—particularly the people of the Ukraine. Today, their lasting influence is evident in *holupchi* (cabbage rolls), *pierogi* (potato or cheese dumplings), *kielbasa* (garlic sausage), and *borscht* (beet soup)—all now quite common in prairie homes and restaurants.

Northern Canada

The Yukon and Northwest Territories which form this vast region have some distinctive foods but also great difficulty in producing them commercially. Gigantic in size but small in population, the north is for the outdoorsman, the pioneer, the adventurer. Game is taken from the land; staples, such as bread, milk, eggs, and vegetables, are shipped in.

Moose, the most plentiful game in this area, is a staple of northern cookery. Prepared in many ways to retain its wild flavor or to disguise it, moose is the meat used for everything from kebabs to pot roast, hash to soup, and is usually accompanied by local vegetables and sourdough bread or biscuits. Dall sheep, mountain goat, caribou, bear, and small game such as rabbit, gopher, porcupine, beaver, and squirrel are also eaten. Wild fowl and fish vary the diet.

Fish cannot be passed over lightly in this region! The Arctic grayling, a small fish weighing about two pounds, not only makes a good meal but is considered good sport among fishermen as it is a "fighter."

The Arctic char or *ilkalu,* as the Inuit call it, is also found in the Northwest Territories. Its rare quality and flavor—not quite trout and not quite salmon—make it a gastronomic delight. The Arctic char is sold commercially by Inuit cooperatives to other parts of Canada for restaurant fare.

No one should visit the north without sampling bread or biscuits made of sourdough, a mixture of flour and water fermented in various ways with natural yeast. Old prospectors were known to store their "starter" or "makins" for the next batch in wooden buckets or hollowed-out logs. Carrying their "makins" on their persons to keep it warm when they traveled, they themselves became known as *sourdoughs.*

Although the growing season is very short in the North, it is long enough to yield many varieties of wild berries—rose hips, cranberries, soapberries, bearberries, mealberries, gooseberries, currants, mossberries, and cloudberries. These are used in preserves, juice, tea, puddings, and pemmican, a unique concoction used by the natives and early white men as survival rations on long journeys. Still used today to some extent, pemmican is made from dried smoked meat which is boiled, pounded to a fine consistency, and then mixed with onions, fat, and berries to form dried meat cakes.

Upper Canada

The early food habits of Ontario, historically known as Upper Canada, were influenced by the American Quakers, the English Loyalists and later, by the Germans and Dutch. While Québec's cookery is distinctly French, Ontario does not have an identifiable cuisine, offering more of a "conglomerate of cookery" although one thinks, somehow, of roast beef and Yorkshire pudding when one is visiting. This vast province incorporates what some call the "banana belt" of the south with the "barrens" of the north. Southern Ontario has extensive orchards and truck farms that supply great quantities of fruits and vegetables throughout all of Canada. The Niagara peninsula here is one of the great fruit-producing areas of North America.

Corn and pumpkins are also grown in large quantities. Corn is truly Canadian, as it was cultivated in Canada long before European colonization. The Indians, who called it maize, valued corn not only as a food but for currency, fuel, and jewelry; it was also incorporated into their religious rites. Today, corn, roasted in butter and seasoned with salt, is a common dish during the fall harvest. Pumpkins are used largely for pie, topped with whipped cream.

From Ontario's many lakes comes a variety of fish, including whitefish, pike, lake trout, and the delicately flavored smelt. At the mouth of the Credit River near Toronto, fisherman gather by the hundreds to take part in the annual salmon derby. At Parry Sound on Georgian Bay, a smelt fry is held in the streets at the peak of the fishing season. Arctic char, although native to the Northwest Territories, is often served in homes and restaurants here because of its distinctive flavor.

Other culinary assets? Ontario has extensive vineyards providing much of Canada's wine; a small maple sugar industry; and it is famous for its cheese, claiming to make the best cheddar in the world. Almost every variety of cheese is available—Danish, Dutch, Swiss, French, English.

Lower Canada

Lower Canada is Québec—an exceptional food experience! French-Canadian cuisine bases itself on the culinary arts of French provincial cooking, brought to Canada over 300 years ago, and handed down, almost intact, through the generations. Simple, plain, and nourishing—and quite different from the aristocratic haute cuisine of the elegant restaurants of Paris—French-Canadian cooking makes much use of fruit, eggs, meat, milk and cream, a tradition of the French settlers who came from Normandy, where these products were plentiful. It is also alleged that the art of French cooking has flourished through the centuries for the reason that a daughter's marriageability often depended on her culinary skills.

French-Canadians are a happy people who thrive on family gettogethers that are lavish productions of food, wine, and song. New Year's Day with its roast suckling pig and goose, the *réveillon* after the Christmas midnight Mass with *tortière* and *cretons,* and *à pendre la crémaillère* or housewarming, are some of the traditional yearly celebrations. The French-Canadian does not like hot spicy foods. Onions, leeks, and shallots are preferred to garlic. Subtle flavorings are used to enhance, not overpower, the food.

Pork has been an important ingredient of French-Canadian cooking since the days of the early French settlers who, by necessity, used every possible bit of the animal. The results, today, are delicious dishes using pigs' feet, cheeks, and tails as well as the more common cuts. Even salt fat pork turns up in many recipes. A very famous dish, traditionally eaten on Christmas Eve, is pork pie or *tortière*. The highly popular *cretons du Québec,* a spiced pork spread, served on bread at breakfast and lunch, is sold commercially.

Soupmaking is another unique French-Canadian skill. Thick, hearty soups were often served in settlers' homes because they made "a little go a long way." *Soupe au chou* (cabbage soup) is served in many areas of Québec with bread and butter as the main course for lunch or supper. Pea soup and onion soup are, of course, distinctly French-Canadian. In Eastern Canada, the use of fish and shellfish in chowder always indicates the influence or presence of the French.

Cipâte (meat pie), *croquignoles* (doughnuts served during Christmas holidays), blueberry *cipâte* (a three-layered pie), *grand-pères au sirop d'érable* (a dumpling dessert using maple syrup), and sugar pie add to the array of dishes found in Québec. The last two were developed to use Québec's famous maple sugar. At present, Québec is responsible for 90 percent of the more than 2,000,000 gallons of maple syrup produced annually in Canada.

For many of the early settlers, maple trees were the only source of sugar. Each spring, the trees were tapped for their sap, which was boiled and formed into brown cakes of maple sugar for the yearly supply. Although maple syrup is now produced commercially, many families still hold "sugaring off" parties each spring when they collect their supply.

Wild game abounds in Québec. Brome Lake ducklings, raised in the Eastern townships, are a world-famous delicacy, exported in large quantity.

Many distinctive cheeses are made in the local monasteries, using secret processes handed down through generations. *Oka* cheese is made at a Trappist monastery near the town of Oka; *Ermite* is made at a monastery at St. Benôit du Lac. Apart from the monasteries, *Fromage de L'Île* is from L'Île d'Orleans. Only ten families share the secret of this process.

Eastern Coastal Region

Food in these provinces (New Brunswick, Prince Edward Island, and Nova Scotia) results from many contributions—native Indian, Acadian (French), English, German, New England, Irish, Scot, and Black.

New Brunswick is famous for seafood. Atlantic salmon, a prized export, has a delicate flavor, and is served with butter, new potatoes (New Brunswick is also known for its potato crop), and fiddleheads (described below). *Buctouche* and *Caraquet* oysters become tasty stews; lobsters, among the finest in the world, are eaten boiled, broiled, or steamed, in soups, or on bunwiches; clams are savored in chowder; and shad adds its special taste to provincial fish dishes.

Homemade baked beans and steamed brown bread are served in many parts of New Brunswick as a traditional Saturday-night supper dish. *Rapée* pie, made with chicken, is an Acadian specialty for Sundays and festive occasions.

Fiddleheads are unique to New Brunswick. These are young fronds of the ostrich fern that grow abundantly in shady moist woods. Their name comes from their tightly curled top which is shaped like the end of a violin. They are marketed fresh during May and June and available frozen or canned year-round. Fiddleheads are usually served with butter and seasoned to taste, or used cold in salads.

Apples turn up in desserts year-round, as do blueberries and cranberries—here and in the rest of the Atlantic Provinces. Blueberries are also an important source of income in this region.

Prince Edward Island, Canada's smallest province, is known as the "Garden of the Gulf" because of its climate and its fertile red soil which yields a superb crop of seed potatoes for home consumption and for export. A favorite local recipe for serving potatoes is to grate them, combine them with pork and finely chopped onions, and then fry the mixture as a pancake.

Throughout the island, which is also famous for its shellfish, lobster is the mainstay of the dinner table, brought in daily, in season, from the deep waters off the coast. They are steamed, boiled, or eaten in casseroles or salads. The "lobster supper" is an island tradition. Seek it out as you travel along the North Shore.

Oysters, another popular island specialty from the famed farming beds in Malpeque Bay, are served in almost every way here—raw on the half-shell with a tangy sauce; deep-fried; in oyster pies; scalloped; in soufflés; and in soups and stews. Soused mackerel, a favorite recipe, consists of mackerel and onions cooked in a spiced vinegar sauce, eaten cold or hot.

Nova Scotia's food traditions date back to the 17th century when the first white settlement was established in 1605 by a "company of Frenchmen" at Port Royal. They formed the "Order of the Good Time"—the first social club in North America—to provide entertainment during the dreary winters and to satisfy their appetites. Each gentleman, taking a turn as host for a day, was responsible for the day's fare. Competition was avid. The participants, however, did not bestow their culinary skills on Acadia for long. They left for other adventures and it was not until the 1630's that French colonists arrived. These Acadians befriended the native Micmacs and learned from them a great deal about living in the new land—and food preparation. Later, succeeding waves of Scots, Germans, English, Irish, and Blacks brought their own traditional recipes.

Here, the famous Annapolis Valley apple is grown and exported in great quantity. Cranberries and strawberries are also commercial produce. Maple sugar, fresh vegetables, dairy products, fish and shellfish are other products of the area.

Fruits of the sea feature large sea-flavored scallops that are French fried, baked, or grilled, and usually served with a tartar sauce. Fish and clam chowders and the herring dish "Solomon Grundy" are also very popular. A variety of smoked fish, including mackerel, herring, cod and eel, as well as the famous salmon, can be found in restaurants and markets.

The German influence is evident in Nova Scotia's Lunenberg sausage as well as in a dish known variously as "hugger-in-buff," "fish and scrunchions," "Dutch mess," or "house bankin' "—whatever its name, this is a tasty combination of potatoes and fish, covered with a cream sauce flavored with onions and salt pork.

Desserts in Nova Scotia make use of the plentiful fruits and berries. "Acadian grunt" uses blueberries, partridgeberries, rhubarb, strawberries and apples, but most popular are the blueberries. The fruit is stewed and dumplings are added. Sometimes called "slump" or "fungy," the dessert gets its names from the sound of the fruit boiling through the dumplings. In early times, this dessert often constituted the entire meal.

Baked apple dumplings are a treat for the visitor. Many years ago, when food was cooked on the hearth, apple dumplings were boiled in a cloth. Now they are wrapped in pastry, baked in the oven, and served with cream and sugar, whipped cream, or lemon sauce.

Newfoundland

Newfoundland has a culinary history all its own. The most homogeneous of all Canadians and the most isolated, Newfoundlanders developed dishes that, for a long time, appeared nowhere else in the country. Theirs is a hearty cuisine that makes full use of fat pork and molasses, salt fish, salt meat, boiled vegetables, and soups. It's a filling, "stick-to-the-ribs" kind of cookery that is tasty and unusual.

Fish is a staple of their diet and fishing voyages to the famous Grand Banks fishing grounds which lie off the coastline have produced a recipe for a delicious stew, easily prepared with fresh fish and vegetables by the fishermen on board their boats. It's important to know that when you ask for fish in Newfoundland, you get cod. Available year-round, it is eaten fresh, dried, and salted. Even the cod's tongue is eaten— buttered and fried, and served as an appetizer with browned scrunchions. You may even overlook its origins. If you want salmon (you must try Newfoundland salmon), trout, halibut, or hake, you must ask for it. Otherwise you will be served cod—cod au gratin, codfish cakes, or a traditional Newfoundland dish known as fish and brewis (pronounced "broos"), concocted of boiled salt cod mixed with hardtack which has been soaked overnight to make it soft. A staple in most Newfoundland homes for many years, it may be sprinkled with scrunchions (bits of fat pork, fried and crunchy).

Flipper pie is another Newfoundland specialty, made from the flippers of young harp seals. Flipper pie suppers are held each spring when the sealing ships return from the northern ice. At that time, pies several feet in diameter, holding 15 to 20 pounds of seal meat and gallons of vegetables and gravy, are served. The secret of making a tasty flipper dish is to remove all the fat that would otherwise impart an unpleasantly strong flavor to the pie.

Fried chicken livers is another special dish, along with damper dogs (a type of fried bread dough). There's also cod sound pie (made from the tough meat near the cod's backbone), crubeens (truly Irish pickled pig's feet), and fat back and molasses dip (a rich mixture of pork fat and molasses for dipping bread). And do not be put off by a "gandy" on the menu; it's a common pancake.

Newfoundland's small area of arable land produces wild berries—partridgeberries, marshberries, and squash berries, as well as bakeapple berries which are yellow, shaped like blackberries, and delicious. Pies, jams, jellies, and puddings are made from these fruits. Another favorite dessert is molasses pie.

Wine and Spirits

Winemaking, as old as civilization, was introduced to Canada by the French who also brought brandy with them. Later, the English imported Malaga and Muscat from Spain and rum from the West Indies. Here, as in many parts of the world, the monks made their own wine, using it not only in the sacraments but also as a food. Laboring long to perfect its quality, they set standards for vintners outside the Church.

Canadian consumption of wine is modest but increasing every year. Roughly 80 percent of Canada's wine is produced and bottled in the Niagara peninsula of southern Ontario, where the main grape-growing centers are Niagara Falls and St. Catherine's. Others include Jordan, Grimsby, and Welland. Each autumn, the Niagara Grape and Wine Festival is held to celebrate the harvest.

British Columbia's Okanagan Valley is the other major wine-producing area in Canada responsible for the remaining 20 percent of the total output of the country. Here, apples and berries as well as grapes are used in the manufacture of the different wines.

Many varieties of grapes are grown in Canada—Concord, Niagara, Agawam, Elvira, Catawba, Delaware, Fredonia, and Labrusca Hybrids, the most popular variety—grown in the peninsula since the mid-1940's. The use of French hybrid varieties, developed by crossbreeding European and Canadian vines, has been an important step in the expansion of the industry. These new vines, with greater resistance to insects and disease, produce a better-quality fruit.

Canadian vintners produce all classes of wines but do not ordinarily produce vintage wines as do their European counterparts. Instead, the product is blended from different harvests to ensure a standard and consistent quality. In Newfoundland, however, a fine, well aged port was the fortuitous result of a shipping problem some 300 years ago. It happened that a British merchant ship, carrying a load of port wine from Oporto, Portugal, to London, was forced to head for St. John's in order to outrun a French privateer. The vessel remained in St. John's for the winter. When the wine reached London the following spring, it was found to have been greatly improved and it was decided that the moist Atlantic air and the process of transporting the wine had caused the change. Large vaults were built forthwith along St. John's waterfront to hold the wine for aging. Although the wine, known as Newman's Port, is still a favorite of Newfoundlanders and Europeans, the vaults are no longer used. A modern storage system now matures the port but the full-bodied flavor has been retained.

Spirit production in Canada includes liquors as well as beer, which was first made in Québec in 1648 in the Boswell Brewery at Sillery. Canadians are great beer drinkers, and breweries, from coast to coast, are increasing production year by year. Most beer is 5 percent alcohol by volume and Canadians drink it as is, with salt, or mixed with tomato juice.

"Native" beverages that may add to your enjoyment of a local meal —in Newfoundland, for example—are calabogus, a mixture of rum, molasses, and spruce beer (definitely not for the faint of heart), and a "wee swallie" of potent Newfoundland screech, a dark rum of dubious ancestry. Once a popular workingman's drink, screech was made by steaming or washing out Jamaica rum barrels with boiling water. The residual liquor was particularly powerful. (In other places, the same drink is known as "swish.") Screech, a name coined by U.S. servicemen stationed in Newfoundland during World War II, refers to the reaction of those who drank too much of it. Since that time, the process has been refined. Screech is now prepared from legitimate Caribbean rum and bottled by the Newfoundland Liquor Corporation.

EASTERN CANADA

ONTARIO

The Heartland of Canada

by
VALERIE ROSS

Valerie Ross has written for most major Canadian publications. She is currently an associate editor at Maclean's *magazine.*

Ontario, an old Iroquois word meaning "the shining waters," offers you 68,490 square miles of it—one quarter of all the fresh water in the world.

The waters of the St. Lawrence Seaway and the Great Lakes bound Ontario for a thousand miles on its populous and affluent southern rim. Here its waterways are plied by hulking ocean tankers, lake cruisers, and pleasure craft. But the majority of Ontario's lakes are wilderness waters, their empty blue expanses crossed by the occasional lone canoe. West of Kenora and Rainy River, the Ontario-Manitoba border runs north through forest, tundra and Arctic plain. Ontario's eastern boundary is the Ottawa River and then a line of ever-diminishing trees straggling up to the barren saltwater shores of James and Hudson Bays.

The sheer immensity of Ontario (an area of almost a half-million square miles) makes it hard to discern a character. Inside one political

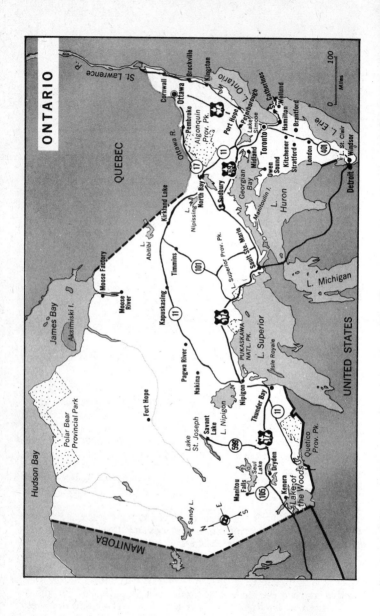

boundary you will find frontier mining towns like South Porcupine, the gentle pastoral scenery of Kitchener's Mennonite farm communities, flashing neon sophistication of midtown Toronto, and gray stone conservatism of townships around Kingston.

The scenery varies tremendously and so do the people. Ontario, with 8,715,800 people, is the most populous province in English Canada. It's home to wealthy industrialists, Indian and Métis trappers, showbiz celebrities, federal politicians, solitary bush pilots, WASP gentry and immigrants of all colors and creeds. It has more Germans than Nürnberg, more Italians than Florence, more Blacks than Bermuda. The province is as big as two Texases, three Japans or France, Germany, and Italy combined. As a traveler in a province this big and this diverse, the best you can do is scratch the edges and marvel at the rest—like the first explorers who glimpsed its vastness more than three and a half centuries ago. Significantly, Ontario's "shining waters" were their doorways.

Greed and God and the First Explorers

In 1610 Henry Hudson sailed through Arctic waters into Hudson Bay and claimed the land for the British Crown. Meanwhile, the French were beginning to explore the Great Lakes shoreline and backwoods river systems in the south. Between those first French and English explorers stretched thousands of square miles of forest, marsh and rock, sparsely populated by farming tribes of Iroquois and Huron, and hunting tribes of Algonquin, Cree, and Eskimo.

A mixture of motives brought these first Europeans: greed for land for their respective crowns; greed for the natural wealth (furs, fish, lumber, and minerals) the region promised; religious zeal; and the simple challenge of curiosity.

Two very different, but very typical, men were French-born Étienne Brûlé and Father Jean de Brébeuf.

Brûlé, a lieutenant of the explorer Samuel de Champlain, was not yet 17 years old when he made his first sortie from the French settlement at Québec into the western wilderness. He is credited with being the first white visitor to Lake Ontario, Lake Erie, Georgian Bay, Sault Ste. Marie, and the north shore of Lake Superior. Rascally and audacious, he traveled extensively with his Indian guides, speaking their language, making love to the women, quarreling with the men, until in 1632 he was murdered and reportedly eaten by some exasperated Hurons.

By contrast, Father de Brébeuf was a calm, dedicated Jesuit who lived for 12 years among the Hurons. He built a mission school and hospital, advised their farmers and ministered to their sick, all the while hoping patiently for converts. The site of the early Jesuit mission has been reconstructed at Ste. Marie Among the Hurons, near Midland.

In 1649 de Brébeuf was captured by the Hurons' enemy, the Iroquois, and horribly tortured and martyred by them. Father de Brébeuf has since been canonized by the Catholic Church.

After the death of de Brébeuf and his fellow missionaries, French settlement in Ontario was limited to the occasional fortified trading post. But exploration continued, and from Ontario trading posts and friendly Indian villages, the expeditions of La Salle, Joliet and Father Marquette set out for the American Midwest and down the Mississippi. The French naturally claimed the land they found for their king, and by the end of the century their claims had almost surrounded the fledgling British colonies of New England. Strategically, this was bad; economically, worse, for it gave the French a huge advantage in the profitable fur trade. The British waited for their chance. When the Seven Years' War broke out in Europe, French forts in Ontario and Québec fell to American-based British officers; in 1756 the western regions of New France passed to the British Crown and became Upper Canada.

Loyalists: the Backbone of Ontario

The American War of Independence had a profound effect in shaping Ontario. Waves of pro-British refugees flooded into the region, bringing their families and slaves, their political conservatism and their staunch loyalty to Britain. The motto of the province is *Ut incepit fidelis sic permanet* ("Loyal she began, loyal she remains"). The colonial government tried to help the Loyalist refugees with grants of land, equipment, and livestock, but there is no doubt that the going was tough for the Germans who settled around Adolphustown (Bay of Quinte) and Berlin (now Kitchener), the Scots at Glengarry, and the British who settled all across the province.

Just as 1776 marks the coalescence of the American spirit, so the British-American war of 1812–14 marks the real beginning of Canada's determination to survive as a country. In truth, the war was simply a series of skirmishes that hardly changed the borders of its participants. Perhaps. But the history of the 1812 war, the uphill charge at Queenston Heights, the British capture of Fort Michilimackinac, the Yankees' burning of York (Toronto) for which Washington, D.C. was burned in retaliation still thrills Ontario school children. Many Ontario forts which saw action in the War of 1812 have now been reconstructed. You may also notice the Laura Secord chain of candy stores throughout the province; they're named after a héroine of the War of 1812, a Massachusetts-born female counterpart to Paul Revere. Laura Secord trekked 20 miles through enemy lines and thick woods at night to warn the nearest British troops that the Yankees were coming—in fact, that they'd put up overnight at her farm at Queenston.

The War of 1812 brought more settlers to the province—Scots and English soldiers and German mercenaries who decided to stay, and soon after them, the Irish. Driven to emigrate by poverty and famine at home, the Irish poured into Canada both from the Protestant north and the Catholic south. But once here the Protestants joined the powerful Orange Lodge, greatly strengthening the pro-British conservatism of the province. Irish Catholics remained poorer and far less influential politically. On July 12, the Orange holiday, you can still see parades of Protestants in some Ontario communities. The old fights live on through the symbolic white horse, orange sashes, Union Jack banners and drum corps, and the descendants of the Irish Catholic immigrants offer pithy partisan observations from the sidelines.

The Fight for Good Government

Surprisingly, it wasn't one of the fighting Irish, but a Scotsman, William Lyon Mackenzie, who led the fight for democratic reform of Ontario's colonial government. The Constitutional Act of 1791 had divided Upper Canada (Ontario) from Lower Canada (Québec), and established an elected legislative assembly with no real power and, over it, a legislative council run by a self-perpetuating clique of rich Anglicans so closely related in philosophy and marriage that they were called the Family Compact. The system was rife with patronage for members of the Compact which Mackenzie, through his outspoken newspaper, the *Colonial Advocate,* attacked vigorously. In retaliation, several young men from Toronto's finest families dumped his printing presses into Toronto harbor.

Mackenzie was elected five times to the Legislature and five times he was expelled—sometimes bodily. Finally, in 1837, coordinating with rebellious democrats in Québec, Mackenzie staged open rebellion. A ragtag group of men marched on Toronto from Montgomery's Tavern at the north end of Yonge Street, only to be dispersed by the muskets of the British army. Mackenzie fled to the States; two other rebel leaders were caught, tried and hanged. It appeared the Family Compact had triumphed.

In a very real sense, however, Mackenzie's revolt succeeded. As a result the colonial government was reformed, elected representatives given real political power and democracy established in Ontario.

Ethnic Diversification

Throughout the 19th century, waves of immigrants kept arriving, settling and adding to the blend of Ontario's character. Many sailed from the British Isles, bringing traditions of beef-and-potatoes cooking, a hardy ambition to make a lot of money, and a taste for whiskey and beer.

A lot of drinking went on in pioneer Ontario. In winter a town's main streets would be lined with barrels of alcohol; as the water content froze the ice was lifted out, and some very strong brew remained! The temperance efforts of Methodist ministers eventually brought in Ontario's famously repressive liquor laws. For a long time, no Sunday drinking was allowed. Many local townships in Ontario are still "dry" and technically, you still cannot picnic with wine in a public place. (Interestingly, Ontario never had full prohibition. From here in the Roarin' Twenties, bootleg whiskey was smuggled to the American underworld, to the chagrin of Elliot Ness.) But later immigrant groups greatly altered Ontario's attitudes to liquor—and, thank goodness, improved the quality of its local wines.

Jews and Eastern Europeans came to Ontario towards the middle of the 19th century (settling in Toronto, Hamilton, and around southwestern Ontario). Chinese and Italians brought out as laborers added to the mosaic of the province's peoples. Of special pride to Ontarians is one group of immigrants who arrived in the 1840's, 50's and 60's—

runaway Blacks from the Southern states. They traveled by the Underground Railroad to freedom in Canada where the slave trade had been outlawed since 1793. In Southeastern Ontario at Windsor and Niagara-on-the-Lake there are plaques commemorating the Underground Railway's "terminals," while near Dresden is the home and grave of Rev. Josiah Henson (on whom Harriet Beecher Stowe based *Uncle Tom's Cabin*).

Confederation and Commerce

Among the Fathers of Canadian Confederation—the men who joined separate British colonies into the independent Dominion of Canada—none were more influential than Ontarians. George Brown (crusading first editor of Toronto's powerful paper *The Globe and Mail*), Oliver Mowat, premier of Ontario and the hard-drinking Kingston lawyer, Sir John A. MacDonald, not only helped midwife the country, they ensured that Ontario would play a dominant role in its politics. John A. MacDonald went on to become Canada's first prime minister and the driving force behind the construction of the transcontinental railway which brought the west into the new Dominion.

The railways changed the lives of Ontario settlers. Previously towns had depended on the waterways for transport and power for their struggling flour and saw mills. Sir John's creation, the Canadian Pacific Railway (which spanned the province by 1888), opened up Ontario's manufacturing, resource, and trade potential. The coming of electricity accelerated Ontario's development. The province has always lacked major fuel resources, but in 1906, Sir Adam Beck established the provincial government-run Hydro Electric Power Commission and soon was providing more than enough cheap power for local industry. Now Ontario Hydro has become one of the world's greatest hydroelectric enterprises. Hydro operates nuclear stations—the two largest are at Pickering (east of Toronto) and near Port Elgin—and coal-based stations which bring the province-run corporation into frequent conflict with environmentalists concerned about acid rain.

Hydro spurred the growth of pulp and paper manufacture (now a major industry), mining, refining and manufacturing. As a result Ontario has continued to grow rich and powerful. It produces almost half the manufactured goods in Canada, including most of the automobiles (at Oakville and Oshawa). The "Golden Horseshoe"—the heavily populated and wealthy semicircle from Oshawa through Toronto to steel-producing Hamilton—is the center of this wealth and industry.

The Land of Precious Metals

Meanwhile, Northern Ontario (dubbed "God's Country" because no one else seemed to care about it) has proved rich in mineral wealth. At the beginning of this century, precious metal discoveries precipitated gold and silver rushes at Cobalt, Kirkland Lake and Porcupine Lake. They are still major mining centers. Sudbury now produces most of the world's platinum and more than a third of the world's nickel output. Rich uranium discoveries around Algoma, Blind River, and Bancroft within the last 25 years have fueled the research and development of nuclear power.

Waterways have always played a major role in Ontario's history, but of unparalleled importance is the 2,000-mile-long St. Lawrence Seaway, handling grain (from the giant terminals at Thunder Bay), ore (from Sault Ste. Marie), and manufactured goods (from the Golden Horseshoe). The seaway, opened in 1961, accounts for a 500 per cent increase in the port of Toronto's overseas consignments alone.

Despite the recent shift of financial power to the oil-rich province of Alberta, Ontario dominates the rest of English Canada culturally, politically, and financially. Here are the headquarters of English-language C.B.C. television, private television and film production; here is the home of the National Ballet, the Canadian Opera Company, the National Gallery. Out of 282 seats in the federal House of Commons, 95 are occupied by members from Ontario. The Toronto Stock Exchange, largest in Canada, is among the top five on the continent.

But its people are the basis of Ontario's wealth. Post-war immigrants have poured into Ontario from Asia and Europe (including refugees from Hungary, Vietnam, and Latin America), swelling the province's population to well over 8½ million. Once Loyal Orange and True Blue, Ontario has become a colorful spectrum—still loyal to its founders' principles of order and respect, but combining with them tolerance, friendliness, and an appetite for life.

EXPLORING TORONTO

"Toronto is not a city generally attractive to the traveller" wrote the great English novelist Anthony Trollope in 1862, while poet Rupert Brooke lamented "the depressing thing is that it will always be what it is, only larger."

Fortunately for the provincial capital, these learned men reckoned without the dramatic changes wrought by time, wealth, and thousands of immigrants. This once dull, staid backwater ("Toronto the Good") is now known as "People City": a city of over 2.9 million souls, of old tree-lined streets, safe pleasant parks, galleries and cafés, low crime rates, renovation and innovation.

Toronto's restaurants (many of them commended by top international critics), clubs, bars, and theaters are lively all year round, but city life might be said to center in the nine-acre Nathan Phillips Square in front of City Hall. Named after the Toronto mayor who backed the project, the square is the center of activity even in winter, when the reflecting pool becomes a skating rink, and is as jammed on New Year's Eve as Times Square in New York City. In summer, Nathan Phillips Square is the site of ethnic festivals, outdoor art shows, free concerts, and people-watching. It's an excellent place to begin a Toronto walking tour.

To your east looms the old City Hall, a pile of Victorian Gothic stones, complete with clocktower, gargoyles (said to be portraits of early city fathers) and the architect's name (E. J. Lennox) carved into stone tracery under the eaves. Built in 1899, it now houses courts.

In front of you is the new City Hall, a clam-shaped design of Finnish architect Viljo Revell which was completed in 1965. Every day of the week City Hall offers conducted tours. There is an information booth and art displays in its front lobby. In front of the main entrance stands "The Archer," a Henry Moore bronze sculpture purchased by some of Toronto's rich to complement Revell's architectural design.

On the west side of the square is the beautifully restored Osgoode Hall, the headquarters since 1832 of the Law Society of Upper Canada. It once housed Ontario's Supreme Court. Particularly beautiful are Osgoode Hall's main lobby (white Corinthian columns, broad double stairways, stained glass) and second-floor library (40-foot vaulted ceilings, paneling, a huge fireplace, and acres of leatherbound volumes). The wrought-iron fences in front still feature the original cow-gates, complexly shaped to keep out wandering cattle.

At the northwest corner of City Hall Square, behind Osgoode Hall, a passageway leads past the New Courthouse and fountains to University Avenue. Here is the American consulate. A plaque (at 555 University Avenue) marks the birthplace of silent screen star Mary Pickford. At 426 University Avenue stands the Royal Canadian Military Institute, a private officers' club with an excellent collection of pistols, sabers, swords, and the cockpit of the Red Baron von Richthofen's Fokker D-VIII (he was shot down by a Canadian flying ace in 1918).

Gentlemen, Scholars and Immigrants

Turn west three blocks on Dundas Street until you reach the Art Gallery of Ontario. Its back entrance—overlooking a small leafy park where old men play chess in summer—is known as The Grange. Built in 1817, The Grange is a Georgian manor home, once belonging to members of Upper Canada's ruling Family Compact. Later it housed Toronto's first public art gallery. The Art Gallery of Ontario has since moved next door, but shares a courtyard restaurant and its hours of opening with The Grange.

East and west along Dundas Street stretches Toronto's Chinatown: first-class restaurants and shops offering candied roses, pickled seaweed, porcelain and jade. Keep heading west and you'll come to Spadina Avenue, the ladder to success of Toronto's immigrants. As the original Anglo-Saxon gentry moved farther up the street, Jewish immigrants moved in at the southern end. One notable site is Switzer's Delicatessen (322 Spadina Avenue). In an upstairs room "Red Emma" Goldman died, the internationally feared (and loved) anarchist and feminist. One block west (between Dundas and College) Kensington, the old Jewish market, teems with live rabbits, smoked salmon, hundreds of local and imported cheeses, old men selling homemade halvah. As groups of immigrants have prospered and moved north, new ones have taken their place. Today Kensington shoppers can also choose from among Portuguese, West Indian, and Chinese goods.

At Spadina and College are clubs and bars offering jazz and blues. They're overshadowed to the north of the intersection by a batlike

Gothic building. Constructed in 1875 as Knox college, this sinister-looking building later became Connaught Laboratories; here the first penicillin and polio vaccine were manufactured.

Turn east from Spadina along College Street. You're entering the campus area. On College Street's north corner is the old Central Library; the corner of College and St. George Street (#33 St. George), boasts the MacDonald-Mowat House. Now the International Student Centre attached to the University of Toronto, 33 St. George Street's airy, high-ceilinged rooms were once home to Canada's first prime minister, Sir John A. MacDonald, and to Sir Oliver Mowat, premier of Ontario at the end of the 19th century. The main campus of the century-and-a-half-old University of Toronto lies east of St. George, north of College Street. University College (which dominates the north side of King's College Circle) was built in 1859. Its leafy quadrangle, gargoyles, vaulted halls, carved bannisters and patterned tile floors give it special charm. The round tower at the west end is reported to be haunted.

To the east of University College is the small domed tower of the old Observatory building. Now that Toronto's David Dunlap Observatory has moved north to Richmond Hill, the old building has become the headquarters of the University's Students' Administrative Council.

To the northeast is Hart House, a Gothic-style student center, with a paneled, Oxford-style Great Dining Hall, built between 1911 and 1919 by the Massey family—"Toronto has no social classes, only the Masseys and the masses." The family also gave Toronto its fine old concert hall on Shuter Street, and a beautiful piece of modern architecture, Massey College at Devonshire Place just north of Hart House.

The University of Toronto, one of the largest and best in the country, is known for research (penicillin, pablum, and the electron microscope were developed here), scholarship, and power. Canadian prime ministers, e.g. the long-ruling Mackenzie King and Nobel Peace Prize winner Lester B. Pearson, are among its graduates.

Yorkville

Avenue Road and Bloor marks the edge of Toronto's shopping and coffeehouse district, Yorkville. An independent village until 1883, Yorkville was Toronto's bohemia in the 1950's and 60's. Its clubs hosted then-unknown folk singers like Gordon Lightfoot and Joni Mitchell. Some of Yorkville's architecture is new (for example the Hazelton Lanes, Cumberland Court, and York Square café-boutique-and-garden complexes). Some of it is sandblasted Victoriana, like the houses and galleries on Scollard Street and Hazelton Avenue. Of special interest is a renovated church-turned-boutique-arcade at the corner of Hazelton and Scollard.

A side trip: 30 minutes' walk northwest of Yorkville is Casa Loma, a millionaire's folly built between 1911 and 1914 by Sir Henry Pellatt. Known in financial circles as "Pellatt the Plunger," Sir Henry spent three million dollars to equip his 98-room castle. He installed one of the first private elevators anywhere plus gold-plated bathroom fixtures, an 800-foot-long underground passageway to huge stables, and por-

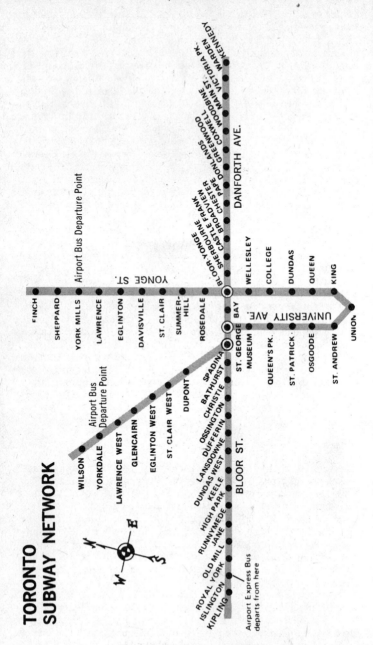

TORONTO
SUBWAY NETWORK

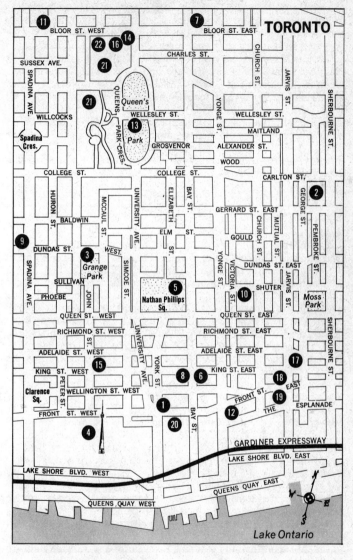

TORONTO

Toronto—Points of Interest

1) Air Terminal
2) Allan Gardens
3) Art Gallery
4) C.N. Tower
5) City Hall
6) Commerce Court
7) Cumberland Terrace
8) Toronto Dominion Centre
9) Kensington Market
10) Mackenzie House
11) Medical Arts Building
12) O'Keefe Centre
13) Parliament Buildings
14) Planetarium
15) Royal Alexandra Theatre
16) Royal Ontario Museum
17) St. James Cathedral
18) St. Lawrence Centre for the Arts
19) St. Lawrence Market
20) Union Station
21) University of Toronto
22) Varsity Stadium

celain troughs for horses. The cost of castle-living broke Pellatt in the 1920's. And except for a brief stint as a hotel, the castle stood empty and deserted until 1937 when the Kiwanis Club took over. During World War II it served as an army intelligence headquarters.

The castle features an organ with 60-foot high pipes in the Great Hall; Sir Henry and Lady Pellatt's bedrooms (totally refurnished); views from the east-end Scottish tower and west-end Norman tower, and a small museum which includes a lock of Métis rebel leader Louis Riel's hair.

A fifteen-minute walk southwest of Casa Loma takes you to Markham Village, another boutiques-and-art-galleries shopping area one block west of Bathurst and Bloor. Or head southeast to Yorkville, Bay Street (Canada's Wall Street of high finance), and Yonge Street, which is probably the most colorful way to get back downtown.

Yonge Street

Yonge Street is billed as "the longest street in the world." It stretches from Lake Ontario 207 miles to North Bay, and as Highway 11 north of town and then (by other names) a further 1,000 miles north and west. Yonge Street was first laid out by Lt. Governor John Graves Simcoe almost 200 years ago. The ill-fated rebels of 1837 marched down this street. Now it's an expensive-to-gaudy shopping strip. Head south from Bloor. Maple Leaf Gardens, at Yonge and College Streets, is the home of the Toronto Maple Leafs hockey team. It has also hosted practically every other sort of entertainment, from Sunday-night wrestling to the Bolshoi Ballet and Bob Dylan. Below College, Yonge Street turns into a strip of bargain book and record stores and raunchy movie houses. Two of Toronto's major department stores are at the intersections of Yonge and Dundas and Yonge and Queen. On the north side, the Eaton Center, a huge glassed-in mall, stretches right up to Dundas Street. The Metropolitan Toronto Convention and Tourist Bureau is headquartered here. Behind the Eaton Center hides the tiny, pretty Church of the Holy Trinity, built in 1847 when an anonymous English benefactress willed the land to the Anglican Church in perpetuity. East across Yonge Street along Dundas a block or two (at 82 Bond Street) is the old Mackenzie House, where the rebel leader died in 1861. The house has been restored to its 1850's finery and includes the flatbed printing press which Mackenzie's ghost is said to haunt.

Still east of Yonge but farther south, a plaque at 60 Richmond Street East marks the site where in 1879 Sir Sandford Fleming read a paper to the Canadian Institute outlining his plan for a worldwide standard time system.

Two of Toronto's major theater complexes are east of Yonge on Front Street: the O'Keefe and the St. Lawrence Centre. From here, looking west, you see the main post office. Beyond it, soaring 1,815 feet, is the world's tallest free-standing structure, the CN Tower (CN is Canadian National, the publicly owned rail and communications corporation). From the CN Tower's 1,100-foot-high revolving restaurant and observation pod visitors can see about 75 miles on a clear day.

East of Yonge on Front Street is the 170-year-old St. Lawrence farmers' market (open Saturdays for the sale of fish, fresh produce, and home preserves). Attached to the market is another of Toronto's early city halls, the St. Lawrence Hall, built in 1844 and recently restored to its former splendor. It was here that Jenny Lind, the Swedish songbird sang, Sir John A. MacDonald boomed out speeches at stormy political rallies and P. T. Barnum once displayed midget Tom Thumb.

Museums, Parks, Art Galleries

Escape from the city via the island ferries. You can catch them just west of the foot of Yonge Street. There are three major island areas. Ward's Island is where a remnant residential community retains private homes. Centre Island has bicycle and boat rentals, outdoor pubs, beaches, a zoo, a children's amusement area and farm, and sailing clubs. Hanlan's Point's beaches are less crowded, and you can watch the planes take off from Island Airport. In summer the islands host ethnic festivals (the biggest is the West Indian community's in late July) and music and theater festivals. The islands may also be seen from cruise boats that depart from the bottom of Yonge Street. For licensed pilots, Island Rent-a-Plane is located at 545 Lakeshore Boulevard.

Back on the mainland, turn west from Bay along King Street. Above you soar the towers of the country's most powerful corporations. Underfoot are miles of shopping malls. Ahead, across University Avenue, on the north side of King Street one eccentric Toronto millionaire has opened a row of good, inexpensive beef and seafood restaurants and financed the resurrection of the grand old Royal Alexandra Theatre. Across from the "Royal Alex" rises Toronto's new concert hall named after the newspaper baron, Roy Thomson. Farther west along King Street are a couple of good restaurants and wholesale clothiers. To the south lie the CN Tower and Old Fort York. At Fort York you can see drills and cannons demonstrated by its scarlet-clad guard. Fort York was the scene of Toronto's fiercest battle in 1813. Seventeen hundred Americans defeated Toronto's 700-man defense force. Retreating, they set fire to the gunpowder barrels lest the fort fall into American hands. The explosion was tremendous. When the smoke cleared, 38 American soldiers lay dead. The American occupation of York lasted less than a week. Though Torontonians remember it for the burning of their legislative buildings, many of the soldiers were gentlemen conquerors, even returning books they had borrowed from local libraries!

Farther west are the grounds of the Canadian National Exhibition (the world's largest annual exhibition, it's open from mid-August to Labor Day in September). The "Ex," as it has been known for almost a century, features craft shows, ferris wheels, butter sculptures, the latest model cars and appliances. Off-season some of the Ex Grounds' attractions are open, like the Hockey Hall of Fame (where the Stanley Cup is displayed), Canada's Sports Hall of Fame, Scadding Cabin, a restored log house (built 1794), and the Marine Museum of Upper Canada. Housed in century-old army barracks, the Museum displays Eskimo kayaks, a fully restored tug, and working models of Ontario's canal systems.

To the south of Exhibition Park is Ontario Place, a waterfront amusement park. Ontario Place has man-made beaches and picnic spots plus the world's largest indoor movie screen (offering spectacular experimental films), a children's playground with climbing ropes, punching bags and dunking pools. And it has the Forum. The Forum is an outdoor amphitheatre where symphony orchestras or rock groups play for 8,000 fans stretched out on the grass under the stars.

West of Ontario Place and the CNE are some small public beaches and landing places for small craft. To reach one of Toronto's most pleasant city parks, turn north at Parkside Drive (subway stops: Keele, High Park). High Park contains a small zoo, floral gardens and abstract sculpture dotted throughout 400 acres of treed, rolling hills. In the heart of the park, you'll find Grenadier Pond. It's named for a Redcoat Grenadier who drowned in it a century and a half ago. Now it's a cheerful, pretty spot, with boat rentals and gardens along its shores. At the Regency-style Colborne Lodge (built in 1836) in the middle of the park you can see sketches and paintings of architect John Howard (the original owner).

Back in downtown Toronto, you'll find other pleasant parks. Queen's Park is one of the main downtown parks, and the well-fed black and brown squirrels who live here think it's just fine. The park has the same name as the pink Romanesque Provincial Parliament Buildings to the south. It is flanked by the Sigmund Samuel Canadiana Gallery, the McLaughlin Planetarium, Victoria University in the University of Toronto, and St. Michael's College. The equestrian statue in the middle of the park is a recent addition; King Edward VII was first unveiled over 60 years ago in Imperial India. He was brought to Canada just decades ago when the independent Indians no longer wanted him.

The Sigmund Samuel Canadiana Gallery (14 Queen's Park Crescent West) contains an early Canadian paneled room, plus a fine collection of drawings, prints, crafts, and antique furniture. Nearby, the McLaughlin Planetarium houses permanent exhibits of the development of astronomy, model solar systems, solar wind, meteorite matter. It also features a domed theater where a 150-lens film projector creates astronomical films-in-the-round.

The newly expanded and renovated Royal Ontario Museum is next door: about 5,000,000 human artifacts and natural wonders, including one of the world's best Chinese collections (20 galleries' worth and, at street level, behind a glass wall, the renowned Ming Tomb Complex); a six-story West Coast Indian totem pole; intriguingly instructive models in the geology and palaeontology galleries (including skeletons of 70-million-year-old dinosaurs); and toy-and-snack shops for children.

Toronto, a major center of the Canadian and international art scene, has many excellent private galleries. They are clustered around Yorkville, north of Queen's Park, Markham Village, Yonge Street and the Art Gallery of Ontario. It also boasts two excellent public galleries, the already mentioned Art Gallery of Ontario and the McMichael Canadian Collection in Kleinburg (a 20-mile drive northwest of Toronto).

The McMichael Collection, a beautiful 30-room log-and-stone gallery, houses major works by the Group of Seven, a movement of early 20th-century landscape painters. In addition to their colorful, dramatic canvases, and those of their associates, you can see carvings and crafts by Indian and Eskimo artists. The setting is perfect: lofty art-lined rooms smelling of warm wood look out on the rolling woods of the Humber River Valley. A recent $9 million renovation has made the gallery fireproof, and climate controlled. All levels are now accessible to the handicapped.

A Mental Mecca

There's another intellectual playground for children and adults in northeast Toronto: the Ontario Science Centre, in whose exhibits you can discover and participate in the operation of television studios, musical instruments, electrical storms, and simulated moon-landings. The center also contains an excellent film library and theater. It's all housed in a spectacular modern building clinging to the slopes of the Don Valley at Don Mills Road and Eglinton Avenue.

Many of Toronto's parks are linked through the city's ravine systems and the Don Valley north of the Science Centre joins some particularly beautiful ones. You can walk from the Wilket Creek–Sunnybrook Park chain (where there are public riding stables) north to Edwards Gardens. Once a private estate, Edwards Gardens is now 35 acres of rustic paths, bridges and flowerbeds; here, too, is the Civic Garden Centre of Toronto with a fine gardener's library.

A bus from Eglinton subway (or a drive west to Jane Street then north to Keele) will take you to Black Creek Pioneer Village, where small-town Ontario of the 1840's has been re-created. Guides in period costume show you around an operating mill, schoolhouse and general store.

The inventiveness manifested by the new Metro Zoo has astonished Toronto. It's really a park for animals; the people are kept apart. Five thousand creatures roam around in 710 acres of forest, plain and river valley where botanists have simulated African savannah, Malayan rain forest and polar tundra. The people, on the other hand, must keep to footpaths or board silent, slow-moving trains so as not to disturb the zoo's full-time inhabitants.

PRACTICAL INFORMATION FOR TORONTO

HOW TO GET THERE. By air: Many major international carriers *(KLM, Air France, Alitalia, El Al, American Airlines, Eastern Airlines)* land at Lester B. Pearson International Airport. *Air Canada* and *Canadian Pacific* link Toronto to international and intraprovincial centers.

By train: *Via Rail* links with *Amtrak* at Montréal, Windsor and Buffalo.

By bus: The bus terminal is at 610 Bay St. Service to all points in Ontario and beyond is provided by *Eastern Canadian Greyhound Lines Ltd., Gray Coach Lines, Voyageur Colonial,* and others.

By car: the MacDonald Cartier Freeway (Hwy. 401) passes through Toronto on an east-west axis. Hwys. 11 and 400 are major routes north. The Queen Elizabeth Way curves southwest from Toronto, linking it to Hamilton, Niagara Falls, Fort Erie, and New York State.

ACCOMMODATIONS. In Toronto, they range from clean budget establishments to royal suites. Recently there has been a trend toward construction of middle-priced hotels with smaller rooms and fewer frills, providing clean, modern accommodation and basic services. Tariffs for double occupancy are categorized as follows: *Deluxe,* over $115; *Expensive,* $85–115; *Moderate,* $60–75; *Inexpensive,* under $50. The Ontario Government has lifted the 7% hotel room tax. That move, coupled with favorable $U.S. exchange rates, means hotel room prices are even cheaper than they seem.

Most places accept the following major credit cards: American Express, MasterCard and Visa; others may also be honored. Not all establishments accept credit cards, therefore we suggest you call for information.

Deluxe

Four Seasons. 21 Avenue Rd. You may see rock star Elton John under the foyer's chandelier or it may be the Prime Minister. Rooms are bright and airy with good midtown views. In summer the outdoor pool is a popular meeting spot. There's an indoor pool, too. All in the fashionable, overpriced Yorkville district.

Toronto Hilton Harbour Castle. 1 Harbour Sq. A spectacular view of Toronto Harbour, an indoor pool, first-class restaurants on the premises, and a jet-setting clientele account for this new complex's prices.

King Edward Hotel. 37 King St. E. It's been splendidly restored since The Beatles and Liz and Dick stayed there in the late 1960's, and is now a palace of marble and mushroom velvet, saunas, first-class restaurants, handy to the best theaters.

The Sheraton Centre. Across from City Hall, has almost 1,500 rooms, some of which look out on the rooftop pool; an indoor waterfall; a shopping arcade; and the longest bar in North America.

Westin Hotel. 145 Richmond St. W. A Trader Vic's. Indoor/outdoor pool, expensive modern décor.

Expensive

Park Plaza Hotel. 4 Avenue Rd. Since the 1930's the quiet quality of this hotel has attracted Prince Phillip, Rudolf Nureyev—quite a range. Great rooftop bar. Some deluxe rooms.

Royal York. 100 Front St. For years it's been Toronto's top-of-the-line. Old but gracious, with a shopping arcade, a huge nightclub and a smaller, but excellent jazz club on the ground floors. Some deluxe rooms.

Windsor Arms. 22 St. Thomas. This small hotel in the expensive Bloor St. shopping district is a real find. The absence of indoor-pool-type frills is more than made up for by individually decorated rooms, some of the best restaurants in the city and an urbane, discreet ambiance.

Moderate

Bond Place. 65 Dundas E. 300 small rooms in a sensible service hotel.

The Carlton Inn Hotel. 30 Carlton St. This central, serviceable hotel, right next door to Maple Leaf Gardens, has 550 rooms, indoor pool and sauna.

The Delta Chelsea Inn. 33 Gerrard St. W. The pleasant rooms are fully equipped with color TV and private bath—some have kitchenettes. The reason they're less expensive is their slightly smaller size. Indoor pool. Right downtown. Some expensive rooms.

Roehampton Place Hotel. 808 Mount Pleasant Rd. An outdoor pool, some rooms with individual saunas, lounge and dining room. Slightly too far north to be central, but handy to public transport, shopping, restaurants.

Inexpensive

Toronto International Hostel. Church St. at Dundas. Open to all ages. Shared rooms; midnight curfew. Lowest rates in town.

Friendship Inns: Seahorse Motel. Ranges from inexpensive to expensive, depending on whether your room overlooks the expressway or the lake. Outdoor pool. A short taxi ride from subways, Ontario Pl., the Exhibition Park.

Neill-Wycik College. Gerrard St. E. at Church St. Open only in summer. Single, double and family accommodations available in this 22-story co-operative residence. Popular roof deck for sunning. Downtown location.

Selby Hotel. 592 Sherbourne St. In a quiet but raunchy area of town (if that seems contradictory, it's the essence of Toronto). Just steps from the subway. Some rooms nicely renovated.

Victoria. 56 Yonge St. No TV, not all the rooms have bathrooms—but it's cheap and clean and has welcomed travelers to downtown Toronto since 1906.

TELEPHONES. Toronto and the Golden Horseshoe cities of Hamilton, St. Catharines, and Niagara Falls are in area code 416. Pay phone booths cost 25¢.

HOW TO GET AROUND. By public transport: Tokens are available at subway stations, cigar stores and sundries stores on bus and streetcar routes. Buses and streetcars will only take exact fares. The subway is fast, clean and relatively pleasant. It crosses midtown on Bloor St.'s east-west axis and runs north and south on Yonge St., and the Spadina–University line. Transfers are free. Call 484–4544 for transit information. If you're staying for a month, do buy a "Metropass"—a photo-identity card that entitles you to unlimited rides—after you've paid the initial $36.50.

By taxi: The rates start at $1.20, increasing by 20¢ each 300 meters. For complaints call: 488–2221. The biggest city-wide companies are *Metro, Diamond* and *Co-op.* Smaller companies are equally efficient.

From the airport: Limousines will take you down in style. They're generally waiting outside the arrival level. Airport buses will take you downtown to the Royal York Hotel for $6.00. Other hotels run buses from the airport; their fares vary. There are also Airport Express buses run by Gray Coach, which for $2.75 will take you from the airport to the Islington Stop on the east-west subway line, for $3.00 to the Yorkdale Stop on the Spadina line, and for $3.75, to the York Mills Stop on the Yonge line.

TOURIST INFORMATION. The *Metropolitan Toronto Covention and Vistors Association* has a good general city map and a quarterly publication on what's happening. Toronto Eaton Centre Galleria, Suite 110, Box 510, Toronto M5B 2H1 (Telephone: 979–3143).

SEASONAL EVENTS. January-February. New Year's Eve is celebrated by crowds skating in front of City Hall. There are weekend sleigh rides at Black Creek Pioneer Village.

The International Boat Show and The Farm Show come to the Coliseum in Exhibition Park. Exact dates may vary yearly.

In **March,** the Coliseum hosts the Quarter-Horse extravaganza, Quarterama, with many riding classes, an auction and a stallion parade, as well as the Canadian National Sportment's Show.

April brings crafts lovers to the Winter's End Craft Show, and do-it-yourself repairmen and interior decorators to the National Home Show in Exhibition Park.

On the **May** 24th weekend, fireworks at Ontario Place celebrate the birthday of Queen Victoria.

In **June,** it's time for the running of the Queen's Plate, the oldest stakes in North America. Metro Caravan begins; it's a 9-day salute to the food, drink, and dance of the city's ethnic communities.

Toronto's West Indians get a weekend to themselves in mid-**July:** it's Cariabana, with parades, music, and mardi-gras atmosphere.

August marks the opening of the Canadian National Exhibition, and also the Players Tennis Championships.

In **November,** the Royal Winter Fair opens. Out at Black Creek Pioneer Village, kids help adults spin, bake, and sing in preparation for Christmas.

TOURS. The *Toronto Stock Exchange* is at 234 Bay St., shadowed by the high office towers of high finance. This exchange handles over two-thirds of the volume of trading in Canada, and offers two guided tours a day, summer weekdays.

Guided tours leave the front desk of the new *City Hall* daily, at frequent intervals. The *Provincial Parliament,* built of pink sandstone Romanesque style are close by Queen's Park subway. There's also a visitors' gallery high above the Debates chamber.

The *Ontario Jockey Club* conducts guided group tours around Greenwood and Woodbine Race Tracks (May–September, Wednesday and Thursday mornings). Visitors get a chance to talk with the track vet, watch the horses train, speak with their trainers. Telephone for details and reservations: 675–6110 or 698–3131.

Molson's Brewery will guide visitors through their plant at 640 Fleet St. W. and explain the entire brewing process. The tour is limited to people above the drinking age (19 years). They request that you call ahead.

University of Toronto tours leave the front door of the University College on summer afternoons.

See Toronto from the air: *Toronto Airways Ltd.* takes off with sightseers aboard from the Buttonville airport, Hwy. 7 and Woodbine Ave. Or you can see Toronto by streetcar (2-hour tour includes Fort York): call 869–1372.

Or see Toronto from a three-masted sailing ship: call *Empire Sandy Cruise,* 364–3244. Glass-topped sightseeing boats also provide 1-hour cruises of the waterfront, and of duck hideaways in the lagoons of Toronto Islands. Board at the foot of Yonge St. *Boat Tours Int'l.* reserves for its one-hour tour of the harbor islands. Telephone: 364–2412.

For a free 3½-mile tour of Toronto's east harbor and headlands call the *Toronto Harbour Commission.* On summer Sundays tours leave from the foot of Leslie St.

The *Pickering Nuclear Plant* offers free tours with well-informed guides and a Star Trek display of computer games, all designed to make you feel more comfortable about nuclear power.

Three guided walking tours of the University of Toronto's midtown campus start from Hart House at Queen's Park and Wellesley St., June through August, at 10:30 A.M., 12:30, and 2:30 P.M.

CHILDREN'S ACTIVITIES. *The Ontario Science Centre,* 770 Don Mills Rd., has the ultimate in toys—millions of dollars' worth of educational, experimental, participatory machines and exhibits, like a computer with which you can play tic-tac-toe, a static electricity machine that is quite literally hair-raising, or a model of the rain cycle.

The exhibits at the *Royal Ontario Museum* and next door to it the *McLaughlin Planetarium* are both imaginatively designed, and bright older children can occupy themselves here quite happily for hours. Children under six are not admitted to the *Planetarium Theatre.* The ROM has a special children's cafeteria downstairs. The McLaughlin Planetarium, the ROM and the Science Centre are more fully described under "Museums and Galleries."

Canada's Wonderland has 370 acres of rather un-Canadian cartoon animals come to life, 5 roller coasters, a saltwater circus with dolphins, and an artificial mountain.

The *CN Tower,* the world's largest freestanding structure, has a futuristic games area at the base.

Harbourfront is great, day or night: craft shows, antique sales, dance (watching or doing), sailing, jazz.

Centre Island has a special children's park where kids can ride swan-shaped boats or an old-fashioned merry-go-round, or play with the animals in the *Centreville Farm.* Take the Centre Island ferry from the foot of Bay St.

The *Toronto Islands* are a great place for children to run off excess energy; so is the *Children's Village Playground* at Ontario Pl., with its ropes to swing on and foam rubber to land in.

Ontario Place is open from mid-May to Labor Day. In its winter season, the *Toronto Symphony* performs special children's concerts: *Peter and the Wolf, Carnival of the Animals,* etc. Call Roy Thomson Hall for details.

Toronto is also the home of *Young People's Theatre,* which coordinates several companies of professional actors who tour schools; their 468-seat YPT Centre opened in the fall of 1977 at the corner of Front and Frederick Sts., the first center for the performing arts for children and teens in Canada. They have also showcased music, puppetry, mime, and dance.

Children can see the 19th century come alive in the general store, blacksmith's shop and 28 other reconstructed buildings at *Black Creek Pioneer Village,* open from March to December. It's at Jane St. and Steeles Ave. W. The admission fee (family maximum $8.00 with children under 16)) is worth it. Weekend events vary with the season.

Historic *Fort York* (east of the Canadian National Exhibition grounds) is a good bet. Better: the 700-acre *Metro Zoo* where animals roam free in faithfully re-created natural environments, which humans tour by silent electric trains, on foot or on cross-country skies in winter.

There are some excellent toy shops in the *Ontario Science Centre* and the *McLaughlin Planetarium.* Among the other good toy stores are *The Toy Shop,* 62 Cumberland; *Little Dollhouse,* 609 Mt. Pleasant, specializing in miniatures; *The Teachers' Store,* for educational toys—Leggo, etc.; and *The Creative Child,* 47A Colborne St.

SPORTS. Professional sports: The *Toronto Blue Jays* bring American Baseball League games to Toronto; the stars of Canadian professional sports, the *Toronto Argonauts,* play Canadian Football League games in the CNE Stadium, which also rocks with the cheers of fans at Toronto's popular *Blizzard Soccer Club* games. *The Toronto Maple Leafs'* games are held at Maple

Leaf Gardens, 60 Carlton St. E., where you can also catch the Ontario Hockey Association's Toronto *Marlboroughs.* **Horse-racing:** *Greenwood Racetrack* at Queen and Coxwell is relatively central, but Toronto's other horse-racing center, *Woodbine Racetrack,* is a brisk drive away at Highway 27 in Malton. **Golf:** Toronto has many public 18-hole golf courses, including *Don Valley Golf Course,* 4200 Yonge Street, and *Dentonia Park Par 3,* at Victoria Park subway station. **Tennis:** Thirty-nine public parks have tennis courts, but at some you must bring your own net. **Swimming:** There are large—and popular—public swimming pools in or near *Christie Pitts* (subway: Christie), *Broadview, Don Valley, High Park, Monarch Park,* and *Eglinton* at Avenue Rd. Swimming in Lake Ontario is supervised on Toronto Island, the beaches in the east end, and Sunnyside west of Ontario Pl. **Boating:** The water is cold; you may be happier sailing. For information about public launching spots call Metro Parks (Telephone: 947–7251). **Winter sports:** In winter, they'll also give you information about the city's 75 outdoor rinks and cross-country skiing on the islands or in the city's ravine systems. **Horseback Riding:** *Central Don Stables* in Sunnybrook Park are municipally operated riding stables. In winter, instruction is available in a heated indoor arena. **Bicycling:** There are some excellent *cycling routes* in Toronto, notably the path in Central Don Park. **Fishing:** In the conservation areas that surround the city, *fishermen* can even get in some decent angling.

 HISTORIC SITES. Toronto was settled by a few French traders as early as 1730; a granite monument in the grounds of the Canadian National Exhibition marks the site of the original *Fort Rouillé.* The *Scadding Cabin,* also on the CNE grounds, is the oldest remaining building in Toronto. Preserved as a late 18th-century residence, open afternoons Wednesday–Sunday, summer. After the 1793 Toronto Purchase, development from wooded ravines to settlers' residences began. The old town was bounded by Ontario, Parliament, Duke and King St. Close to these original city limits is the *Old City (St. Lawrence) Hall,* a graceful classic with ornamental plaster and glittering chandeliers built in 1850, many years after the town had grown. At King St. E. is historic *Little Trinity Church,* which was built in 1844 for Irish immigrants.

None of the original buildings survive but the southeast downtown area has many old architectural and historic curiosities: among them *The Enoch Turner Schoolhouse* (1848), 106 Trinity St., behind Little Trinity Church. The school provided Toronto's first free education. A small admission price treats you to a typical 13th-century Toronto schoolday. Open weekdays.

Many early Toronto residences, such as the *Parshall Terry House* at Todmorden Mills and *Colborne Lodge* (1836), have been restored and opened to the public. *The Grange,* behind the Art Gallery at 317 Dundas St. W., is a gentleman's manor in the style of the 1830's—polished wood and delicate wallpaper— where English man of letters Matthew Arnold was once entertained. For many years it was Toronto's art gallery. The Parshall Terry House dates back to 1798, although it has been refurnished in the 1830's style. Colborne Lodge was the home of surveyor, architect, and art teacher John Howard and his watercolors are on the walls of this Regency-style house in the middle of High Park.

Osgoode Hall (Queen St. at University Ave.) has been the home of the Law Society of Upper Canada since 1832. But its serious occupants haven't dimmed the airy, chandeliered, Corinthian-pillared charm of this impressive public building. *Montgomery's Inn* (Dundas and Islington) once served travelers journeying from the west into Toronto. Now open daily, its Loyalist-era comforts have been restored. *Cornell House* (Brimley Rd. and Lawrence Ave.) was built in 1850. The clothes and kitchen utensils of its 19th-century occupants, on display, make Cornell House a disarmingly personal museum. Open late May to mid-October, Wednesdays, Saturdays, and Sundays. *Gibson House,* at 5172 Yonge St., features daily demonstrations of crafts and cooking from the 1830's. Its original owner was one of the rebels who supported William Lyon Mackenzie, and was forced to spend a decade in exile in the United States. The ghost of the man responsible for the rebellion of 1837 is said to haunt *Mackenzie House,* 82 Bond St. Furnishings of the 1850's, plus Mackenzie's former printing press in the basement, would make the journalist-turned-rebel feel right at home.

Many of the fathers of Canadian Confederation lived in Toronto. Their homes are commemorated by Provincial Plaques. Editor and politician *George Brown's house* on Beverly St. is now the home of the Metropolitan Toronto Association for the Mentally Retarded; the mansion in which *Sir John A. MacDonald* and *Sir Oliver Mowat* lived at 63 St. George St. is now the International Student Centre. You're welcome to look in.

LIBRARIES. Every book in the University of Toronto's enormous system of colleges, schools and institutes is catalogued in the main *John Robarts Library.* The students call this lofty modern $48 million pile dominating the corner of St. George and Harbord Sts. "Fort Book." Here too is the *Thomas Fisher Rare Books Library,* with over 200 books inked before the year 1500. You need a special permit to get in. The Metropolitan Toronto Public Libraries system boasts among other things an excellent multilingual collection and one of the most complete collections of Sherlock Holmes tomes and the works of his creator, Sir Arthur Conan Doyle. You'll find them at the *Metropolitan Toronto Library,* one block above Yonge and Bloor.

The country's largest military library is hidden away in the *Canadian Military Institute,* 426 University Avenue. Gardeners may find the books they need at the *Civic Garden Centre* in Edwards Gardens. The *Law Society of Upper Canada's Library,* on Osgoode Hall's second floor, is a neoclassical paneled room with fireplace, squeaking floors and books.

MUSEUMS AND GALLERIES. Recently imaginative administrations, charged with the new spirit of civic enthusiasm, have made Toronto's museums and galleries come alive as well-loved and well-used focal points of community cultures.

Museums. The *Royal Ontario Museum,* at Avenue Rd. and Bloor (subway: Museum) has one of the finest Chinese collections in the world; its Ming Tomb Complex, relocated behind a glass wall, is dramatically illuminated and visible from Bloor St. There's also a good Egyptian collection which includes 2,000-year-old jewelry, mummies, and models; rooms of European furnishings and musical instruments and a well-organized ethnology section. A children's store, a gift shop with reproductions, and two cafeterias on the premises offer a pleasant tour break. Don't overlook the well-presented geology, minerology, or ethnology displays, or the West Coast totem poles which soar on either side of the central staircase. Massive renovations were completed late in 1983.

The *Sigmund Samuel Canadiana Gallery* specializes in early Canadian furniture and antiques. Silver, glass, coins and wooden sculpture complement the paneled rooms of rich wooden furnishings. It's at 14 Queen's Park Crescent and is open seven days a week, admission free.

The *McLaughlin Planetarium* is next door to the Royal Ontario Museum, north of the Sigmund Samuel Museum. Open daily, it familiarizes visitors with the development of astronomy through a tunnel that leads past exhibits and diagrams into a huge domed theater. Here hour-long films broadcast the heavens onto a curved screen. You tilt back in your chair and marvel. The planetarium admission price includes theater entrance.

The *Marine Museum of Upper Canada* is housed in officers' quarters that date from 1841. The atmosphere is nautical, the exhibits entertaining—everything from an old Eskimo kayak to a tug in dry berth. Open daily. Because the museum is on the grounds of the Canadian National Exhibition, it's best to drive there. Go along Lakeshore Blvd. and turn into the CNE Grounds. While you're there, the *Sports and Hockey Halls of Fame* are close by. The latter is the permanent home of the Stanley Cup and fans can also view hockey memorabilia like Bobby Hull's stick.

The HMCS *Haida,* a destroyer that served Canada in World War II and the Korean War is yet another museum near the CNE. It's afloat off the east end of Ontario Pl.

The *Museum of the Queen's Own Rifles of Canada* is not a large museum, but if the fanciful architecture of Casa Loma has attracted you, it's worth a visit to the castle's third floor to look at the museum's weapons, medals, and memorabilia of the 1885 Northwest Rebellion, including rebel Louis Riel's moccasins and the hood he wore at his hanging. Open daily. Casa Loma also houses an antique car collection.

Todmorden Mills Museum, 67 Pottery Rd., is a four-building complex on the site of an early mill. The old brewery has changing exhibits; there's a collection that will delight the hearts of old railway buffs in the Don Station building; and the Parshall Terry House has been refurnished the way it looked in 1837 when Toronto rebels marched against the local government. The fourth building is a restored house circa 1867. Closed Mondays, open May through December, Tuesdays to Sundays.

Historic *Fort York* northeast of the CNE grounds is a living museum. The scarlet-clad guards drill, parade and fire their cannon daily, all year. In the original buildings, maps, films, models, uniforms and equipment recall the fort's heyday when it guarded Toronto during the War of 1812.

A Henry Moore bronze dominates the southwest corner of Dundas and McCaul Sts. That's your introduction to *The Art Gallery of Ontario,* expanded in the 1970s to include the world's largest public collection of Henry Moore's work (plasters, sketches, and bronzes). Expansion also permitted exhibition of the important Zacks Collection of 20th-century painting and sculpture and the evocative works of Tom Thomson and the Group of Seven school of Canadian landscape painters; Tintoretto's "Christ Washing His Disciples' Feet," Rubens' "The Elevation of the Cross," some rosy Renoir women, an Augustus John portrait of a vivid woman with amazing red hair, a Rodin nude, Claes Oldenburg's giant soft "Hamburger." There's a good licensed restaurant in the back which in summer expands into a sunny courtyard. 317 Dundas St. W. Closed Mondays.

Galleries. There are many private galleries in Toronto, from pillars of the international art establishment to offbeat emporiums of the avant-garde; here are some you might want to visit.

Babbin Saul Galleries, 217 Queen E., specialize in 19th-century oils, watercolors, and etchings. Try *Mira Godard Gallery* at 22 Hazelton, for internationally acclaimed moderns (Ben Nicolson, Jean McEwen); *Moos Gallery* at 136 Yorkville (Canadian modern); *Albert White Gallery* (25 Prince Arthur).

Nancy Poole's Studio, 16 Hazelton, features exclusively Canadian work—like the nostalgic works of magic realist John Boyle, Tony Urquhart's fanciful sculptures or Kim Ondaatje's cool prints. Closed Mondays.

A Moment in Time, 620 Richmond W., and the *Jane Corkin Gallery,* 144 Front St. W., are galleries of photographic art. The *Innuit Gallery,* 30 Avenue Rd., specializes in Eskimo art. *Limited Editions,* 136 Yorkville, sometimes carries Dali, Delacroix, and Miro prints.

More avant-garde works are to be found at *YYZ Artists' Outlet* 116 Spadina Ave., and *The Funnel,* 507 King St. E.

The Isaacs Gallery, 832 Yonge St., is one of the guardians of contemporary Canadian art. Here you'll see anything from William Kurelek's almost primitive realism to Denis Burton's word and image fantasies. Closed Mondays.

Toronto Fine Arts Gallery, 145 King St. W., carries fine French lithographs, Aubusson tapestries, limited-edition prints. Monday to Friday.

Not quite a museum and not exactly a gallery, *The Ontario Science Centre* houses over 500 fascinating exhibits in a striking modern complex that descends the slope of the Don Valley. How musical instruments make sound; how a TV studio works; what causes genetic mutation; computers, ant colonies, geiger counters, miniature rain storms—they're all here. Open daily. Don Mills Rd. and Eglinton Ave.

 MUSIC AND DANCE. If you've checked the local papers or magazines, it hasn't escaped you that Toronto is a musical city. It's home base of the *National Ballet, The Canadian Opera Company,* the *Toronto Symphony,* and many smaller but excellent companies and groups.

For over a decade the active *Guitar Society* has been bringing the world's best concert guitarists, lutenists, and groups to Toronto audiences.

The *Royal Conservatory of Music,* 273 Bloor St. W., is an old neo-Gothic pile of stone where solo concerts and workshops are regularly held.

The *Edward Johnson Building,* partially hidden by the McLaughlin Planetarium south of Avenue Rd. and Bloor is the home of the University of Toronto's *Faculty of Music.* Its two theaters, *Walter Hall* and the *MacMillan Theatre* have esoteric concerts—renaissance songfests or electronic sounds, for example, for its learned audiences. The Edward Johnson Building also runs an excellent chamber music program. You may hear Toronto's well-known *Orford Quartet* or the *Camerata Chamber Orchestra.*

Massey Hall may not be beautiful, but acoustically it's one of the best concert halls in North America. It has been replaced by the huge new *Roy Thomson Hall* as the winter home of the *Toronto Symphony.*

In summer, the Toronto Symphony moves to the *Ontario Place Forum,* where the *Hamilton Philharmonic* is also a regular guest. The acoustics are not great at the Forum unless you can get one of the 2,000 amphitheater seats; but you can still hear the music while you gaze at the night stars if you sprawl out on the grassy hills that surround the Forum.

During the academic year, York University runs concerts at the *Burton Auditorium* and in its college theaters.

The *National Ballet,* headquartered in Toronto, performs at the *O'Keefe Centre* in winter. The O'Keefe also showcases musicals, opera (*The Canadian Opera Company* is here in early fall) and the likes of Tony Bennett and Harry Belafonte.

Next door to O'Keefe Centre, are the two stages of the *St. Lawrence Centre for the Performing Arts.* Lavishly renovated, the new main theater is home to

CentreStage Company, which produces dramatic and comedic works. The smaller *Town Hall* hosts solo musicians, chamber groups and dance companies.

Consult newspaper listings for the performances of the active modern troupe, *The Toronto Dance Theatre.* For experimental dance/art, check out *The Funnel,* on King St. E. at Parliament.

In summer, try Toronto island ferries' *Jazz-on-the-Lake* cruises for a lively evening of drinking and listening to good Dixieland. For information on the free jazz, folk, pops and classical summer concerts in the parks, Harbourfront Park, and City Hall Square, consult newspaper listings.

 THEATER AND REVUES. The twelve-million-dollar *O'Keefe Centre* is a 3,155-seat cavern, a regular off-Broadway tour stop. The O'Keefe Centre, owned by Metropolitan Toronto, is next door to the *St. Lawrence Centre,* a publicly supported showcase for Canadian theater, community forums, small concerts.

Another major theater, the *Royal Alexandra,* is privately owned and has been lovingly restored to its turn-of-the-century splendor. Its booking policy is aggressive and often its Broadway-destined plays star international talents like Liv Ullmann and Laurence Olivier. It's at 260 King Street West, across from Toronto's new concert hall, *Roy Thomson Hall.*

Some of the most exciting theater in North America is showcased at *Theatre Passe Muraille,* 16 Ryerson Ave., the *Toronto Workshop Productions,* 12 Alexander St., and the *Tarragon Theatre,* 30 Bridgman St. Good talent and powerful scripts also come to the *Bayview Playhouse,* 1605 Bayview, *Toronto Free Theatre,* 26 Berkeley (where George F. Walker premieres his work), and *Bathurst Street Theatre,* 736 Bathurst St. *Young People's Theatre,* 165 Front St. E., specializes in puppet shows, concerts, musicals, and plays for children. Major ticket agent: Bass, Telephone: 698–2277.

Second City Fire Hall, 110 Lombard, is the home of Toronto's satirical Second City Revue. Other revues entertain after-dinner audiences at restaurants like *Old Angelo's,* 45 Elm St., *The Teller's Cage,* in the Commerce Court complex at King and Bay Sts., and *Theatre-in-the-Dell,* 300 Simcoe St.

 SHOPPING. You can get pretty well everything in Toronto, from antique radio parts to bathrobes lined in ranch mink, if you've got the money and the time to hunt. The biggest retail stores are *Eaton's, Simpson's* (both are on Yonge between Queen and Dundas Sts. and in suburban shopping plazas), and *The Bay,* better known as The Hudson's Bay Company. Its biggest store is at Yonge and Bloor Sts. *Yorkdale, Sherway Gardens, Square One,* and *Scarborough Town Centre* are among the biggest suburban shopping centers, but you can shop in underground plazas in the heart of the city, too. The *Toronto Dominion Centre* at King and Bay Sts. has 54 stores, a cinema and restaurants; it links up to the *Commerce Court Mall, First Canada Place,* the *Richmond-Adelaide Centre* and the *Four Seasons Sheraton.* Most chic and expensive: *Hazelton Lanes,* Yorkville at Avenue Rd.

Toronto's villages come alive in summer. *Yorkville* and *Markham Villages* (the former at Bloor St. and Avenue Rd., the latter at Bloor and Bathurst) are colorful streets of renovated Victoriana with art galleries, gourmet shops, antique stores, and outdoor cafés. Markham Village has a shop devoted to art books at bargain prices; Yorkville, a sex store, several bath boutiques, expensive toy shops, and women's clothing stores with used and new high fashion. A new shopping strip has taken over the run-down Queen St. Strip west of University

Ave. Collectors' comic books, punk rock dayglo leather, sci-fi bookstores, and several good cafés are scattered amid the area's greasy spoon eateries and office supply warehouses.

In the ManuLife Centre (south corner of Bay and Bloor Sts.) *Birk's* and *Creed's* cater to Toronto's wealthy. Birk's sells mainly jewelry; Creed's carries designer clothes (Sonia Rykiel, Missoni), furs, and a small line of Maud Frizon's extraordinary shoes. Diagonally across from the ManuLife Centre is *David's,* Toronto's best and probably most expensive shoe store. For bargains in clothes or anything else, you'll do better on *Spadina Ave.,* the garment and warehouse district, *Chinatown* (Dundas St. east of Spadina), *Hercules* army surplus, 577 Yonge St., *Import Bazaar,* 24 Wellesley St. W., or the incredible *Honest Ed's* at Bathurst and Bloor. The Queen-Jarvis-King area abounds in antique and junk stores. The *Jazz & Blues Record Centre* at 337 King St. W. is a mecca for serious buffs. *Bakka,* 282 Queen Street West, carries only science fiction, albeit broadly defined.

 DINING OUT. Toronto used to close its sensible meat and potatoes eating establishments early—perhaps because people were so bored. But in the last decade, with the influx of immigrants, money and education about such matters, fine food has become a passion for Torontonians. Good restaurants in all price ranges and all types of cuisines still meet with the approval of an increasingly educated, critical palate. Critics (like *Esquire* magazine's Roy Andries de Groot or France's *Gault et Millaud*) rate Toronto as one of the best dining cities on the continent.

Restaurants have been categorized on the basis of a typical dinner with appetizer, entrée, and dessert. Drinks, tax and tips are excluded. *Deluxe* costs over $40 per person; *Expensive,* $25–40; *Moderate,* $15–25; *Inexpensive,* under $15.

Most places accept the following major credit cards: American Express, MasterCard and Visa; others may also be honored. Not all establishments accept credit cards, therefore we suggest you call for information.

Canadian

Moderate

Montréal Bistro. 65 Sherbourne St. French-Canadian favorites like *Tortière* (pork and herb pie) in a charming country atmosphere. Great bar adjacent.

Inexpensive

Newfoundlander. 185 Danforth Ave. "Newfie" dishes like "brewis" (cod and fried potatoes) and "screech" (dark, overproof rum).

Chinese

Moderate

The Pink Pearl. 142 Dundas Street W. Authentic Hong Kong cuisine, comfortable elegance. Try the fried stuffed crab claw; Rainbow in Crystal Fold, shark's fin soup. Licensed. Can become expensive.
Kowloon Dim Sum. 187 Dundas West.

Inexpensive

Ho Yuen. 105 Elizabeth St. If you're serious about Chinese food, this gritty, unlicensed basement is for you. The setting is horrible, the line-ups a bother, the lobster in ginger and garlic is breathtaking. A find, an adventure, a gem. Can be more expensive.

French

Deluxe

Auberge Gavroche. 90 Avenue Rd. The atmosphere is elegant-rustic, the entrées famous for their smooth herbed sauces, the waiters very French.

Expensive

Gaston's. 35 Baldwin St. The rooms are steeped in French atmosphere and the mussels, rabbit and seafood can be delicious. There is a charming backyard patio for open-air dining on hot summer nights.

Les Copains. 48 Wellington Ave. E. Sandblasted brick, sophisticated graphics, *pommes frites,* informal elegance.

Maison Basque. 15 Temperance St. Service can be frustrating, but salmon, grouper, lamb, inexpensive wines, and rich Basque cake make up for it.

Moderate

Le Select. 328 Queen St. W. Casual atmosphere, jazz, *coq au vin,* good salads, and a clientele of local Francophones.

Le Pigalle. 315 King St. W. Very popular because of its grilled lamb, bourgignons, moderate prices and ambience. Expect lineups.

Raclette. A wine bar, really, with peasant regional specialties of France (fondues, smoked beef) to accompany your bottle.

Greek

Expensive

Kosta's. A gorgeous indoor garden, whose rugs, balconies, trees could be in Corfu. A delicate, spicy menu of bean soups, spinach pies, grilled lamb, squid, rabbit.

Moderate

Ellas. 702 Pape Avenue. Visit the kitchen and choose moussaka, roast lamb, spicy vegetables and a feta salad. Licensed.

The Round Window. 729 Danforth Ave. A Greek seafood restaurant. Tarama, grilled fish. Pleasant, cozy, tasty. A real find. Crowded.

Indian

Moderate

Rajput. 376 Bloor W. Bombay chicken, stuffed parathas, condiments, and a license.

Inexpensive

Sher-E-Punjab. 341 Danforth Ave. A good curry house. No license, no décor to speak of.

International Cuisine

Deluxe

The Restaurant, Three Small Rooms. 22 St. Thomas St. Its low-key comfort, extensive wine list and classic cooking have earned it an international reputation.

The Royal Hunt Room, Sutton Place Hotel. Its executive chef captained the medal-winning Canadian team at the International Culinary Olympics 1976. Try its salmon in sorrel, cuisine minceur, strawberries in chocolate. Excellent service.

Fenton's. 2 Gloucester St. Gorgeous décor: one room has an open fireplace, another is a courtyard full of trees hung with lamps. The food is inventive if a bit pretentious: cold Stilton soup, chicken stuffed with ginger, syllabub. Good wine, liquor list.

Italian

Expensive

Noodles. As with a Fellini film, you will either love Noodles or hate it. A pink neon and chrome décor works a warm magic in this futuristic Italian restaurant. Soups like cream of watercress or iced cucumber, followed by rich linguini, basil and garlic-tinged ravioli, imaginative spinach, endive or celery root salads, good veal, plump fowl and seductive desserts have built up a regular, rather arty, clientele. Entrance on Bay St., north of 60 Bloor St. W.

Pronto. 692 Mt. Pleasant. A grand piano, wallful of Italian art posters, an uptown clientele. The delight of the nouvelle cuisine is as much in the presentation as in the taste. Their bread is poor and service can be slow—otherwise a delight.

Vittorio's Osteria. 2637 Yonge. There are always lineups because the pasta is homemade, light and perfect, and the veal unbeatable.

Moderate

Portofino. 600 The East Mall. Worth a trip into darkest suburbia. Splendid seafood, grilled with garlic; accordion players and succulent pasta to accompany. Very crowded, no reservations; arrive early.

Inexpensive

Porretta's Pizza. 97 Harbord. Best pizza in town. Unlicensed.

Jewish-Middle Eastern

Moderate

Balkan. 12 Elm St. Try one of the set dinners for two—the courses never stop coming. Spicy bean soup, deep-fried mushrooms, stuffed grape leaves, shish kebab, baklava. As you leave, a waiter discreetly rings a bell; it's good luck.

Inexpensive

Jerusalem. 955 Eglinton West. Middle Eastern delights like hummus and shish kebab. Licensed.

Scandinavian

Moderate

Copenhagen Room. 101 Bloor West. Lunch here is a joy: tartar with caviar and fried Camembert open-faced sandwiches. In the evening, prices shoot up for the Indonesian and Danish entrées. Stick with the sandwiches and you'll be full and happy. Can become expensive.

Seafood

Moderate

Ed's Seafood. 276 King St. W. King crab legs, lobster tails, lots of atmosphere. No blue jeans. Gentlemen must wear jacket and tie.

The Old Fish Market. 12 Market St. Big brick rooms accommodate all the people who are attracted by conch, crab, mussels and salads at reasonable prices.

Spanish-Latin American

Moderate

Don Quijote. 300 College St. The chicken is rich, the squid delicate, the mussels, shrimps, and paella delicious. Afterwards go upstairs for Spanish coffee and flamenco dancing. Licensed.

Steak Houses

Expensive

Hy's. 73 Richmond W. A library atmosphere and delicious appetizers (*e.g.*, chopped liver, ribs). The steaks are good too. Businessmen love it. There's another Hy's at 133 Yorkville where the crowd is jet-set, sort of.

Moderate

Barberian's. 7 Elm Street. It's cozy, attractive and practically an institution. It's open late, too. Can become expensive.

The Keg Mansion. Jarvis at Wellesley. The setting—the former mansion of the Massey family—outshines the food. The steaks and ribs are good value and the service young and excessively cheerful.

Other

Moderate

The Hop and Grape. 14 College St. A wine bar upstairs, pub downstairs, with savory fare. Smoked goldeye, salmon mousse, steak'n'kidney pie.

The Parrot. 325 Queen St. W. Another hangout. Punk waiters, good music, vegetarian food, licensed.

Inexpensive

Bregman's The Bakery Restaurant. 1560 Yonge. Particularly popular with crowds coming out of the area's four movie theaters. A meal at Bregman's means crisp salads, terrific pastry and croissants and swift service. Can be more expensive.

 NIGHTCLUBS AND BARS. Toronto is a good jazz and blues town, but has its share of dark, comfortable, quiet places to talk. Best known—and darkest—of these is *The Twenty Two*, 22 St. Thomas St., which features piano entertainment in the evenings.

Malloney's, 85 Grenville, has a young singles scene. It also has soft comfortable couches, barnboarded walls and one of Toronto's few stand-up bars.

The *SRO* bar in the Four Seasons Hotel, 21 Avenue Rd., is extremely popular —which means it's not so quiet after all.

Single's bars like *Brandy's*, 58 The Esplanade, *Thank Goodness It's Friday*, 204 Eglinton East, and the *Duke of York*, 39 Prince Arthur are popular.

The bilingual crowd at the Auberge Gavroche's *Rélais de l'Auberge,* 90 Avenue Rd., is cliquish. But the *Rélais* is comfortable, with quiet entertainment.

The town's hottest jazz spots are *George's Bourbon Street,* 180 Queen St. W., *George's Spaghetti House,* 290 Dundas St. E., *Lites,* in the Royal York Hotel, and the *Brunswick House,* 481 Bloor St. W., where the Dixieland may not be technically pure but always comes on strong.

Upstairs at *El Mocambo,* 464 Spadina Ave., is a mecca for blues fans. Since The Rolling Stones played here some years ago, the "Elmo" has attracted big-name groups. Get tickets early.

Stagger Lee's, on Queen St. just east of Spadina, changes its style often. Formerly country music, it has presented punk and feminist performers and now offers 50s and 60s nostalgia bands.

Flamenco dancers and Spanish guitars entertain the Latin patrons of *Don Quijote,* 300 College Street.

Another font of Canuck culture: *The Newfoundlander,* a restaurant, bar, and, on weekends, Maritime country music spot. On Danforth east of Broadview.

Toronto's skyscrapers are usually topped by quiet, polished roof lounges. Among the most popular are *Aquarius 51,* 55 Bloor West; *The Pinnacle,* 123 Queen Street West; and *Runway 23,* in the Skyline Hotel at 655 Dixon Road, from which you can watch the planes take off from Pearson International.

There are big, expensive nightclubs in town and frequently they feature big, expensive entertainers. One of the most popular is the Royal York Hotel's huge, elegant old *Imperial Room,* which features the likes of Ella Fitzgerald and Tina Turner.

Punk disco for under-25-year-olds can be found along the Queen St. Strip.

EXPLORING OTTAWA

In 1858, Queen Victoria astounded Canada by choosing Bytown, a backwoods lumbering town, to be the capital of the new Dominion. Typically, her compromise site pleased neither French-Canadians (who were arguing for Québec City) nor English (who supported Kingston and Toronto). At any rate, Bytown was renamed Ottawa, an Indian word meaning "a place of buying and selling." The name is perhaps a caution to the city's thousands of federal politicians and civil servants.

From a remote village with a population of 7,500 at the time of Confederation, "Westminster in the wilderness" has blossomed into a lively cosmopolitan capital of over 650,000 people. The verb "blossom" is in Ottawa's case quite literal: the city is full of gardens and parks. Every May, to commemorate Canada's hospitality towards the exiled Dutch royal family during World War II, the government of Holland sends three million gorgeous tulips, 600,000 daffodils, and half a million crocuses to paint Confederation Square, the banks of the Rideau Canal and Parliament Hill.

When Bytown became Canada's capital, land values were modest, to say the least. The government paid $3,750 for the original 29-acre site which became Parliament Hill. A quick decision was made to award an $800,000 contract to architects Thomas Fuller and Chilion Jones, and the neo-Gothic Parliament Buildings were erected on a 150-foot promontory overlooking the Ottawa River by 1700 laborers whose pay ranged from 80¢ to $2.45 a day.

The Peace Tower, in the center block of the complex, is the natural place to begin a walking tour of Ottawa. The tower is a 291-foot-high neo-Gothic structure which replaced the original Centre Block after it was gutted by fire in 1916. Ten-foot gargoyles project from each corner of the tower under the four-faced clock. Inside, there's a monument to Canada's war dead, a lookout and a 52-bell carillon. The 22,400-pound Bourdon Bell strikes the hour.

Changing of the Guard

Around the Peace Tower stretch Parliament Hill's acres of brilliant lawn. The Eternal Flame in the center symbolizes Canadian unity; it's rumored to have gone out six times since it was first lit in Canada's centennial year, 1967. All coins tossed in the surrounding fountain are given to charity. Every summer day in front of the Peace Tower—weather permitting—the 30-minute-long changing of the guard ceremony is performed at 10 A.M., complete with pipes, drums, bearskin hats, and the flashing red coats of the Governor General's Foot Guards and the Canadian Grenadier Guards of Montreal.

To the sides of the Peace Tower and Centre Block are the East and West Blocks, their copper roofs oxidized to blue-green above gray sandstone. Both are part of the original complex which first housed Parliament in 1866 (a year before Nova Scotia and New Brunswick joined Québec and Ontario in Confederation). They partially escaped the fires half a century ago which devastated the Centre Block. Above the doorway of the East Block's main (150-foot-high) tower are carved the Coats-of-Arms of the two provinces of United Canada. On the western façade a carriage porch of cut freestone stands out from the building. At the northern end of the East Block is the entrance to the prime minister's office. The East Block is open to the public on Sundays only.

The Senate, the House of Commons, and the office of the leader of the opposition are all located in the Centre Block. Austere, dignified, the limestone-and-oak hall of the House of Commons is the scene of the debates of Canada's 282 elected members of Parliament. The public is welcome to observe House debates and Question Period (usually the liveliest part of the proceedings) which take place daily when the House is in session. In the Centre Block's blazing gold-and-crimson Senate Chamber the Governor-General (the Queen's representative in Canada) reads the speech from the Throne at the opening of each session of Parliament. The Centre Block also houses the Library (completed 1876) with its rich paneling, echoing 132-foot dome and white marble statue of Queen Victoria.

Commons Committee meetings which are held in the West Block are also open to the public, but the rest of the building is not (except public washrooms in the northeast corner). The West Block houses the offices of members of Parliament.

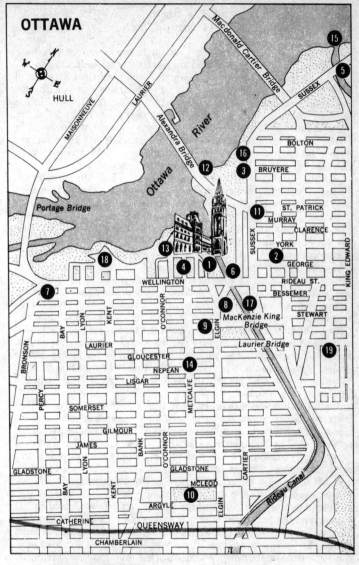

OTTAWA

HULL

Macdonald Cartier Bridge

LAURIER

MAISONNEUVE

Alexandra Bridge

Ottawa River

SUSSEX

Portage Bridge

BOLTON

BRUYERE

ST. PATRICK

MURRAY

CLARENCE

YORK

GEORGE

RIDEAU ST.

BESSEMER

STEWART

KING EDWARD

WELLINGTON

BRONSON

BAY

KENT

LYON

O'CONNOR

ELGIN

MacKenzie King Bridge

Laurier Bridge

LAURIER

GLOUCESTER

NEPEAN

LISGAR

SOMERSET

PERCY

GILMOUR

JAMES

BANK

O'CONNOR

GLADSTONE

METCALFE

CARTIER

Rideau Canal

GLADSTONE

BAY

LYON

KENT

MCLEOD

ARGYLE

ELGIN

CATHERINE

QUEENSWAY

CHAMBERLAIN

Ottawa—Points of Interest

1) Bytown Museum
2) Byward Market
3) Canadian War Museum
4) Centennial Flame
5) City Hall
6) Chateau Laurier
7) Garden of the Provinces
8) National Arts Centre
9) National Gallery
10) National Museum of Man

11) National Ski Museum
12) Nepean Point
13) Parliament Buildings
14) Place Bell Shopping Mall
15) Rideau Falls
16) Royal Canadian Mint
17) Sightseeing Boat Cruises
18) Supreme Court of Canada
19) University of Ottawa

Statues of Founding Fathers

The grounds of Parliament Hill abound in statues. Among the more notable figures here immortalized are two fathers of Confederation who were assassinated: behind the Centre Block's northwest corner is George Brown, a Toronto newspaper editor who was shot by a disgruntled employee. Diagonally across from him is Thomas D'Arcy McGee, shot by Irish Fenians in 1868. The statue of Sir Wilfred Laurier, Canada's first Francophone (French-speaking) prime minister, can be found in the extreme east corner of the grounds. At the southeast corner of Centre Block, is the statue of the hard-drinking visionary, Sir John A. MacDonald, Canada's first prime minister.

Across Wellington Street from the Parliament Buildings are some of Canada's unofficial policy-influencing institutions—the Rideau Club (the haughty preserve of senior civil servants and *eminences gris*), the National Press Building (150 Wellington), and the United States Embassy. Continuing along Wellington across Bank Street, you pass the Justice Building and the Supreme Court on your right. Here the public can watch Canada's highest court make final and far-reaching decisions on constitutional, criminal, and civil cases. The Bank of Canada (and Canada's gold reserves) are on your left.

The Memorial Arch over Lyon Street joins the neoclassical Veterans' Affairs and the Trade and Commerce Buildings. Straight ahead is the Garden of the Provinces, flanked by St. Peter's Lutheran Church and Christ Church Cathedral. Across from the garden are the Public Archives and the National Library (with 400,000 volumes and 100,000 more in microcopy). The rounded bronze form of a Henry Moore sculpture stands in the foyer; etched glass windows on the first floor are by John Hutton who created the windows of Coventry Cathedral in England.

Walk two blocks south on Bay and turn east (past Place de Ville, a large office and commercial site with an underground mall of boutiques) to 150 Kent Street, headquarters of the National Film Board of Canada. The National Film Board's Photo Gallery has excellent photography exhibitions; film and slide shows are also offered. North again is the Sparks Street pedestrian mall, where fountains, sculpture and café tables have replaced automobiles, bringing thousands of browsers and tourists to shop on balmy summer days.

Emerging from the Sparks Street Mall you'll face Confederation Square, and the dense, heroic bronze figures of Canada's War Memorial. Unveiled by King George VI in 1939, the Memorial commemorated the 66,655 Canadian dead of World War I. Ironically, the Memorial was completed on the eve of World War II. The 70-foot-high Memorial is the work of Vernon March. To your left is Parliament Hill; to your right one of Canada's grand old hotels, the Château Laurier, which looks like an oversized, gray-turreted baronial castle; straight ahead of you is a deep gorge where manual locks can lift boats 79 feet up from the Ottawa River to the Rideau Canal. Follow the steps down the gorge to Bytown Museum in Ottawa's oldest stone building, erected 1826–27. A pedestrian and bicycle path has been built around the base of Parliament Hill on your left. It's a recent addition: the original pathway, Lovers' Walk, was closed in the 1930's because the earth moved—landslides.

Civil Servants on Skates

The old railway station (now the Government Conference Centre) and the National Capital Commission, the federal agency responsible for enhancing Canada's capital (and incidentally a good place to get information on the city) face you from the far side of the Rideau Canal. Closer are the 2,300-seat opera house, 800-seat theater and experimental stage of the National Arts Centre, a complex modern building hung with vines and gardens. Home of the National Symphony, the Arts Centre also features a pleasant waterside café where on winter days you can watch the unusual but typically Ottawan sight of briefcase-carrying civil servants skating to work along the Rideau Canal.

Two blocks after Wellington Street becomes Rideau Street, turn north (on William) to the Byward Market, where, since 1846, local farmers have hawked cheeses, pickles, fresh produce, and cut flowers. Head up Sussex Drive. Here the National Capital Commission has restored many of the original Georgian and Victorian shopfronts. Now they are boutiques, art galleries, and cafés.

If you turn left off Sussex Drive towards Alexandra Bridge, you'll find yourself at Nepean Point, a small public park with a big beautiful view. The view encompasses the odd duality of the capital's character. Behind you, on an imposing bluff rising out of the Ottawa River are the gray spires and distinguished blocks of Parliament Hill; across the river, a tangle of industrial buildings and neon: Hull, Québec, which for a long time was, frankly, the most interesting part of Ottawa, Ontario. Ottawa's relationship with Hull is symbiotic. It has relied on the Québec lumbering town to alleviate its burdens of state—and in fact Hull still has many of the capital's finest French restaurants and liveliest nightclubs.

In Ottawa, Notre Dame Basilica (1841–46) stands on the corner of Sussex Drive and St. Patrick. The beautiful wooden decorations inside were executed by Philippe Parizeau, who also worked on the National Library. The Canadian War Museum at 330–350 Sussex Drive is next door to the Mint (which produces all of Canada's coin currency). The Mint also has a good display of historic coinage. Tours are available by appointment.

Ballroom, Rink and Cricket Pitch

Sussex Drive skirts the Ottawa River above limestone bluffs. Monumental institutional architecture gives way to the elegant leafy streets of Rockcliffe Park, the home of many governmental officials, embassies, and official residences. The prime minister's residence (24 Sussex Drive) is a gray stone mansion built in 1868. It was acquired by the government in 1943 and Prime Minister Louis St. Laurent became its first prime ministerial occupant in 1950.

Government House (or Rideau Hall), the official residence of the Governor-General, is across a park from the prime minister's residence, on MacKay Street. Built in 1838, it has its own ballroom, skating rink and cricket pitch.

Final stop: the Central Experimental Farm, where the government conducts cross-breeding and fertilization projects, and where you can wander among 1,200 acres of flowerbeds, gardens, brand-new plants and an arboretum of approximately 1,700 different trees and shrubs. They even grow marijuana here, but not for public consumption! The farm is closed on weekends.

Although Parliament recesses for the summer, Ottawa goes about its political business all year long. To really get a sense of this city you have to be plugged into its humming gossip network, its energy centers like the private offices on the Hill that stay lit late into the night; corner tables at a few favored Hull restaurants, cocktail parties in Rockcliffe. Ottawa is fascinated by its own politics. But Ottawa has charms for the apolitical tourist, too. In May, the city astounds with its millions of flowers. In late August, the Central Canada Exhibition brings a horse show, a grandstand show and a midway to town. In winter, skaters swarm on the Rideau Canal, Parliament Hill is floodlit on frosty nights, theatergoers glitter in the foyer of the National Arts Centre and skiers escape to the snowy slopes of the Gatineau Hills.

PRACTICAL INFORMATION FOR OTTAWA

HOW TO GET THERE. By air: Ottawa Uplands Airport is an international airport. There are direct flights from New York via *Eastern Airlines,* from Montréal via *Nordair, Canadian Pacific* and *Air Canada,* and from Toronto via *Canadian Pacific* and *Air Canada.*

By train: *Via Rail* runs day, express and overnight trains from Toronto; it also operates an Ottawa-Montréal route. The train station is at the Alta Vista interchange off the Queensway.

By bus: *Voyageur Colonial* is the major inter-city service. Its terminal and the Ottawa bus station are at 265 Catherine St.

By car: The *Trans-Canada Highway* links Ottawa with Montréal from the east and goes west through Sault Ste. Marie, Thunder Bay, and into Manitoba. *Highway 7* is the scenic central route between Ottawa and Toronto.

ACCOMMODATIONS. Most of Ottawa's hotels serve a governmental clientele. They therefore tend to be a little more expensive, with an emphasis on quiet comfort, than hotels in other Ontario centers. But there are hotels and motels to suit all pocketbooks in the area, most of them within walking distance of major sights and museums. Rates for double rooms are categorized as follows: *Deluxe,* $90 and higher; *Expensive,* $75–100; *Moderate,* $50–75; and *Inexpensive,* under $45.

Most places accept the following major credit cards: American Express, MasterCard and Visa; others may also be honored. Not all establishments accept credit cards, therefore we suggest you call for information.

Deluxe

Château Laurier. Major's Hill Park at Elgin St. It's old, gracious and very much a Canadian institution. The large, airy rooms have recently been refurnished but the dark paneled lobby has been allowed to retain its nostalgic elegance. Right beside Parliament Hill and the Rideau Canal, the Château has an indoor pool, boutiques, and lounges with entertainment.

Four Seasons Hotel. 150 Albert St. Modern, with rich brown velvet carpeting and elegant lighting. The attractive rooms are favored by out-of-town visitors for their comfort. Indoor pool.

Holiday Inn Centre. 100 Kent at Queen St. The rooms are modern and attractive, large and comfortable. The lobby, too, has an expensive yet relaxed atmosphere. Indoor pool.

Skyline Hotel. 101 Lyon St. Another high-rise hotel with indoor pool, the Skyline has a slightly more lively atmosphere than the above two and a great roof lounge.

Expensive

Chimo Inn. Corner Queensway and St. Laurent. This hotel has reasonably priced weekend rates, plus indoor pool, sauna, and whirlpool. Can be expensive other times.

Talisman Motor Hotel. 1376 Carling Ave. Surburban. An outdoor pool, golf nearby, babysitting, comfortable rooms and a popular, but relaxing bar.

Moderate

Lord Elgin. 100 Elgin St. Because of its reasonable prices, its pleasant, older atmosphere and its downtown location, this hotel remains extremely popular. The rooms are smaller but comfortable and fully serviced.

Macies Ottawan Motel. 1274 Carling Ave. Family operated, 116 rooms, with sauna, whirlpool and exercise area.

Inexpensive

Albion Motor Hotel. 1 Daly Ave. Its 50 rooms are old and small but clean. The Albion's pub is popular with university students because of its proximity to the campus.

L'Auberge du Voyageur Inn. 2200 Montréal Rd. Small, suburban, with 39 rooms and TV.

TELEPHONES. Ottawa, Kingston, and the cottage country between—including the Rideau Lakes district —all lie within area code 613. Some government telephones, on local call rates with Ottawa, actually lie in area code 819—because their offices are on the Hull, Québec, side of the Ottawa River.

HOW TO GET AROUND. By bus: There are two bus systems in Ottawa, the *Rideau-Carleton Regional Transit Commission,* and *La Commission de Transport de la Communaute Regionale de l'Outaouais;* a bus loop joins Ottawa, Hull, and the two systems. Tickets must be purchased in specially designated neighborhood stores, or a cash fare is required (no change given). For further information and a public transportation map contact the Ottawa-Carleton Transportation Commission at 294 Albert St. (613-741–4390).

By taxi: Major cab lines, like *Blue Line* and *Diamond,* run a good citywide service.

From the airport: An airport limousine bus service run by *Blue Line* takes visitors to and from the airport and major downtown hotels. Taxi fares from the airport are a good deal more expensive, but should stay under $10.

TOURIST INFORMATION. Canada's Capital Visitors and Convention Bureau is in 222 Queen St., 7th floor, a block south of the Sparks St. Mall. Telephone: (613) 237–5158.

SEASONAL EVENTS. Winterlude, each **February**, culminates a week of speed skating, snow sculpting, horse races on ice and bed races (?!) with fireworks. The Festival of Spring in **May** brings musical events, parades, beer gardens, and more fireworks. **July** 1 is the celebration of Canada Day, culminating a variety show televised from Parliament Hill, with fireworks, of course. Festival Ottawa is a midsummer performing arts festival. In late **August,** the Central Canada Exhibition opens its midway, horseshow, and agricultural exhibits.

TOURS. The Rideau Canal winds through the heart of the city and falls to the Ottawa River below Parliament Hill. Two of the most pleasant sightseeing expeditions are run by *Paul's Boat Lines,* which take visitors on 1¼-hour cruises of the canal or ½-hour cruises of the Ottawa River. Riverboats can be boarded below the Bytown Museum; canal boats dock across from the National Arts Centre at 3244 Riverside Dr., Ottawa. Tours are available in English or French, and are operated from mid-May to mid-October. Or take a 3-hour cruise of the Rideau Lakes (Saturday-night Dinner Dance Cruises available in mid-summer). Contact *Ottawa Riverboat Company,* 316 Dalhousie (613-232–4888), for 1¾-hour cruises on the Ottawa River.

Double-decker buses cover a 27-mile sightseeing circuit leaving from Confederation Square, mid-May to the end of October. In the fall, special trips are offered into the Gatineau Hills in Québec to see the brilliant autumn colors. For further information contact *Gray Line Sightseeing Tours,* (613-741–6440). From April to October, their 2-hour National Capital Tour shows visitors Parliament Hill, the Central Experimental Farm, Hog's Back Falls, various embassies, etc. From July to early September, the tour is expanded to include an optional viewing of the Changing of the Guards on Parliament Hill. The *Ottawa-Carleton Transportation Commission* runs seven daily bus tours around the capital from May to October. You can take a horse-drawn wagon ride through the Central Experimental Farm, weather permitting.

GARDENS AND PARKWAYS. The 3½-mile-long parkway which runs beside the Rideau Canal—it's called *Queen Elizabeth Driveway*—has cycle paths, shady spots to stop and watch the water, and in May, Ottawa's famous tulips. The largest flowerbeds are at Dow's Lake.

There is a two-mile parkway through the *Central Experimental Farm,* which connects with scenic, residential Island Park Drive. The farm has ornamental gardens and an arboretum with over a thousand different trees and shrubs among its 1,200 acres. Open May to September.

Rockcliffe Driveway runs along river cliffs to garden rockeries. Here you can picnic in Rockcliffe Park.

The 8.2 acres of *Nepean Point* offer a splendid view of Parliament Hill and the river.

Hog's Back Park, 54 acres, contains the pretty Hog's Back Falls.

Right behind Château Laurier there's a small park, *Major's Hill,* and across the canal, a path leads around the base of Parliament Hill.

CHILDREN'S ACTIVITIES. Ottawa's *Museum of Science and Technology* is for children of all ages who want to twist knobs, pull levers, turn dials and watch the laws of physics, astronomy and meteorology come to life. There are locomotives, vintage autos, and model ships too. The Museum is on 35 acres of parkland, 1867 St. Laurent Blvd., and is closed Mondays from mid-September to mid-May.

The Ottawa Parks Recreation Branch organizes children's activities—*puppet shows, theater groups* and *celebrations* in its parks. Other regional administrations run similar programs: *Nepean Parks and Recreation* and *Gloucester Recreation and Parks.*

The public *libraries* offer story hours, puppet shows, and films. Also check with Gloucester Public Libraries and Nepean Public Libraries.

The *Museum of Canadian Scouting,* 1345 Baseline Rd., is full of artifacts of interest to those members and ex-members of packs.

Children also enjoy the daily 10 A.M. changing of the guards on Parliament Hill.

Slide-A-Ride is a 350-foot-long flume, just 8 miles south of town on Hwy. 31 at Poplar Grove. Mini-golf, too.

SPORTS. Ottawa has been a sports-minded town since its lumberjack days. **Spectator sports** (especially the games of Canadian Football League pros, the *Ottawa Roughriders*) are popular, but participatory sports are even more so.

Boats can be rented at Dow's Lake on the Rideau Canal, rowboats at the corner of Fifth Ave. and Queen Elizabeth Driveway. There is good **swimming** at Gatineau Park in Quebec, but swimming in the Ottawa River is not advised. *Cycling* is extremely popular. It seems that everyone from cabinet ministers to kids takes advantage of the city's 65 miles of bicycle paths. Path maps are available from the National Capital Commission, 48 Rideau, near Parliament Hill. In winter, the paths become urban **cross-country ski** trails. The hills around Ottawa offer good **downhill skiing.** One of the major Ontario resorts is at Mount Packenham, Highways 17 and 29. On sunny winter weekends, it's possible to see 50,000 **skaters** on the Rideau Canal. Public **golf** courses in the National Capital region include National Capital Commission Golf Centre and Pine View Municipal Golf Course. There are public **tennis** courts at City View and West Ottawa, but don't be surprised to find them heavily subscribed. Ottawa has two **racetracks.** When the Connaught Park is closed, chances are you can still find some action at the Rideau-Carleton Raceway on Albion Rd.

HISTORIC SITES. Ottawa is a relatively young city. Settlement began here in 1809, but until 1867, when Queen Victoria chose it as Canada's capital, it remained a tiny lumbering town. Consequently, its historic sites are only a couple of generations old.

Laurier House, 355 Laurier Ave. E., residence of two Canadian prime ministers, was built in 1878. It has been refurnished in period style. Closed Mondays all year.

At *Kitchissippi Lookout* on Island Park Dr., a plaque commemorates the Canadian rivermen who were recruited in 1884 to negotiate the dangerous cataracts of the Nile River and relieve British General Charles Gordon in the siege of Khartoum.

A statue of Samuel de Champlain, the French explorer, geographer, and governor of New France, gazes across the city from *Nepean Point.*

You can tour Ottawa's 8 locks where the Rideau Canal pours into the Ottawa River, simply by scrambling down the north side of the Château Laurier Hotel grounds.

There are many old, charming villages within the National Capital Region. At Almonte, west of the city, an old gristmill has been restored and now contains a fine collection of pioneer artifacts. The *Mill of Kintail* is closed from October to May and Tuesdays.

Moorside, the summer home of Canada's longest-serving prime minister, the occultist MacKenzie King, is open to the public. It's in the middle of Gatineau Wilderness Park.

At Manotick, *Watson's Mill* dating from 1859 has been restored and opened to visitors.

Nearby, at Richmond, there's an old church, *St. John's Anglican,* which was built in 1823 and old stone houses, one built in 1828.

  MUSEUMS AND GALLERIES. Museums. *The National Gallery* is waiting to move out of its office building at the corner of Elgin and Slater Sts. and into something more suitable for its work by Rembrandt, Van Gogh, Picasso, and contemporary Canadian masters. The Gallery boasts the largest collection of Canadian art and sculpture in the country. Open daily except Christmas Day.

The National Film Board, 150 Kent St., has an excellent photographic arts gallery. Open daily during exhibitions only.

The Bytown Museum is a stone commissariat store constructed in 1827. It's between Château Laurier and Parliament Hill and is open from May to September. Most of its 3,500 artifacts relate to the building of the Rideau Canal, the development of Ottawa, and the personal history of Colonel By, an engineer in charge of the building of the canal. Open May to September except Sundays and holidays.

At the *Museum of Canadian Scouting,* 1345 Baseline Rd., the lives of Lord Baden-Powell and his movement in Canada are remembered through old photos, insignia and so forth, which should be of interest to scouts and former scouts. Open all year, Monday–Friday except holidays.

The National Museum of Natural Sciences is in the same building as the *National Museum of Man*—a converted warehouse at the corner of Metcalfe and McLeod Sts. In the Museum of Natural Sciences, there are over two million items, from prehistoric monsters to precious minerals. The National Museum of Man has excellent North American folklore and native peoples sections. Both museums are closed Mondays, September to April.

At the *National Museum of Science and Technology,* 1867 St. Laurent Blvd., you can participate in many of the displays of meteorology, physics, and astronomy. From mid-September to mid-May, the museum is closed on Mondays.

The *National Aviation Museum* has over 100 aircraft inside three World War II hangars at Rockcliffe Airport, including the early Canadian "Silver Dart." Closed Mondays from mid-September to mid-May.

Some of the specimens date back three hundred years to the French-Indian bush wars at the *Canadian War Museum,* 330 Sussex Dr. Photos, maps, flags, models, a Sopwith Camel, Indian clubs, and one of the finest medal collections in the world can be seen daily all year except Mondays, Labour Day to April.

Philatelists will enjoy the *National Postal Museum* at 180 Wellington Street. Old photographs, old mailbags and pouches, ornate brass letter balances, hand canceling hammers, and a priceless collection of stamps make this an intriguing place to browse even for non-philatelists. There's even an old general store and post office, circa 1885, reconstructed right down to the weathered floorboards, tin boxes of medicinal herbs, glass jars, crocks and earthenware. At the counter of the store you can buy the latest mint stamps, first-day covers, and postcards. If you mail one from the store's Victorian mailbox, it will receive the special Postal Museum cancellation. Open all year daily except Christmas Day.

There are old photographs and ancient skis at the *Canadian Ski Museum,* 457A Sussex Dr. Open all year Tuesday to Saturday, afternoons.

The *National Library* and *Public Archives* displays its books, films, paintings, watercolors, engravings, photographs, and maps at 395 Wellington St.

Galleries. Among the private art galleries are *Wells Gallery,* 459 Sussex Dr., for contemporary painting, graphics, and sculpture, the *S A W Gallery,* 55 Byward Market, for representational works by local painters and watercolorists. You might also try the *Wallack Gallery,* 203 Bank St., and *Robertson Galleries,* 162 Laurier W., for moderns.

MUSIC AND THEATER. The three-theater complex of the *National Arts Centre* is the focus of the city's cultural life. Here you can enjoy dinner before a ballet or symphony in the 2,300-seat opera theater, drama in an 800-seat, thrust-stage theater, or something more avant-garde in the 300-seat experimental studio. Music, dance, and two resident (French and English) drama companies play here. The *National Arts Centre Orchestra* is a 45-member symphony conducted by Franco Mannino of Italy. The Centre stands among gardens and walkways by the side of the Rideau Canal just south of Confederation Square.

The popular *Ottawa Little Theatre* has a resident drama troupe which performs all year round.

The University of Ottawa's music department sponsors concerts throughout the academic year.

SHOPPING. *Sparks Street Mall* is a traffic-free shopping street in the heart of the city, and in summer its crowds are attracted as much by the rock gardens, fountains, outdoor tables and art exhibitions as they are by the shops. Eskimo sculpture and Eskimo and Indian prints and crafts can be purchased at *Snow Goose Handicrafts,* 40 Elgin St. *Canada's Four Corners,* 93 Sparks St., carries native and Canadiana crafts. *Pierre l'Artisan* (at the St. Laurent shopping mall) offers jewelry, crafts, Canadiana. Look at the jewelry, furniture, pottery, leatherwork, and prints; they are the work of excellent local craftsmen. The *Wells Gallery,* 459 Sussex Dr., sells quality ceramics, glass, and fine art. *Byward Market,* just around the corner on York St., is one of the most colorful places to shop for fresh fruit, vegetables, and cheeses. The *Bayshore Shopping Centre* is a two-level mall with over 100 shops.

Embassy wives buy their finery at expensive import shops like *Peacock Imports,* 219 Bank St., *Capune Ltd.* (for imported knitwear), and *Puchi Mode Internationale,* both at Place de Ville. Richard Robinson, whose boutique, *Maison de Haute Couture,* is at 423 Sussex Dr., has designed for the Prime

Minister's ex-wife. Also try *Sarah Clothes,* 46 Elgin, for more off-beat, Asian imports.

Downtown Ottawa has been restructured by the *Rideau Centre,* a new development of 200 stores and shops. Rideau and Sussex Sts. don't look the same, now that the two-level complex is linked by an overhead walkway to *The Bay* and adjoins *Ogilvy's. Eaton's, Simpson's,* and *Holt Renfrew* are other popular stores.

DINING OUT. For many years Ottawa's restaurants shared the fate of local cultural and night life—they struggled along in the shadow of Hull. While Hull still boasts many of the finest French and international cuisine restaurants—like La Ferme Colombia or L'Echelle de Jacob—now Ottawa has many restaurants to be proud of too. And if you are planning a summer picnic, you couldn't do better than to drop by the *Kardish Delicatessen,* 979 Wellington St., for smoked meat and strong dill pickles, or the *Byward Market* and surrounding bakeries.

Cost categories per person are for dinner including hors d'oeuvre, entrée, and dessert. Drinks and tips are not included. *Expensive,* over $15 per person; *Moderate,* $9–15; *Inexpensive,* under $9.

Most places accept the following major credit cards: American Express, MasterCard and Visa; others may also be honored. Not all establishments accept credit cards, therefore we suggest you call for information.

Central European

Moderate

A Touch of Europe. 1792 Bank St. Noted for Stroganoff, thick goulash soup, and bratwurst and sauerkraut. Can be expensive.

Little Hungarian Village. 164 Laurier, West. A licensed Central European restaurant with violinist.

Chinese

Moderate

Golden Dragon. 176 Rideau. Standard Cantonese food beloved by local civil servants.

Mandarin Court. 1374 Baseline. Authentic Szechuan, Malaysian food.

Pine Tree Village. 354 Elgin. Northern Chinese cuisine features delicious Peking duck, hot and sour soup, curry-style dishes. No license.

Shanghai. 651 Somerset St. W. Specialties include pickerel fried with almonds and shallots, soft noodle (chow mein), and chicken fried with ham. Licensed for wine and beer.

French-International

Expensive

L'Artisan. At the Delta Ottawa Hotel. A small, high-tradition French restaurant in formal blue and white, with haute cuisine to match.

Le Jardin. 127 York St. Award-winning cuisine.

Le Restaurant. The National Arts Centre's upstairs restaurant has deep, comfortable, burgundy upholstered booths, specialties like watercress soup and duckling and a graciously paced service.

Moderate

La Bonne Fourchette. 442 Gilmour. Rated highly by local Francophones. Can be expensive.

Café Casa Blanca. 87 George St., Market Mall. French-Moroccan food: couscous, cornish hen with prunes, hot pepper salads with cumin. Great waiters and French chansonnier tapes, but a rather dull setting.

Inexpensive

Le Café. The Arts Centre's other restaurant is an informal but charming place to eat, especially near the windows overlooking the Rideau Canal. Light meals, leafy salads and delicate quiches. Licensed. Open only in summer.

Italian

Moderate

Calabria. 193 Bell N. Local Italian-Canadians love it for its excellent pizza, but the menu is extensive. Licensed.

House of Caesar. 1066 Somerset St. W. Wide selection of Italian dishes.

Mamma Teresa. 281 Kent St. It's extremely popular because its veal dishes (with wine sauce, or vermouth or lemon or cheese or . . .) are invariably good. Mamma's zabaglione is also recommended.

Japanese

Expensive

Japanese Village Steak House. 170 Laurier Ave. W. There's something about the lightly fried shrimps, teriyaki chicken, steak and lobster that make them particularly good here. Maybe it is because they are cooked in front of you by showman chefs.

Moderate

Suisha Gardens. 208 Slater. One of Ottawa's many popular Japanese restaurants.

Japanese Yakitori House. 544 Rideau. Costumed waitresses serving authentic dishes. Can be expensive.

Mexican

Moderate

Guadala Harry's. 18 York St. Mexican furniture and a re-created Spanish-style streetfront. Tacos and tequila.

Mexicali Rosa's. 895 Bank St.

Other

Expensive

Atlantic Pavillon. 253 Slater. More upscale seafood.

Moderate

Friday's. 150 Elgin. So popular with the civil servants at lunch it should be listed in the government telephone directory. Roast beef, steak, seafood. Can be expensive.

Hayloft Steak House. 200 Rideau. It's part of a chain which handles big flavorful steaks in a cheerful barnboard atmosphere.

The Old Fish Market. 54 York St. Fresh fish in a rapid-service, funky setting. Cooking is simple-grill or pan-fry techniques.

BARS AND NIGHT LIFE. Château Laurier's warm, dimly lit *Cock and Lion Club* features live entertainment nightly, except Sundays.

The Quadrille, in the Delta Ottawa Hotel, is a discothèque with live music. It is lively, friendly, and very popular with fans of big beat rock.

You can enjoy a fine view over drinks at the Skyline Hotel's *Stop 26,* where the music and the atmosphere are subdued and sophisticated.

Brandy's, on the Byward Market, is a popular disco.

Molly McGuire's is an Irish pub on Rideau St.

Stoney Monday's is a popular rock and dance spot in the Byward Market, at 62 York St.

Le Castor at 449 Sussex has a late 20's crowd, folkier music.

Try *Houlihan's,* 110 York St., for dining and dancing.

The Beachcomber Room at the Talisman Motor Inn has Polynesian sculptures, a live dance band which plays sedate cha-chas and requests, and an older clientele.

Some of Ottawa's most popular clubs are in Hull, on the Québec side of the river.

EXPLORING SOUTHERN ONTARIO

Most of Ontario's first French, English, and Loyalist settlers entered the province from the southeast. You can retrace some of their routes on Southern Ontario's Heritage Highways. Highway 2, parallel to Highway 401, is smaller than the cross-Ontario freeway but more picturesque. It's the original nineteenth-century route that linked Québec and Kingston to "Muddy York" (Toronto) in the west. And with appropriate detours it can afford you a good glimpse into Southern Ontario's attractions.

Cornwall, headquarters of the St. Lawrence Seaway, is a bilingual city of 45,900, which connects via the international bridge to Rooseveltown, New York State. For pedestrians only: Pitt St. Mall, whose pools and fountains are built of local limestone. West on Highway 2 before Morrisburg is Upper Canada Village, a faithful re-creation of an Ontario community in the early 1800's. When the construction of the St. Lawrence Seaway flooded some old riverside communities, the historic buildings were moved to the site of the Battle of Crysler's Farm, a dramatic military engagement. It was a British victory or an impasse, depending on who tells the tale. Twenty-five hundred Americans arrived on the Canadian shore in the autumn of 1813 and were met by 800 Redcoats sent down from Kingston. After what historians have called a "smart but indecisive action," 181 British lay dead, while 300 Americans were killed or wounded. There is no echo of musketry in the peaceful, mid-19th-century Upper Canadian town that has been re-created at Crysler's Farm. Oxcarts, horse-drawn boats or shank's mare take you past a bustling general store, a church, a tavern, a schoolmaster's house. Cheerful costumed occupants give you a wave. (Upper Canada Village is open from mid-May to mid-October.) Morrisburg also has an antique car museum (one mile west of Upper Canada Village on Highway 2) and the Upper Canada Migratory Bird Sanctuary, a 3,500-acre refuge, nine miles east of the town. It is open daily from April to November.

Highway 2 runs beside the St. Lawrence River section of the 2,300-mile-long Seaway. Sixty-five hundred homes had to be moved, along with 18 cemeteries and 35 miles of highway, to accommodate the flood of water along this particular stretch of Seaway. Iroquois, a tiny village, of 1,211, now boasts a major set of locks, through which massive lakers carry tens of thousands of tons of grain and ore.

Farther on, at Prescott, Fort Wellington and the Old Lighthouse (both of which saw action in the War of 1812) are now restored and open to the public. Canadian, American, and French regiments perform period drills dressed in period costume in mid-July. You can also visit Prescott's old wooden chapel (the Blue Church, built 1845). In its cemetery are the graves of many early settlers, including Barbara Heck, founder of Methodism in North America.

Brockville (named after Sir Isaac Brock, hero of the War of 1812) is an entry point to the St. Lawrence Parks Commission's Islands Park. The park offers both mainland campgrounds and island camps accessible by boat. You can rent boats at Brockville, or take a boat tour from Rockport, Kingston, Gananoque or Ivy Lea through the Thousand Islands. Hill Island, near Ivy Lea, features Never Never Land, a children's playground. Adults have their playgrounds too. Boldt Castle, once the summer residence of a nostalgic and wealthy German, rises like a Rhine Valley château on an island near Gananoque.

The Spirit of Colonialism

The city of Kingston, solid and enduring like the gray limestone of which it is built, is over 300 years old. It was founded in 1673 by Count Frontenac, the governor of New France, and was guarded by Old Fort Henry, once the principal military stronghold of Upper Canada. Here from mid-May to mid-October you can see a splendid display of infantry, cavalry, artillery, and naval equipment. Muzzle-loading cannon cast in 1874 blast salutes, and red-coated army cadets execute the traditional changing of the guard.

There is a real spirit of Upper Canadian colonialism about the city. Savor the title of a local newspaper, *The Kingston Whig-Standard;* the strong Martello towers rising above the harbor; the confident monumentality of Kingston's 19th-century stone architecture. The "Limestone City" is the home of Canada's Royal Military College, the Military College Museum (housed in a Martello tower in the city's other military defenses at Fort Frederick), the old and venerable Queen's University, and Bellevue House, a Tuscan-style villa, once the home of Canada's first prime minister, Sir John A. MacDonald. This staunch old town has other surprises. You'll find a Hockey Hall of Fame, a Canadian Forces Communications and Electronic Museum (with kit shop) at Vimy Barracks, Highway 2 East, plus bookshops, cafés, art/craft galleries and lively local theater, all patronized by Kingston's university community.

Situated at the point where the Rideau Canal system and Lake Ontario join the St. Lawrence River, Kingston is very much a harbor town. In 1976, it was the site of the XXI Olympiad's yachting events. In late August, the former Olympic site becomes the site of North American training regattas. Its 19th-century naval glory is recalled at the old shipbuilding yards (now on Royal Military College grounds), the century-and-a-half old Rideau Canal locks at Kingston Mills and the bright sails and riggings of the pleasure craft clustered in the city's harbor. From Kingston, boat lovers can also enjoy paddlewheel tours on the licensed, three-tiered *Island Queen* (trips daily, mid-May to September) and motor launch tours through the Thousand Islands.

Don't leave Kingston without dropping by the Pump House Steam Museum. The museum, housed in an imposing pile of Victorian limestone on the waterfront, has the biggest working-order steam exhibit in the world (open June 15 to Labour Day, daily, except Fridays).

North of Kingston is resort country—the Rideau Lakes. Mallards and blue-winged teal skim the warm water; boats cruise through the Rideau Canal. In the heart of the Lake district, Perth is the site of Ontario's last fatal duel, fought in 1833 over the honour of one Miss Hughes. Her fiancé, Robert Lyon, died in the exchange of shots.

The White House

Take Highway 33 west and stop by the White House at Collin's Bay. Built in 1793, it is one of the best remaining examples of a Loyalist home. There's another, near Bath, built in the 1780's by Loyalist Jeptha Hawley. Then drive on into the out-of-the-way pastoral countryside of the Prince Edward County Peninsula. Much of the peninsula was settled by German refugees from the American War of Independence; their early tribulations in the half-surveyed wilderness are recalled at the Loyalist Museum at Adolphustown. Two-and-a-half miles north, at Hay Bay, is a Quaker Burying Grounds which dates from 1784.

Picton (population 4,300) is the county center. Its original Greek revival courthouse, built in 1832, where Sir John A. MacDonald once practiced law, is still in use. The Prince Edward County Peninsula is rich in historic sites; it also offers some beautiful lakeside campsites, like the breezy dunes of Sandbanks and North Beach Provincial Parks (11 miles west of Picton).

Belleville has a fine yacht harbor on the Bay of Quinte, plus golf, swimming, even a local flying club.

In Belleville you can visit the handsome Hastings County Museum at Glanmore, a French rococo-style Victorian mansion. The museum displays European and Oriental furniture and a rather unusual assembly of lighting devices that date back to the Stone Age (257 Bridge St. E.). Belleville also produces some first-rate Canadian cheddar cheeses.

Highway 62 north from Belleville takes you into mining and lumbering country. Seventy miles on is Bancroft, a geologists' paradise, with its quality rock shops, its annual early-August "Gemboree" and its abundance of local amethyst, beryl, garnet, magnetite, rose quartz, tourmaline, and zircon mineral deposits. River raft trips on white water (i.e., rough water) are available for the intrepid. So's a gorgeous picnic spot at Eagles' Nest Lookout, 600 feet above the town of Bancroft.

Back on Highway 2, and heading west, there's a licensed restaurant in the century-old home of silent movie star Marie Dressler at Cobourg. Here you can follow a swim with a summer afternoon band concert in the town park near Cobourg's restored Palladian-style Victoria Hall.

You can take another interesting side trip off Highway 2, up Highway 28, west of Cobourg. Traveling through the Great Pine Ridge and Kawartha Lakes vacation regions, you'll come to Peterborough, a university town of 61,000 people. Besides the intricate modern architecture of Trent University, Peterborough offers the Kawartha Downs standardbred racetrack, the second highest hydraulic lift locks in the world on the Trent-Severn Waterway and the annual Peterborough Summer Festival (aquatic events, music and theatre, early July). On Saturday morning, pick up some fresh fruit and baked goods at the local Farmers' Market in Morrow Park, then drop by Century Village (a restored pioneer village) to picnic and swim in the Indian River.

Six-Foot Mound Snakes

Picnickers mingle with archeologists at the Serpent Mounds Provincial Park (south of Peterborough at Keene). Here a mysterious six-foot-high man-made mound snakes across the landscape. Northeast of Peterborough at Nephton are unusual black symbols painted on the white rock. Both sites are believed to have been left by prehistoric Indian peoples 2,000 years ago. The parks are open mid-May to mid-September.

Farther north are the Kawartha and Haliburton Highlands, unsurpassed camping and cottage country culminating in the wilderness of Algonquin Provincial Park. In between are pretty little towns like Lakefield, where Prince Andrew of the British Royal family attended the prestigious local boys' school. In summer, theatergoers flock to Lindsay's Academy Theatre, which specializes in comedy. Haliburton has four 9-hole golf courses.

Sixty-five miles east of Toronto, Heritage Highway 2 merges with the fast-moving MacDonald-Cartier Freeway (Highway 401). The traffic thickens as you approach Oshawa. Oshawa's General Motors plant is the biggest automobile manufacturing center in the country. Adults and accompanied children can tour the plant, then drop by the Canadian Automotive Museum (99 Simcoe Street, South) to view a collection of 50 motor vehicles, some dating back to 1900. Around that time Colonel Sam McLaughlin was designing his own version of the horseless carriage; later he became president of General Motors of Canada. His 55-room estate, Parkwood, is open June–August except Mondays, September–November and April–May except Saturdays and Mondays. Although the mansion has opulent touches (an indoor pool, a tiled private barbershop, a gilded Steinway grand piano, and an organ hidden by silk-paneled walls), the real attractions are the greenhouse and gardens.

The Grand Prix of Canada

If Oshawa is the commercial car capital of Canada, Mosport to the north has become synonymous with auto racing. The Canadian Grand Prix has been held on its ten-corner 2½-mile wooded circuit. On race weekends, expect crowds of up to 50,000.

Highway 401 west brings you past the mammoth nuclear power station at Pickering into Toronto. Many towns of the surrounding area (like Newtonville, Uxbridge, Sutton, Aurora, Cheltenham, Caledon) are known to antique collectors as great places to browse. Others, like Bradford in Holland Marsh, are farming and produce centres. Farther out from Toronto are small cities: Orillia, Barrie, Midland, Guelph and Kitchener.

Barrie, a thriving city of 44,000, is situated on the shores of Lake Simcoe, less than an hour's drive from Toronto. Barrie is another lake-oriented town. In winter, it attracts ice fishermen and, at its Winter Carnival, ice motorcyclists, dog sledders, and other winter-sport sensation seekers. There's good summer stock at the Gryphon Theatre, floodlit harness racing at Barrie Raceway, and lakeside regattas for its thousands of visitors.

Highway 27 leads you to other local attractions: scenic caves and a summer slide at Collingwood, Ontario's largest ski center. Indian crafts and pioneer artifacts on exhibition at the Simcoe County Museum and an old log house next door. At Shanty Bay you can see an unusual rammed-earth construction church built in 1838.

Leacock and Orillia

At the turn of the century Orillia, Barrie's sister city at the junction of Lakes Simcoe and Couchiching, was a flourishing resort drawing regular vacationers from as far away as Memphis, Tennessee. Humorist Stephen Leacock immortalized Orillia's golden years in *Sunshine Sketches of a Little Town,* still recommended reading for ramblers through small-town Ontario. Leacock is buried at Sutton, in St. George's Church, along with novelist Mazo de la Roche. You can visit Leacock's summer home, a lovely white colonial-style house off Highway 12B, from June to September. Children might prefer to visit elk, moose, and deer at the Buffalo Ranch and Game Preserve, 7 miles north on Highway 11 (summer, open daily).

North of Orillia, the gentle landscape changes to the granite-and-pine scenery of the Canadian Shield. You are in Muskoka, a resort region whose population triples in summer. Among Muskoka's sights are Santa's Village (at Bracebridge, open all summer); the 40-foot totem pole on Canoe Lake (a memorial to artist Tom Thomson, who disappeared here half a century ago), and Muskoka Pioneer Village at Huntsville.

Gravenhurst, a holiday town on Lake Muskoka, is the unlikely birthplace of Norman Bethune, a Canadian doctor who treated Mao Tse-tung's army of peasant revolutionaries and became a hero in the Peoples' Republic of China. Visitors from China make a pilgrimage to

Bethune's birthplace. North American visitors to Gravenhurst are attracted by summer theater at its restored Opera House, by lakeside Sunday evening concerts and by cruises aboard the *S.S. Segwun.*

Midland, on the south shore of Georgian Bay, is another pretty port town. It's also the site of the original French mission, Ste. Marie Among the Hurons. Jean de Brébeuf and five other Jesuit priests were murdered near here by Iroquois; they were canonized by the Catholic Church (which did not bestow the same honor on the hundreds of Huron Indians who died with them). Thousands of Roman Catholics attend the daily masses at Martyrs' Shrine, the twin-spired church which overlooks a reconstruction of the Jesuit mission. At Midland's Little Lake Park, a full-scale replica of a Huron village adjoins the Historic Huronia museum (late May to mid-October). The Wye Marsh Wildlife Centre on the outskirts of Midland is a 2,500-acre wildlife haven. Naturalists will guide you through (late May to Labour Day).

Home of the British Navy

At Penetanguishene, 3 miles northeast of Midland, British forces established a naval headquarters in 1817. Guides costumed as sailors and soldiers show you through officers' quarters, garrison reserve and work areas (late May to Labour Day). Boat cruises through (some of) the 30,000 islands of Georgian Bay are available from the foot of the Penetanguishene Town Dock. West of Penetanguishene, 9-mile-long Wasaga Beach stretches in the curve of Nottawasaga Bay. It's both a wonderful place to sun and swim; and an Ontario version of Coney Island, complete with hot dog stands and pinball arcades. At Wasaga's Nancy Island Historic Site, you can watch the recreation of an 1814 naval battle in an electronic theater. The schooner *Nancy,* once called the most beautiful ship on the Great Lakes, was a vital supply ship in the War of 1812. In 1814, an American naval squadron discovered the *Nancy* hidden up the Nottawasaga River and set her on fire. Her charred hull and the complete wheelhouse of a Great Lakes steamer are among the artifacts displayed.

Collingwood, past the far end of the beach, is a major ski resort in winter. The Blue Mountain chairlift affords you a superb view of Georgian Bay, and there is a 3,000-foot sled-run descent. The Collingwood area is also noted for its Blue Mountain pottery (you can tour the pottery works) and for good antique hunting.

The next big port town along Georgian Bay is Owen Sound. Worth a visit are the County of Grey and Owen Sound Museum, with its Algonkian Indian and pioneer artifacts, and the Tom Thomson Memorial Art Gallery, featuring oils, drawings, and mementos of the influential Canadian landscape painter. Inglis Falls, 80 feet high, and a local beauty spot, can be reached by taking Highway 6 south from Owen Sound.

Georgian Bay is enclosed by the limestone spit of the Bruce Peninsula. Hikers on the 430-mile Bruce Trail which runs along the Niagara escarpment from Niagara Falls to the Bruce Peninsula discover Tobermory, a tiny fishing village at the peninsula's tip. Here scuba divers can explore old shipwrecks in the Fathom Five Provincial Park, or scramble among weird, wind-shaped rock formations on Flower Pot Island. From late April to Labour Day, a ferry connects Tobermory to Manitoulin Island (discussed in "Exploring Northern Ontario"). The trip aboard the 600-passenger *Chi-Cheemaun* ("Big Canoe") should take under 2 hours.

From Tobermory to Sarnia, Lake Huron washes against quiet beaches and resort towns like Port Elgin, Grand Bend (with excellent summer theatre at the Huron County Playhouse) and Goderich. Kincardine has pipe band concerts in summer. At Douglas Point visitors can tour the Bruce Nuclear Power Development. At Sauble Beach they can swim off a 7-mile strip of fine sand. Sarnia, which connects via international bridge to Port Huron, Michigan, is an oil refining and petrochemical center.

The Golden Horseshoe

The Ontario that lies between Lake Huron, Lake Erie, and Lake Ontario is rich—economically, culturally and historically. The Golden Horseshoe, stretching from Oshawa east of Toronto to Oakville, Hamilton, St. Catharines and Welland around the western end of the Lake, is where much of the cultural and economic wealth is concentrated. Oakville, just west of Toronto on the Queen Elizabeth Way (the Golden Horseshoe's main artery), is one of the wealthiest communities in Canada. The reason for Oakville's yachts and stately homes is the presence of the Ford Motor Company. You can tour the Ford plant (by reservation 416–845–2511). Bronte Creek Provincial Park, with its bicycle paths, playgrounds, hiking trails and tractor tours and a restored turn-of-the-century farmhouse, is also worth a visit.

Hamilton is Canada's steel capital. The city's spectacular entrances —over the Burlington Skyway from the north, or via the Royal Botanical Gardens on the south—make Hamilton proper look gritty and industrial by contrast. But Hamilton is a tough, vital city with strong traditions. Among them are football (you can visit the Canadian Football Hall of Fame in City Hall Plaza); steel (the bay area is dominated by the huge Dofasco and Stelco plants); and, surprisingly, it's also known for gardens: the Royal Botanical Gardens in the north end, whose nature trails cross over 2,000 acres of garden and parkland. Strollers stop for refreshment at the Tea House overlooking the rock garden. Nearby, the marshes and gullies of Cootes Paradise provide a sanctuary for wildlife. Dundurn Castle, built between 1832 and 1835 by a pre-Confederation Canadian prime minister, Sir Allan Napier McNab, has gardens where in summer you can enjoy concerts and children's theater. Hamilton's McMaster University recently acquired the papers of 20th-century philosopher Bertrand Russell. Tuesdays to Saturdays the Central (farmers') Market bustles with local produce. Hamilton, which has lived with the reputation of being a tough industrial city, is also proud of its glittering performing arts center, Hamilton Place, home of the Hamilton Philharmonic Orchestra, and its boutique and restaurant shopping area, Hess Village.

St. Catharines, in the heart of Canada's fruit belt and major wine-producing region, celebrates the harvest with the ten-day Niagara

Grape and Wine Festival at the end of September. An old city, it was originally settled by the Loyalist troops of Butler's Rangers, who disbanded here in 1784. Loyalist nostalgia for Britain is also recalled in the Royal Canadian Henley Regatta, North America's largest rowing regatta which St. Catharines hosts in early August. The city has its attractions throughout the year, among them the locks of the Welland Canal and Rodman Hall's Art Gallery of graphics, sculpture, and tapestries at 109 St. Paul Crescent.

Tecumseh and General Brock

From St. Catharines, it's just a short drive to Queenston. Queenston, a typically pretty Southern Ontario town won its place in history during the War of 1812. The invading American forces landed here, securing Queenston Heights. British General Sir Isaac Brock scanned the Heights, and believing them to be held by only a handful of Yankee gunners, cried "Follow me, boys!" and led his cheering militiamen in a charge uphill. Of course, the attempt failed. Brock, the hero who had captured American Forts Detroit and Michilimackinac, was shot and killed; the 210-foot Brock monument commemorates the place on which he fell. At one point in the 1812 War, the Stars and Stripes flew over the Heights. They were later recaptured by the British with the help of Indian allies. Brock, in spite of his uphill charge, was regarded as the most competent general on the British side, which may not speak well of their competence. There's another souvenir of the War's skirmishes near Queenston. The Laura Secord home has been restored to the condition in which she left it on the night she warned British troops of a surprise attack by the Americans. North of Queenston, at Niagara-on-the-Lake, the Shaw Festival and Canadian Mime Theatre delight audiences each summer. You might be tempted to follow a weekend concert or play with a look through the Niagara Apothecary shop, a pharmacology museum where apothecary glass is lined up above old-fashioned walnut and butternut fixtures. Stroll past outdoor cafés and curio shops, and explore the Niagara Fire Museum, where some of the fire-fighting equipment displayed dates back to 1816. Fort George (1797) and the McFarland House, a Georgian brick home built in 1800, both restored, are nearby on the Niagara Parkway.

Don't confuse the pretty 19th-century charms of Niagara-on-the-Lake with the commercial glories of Niagara Falls, once a honky-tonk paradise for publicity seekers (who tight-roped across the Falls or went over in barrels) and honeymooners, who watched hand-in-hand from the side. The honeymooners still come, but now it's to visit the Wax Museums, the 520-foot-high Skylon Tower with its revolving restaurant, the palatial mansion Oak Hall, fountains and gardens and, of course, the magnificent white curve of the 186-foot-high falls themselves. At night the Falls are illuminated. Horseshoe Falls on the Canadian side is separated from the American Falls by Goat Island. Take the *Maid of the Mist* boat tour under the falls from 5920 River Road or descend by elevator and tunnel to the water's edge at 4330 River Road—it's called the Niagara Daredevil Gallery and is open May to October.

Outside Niagara Falls, stop and visit the dolphins at Marineland and Game Farm (7657 Portage Road South). If weather permits you'll be able to enjoy the whale show, which stars a killer whale.

Old Fort Erie, with its drawbridge, moat and cannon, guards the town of the same name 20 miles south of Niagara Falls. Fort Erie also offers some of the best thoroughbred racing in Ontario. Crystal Beach on Lake Erie is a beachside carnival town; shrieks of laughter from its Comet Coaster riders can be heard for miles. Port Colborne handles the area's serious business. At Port Colborne, one of the world's largest single locks, marks the southern end of the Welland Canal. In the country north of the Erie shore, tobacco is grown.

Home of Alexander Bell

Brantford, northeast of Port Dover on Highway 24, is named after Joseph Brant, the loyalist Mohawk chief who brought the Six Nations Confederacy into Canada after the American War of Independence. Brantford's other famous son is Alexander Graham Bell, whose homestead is open to the public all year, daily, except Mondays from Labour Day to mid-June. Canadians claim he invented the telephone and made his first long distance calls here in Southern Ontario.

Brantford is rich in Indian traditions. The oldest Protestant church in Ontario, Her Majesty's Chapel of the Mohawks, was built here in 1785. The Brant County Museum has an excellent collection of Six Nations artifacts. Another attraction is Chiefswood, the classical-style 1850's home of Mohawk chief George Johnson; now it's also a literary shrine to Indian poet Pauline Johnson. In June, at Alberton, near Brantford, there's a major archery competition. In August, the nearby reservation hosts a Six Nations Indian Pageant.

West of Brantford is London, a city of about 266,000. Chosen by Colonel (later Lieutenant Governor) John Graves Simcoe as Upper Canada's future capital, it has turned instead into an academic, industrial and commercial center. London's got attractions for all tastes, from a pioneer brewery to a 75-year-old Opera House housing its local live theater company. Paddlewheel boats lined with tourists cruise the placid Thames River. Fanshawe Park with its dam, reservoir, Pioneer Village, swimming, hiking, golfing and sailing is also on the banks of the Thames. Eldon House, built in 1834, has been restored and is open from March to November; if you have children, you should also drop by Ska-Nah-Doht, a reconstructed long house Indian Village (Longswoods Road Conservation area) and Storybook Gardens in Springbank Park, complete with miniature trains and Old MacDonald's Farm.

St. Thomas, south of London, is known as "the Garden City"— visitors to the floral displays and fountains of Pinafore Park and Waterworks Park can see why. Nearby, at the Southwold Earthworks, is the only double-walled Indian village and fort in Canada.

The swans on Stratford's Avon River ignore picnickers and canoers. When the theaters open, the crowds disappear to enjoy some of the finest productions of Shakespearian drama in the world. Stratford is a pleasant old town with leafy streets, cafes, gift shops and an art gallery (on Romeo Street). Fryfogel's Inn (1844), 8½ miles east of Stratford on Highway 8, was a stop over for stagecoaches on the old Huron Road.

East of Stratford are the twin towns of Kitchener and Waterloo. Original German settlers have left their stamp on the city. Kitchener's ten-day Oktoberfest is an annual beer-drinking, tuba-thumping, roaring success. Here and in Elmira you can still catch glimpses of black-bonneted women and soberly dressed men—Amish and Mennonite farmers. Strict Mennonites still drive horse-drawn buggies; conveniences of all kinds are antithetical to their defiantly self-sufficient way of life. The baked goods, delicious preserves, and handicrafts of the Mennonite women are plied among the other produce at the Kitchener Farmers' Market on Saturdays.

Travel west of Kitchener on Highway 401. And don't overlook the town of Aberfoyle as you turn off on Highway 6. Aberfoyle's century-old grist mill is now restored, and houses a very successful dining lounge. Every summer Sunday, bargain hunters flock to Aberfoyle's flea market, where acres of stalls crammed with junk produce some surprising bargains.

Guelph, a lovely old gray stone university and manufacturing town, is dominated by the spires of its Church of Our Lady Cathedral (modeled after the Cathedral of Cologne). Guelph has a waterfowl park, an electric railway museum, a museum for poet John McCrae (*In Flanders Fields*), plus the usual university town's complement of bookstores and cafés. Just north of Guelph is Elora. It's a picturesque village clinging to the sides of a limestone gorge. Many of its 19th-century shops have become antiques and crafts stores.

Highway 401 slices through southwestern Ontario. It will take you the 185 miles from Guelph to Windsor on the border in just over three hours. It's worth a detour to visit Dresden (16 miles north of Chatham), where you can visit the home of Reverend Josiah Henson, a runaway slave. Henson, who founded Canada's first vocational school as a rehabilitation service for other runaway slaves, is supposedly the model of Harriet Beecher Stowe's *Uncle Tom's Cabin*. At any rate, that's what the Dresden slave museum is called.

The Route of Rum-Runners

Windsor is Canada's southernmost city. In the roaring twenties it was a main rum-running route to Prohibition America. Now it's a heavily industrialized center with close ties to Detroit's automobile industry but the verve of its earlier days lives on in its restaurants and nightclubs. The city has a good art gallery (with an excellent collection of Inuit art), an all-seasons harness raceway, and an abundance of industrial tours (Bell Canada, Ford Motor Company and the Hiram Walker Distillery, which produces Canadian Club rye). Don't miss the Sunken Gardens and fountains at Jackson Park. They are especially beautiful by night when the ornamental lighting goes on. François Bâby House, now the Hiram Walker Historical Museum, was the headquarters of the invading American army in 1812. It has been handsomely restored. South of Windsor, at Leamington, you can enter Point Pelee National Park. Canada's southernmost point, it is on the same latitude line as the French Riviera. It's a 4000-acre marsh and forest sanctuary for over 300 species of birds. You can explore the park by taking a boardwalk stroll for over half a mile past thick marsh grass to an observation tower. From here you can birdwatch in silence or enjoy the sunsets for which Point Pelee is famous. However, its most astoundingly beautiful sight probably occurs in late September when tens of thousands of orange Monarch butterflies rest at Point Pelee before migrating south.

EXPLORING NORTHERN ONTARIO

Northern Ontario, its inhabitants will proudly tell you, is a province unto itself. The line from Ottawa to Kenora that roughly separates north from south is over 1,000 miles long. Most of the land in between is the rugged, 2½-billion-year-old igneous and metamorphic rock-face of the Canadian Shield, dotted by innumerable freshwater lakes. People here are tough frontiersmen, descendants of native hunting peoples, French and English traders, Italian laborers, Scandinavian trappers. Northern Ontario's winters are long and harsh, its summers balmy, and its autumns brilliant. The area is a paradise for hunters, fishermen, or people who simply yearn for isolation and austere grandeur.

The best way to see northern Ontario is probably by canoe or bush plane. But to get there, you'll be taking the Trans-Canada Highway. Although the roadside scenery can be dazzlingly beautiful in fall, winter and spring, please bear in mind that many museums and other attractions are open only between May and September.

From the nation's capital, Highway 17 follows the route of the early *coureurs de bois* north beside the Ottawa River. The Ottawa is now a major logging river, down which log booms are transported from lumber camps to the pulp mills at Hull. At Almonte (a short detour south of Highway 17 on Highway 44), you'll find the Mill of Kintail, a picturesque stone mill dating from 1830. A century after it was built it became the home of sculptor and fitness educator Dr. R. Tait McKenzie, who designed the medallions that are awarded in Olympic Games. Many of his sculptures of athletes in action are displayed here alongside the older pioneer artifacts.

In summer, cottagers flock to Renfrew, 61 miles west of Ottawa on Highway 17. Children can play among life-sized fairytale figures at Storyland (open May to October), while their parents browse in the Cross Canada Craft Shop. Native crafts for sale include basketry, prints and carvings from the Golden Lake Reserve (July–August). Near Renfrew, from the Champlain Lookout, miles of surrounding woods and water are visible—but it isn't until you get to Cobden, 20 miles farther on, that your path crosses that of the 17th-century French explorer. Here a plowboy stumbled across what historians agree was Champlain's astrolabe, a navigation instrument his party lost almost four centuries ago.

Heading west, you'll pass Pembroke (its small zoo is open in summer), a Canadian Forces base at Petawawa, and Chalk River, site of one of the first atomic fission stations in the world. You can tour Chalk River's Nuclear Laboratories (open from June to Labour Day) and see an atomic reactor at work.

A hundred and ninety miles northwest of Ottawa lies Mattawa, a bilingual town of about 3,000 people. Mattawa was once a major portage on the Ottawa River route of the fur traders. The next big community is the city of North Bay. Each February, North Bay holds a dog-sledding, log-chopping, sleigh-riding extravaganza which culminates in the Fur Trappers' Ball. The rest of the year, its population of 50,000 is swelled by vacationers attracted to its golf courses, its mile-long sand beach, and its reputation for great hunting and fishing.

The Trans-Canada Highway splits at North Bay. If you follow the Superior Route, you'll find the landscape more hilly, varied and beautiful, the food and lodging more sophisticated. The rather barren Northern Route is for the curious.

The Northern Route

Ninety miles north of North Bay, in 1903, Fred Larose threw his hammer at a passing fox and struck silver ore instead. He precipitated a Silver Rush now celebrated by the town of Cobalt in its 10-day-long Miners' Festival (held each July). Cobalt also has an excellent Mining Museum, open from May to October.

A tiny town just after Kirkland Lake illustrates the cocky independence of Northern Ontarians' character: during World War II, when patriots suggested Swastika change its name from Adolf Hitler's hated symbol to something more Canadian, inhabitants demanded, "Why? It's been ours longer. Let *him* get a new symbol."

Timmins, to the southwest, is Canada's biggest city—at least in area (1,260 square miles). Timmins is centered in one of the most productive zinc and silver regions in the world. You can tour the mines in summer months. Nearby, the town of Porcupine has an outdoor mining museum. Cochrane is a major outfitting center for sportsmen and the southern terminal of the famous Polar Bear Express.

The train from Cochrane is the only land access to Moosonee, 186 miles north on the shores of James Bay. The Polar Bear Express follows the route of a French soldier, the Chevalier de Troyes. In 1668, he led a tiny expedition up chilly northern rivers and captured the unsuspecting English trading post at Moosonee's twin city, Moose Factory, for the French Crown. The train from Cochrane takes you through Northern Ontario's fertile Clay Belt, past the massive Hydro Dam at Otter Rapids, through muskeg and forest. As you approach the Tree Line, the scraggly pine get smaller and smaller, then disappear.

Moosonee and Moose Factory, founded more than 300 years ago by the Hudson's Bay Company, are both genuine frontier towns, and some of their buildings date back to the early 18th century. St. Thomas Church has a beaded moosehide altar cloth and hymn books in the Cree language. Moosonee is also the gateway to Ontario's largest and most rugged park, Polar Bear Provincial. To visit it, you'll require a special permit and a chartered plane. Polar and black bear, moose, caribou, and Artic fowl abound in the park. Not observing the boundaries around its 9,300 square miles, the rest of this barren country is theirs too.

West of Cochrane on Highway 11, are the pulp and paper town of Smooth Rock Falls, Kapuskasing (the Kleenex capital), and Hearst, a sawmill town with a lively French-speaking population. Hearst is also noted for moose hunting and for the pickerel (walleye) that teem in its local waters.

Hundreds of miles of forest, deserted beaches, and rock (where rockhounds can find agate, quartz, fool's gold, flint and fossils) dominate the scenery to Nipigon, where the Northern and Southern routes merge again. The last few miles of the Northern route skirt Lake Nipigon by tall cliffs. From the Nipigon River, west of the highway, 14-pound brook trout and 30-pound lake trout have been taken.

The Southern (Superior) Route

Take Highway 17 west from North Bay. As you approach Sudbury, the landscape becomes positively lunar—in fact, American astronauts trained for their moon walk here. (Outsiders joked that the astronauts were in town to see what the moon looked like; in fact, they came to see "shatter cones"—geological formations that resulted from a giant meteorite's crashing into the earth's surface here. The mineral wealth of the Sudbury Basin—nickel, cobalt, copper, gold, and platinum—is believed to be the result of that meteorite crash.) Sudbury is noted for its polluted air, the orange glow of molten metal on its slag heaps, and its nickel production (commemorated by a 30-foot-high Canadian 5¢ piece, made, oddly enough, of stainless steel).

West of Sudbury, the "World's Nickel Capital," is Elliot Lake, which styles itself the "World's Uranium Capital." Early in 1953, prospectors, geologists, and bush pilots flew a secret mission into the area. When news of their uranium discovery broke, Elliot Lake's mines were contracted to produce over a billion dollars' worth of the metal. A well-planned model community sprang out of the wilderness, but by 1960, when the uranium boom was over, it nearly became a well-planned model ghost town. Recent contracts with the Ontario government may revitalize operations.

You might also want to take a detour from Espanola (30 miles before Elliot Lake). From Espanola, you can head south to Manitoulin Island. "Manitou-lin" ("God's home") is quite literally a vacationer's heaven. There are over a hundred freshwater lakes on this, the world's largest freshwater island. Manitoulin has tent and trailer parks, pretty little port towns, waterfalls and beaches, restored jailhouses, lighthouses, churches and other museums, and two culturally active Indian Reserves. Both Ojibwa communities hold summer festivals. The area is rich in Indian history and artifacts. Archeologists working at Sheguiandah have suggested that Manitoulin was the site of one of North America's earliest native cultures.

Next is Sault Ste. Marie, a city of about 82,000 people. The "Soo" derives its name from *sault*, the French word for rapids—and from which the English expression "shoot the rapids" comes. Across the St.

Mary River rapids lies Sault Ste. Marie's twin city, Sault Ste. Marie, Michigan; they're joined by the International Bridge.

Even before explorer Étienne Brulé arrived here in 1622, the rough water between Lake Superior and Lake Huron was a meeting and trading center for the Ojibwa Indians. For the early trader-explorers, the Soo was the gateway to the west. In fact one Frenchman, figuring he would shortly reach China, arrived here wearing "damask silk robes." On seeing the hilly wilderness around him, he discarded his finery for buckskin. The French explorer, Father Marquette, established a mission here in 1689. Later it became a major post of the Nor'West and Hudson's Bay Companies. During the War of 1812, the men of Sault Ste. Marie, with the crucial support of their Indian allies, aided in the capture of the American Fort Michilimackinac. In retaliation, the Canadian settlement was destroyed by American naval forces in 1814. The oldest stone house in Northern Ontario, the Soo's Ermatinger House, was built that year after the departure of the Americans by fur trader Charles Oakes Ermatinger for his Ojibwa wife, Charlotte Kallawabide, and has been beautifully restored.

The Soo locks on the Canadian side of the St. Mary River were built in 1870 to facilitate the movement of troops west to crush Louis Riel's second rebellion. The building of the locks increased the city's wealth in trade; following the discovery of iron ore in the Algoma district, the first steel plant in Ontario opened here in 1902. Italian laborers (paid at the rate of 17¢ an hour) were brought in to man the mills. Their descendants include talented local restaurateurs, delicatessen operators, and hockey superstar Phil Esposito.

The Soo is the place to begin Northern Ontario's other great rail adventure, the Agawa Canyon Tour. You catch the Algoma Central Railway train before breakfast (in peak summer months, its served aboard the train), then settle back and watch as the train twists around great hulking hills and slopes of river gorges, rattles over 130-foot-high trestle bridges and then, four hours later, plunges into the Agawa Canyon. In winter, the frozen lakes are crisscrossed by the tracks of otters' slides across the ice. Waterfalls, frozen into white sheets, are streaked with yellow and blue mineral deposits. Trappers and skiers flag down the train and jump aboard. In autumn, the hillsides blaze with scarlet and gold. Any time of year, it's a colorful trip, and if you make arrangements with the railway personnel in advance, you can be dropped by the side of the track to head off into the bush and camp. The train makes the trip six days a week and will pick you up again at an appointed time.

North of the Soo is some of Ontario's most spectacular scenery as the highway winds along the hilly north shore of Lake Superior. You can find Indian pictographs painted on the rock north of Agawa Bay Scenic Lookout, in Lake Superior Park.

A huge statue of a Canada goose welcomes you to Wawa ("Wild Goose"), the center of Algoma's iron mining industry. Here you can tour the pit heads of abandoned mines, watch the Magpie River drop 75 feet at Magpie High Falls, or poke around the area's Indian sites. There's an outsized thermometer by the highway at White River (population 847) proclaiming it the most frigid spot in Canada where the mercury once fell to $-72°F$ (or $-58°C$). Why White River should covet this uncomfortable distinction is unclear, but it's hotly (or coldly) contested by Hawk Junction, just north of the Agawa Canyon near Wawa. Incidentally, White River, Hawk Junction, and Chapleau (a bush pilot center) are all jumping-off points for sportsmen bound for the bush.

From scenic Aquasabon Gorge near Terrace Bay, it's another 130 miles to Thunder Bay. Before you arrive, take another detour to Silver Islet (41 miles east of Thunder Bay) and visit a tiny abandoned mining community. Once the site of one of the world's richest silver mines, it is now inhabited by cottagers. The old general store is open for business in summer.

Now the sight of Thunder Bay's huge grain elevators greets you. Thunder Bay is in the geographical center of Canada. A billion bushels of prairie wheat are stored here, then shipped east through the St. Lawrence Seaway. Across from the grain and freight bustle of Thunder Bay's waterfront looms Nanibijou, the Sleeping Giant. Once an Ojibwa god, Nanibijou was, according to legend, turned into stone because of the ungrateful treachery of his people.

Thunder Bay offers first-class skiing. At Big Thunder Jump there are 70- and 90-meter jumps—the second highest jumps in the world. One of five local ski areas, Mount McKay, is operated by the Fort William Indian band. If you visit in summer, you can gather gemstones at an amethyst mine (open May to October), or visit Fort William, a fur-trading community which has been restored to its early 19th-century state. Costumed artisans work in the blacksmith's shop, candle factory, bakery, and canoe repair sheds. Thunder Bay's other attractions include Centennial Park's replica of a logging camp, a good local museum with Indian and early military artifacts, and harbor cruises. The International Friendship Garden, colorful in many senses of the word, is really a series of gardens reflecting the characters of the city's different ethnic groups. Eighteen miles beyond Thunder Bay is Kakabeka Falls. According to legend, an Ojibwa princess once led a band of Sioux warriors over the 128-foot drop and saved her people. Legend notwithstanding, it's a beautiful site for a picnic or overnight camping.

At Shabaqua Corners the Trans-Canada Highway splits again. The Southern Route (Highway 11) goes through Atikokan, the access point to Quetico Provincial Park. Nearby, a whole lake has been drained and turned into open pit iron mines. The highway travels through forest, followed by a three-mile causeway which leapfrogs across Rainy Lake's islands to bring you into Fort Frances. Fort Frances has an official museum, a reconstructed trading fort at Pither's Point Park, and paper-making tours of the Boise Cascade Canada Ltd. plant.

After Nestor Falls, the water to your west is Lake of the Woods, whose shoreline twists through so many peninsulas and indentations that, it is longer than the Lake Superior shore. This makes Lake of the Woods a natural site for the International Sailing Association Regatta (held every summer in Kenora).

At Kenora, the southern Highway 11 links up with the northern Highway 17 route. If you have followed 17, the way has been flatter, less scenic. But Highway 17, too, has its points of interest; for example the fascinating bush pilot museum at Ear Falls or other bush pilot towns like Sioux Lookout and Red Lake. At Kenora, ½-hour's drive to the Manitoba border, you're 1,280 miles west of Cornwall in eastern Ontario. Set your watch back an hour—you've traveled into a new time zone.

PRACTICAL INFORMATION FOR ONTARIO

HOW TO GET THERE. By air: Pearson International and Ottawa Uplands are major international airports, served by most international carriers as well as *Canadian Pacific* and *Air Canada*.

By car: Ontario is easily accessible by car. From Michigan in the southwest, the MacDonald-Cartier (Hwy. 401) connects Windsor, London, Toronto and Kingston. From New York State, the Queen Elizabeth Way connects Fort Erie and Niagara Falls with Hamilton and Toronto. Ontario is connected to Québec via Hwys. 401 and 417 (Québec Hwy. 40, which splits at Dorion). Hwys. 17 and 11 cross northern Ontario. Hwy. 17 exits via Manitoba, Hwy. 11 via Minnesota.

By train: Ontario is served by cross-Canada *Via Rail* service. There are rail connections with the United States at Windsor/Detroit and Fort Erie/Buffalo.

By bus: *Greyhound Lines* link Ontario to other provinces and to the United States.

ACCOMMODATIONS. Hotel rates vary greatly in Ontario. Bear in mind that rates will go up as you get closer to (or in) large cities and may depend on season, as well. Because it is such a large province, we are breaking it down by Southern Ontario and Northern Ontario. Most places accept the following major credit cards: American Express, MasterCard and Visa; others may also be honored. Not all establishments accept credit cards, therefore we suggest you call for information.

SOUTHERN ONTARIO

Southern Ontario has everything from lush resorts to serviceable motels to antique-filled inns. Information at time of writing has been checked, but vacationers are warned to inquire in advance about rates and services. Where hotels are unlicensed it is sometimes permissible to provide your own liquor. These categories indicate price only and are daily rates for two people in double occupancy. *Deluxe,* $90 a day and over; *Expensive,* $70–100; *Moderate,* $40–70; *Inexpensive,* under $40.

ALGONQUIN PARK. *Deluxe.* **Arowhon Pines.** On Little Joe Lake. Artist Tom Thomson was entranced by the scenery. So are the guests, but they also return for the beach, boat rentals and comfortable rooms and cottage units furnished in pine. Guides are available for longer canoe trips. Not licensed. Meals included in the price. The kitchen is first-rate—the owner's daughter is one of Canada's leading food critics.

ALTON. *Deluxe.* **The Millcroft Inn.** A beautiful job of restoring an old mill overlooking the water. This 42-room inn has fireplaces in its rooms, an outdoor pool, golf, tennis, and first-rate food. Licensed. Very popular; reserve ahead.

APSLEY. *Inexpensive–Moderate.* **Harbour Hill Cottages.** High on a hill overlooking Chandos Lake, these simple, older housekeeping cottages offer good summer and winter accommodation for families. There's a sandy swimming place for kids; nearby golf, cross-country ski or hiking trails.

BALA. *Moderate.* **Roselawn Lodge.** A pretty clapboard complex of lodge and cottages with a beach on the Moon River, boat rentals and an unlicensed dining room.
Inexpensive. **Hacienda Motel.** Housekeeping units available in this 7-room roadside motel.

BANCROFT. *Moderate.* **Sword Motor Inn.** It's one of the larger complexes in the area with TV, licensed dining room, and golf nearby. On the property, facing the water, there's a beach, and an outdoor pool for folks who prefer less natural water.

BARRIE. *Moderate.* **Bayshore Motor Hotel.** Overlooking Kempenfelt Bay, this modern two-story motel has a licensed dining room on the water, TV, and golf nearby.
Inexpensive. **White Towers Motel.** Small, clean housekeeping units, facilities for people in wheelchairs. Golf nearby.

BAYFIELD. *Moderate.* **The Little Inn.** Built around 1830, this Victorian hotel has 13 guest rooms and a marvellous licensed dining room. It's handy to tennis, swimming, and walking by the Lake Huron shore.

BELLEVILLE-PICTON. *Expensive.* **Lake on the Mountain Resort.** East of Picton on Lake on the Mountain Rd. Natural shoreline, boat rentals, TV in the lodge or one of the seven housekeeping cottages make this place pleasant and popular.
Four Seasons Hotel. With 125 air-conditioned rooms with TV, it's a large modern hotel with an outdoor pool and a beach. Overlooking fields and water, it's quiet with decent views.

BENMILLER. See **GODERICH.**

BRACEBRIDGE. *Deluxe.* **Aston Villa.** Six miles west of Bracebridge on Hwy. 118. You can swim at the beach or take a plunge in the outdoor pool. There's tennis and a licensed dining lounge. Modified American Plan.
Tamwood Lodge. Also six miles west on Lake Muskoka, it's a rustic complex of lodge and cottages built of logs. An indoor pool substitutes for the beach on rainy days.
Inexpensive–Moderate. **High Falls Motel.** 9 cottages, 6 motel rooms, and a beach for the kids.

BRANTFORD. *Inexpensive.* **Bell City Motel.** The twenty air-conditioned rooms have TV. The hotel is small, but clean and pleasant, and has an outdoor pool.

BROCKVILLE. *Moderate.* **Skyline Hotel.** Seventy-four rooms, outdoor pool, TV, air conditioning, a licensed lounge make it one of the area's most popular facilities.

White House Motel. Two miles east of Brockville on Hwy. 2, it's a quiet family-operated, riverside motel with outdoor pool, TV and good licensed dining room.

BURLEIGH FALLS. *Inexpensive–Moderate.* **Stricker's Cottages.** Among the birches, you'll find eleven housekeeping cottages on a beautiful stretch of water.

CHATHAM. *Moderate.* **Holiday Inn.** This 160-room inn is right on the Thames River. There are even docking facilities along with an outdoor pool, indoor pool, lounge and TV.

Wheels Inn. The building is designed around indoor gardens. The licensed dining room has a Victorian flavor to it. The 354 rooms are air-conditioned and have TV. There are indoor and outdoor pools, golf, and tennis. Families come here for exercise facilities as much as for relaxation.

COLLINGWOOD-KIMBERLEY. *Moderate–Expensive.* **Blue Mountain Inn.** The inn has been a popular spot for almost a generation of skiers. Its rooms are older, but have a rustic flavor.

Moderate. **Beaconglow Point Cottages.** 12 cottages by Georgian Bay's magnificent beaches.

Inexpensive. **Inn in the Valley.** A small, old inn, backed up against the huge Niagara Escarpment. Seven rooms, dining room, outdoor pool, great hiking and skiing nearby.

CORNWALL. *Inexpensive–Moderate.* **Anchor Motel.** Its 42 rooms are air-conditioned with TV, and it has an outdoor pool. Business travelers find it comfortable and reliable.

DORSET. *Moderate.* **Nordic Inn.** The inn is owned by a Finnish family and specializes in cross-country skiing. It also has licensed dining facilities and rooms with TV.

ELORA. *Moderate–Deluxe.* **The Elora Mill Inn.** The roar of a waterfall is muffled in 22 tastefully renovated rooms, licensed dining.

FERGUS. *Moderate.* **The Breadalbane Inn.** The six rooms are small, but comfy places to read the Inn's tattered old copies of *Country Life.* Sauna, excellent dining room, splendid garden in which to sip your before-dinner apéritif.

FORT ERIE. *Inexpensive.* **Queen's Hotel.** With a view of the Niagara River, fronting on Lake Erie, its 20 rooms have TV. There are two licensed lounges, one a pub, the other with live entertainment for an older clientele. Beach nearby.

GANANOQUE. *Moderate–Expensive.* **Gananoque Inn.** On the St. Lawrence River. A 90-year-old renovated mansion overlooking the water. There are 37 fully serviced rooms and 3 cottages.

Inexpensive–Moderate. **The Athlone Inn.** Built in 1874, it was called Woodview Villa because of the leafy trees surrounding it. The eleven rooms are furnished with antiques and have fireplaces. They also have TV, and air conditioning. The dining room is licensed.

GODERICH. *Deluxe.* **Benmiller Inn.** Two mills on the banks of Sharpe's Creek have been expensively restored. The beamed sitting rooms look out on gardens or, in winter, cross-country ski trails. Reservations a must.

HALIBURTON. *Deluxe.* **Sir Sam's Inn.** In winter, skiiers gather in the parlor for singsongs. In the summer, people come for the beach on Eagle Lake, the fishing, the tennis. Intimate (only 10 rooms, 10 cottages).

Inexpensive. **Haliburton Forest Reserve.** On Kennisis Lake. A lodge in the middle of the wilderness with spartan bunkhouse-type accommodation on the edge of Algonquin Park. Swimming, boat rentals and simple dining.

HALLS LAKE. *Moderate.* **Cherokee Resort.** Well-equipped housekeeping cottages amid the pines overlooking a waterfront full of swimming kids and boaters. Good hiking, cross-country skiing nearby.

HAMILTON. *Moderate–Expensive.* **Royal Connaught Hotel.** Hamilton's grand old hotel has catered to conventions, football fans and honeymooners for several generations. Two hundred and eight rooms have TV and all facilities. Licensed lounges, dining room.

HUNTSVILLE. *Expensive.* **Billie Bear Lodge.** On Bella Lake. There are 6 rooms in the main log-built lodge, but Billie Bear's real charm is its 21 cottages with fieldstone fireplaces. Aircraft charter service and fly-in fishing are provided. Beach, boat rentals.

Ox-bow Lodge. American Plan, i.e., three square meals included in the price. Rooms, cabins with fireplaces. Beach.

Moderate. **The Empire Hotel.** Large (101 rooms), licensed and a local institution, it has been immortalized in one of folksinger Joni Mitchell's songs.

JONES FALLS. See **RIDEAU LAKES.**

KIMBERLEY. See **COLLINGWOOD.**

KINGSTON. *Expensive–Deluxe.* **The Opinicon.** An old-fashioned resort, its outdoor pool is almost superfluous in its beautiful setting by the Rideau Canal. Boat rentals, good dining facilities. 18 rooms and 17 cottages with fireplaces, TV. A 20-minute drive north of Kingston.

Moderate. **Best Western Capri.** The fireplace and lounge paneled in logs add to its charm. There's also an outdoor pool, TV and a good dining room.

The Prince George A real find, this renovated 100-year-old hotel overlooking the waterfront has antique pine in the rooms, balconies, and saunas, and a good restaurant.

Inexpensive–Moderate. **La Salle Motel.** Has an outdoor pool which is beloved of families with children. One-hundred and nine rooms. Air conditioning, TV. Golf nearby.

KITCHENER. *Moderate.* **Valhalla Inn.** Indoor pool, 130 rooms, and a superb brunch make this a favorite stopping place for families enroute to the Stratford Festival.

LONDON. *Expensive–Deluxe.* **Holiday Inn Centre and Tower.** An indoor pool, an outdoor pool and all the usual contemporary comforts in this huge (632-room) complex.

Park Lane Hotel. A businessman's hotel; 156 rooms and all conveniences.

Inexpensive. **Rainbow Motel.** An outdoor pool, golf nearby, and 23 quiet rooms. It's rated very highly among travelers to the area.

MAGNETAWAN. *Inexpensive.* **Lockview Cottages.** Three little housekeeping cottages with a nearby beach.

MINDEN. *Expensive–Deluxe.* **Hart Lodge.** (Modified American Plan.) On Mountain Lake. There are 12 rooms in the main lodge plus 21 cottages. An outdoor pool, beach, boat rentals, TV, and fireplaces, add to the relaxed charm of the place. Not licensed.

MINETT. *Expensive.* **Clevelands House.** On Lake Rosseau. Golf, outdoor pool, rooms with TV, a licensed dining room known in the area for its good food and service. Tennis and boating are specialties. It's an older resort on spacious grounds.

NEWBORO. *Expensive.* **The Poplars.** On Newboro Lake. This 26-room lodge, 2-cottage complex is known for good fishing, marine services, beach and boat rentals. Guides are available. The unlicensed dining room is good. Really moderate, considering that American Plan meals are included in your $76 a day.

NIAGARA FALLS. *Moderate–Expensive.* **The Brock Sheraton Hotel.** A popular place to stay, with an outdoor pool, golf, babysitting services, licensed dining room and TV in its 248 air-conditioned rooms.

Inexpensive–Expensive. **Michael's Inn.** Overlooks Niagara Gorge and Rainbow Bridge. Pubs on the premises are popular. Its 130 rooms have air conditioning and TV, and there's an indoor pool.

Inexpensive. **Old Stone Inn.** A 1904 flour mill, now a quiet, luxurious, sunken-baths retreat. Outdoor pool, licensed dining rooms with antique furniture.

NIAGARA-ON-THE-LAKE. *Moderate–Expensive.* **Prince of Wales.** An old hotel, renovated with real charm—tasteful graphics, ornate wallpapers, a comfortable elegant lounge and dining room, and TV in its 94 rooms.

Moderate. **Oban Inn.** From the Oban's spacious front porch you can gaze out over the Niagara River and Lake Ontario. It's a gracious old small-town inn with good dining facilities and modern conveniences (TV, air conditioning, convention facilities).

PICTON. See **BELLEVILLE.**

PORT COLBORNE. *Moderate.* **Rathfon Inn.** This house was built in 1797; Governor-General Lord Elgin slept here. Its 17 rooms are filled with Victorian charm. The dining room is very good, and there's a beach with boat rentals.

PORT DOVER. *Inexpensive.* **Erie Beach Hotel.** You're in a time warp here, lost in the early 1950's decor, with the honkytonk midway and beach just out the front door. 18 rooms, real charm.

PRESCOTT. *Inexpensive.* **Isle of Rest Motel.** 6 rooms, 5 cabins, some with fireplaces, TV. Beach nearby.

RIDEAU FERRY. *Expensive–Deluxe.* **Hotel Kenney.** In Jones Falls on Whitefish Lake. There's a view of the locks from the licensed dining room, an outdoor pool, boat rentals, babysitting, 37 rooms with TV, and one cottage. The setting is especially pleasant.

Inexpensive. **Rideau Ferry Inn.** Near Perth on Big Rideau Lake. The view through the colonial-style licensed dining room adds to the middle-aged clientele's enjoyment of this comfortable resort's features: outdoor pool, natural shoreline, boat rentals, guides available for fishing expeditions, and 16 rooms, 3 cottages with TV. Modified American Plan available.

SARNIA. *Inexpensive–Moderate.* **Laurentian Motel.** An indoor pool, golf nearby, TV in its 50 rooms and a licensed lounge recommend this hotel to business travelers, while families make use of its babysitting, wheelchair facilities.

STRATFORD. *Moderate–Expensive.* **Victorian Inn.** Only one block from the Festival Theatre, it overlooks a parking lot. But beyond lie a golf course and the Avon River. The lounge has a small fireplace and there's also an indoor pool and sauna. Reservations essential in Festival season.

Inexpensive. **Queen's Hotel.** Big soft wing chairs greet you in the lobby of this century-old hotel. The 32 rooms are air-conditioned with TV, and the lounge is dim panelled and cozy. Reservations essential in Festival season.

TOBERMORY. *Moderate.* **Tobermory Lodge.** Lodge rooms or semi-detached chalets. Modern, well-appointed, with outdoor pool, by scenic Tobermory Harbour.

WASAGA BEACH. *Moderate.* **Hotel Waldhorn.** Welcome to Bavaria West. The fact that the rooms are adjacent to a popular beer garden and a highway mean it's not peaceful; but its 21 rooms are well-equipped and just a short stroll from the world's largest freshwater beach.

WINDSOR. *Moderate.* **Richelieu Inn.** Its spaciousness plus a generous use of red and mirrors give this 150-room hotel its opulent atmosphere. Indoor pool.

Wandlyn Viscount Hotel. A 203-room hotel with indoor pool, TV, babysitting, golf nearby.

Inexpensive. **ABC Motel.** 47 air-conditioned rooms, TV. An outdoor pool, basic modern décor.

NORTHERN ONTARIO

Although there are modern and even deluxe accommodations available in northern Ontario's larger centers, many communities can only promise you comfortable clean quarters—no frills such as air conditioning and television. Remember, many tourists bring their own accommodation, *i.e.,* camping gear, with them. The categories used in this survey are price categories only. They are for double occupancy: *Deluxe,* over $60; *Expensive,* $45–$55; *Moderate,* $35–$45; *Inexpensive,* under $35.

ALBAN. *Deluxe.* **Lift the Latch Lodge.** Dining facilities serve 13 cottages, fireplaces, beach, boat rentals, golf nearby. Guides available. Good value considering that the price includes Modified American Plan.

Moderate–Expensive. **French River Lodge.** A main lodge with dining room plus 10 cottages with fireplaces and private bathrooms overlooking the French River. Boat rentals. Modified American Plan.

ATIKOKAN. *Deluxe.* **Tip Top Lodge.** A fly-in lodge on Sandford Lake, it offers guided fishing and hunting trips, 8 cottages with fireplaces, dining facilities, beach and boat rentals. Not licensed.

Moderate. **Perch Lake Resort.** Six housekeeping cottages with fireplaces overlook a beach on Perch Lake.

Inexpensive. **Hillcrest Resort.** On Duncan Lake, it has a beach, boat rentals and guides. Five housekeeping cottages open May to October.

BLIND RIVER. *Moderate–Expensive.* **North Shore Motel.** Bavarian atmosphere, licensed dining lounge plus an indoor pool, sauna, 25 air-conditioned rooms with TV and 2 cottages.

Old Mill Motel. Its 39 rooms overlook Lake Huron.

Moderate. **Abernot's Camping and Cottages.** Four cottages, not all of which have private bathroom facilities, overlooking Lake Duborne.

BRUCE MINES. *Moderate.* **Bavarian Inn.** Eighteen rooms with TV, a view of the water, plus a licensed, German-atmosphere dining lounge on the premises.

BURKS FALLS. *Moderate.* **Pickerel Lake Lodge.** Eleven rooms, 11 cottages with fireplaces. It's a pretty setting and handy to a beach. Hunting and fishing packages available.

COCHENOUR. *Deluxe.* **Sabourin Lake Lodge.** (American Plan.) Fly-in on Sabourin Lake. Five rooms, eight cottages, and dining facilities; beach, boat rentals, guides and fishing and hunting trips.

COCHRANE. *Expensive.* **James Bay Outfitters.** They operate a fly-in service to hunting and fishing resorts and a goose hunting camp, with food and guides provided.

Moderate–Expensive. **Northern Lites Motel.** Forty-one rooms have private bath, air conditioning, TV. There's golf nearby.

DRYDEN. *Moderate.* **Lenver Inn.** Thirty rooms have TV, babysitting, air conditioning. Dining room on the premises; golf nearby.

Timberland Motel. Thirteen rooms with TV. Clean and cheerful.

Inexpensive. **Riverview Lodge.** Sixteen rooms overlooking the Wabigoon River.

EAGLE RIVER. *Deluxe.* **Lindmeier's North Shore Lodge.** Fly-in to Eagle Lake. Rustic décor in the main lodge and 20 cabins. Dining facilities plus a complete outdoor program: boat rental, beach and guides available for hunting and fishing expeditions. European Plan available.

EAR FALLS. *Moderate.* **Trillium Motel.** Thirty-nine rooms with closed-circuit TV available. Saunas.

Inexpensive. **Canada North Lodge.** A dozen cottages overlook Little Bear Lake and beach.

ENGLISH RIVER. *Moderate.* **Meade's of English River.** Fourteen rooms and 7 cottages overlooking the river. Dining room, boat rentals, guided fishing trips.

ESPANOLA. *Moderate.* **Goodman's.** Nineteen rooms with TV and a licensed dining room with German atmosphere.

FORT FRANCES. *Deluxe.* **Bill Zup's Fishing Camp.** (European Plan.) A fly-in resort. The large main lodge has a big fireplace, artifacts to add to woodsy atmosphere. Six housekeeping cottages, plus boat rental and guided fishing-hunting trips.
Inexpensive–Deluxe. **Campbell's Cabins.** (European Plan.) Fly-in to Lac La Croix and stay in "boatels," hotel units built on the water. Coffee shop, dining facilities, boat rentals, guided trips.
Moderate. **The Fisheries.** Six cottages, with fireplaces, by Rainy Lake. Hunters and fishermen are the main customers.
Inexpensive. **Makabi Inn.** This 26-room modern motel has a central location.

FRENCH RIVER. *Moderate.* **French River Trading Post Motel.** Ten rooms have private bath, TV. There's golf nearby.

HEARST. *Moderate–Expensive.* **Queen's Motel.** Fifty rooms, air conditioning, TV, and pleasant service.
Moderate. **Northern Seasons Motel.** There's an indoor pool here, babysitting, 52 air-conditioned rooms with TV, and golf close by.

IGNACE. *Inexpensive.* **Cobblestone Resort.** On Raleigh Lake. Seven cottages are built of round stones—the construction is quite unusual. There are also 24 rooms, a coffee shop, a beach and boat rentals.

KAPUSKASING. *Moderate.* **Apollo Motel.** A 38-room motel (with TV, air conditioning, sauna) plus 9 cottages, an indoor pool, and golf nearby. Near an amusement park, it is very good for children.
Kapuskasing Inn. It's large (178 rooms), and has a licensed dining lounge which is a popular place to eat. TV in rooms.
Mattagami Motel. Fifty-eight air-conditioned rooms with TV, private bath.

KENORA. *Deluxe.* **Clinton's Ash Rapids Camp.** Access by boat only to these 12 cottages overlooking Lake of the Woods. Hunting and fishing packages a specialty, or you can simply rent a boat and putter around off the beach.
Expensive–Deluxe. **Travel-Inn Resort Motel.** Its 34 air-conditioned rooms have TV's and there's a licensed dining room, outdoor pool and indoor pool and sauna.
Moderate. **Kenricia Hotel.** Seventy-five rooms, air conditioned, with TV, above a licensed bar. Central.

KIRKLAND LAKE. *Moderate.* **Bon Air Motor Inn.** Sixty-eight air-conditioned rooms with TV, coffee shop, dining.
Commodore Motel. Twenty-seven rooms with TV, coffee shop.

MATTAWA. *Moderate–Expensive.* **Turcotte Park.** Six cabins with beach nearby.

Inexpensive. **Papineau Lodge.** European Plan available. 5 cottages on natural shoreline. Some toilets are outdoor, separate.

MORSON. *Expensive.* **Buena Vista Resort.** On Lake of the Woods. Five rooms, 7 cabins with air-conditioning, dining, beach, boat rentals.

NESTOR FALLS. *Moderate.* **Green's Camps and Tavern.** Eleven cottages by Lake of the Woods. American Plan. Babysitting available.

NEW LISKEARD. *Moderate.* **Breault's Motor Hotel.** French-Canadian wood furniture in lobby. Indoor pool, sauna, whirlpool. Dining room and cocktail bar. Rooms have color TV.

All Seasons Motor Inn. Sixty rooms with TV, entertainment in the cocktail lounge, indoor pool, golf nearby.

NORTH BAY. *Moderate.* **Pinewood Park Motor Inn.** The décor leans to russets, golds, and browns, Canadiana furniture in this comfortable modern hotel with pool and sauna, golf nearby.

Inexpensive. **Camp Conewango.** Cottages with fireplaces by the week. Beach on Lake Talon.

Friendship Sands Motor Inn. Thirty-three clean and simple rooms with TV.

PERRAULT FALLS. *Deluxe.* **Manotak Lodge.** American Plan, weekly rental, housekeeping cottages all available. On Perrault Lake. The 16 cottages and main dining hall overlook the water. Boat rentals, guides, hunting-fishing packages.

RED LAKE. *Deluxe.* **Echo Lake Lodge.** (American Plan.) Housekeeping cabins with outside toilets available, dining, fish-hunt packages, beach, boat rentals.

SAULT STE. MARIE. *Expensive–Deluxe.* **Sheraton Caswell Inn.** Seventy-three rooms, a plush lounge, coffee shop, dining, outdoor pool, golf nearby.

Water Tower Inn. 153 rooms, sauna, indoor pool, babysitting, fireplaces in rooms.

Inexpensive. **Royal Hotel.** It's old, but its 30 rooms are air conditioned, with TV's. Good dining, drinking on the premises.

SIOUX NARROWS. *Moderate.* **Rod and Reel.** Six rooms, 10 cottages overlooking a beach by Whitefish Bay. Fireplaces round which to gather and listen to tales of other hunters, fishermen.

SMOOTH ROCK FALLS. *Moderate.* **Moose Motel.** Its 30 rooms with private bath and TV don't seem remarkable, but the proprietors are scrupulous and thoughtful.

SUDBURY. *Expensive–Deluxe.* **Peter Piper Inn.** Some of its 45 rooms have private sauna. Good licensed dining room, central location; "the Prime Minister's Suite," too.

Moderate. **Cassio's Hotel.** Thirty-six rooms, hearty restaurant, facilities for wheelchairs.

Inexpensive–Moderate. **Ambassador Motor Hotel.** Forty-five rooms, saunas, indoor pool.

TEMAGAMI. *Inexpensive–Deluxe.* **Papa John's Place.** Six cottages overlooking a beach on Herridge Lake.

Moderate. **Ravenscroft Lodge.** European or American Plan available. Three rooms, 6 cottages with beach on Jumping Caribou Lake.

THESSALON. *Expensive.* **Melwel Lodge.** Fourteen miles northeast on Big Basswood Lake, the big, rustic lodge with its good dining facilities plus 11 comfortable cabins with TV and fireplace look out on a beach and boating facilities. Guided trips available. American Plan.

THUNDER BAY. *Expensive.* **Red Oak Inn.** One hundred eighty-two rooms with indoor sauna, near airport, routes to skiing. Regarded locally as the best restaurant, businessman's and family hotel.

Moderate. **Crossroads Motor Inn.** Sixty rooms with TV, air conditioning, golf 1 mile away.

Prince Arthur Hotel. Nicely renovated old railway hotel. View of Thunder Bay's harbor. Inuit prints in comfortable rooms. Central, too. Great restaurant attached.

TIMMINS. *Expensive.* **Ramada Inn.** One hundred twenty rooms with TV, air conditioning, indoor pool, licensed dining room, babysitting.

Moderate–Expensive. **Bon Air Motel.** One hundred one rooms with TV, plus a licensed pancake house on the premises make it fine for families.

VERMILLION BAY. *Moderate–Deluxe.* **Stanley's West Arm Camp.** On Eagle Lake, which is famous for muskellunge fishing. Twelve housekeeping cabins, beach.

WAWA. *Moderate.* **The Wawa Motor Hotel.** Eighty rooms with TV, coffee shop, licensed dining room, fireplace. Ten log cottages accommodating 12 guests. Indoor pool and sauna.

Inexpensive. **Holiday Cottages.** Four cheerful little cottages and 3 rooms overlooking a pretty body of water with an unfortunate name—Fungus Lake.

Sportsman's Motel. In town. Thirty-six rooms with TV, golf nearby, and advice on outfitting a fishing or hunting trip next door.

HOW TO GET AROUND. By car: An excellent road map with index on top is available at Tourist Information Offices. Twenty-four-hour road condition information is available at (416) 248–3561 and could be vital in winter driving conditions. U.S. drivers' licenses are valid in Ontario, but you should bring your owner's registration or copy of rental contract. The U.S. AAA is affiliated with the Ontario Motor League, which has offices in 28 centers across the province. Speed limits: 60 mph or 100 km./hr. on freeways; 50 mph or 80 km./hr. on two-lane highways; 30 mph or 50 km./hr. in urban areas. Also bear in mind that many gas stations close at 7 P.M. and on Sundays. And that wearing seatbelts in automobiles is compulsory for all passengers for whom belts are available.

The Trans-Canada Highway crosses Northern Ontario. Major links are Highways 11 (from Toronto) and 417 (from Montréal).

By train: *Via Rail* operates all across the province. In addition, the *Ontario Northland Railway* connects Cochrane to James Bay and the *Algoma Central Railway* serves the Algoma District north of Sault Ste. Marie. The *Polar Bear Express* connects Cochrane with Moosonee.

By bus: *Voyageur Colonial, Trailways* and *Gray Coach* are among the major carriers in Southern Ontario. *Gray Goose* and *Ontario Northland Transportation Commission* cross the north.

By air: *Air Canada* and *CP* fly intraprovincially. Northern Ontario is serviced by *Air Canada* which serves North Bay, Sudbury, Sault Ste. Marie, Timmins. *NorOntair, Austin Airways, Transair* and *Bradley Air Service* fly into smaller communities and fishing and hunting resorts. *Bush pilots* may be hired in northern centers like Ear Falls, Chapleau, Fort Frances, Hearst, North Bay and Temagami.

 FACTS AND FIGURES. The name *Ontario,* adopted in 1867 when the province joined the Confederation, is an Iroquois word which means "the shining waters" or "beautiful lake." The provincial flower is the white trillium. The Provincial Coat-of-Arms is a green shield with three maple leaves surmounted by the Red Cross of St. George. Above the crest stands a black bear; the sides are supported by a moose and a deer. Beneath the shield is a scroll bearing the provincial motto; *Ut Incepit Fidelis Sic Permanet* ("Loyal she began, loyal she remains"). The Provincial capital is Toronto. The population of Ontario is over 8,700,000. The province covers 412,582 square miles.

Ontario's winters can be extremely cold in the north to cool in the extreme south. Its summers are warm, but in the north temperatures drop after sunset.

 TOURIST INFORMATION. The central clearing house of tourist information is the *Ministry of Tourism and Recreation.* In Ontario you may contact its Ontario Travel division, Queen's Park, Toronto, Ontario M7A 2R9 (telephone: 416-965-4008).

Travel Information. In *Southern Ontario,* Ontario Travel Information beside Hwy. 400 at Barrie is open year-round. So are travel information offices on Brookdale Ave. in Cornwall, at 5355 Stanley Ave. in Niagara Falls, at 110 Park St. E. in Windsor, at the Garden City Skyway and QEW in St. Catharines and at Blue Water Bridge in Sarnia.

In *Northern Ontario,* there are travel information offices open all year in Fort Frances, 400 Central Ave. and Sault Ste. Marie at 120 Huron St.

Year-round travel information centers are open from 9 A.M. to 4:30 P.M. (4 P.M. Saturdays), later in summer.

Ski information is available from the *Ontario Ski Resorts Association,* 17 Mill St., Willowdale, Ontario M2P 1B3, and from *Ontario Travel,* Queen's Park, Toronto M7A 2E5. Up-to-the-minute snow condition reports are available from Central Ontario (705) 726–0932 or (416) 364–4722 Central and Southern Ontario. The *Canadian Ski Instructors Alliance* supervises most ski instruction in Ontario; most areas are patrolled.

Fishing and **hunting** enthusiasts flock to Ontario for its muskie, trout, goose, pheasant, moose, deer, and bear. Fishing and hunting are seasonal however. For fishing information contact the *Sport Fisheries Branch, Ministry of Natural Resources,* Queen's Park, Toronto. Information about fishing in lakes which may be polluted is available at *Ministry of the Environment,* Information Services Branch, 135 St. Clair Ave. W., Toronto M4B 1P5. Fishing and hunting maps available from *Ministry of Natural Resources,* Public Service Centre,

Toronto M7A 1W3. Hunting licenses are available at over 40 Natural Resources District offices or can be purchased at some sporting goods stores or outfitters. Hunting dogs from the U.S. need certification from a licensed vet of rabies vaccinations at least 30 days before entering.

Campers can obtain camping permits at the entrance to Ontario's 128 provincial parks. To plan a trailer trip contact the *Ministry of Tourism and Recreation,* Queen's Park, Toronto M7A 2R9. There are size limits for trailers traveling on Ontario highways (maximum length, car and trailer, 65 feet). The Province of Ontario has a Human Rights Code, providing for fair and equal treatment of all visitors by public resorts, restaurants, hotels, motels, beaches pools, parks, and campsites. Contact *Ontario Human Rights Commission,* 400 University Ave., Toronto (telephone: 416–965–6841) for inquiries.

TIME ZONES. Ontario spans two time zones. West of Thunder Bay, the province runs on Central Standard Time. East of and including Thunder Bay, it is on Eastern Standard Time (the same zone as New York City, Miami, and Montréal).

BUSINESS HOURS AND HOLIDAY CLOSINGS. Bank hours are 10 A.M. to 3 P.M., Monday–Thursday, 10 A.M. to 6 P.M. on Friday. Many banks offer self-serve, automated tellers for simpler transactions; customers with clearance use special cards to gain access to accounts. Many post offices are open 9–5 and on Saturday mornings (smaller ones run by one person may close for lunch). Small shops close Sundays and Mondays. Larger shops are open 6 days a week, and Thursday nights until 9. Some government ministries are on staggered hours (8:30 A.M. to 4:30 P.M. or 9:30 A.M. to 5:30 P.M.). Almost *nothing,* except convenience stores, restaurants and theaters, opens in Ontario on Sundays.

SEASONAL EVENTS. January–February: Cross-country skiers compete in the *Muskoka Loppet* (snow conditions permitting). In mid-January *Niagara Falls* holds its Winter Festival (broomball, arts and crafts, Old Timers Hockey Tournament). In late January or early February, the Canadian Ski Jumping Championships are held at Thunder Bay. From *Sault Ste. Marie,* the Agawa Canyon snow train takes you into a wilderness of frozen waterfalls and forests hung with icicles. The *Bon Soo Winter Carnival* (Sault Ste. Marie) opens with a torchlight parade, followed by polar bear swimming, sled dog races at the end of January and early February.

North Bay holds its Winter Fur Carnival in late February. Near the end of the month *Georgian Peaks* hosts the Pontiac Cup ski races.

March: *Kenora* holds winter festivities.

April: Join in a "sugaring-off" at the Algoma Maple Festival, *St. Joseph's Island.* Or take a hayride into the maple bush at the *Elmira* Maple Syrup Festival (mid-April) then sample syrup and pancakes or Mennonite cooking.

May: Early in May the *Niagara region* bursts into bloom, and you can celebrate spring at the Niagara Falls Blossom Festival (parades, ethnic dances, sporting events). *Ottawa's* flowers follow later—three million tulips set off the Ottawa/Outaouais Festival of Spring (fireworks, flea market, regattas). Early in May, the *Guelph* Spring Festival schedules first-class opera, concerts, films, and art exhibitions. *St. Catharines* throws an ethnic extravaganza—its Folk Arts Festival in late May. The Shaw Drama Festival season begins at *Niagara-on-the-Lake.* The last Saturday of the month, the Mennonite communities near *Kitch-*

ener-Waterloo and *New Hamburg* sell food and crafts for overseas relief. The 24th of May, Queen Victoria's birthday, is celebrated with fireworks.

June: *Welland* celebrates its Rose Festival with parades, boat races and fiddle contests. The internationally acclaimed *Stratford* Shakespearean Festival begins its season. *Fort Frances* hosts a "Fun-in-the-Sun" festival, bathtub derby, water skiing contest, parade and horse show.

July: Across Ontario, fireworks mark the national Canada Day (July 1). It's also the beginning of the *Windsor/Detroit* International Freedom Festival and *Ottawa's* cultural Festival Ottawa. At *Mosport,* the Canadian Grand Prix brings world championship motorcycle racers to Southern Ontario.

August: Participants have the most fun at the *Lake of the Woods* International Sailing Regatta (beginning of the month). *Cobalt's* Miners Festival (first week in August) features French-Canadian step-dancing and a canoe marathon. Also check the Bancroft Gemboree, in *Bancroft,* and the Wikwemikong Pow Wow on *Manitoulin Island.* There's sweet music at *Shelburne's* Canadian Open Old Time Fiddlers' Contest—antiques, crafts and a parade, too. A forest amphitheater in the *Brantford Reserve* turns into the Six Nations Pageant mid-August weekends. The Glengarry Highland Games in *Maxville* are the largest such celebration in North America. The Royal Canadian Henley Regatta, the largest rowing course in North America, is seen in *St. Catharines* in early August. A second Highland Festival is held in *Fergus* later in the month.

September: Clowns and musicians stroll among the crowds and industrial exhibits at *London's* century old Western Fair. Wine-tasting parties headline *St. Catharines'* Grape and Wine Festival (mid-September) along with steel bands, ethnic dancing, art displays and parades. The *Algoma* Arts Festival brings music, theater and displays to Sault Ste. Marie (mid-September to the end of the month). The Canadian Grand Prix for formula cars is run at *Mosport.*

October: Gemutlichkeit Uber Alles: oompah bands, beerhalls and dancing at Oktoberfests in *Kitchener-Waterloo* and *London.* The Canadian Thanksgiving weekend is the best time to enjoy the *Muskoka* and *Haliburton* Cavalcades of Colour (parades and fairs throughout the regions).

November: Early in November, 240 varieties of flowers bloom at Parkwood's Fall Flower Show (*Oshawa*).

December: Celebrate an Old Tyme Christmas at *Port Hope* (antique show, carolling, sleigh rides). Victoria Park blazed with lights for skaters and strollers in *London's* Winter Wonderland. And colored lights illuminate *Niagara Falls* and its usual winter formation, the Ice Bridge.

TOURS. There's a wide choice of tours waiting to show you Ontario—everything from cultural sorties into the theaters of Festival country to whitewater kayak trips down wild northern rivers. All tour operators must be registered with the Ministry of Consumer and Commercial Relations. Packages available include weekend specials from Windsor to Toronto or Niagara Falls which include rail transportation, accommodation, and Continental breakfast. Contact *CanAm Travel Ltd.,* 1575 Ouellette Ave., Windsor N8X 1K5. *Canada Coach Lines Ltd.* (18 Wentworth St. N., Hamilton, Ontario L8L 5V1) runs weekend packages to Ottawa's Tulip Festival and tours to the spectacular north-of-Superior Agawa Canyon. *Hiawathaland* runs 5 sightseeing tours through Sault Ste. Marie. A five-day "Discover Ontario" tour takes you through the rock-and-lake scenery of the Muskokas and the historical sites of the south and southeast. Contact *Charterways,* ground floor, City Centre, 380 Wellington St., London, Ontario. *Gray Coach,* 610 Bay St., runs tours around Toronto plus excursions to the Kitchener Mennonite Farmers' Market or Georgian Bay's 30,000 islands.

You can cruise Trent Severn Waterway by private cruiser houseboats. Contact *Canadian Holidays Afloat Inc.,* 255 Gerrard St. E., Toronto M5A 2G1. And of course you can always enjoy northern Ontario's two well-known, well-loved rail adventures. The *Algoma Central Railway* 212 Queen St. E., P.O. Box 814, Sault Ste. Marie, carries passengers year-round into the spectacular Agawa Canyon. The day-long trip is most colorful in late September. Dining facilities are available in peak seasons. The *Polar Bear Express* from Cochrane to Moosonee is a longer trip, but can still be made in a day. Aside from the barren grandeur of the tundra and muskeg scenery, and the curiosities of Moose Factory and Moosonee, the excitement of the trip is often provided by local hunters, trappers, and Métis who spin stories to pass the time aboard the train.

For the adventurous: *Wildwaters,* RR #4, Thunder Bay; *Sioux Narrows Air Tours,* North Central Airlines, 7500 Northliner Dr., Minneapolis, MN 55450; and, for trail rides, *Almaguin Trails,* which also operates escorted 6- and 12-day packages, c/o Box 356, Bolton, Ontario L0P 1A0.

For a complete list of tours available throughout the province write to the *Ministry of Tourism and Recreation,* Queen's Park, Toronto, Ontario M7A 2R9.

 NATIONAL PARKS. Boat services from Honey Harbour take you to the 50 islands of *Georgian Bay Islands National Park* in the heart of historic Huronia. There is also boat access from Tobermory, only 3 miles from the weirdly-shaped rock pillars of Flowerpot Island. Scuba divers can explore the wrecks of sunken lake vessels, while naturalists will enjoy the abundance of wildfowl (wood ducks, black ducks, coots, mergansers and scaup), and wildlife. The fishing is good and many of the beaches deserted. Admission is free. Camping is by permit only and is limited to 14 days. Contact the Superintendent, Georgian Bay Islands National Park, Box 28, Honey Harbour. Open May through September.

Point Pelee National Park is the southernmost mainland point in Canada—on the same latitude as Northern California or the French Riviera. Four thousand acres of rolling dunes, virgin forest, and marshland attract thousands of visitors each year—from naturalists to over 350 species of migratory birds. In late September Point Pelee is a stopover for thousands of brilliant Monarch butterflies. The sight is dazzling. A boardwalk winds 3,100 feet into the marsh to a 20-foot observation tower—or you can rent rowboats and canoes to discover the park's wildlife. In summer a park naturalist is on duty to answer your questions about the woodland nature trail. Maps, sketches, and displays offer further explanations at the Park Nature Centre. Point Pelee Park is six miles south of Leamington. No family camping; group camping for organizations. Contact Superintendent, Point Pelee National Park, R.R.1, Leamington. Open from April to Labor Day.

Pukaskwa National Park, 725 square miles, is the largest national park in Ontario. Near Marathon, on the north shore of Lake Superior, the park encompasses Tip Top Mountain, whose 2,120-foot elevation makes it one of the highest points in the province. Through typical Canadian Shield landscape—rocks, rugged islands, wild rivers and lakes—roam caribou, moose, deer, mink, otter, marten, lynx, bobcats and wolves. Archeologists are also investigating the sites of prehistoric pit culture Indian inhabitants. The park is still being developed. For information apply to the Park Superintendent, Pukaskwa National Park, P.O. Box 550, Marathon, Ontario P0T 2E0. Season: from June through September.

St. Lawrence Islands National Park consists of 17 islands, 80 rocky islets, and a mainland base. At the Mallorytown Landing (between Kingston and Brockville) you can explore the Nature Exhibit or the Brown's Bay wreck exhibit before boarding a boat for the islands. The park offers a naturalist program during summer months to help you discover the wildlife of the area—ring-billed gulls, blue herons, a variety of ducks. Boats can be rented, water taxis hired, or docking facilities are available. Serviced camping at Mallorytown Landing and Central Grenadier. Campgrounds open mid-May to mid-October, park open all year. Contact: Superintendent, St. Lawrence Islands National Park, Box 469, R.R. #3, Mallorytown, Ontario K0E 1R0.

PROVINCIAL PARKS. The province operates 128 parks; 98 have campsites available on a first-come, first-served basis. Permits are available at park entrances for a fee. Some parks have facilities for mobile homes; all have some form of sanitation provisions. Frequently there are sheltered cooking and dining areas. Electric power costs a small additional sum at those parks which offer it. Riders of motorcycles and trail bikes must wear helmets and keep to the main park roads. Some provincial parks ban liquor in spring.

Algonquin Park was first designated a protected area in 1893. It is still a virtually untouched wilderness. Although Hwy. 60 crosses the southwest corner of the park, most of its 2,955 square miles of forest and lake are accessible only by canoe or on foot. On Hwy. 60 near the East Gate Entrance, the Logging Museum illustrates lumber activities in the area. Canoe outfitting, stores, restaurants and some excellent lodgings are available within the park. Camping, fishing. Admission charges. Season mid-May through mid-October. For information, apply Superintendent, Algonquin Provincial Park, Algonquin P.O., Ontario.

Arrowhead: 2,162 acres near Huntsville on Hwy. 11. Year-round camping, swimming, hiking, snowshoeing, and cross-country skiing. Spectacular lookouts at Big Bend, Stubb's Falls.

Batchewana: 418 acres north of Sault Ste. Marie on Hwy. 17. Day-use only (no camping). One mile of sandy beach along Lake Superior.

Blue Lake: 873 acres on Hwy. 17 west of Dryden. Fishing, swimming, 70-mile canoe loop. In spring the park blooms with moccasin flowers.

Bon Echo: 16,417 acres on Hwy. 41 north of Napanee. Camping facilities range from drive-in spots with showers to remote campsites accessible only by canoe or overnight hike. Swimming, fishing. Granite cliffs 375 feet high at Mazinaw Lake, which can throw back a loud echo, give the park its name. Indian rock paintings.

Chutes: 270 acres on Hwy. 17 west of Espanola. By the Aux Sables River waterfalls. Swimming, hiking, trout fishing nearby.

Craigleith: Small (126 acres) shoreline park on Hwy. 26 in Blue Mountain area near Collingwood. Swimming is dangerous because of rocks, where fossils and formations delight geologists.

Darlington: 360 acres. Hwy 401 east of Oshawa. Camping and picnicking. Duck hunting and waterfowl weekends in fall.

Devil's Glen: 150 acres. Take Hwy. 24 south from Collingwood. The ¾-mile Mad River Trail connects with the Bruce Trail.

Esker Lakes: 7,680 acres on Hwys. 11 and 66 north of Kirkland Lake. Many lakes afford good canoe routes. Beach, hiking trails, rock-collecting.

Ferris: 503 acres on Hwy. 30 and on Trent Severn Waterway near Campbellford. Campgrounds in open and wooded areas which form part of the large Peterborough Drumlin Field.

Fitzroy: 435 acres on Hwy. 17 west of Ottawa. Swimming at sandy beach, boating, angling for smallmouth bass and yellow pickerel. Small pioneer cemetery.

Holiday Beach: 521 acres on Lake Erie. Take Hwy. 18A south from Windsor. Good beach, picnic grounds, some camping. Stocked fish pond. Waterfowl hunting in season. Canada goose sanctuary nearby.

Inverhuron: 545 acres. Take Hwy. 21 south from Port Elgin. Day-use only (no camping). Trails, beach, swimming, boating. Site of prehistoric Indian camps and pioneer town.

Ipperwash: 201 acres. Take Hwy. 21 north from Sarnia. Children's programs, family campgrounds, sandy beach.

Ivanhoe Lake: 3,000 acres. Take Hwy. 101 west from Timmins. One of the best sandy beaches in northeastern Ontario. Swimming, boating.

Lake-on-the-Mountain: 256 acres. Take Hwys. 401/14/33 to Prince Edward County. Day-use only, no swimming. A spring-fed lake with a mysterious source and a spectacular view.

Lake Superior: Large (512 square miles) and accessible via Hwy. 17 north from Sault Ste. Marie. Camping and picnic grounds and Indian rock paintings near Hwy. 17. Interior camping accessible by canoe or on foot.

Long Point: 849 acres. Take Hwy. 3 south from Tillsonburg then 59. Sandy beach, picnic area, bass fishing, viewing of waterfowl migration.

MacLeod: 200 acres. Take Hwy. 11 east from Geraldton. This former gold-mining area is ideal for viewing moose and collecting rocks. Swimming, fishing for pike and pickerel (walleye).

Marten River: 1,034 acres. Take Hwy. 11 north from North Bay. Boating, game fishing, children's wading pool. Sawmills and exhibit of early logging industry nearby.

Missinabi Lake: 157,334 acres. Take Hwy. 11 from Chapleau, then north. Rough access road, bad for trailers. Indian rock paintings, large lake with good beaches.

Neys: 8,150 acres. Take Hwy. 17 west from Marathon. In spite of the fine beach, Lake Superior is cold for swimming. Fishing is excellent. Good hiking, great lookouts. Caribou herd in the park.

Pancake Bay: 1,151 acres on Hwy. 17 north of Sault Ste. Marie. The swimming is cold at good Lake Superior beach, but rainbow trout attract fishermen.

Petroglyphs: 2,500 acres on Hwy. 28 north of Peterborough. Day-use only (no camping). Hiking trails to waterfall, large concentration of prehistoric Indian rock paintings.

Point Farms: 582 acres. Take Hwy. 21 north from Goderich. Enjoy barn dances, sing-alongs, horseshoe tossing in the restored barn or try out the fitness trail, baseball diamond, and beach.

Polar Bear: 9,300 square miles, accessible only by charter aircraft from Moosonee (250 miles to the south). All provisions and equipment must be carried in. There are no means of outside communication. Access points and travel areas within the park have been chosen to minimize disturbance of abundant wildlife—polar bear, black bear, red fox, Arctic fox, wolf, bearded seal, moose, caribou, Arctic loon, Canada goose, snow goose, northern phalarope. The weather varies from the surprisingly balmy odd day in summer to severe winters. Chilling sea fog frequently engulfs the land and has discouraged tree growth near coast of Hudson Bay. Polar Bear Provincial Park is open in summer only; to get a special permit of admission, contact the District Manager, Ministry of Natural Resources, P.O. Box 190, Moosonee, Ontario P0L 1Y0.

Presqu'ile: 2,170 acres. Take Hwy. 401 west from Cobourg, then Hwy. 30. Migratory birds displayed in small museum, and good birdwatching in spring and fall. Picnicking, boating and swimming on long sandy beach.

Quetico: 1,750 square miles of wilderness accessible via Dawson Trail Campgrounds, Hwy. 11, 30 miles east of Atikokan. Quetico is a favorite for canoeing. Local outfitters offer comprehensive service. Game fishermen are attracted by lake trout, northern pike and pickerel (walleye), bass and some sturgeon. Resident mammals include black bear, moose, wolves and white-tailed deer. A natural history museum outlines the park's flora and fauna. Season: June through September. Contact: District Manager, Ministry of Natural Resources, Atikokan, Ontario.

Rondeau: 11,456 acres. Take Hwy. 3 west from Leamington, then Hwy. 51. At the interpretive center, the Carolinean forest (walnut, sassafras, and tulip trees) and the park's animal inhabitants are explained in exhibits. Swimming, boating, cycling, hiking, waterfowl hunting in season.

Sandbanks: 1,802 acres. Take Hwy. 401 to Trenton, then Hwy. 33. A 5-mile sandbar between Lake Ontario and West Lake. Spectacular dunes, beach, swimming, and boating.

Serpent Mounds: 70 acres. Take Hwy. 7 to Peterborough then south to Keene. Campsite overlooks Rice Lake. Archeological exhibits, prehistoric Indian burial mounds, fishing, access to Trent-Severn Waterway.

Wasaga Beach: 344 acres. Take Hwy. 27 then 92. Day-use only (no camping). Museum of the Upper Lakes on Nancy Island outlines naval history, local battles of War of 1812. Swimming, cross-country skiing, boating.

Windy Lake: 293 acres. Take Hwy. 144 north from Sudbury. Long beach, swimming, boating, fishing, golf course adjacent to park.

This is only a partial list of Ontario's parks. There are also recreational areas operated by 38 conservation authorities, and 3 parks commissions, plus roadside picnicking, camping, and public recreation centers.

For more information: a complete list of parks, campsites, and picnic grounds is available from: Provincial Parks Information, Whitney Block, Queen's Park, Toronto, Ontario M7A 1W3 or contact a District Tourism Office.

FARM VACATIONS AND GUEST RANCHES. Ontario has many working farms that take in guests. Some specialize in holidays for children, others attract adults with their home-cooking, crafts facilities or proximity to cultural events and country auctions. For up-to-date information listing host farms, write to the *Ontario Vacation Farm Association,* RR #2, Erin, Ontario N0B 1T0.

Specific questions, reservations and vacation arrangements can only be made directly with your host. Usually a nonrefundable deposit of 10 per cent is payable when you make your reservation. Meals are usually included with rates and at most farms children over 12 are charged the adult rate. Your host may prefer to limit the consumption of alcohol on his premises. That's his perogative —check with him.

CHILDREN'S ACTIVITIES. Children seem to be happiest when they're participating with their bodies as well as their minds. In Ontario you can provide them with a wide range of activities, happily exhausting and pleasantly instructive. Some provincial parks run special youth programs or offer children's playground facilities.

At **Bronte Creek,** 25 miles west of Toronto, there's a farm where children can see and touch the donkeys, sheep and cows or play in a hay-filled barn, fully equipped with ropes to swing on. Here you can take them on a tractor or wagon ride through the park, or introduce them to turn-of-the-century life at the park's *Spruce Lane Farm.* You're welcomed into the farmhouse by the smell of baking bread or the strains of the parlor organ.

There's a children's playground and snack shop at *Blue Mountain Scenic Caves,* 5 miles west of **Collingwood** on Hwy. 26. The caves, once the home of an early Huron tribe, can also be reached by chairlift.

More caves outside **Eganville** (21 miles south of Pembroke); the *Bonnechere Caves* are full of fascinating fossils and stalactites. While you're in the area, Ontario's only *"magnetic hill"* is at **Dacre,** at the junction of Hwy. 132 and 41. Be ready for questions about the behavior of your car. If you point your car downhill and release the brakes, it will roll back up.

There are special facilities for children at some provincial parks, including *Ipperwash* on **Lake Huron.** Take Hwy. 21. Farther north on Hwy. 21, at *Point Farms,* a restored barn, a baseball diamond, and a horseshoe pitch keep children happy and busy.

Rushing River east of **Kenora** in the heart of Canadian Shield country has a playground; so does *Sioux Narrows* to the south, where you can also show children Indian pictographs or take them boating on *Lake of the Woods.* **Wasaga Beach** is a superb stretch of sand for running, jumping or flopping down in the sun. Drivers get there via Hwy. 27 and 92. Nearby is a sound and graphics recreation of the War of 1812 at the *Museum of the Upper Lakes.*

Provincial parks with "themes"—bird-watching, Indian culture, skills programs in camping or canoeing—have visitor service centers which provide interpretive information about the parks. For example, *Sibbald Lake* and *Balsam Lake* have star-watches; there's a 38-foot replica of a Canoe d'Maître and a small fur trade museum at *Samuel de Champlain Park,* while at *Quetico* and *Point Pelee,* naturalists are on duty to answer your child's questions about the wildlife.

At **Rockton,** 11 miles northwest of Hamilton, there's a different sort of park—the *African Lion Safari,* which also features an elephant compound, an ostrich pen, and a pet's corner where children can pet the pets. *Marineland and Game Farm* in **Niagara Falls** (open all year) is famous for its trained dolphins. Its summertime aquarium show also stars a killer whale.

Niagara Falls appeals to grown-up children; small ones will also get a kick out of climbing into raincoats for the *Maid of the Mist* boat trip. The boat passes directly in front of the Falls. Helicopter rides over the Falls cost $10 per person for a 12-minute trip. Children under 3 are free. If they are accompanied by adults, children can get into Niagara Falls' Panasonic Centre and Marine Museum free. High-speed elevators whisk visitors to a tower 665 feet above the Falls, where a wax museum and dining rooms compete with the spectacular view. Niagara Falls' other joys for kids include waxworks, fantasy museums, and a *Daredevil Hall of Fame* in the City Museum.

Niagara Falls doesn't have a monopoly on fantasy; another version of it is available at **Niagara-on-the-Lake.** The *Canadian Mime Theatre* is Canada's only professional mime group and can be enjoyed from mid-May through August at the Royal George Theatre.

There are many children's gardens throughout Ontario. In **London's** *Storybook Gardens,* children can take rides in a miniature train or meet fairytale characters and live animals of Old MacDonald's Farm. **Stratford's** *Shakespeareland* features 60 large-scale replicas of famous buildings from England's Stratford-upon-Avon (open mid-May through September). **Ivy Lea,** near

Gananoque has its *Never Never Land* (Victoria weekend in late May–Labor Day in September); more fairytales come to life at **Renfrew's** *Storyland*. Here a telescope on top of the lookout provides a great view of the surrounding woodlands. In **Dorset,** there's a 100-foot *observation tower* from which children can scan the Haliburton Highlands. Not far away, in **Bracebridge,** they can take miniature trains, paddle wheel boats or covered wagons through *Santa's Village*. These parks' seasons run from mid-June to September.

Windsor's *Bob-Lo* is a large amusement park with 40 rides and attractions. On an island in the Detroit River, it is accessible by ferry. Canada's largest amusement park is outside **Fort Erie** at *Crystal Beach*. The gigantic Comet Coaster is among 40 rides featured. *Old Fort Erie,* nearby, has the original ditches, drawbridge and guns. Guards in 19th-century uniforms drill daily.

Meanwhile, at the other end of the province, the soldiers are also drilling at **Kingston's** *Old Fort Henry*. While you're in the area, your child can experience the life style of a century ago at *Upper Canada Village* in **Morrisburg.** Oxcarts, miniature trains or horse-drawn boats take them past the church, bakery, smithy, and even an old hotel where meals are served.

Older children will never forget a trip through the glowing red and black interior of a *steel plant*. In **Hamilton,** *Stelco* guides visitors through the stages of steelmaking. (Visitors must be 15 or older.) Telephone in advance to confirm your visit. If they enjoyed that, they may also take themselves on a tour of the *Hershey Chocolate plant* in **Smiths Falls,** or a 7½-hour tour, with lumberjack lunch, through the *Abitibi pulp and paper* operations in **Iroquois Falls.** (Children under 8 not allowed, but babysitting services are available.)

There are *Indian pow-wows* in **Sumer, Brantford** and **Manitoulin Island.** Another great way to introduce native culture is to visit *Ska-Na-Doht,* a reconstructed Indian Village with 70-foot long bark-covered long houses, or the timber palisaded *Huron Village* in **Midland.**

Sportsminded kids will get a kick out of visiting **Hamilton's** *Canadian Football Hall of Fame,* the *Hockey Hall of Fame* in **Toronto** and the *Canadian Ski Museum* in **Ottawa.** If they have ever asked you what a *gelandesprung* is, you can find out here.

SUMMER SPORTS. In summer, Ontario lives out-of-doors. Campers, hikers, and hunters find wildlife and the wide-open spaces that keep bringing them back. **Canoeing:** If you don't own a canoe, you can rent or buy one, along with all the other supplies needed for a trip. Complete outfitting services provide canoes, life jackets, camping and cooking equipment, food supplies, maps, fishing licenses and tackle, and guides. The canoeing season runs from the May thaw or breakup to the November freeze-up. Lists of outfitters should be available at regional tourism and Ministry of Natural Resources offices. Packaged canoe trips are also offered. Contact: *Wilderness Canoe Tours,* Box 661, Pembroke, Ontario; *Canoe Canada Outfitters,* Box 388, Atikokan, Ontario; *Headwaters,* P.O. Box 288, Temagami, Ontario; or *Outfittings Coordinator, National and Provincial Parks Association of Canada,* 69 Sherbourne St., Toronto (416-366-3494). Some provincial parks specialize in wild river routes.

Package holidays: Experienced bush pilots, usually flying prop planes capable of lake landings, provide a province-wide air service to take you to the best fishing and hunting spots. For further information, contact *NorOntair,* 195 Regina St., North Bay, Ontario, P0B 8L3, *Austin Airways,* Timmins Airport, Box 1160, or *On Air Ltd.,* Thunder Bay Airport, P7E 3N9.

Package fly-in holidays are also available and there are many excellent fly-in lodges from which to base your swimming, fishing, sailing, canoeing vacations. Hunting and fishing licenses are available at Natural Resources district offices.

Cycling: Some bicycle shops will rent cycles for cross-Ontario exploration, and as cycling becomes more popular, more metropolitan regions are providing cycling trails.

Horseback riding: There are over a hundred horseback riding establishments in Ontario, not counting the private pony and hunt clubs whose red-coated, blue-blooded members may flash across your trail in pursuit of fox. Among those establishments that provide horse rentals and trails: (in Central Ontario) *Skyline Tourist Park,* R.R. #1, Ennismore, near Peterborough; *Lakeview Farm* R.R. #3, Port Carling; *Rouge Hill Stables,* Port Union Rd. and Hwy. 2 on the beautiful Rouge Valley near Toronto; *Palomino Ranch,* Carlisle. In Eastern Ontario, similar facilities are available at *Valhalla Riding Schools,* Hwy. 2, R.R. #3, Gananoque, Ontario; *Circle "N" Ranch,* R.R. #3, Pembroke. In Northern Ontario, *Wagonwheel Ranch,* R.R. #1, St. Charles, near Sudbury; *Noront Equestrian,* 20 miles north of Sudbury in Chelmsford; *Centre Equestre de Hearst* and *Ferme d'Equitation,* both in Hearst, and *The Royal Ranch,* R.R. #2, Timmins, all offer offer rentals and other services.

Golfing: There are over 300 golf courses in Ontario. Some larger public ones are *Ava,* in Brantford; *Tyandaga Municipal Golf and Country Club,* Burlington; *Lee* in Cochrane; *Kitchen Creek Golf and Country Club* in Fort Frances; *Chedoke Civic* in Hamilton; *Doon Valley* near Kitchener; *Thames Valley* in London; *Upper Canada* in Morrisburg; *Countryside* in Sudbury; *Chapples* in Thunder Bay.

Racing: Southern Ontario's two major drag strips are at Cayuga and St. Thomas, but Mosport, north of Bowmanville, is Canada's capital of car racing. The *Canadian Grand Prix* brings Formula I World Champions to the hilly, well-serviced woodlands of Mosport Park. Here fans can also enjoy *Can-Am* and motorcycle races on most weekends in summer and early fall. Stock car enthusiasts watch the rubber burn at Delaware International Speedway in London.

Horse-racing: The *Queen's Plate* is to Canada what the Kentucky derby is to the United States—venerable tradition and heady excitement. It kicks off the racing season at Toronto's Woodbine Racetrack in June. Other racetracks throughout the province are Ottawa's *Rideau Carleton,* the picturesque track at *Fort Erie* which opened in 1897; the modern, glass-enclosed *Flamboro Downs* near Hamilton; *Sudbury Downs;* Peterborough's *Kawartha Downs,* which holds standardbred racing virtually all year long.

Boating: St. Catharines' *Royal Canadian Henley Regatta* is one of North America's largest rowing regattas. Many yacht clubs run sailing schools in summer and often marinas will rent sailboats, powerboats, and water ski equipment.

Scuba diving: Local outfitters in Tobermory will equip you for scuba diving among Georgian Bay wrecks.

Professional sports: The recently established *Toronto Blue Jays* are members of the American Baseball League, and they are building up Ontario's appetite for pro **baseball. Football** has a longer tradition in this country. The *Hamilton Tiger Cats* and the *Ottawa Roughriders* were the stars of the Canadian Football League, recently eclipsed by the hard-working *Toronto Argonauts.* The *Toronto Blizzard* is one of the top teams in the North American Soccer League. Strong semi-pro **soccer** teams have sprung up in other centers, among them Hamilton, Kitchener, and Windsor.

Other sports: You can enjoy tennis, squash, table tennis, badminton, kayaking, scuba-diving or sky diving in Ontario if you've got the energy and the inclination. For more information, contact the *Sports Centre Inc.,* 1220 Sheppard Ave., E, Toronto telephone: 416 495-5000.

PRIVATE CAMPGROUNDS AND TRAILER SITES.
There are over a thousand privately owned campgrounds and trailer sites. All are inspected and licensed by the provincial government or municipal authorities. For a comprehensive booklet listing private campgrounds, write to *Travel Information, Ministry of Tourism and Recreation,* Third Floor, Hearst Block, Queen's Park, Toronto M7A 2E5.

At private campgrounds daily rates vary depending on the facilities available. Although trailers' size is limited on Ontario highways (65 feet long including car), oversize permits are available from *Oversize-Overweight Permit Section,* Ontario Ministry of Transport and Communications, Queen's Park, Toronto, Ontario. Many provincial parks and private campgrounds have sewage and pump-out facilities.

HIKING TRAILS. Day and weekend hiking trips are becoming increasingly popular with Ontarians and visitors. On Saturdays and Sundays the trails can be relatively crowded with hikers, campers, picnickers, and naturalists. At all times, people are asked to remember that since many trails cross private property, you are only crossing it on the goodwill of the farmers.

Algonquin Park Highland Hiking Trail: A 22-mile loop with a shorter 11-mile loop, suitable for snow shoeing and cross-country skiing in winter, guides you through the woods of Algonquin Park. The park also features the Western Uplands hiking trail. Contact the Ministry of Natural Resources, Box 219, Whitney, Ontario K0J 2M0.

Arrowhead Park north of Huntsville has miles of cross-country ski trails, good for summer hikes.

The Bruce Trail: White blazes on trees, fenceposts, and rocks mark the trail. Blue blazes indicate campsites and lookouts. The Trail's 430 miles (680 km.) stretch along the limestone Niagara Escarpment from the orchards of Niagara Falls to the cliffs and bluffs at the end of the Bruce Peninsula. Write to: Bruce Trail Association, 33 Hardale Crescent, Hamilton, Ontario L8T 1X7.

Ganaraska Trail: A geologist's wonderland, the trail extends northwest from Port Hope to connect with the northeast section of the Bruce Trail. Through historic Huron, French, and English pioneer country, the trail's access points are marked by a brown arrowhead symbol on a white square. It's also ideal for cross-country skiing and snow shoeing. For information write to Ganaraska Trail Association, Box 1136, Barrie, Ontario L4M 5E2.

Grand Valley Trail: This trail, suitable for day hikes only, stretches 80 miles (128 km.) from the Scottish-flavored village of Elora through Mennonite country to Brantford, and the famous Mohawk's Reserve. There is overnight camping at Conservation Parks only. Contact Grand Valley Trail Association, Box 1233, Kitchener, Ontario N2G 4G8.

Rideau Trail: The trail stretches 241 miles (406 km.) from the marshes of Little Cataraqui near Kingston to the Chaudière Falls, Ottawa along the route of the historic Rideau Canal. Access points from the highway are marked with orange triangles. Blue triangles indicate loops and side trails. Contact the Rideau Trail Association, P.O. Box 15, Kingston, Ontario K7L 4V6.

Voyageur Trail: In the process of being constructed, this trail will stretch from Manitoulin to Gros Cap, west of Sault Ste. Marie. Three sections of the trail have been completed. For further information contact Voyageur Trail Association, Box 66, Sault Ste. Marie, Ontario P6A 5L2.

Other trails in Ontario are as follows: *Thames Valley Trail,* c/o Thames Valley Trail Association, 403 Lansing Ave., London, Ontario N6K 2J2; *Guelph Trail,* c/o Guelph Trail Club, Box 1, Guelph, Ontario N1H 6J6; *Quinte-Hastings Recreational Trail,* stretches 250 miles from Outlet Provincial Park to Lake St. Peter. Contact Quinte-Hastings Recreational Trail Association, R.R. #7, Belleville, Ontario K8N 4Z7.

 WINTER SPORTS. You can always pass a pleasant Ontario winter sipping hot cider by a roaring fire—but remember, there's also a world of Alpine skiing, cross-country skiing, snowmobiling, hockey, sleigh riding, ice-fishing, curling, even winter camping awaiting you outside. Don't forget these telephone numbers for up-to-the-minute snow condition reports: (705) 726–0932 or (416) 364–4722.

Skiing: The Canadian Ski Instructors' Alliance standardizes the high quality instruction available at many resorts and slopes. Commercial slopes are patroled by the Canadian Ski Association. A complete list of Ontario's more than 400 slopes is available from *Ontario Travel,* Queen's Park, Toronto M7A 2R9. Major sites in the southern part of the province are near Ottawa, Collingwood, Huntsville, Barrie; major northern sites are at Kirkland Lake, Sault Ste. Marie, and Thunder Bay, which also features two of the world's largest (70- and 90-meter) ski jumps. Remember, 90 meters is about 300 feet—just watching the professional jumpers can be an exhilarating sport.

Cross-country skiing is becoming increasingly popular, and at many ski centers is complemented by snow shoeing and tobogganing facilities. Rented equipment and snacks are available at most centers. The *Muskoka Loppet* in early January is one of Canada's largest cross-country ski events.

Snowmobiling as a sport was invented here, and many international snowmobile races are held at Owen Sound and Lindsay (mid- to late January), and Eganville, Orangeville, and Jordan (February). For your protection the law requires that you wear a safety helmet whenever you board a snowmobile.

Winter camping, skiing, snow shoeing: Half of Ontario's parks remain open in winter for winter camping, skiing, and snow shoeing. Most are clustered in the southern part of the province. Write to the *Ministry of Natural Resources,* Parks Branch, Queen's Park, for a complete list.

Ice-fishing, people are discovering, can mean sitting comfortably in a stove-heated hut waiting for the trout, whitefish, perch, and pike to nibble. Major fishing centers are Lakes Simcoe and Couchiching (near Barrie), Lake Nipissing (near North Bay), Boshkung and Kennesis Lakes (near Haliburton), and Manitoulin Island.

Hockey: Winter is hockey time in Canada—*Toronto's Maple Leaf Gardens* is the place to catch the National Hockey League stars in action. When you watch the games of Ontario's Junior A Leagues you are probably watching the Wayne Gretzkys and Phil Espositos of tomorrow—that's where they got started.

Ice skating: Most municipalities have skating rinks or natural facilities; among the most picturesque places to skate are Ottawa's Rideau Canal (stroking side by side with the civil servants), Toronto's City Hall Square and London's Victoria Park.

Curling bonspiels are held throughout the province from December to February.

Racetracks are open in winter at *Windsor Raceway* (harness racing), London's *Western Fair Raceway* (harness), and Campbellville's huge *Mohawk Raceway*. For a list of winter carnivals, races, and events—don't forget the *Canadian National Sportsmen's Show* in March in Toronto—write to *Ontario Travel*, Queen's Park, Toronto M7A 2R9, or call (416) 965–4008 for information.

 MUSEUMS AND PUBLIC GALLERIES. Almonte: R. Tait McKenzie sculpted the athletes you see on Olympic medallions. He was also a great Canadian surgeon and the father of physical education in Canada. His words are displayed in the 1830's mill he restored and made his home, *Mill of Kintail Museum and Conservation Area* off Highway 29, north of Almonte. Open mid-May to mid-October daily.

Amherstburg: After the British evacuated Detroit in 1796, they constructed earthwork defenses and fortifications at Amherstburg's *Fort Malden*. The fort saw action in the War of 1812, and for years after continued to be Canada's main military base in the southwest. Open all year except December 25–January 1.

In King's Navy Yard visit the *Park House Museum*, the oldest (1799) house in the area. It was moved from Detroit to its present site and refurnished. The *North American Black Historical Museum*, adjacent to the Nazery AME Church (one of the first Black parishes in the area), is at 281 King St., west off Hwy. 3 (Sandwich St.). The museum contains old slave shackles, early farm implements, and songbooks.

Belleville: In the grandeur of a restored Victorian mansion you can browse through the *Couldrey Collection* of furniture and art, or pore over an unusual collection of lighting devices from prehistoric times to gas lamp days. *Hastings County Museum*, 257 Bridge Street, Belleville. Open all year daily, except Mondays.

Bowmanville: *Bowmanville Museum* (37 Silver Street) has a collection of century-old toys that will delight children of all ages. At the 1861 residence-turned-museum there are also displays of musical instruments, arts and crafts, and room after Victorian room of period furnishings. Open mid-April–mid-December, Tuesday–Saturday.

Brantford: At the *Brant County Museum*, the history of the Six Nations loyalist Indians Joseph Brant led to Canada after the American War of Independence comes alive. The museum also illustrates the lives of Alexander Graham Bell, the Mohawk poetess E. Pauline Johnson, and novelist Thomas B. Costain. Drop by 57 Charlotte St. It's open all year Tuesday–Saturday except holidays; May–Labour Day closed Mondays.

Base Borden/Barrie: The *Canadian Forces Base* at Base Borden is open to visitors all year, daily except Monday. Huge Allied Sherman Tanks and German panzers from World War II line the roads and there are more guns and vehicles at the museum. (Hwy. 90, west from Barrie.)

Cochrane District: The *Cochrane Railway and Pioneer Museum* displays model trains, photos and Indian and Eskimo handicrafts in old Ontario Northland and Canadian National Railway cars. Open mid-June to Labour Day, daily.

Cornwall District: Thomas Edison installed the electrical equipment you can see at the *United Counties Museum*. Settlers produced the maps, toys, and early local pottery. There are also Indian artifacts from the flooded Sheik Island site on display. Open May to October.

Other museums: The *Invarden Regency Cottage* is the finest Regency (1816) cottage architecture in the province. You'll find its 14 rooms on Hwy. 2 at Boundary Rd. (April–November). The *Living Museum and Indian Village* was built by the North American Indian Traveling College on Cornwall Island. Mid-May–September.

Elliot Lake: Models of uranium mines can be seen at the *Elliot Lake Mining and Nuclear Museum,* 45 Hillside Drive North, Elliot Lake. Open June to September, daily; October–May, Monday–Friday.

Elmira: Handmade doll costumes and antique dolls are on display at *The House of Dolls,* 28 South St. W. Open all year.

Guelph: The *University of Guelph Art Gallery,* open daily September to mid-July. In the permanent collection are over 400 items—paintings, graphics, and prints from 1800 to the present. *Halton County Streetcar and Electric Railway Museum,* 9 km. north of Hwy. 401 on Guelph Line. You can ride some of the old streetcars.

Hamilton: A gorget presented to a loyalist Mohawk chief (Joseph Brant) by an English king (George III) is among the Indian artifacts from 10,000 B.C. to the present day exhibited at the *Joseph Brant Museum,* Burlington. Open all year daily. Open Sundays in July and August only. A special children's collection of toys and dolls can be seen at the *Dundas Historical Society Museum,* 139 Park St. W. in Dundas. Open Monday to Friday. In Hamilton, check out the adults' toys at the *Canadian Football Hall of Fame,* City Hall Plaza. Open daily. Hamilton also has two art galleries. At 123 King St. W., the *Art Gallery of Hamilton's* permanent collection of Canadian, American, and European painters is worth a visit. Open all year daily except Mondays and statutory holidays. The *McMaster University Art Gallery* is noted for its excellent collection of German Expressionist prints. Monday to Thursday, closed Fridays and weekends. *Dundurn Castle,* a 19th-century mansion with adjacent gardens and aviary, is open all year, afternoons. On summer nights there is a Son-et-Lumière display. *Whitehern,* built in the 1840's, has been carefully restored to its upper-middle-class stuffy splendor. Ask the guide to tell you the story of the McQuesten family who lived here.

Kapuskasing: *Ron Morel Memorial Museum:* More railway coaches, this time including steam engines and 19th- and early 20th-century railway memorabilia. Open mid-June–Labour Day, daily, afternoons.

Kenora District: *Lake of the Woods Museum* by Memorial Park houses Indian and pioneer artifacts. But the museum in **Ear Falls** has an intriguing collection of artifacts from pioneer bush pilot days, housed in an old log building. Open mid-May to September, daily.

Kingston: There are many museums in Kingston, among them Sir John A. Macdonald's home, *Bellevue House* on Centre St. Open all year daily, except holidays from October to April. The *Pump House Steam Museum* holds a collection of intricate machines, model engines, and two monster pumps, circa 1892. The museum is at 23 Ontario St, open June 15 to Labour Day, daily. *The Canadian Forces Communications and Electronic Museum* has equipment displays and a kit shop. At Vimy Barracks, Hwy. 2 E. At the *Royal Military College Museum,* the Douglas Small Arms and Weapons Collection is displayed. The Museum is located in the Martello Tower, Fort Frederick, and is open June to Labour Day. *Old Fort Henry* is a living museum, where infantry cadets perform daily drills and, Mondays, Wednesdays and Saturdays in July and August (weather-permitting), execute the colorful "Sunset Ceremonial." May 15 to October 15. The *Agnes Etherington Art Centre* on the old gray stone campus of Queen's University has circulating exhibitions on view. Open all year, daily except Mondays and holidays. It has also inherited part of the excellent Zacks collection of contemporary Canadian sculpture and nonfigurative art.

Kitchener–Waterloo District: The little town of **Doon** on a wooded hilltop near Kitchener has its own school of fine arts. It also has the *Doon Pioneer*

Village, open May to October. *Enook Galleries,* 16 Young St., features Indian and Eskimo prints. At the University of Waterloo, there's a *Museum of Games* —over 1,000, including Indian bone games and Japanese drinking games.

Lindsay: *Victoria County Historical Museum* features an apothecary shop, a toy store, a doctor's office, and early Canadian glass and oil lamps. May 24– Labour Day, daily except Mondays. Afternoons only.

London: *Eldon House* at 481 Ridout St. dates from 1834. In summer, its old garden is open, too. The *Labatt Pioneer Brewery,* 150 Simcoe St., shows early methods of beer-making. The *London Regional Art Gallery,* 421 Ridout St., is a beautiful modern structure overlooking the Thames River. It houses changing national and international exhibitions.

Moosonee: *Moose Factory Museum Park:* This museum has been built on the site of an early trading post. A forge, a gun powder magazine, and Hudson's Bay Company exhibits chronicle the development of the 300-year-old trading center. Open June–October daily.

Morrisburg: *Upper Canada Village*'s more than 40 buildings make it a living museum. You can travel by oxcart to candlemaking or bread baking demonstrations, sample the atmosphere of early 19th-century churches and taverns, visit lovingly refurnished residences of the period 1785–1865. Open May 15 to October 15.

Niagara Falls: A 6 × 28 foot mural, "The Canadian Pioneer," and a 160-panel series, "The Passion of Christ," bring the sharp lines and vivid colors of Canadian master William Kurelek to the *Niagara Falls Art Gallery and Museum.* The five-level gallery also has changing exhibitions and art films. Queen Elizabeth Way. Open all year, closed Tuesdays. Admission charge.

Oshawa: Over 50 vintage cars, some Canadian-designed, are on display at the *Canadian Automotive Museum* (99 Simcoe St., S.). Open all year, daily.

The works of one of the most influential movements in nonfigurative painting in Canada, "Painters Eleven," form just part of the *Robert McLaughlin Gallery's* collection. Modern Canadian works are complemented by changing exhibitions of internationally known artists. Civic Centre. Admission free. Open daily all year.

Parkwood, mansion of the Canadian auto manufacturer R.S. McLaughlin, who sold out to General Motors, is magnificent. Gardens open, too, June– Labour Day daily except Mondays.

Owen Sound: A 26-foot birchbark Express canoe is part of the Indian and pioneer collections displayed at 975 Sixth Street East—the *County of Grey and Owen Sound Museum.* Open mid-January to mid-December, Tuesday through Sunday. The brilliant, thick-stroked canvases of the influential Canadian landscape painter Tom Thomson, and his sketches, letters, and drawings are hung in *Tom Thomson Art Gallery,* 840 First Ave. W., Owen Sound, and can be seen afternoons except Mondays in July and August.

Peterborough: Rare pioneer homespun, toys, photos, fossils, and an animated model of the Trent-Severn Waterway are just part of the collection of the *Peterborough Centennial Museum* on Hunter St. E. Open all year, daily. Fourteen restored pioneer buildings comprise Peterborough's other museum, *Century Village.* Open mid-May to Thanksgiving; special demonstrations on Sundays. July and August, daily. Other times, Wednesdays, Saturdays, and Mondays. Peterborough's *Art Gallery* is at 2 Crescent St. by Little Lake.

St. Catharines: *Rodman Hall,* 109 St. Paul Crescent, features tapestries, glassware, paintings, and graphics as well as exhibitions of Canadian and international artists. Open Tuesday, Thursday to Sunday. More china and weaving are displayed at the *St. Catharines Historical Museum,* 343 Merritt St., along with prints and relics from the War of 1812, and old photos and scale models relating to the construction of the Welland Canal.

St. Thomas: Colonel Thomas Talbot, an English backwoods despot, ruled the settlers on his grant of land with an iron fist in an iron glove. His life is recorded in exhibits on display at 32 Talbot St., in the renovated residence of a pioneer physician. Open all year daily.

Sarnia: You can clamber around a former Great Lakes oil tanker's center castle and explore the officers' quarters, masters' quarters, wheelhouse, signal flag locker, etc. in the *Pilot House Museum* in Corunna on Hwy. 40 south of Sarnia. Open mid-May to October, daily.

Sault Ste. Marie: A century-old church, a pioneer log cabin, a barn and a school make up the *St. Joseph Island Museum* complex just east of Sault Ste. Marie. Open June through September, Wednesdays, Saturdays, and Sundays, 2 to 5 P.M. July and August. Also visit the 1814 *Ermatinger House,* built by a fur trader for his Indian princess wife.

Remnants of the fur trade canoes, battleships,and freighters that plied the Great Lakes are on display at Sault Ste. Marie's *Marine Museum,* 41 Lake St., Bellevue Park, open July 1 to Labor Day. The *Art Gallery of Algoma* is at 10 East St.

Stratford: Every month a new and impressive exhibition is mounted by *The Gallery,* 54 Romeo St. North. Open May to September, daily; closed Mondays from Labour Day to May. Also features films, lectures, and concerts.

There's a 1/10-scale reproduction of Stratford-upon-Avon—including the Garrick Inn and Anne Hathaway's cottage—at *Shakespeareland. Fryfogel's Inn,* 8½ miles east of Stratford on Hwy. 7, has been made into a museum. Costumed hostesses guide you through the stagecoach inn past 5 rooms of exhibits. Open July to Labour Day, daily, noon to 6 P.M., except Monday.

Sudbury. *The Laurentian University Museum and Art Centre,* John St. at Nelson, consists of 3 galleries and a restored 1906 home.

Thunder Bay: A wide assortment of old stoves, player pianos, outboard engines, Edison record players—if it sounds like a general store, that's part of the *Thunder Bay Founders' Museum,* too. Hwy. 61. Open June 15 to September 15, daily. *Lakehead University* has an art gallery, open daily. *The National Exhibition Centre,* Keewatin at Red Lake Rd., features Indian art.

Wasaga Beach: A sound and graphics show dramatizes the American's burning of the *Nancy,* a supply schooner which served the British in the War of 1812 at the *Nancy Island Historic Site.* There are models and artifacts inside the museum, and the charred hull of the *Nancy* outside. Open late May to Labour Day.

Whitby: The former *Grand Trunk Railway Station* (early 1900's) has become Whitby's Art Gallery. "The Station" features traveling exhibits from the Art Gallery of Ontario plus a good display of local crafts. Open daily except Monday.

MUSIC. There are over 30 symphony orchestras plus 18 youth orchestras in Ontario. The largest and most polished are the excellent *Toronto Symphony,* the *Hamilton Philharmonic,* the *London Symphony Orchestra,* and the *National Arts Centre Orchestra of Ottawa.* The *Guelph Spring Festival* is an annual event held in late April and early May in **Guelph.** In the past the festival has featured chamber and solo concerts by ranking musicians from violinist Yehudi Menuhin to jazzman Moe Koffman. Ticket prices vary. International and local jazz, opera and pops artists are showcased in the concert series of the **Stratford** and **Shaw** Festival programs. Check **Ottawa** and **Peterborough** Festivals (spring-summer) for quality concerts. The *Shaw's Festival Theatre* at **Niagara-on-the-Lake** also runs a winter weekends concert series. Early August is the time to catch fiddlers at the *Open Old Time Fiddlers' Contest* in **Shelburne** and the pipe bands at **Kincardine.** Out-of-door summer concerts at **Hamilton's** *Dundurn Castle* and *Toronto's Ontario Place* range from pops to classical. There are bluegrass festivals at **Carlyle** and Burk's Falls. Fall brings symphony season to **Toronto, Hamilton** and **Ottawa;** late fall, the performances of the *National Ballet* and the *Canadian Opera Company.*

 SHOPPING. Canada's richest province naturally has some of the best shopping—everything from native crafts to antique junk to tens of thousands of dollars' worth of fur coats. Major retail stores are *The Bay* (The Hudson's Bay Company), *Eaton's, Simpson's, Ogilvy's,* and *Holt Renfrew.* They are clustered in major urban centers and their suburban branches carry the same lines of manufactured clothes and goods.

Native arts and crafts. Eskimo soapstone carvings and prints are available at Toronto's *Innuit Gallery of Eskimo Art,* 9 Prince Arthur Ave., which sells soapstone sculpture (from $50), prints, wall hangings, scrimshaw—or etched ivory—and other Eskimo antiquities. *Inukshuk Gallery,* in Waterloo, also specializes in Eskimo art. At *The Three Bears,* Niagara Falls, *The Canadian Craft Shop,* Kingston, and *The Snow Goose,* Ottawa, you can find both Eskimo and Indian work.

Indian crafts (moccasins, beadwork, traditional basketry often fashioned from fragrant sweet grass, silverwork, wood carvings, and Native prints) are available at centers like *Courtney's* on St. Joseph Island, east of Sault Ste. Marie. The *Cross Canada Craft Shop,* 11 miles west of Renfrew, carries Eskimo and Golden Lake Reserve Indian carvings and crafts. In Sault Ste. Marie's *The Loon's Nest,* quilts, dolls, puppets, homemade jams, weaving, pottery, Indian mittens and moccasins, and fine batiks are improbably jumbled in a modern shopping mall.

Canadian crafts. Many excellent Canadiana crafts centers are dotted across the province. Check Gananoque, Packenham, Perth, and Westport in eastern Ontario. In Kingston, the *Canadian Shop of Kingston and Gallery* carries glass, ceramics, tapestries, jewelry, toys, and Native crafts. There's a café behind the store where you can relax after browsing. *Chez Piggy* is a restaurant off King St. with boutiques all around the courtyard. *Cooke's Olde World Shop* on Lower Brock St. is a century-old general store with wood floors carrying gourmet teas, coffees, etc. *The Peanut Gallery* in Burk's Falls is the place where Northern Ontario craftsmen display their ceramics, metal, and woodwork.

In central Ontario, quilts, rugs, needlework, and crafts are sold in Cookstown, Dwight, Bond Head.

Elmira is in real Mennonite country. At *The Sap Bucket,* double-bed, down-filled quilts go for about $200, for a tiny fraction of that price you can take some Mennonite tradition home in the shape of an odd, charming little apple doll. The Sap Bucket also carries stained glass, wooden toys, and works by the Waterloo Potters' Guild. In London *The Canadian Craftsman* carries some jewelry and ceramics. Also check crafts shops in Bronte, Campbellville, Beamsville, and Dundas when in southwestern Ontario. At the *Pillar and Post Shoppe* in Niagara-on-the-Lake you can find work by over 150 local craftspeople. There's even a carpentry workshop and smithy on the premises, where pine replicas of traditional furniture, hardware and lighting fixtures are produced.

Gems and minerals. Bancroft is a center for geologists and in its two local rock shops you can pick up rose quartz, garnet, zircon, and beryl. You'll also find the books, tools, and advice you need to go out hunting for your own. In Thunder Bay's *Amethyst Mines,* you either chip your own gems and pay for what you take with you, or browse for already polished gems and jewelry in the mine's rock shop.

Antiques. Antique hunters are more common in Ontario than game hunters. They flock to *flea markets* in Burlington (weekends at 1400 Plains Rd. E.), Aberfoyle (Sundays in spring, summer, and fall) and Hamilton (on Sundays). The little towns of southeastern Ontario are a treasure trove for people in search of pressback chairs, dry sinks, oak tables; sharp-eyed collectors can even find relatively rare pieces of Ontario pine. Some of the best antiques are to be found in roadside, family-owned stalls around Cobourg, Peterborough, Marmora, Hastings, and Belleville. Another good bet—and a lot of fun—is to get a list of country auctions from local papers and general stores. If Elora's turn-of-the-century antique stores don't have what you're looking for, *Bon Accord Farm and Antiques* nearby makes fine reproductions. Hamilton's *Hess Village* is a restored area of specialty shops, galleries and restaurants, as entertaining an afternoon's stroll as Toronto's *Yorkville, Markham Village,* and the east and west Queen St. strips.

 DRINKING LAWS. Anyone over 19 may buy liquor. Liquor is sold in Provincial Liquor Control Board Outlets. Domestic beer is available at Brewers' Retail. Domestic wines are sold through company stores. On Sundays, alcohol is served from noon to 11 P.M. On other days drinking hours are 11 A.M. to 1 A.M.

 DINING OUT in Ontario means big helpings of plain food of the meat and potatoes variety, and, if you're lucky, fish or home-baked goods. You can also find tasty ethnic cooking in an area not otherwise noted for its cuisine. In both Southern and Northern Ontario, price categories for a dinner for one of appetizer, entrée and dessert, are: *Deluxe,* over $20; *Expensive,* $15–20; *Moderate,* $12–15; *Inexpensive,* under $12.

Most places accept the following major credit cards: American Express, MasterCard and Visa; others may also be honored. Not all establishments accept credit cards, therefore we suggest you call for information.

ALGONQUIN PARK. *Expensive.* **Arowhon Pines.** You can take second helpings in this pine-paneled rustic dining room, and you may very well want to: the chef, imported from Toronto for the summer, concentrates on a choice of three entrées each night and gives them his full attention. Roasts especially good. Not licensed. Season: May to October.

ALTON. *Expensive.* **The Millcroft Inn.** Imaginative soups and entrées, fresh fish, herbs from the garden, good wine list. Overlooks a waterfall.

BARRIE. *Expensive.* **Maude Koury's.** An old home turned into a restaurant, this is a cozy place to enjoy steak and seafood. Lunch is also excellent and less expensive. Licensed.

BELLEVILLE. *Expensive.* **Inn on the Bay.** Outside Picton, southeast of Belleville. A fireplace, antiques, and the ambience of a house built in the early 1800's add to your enjoyment of surf'n'turf, chicken cordon bleu, Rouladen, homemade desserts. Licensed.

BROCKVILLE. *Moderate.* **The White House Motel.** Canadiana cooking like maple-and-rum-baked beans for lunch. Colonial atmosphere. Licensed.

CALEDON. *Expensive.* **Caledon Inn.** The dining room has cedar beams and an old stone fireplace. Menu limited. Roast beef, homemade pies, high tea. No license. Reservations necessary.

COBOURG. *Deluxe.* **Marie Dressler House.** Continental menu, complemented by good vichyssoise, rum and walnut pie, served in a late Victorian atmosphere. Licensed.

COLLINGWOOD. *Expensive.* **The Spike and Spoon.** Fresh flowers, a prix fixe menu, gazpacho, Stroganoff, Dutch apple pie. Licensed.
Moderate–Expensive. **Hampton House.** An old stagecoach inn with winding staircase, stained glass, French cuisine, and informal atmosphere. Licensed.

CORNWALL. **Miss Cornwall.** *Expensive.* Because the menu is large, the restaurant is very popular with families. Between Italian, Chinese, steak, and seafood, there should be something for everyone. Licensed.

GANANOQUE. *Moderate.* **Golden Apple.** Highly recommended, but very popular, so reserve. In summer, a lovely garden is your first introduction to this old and much-loved restaurant. Fresh vegetables complement good homestyle entrées (beef, lamb, fish). Relishes and desserts especially good. Licensed.

GEORGETOWN. *Expensive.* **Spot on 7.** Everything is fresh, tasty, and cooked to order by the proprietress. Some of the vegetables come from the garden outside. A choice of three entrées, usually steak, poultry, and lobster. Although it's not licensed it has many enthusiastic fans; you must reserve.

GODERICH. *Deluxe.* **Benmiller Inn.** Overlooking Sharpe's Creek. There's a view of water and gardens outside; inside, a stone-floored dining room in a restored, 100-year-old mill serves rainbow trout, sirloin, fresh vegetables. Licensed.

HAMILTON. *Expensive.* **Lo Presti's.** A flock wallpaper décor, but very sophisticated Italian cuisine. Licensed.

KINGSTON. *Expensive.* **Firehall.** A greenhouse, glassed-in view of the harbor enhances the local pheasant, trout. Fireplace and license to warm you.
Moderate. **Rousseau's.** 200 Ontario St. A ribs 'n' sirloin spot, with Tiffany lamps and a young, good-times atmosphere. Open for breakfast. Great sausages.
Chez Piggy. Fresh vegetables, sophisticated but light menu, homemade desserts. A courtyard setting and a license. Operated by rock musician Zal Yanofsky, formerly of The Lovin' Spoonful.

KIRKFIELD. *Expensive.* **Mackenzie Historic Home.** A stately, 40-room mansion. Veal, sole, and B.C. salmon. Licensed.

KITCHENER. *Expensive.* **Café Mozart.** Wonderful tortes and pastries with coffee.

KLEINBURG. *Deluxe.* **The Doctor's House and Livery.** Roast duckling, sweetbreads, old-fashioned service. Licensed.

LEAMINGTON. *Expensive.* **Thirteen Russell Street.** The address turns out to be a charming old house where steaks and seafood are served. Licensed.

LONDON. *Expensive.* **Auberge du Petit Prince.** A reputation for good French cuisine, but it has recently changed owners.
Sorrenti's. Right across from Theatre London in renovated old building. Varied international cuisine, popular with theater people.

MOUNT PLEASANT. *Moderate–Expensive.* **The Heritage Inn.** A country inn with cozy dining room.

NEWBORO. *Moderate.* **The Poplars.** The rustic dining room with old stone fireplace overlooks Newboro Lake. Roast beef, fresh local vegetables all summer, homemade desserts. Not licensed. Season: May–October.

NIAGARA FALLS. *Moderate.* **Betty's One.** In Chippewa. This is no-nonsense, no-frills, dependably good home cooking. Steak or turkey dinners, real whipped cream in the desserts. Licensed.
Falls Manor. Barnboard panelling, roasted chicken, steak, homemade pies. No license.

NIAGARA-ON-THE-LAKE. *Deluxe.* **Prince of Wales.** In summer the airy, elegant restaurant expands into a greenhouse. The menu is imaginative (*e.g.*, watercress soup) and tasty (*e.g.*, fresh trout). A good wine list complements your dinner and there is a comfortable lounge next door.
Expensive. **The Oban Inn.** Pine furniture in a warm old-fashioned dining room. Classic beef and poultry entrées. Licensed.

PETERBOROUGH. *Moderate–Expensive.* **The Burnham Mansion.** Country inn dining. Steak, seafood, entertainment.

PRESCOTT. *Expensive.* **Grenville Motor Lodge.** The dining room looks out on the river. Steaks, surf 'n' turf. Homemade soups, salad bar. Licensed.

RIDEAU LAKES. *Expensive.* **Hotel Kenney.** In Jones Falls. A view of Whitefish Lake and the locks. Fish, beef entrées. Licensed. Season: May–October.
The Opinicon. In Chaffey's Locks. In a late-Victorian house surrounded by gardens fronting on the lake you can enjoy fresh fish and fresh vegetables, traditional entrées like roast beef and turkey. Not licensed. You must reserve ahead. Season: April–November.
Moderate. **Rideau Ferry Inn.** On county road between Perth and Lombardy. Neo-colonial dining room with fireplace faces the river. Broiled steak, chicken, and duck. Licensed. It's a good idea to telephone ahead.

ROSEMONT. *Moderate.* **Globe Restaurant.** Canadian standards (roast beef, steak-and-kidney pie) served before one of the inn's two fireplaces. Licensed.

SHARBOT LAKE. *Moderate.* **Sharbot Lake Hotel.** A licensed dining room with homemade desserts, pleasant view, the usual fish and beef.

STRATFORD. *Expensive.* **The Church.** One-hundred-year-old church has been beautifully converted into a restaurant offering pâté of fresh lamb, lake trout, veal, sweet soufflés. Licensed. The Church is heavily subscribed; book ahead.

TERRA COTTA. *Expensive.* **Terra Cotta Inn.** Terrace, 4 dining rooms, pub, country setting. Open for lunch, afternoon tea, dinner. English and Victorian décor.

WATERLOO. *Moderate.* **Stone Crock.** In the little country town of St. Jacobs. Good, plain Mennonite cooking is served in bowls and platters; you help yourself to roast turkey, farmer's sausage, roast beef. Then go to the salad bar. They also have fresh pan-fried trout, home-baked rolls and pastries. Not licensed.

WILLIAMSFORD. *Moderate.* **Ye Old Stone Inn.** Teas with scones, English roast beef dinners. On Hwy. 6.

WINDSOR. *Expensive.* **The Other Place.** Fish, spareribs, veal-and-chive quiche are served in a dining room with fireplace, wooden beamed ceilings, candlelight. Popular, so it's best to book ahead. Licensed.
Moderate. **Ye Old Steak House.** Filets, French onion soup, garlic shrimp. An old English pub décor. Licensed.

NORTHERN ONTARIO

BLIND RIVER. *Moderate.* **North Shore Motel.** Bavarian atmosphere right down to the cuckoo clocks, and, of course, Wienerschnitzel, Rouladen, and a license.

BRUCE MINES. *Moderate.* **Bavarian Inn.** More German country cooking. Copper pots, peasant artifacts decorate the licensed dining room. Wienerschnitzel. Licensed.

ESPANOLA. *Moderate.* **Goodman's Motel.** Homemade soup and home-fries to go with the German cooking. Licensed.

FORT FRANCES. *Moderate.* **Rainy Lake Hotel.** Local pickerel (walleye) is a speciality in this older hotel dining room, but there is also seafood, beef. Licensed.

KAPUSKASING. *Expensive.* **The Kapuskasing Inn.** A good place for lunch, when there's a smorgasbord buffet, some home baking. Licensed.

KENORA. *Expensive.* **The Captain's Table.** In Kenwood Hotel. Large helpings of steak or local walleye pickerel in a comfortable room with nautical decor. Licensed.
English Inn. In Kenricia Hotel on Main St. There's a painting over the fireplace which adds to the atmosphere of this older hotel dining room. Prime rib, Lake of the Woods walleye pickerel, steak plus a salad bar. Licensed.

MANITOULIN ISLAND. *Moderate.* **Huron Sands Motel.** In Providence Bay. Home cooking with fresh local ingredients in a bright, comfortable room. Not licensed.

MATHESON. *Expensive.* **Kiss Motel.** In town. Central European dishes like paprikash, spicy pork. Not licensed, but very popular.

NEW LISKEARD. *Expensive.* **Breault's Motor Hotel.** Highbacked chairs and a spacious green and white dining room. Menu changes, but expect straightforward beef, seafood entrées from the French-Canadian chef. Licensed.

NORTH BAY. *Expensive.* **Pinewood Park Motor Inn.** Rich warm wood is the setting for prime rib of beef, char-broiled steak, salad bar dining room. Dessert cart. Licensed.
Traditions. Elegant, renovated older home. Varied menu, licensed.
Moderate. **Golden Dragon.** Canadian and Chinese menu—sweet "n' sour, breaded shrimp. Overlooking Lake Nipissing. Licensed.

SAULT STE. MARIE. *Expensive.* **King's Table.** In Royal Hotel. A fireplace and dark, cozy olde pub atmosphere. Salad bar and large portions of prime rib. Licensed.
New Marconi. Italian cuisine—homemade lasagna, gnocchi; they're also famous for their barbecued ribs. Wood panelling and cheerful red tablecloths. Licensed.
Rico's. Popular with families. Italian cooking, seafood.
Moderate **Rib Room.** In Sheraton Caswell. Plush décor, and as the name implies, a menu devoted to beef. Licensed.

SUDBURY. *Expensive.* **Marconi's.** Popular Italian food, steaks. Formerly a motel.
Moderate. **The Peter Piper.** Fresh fish, Italian and Greek items on the menu. It is a local favorite. Licensed.
Inexpensive. **Casey's Road House.** Licensed, popular spot serving chicken wings, hamburgers, steaks.

THESSALON. *Expensive.* **Melwel Lodge.** On Big Basswood Lake. Home cooking, fresh fish, and good fresh-baked pies served in a woodsy dining room. Licensed. Season: May to November.

THUNDER BAY. *Expensive.* **Airlane Motor Hotel.** Fresh Lake Superior trout, fresh vegetables, steaks. Licensed.
Uncle Frank's Supper Club. He cuts his own steaks and serves them up with some fine home cooking in this comfortable, popular restaurant. Licensed.
Inexpensive. **Hoito.** Finnish cooking (mojjaka, a fish soup, and smorgasbord sandwiches) in an unpretentious and unlicensed setting.
Kanga's. First and foremost, a sauna, with restaurant attached, for after-sauna soups and chocolate cheesecakes.

TIMMINS. *Expensive.* **Empire Hotel.** Buffets are a specialty, and they're popular. Licensed.
Moderate. **The Highgrader.** A popular steakhouse, with a mining decor.

WAWA. *Moderate–Expensive.* **The Wawa Motor Hotel.** Wide menu, relative to the area.

QUÉBEC

Beauty, Variety, Prosperity, Adventure

by
STEVE COLLIER
and
MONIQUE NUYTEMANS

Steve Collier, veteran travel and business writer, and partner in a communications company in Western Canada, was born and raised in Montréal, and spent the first ten years of his career as a journalist and public relations consultant in Québec.

Monique Nuytemans, who lives in Montréal, is a well-known award-winning travel writer in Québec and a regular contributor to numerous publications both in French and in English.

Québec is an experience—special—intriguing—different. Here, history, culture, natural beauty, and a people proud of their heritage combine to yield a quality of life that is as enchanting to the visitor as it is satisfying to the lifelong resident. The largest of Canada's ten provinces, Québec offers a wide variety to its visitors. Mountains and forests, lakes and rivers, farmlands and villages seemingly sleep under the white-and-blue Québec flag and offer a vivid contrast to the bustling metropolis of Montréal and the old French atmosphere of Québec City. But the natural beauty of the land is not its only charm.

The people of Québec are also special. Determined to maintain the legendary warmth and hospitality of Québec even as the contemporary issue of separation from Canada causes tempers to flare, Québecers, French and English alike, are open and at ease with visitors, offering friendship and respect. And all who visit are enriched by the experience.

A Bit of History

Although the Vikings may have been Québec's earliest European travelers, an Indian town, Stadacona, had long existed on part of the present site of Québec when Jacques Cartier discovered and explored the St. Lawrence River in 1535. It was not until 1608, however, that Samuel de Champlain established a trading post in the area and named it Québec. Twelve years later, in 1620, Québec's first settlement had a population of 60.

All of North America offered a new world for adventurers and traders, political and religious refugees, kings and commoners. With them came missionaries from many sects. In the Québec area, the Récollets were first. They were closely followed, in 1625, by the Jesuits who, from that time to the present, have played a major role in the history of Québec.

For many years, New France, as Québec was then known, remained undeveloped as a commercial or agricultural settlement, subsisting entirely on the fur trade as a means of support. It was not until the time of Louis XIV of France that a systematic effort was launched to exploit the colony as a French and Catholic empire that would embrace the whole of North America. The result of this policy was a lengthy struggle between the English and French which began in 1689 with the return of Count Frontenac as governor of New France, and ended in 1759 with the capture of Québec by the British army under General Wolfe. The capitulation of Montréal in 1760—28 years after its founding by de Maisonneuve—completed the English conquest of Canada which, with all its dependencies, was ceded to the British Crown in 1763.

The liberal policy of the conquerors toward New France was formalized in 1774 with passage of the Québec Act by the British Parliament. This Act assured French-Canadians of religious freedom, enjoyment of civil rights, and protection of their own civil laws and customs. French civil law still prevails in Québec. The Québec Act also annexed large territories to the province of Québec, provided for a governing council with representation of the Catholics, and called for administration of the criminal code practiced in England.

But constant strife existed between the conquerors and the conquered over the issue of the predominating culture. Was it to be French or English? Seeking to end the conflict, Parliament divided Canada into two provinces in 1791—Lower Canada, or Québec, for the French, and Upper Canada, now Ontario, for the English, each with a governor

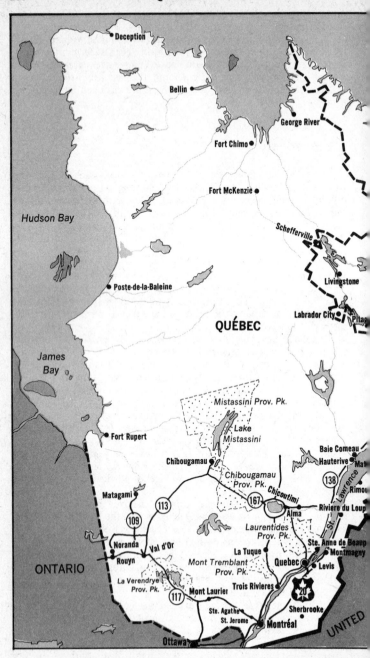

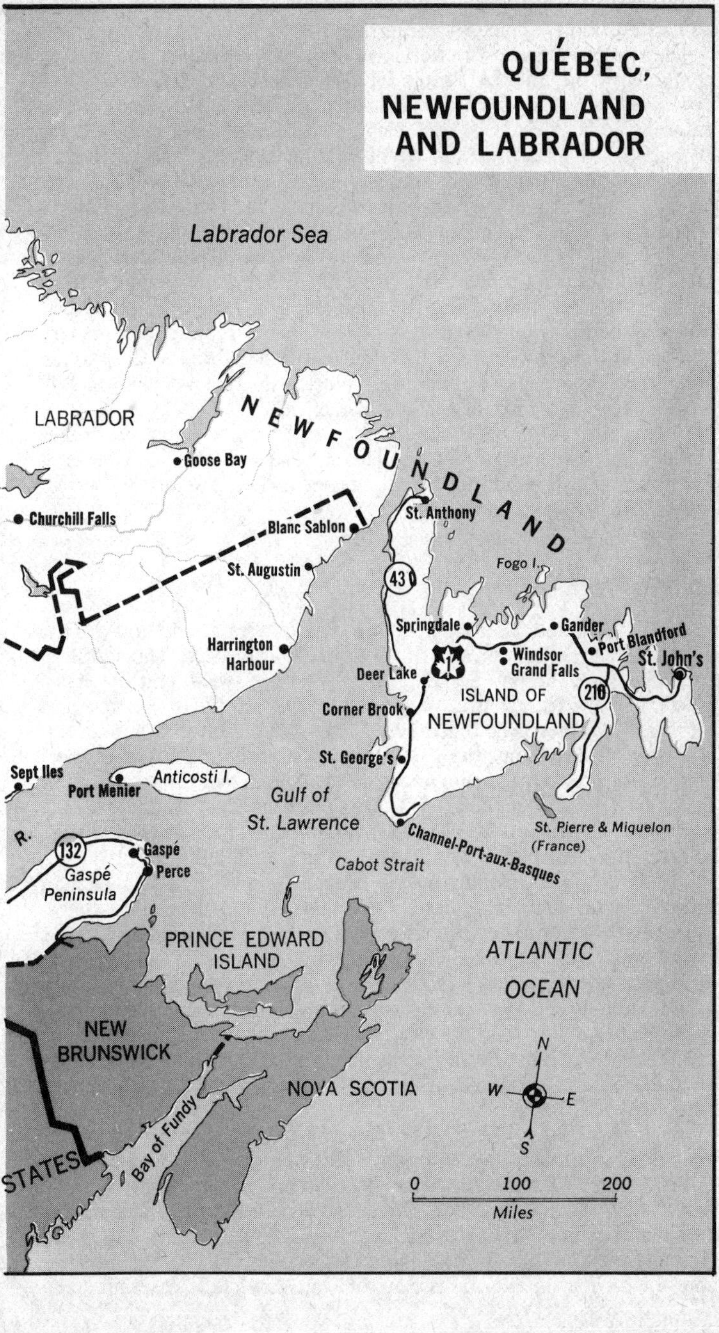

QUÉBEC,
NEWFOUNDLAND
AND LABRADOR

Labrador Sea

LABRADOR

NEWFOUNDLAND

● Goose Bay

● Churchill Falls

● Blanc Sablon

St. Augustin

● St. Anthony

Fogo I.

43

Springdale ● ● Gander

Harrington
Harbour

Port Blandford
St. John's

Deer Lake ● Windsor
Grand Falls

216

Corner Brook

ISLAND OF
NEWFOUNDLAND

St. George's

Sept Iles
Port Menier ● Anticosti I.

Gulf of
St. Lawrence

St. Pierre & Miquelon
(France)

R.

132

Gaspé
Perce

Gaspé
Peninsula

Channel-Port-aux-Basques

Cabot Strait

PRINCE EDWARD
ISLAND

ATLANTIC

OCEAN

NEW
BRUNSWICK

NOVA SCOTIA

N

W ● E

S

STATES

Bay of Fundy

0   100   200
Miles

representing the Crown, a legislative council appointed by the Crown, and an assembly elected by the people for four years.

The two nationalities, however, were neither separated nor pacified by the division. In 1841, after long and stormy agitation, the two provinces were reunited as the Province of Canada. The reunion also marked the beginnings of responsible and responsive government for Canada. The legislature consisted of a council and assembly, with each of the two old colonies to be represented in the assembly by 42 members, 84 in all, elected by the people; the council numbered 20 members appointed by the Crown. It was not until October 1864 that a convention was held in Québec for representatives from all the provinces to establish a confederation. The representatives unanimously adopted a set of resolutions embodying the conditions on which the provinces, through their delegates, agreed to federal union. Finally, in February 1867, after the provinces had put their position before the Crown, the British Parliament passed the British North America Act and, on July 1, 1867, the Dominion of Canada was born.

The recent (1982) proclamation of Canada's new Constitution has met with opposition from Québec citizens and French minorities elsewhere who fear it will limit their rights and endanger efforts to protect their French culture.

The Lay of the Land

Québec is bounded on the north by Hudson Strait and Ungava Bay, on the east by Labrador and the Gulf of St. Lawrence. The southern boundaries are the Bay des Chaleurs, New Brunswick, and the states of Maine, New Hampshire, Vermont, and New York. In the west and southwest, Québec is bounded by the Province of Ontario, James Bay, and Hudson Bay. Since the 1912 annexation of the district of Ungava doubled its area, Québec embraces nearly one fifth of the total area of Canada—1,539,843 sq. kms. (594,534 square miles) of land and water. Its breadth is nearly 1,600 kms. (1,000 miles) on a due east-and-west course; its length (north to south) is 1920 kms. (1,200 miles).

The Notre-Dame Mountains, a continuation of the Appalachian Range, extend along nearly the whole south side of the St. Lawrence, running at varying short distances from the river, crossing the frontier into the state of Vermont, and joining the Alleghenies. The highest altitude in the province is Mont D'Iberville in Matane County, 5,419 feet (1,652 metres). The Laurentian Mountains skirt the northern bank of the St. Lawrence and Ottawa Rivers. At a point some 208 kms. (130 miles) west of Montréal, they cross the Ottawa River and curve in the direction of Kingston, where they run westward to the shores of Lakes Superior and Huron.

Heading the list is the great St. Lawrence, 3,058 kms. (1,900 miles) long, flowing almost the entire length of the province. A short distance from Montréal, the St. Lawrence receives the waters of the Ottawa River, 1,271 kms. (790 miles) in length. The Ottawa, more abundant in water than the Nile or the Rhine, has large tributaries: the rivers Gatineau and Lièvre and three others extend north. The St. Maurice, noteworthy for its enormous flow of water and falls, rises in Lake

Oskelaneo and empties into the St. Lawrence at Trois-Rivières. Among the many rivers that enter the St. Lawrence, the Saquenay is one of the most remarkable bodies of water in the world, varying in depth from 100 feet to 1,000 feet.

The principal lakes of the province are Mistassini, 2,336 sq. kms. (975 square miles); Payne, 1,935 sq. kms. (747 square miles); and Saint-Jean, 1,002 sq. kms. (350 square miles). At three places the St. Lawrence enlarges to form Lake Saint François, Lake Saint-Louis, and Lake Saint-Pierre.

The principal islands in the St. Lawrence are Montréal; Orléans, near Québec; Anticosti and the Magdalen Islands, in the Gulf of the St. Lawrence.

Lumber from the forestlands, covering more than 259,000 sq. kms. (100,000 square miles), is easily handled as a result of Québec's countless rivers and their extensions. It is on the north side of the St. Lawrence that the forests give their best yield.

Winter in Québec means steadily cold weather with the thermometer often registering −30°C. (−22°F.). Snow, usually over 100 inches, lies on the ground from November to April. Summers are warm and pleasant, with temperatures seldom rising above 33°C. (91°F.). Autumn, which lasts six to eight weeks, is the finest season of the year.

Montréal: Canada's Largest City

Montréal is a cosmopolitan and culturally rich city that seems always to be striking out in new directions as it maintains its position as Canada's largest metropolis. With a population of over 1 million people (2.5 million in Greater Montréal), it is the second-largest French-speaking city in the world. Montréal is situated on an island and built around the awesome Mount Royal, from which the city and the island derive their name "Montréal," a variant form, reminiscent of Southern France (Réal). The western half of the island lies between two magnificent bodies of water—Lac Saint-Louis and Lac des Deux-Montagnes—a paradise for aquatic sports, including all-season fishing.

An Ideal Location

Jacques Cartier was the first known European to recognize the advantages of the site. In 1535, when he discovered the archipelago at the junction of the Outaouais and St. Lawrence Rivers, he was greeted by thousands of natives. The settlement included some 50 wooden houses, built of logs and covered with long sheets of bark. It has been estimated that the population at the time was 3,500—very large for an Indian village.

As with Stadacona where Québec City stands today, this settlement was gone in less than a century. When Champlain arrived, 75 years later, all that remained was a large tract of meadow. Well aware of the advantages of the location, Champlain wanted to set up a permanent post at the site but was never free to do so.

In describing Montréal, one writer noted: "We have here one of the most remarkable junctions of waterways in North America, a junction situated at the heart of a rich countryside on a fertile plain over which travel is easy and where a climate less harsh than elsewhere furthers the efforts of man." Here, then, was a natural point of interchange for communications and transport by water and by land—all in the midst of a plain through which roads—and later a railway—would be built. Assuring navigation to the very heart of the continent, the St. Lawrence offered smaller craft an avenue to the southwest and the Great Lakes; the Outaouais River did the same to the north and northwest; the Richelieu River pierced straight south to Lake Champlain and the headwaters of the Hudson.

In the 17th century, the upper circles of French society were keenly receptive to missions evangelizing foreign lands. The Jesuit missionaries instilled in the hearts and minds of the French élite the spiritual aspects of the Canadian venture.

In 1640, the first shipment of supplies and tools was sent across the sea and entrusted to the Québec Jesuits for safekeeping. The following summer, some 40 settlers, from all over France (selected for fortitude and skill), arrived in Québec.

Although the authorities of New France, well aware of Iroquois hostility, tried to keep the new arrivals in Québec, the group settled a little west of what is known today as Old Montréal. Soon, a fort, chapel stores, and some homes were standing. Within a year, the first party of Iroquois attacked. A bitter half century of alarms, raids, and massacres was to follow. Remarkably, the little settlement not only survived, but flourished. By 1701, when the Iroquois finally made peace, the population was approaching 2,000 and Montréal had become the gateway to the west.

The Fur Trade

Throughout the 18th century, the city's economic life was completely dominated by the fur trade. Because of the excellent land surrounding it, Montréal needed no outside support to meet its basic needs. Furs made it prosperous, self-confident, and active. Yet in 1760, besieged by British forces under General Amherst, the town capitulated at once. Perhaps this was because Montréal, unlike Québec, was bereft of strong, natural defenses. Indeed, fifteen years later it again yielded to a besieging army without striking a blow, this time to the Continentals under Montgomery, and remained in American hands for several months.

The British conquest created little change in lifestyle within the town. A small group of English-speaking people took up residence and then proceeded to appropriate and reorganize the fur trade. Instead of relying on the Indians to bring their pelts to Montréal, the traders sent out their *coureurs de bois* and *voyageurs* to scour the wilderness and often conduct their own expeditions.

By 1784, almost a generation after the conquest, the need to unite these efforts and eliminate costly competition induced several canny Scotsmen to organize the North West Company which, for almost half a century, was to be the main cog of Montréal's economic life. Its intrepid leaders left their mark from the Pacific to the Arctic Oceans.

The supremacy of Montréal's fur trade, however, was short-lived. Competition from the ancient Hudson's Bay Company, that had established posts close to shipping points on James Bay and could dispense with the long island haul to Montréal, became more and more insurmountable. Finally, in 1821, the North West Company was absorbed by its older rival and Montréal was forced to look elsewhere for an economic mainstay.

Development of Communications

By the end of the American Revolution, settlers had been trickling into what is now Ontario, along the shores of the upper St. Lawrence, the Outaouais, and Lake Ontario. By 1880, the trickle had become a stream. Since all this traffic passed through Montréal, the young metropolis thus became a gateway to new lands, not only for people but for goods.

Downstream from Montréal, the St. Lawrence presented major problems. In the days of sails, only small vessels could navigate between Montréal and Québec. The advent of steam, however, improved the situation. As early as 1809, Molson's *Accommodation*—Canada's first steamboat—was in service between the two cities; but the waters of the river were sinuous and at many places very shallow, causing constant hazards. Men of vision went to work. Gradually the mud was dredged, hidden dangers removed and the channel straightened. Larger and larger vessels were able to use the waterway until all but the giant ships can now pass safely from the Atlantic to Montréal's 14 miles of berthing space, and continue on to the Great Lakes.

Meanwhile, railways began to weave an ever-widening circle around the city, linking it to the Richelieu River, to Portland, Maine, to New York, Toronto, the lower Saint Lawrence, Québec, Ottawa, and Vancouver. This rapid development, directly and indirectly, gave Montréal its real and continuing economic basis—industry and finance. Thus, the Lachine Canal, supplying power as well as transportation, became the first major area of concentration for manufacturing. As the city gained in importance, its surrounding regions provided an ingenious and industrious labor force to maintain its progress.

The People

The history of Montréal's people is unlike any other on the North American continent. In 1760, the vast majority of the population (5,000) was French. After the conquest, the English-speaking element increased, slowly at first, then rapidly after 1820. By 1830, the two groups were roughly equal in population. Massive immigration from Ireland, however, tipped the balance. Montréal became "Anglophone" (English-speaking) and remained so for a generation.

Towards 1860, the situation was reversed and the French-Canadians came back into their own. Gradually, the present-day situation was established—two-thirds French-Canadian and one-third fairly evenly split among recent immigrants and people of British origin. This makes Montréal the largest French city outside of France; yet some say it is more cosmopolitan than any city in the world, and more homogenous in its background than any place its size in North America.

Industry, Transportation, and Finance

A thousand miles from the ocean, Montréal is now one of the world's greatest inland ports and the key to the St. Lawrence—the world's greatest inland waterway. Perhaps, in the beginning, the port created Montréal's industry. Today, the city's industry far outranks the port. As one of Canada's main commercial and industrial center, the city leads the entire country in storing general merchandise both in scope and diversity of its installations. The range of manufacturing is boundless. In dollar value, petroleum products have, for some time, ranked first. But you name it—cigarettes, locomotives, textiles, automobiles, foodstuffs, aircraft, pharmaceuticals, whiskey, beer—Montréal makes it! Its harbor receives from 5,000–6,000 vessels annually; huge transatlantic liners bring both visitors and new Canadians into Montréal's port by the thousands; and countless cruise ships berth at its harbor.

The city also houses the headquarters of two of the world's greatest railways—the Canadian Pacific and the Canadian National; both operate hotels, telecommunications, ships, and trucks and obtain their rolling stock from Montréal industry.

In air transport, Montréal more than holds its own. It serves as headquarters for Canada's largest airline, Air Canada, as well as the International Civil Aviation Organization, and the International Air Transport Association. Montréal's international airport at Dorval, 24 kms. (15 miles) west of the city, receives and dispatches hundreds of flights daily, handling all domestic and United States flights. Mirabel, a second airport handles all other international flights, as well as transfer flights and air cargo.

Supplementing the city's network of ultra-modern express traffic arteries is Montréal's Métro, widely recognized as one of the world's most sophisticated and effective underground traffic systems with its 52 stations covering 51 kms. and still expanding. Enhanced by beautifully decorated indoor stations featuring works by Québec's most gifted artists, the system also offers an intriguing underground city of miles of interconnecting arcades and malls, lined with shops, restaurants, theaters, and other services. These link up with hotel accommodations, parking garages, exhibition facilities, office space, and panoramic lookouts. In inclement weather, a whole city is within comfortable reach, with rapid transport at every turn, and no need to venture outdoors.

Urban Renewal

New life was injected into this booming metropolis at the end of World War II when much of Montréal's central section was in a state of decay. Today, wide boulevards replace tiny cobblestone streets and a new skyline of vast and well integrated buildings has been created—a change as dramatic as the underground city below.

Keeping pace with modern trends and needs, Montréal still remains conscious of a rich cultural heritage. Even with its contemporary look,

Montréal cherishes the treasures of yester-year. Many millions of dollars were invested in the restoration of "Old Montreal" (*le vieux Montréal,*) to bring that part of the city into harmony with the entire island's cosmopolitan charm.

EXPLORING MONTRÉAL

Place d'Armes between Saint-Jacques and Notre-Dame Streets join Old Montréal in the heart of the financial district. The de Maisonneuve Monument dominates the area. To the south stands the magnificent Notre-Dame Basilica, of neo-Gothic design, built by James O'Donnell, an Irish-born American Protestant who later converted to Roman Catholicism. The church was opened in 1829, but its history dates to the origins of the colony. Beautiful works of art enshrined here include the main altar and pulpit by Victor Bourgeault. Its main bell, known the world over, weighs 24,780 pounds. A museum is also located in the church, the chapel of which, rich in artistic works, was heavily damaged by fire in 1979 but restored and reopened in 1983.

West of Notre-Dame Church is the Séminaire de Saint-Sulpice—founded in Paris in 1641 by Jean-Jacques Olier, established in Ville-Marie (Montréal) in 1685, and noted for its fine woodwork clock which dates to 1710.

Opposite Place d'Armes is a fascinating structure, a classic 19th-century building that houses the Bank of Montréal, Canada's first bank, which opened its doors in 1817. The hypostyle vestibule surmounted by a cupola and the main exchange lobby are of particular interest. The building takes a proud stand beside the modern Banque Nationale du Canada to the west and the Société de Fiducie and the Royal Bank to the east. In the Bank of Montréal's main office is a museum collection of old coins, documents and banking memorabilia. Take Saint-François-Xavier Street southwest to number 440 where you will find the first Montréal Stock Exchange Building, now home for the Centaur Theatre Company. Turn left towards Saint-Nicolas where Place d'Youville comes into view. You'll find a recently restored center, grouping boutiques and offices around a quaint inner court. The former d'Youville stables also features a restaurant, Gibby's, with an international reputation for its historic period décor.

The next point of interest is Pointe à Callières, named after the first governor of Montréal (1684), who also served as governor of New France from 1698 to 1703. By an adroit treaty of peace in 1701, he brought an end to the war with the Iroquois which had lasted fourteen years. His château was built at the corner of rue du Port.

This course takes in the colorful harbor district, flanked on the south by rue de la Commune and the Alexandra wharf. In the center of this area there is a fountain and a monument to John Young "through whose foresight, public spirit and energy, Montréal has become the national port of Canada." The corner witnessed its share of lively times when seamen on leave would strike out on a spree. The old Joe Beef Tavern at the corner of rue de la Commune vividly recalls these times.

Place Royale, the oldest landmark in the city, is readily identified by an obelisk declaring this place to have been named by Champlain. On May 8, 1642, Paul Chomedey de Maisonneuve laid the foundations of the city of Montréal here, erecting the first homes, a fort, chapel and cemetery. On February 23, 1642, Montréal was dedicated to the Blessed Virgin Mary and given the name Ville-Marie. Also to be seen here are the names of Montréal's first settlers.

Rue Saint-Sulpice, rich in history, warm, narrow, and lined with small, romantic restaurants, is an inviting way to return to Place d'Armes. Pierre Lemoyne, Sieur d'Iberville, one of the most outstanding figures to emerge from New France, was born here in 1661. Farther on, in the area encompassing the eastern façade of Notre-Dame, once stood the house of Pierre Gauthier de la Vérendrye, who discovered the Rocky Mountains in 1743. Across the way, near rue Le Royer, was the location of Hôtel-Dieu, founded by Jeanne Mance in 1644 and later moved to Pine Street in 1861. This pioneer was well supported in her efforts by other valiant women, such as Judith Moreau de Brésoles, who left her name to a small street. She was the first nursing sister to come to this site (1659). Another building, at 451 Notre-Dame, now used for boutiques and offices, encloses the original arch (1788) of the first hospital founded by the Grey Nuns. Finally, at the last corner of rue Notre-Dame, the first private school of New France was opened in 1683.

Returning to the Place d'Armes, rue Notre-Dame now heads toward the eastern part of Old Montréal. At the corner of Saint-Laurent, is the Montréal Court House, called "Palais de la Justice," a new, modern, steel and dark glass high-rise building. And right across Saint-Laurent looking west, joining the parallel Saint-Jacques and Saint-Antoine Streets, stand two linked buildings—one dating 1899, the other 1959— which house *La Presse,* one of the most important French daily newspapers in America.

Eastern Part of Old Montréal

Rue Saint-Gabriel (lined with old dwellings—Nos. 420, 426 and 428, of which one has been converted into a picturesque inn) leads to Sainte-Thérèse, where the National Archives of Québec are situated. Along rue Saint-Vincent, there are lovely old Québec homes (Nos. 427–437) that are now converted into small bars and restaurants, handsomely combining modern life and yester-year. Then rue Saint-Amable, a summer rendezvous for artists, opens onto Place Jacques-Cartier, a former outdoor marketplace. Moving slightly downhill, you see a colorful rectangle formed by rows of establishments which have been neatly converted out of historic buildings. The population here is cosmopolitan and multinational in character. Sidewalk terraces, flower merchants, and calèche (horse-drawn carriage) drivers add to the quiet Old World charm of the Place. Here you will find the Nelson Column—the oldest monument in Montréal—erected in 1809 in memory of the famous British admiral.

Even without a map it is easy to find your way in Old Montréal. On the south side it is bordered by the harbor. On the north side, one cannot miss either the Nelson Column or the City Hall. Furthermore, all the street names in this section have been painted on red plaques affixed to the corner buildings.

Along East rue Saint-Paul is the first City Hall (prior to 1879) and the church of Notre-Dame-de-Bonsecours (1772). The first building, which later burned, was started by Marguerite Bourgeois. A wooden sculpture of the Virgin Mary, with arms stretched out toward the river, was installed on the roof. A bronze statue has now replaced the wooden figure that was stolen. An octagonal tower, two stories high and raised on the apse, offers a superb view of the St. Lawrence, Montréal's harbor, Man and His World, and the downtown skyscrapers. The church also houses a small museum.

At the corner of Bonsecours and East Saint-Paul, is du Calvet House (1770). Once the property of a wealthy merchant, it now houses a collection of Québec furnishings belonging to the Beaux-Arts Museum. On Place Bonsecours, No. 440, is a fine old home, Papineau House, that once belonged to Louis-Joseph Papineau (1786–1871), one of the initiators of the 1837 rebellion against British rule. At the Beaujeu House, 320 East rue Notre-Dame, you will find an excellent restaurant and an experimental theater. At the corner of rue Saint-Claude stands the Château Ramezay, rich in history. Located at 290 East Notre-Dame, it was constructed in 1705 by Claude de Ramezay, Knight of Saint-Louis and governor of Montréal from 1703 to 1724. The home was bought by the West Indies Company, came into the hands of English governors after the conquest, and was appropriated by American generals and envoys during the invasion. Benjamin Franklin stayed at the stately château. From that time, the château became headquarters for a succession of institutions and it now houses the Archeology and Numismatics Society, one of Montréal's finest historical museums.

City Hall, an outstanding example of Renaissance architecture adapted to 19th-century needs, rises at the site of the Jesuit's Garden. Overlooking Place Vauquelin is Champ-de-Mars, now converted into a parking lot, but once used as a military training ground. The old Court House (1849) is the home of CIDEM, the economic development department of the City of Montréal. Farther along is the Palais de la Justice and from there it is an easy return to Place d'Armes.

The Underground City

The pulse of Montréal is Centre Town. and Centre Town is Sainte-Catherine Street, with shoppers streaming into the bright ultramodern department stores by day, and enjoying theater, movies, and nightspots by night. Montréal's Centre Town is Sherbrooke Street for high fashion and luxurious windowshopping. It is Crescent and Mountain and Stanley Streets where one shares laughter from terrace-cafés and listens to the exciting disco beat. And Montréal is Saint-Denis Street with its cabarets and day-into-night excitements. Throughout the entire sector, contemporary life flirts unabashedly with the stately and historic.

A vast system of underground passages links Centre Town's great business complexes. Visitors will find this challenge to the city's winter climate a fascinating labyrinth in which to windowshop, eat, drink,

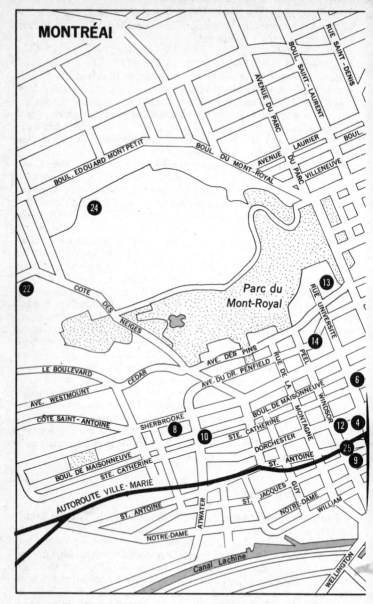

MONTRÉAL

Montreal—Points of Interest

1) Aquarium
2) Bonsecours Market
3) Botanical Garden
4) Central Station
5) Chateau Ramezay
6) Christ Church Cathedral
7) City Hall
8) Congregation Notre-Dame Mother House
9) Dow Planetarium
10) Forum
11) Garden of Wonders
12) Marie-Reine-du-Monde Cathedral

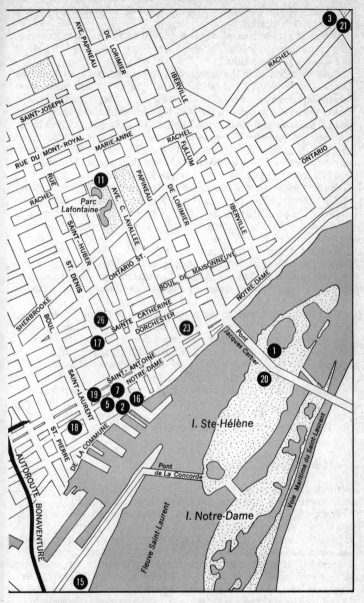

13) McGill Stadium
14) McGill University
15) Museum of Contemporary Art
16) Notre-Dame-de-Bonsecours Church
17) Notre-Dame-de-Lourdes Church
18) Notre-Dame Church
19) Old Court House

20) Old Fort
21) Olympic Stadium
22) Oratoire St.-Joseph
23) Post Office
24) Quebec University
25) Radio Canada Building
26) University of Montreal

enjoy theater and cinema . . . in short, watch the world go by in a bustling city beneath a city.

Montréal's underground city has evolved along two main axes running from north to south. The two focal points are Place Ville-Marie and Complexe Desjardins.

Place Ville-Marie, in the downtown core, is bordered to the south by Dorchester Boulevard and to the north by a little plaza opening on Sainte-Catherine St. which offers open-air art displays in summer. The first of the new ultramodern tall buildings that started changing Montréal's skyline around 1960, Place Ville-Marie is a huge cruciform tower built atop a four-acre shopping plaza complete with restaurants and cinemas. It is linked to Central Station (Via Rail) and the Queen Elizabeth Hotel, Place Bonaventure, Place du Canada, Windsor Station (CP), and the Château Champlain Hotel (CP).

In the same district is a separate underground development around McGill Métro Station. It links two of Montréal's greatest department stores on Sainte-Catherine St., the Bay and Eaton. Eaton features a boutique gallery, Les Terrasses, which also houses one of Montréal's best restaurants, René Varaud.

At the bottom of this axis is Place Victoria. This 47-story tower houses the Montréal Stock Exchange and a shopping plaza. Place Victoria is connected to the Métro by an entrance given by the city of Paris, but it is not linked yet to other parts of the underground pedestrian network.

Complexe Desjardins, in the eastern section of the downtown area, is the focal point of the second main underground development. Complexe Desjardins is made up of two large office towers and the Meridien Hotel, built around an inside plaza lined with boutiques, restaurants, and cinemas. It opens both on Dorchester Boulevard and Sainte-Catherine Street and is linked to the Place des Arts and the Métro. Plans are underway to extend the underground network of this section to the Guy Favreau Centre, a large Canadian Government office building nearing completion, and the new Convention Centre which straddles the Ville-Marie Autoroute and opened in June 1983.

Around Mount Royal

Among the many parks covering one-tenth of the land surface, the most cherished is Mount Royal (Mont-Royal, in French).

Wooded slopes, gently undulating lawns, and man-made Beaver Lake help make 530-acre Mount Royal Park a favorite year-round recreational area. Stroll through the park or enjoy a calèche ride; cars are permitted only on one major parkway. And don't neglect the Museum of Hunting and Nature, which holds exhibitions in an old stone farmhouse. The mountain, a former volcano that rises 752 feet above sea level, affords a panoramic view of the city. In winter, Beaver Lake becomes a skating rink; there are also ski trails, toboggan hills, and horse-drawn sleighs. The park's 100-foot illuminated cross is a landmark that can be seen for 50 miles. It commemorates a wooden cross planted there in 1643 by religious explorer Paul de Chomedey, Sieur de Maisonneuve, after Ville-Marie was spared from a great flood.

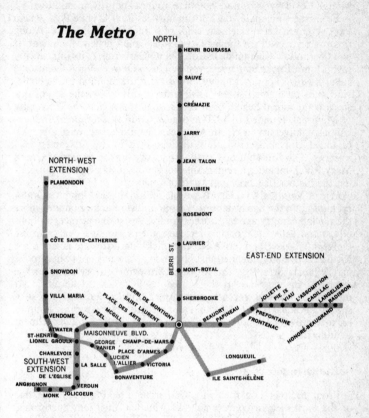

The Metro

This rocky and wooded eminence named Royal by Cartier in honor of François I, King of France, towers over the heart of the city—its two summits well preserved in their natural environment. The highest, Mount Royal, 230 m. (752 ft.) is separated from the other, Westmount, by a shallow cleft. Almost all roads lead here. You can also reach Mount Royal by two more common routes—both from midtown.

From rue Université you will run into des Pins Avenue East, where Park Avenue, which skirts the slope of Mount Royal, is joined. Along this route you will see the Sir Georges-Etienne Cartier Monument. If you then follow Chemin de la Côte Sainte-Catherine to its intersection with Mount Royal Boulevard, you will be in Outremount, a handsome suburb, which appears to have sprung from the mountain. The boulevard ends on a small street called Vincent-d'Indy. At the top of this street is the famed School of Music. Also in this area is the University of Montréal, founded in 1920 and now the most prominent French-language university in North America. The university, once a branch of Laval University, is mainly distinguished in the arts and social sciences. The Museum of Canadian History, at the corner of Queen Mary Road, includes a remarkable collection of wax figures, illustrating the history of Christianity and of Québec.

One of Montréal's highlights, visible for miles, is St. Joseph's Oratory, built upon the north slope of Westmount Mountain. Founded more than a half century ago by Brother André, this shrine attracts millions of visitors each year. For an alternate route to Mount Royal from rue Université, take Sherbrooke Street, which offers you a chance to see McGill University, founded in 1821. Also at the corner of Sherbrooke and Victoria Streets is the McCord Museum (history), and at the corner of Bishop Street is the Musée des Beaux-Arts, the oldest art museum in Canada, recently redecorated and expanded at a cost of several millions. Also to be found along Sherbrooke Street are churches, attractive boutiques, art galleries, elegant hotels, and apartment buildings.

The Olympic Village

From midtown take rue Sainte-Catherine to see Place des Arts, one of the most elegant concert halls in America, then join Sherbrooke Street East, a long artery that extends from Ville Saint-Pierre to Bout-de-l'Île. Lafontaine Park, between Parc Lafontaine and Papineau Streets, a green oasis in the heart of the city, is well worth exploring. It offers a place for picnicking, strolling, or relaxing. There are small boats for rent and outdoor concerts.

The Olympic Village and Stadium at the corner of Pie IX Boulevard is a sports complex designed with flexibility to accommodate athletic competitions and other sports events. The design of the seating areas assures 70,000 spectators a clear view of the competition. The stadium also houses kitchens, restaurants, bars, offices, libraries, post offices, communications outlets, and a sports museum. Guided tours are available daily.

The Olympic Park is linked by tunnel to the Botanical Garden, the lasting achievement of Brother Marie-Victorin, famed Québec naturalist. It contains some 23,000 species and varieties of flora with special sections featuring perennials, fruit trees, medicinal plants, shrubs, and aquatic plants. The garden may be toured on foot or by miniature train. The 9-hole Village Golf Course, situated behind the Olympic Village, spreads along the opposite side of the Olympic Stadium, north of Sherbrooke Street.

Sherbrooke Street East leads as far as Lebrun Avenue, which heads down south as far as Bellerive, where there is a lovely view of the river and the Boucherville islands. The direction is upwards now toward Notre-Dame to reach Montréal-East, where harbor installations and giant oil refineries come into view. The scenery softens as you enter Pointe-aux-Trembles. Close by, the Saint-Laurent sparkles around the islands of Mastaï, Saint-Patrice, au Veau, Sainte-Thérèse, and aux Asperges, dotted with handsome villas.

Island Tour

A tour of fascinating Montréal Island will require a few hours as you wander through varied settings of city and suburb, village, and town. From the Bout-de-l'Île (Montréal-North), where harbor installations and huge oil refineries come into view, take Gouin Boulevard which follows the des Prairies River, a branch of the Outaouais River. The ancient stone houses here are still occupied. Sparkling vistas of river and islands frame a splendid panorama.

At Rivière-des-Prairies, now part of Montréal, the bank becomes more populated; l'Île de Laval appears and, at Montréal-Nord the highway skirts the river. The Ahunstic municipality recalls the drowning of a Franciscan missionary, Father Nicolas Viel, in 1625, along with a young Indian neophyte. A plaque at l'Église de la Visitation, 1751, marks the occurrence. Another plaque recalls that Cartier stopped here in October 1535, and that Mass was celebrated 50 years later in the presence of Champlain by Father Joseph Le Caron, a Récollet priest.

Passing through the two communities of Bordeaux and Cartierville, again now part of Montréal, the road takes you back into the countryside. It crosses hamlets, such as Saraguay (Montréal), where truck gardening is a primary enterprise. The Indian name means "floaters road" and is a concrete reminder of old logging days when supplementary local raftsmen were required to get the timber over the rapids which obstructed Rivière-des-Prairies. At Pierrefonds, an elegant suburb spreading along the river, a bridge is taken which leads to Île Bizard.

Circled by a narrow, winding road which lends itself to gentle, leisurely driving, the island is linked by ferry to Laval-sur-le-Lac. Stone houses and prosperous farmlands indicate the area's productive agricultural pursuits, while marinas, golf courses, picnic, and camping areas reveal its recreational features. The panorama of lac des Deux-Montagnes with its sharply rising mountains is a natural and endless expression of beauty.

Returning to Pierrefonds, continue west on Gouin Boulevard. A lovely road, lined with trees, gives way to elegant farming estates and leads to l'Anseà-l'Orme (Pierrefonds), where Rivière des Prairies opens the way to lac des Deux-Montagnes.

The tour has now reached the western point of the Island of Montréal. A tablet on a cairn commemorates the battle of lac des Deux-Montagnes, 1689, in which French forces under du Luth and d'Ailleboust Dumontet defeated the Iroquois. Communities and vast estates spread out from Senneville.

From this point, the new route to take after leaving Gouin Boulevard will be found in streets named after the localities they cross. Sainte-Anne-de-Bellevue is situated on one of the narrow straits connecting lac des Deux-Montagnes and lac Saint-Louis. Because of its location, the town played a major role in the development of the fur trade. Some of the leaders in the business took up residence in Sainte-Anne so they could catch an early glimpse of canoe flotillas coming down the Outaouais from the northwest. The Simon Fraser House, dated 1798, is a major attraction. MacDonald College School of Agriculture, affiliated with McGill University, features the splendid Morgan Arboretum with its hundreds of species of native and foreign trees. The Blacksmith Shop Museum is a genuine reproduction of a blacksmith and carpenter's shop of the early 19th century. A good stretch of ecology trails invites walkers.

Île Perrot, close by, attracts interest. Named after a French officer and early governor of Montréal, it was later bought by Charles Le-Moyne. It also served as a stage for the fur trade and acquired a dubious reputation as a smugglers' nest. An old mill stands at its southeast point.

At Sainte-Anne-de-Bellevue the road turns east and skirts lac Saint-Louis. Beautiful marinas serve the communities of Baie d'Urfé, Beaconsfield, and Pointe-Claire as well as Dorval where one of Montréal's two international airports is located. The next two localities are Lachine and La Salle. Lachine was the scene of the worst Indian raid ever suffered by the French when, in 1689, some 1,400 Iroquois warriors converged upon Lachine, killing 200 settlers and capturing another 100. Lachine is the western terminus of the first canal along the Saint-Laurent and of the present Montreal Water Works canal. Close to Saint-Joseph Boulevard, which turns on to a magnificent park along the lakeshore, is Manoir Lachine, 100 chemin La Salle, an old residence converted into a museum. At 9675 La Salle Boulevard stands a stone mill dating back to 1816. (Not open to visits.) In Verdun, the last city before Montréal, the road passes through a park. Here La Salle Boulevard runs into Wellington Street, which takes you downtown to Montréal.

Other Points of Interest in Montréal

Molson Brewery, founded in 1786, is Canada's oldest operating brewery. The original vaults still remain but are closed to visitors. Industrial tours can be arranged on request. The brewery is located at 1535 rue Notre-Dame East.

Mary Queen of the World Basilica, a smaller version of St. Peter's in Rome, was built in 1870–1894. The church is the heart of the Montreal Roman Catholic Archdiocese.

Grand Seminaire is located on Sherbrooke Street West on the exact spot where the Messieurs de Saint-Sulpice had constructed a fort to protect the early settlement from the Iroquois. Two of the original four towers are still standing and may be listed among the city's oldest structures.

The Monument to Patriots, commemorating the fort used by the rebels of 1837, is located at Pied-du-Courant under the Jacques Cartier Bridge at the corner of Notre-Dame and de Lorimier Streets. Maison Saint-Gabriel, the oldest house standing in Montréal, dates to 1685 when it was built by Marguerite Bourgeois upon the foundations of an even older structure (1668). Used as a school, the building has now been completely restored and is accessible to the public.

The Immigrant Rock, located at the foot of Victoria Bridge, is dedicated to the memory of the Irish who died of typhoid fever in 1847–48.

Along the Banks of the St. Lawrence

Montréal is filled with resources, varied and rich, which will astound even the most sophisticated traveler. Its many landmarks, planned for cultural as well as pragmatic reasons, share a quality of originality, typical of the thinking of its people. Here is a tour which should take most of the day on a comfortable schedule.

Leaving midtown, on St. James Street, the first stop is No. 1000, the Dow Planetarium, at the corner of Peel Street. Under this giant dome, the Theatre of the Stars presents a spectacle of cosmic dimensions: astronomy, meteorology, and space-age programs.

Head down Notre-Dame Street East as far as University and the Bonaventure Expressway. On the east side of the road are Cité du Havre, the Museum of Contemporary Art, the International Centre of Television and Habitat 67. Habitat was constructed for Expo '67 and serves as a housing complex. This unusual construction of block-assembled apartments is unmistakable. Here, during the summer months, the Concorde Bridge takes visitors to the islands of Sainte-Hélène and Notre-Dame. Well worth the extra time is a view of the St. Lambert Lock of the St. Lawrence Seaway, accessible from Cité du Havre, the Bonaventure Expressway, Wellington and Bridge Streets, and the Victoria Bridge. Actually the forerunner of all bridge structures in Montréal, it was inaugurated in 1859 to cater to railway travel. A modern drawbridge, it is raised regularly to allow large ships to pass.

The St. Lawrence Seaway is a network of navigable waters, totaling some 2,300 miles of water on the river and five vast lakes, and providing access to ocean-going vessels right to the heart of the continent. It has been of great benefit to the economy of North America. At the head of the seaway, the water level is about 600 feet (183 metres) higher than at sea level. Three Québec locks, the St. Lambert, Côte Sainte-Catherine, and Beauharnois, allow a gradual rise for ocean-going vessels. From the lower level, the ships sail through the open gates into the lock. The vessels then secure themselves to the bollards on the side of the lock and the gates are closed. Valves are opened and the water is allowed to enter and raise the ships. When the vessels reach the upper level, the gates are opened again and the ships sail out.

Leaving the St. Lambert Lock, head east via Highway 20 towards the Jacques Cartier Bridge, a 1934 structure. Longueuil, a seigniory granted in 1657 to Charles Le Moyne, is worthy of a visit. Historic monuments of particular interest include: Charles Le Moyne Museum, Ateliers du Vieux Longueuil, and Labelle and des Oeuvres houses.

Man and His World: A New Concept

Man and His World is one of the most fascinating features of Montréal. Spread over three islands in the St. Lawrence River between Montréal and the south shore, it traces its birth to Expo '67, the international exhibition which marked Canada's 100th birthday as a Confederation. Since 1968, Man and His World has been receiving millions of visitors, on the exhibition grounds on Sainte-Hélène Island and Notre-Dame Island and its amusement park, La Ronde.

Beginning in 1982, Man and His World has been undergoing a major renewal operation. Under the new concept, the focal point will be Notre-Dame Island, the largest of the three islands. Beautifully landscaped and laced with canals and bridges, it features Regatta Lake and impressive pavillions such as the former France and Québec pavillions. There are also huge green spaces and picnic grounds. New developments include the Grand Prix auto track and 98-acre Floral Park, an inheritance of the 1980 International Floralies.

Notre-Dame Island offers free entrance, with access via the Sainte-Hélène Island Métro or over the Concorde Bridge from Montréal by car. Roving musicians, dancers, singers, and clowns accent the joyful spirit here. You'll also find concerts, summer theater and movie houses, not to mention sport competitions and leisure activities such as bicycling, sailing, picnics, popular dances, fireworks. Cafés, terraces, and restaurants will be in operation at all major points. Two of the most popular pavillions are the Children's Garden from Czechoslovakia and the Pioneer Village, transferred from Sainte-Hélène Island to Notre-Dame. All attractions are reasonably priced for the family.

As for Sainte-Hélène Island, although its pavilions will be closed this year, it will continue to offer such features as the Old Fort and Museum, the Hélène de Champlain restaurant, and the La Poudrière Theatre.

For an evening of fun and excitement, visit La Ronde's amusement park. An entrance fee is charged and there are other fees for its numerous attractions.

Country City: Île Jésus

Île Jésus, second largest island in the Hochelaga archipelago, lies north of Montréal Island. It is 20 miles long and 7 miles across at its widest point. Its most remarkable characteristic has been a rapid transition from quiet country to sleek suburb. It is indeed strange that, despite its proximity to Montréal, no mention of Île Jésus appears in historical records until 1675, when Québec's first bishop traded it for Île d'Orléans. Until a generation ago, except for some still-active quarries, the island was wholly devoted to farming—field crops, truck gardening, and dairy cattle. Today, all its little villages and towns have been amalgated into the City of Laval.

The first communities encountered, east of the highway, are largely suburban. Saint-Vincent-de-Paul has a character all its own, due to the presence (for more than a century) of a large walled penitentiary with extensive farms and watchtowers. The center of the village is on a bluff overlooking Rivière des Prairies and affords a spectacular view of Montréal. A number of stately old homes have been maintained in beautiful condition. From here the road continues east through farming area, then turns sharply north across the island's tip and doubles back toward Saint-François-de-Sales, the oldest center on Île Jésus, where many stone homes and farmhouses captivate lovers of antiquity.

Terrebonne, across Rivière des Mille-Îles, is well worth a side trip. In the late 18th and early 19th centuries, Terrebonne was a major contributor to the fur trade. Already a successful agricultural center, it quickly became a storage center for canoes laden with furs from the northeast; in its warehouses, furs were stored prior to their shipment abroad; its mill produced flour and its bakery the "sailor's biscuits" which hardy canoemen carried on their long journeys across half the continent. Many houses dating back to these early days are still serving as residences.

Continuing to Laval, it becomes evident how Rivière des Mille-Îles got its name. The area is dotted with islands, some only a few feet long, most of them wooded and all of them enhancing the landscape. Fertile farming estates stretch from the rural center of Sainte-Rose to the western extremity of the island. At Laval-West, Highway 148 leads to a pleasant excursion to Saint-Eustache. Saint-Eustache Church is highly recommended if only for the parish façade which was scarred by British artillery during the 1837 uprising. Chénier, a leading patriot at the time, died here and his home has been preserved. Highway 148 to Hull and Ottawa and Highway 344 to Oka intersect at Saint-Eustache.

From Laval-West, the route continues to the opulent suburb of Laval-sur-le-Lac, with its stunning view over the Lake of Two Mountains, then turns sharply east, again following Rivière des Prairies. When the river is free of ice, a small ferry boat carries passengers and cars from Laval-sur-le-Lac to Île Bizard. The last lap around Île Jésus traverses luxuriant garden areas, past rapids that gained fame when the great log rafts were on their way from the upper Outaouais toward Sillery Coves near Québec City.

Around the Lake of Two Mountains

The Lake of Two Mountains, or lac des Deux Montagnes, is a surprise-filled excursion. A marvelous area for aquatic sports, the Lake of Two Mountains is put to good use in the warm months. Shaped something like a boomerang, with its banks flanked by mountains rising from the level plain, the lake is alive with pleasure craft today, no longer recalling the highway it offered fur traders, raftsmen, and river steamers in bygone times.

Highway 20 leaves central Montréal, transects Île Perrot from Sainte-Anne-de-Bellevue, and reaches Dorion. Dorion is the first mainland town to be reached from Montréal in this direction. Vaudreuil is a twin to Dorion. Access is gained via rue des Bois-Verts, which separates the two cities. The Vaudreuil Historic Museum, founded in 1857, is one of Québec's finest regional museums. A small road leads to Rigaud. Here you may visit the famed Rigaud Sanctuary, dedicated in 1950 to Our Lady of Lourdes. In summer months, the Sanctuary offers, in its rare natural beauty, an impressive Sound-and-Light presentation, the only one of its kind in Canada, commemorating the apparition of the Virgin Mary to Bernadette Soubirous in Lourdes, France, in 1888. There you can also visit Devil's Field, where a farmer once tended his field on a Sunday and his crop of potatoes was turned into stone—or so the legend goes. Farther on, another secondary road leads to Pointe-Fortune near the Ontario border. A ferry crosses to Carillon just below the immense power dam confining the waters of the Outaouais.

Carillon has a fine local museum, built in 1829 by General Forbes. A huge monument is located here in honour of Dollard des Ormeaux who, with a company of 16, succeeded in holding off an Iroquois attack at Long-Sault, now Sault Sainte-Marie. Highway 344 passes by Saint-André-Est, the site of the first paper mill in Canada. The highway swings east of the lake and meets Saint-Placide, smartly dotted with picturesque stone dwellings. A secondary road leads to Belle-Rivière, one of the few French-Protestant communities in the province, then continues on to Mirabel, where the Mirabel International Airport of Montréal is located. A little more than 20 miles from midtown Montréal, Mirabel has the largest airport surface in the world. It receives international flights as well as border and national transfers.

Continuing on Highway 344, you arrive at Oka, known the world over for the Trappist monastery located here and for the gourmet cheese formerly produced by the monks. Also located here are the Seven Chapels of Stone (1740), which form a mountainside Way of the Cross. After continuing on through Saint-Eustache again, Highway 344 joins up with Highway 148 back to Montréal through Île Jésus and Cartierville.

PRACTICAL INFORMATION FOR MONTRÉAL

HOW TO GET THERE. By air: One of the 10 busiest airports in North America, Montréal has flights arriving at Dorval Airport and Mirabel from all over the world. Private aircraft may land at many smaller fields including St. Hubert and Cartierville. Check with Transport Canada or the Montreal Flying Club (514) 861–5878.

By rail: From Western Canada via either *Via Rail* or *Canadian Pacific Railways*. From the U.S. east coast, *Amtrak* trains depart once daily from Grand Central Station, New York City, arriving at Windsor Station, and once daily from Pennsylvania Station, New York City, arriving at Central Station. Call (800) 361-6142 (toll free).

By boat: Montréal, an island, has a vast number of areas for docking, storing, and repairing boats. From the U.S., you can reach Montréal via the Richelieu River, Lake Saint-François and the Beauharnois Canal or, from the west, via the Ottawa River, the Lake of Two Mountains and Lake St. Louis. There is also the St. Lawrence River from Québec.

By car: From Toronto, make either the 401 connection to No. 20 in Québec or, from the Ottawa area, drive via No. 417 or 17 connecting to No. 40 in Québec. From the eastern U.S. coast take I-87 to No. 15 at the Québec border. From Québec City take the high-speed No. 40 autoroute on the north side of the St. Lawrence. On the south side of the river, take No. 20. From Sherbrooke, Québec take the new Eastern Townships Autoroute No. 10.

The speed limit on highways is 100 kmh (70 mph).

By bus: Full *Greyhound* and *Voyageur* service. Call (514) 842-2281.

ACCOMMODATIONS. The price categories are based on double occupancy, as follows: *Deluxe,* $90 or more; *Expensive,* $75-90, *Moderate,* $60-75, *Inexpensive,* $60 and under. CN = Canadian National Hotel; CP = Canadian Pacific Hotel.

Most places accept the following major credit cards: American Express, MasterCard, and Visa; others may also be honored. Not all establishments accept credit cards, therefore we suggest you call for information.

Deluxe

Hotel Bonaventure (Hilton). Place Bonaventure, just east of Château Champlain and just south of the Queen Elizabeth 878-2332. This excellent, comfortable hotel has some of the finest convention facilities in Canada. 395 rooms; parking, sauna, outdoor heated pool, indoor pool, and a unique layout. Upon entering the building you must take an elevator to the lobby; however, a costumed doorman is always available. Fine restaurants; cheerful staff. Major credit cards.

Château Champlain (CP). Place du Canada 878-1688. 612 rooms, parking. A beautiful hotel with several of Montréal's best restaurants. Has many services —drugstores, clothing stores, flowershop, art, theaters, newsstand; great 360° view from top floor. Possibly the best hotel in Montréal. Major credit cards.

Hotel du Parc. 3625 Avenue du Parc 288-6666. 500 rooms, located in La Cité complex next to Mount Royal Park, about 10 minutes from center of Montréal. Excellent *Puzzles* restaurant, easy access to complex of boutiques, shops, and whatever above and below ground. Indoor and outdoor pools, tennis, squash and handball courts, saunas, whirlpools, exercise rooms. Major credit cards.

Holiday Inns. There are eight locations offering moderate to deluxe accommodations: **Downtown.** *Deluxe.* 420 Sherbrooke W. 842-6111. 489 rooms, parking, indoor pool, sauna. **The Châteaubriand.** *Moderate.* 6500 Côte-de-Liesse 342-2262. 278 rooms. **The Seigneurie.** *Moderate.* 7300 Côte-de-Liesse. 731-7751. 199 rooms. **The Place Dupuis.** *Expensive.* Downtown at 1415 St-Hubert St. 842-4881. 359 rooms. **The Pointe-Claire.** *Moderate.* 6700 Trans-Canada Hwy. 697-7110. 312 rooms. **The Seville.** *Moderate.* 4545 Côte Vertu W. 332-2720. 93 rooms. **The Richelieu.** *Expensive.* 505 Sherbrooke E. 842-8581. 330 rooms, free parking, sauna. **The Longueuil.** *Moderate.* 50 de Serigny St. 670-3030. All major credit cards accepted at all Inns.

Hôtel de la Montagne. 1430 de la Montagne (288-5656). 140 rooms, color TV, 24-hour room service. The newest addition to the downtown scene. Features a fine restaurant, *Le Lutetia.* All major credit cards.

Méridien. Desjardins Center. 285–1450. 616 rooms. Lavishly decorated, comfortable. Two pools. Situated in a lively enclosed complex of boutiques, restaurants, promenades, and offices. Excellent restaurant *La Rôtisserie*. Major credit cards.

Le Quatre-Saisons. 1050 Sherbrooke W. 248–1110. 320 rooms, excellent restaurant *Pierre de Coubertin*. Beautiful decoration. All major credit cards.

The Queen Elizabeth Hotel (CN). 900 Dorchester W. 861–3511. 1,167 rooms, parking, sauna. In the heart of downtown Montréal; connected to the underground system of stores and the subway. Many fine restaurants including *Altitude 737* and the famous *Beaver Club*. All major credit cards.

Ritz Carlton Hotel. 1228 Sherbrooke St. W. 842–4212. 249 rooms, parking, sauna. Beautiful décor; very good reputation. Truly fine hotel in the heart of Montréal's shopping district. All major credit cards.

Expensive

Centre Sheraton Montréal. 1201 Dorchester W. 878–2000. 832 rooms. Major credit cards.

Hyatt Regency. 777 University St. 879–1370. 768 rooms, parking, revolving restaurant on top appropriately named *Le Tour de Ville*. Hosts famous *Chez Régine* club. All major credit cards.

Maritime TraveLodge. 1155 Guy St. 932–1411. 222 rooms, free parking, indoor pool, sauna. All major credit cards.

Montréal Airport Hilton. 631–2411. 500 rooms. Situated within walking distance of Dorval International Airport. Good staff; French restaurant. All major credit cards.

Ruby Foo's Hotel. 7655 Décarie 731–7701. Minutes from downtown by expressway. 118 rooms. Well-established restaurant. All major credit cards.

Mount Royal. 1455 Peel 842–7777. 1,050 rooms, parking, sauna, huge lobby. This hotel, just north of St. Catherine St., is located in the shopping and business district. Home of the *Kon Tiki* restaurant and the Montréal Press Club. All major credit cards.

Moderate

Château de l'Aéroport. (CP). Connected to Mirabel International Airport 476–1611. 361 rooms. Restaurant *Le Mirabel* featuring international cuisine. All major credit cards.

Château Versailles. 1659 Sherbrooke W. 933–3611. 79 rooms, free parking. All major credit cards.

Sheraton Saint-Laurent. 2405 Île Charron 651–6510. Longueuil, right across Montréal. 130 rooms. All major credit cards.

Wandlyn Motel. 7200 Sherbrooke E. 256–1613. 124 rooms, free parking, indoor pool, color TV in some rooms. All major credit cards.

Inexpensive

Le Sherbourg. 475 Sherbrooke W. 842-3961. Indoor pool, free parking. All major credit cards.

Le Herlion. 1240 Drummond St. 866–6482. 176 rooms, parking. All major credit cards.

Le Royal Roussillon. 1610 St. Hubert St. 849–3214. 107 rooms. All major credit cards.

Ramada Inns. There are four locations. **Downtown.** *Moderate.* 1005 Guy St. 866–4611. In the heart of all the Montréal excitement. 205 rooms, good service. **Décarie.** *Moderate.* 6445 Décarie. 739–2771. In the northwest section of Montréal, but minutes from downtown by connecting expressway. 104 rooms. **Olym-**

pic Park. *Moderate.* 550 Sherbrooke E. 256–9011. 240 rooms. **Aéroport.** *Moderate.* 342–2262. 220 rooms. All major credit cards accepted at all inns.

TELEPHONE AND EMERGENCY. The Montréal telephone area code is 514. In cases of **emergency:** dial "0" (zero) and say "THIS IS AN EMERGENCY." The operator will attempt to connect you with the appropriate number.

Montréal Urban Community (MUC) Police: (514) 934–2121; Québec Provincial Police (Sûreté du Québec): (514) 395–4141; Montréal Children's Hospital: (514) 937–8511.

HOW TO GET AROUND. By bus: *MUCTC,* the *Montréal Urban Community Transport Commission,* supplies bus service all over the island. The fare is 85¢ for a single passage; exact change required. You can also buy 14 tickets for $10. A new monthly pass ($25) has just been introduced, valid both on buses and subway.

Through *Autocar, Inc., Transports Canada* has introduced bus service between Mirabel and Dorval Airports. Adults $9, children $4.50. From Dorval to Montréal (terminus at Lagauchetiere St., behind Central Station), $5. Also available is *Laval Transit* from Mirabel to Henri Bourassa Métro Station from 5:40 A.M. to 10:40 P.M. for $5.

By métro: Montréal's superlative subway takes transfers from buses and covers the main downtown core. The cost is the same as for the bus; use change or tickets. West and Northwest sections are rapidly expanding, with two new stations opening up recently.

By taxi: Minimum fare is $1.20 plus 70¢ a km. From Dorval Airport to downtown, $15. From Mirabel Airport, $35. Between Dorval and Mirabel Airports, $25.

By calèche. Horse-pulled carriage—available at Dominion Square downtown or at Beaver Lake atop Mount Royal.

TOURIST INFORMATION SERVICES. The Convention and Tourist Bureau of Greater Montréal will be helpful on all information requests regarding Montréal. Their offices are at Place Bonaventure (514) 871–1129.

For the rest of Québec, contact the Montréal reception center of Tourisme-Québec, 2 Place Ville-Marie, or write to Ministère de l'Industrie, du Commerce et du Tourisme (MICT), Place Ville-Marie, 24th floor (Room 2433) (514) 873–2308.

LOCAL TIME AND BUSINESS HOURS. Québec is in Eastern Standard Time.

Banks are generally open from 10 A.M. to 4 P.M., with some branches opening up to 7 P.M. on Friday. Closed Saturday and Sunday. You can count on government and municipal offices, as well as banks, to be closed on holidays.

SPECIAL INTEREST SIGHTSEEING. Group tours of the *CBC* studios (Radio-Canada), 1400 Dorchester Blvd. E., are available Monday through Friday. Reservations required (285–2690).

The *Montréal Stock Exchange,* 800 Place Victoria (871–2453). Exchanges on the floor visible from the visitors' balcony from 10 A.M. to 4 P.M., Monday through Friday. Free admission. Also guided tours for groups of from 20 to 60 (cost: $1.50 per person) by reservation (871–2430).

The *Postal House* (Maison de la Poste), 640 Ste.-Catherine W. Guided tours on the Canadian postal system, with stamps exhibits, Monday to Friday, by reservation only (283–4185). Free admission.

GARDENS. The *Botanical Garden,* 4101 Sherbrooke St. E. (872–3455), every day from 9 A.M. to 6 P.M. Adults $2, children $1. The third largest botanical garden in the world (after Berlin and London) is noted for its cactus and begonia collections. There are also rock, shrub, and aquatic gardens, with some 15,000 species from around the world.

 CHILDREN'S ACTIVITIES: Young people are easily occupied in Montréal with its swimming pools, parks, amusement parks, and calèche rides through downtown or atop Mount Royal. Most of the permanent exhibitions and tours mentioned earlier will also interest them. But of special appeal are:

Dow Planetarium, 1000 St.-Jacques St. (872–4530), featuring shows in French and English on the Universe. Every day from 1 P.M. to 7:30 P.M. Closed on Monday. Regular shows: adults $2.50; children under 13 $1.25. Special Monday feature: The Sky Over Montréal.

Lafontaine Park, bordering Sherbrooke St. E., with its picnic and amusement grounds, the Garden of Wonders, the Children's Zoo, and boat rides in gondolas. Free.

La Ronde, Montréal's favorite amusement park in summer, on one of the three St. Lawrence Islands which were host to Expo '67. From June 1 weekends only; from June 14 to September 3, every night till 2 A.M. One-day super-visas, access to all entertainments, adults $13, children $8, one-day visas, entry only, $4 adults, children free.

The *Montréal Aquarium* at the Alcan Pavilion on Sainte-Hélène Island (872–4656). Kids' favorites: the shark tank and the penguin pool, especially at feeding times. Open every day from 10 A.M. to 5 P.M. Adults $2.00, children and senior citizens $1.00.

Angrignon Park, 3400 boulevard des Trinitaires (872–2815), open every day from 10 A.M. to 6 P.M. In a Mother Goose décor it harbors the zoo animals and features marine circus presentations during the day, along with winter activities as skating and sliding. Free admission.

 PARTICIPANT SPORTS. Winter sports. There are many and excellent opportunities for winter sports: *skiing* (downhill and cross-country), *snowshoeing* and *snowmobiling,* in the many parks, reserves, and resort areas of Québec. These are described in more detail in the sports section of *Practical Information for the Rest of Québec* at the end of this chapter.

In Montréal itself, the Mount Royal offers skiing facilities for all the family on its gentler slopes around Beaver Lake, some with lifts. There is also skating on the lake itself.

Summer Sports. The Village Golf Club (872–4199), bordering the Botanical Garden on Sherbrooke St. E., offers a 9-hole course of challenging caliber. There are over 40 other first-rate *golf* clubs in the Montréal metropolitan area, and in most cases reservations can be made by phone from Montréal (consult the phone book under the listing *Club de golf*).

Throughout the city, there are *swimming* pools operated by the Municipal Parks Service (872–3455) as well as *tennis* in 10 different parks (reservations individually made at each park, telephone numbers in the phone book under the listing: *Montréal, City of*). *Water skiing, sailing, boating,* and *fishing* are also within easy reach. The marine facilities at Terre des Hommes are open to the yachting fraternity, and *equestrians* are welcome at stables scattered about the island. One of the best is at the top of Mount Royal.

SPECTATOR SPORTS. Team sports. Each winter, Montréal's Forum welcomes enthusiastic hockey fans supporting the home team, the *Montréal Canadiens,* or its rival from Québec City, the *Nordiques.*

In the fall, professional football is played by the Montréal *Concordes,* member of the Canadian Football League, who occasionally reach the Grey Cup finals. Baseball fans root for their home team, the Montréal *Expos.* Soccer is picking up wide popularity with Montréal's club, the *Manic,* becoming the idol. All three sports use the gigantic, 70,000-seat Olympic Stadium in the Olympic Park (direct access to subway), in the eastern part of the city.

Racing. Harness racing is a perennial favorite among Canadian sports fans. Montréal's outstanding track, Blue Bonnets, is on Decarie Blvd. (739–2741).

The latest addition to the Montréal sport scene is auto racing. On a brand-new, international caliber track of 4.6 km (2¾ miles) on Notre-Dame Island, it now offers an annual Grand Prix during the second week of June, which attracts some 75,000 spectators.

MUSEUMS AND SITES. There are numerous museums, galleries and historic sites in Montréal. The following are among the most outstanding. The *Montreal Museum of Fine Arts,* 3400 Ave. du Musée (corner of Sherbrooke St.; 285–1600). European and Canadian masters and furniture, ancient Greek, Egyptian and Oriental art. Open Tuesday to Sunday, 11 A.M. to 5 P.M. Admission: adults $2.00; students 75¢.

The *Museum of Contemporary Art* (Musée d'art contemporain), at the Cité du Havre (873–2878). Features international and Québec artists in rotating exhibitions highlighting the best in modern art. Open Tuesday to Sunday from 10 A.M. to 6 P.M. Free admission.

The *Montreal Museum of Decorative Arts* (formerly Château Dufresne), corner of Sherbrooke St. E. and Pie IX Blvd., right across the Botanical Garden (259–2575). Features a permanent exhibition of decorative arts and special exhibits. Open Thursday to Sunday, noon to 5 P.M. Admission: adults $1.00; students and senior citizens 50¢; accompanied children free.

The *Musée d'art de Saint-Laurent,* 615 Ste.-Croix Blvd. (747–7367). Permanent and special exhibits. Group-guided tours on request. Free admission.

The *McCord Museum,* 690 Sherbrooke St. W. (392–4778). Unique collection of photographs of Montréal's life. Open Friday, Saturday, and Sunday, 11 A.M. to 6 P.M. Free admission.

The *Royal Canadian Mounted Police Museum,* 6560 Hochelaga St. (255–8811). Features military exhibits. Open Monday to Friday, 9 A.M. to 3 P.M. Free admission.

The *Saidye Bronfman Centre,* 5170 Côte Ste.-Catherine Rd. (739–2301). Permanent and special exhibits. Open from Sunday to Thursday, 9 A.M. to 9 P.M., and from 9 A.M. to 3 P.M. on Friday. Free admission.

The *Sir George Williams' Art Gallery*, Concordia University, 1455 de Maisonneuve Blvd. (879–5917). Permanent and special exhibits. Open 11 A.M. to 9 P.M., Monday to Friday; 11 A.M. to 5 P.M., Saturday; closed Sunday. Free admission.

The *Montréal Military and Wartime Museum*, in the Old Fort on Sainte-Hélène Island (861–6738). Over 20,000 items from Colonial times; military drills and parades in summer. Open every day, from May to October, 10 A.M. to 5 P.M.; closed on Monday from October to May. Admission free from September 7 to May 1. From May 1 to September 6, adults $1.50, children $1.00.

The *Canadian Rail Museum* (Musée ferroviaire canadien), 122A, rue Saint-Pierre, in Saint-Constant (632–2410). More than a hundred pieces of rail engines and cars. Open from May to September every day, 10 A.M. to 5 P.M.; Saturday and Sunday till October, 10 A.M. to 6 P.M. Admission: adults $3.00; students, $1.50 and $2.00, depending on age.

The *Canadian Historical Museum* (Wax Museum), 3715 Queen Mary Rd. (738–5959). Intriguing exhibits highlighting historic and religious themes. Open every day from 9 A.M. to 5 P.M. Admission: $4.50 adults; children under 12 $1.75; students $2.50.

The *Bank of Montréal Museum*, 129 Saint-Jacques St., Place d'Armes (877–6892). Every day, Monday to Friday, 10 A.M. to 4 P.M. Free admission.

The *Calvet House* (Maison du Calvet), 401 Bonsecours St. in Old Montréal (845–4596). Old Québec furniture. Open from Tuesday to Saturday from 10 A.M. to 4 P.M.; on Sunday, from noon to 4:45 P.M. Free admission.

The *Notre-Dame Church and Museum*, on Place d'Armes (949–1070). Open every day from 6 A.M. to 6 P.M. Free admission.

The *Château Ramezay*, 280 Notre-Dame E. (861–3708). Ethnographic museum; open every day, except on Monday, from 10 A.M. to 4:30 P.M. Admission: adults $1.00; children 50¢.

The *Museum of Hunting and Nature*, 1260 Remembrance Rd., in a century-old farmhouse, on top of Mount Royal (872–3455). Features rotating exhibits every month of the year. Open every day from 10 A.M. to 8 P.M. Free admission.

The *St. Joseph's Oratory Museum*, 3800 Queen Mary Rd. (733–8211), featuring mostly religious art. Open every day from 10 A.M. to 5 P.M. Admission: adults 50¢; children 25¢.

The *Vaudreuil-Soulanges Regional Museum*, 431 Roche Blvd. in Longueuil (455–2092), featuring Canadiana and historical exhibitions. Admission: adults $1.50; children 50¢.

The *André-Benjamin Papineau House*, 5475 Saint-Martin Blvd. W. in Laval (north of Montréal). Contemporary art exhibitions. Open every day from 1 P.M. to 9 P.M. Reservations for group visits: 681–6323. Free admission.

The *Electricity Historical Museum*, 440 Chambly Rd. in Longueuil, on the south shore (677–5733). From Tuesday to Friday, 10 A.M. to 5 P.M. (closed from noon to 1 P.M.). Admission: adults $1.00; children 50¢. Reservation required for groups and guided tours.

The *Montréal Holocaust Memorial Centre of Allied Jewish Community Services*, 5151 Côte Ste.-Catherine Rd. Historical exhibits and audiovisual presentations on World War II. Open Sunday from 11 A.M. to 4 P.M., and Tuesday to Thursday from 1 P.M. to 4 P.M. Reservations for group visits: 735–3541, local 221.

THE PERFORMING ARTS. A focal point of cultural life in Montréal is the **Place des Arts** (842–2112), with its three halls for concerts, ballet, theater, opera and other entertainment of the highest caliber. The largest of the three halls, *Salle Wilfrid-Pelletier* (3,000 seats), named after the famous former conductor of the New York Metropolitan Opera orchestra, is the home of the Montreal Symphony Orchestra and the Montréal Opera Company. Although a relative newcomer (1953), this orchestra has made its mark on the world of fine music. Its tremendous success continues under the direction of present conductor, Charles Dutoit. The Orchestra presents concerts on Tuesdays and Wednesdays (ticket prices from $8.50 to $25), with a popular series on Sunday afternoons (tickets from $4 to $6). The 1,300-seat *Maisonneuve Theatre* features chamber music, plays and variety shows. The smallest hall, the *Port-Royal Theatre* (823 seats), houses the Jean Duceppe Company, one of Quebec's best-known drama groups.

There are numerous performing theater groups in the Montréal region. Among them:

The 440-seat *Centaur Theatre*, 453 St.-François-Xavier in Old Montreal (288–3161), plays in English only, from October to June.

The *National Theatre School of Canada*, 5030 St-Denis St. (842–7954), offers plays in French and in English at the Monument National, 1182 Saint-Laurent Blvd. (861–4638).

The *Children's Theatre*, in existence for over 40 years, offers plays by children from October to May at the Victoria Hall, in Westmount, 4626 Sherbrooke St. West (935–8531).

The 300-seat *Saidye Bronfman Centre*, at 5170 Chemin de la Côte Ste-Catherine (739–7944), is sponsored by the Jewish Community and offers both English-language and Yiddish plays.

For amateurs of French plays, there are:

the *Théâtre d'Aujourd'hui*, at 1297 Papineau St. (523–1211);

the *Théâtre du Nouveau-Monde* (TNM), 84 Ste-Catherine St. West (861–0563);

the *Rideau Vert*, 4664 St-Denis St. (844–1793);

the *Théâtre Denise-Pelletier*, 4353 Ste-Catherine St. East (253–8974);

the *Théâtre de Quat'Sous*, 100 Pine St. East (845–7277);

the *Théâtre Populaire du Québec*, 5015 Boyer St. (849–2285);

the *Salle Fred Barry*, 4353 Ste-Catherine St. East (522–7012);

the *La Poudrière Theatre*, on Sainte-Hélène Island, (861–0938).

The two large newspapers, *The Gazette* (English) and *La Presse* (French), give detailed information on what is going on in Montréal in their weekend editions.

SHOPPING. Shopping is great along Ste.-Catherine St., mainly between Phillipps Sq. and Guy St., with large department stores featuring up-to-date imports from France and England. There are also countless boutiques, with goods and prices to suit all tastes and means, in the Underground City. The Viaduc, in Place Bonaventure, has over 60 stores. Most will accept major credit cards, particularly American Express and Visa.

Most stores are open from 9:30 or 10 A.M. to 6 P.M., Monday to Wednesday, and up to 9 P.M. on Thursday and Friday. Closing time on Saturday is 5 P.M.

DINING OUT. There are over 3,000 restaurants in Montréal and most of them serve very good food. Choices are hard to make, Price ranges per person, which do not include wine, sales taxes or gratuities, are as follows: *Deluxe,* over $30; *Expensive,* $20–$30; *Moderate,* $10–$20; *Inexpensive,* less than $10.

Most places accept the following major credit cards: American Express, MasterCard, and Visa; others may also be honored. Not all establishments accept credit cards, therefore we suggest you call for information.

Hotel Restaurants

Over the past several years, the major hotels have developed restaurants of excellent quality which, in inclement weather, is to be appreciated. But any time of the year the visitor will find in their lavish décors, the distinctive food for which Montréal is famous. All accept major credit cards.

Deluxe

Café de Paris. At the Ritz-Carlton Hotel, 1228 Sherbrooke St. W. 842–4212. Food and service strictly classical.

Le Castillon. At the Bonaventure Hotel, Place Bonaventure. 878–2332. Beautiful setting at top of the hotel.

Le Neufchâtel and **Le Tournebroche.** Both at the Château Champlain Hotel, Place du Canada. 878–1688. *Le Neufchâtel* is considered one of the top five French restaurants in Montréal and *Le Tournebroche* (ground level) offers fresh bread baked daily.

Pierre de Coubertin. At Le Quatre-Saisons Hotel, 1050 Sherbrooke St. W. 284–1110. Dancing Friday–Saturday nights.

Restaurant de France. At the Méridien Hotel on Ste.-Catherine St. (Desjardins Center). 285–1450. The former *La Rôtisserie.* Has kept all its charms.

Salle Bonaventure and **The Beaver Club.** Both at the Queen Elizabeth Hotel, 900 Dorchester Blvd. W. 861–3511. French and original menus in elegant surroundings.

Expensive

L'Escapade. A buffet restaurant on the top floor of the Château Champlain Hotel. 878–1688. Recently decorated. Splendid view of the city below.

Downtown

Deluxe

Festin du Gouverneur. Old Fort, Saint-Hélène Island. 879–1141. Beautiful setting; Canadian, but touristy (the 17th-century banquet bit).

Les Chenêts. 2075 Bishop St. 844–1842. Offers a choice of 60 cheeses and a wine list including some bottles at $6,000. Gastronomic dinner for two on reservation.

René Varaud. Les Terrasses, 705 Ste.-Catherine St. West. 843–8592. Listed by many as first in Montréal. Truly superb food, menus designed to season. Elegant decor.

Troika. 2171 Crescent St. 849–9333. Russian and French cuisine.

Expensive

Altitude 737. Place Ville Marie. 861–3511. Buffet with panoramic view of Montréal.

Angelo Il Cacciatore. 1184 Crescent St. 861–8791. Fine Italian food, unique wine list.

The Bluenose Inn. Place Ville Marie. 861–3511. French cooking and seafood.

Chez la Mère Michel. 1209 Guy St. 934–0473. A fine old establishment in an old house, with French cuisine from many French regions and a notable wine list.

Darwin's. 1187 Bishop St. 871–9808. A gazebo bar and restaurant featuring leisurely brunches in a leafy courtyard.

Jardin du Ritz. Ritz-Carlton Hotel. 842–4212. French. Summer months only.

La Chamade. 1453 Bélanger St. East. 747–7040. French, informal, and warm. Superb entrées.

Le Lutétia. In the Hôtel de la Montagne, 1430 rue de la Montagne, downtown. 288–5656. Brand-new, but already establishing a solid reputation, both for its food and its service.

Le Pickwick *(Chez Jean Cayer)*. 1414 Drummond. 849–4551. It is a small restaurant for *habitués,* on the second floor of a medical building. A reputation way over its size.

Le Vert Galant. 1425 Crescent St. 844–4155. French in exquisite setting.

Les Beaux Jeudis *(Thursday's)*. 1449 Crescent St. 849–5634. The "in" place for the jet-set.

Les Halles. 1450 Crescent St. 844–2328. Everything you would wish of a Paris restaurant, including the atmosphere. A bit crowded, though.

Moderate

Katsura. 2170 de la Montagne St. 849–1172. Japanese with all the style.

Kon-Tiki. Mount Royal Hotel. 842–7777. Polynesian.

L'Entrecôte Bordelaise. 1458-A Crescent St. 844–2620. Parisian-style bistro.

Le Paris. 1812 Ste.-Catherine St. W. 933–4898. French.

Old Montréal
Deluxe

Gibby's. 298 Place d'Youville. 282–1837. Seafood and steaks in an historic setting.

Le Saint-Amable. 188 St.-Amable St., Place Jacques-Cartier. 861–4645. One of Montréal's top French establishments, in fine old house, loyal clientele. Classic dishes, including game specialties.

Expensive

Le Fadeau. 423 St.-Claude St. 878–3959. The chef is a master at "nouvelle cuisine," and on a 24-hour reservation will prepare a gastronomic dinner.

Les Filles du Roy. 415 Bonsecours. 849–3535. Features Québec cooking in traditional Québec décor.

Moderate

Auberge la Belle Poule. 406 St.-Sulpice St. 288–7770. French, Maritime décor.

Auberge Le Vieux St-Gabriel. 426 St.-Gabriel St. 878–3561. Continental. Old Canadian décor.

Delmo's. 211 Notre-Dame St. W. 849–4061. Mostly seafood in a 1900 décor. Excellent.

Le Muscadin. 100 St.-Paul St. W. 842–0588. Excellent Italian cuisine.

Le Navire. 429 St.-Vincent St. 866–8307. French, cozy, and warm, with accordion music.

Le Petit Havre. 443 St.-Vincent St. 861–0581. Tasty French food, diligent service.

Le Soleil d'Italie. 111 St.-Paul St. E. 861–4562. Classical Italian.

Intermediary Zone
Moderate

Auberge Chez Henri. 3715 Saint-Laurent Blvd. 849–9356. French.

Au Quinquet. 354 St.-Joseph Blvd. 272–4211. Typical Québec cuisine.

La Lucarne. 1030 Laurier St. W. 279–7355. French.

West End

Deluxe

Les Trois Arches. 11,131 Gouin Blvd., Pierrefonds. 683–8200. French food in a truly unique décor. Excellent service.

Le Vieux Saint-Charles. 3872 St.-Charles Road, Pierrefonds. French food in beautiful old Canadian house.

Expensive

Abacus. 4230 St.-Jean Blvd. 620–6333. Excellent Cantonese and Szechwan cuisine.

Lanterna Verde. 1560 Herron (Dorval). 631–6434. Continental and Italian specialties.

L'Habitant. 9656 Gouin Blvd., Pierrefonds. 684–4398. Old house. French.

North End

Expensive

Bill Wong's. 7965 Décarie Blvd. 731–8202. Chinese.

Peking Garden. 5339 Queen Mary Rd. 484-9139. Spicy and Szechwan cuisine is a specialty.

Moderate

Bellavista. 88 Montée Masson (Duvernay). 661–2544. Italian.

Bianca & Franco. 7143 St.-Dominique St. 274–1122. Italian.

La Tour de Pise (formerly *Magnani*). 9245 Lajeunesse St. 387–6438. Italian with a top reputation.

South End

Deluxe

Au Tournant de la Rivière. 5070 Salaberry St., Carignant (South Shore). 658–7372. Most exquisite "nouvelle cuisine" dishes. A little out of the way (inquire for directions), but worth it.

La Saulaie. 1161 Marie-Victorian Blvd., Boucherville. 655–0434. French. High class.

Les Trois Tilleuls. 290 Richelieu, St.-Marc. 584–2231. French.

Moderate

Auberge Handfield. St.-Marc-sur-le-Richelieu. 670–0284. Canadian.

Vieux Longueuil. 43 St.-Charles St. W. 670–0284. French.

Latin Quarter

The new setting of the Québec University Campus on St.-Denis St., just east of dividing St.-Laurent Blvd., has given birth to a new and lively Latin Quarter in Montréal. St.-Denis St. is its main artery, between Dorchester and Sherbrooke Sts. It features the Québec University buildings, of course, and a number of restaurants and small cafés, most of them in the inexpensive category.

Jardin St.-Denis. 1615 St.-Denis St. 288–2023. Offers dietetic cuisine as well as very delicate sauces, thanks to its Laotian chef.

La Picholette. 1020 St.-Denis St. 843–8502. One of the most elegant on the street.

La Sila. *Moderate.* 2040 St.-Denis St. 844–5083. Good Italian dishes.

Le Bercail. 1238 St.-Denis St. 288–4504. A long-time favorite.

Le Mazot. 1670 St.-Denis St. 844–7171. A Swiss restaurant which was one of the first favorites and has kept on.

Le Relais St.-Denis (formerly *Le Cévenol*). *Expensive.* 2035 St.-Denis St. 849–8802. It has kept items from its original menus such as wild boar and buffalo.

Le Saint-Mâlo. 1605 St.-Denis St. 845–6327. One of the original eating places on the street.

L'Express. 3927 St.-Denis St. 845-5333. New, Paris-style bistro crowded with chic regulars; excellent wine list.

In summertime, many of the restaurants and cafés along St.-Denis St. have terraces where you can eat while watching the people go by. And for a little bit of excitement, try *Le Vieux Munich,* on St.-Denis St., near the corner of Dorchester Blvd., for German cuisine, schnapps, and the contagious beat of Bavarian music. No reservations necessary.

Chinese Quarter

There are some 25 Chinese restaurants in Montréal. About half of them are in the tiny but picturesque Chinese Quarter, bordering Saint-Laurent St. just north of the Old Montréal section. With prices ranging from inexpensive to moderate, they feature Cantonese, Peking, and Szechwan cuisine. Cantonese, more subtle than the others, uses very light soya sauces. It used to be the main fare of Chinese cuisine in Montréal. Peking cuisine uses wheat instead of rice, is light and features a wide variety of sweet-and-sour dishes. As for the Szechwan, recently introduced, it is more heavily spiced than the other two and features well-seasoned dishes.

The Chinese Quarter is bordered on its west side by the new Montréal Convention Centre, opened in 1983. The restaurants are mainly found on Lagauchetière, Clark, Saint-Urbain, and Saint-Laurent Sts. Major credit cards accepted.

Hee Lum Mon. 1002 Saint-Urbain St. 871–1019. Cantonese.

Hu-Nan. 1092 Saint-Laurent Blvd. 866–8108. Hunan and Szechwan.

Jasmine. 62 Lagauchetière St. West. 861–4501. Cantonese. One of the oldest in this section.

Joy Inn. 1017 Saint-Laurent Blvd. 866–9744. Peking with a few specialties as fish lips . . . .

La Maison Kam-Fung. 1008 Clark St. 866–4016. Features a Cantonese brunch served at your table; 500 places . . . but come early!

Nanking. 50 Lagauchetière St. West. 866–4815. Cantonese and Peking. A favorite for 50 years.

New Lotus Café. 1050 Clark St. 866–8356. Cantonese.

Sun Sun. 1023 Clark St. 861–4851. Cantonese. Originally a Chinese restaurant for the Chinese. Imaginative cuisine.

Wong Kung. 1051 Saint-Laurent Blvd. 871–9282. Cantonese, with a daily menu of some 200 dishes.

NIGHT LIFE. Clubs have proliferated in recent years in Montréal. The main hotels all provide for some form of entertainment, be it full-size shows, cabarets, or discos. Among the notable ones:

The Caf'Conc'. At the Château Champlain, a Paris-style show in a Toulouse-Lautrec décor. 878–1688.

The Salle Bonaventure. At the Queen Elizabeth Hotel, 900 Dorchester St. Lavish shows. 861–3511.

Disco Constellation. At the Four-Seasons (Quatre-Saisons) Hotel, 1050 Sherbrooke St. W. 248–1110.

Most of the best clubs and bars are to be found in the downtown section around Ste.-Catherine St. and Crescent, Bishop, Drummond, and De la Montagne Sts. Nearly all bars feature a "happy hour," usually between 5 P.M. and 7 P.M., offering free hors d'oeuvres. Among the most popular:

Thursday's. 1449 Crescent St. 849–5635.
Déjà-Vu. 1224 Bishop. 866–0512.
L'Air du Temps. 191 St.-Paul, in Old Montreal. 842–2003.
The Rising Sun. 1251 St.-Antoine St. 875–6232 or 875–6227.
Woody's. 1238 Bishop St. 861–2016.
The Longest Yard. 1238 Bishop St. 866–4260.
The Cock'n Bull. 1944 Ste.-Catherine St. 933–4556.
Le Bijou. 300 Lemoyne St. in Old Montréal. 288–5508.
Troïka. 2175 Crescent St. Russian. 849–9333.
La Marie du Port. 408 St.-François-Xavier, in Old Montréal. 849–0937.
Winnie's. 1455 Crescent St. 288-0623.
Darwin's. 1187 Bishop St. 871-9808.

QUÉBEC CITY—Gibraltar of America

Québec, the cradle of French civilization in North America, resembles no other city in the world. Founded in 1608, it is a city steeped in history. "The place where the water narrows," Québec takes its name from the language of the Indians who once lived there. Now, the city's French character, its culture (96 percent of the population of 480,000 are French-speaking), and its lifestyle have made this capital an international tourist mecca.

A natural citadel, perched high above the majestic St. Lawrence River, Québec City, often called "the Gibraltar of America." It is the only walled city north of Mexico, and is really two cities in one. Its old part is nestled high upon a promontory within the walls, while its newer part stands outside the fortifications. Québec is also one of two hubs of travel within the province; Montréal, of course, is the other.

Québec is the starting point for delightful excursions into some of the province's most colorful and picturesque tourist regions: the Beaupré Coast, the Laurentians, La Beauce and the Lower St. Lawrence.

The rare natural assets of Québec have forged its destiny. Its geography is its most striking feature: it lies at the point where the St. Lawrence becomes an estuary, with broad deep waters accommodating the world's largest vessels. Upstream the river narrows and is relatively shallow. Northeast of Québec, mountains skirt the water while the rugged Laurentians veer west and the Appalachians south, leaving a wide flat area for agriculture.

A distinctive attribute of the city is its 8-mile-long ship-like plateau, atop solid rock, varying in width from a few hundred yards at its bow to three miles at its stern. Québec completely dominates the river. Its highest point is Cap Diamant, 360 feet above the St. Lawrence and site of the famed Citadel. This is a natural fortress commanding water access as far as the Great Lakes. At the base of the Québec City cliffs and at Lévis, half a mile directly across the river, is a continuous rock edge, constituting a vast natural berthing place.

Québec's Early History

In 1541, Cartier tried, without success, to establish a permanent settlement near Stadacona (now Québec City), at the site where suburban Cap-Rouge is situated. Toward the end of the century, France became interested in the fur trade and tried to develop it from the Gulf of the St. Lawrence. But this base proved too far from the rich pelt regions, and it became clear that an interior post was needed. When Champlain saw Québec in 1603, he envisioned its true potential for the fur trade, noting also that its cove afforded a safe landing for boats. In 1608, he founded Québec City. Twelve years later, he realized that this colony, with its back to the cliff, was vulnerable to attack from above. He built a fort at the top of the cliff on the eastern end of what today is Dufferin Terrace. In 1626, this fort was rebuilt and enlarged.

Slowly, Québec began to take permanent form: a lower town for fur trade and commerce, an upper town for administration, defense and, in its early years, market gardening. But it remained small as a colony —so small and defenseless that in 1629 it surrendered to a British fleet commanded by Admiral David Kirke without firing a shot. Three years later it was restored by treaty to France. Yet Québec's natural geographic advantages had already fired the imagination of the Western world.

From 1632 to 1688, France and England were at peace and the military problems of New France focused on the Iroquois Indians. Most of the Indian activity however, centered around Montréal. As a result, Québec was rarely threatened and the city continued to grow and expand as a commercial center for the mother country. Commercial activity was matched by religious enterprise. In Sillery, the Jesuit missionaries were frustrated in their attempts to attract nomadic Indians into permanent settlements. Their missionary works and explorations, however, spread across half the continent. In Upper Town, space was allowed for the construction of Hôtel-Dieu Hospital, Ursulines Convent, the Seminary, and the Cathedral, all built between 1638 and 1678 where they still stand. They also founded a college for young men in 1635 on the site where City Hall now stands, and Monseigneur de Laval was named bishop of the diocese, which extended as far as the Pacific and south to the Gulf of Mexico.

But Québec remained unfortified as it had been assumed for 150 years that the settlement's natural defences were sufficient. After destructive French raids in New York and New England, however, the British colonies decided to eliminate New France, pinning their hopes on a fleet under Sir William Phipps. When his expedition arrived in 1690, Frontenac, probably New France's most illustrious governor, issued one of the most memorable statements in Canadian history. To

Phipps messenger, Frontenac answered, "Tell your lord that I will reply with the mouths of my cannons." So ended the siege.

By 1690, Québec had only 1,500 residents, and barely 2,300 by 1715. Yet the town's stature ranged far beyond its size. War with Britain was intermittent during the 18th century and many beginnings were made to fortify Québec properly. In 1711, another fleet, dispatched against Québec under Sir Hovenden Walker, was in large part shipwrecked on the lower North Shore of the Gulf.

The Conquest

England was more determined than ever to conquer the French in North America. William Pitt, the Prime Minister of England, hurried an expedition towards Québec. The naval forces under Sir Charles Saunders numbered some 28,000 men, 43 warships, and almost 2,000 cannons. The army, 9,000 strong, was under the command of a young and brilliant general, James Wolfe.

Compared with the British forces, France's defense system was pitiful. While the French had the advantage of Québec's natural defences, there was no navy and only 12,000 troops commanded by Marquis de Montcalm.

The siege began on June 26, 1759. Most of the French forces were posted along the Beaupré shore where they expected the next main British assault. Wolfe had to risk everything on one bold stroke, or face withdrawal due to the onslaught of winter.

Wolfe learned of a feasible path up the slope at Anse-au-Foulon (Wolfe's Cove) near the present Champlain Maritime Terminal. He succeeded—on the morning of September 13—in moving some 5,000 men up the slope, up river from the French forces, and onto the Plains of Abraham, directly opposite the French forces. General Montcalm, surprised by Wolfe's move, decided to do battle rather than withdraw behind his defences. The engagement lasted only 20 minutes, with the British firing only at pointblank range. The French retreated, both generals were mortally wounded, casualties were heavy on both sides, and one of history's most important battles had been fought.

Five days later the English took over the city. The remaining French forces under the command of Lévis retired to Montréal for the winter. The English fleet returned to home waters, leaving Québec with a garrison under General Murray. The following spring, Lévis returned from Montréal with 10,000 troups and engaged Murray in a battle at Sainte-Foy, a short distance from the Plains of Abraham. Once again the city was under siege—this time by the French. Everyone knew, however, that aid from the Mother Country—France or England—whichever came through first—was critical to resolution of the struggle. And so it was. The arrival of British vessels on May 9, 1760, heralded the end of French rule in New France. The Treaty of Paris in 1763 confirmed the victory.

British rule brought little change. Fur, fish, lumber, shipbuilding, and certain small industries continued to activate the economy. A number of English-speaking settlers—apart from the garrison—took up residence in Québec, but even after 20 years they still numbered less then 1,000. And it was not until 40 years after the Treaty of Paris that a Protestant church was built in Québec.

The American Invasion

It remained for the American Revolution to disturb Québec's provincial tranquility. Unrest in the English colonies along the Atlantic seaboard had already induced authorities in London to pass the Québec Act of 1774, which guaranteed the religious rights of French-Canadians in an effort to keep them on the British side in the event of a revolution by the predominantly Protestant-American colonists. Even before the Declaration of Independence, the Patriots, furious over the Québec Act, decided to try to seize Canada.

In 1775, two expeditions were mounted: one, under General Richard Montgomery, proceeded up the Hudson Valley and Lake Champlain; the other, commanded by Colonel Benedict Arnold, moved up to Kennebec, through Maine, then overland and down the Chaudière River to Québec.

In November 1775, Montréal fell to Montgomery (a British officer stationed at Québec before joining the Continentals), who continued downriver to join forces (on December 1) with the other invaders at Québec. He established headquarters at Holland Farm at the site of present day Holland Street, while Arnold took shelter near Scott Bridge. The British, just as the French before them, relied on Québec's natural strength and neglected to fortify the city. The American alarm resulted in the construction of gates (long since demolished) atop de la Montagne and de la Canoterie hills. Arnold, after trying to enter through Saint-Louis Gate, took up a position to the southeast from which he could shell the city. Finally, as the Continental troops' enlistment was to expire on January 1, both American forces attempted an attack on Lower Town. The attack took place on the morning of December 31, the Americans were defeated, and Montgomery was killed.

The 19th and 20th Centuries

The American Revolution injected new life into the Canadian economy. Thousands of Loyalists were granted lands for settlement, first in Nova Scotia, then in what is now Ontario and in unsettled areas of Québec. Pot- and pearl-ash, a valuable byproduct of this migration (produced by burning the wood cleared from the new lands), was shipped in great quantities to England.

As a port, Québec prospered for the next three generations. The two main cargos, wheat and lumber, were greatly stimulated by Napoléon's continental system which cut Britain's European supplies. Good lumber was abundant, but only long distances inland from Québec. As overland shipments would have been too costly, Québec became the port farthest upstream where wood could be loaded on large sailing vessels bound for overseas destinations. Lumber remained the key export feature of Québec until 1890.

Shipbuilding had existed in Québec City since the days of Jean Talon, first intendant of New France. There had always been some yards on the Saint-Charles estuary and the Lower Town waterfronts. Their number multiplied with the arrival of plentiful raw materials and the increase in international trade.

Between 1797 and 1897, Québec City shipyards turned out more than 2,500 ships for a gross tonnage of 1,377,099. Most vessels were small, but many passed the 1,000 ton mark. The *Royal William,* launched in 1831, was the first vessel to cruise the Atlantic in 25 days entirely under steam. When steel replaced wood and steam overtook sail, the shipbuilding industry declined rapidly. But, even today, one of the world's largest shipyards is located at Lauzon.

A great many French-Canadian businesses were established in Québec City. For example, the city became the shoe manufacturing center of Canada. This French-dominated secondary industry is typical of the activities which gradually absorbed the labor force formerly concentrated in the shipyards and eventually created opportunities for a much larger labor force.

EXPLORING QUÉBEC CITY

Québec, the capital of Canada's largest province, is the most European city on the North American continent. There are many ways to visit the old part of this city, but the most rewarding is a walking tour. Streets, buildings and historic sites seem to spin a web of magic around travelers to Québec. Days on end can be spent exploring the past and enjoying contemporary life.

All that is really needed to tour Québec City is a comfortable pair of walking shoes. If you are more romantically inclined, try a calèche which may be hired inside the city wall on d'Auteuil Street. The cost is $20 and the drivers switch from French to English as they take you through the more interesting sections of Québec, meeting their friends along the way.

The Heart of Old Québec

Old uptown Québec is at its liveliest at Place d'Armes. Called Grande Place during the French Regime, this area was encircled with a large chain. Once a meeting place of European settlers and Indians, Place d'Armes is now an ideal spot to sit and relax.

Castlelike Le Château Frontenac dominates the square, with its turrets and towers visible for miles. The Château was constructed as a hotel in 1892 and is still owned by the Canadian Pacific Railway Company. It remains one of Canada's most beautiful hotels, commanding a matchless view of Québec City. It was here that Franklin D. Roosevelt, Winston Churchill and Mackenzie King met in 1943 and again in 1944 to plan strategies for World War II.

Just a few feet south of the Château Frontenac is Dufferin Terrace and the Champlain Monument as well as North America's oldest elevator. This beautiful old lift takes you down the escarpment to Lower Town for 55 cents. Below Place d'Armes lies Sainte-Anne Street. A small fortresslike building featuring an electronic reenactment of Québec's military history, Musée du Fort is to be found on the east corner. Opposite rue du Fort, at 12 rue Sainte-Anne, is the old Union Building (1805). It served as a hotel, a theater, church, and store before being renovated and now houses the Tourism Department. This should be your first stop in Québec City. Everything you will need in the way of information on Québec may be obtained here. At the corner of rue Sainte-Anne and the tiny rue du Trésor is the Vallée House (1732), dating back to the French regime and presently housing a wax museum.

West of here, on the site of the Anglican Cathedral of the Holy Trinity (main entrance on Desjardins Street) is the Court House, formerly a Récollets church and monastery. The Monument of Faith, with its refreshing fountain was erected to mark the tercentenary of the arrival of the Récollets Order to New France (1615).

Rue Saint-Louis has the distinction of being one of the first streets laid out by Governor Montmagny. From Place d'Armes, this street is marked with tablets indicating historic houses. The Maillou House, 1736, has been restored and now serves as the headquarters for the Québec District Board of Trade. Next door is the famous Kent House, one of the oldest in Québec—the residence of Governor d'Ailleboust, as early as 1648. In 1759, Governor de Ramezay signed the capitulation of Québec in this house. The Duke of Kent, father of Queen Victoria, used the house as a dwelling place between 1792 and 1794.

The Jacquet House, at the corner of Saint-Louis and des Jardins Streets dates back to 1675. From 1815 to 1824, the house was a residence for Philippe-Aubert de Gaspé, author of the classic *Anciens Canadiens*. Today, this house is one of Québec City's most delightful restaurants, Aux Anciens Canadiens.

A turn onto du Parloir Street leads to the Ursulines Monastery (1641), first school for girls in America. At the center of the garden, a monument to Marie de l'Incarnation smiles upon the community she founded there. A gateway to Ursulines Lane leads to an area where the view is at its finest. The magnificent chapel is in the Louis XIV style. The museum, located at 12 Donnacona Street, is open to the public, and houses, among other rare findings, the skull of General Montcalm. The story goes that after Montcalm died of wounds received during the battle with the English on the Plains of Abraham, his officers, fearing to alarm the people, dragged his body to the convent and hid the general in a hole in the countryside where a British cannon ball had exploded. The burial was witnessed by a young school girl who, some 70 years later, identified the burial site to local officials who recovered the body and claimed it to be that of Montcalm.

Now on to des Jardins Street where the Anglican Cathedral of the Holy Trinity comes into view. This is the first church of its kind to be constructed outside the British Isles (1804). Then to Sainte-Anne Street, lined on one side with interesting buildings and on the other side with wrought-iron gates surrounding the cathedral. Returning to Place

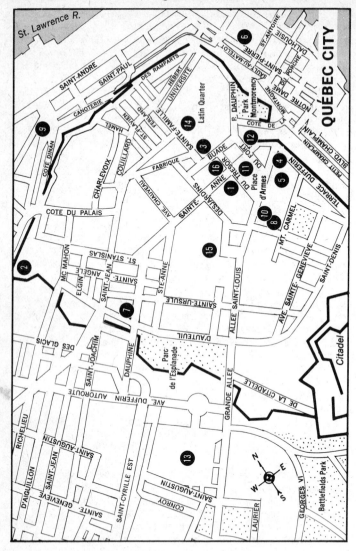

Points of Interest

1) Anglican Cathedral of the Holy Trinity
2) Artillery Park
3) Basilica Notre Dame
4) Champlain Monument
5) Chateau Frontenac Hotel
6) Fargues House
7) Jesuits' Chapel
8) Kent House
9) Laval Monument
10) Maillou House
11) Monument of Faith
12) Musee du Fort
13) National Assembly
14) Quebec Seminary
15) Ursulines' Convent
16) Wax Museum

d'Armes, a short visit to du Trésor Street provides a glimpse of the outdoor world of art.

At Buade Street and the corner of de la Fabrique stands the Basilica of Notre-Dame. Its first stone was laid in 1647. It was bombarded and burned in 1759; rebuilt in 1774; renovated in 1844–47 then struck by fire in 1921. In the church crypt lie the remains of many important figures of the French regime. Beside the Basilica, a wrought-iron gate identifies the old Québec Seminary founded in 1663 by Monseigneur de Laval, whose remains lie in the crypt outside the chapel. During the summer, open-air concerts are held in the Seminary courtyard, while a sundial, dating back more than 200 years, keeps time with a new generation.

Buade Street glitters on one side with smart shops and bright boutiques, surrounding the place where the first parish church in Québec, Notre-Dame-de-la-Recouvrance, once stood, and where Champlain is said to be buried.

Then head east to historic rue du Fort. Uptown on this street is the Post Office building which occupies the site of the ancient Chien d'Or House, immortalized by the classic which describes life in Québec toward the end of the French regime. A plaque in ancient graphics reads:

> Je suis un chien qui ronge lo
> (I am a dog that gnaws his bone)
>
> En le rongeant je prends mon repos
> (I crouch and gnaw it all alone)
>
> Un tems viendra qui n'est pas venu
> (A time will come which is not yet)
>
> que je mordray qui maura mordu
> (When I'll bite him by whom I'm bit.)

Facing the post office stands the monument to Québec's first bishop, Monseigneur de Montmorency Laval. Next is the Archbishop's Palace, and behind it the Québec Seminary buildings (1663). To the right and on the opposite side of the street is Montmorency Park, once the property of the illustrious intendant Talon. Later, Québec's second bishop, Monseigneur de Saint-Vallier, chose the site for his residence.

Québec's first legislature assembled here and successive buildings were used for meetings of the legislators and the Fathers of Confederation. The last structure was destroyed by fire in 1833. Peering towards the St. Lawrence are rows of virtually indestructible ancient cannons, flanking the rue des Remparts, proud reminders of the military exploits of Québec of yesteryear. The park opens into the abrupt and winding Côte de la Montagne (Mountain Hill) where the Prescott Gate once stood. A staircase heads off from narrow Sous-le-Fort and here you may choose either to return to midtown onto Dufferin Terrace by the cliff-side cable car, or to take on the discovery of Old Québec lower town, starting with Place Royale.

Place Royale and the Latin Quarter

From the heights of Dufferin Terrace, some 200 feet above the St. Lawrence and expanding west towards Cap Diamant, it is easy to recapture the early years of Québec. Here Champlain built his fort in 1620. It was also in this area that he died on Christmas Day in 1635. The fort was turned into the Château Saint-Louis which, for two centuries, served as a residence for governors. The terrace offers an exceptional view of the river's south shore. On a clear day, you may see as far as the western tip of Île d'Orléans.

The cliffside cable car from Dufferin Terrace reaches its terminal point at Jolliet House (1684), which contains an interesting display of natural history. It is situated at the corners of Sous-le-Fort and Petit-Champlain Streets. Following Petit-Champlain Street, an old and narrow "rue," you come on the right to a monument to Jolliet, who discovered the Mississippi River. Further along is Marché-Champlain, formerly a market place. Here, facing Place Champlain, are three famous old Québec houses: Chevalier, Frérot and Chenaye (1752), which have been beautifully restored, housing original furnishings, copper works, porcelain, enamels, and paintings.

The heart of Old Lower Town Quebec, along the riverfront, is crowded with small streets studded with many architectural gems of the 17th and 18th centuries. From Place Champlain, rue Notre-Dame veers to Place Royale, a special area which has been carefully and completely restored. Focal point of the area is Notre-Dame-des-Victoires Church, the oldest standing house of worship in North America.

Nearby is the old Finlay Market where remnants of the Royal Battery (1691) whisper from the depths of the soil. You may now wish to take a short boat trip on the Lévis ferry. In past days, crossing the St. Lawrence was done by small boat. During the winter, when the ice was thick, carriages were used. When the ice began to thin, canoes were used to make the trip to Lévis. This event is still relived today in the famous Québec Winter Carnival Canoe Race. The Carnival is held the first two weeks of February. The ferry trip offers a spectacular view.

In this area, on Côte du Palais, is Hôtel-Dieu Hospital, the oldest institution of its kind north of Mexico (founded in 1644). A highly acclaimed modern day medical center, the hospital houses a museum that proudly displays the vaults in which the community and its patients found refuge during two sieges of Québec. It is open to visits with advance notice. To the right is McMahon Street, where old fortifications and barracks of Artillery Park remain. These buildings have now been restored by the Canadian Government and are open to the public. The visit features an audio-visual presentation on the military history of Québec.

The defense system for Québec City was the brainchild of Chaussegros de Léry. The park, with a surface area of 8.2 acres, is part of the city's fortifications. The Dauphine barracks, started in 1712, became known in 1749 as the "new barracks" and were the longest structures ever erected by the French regime in North America. They have been preserved, partly in their original state, and are now the property of the

Government of Canada. Visits are scheduled during the summer and guides are on hand.

The heart of the Latin Quarter may be reached by rue de l'Université, where the original building of Laval University, founded in 1852, is located. An art gallery here stores works by masters.

The beauty of this section of Old Québec surrounds you—no matter where you turn or where you walk. And there is always something to challenge the lover of history for everything here is history.

The Walls of Old Québec

One of the more moving sites inside the walls of Old Québec is a monument located in front of the Château Frontenac Hotel in the Jardin des Gouverneurs. This monument is perhaps unique in that it honors two opposing generals, Wolfe and Montcalm. Its inscription states: "Valour gave them a common death, history a common fame and posterity a common monument."

Rue Saint-Louis and the Citadel

Rue Saint-Louis has the distinction of being the first street laid out in Québec. Beautifully restored old homes line both sides. Most of these have been converted into rooming houses (very reasonable), some into boutiques (expensive), others into restaurants where dining is elegant and the atmosphere warm. The food is truly excellent and prices are moderate to expensive.

Opposite 59 Saint-Louis is the house where the Québec poet and patriot Octave Crémazie lived. He died in exile in 1879. The Gaubert house, 72 Saint-Louis, is where the body of the American General Montgomery was brought to rest on December 31, 1775. Near the approach to Saint-Louis Gate, main entrance to the Walled City, is the Sewell House, formerly the residence of the Chief Justice of Lower Canada. Close by the gate, on a hill which leads to the Citadel, a tablet marks the spot where General Montgomery, two aides-de-camp, and 13 American soldiers were buried on January 4, 1776, during the last siege of Québec. The Citadel has the shape of a star surmounted by four bastions. The first building erected on this site dates back to 1693. It was expanded and re-enforced a number of times, the last in 1820. Guides are always on hand to escort visitors on tours. There is an admission fee of $2.25 for adults, $1 for young people. During the summer, the changing of the guard is performed at 10 A.M. every morning (weather permitting) by the famed Royal 22nd Regiment. The Citadel is only a ten-minute walk from Place d'Armes.

Grande-Allée

One of the most agreeable routes to explore in Québec is the broad and breezey Grande-Allée, which is a continuation to the west of Saint-Louis Street, with a return by way of the green splendor that identifies Battlefields Park. Heading under the Saint-Louis Gate, it is interesting to note that the current gate dates back to 1873. The first

Saint-Louis Gate was built by Frontenac in 1692, demolished and
rebuilt in 1721 and again in 1873. Beyond the gate, lies Grande-Allée,
long Québec's most fashionable thoroughfare. Farther on, a Cross of
Sacrifice pays tribute to the men who died on the battlefields of two
World Wars. Handsomely landscaped grounds surround the Québec
Government buildings, seat of the National Assembly.

The government center, built in 1886 in Renaissance style, welcomes
visitors, and guides are at their disposal. Parliament City is a study in
contrasts with huge new buildings on both sides of Grande-Allée. The
great bronze statues that ornament the circular fountain facing the
main entrance of the Parliament Buildings are Québec's tribute to the
aboriginal tribes of Canada. (An impressive totem pole stands tall, a gift
to Québec from the Indians of British Columbia.) While in the Parliament Building area be sure to visit the 31st floor of Complex 'G' for
the view.

Grande-Allée, wide and relatively level, makes for a pleasant stroll.
Continue along and you will come to Claire-Fontaine Street where
Québec's elegant Grand Théâtre is located. This ultra-modern culture
center has a variety of first-rate concert halls. Guided tours are provided during the summer months. There are also a number of beautiful
churches along Grande-Allée.

Battlefields Park

Although there are entrances to the park all along Grande-Allée, the
entrance near Bourlamaque is closest to the Québec Museum, which
you must visit. Dedicated to Québec's fine arts and crafts, the museum
frequently features collections from international and national galleries.

As for the park, it is one of the largest (235 acres) of its kind in
America, offering a resting place in the heart of the city. Battlefields
Park extends along the bluffs from the Citadel to Gilmour Hill where,
in 1759, Wolfe's troops clambered to the top of the rocky slope to reach
the Plains of Abraham. (The Plains took their name from Abraham
Martin, King's pilot, who grazed his sheep there.)

A number of monuments gracing this panoramic urban park immor-
talize heroes of bygone days. The many pathways of the park will ease
the visitor's way to the Earl Grey terrace lookout and the two Martello
Towers, built between 1804–06. Plaques located throughout the park
describe the historic events of the area and the battle which, in a matter
of 20 minutes, decided the fate of a nation.

The Outskirts of Québec

Apart from its fascination as the only walled city in North America,
Québec offers a host of other attractions in its outlying districts. Easily
accessible, these areas are not always included in organized tours.

Starting from Place Champlain in Old Lower Town, Boulevard
Champlain extends west along the river at the foot of Cap Diamant.
It is along this route that the General Montgomery was defeated and
killed.

Sillery (population 15,000), with its elegant homes and wide stretches of green land is one of Québec's most attractive suburbs. It links up with the City of Sainte-Foy (population 75,000).

Sainte-Foy has grown at a spectacular rate. A modest village just a quarter of a century ago, Sainte-Foy today is Québec's major residential suburb. Also to be found in Sainte-Foy is the famous Université Laval. Ultramodern buildings house more than 20,000 full-time students at the University, which received its Royal Charter in 1852.

PRACTICAL INFORMATION FOR QUÉBEC CITY

HOW TO GET THERE. By air: Québec City's airport in the suburb of Sainte-Foy is served by two major airlines, *Air Canada* and *Québecair.*

By car: From the U.S. northeast, take Québec Highway No. 73. From Montréal, No. 20 is an express route on the south shore or take No. 40 on the north shore of the St. Lawrence from Montréal. From Gaspé take No. 132.

By bus: Full service from *Greyhound* and *Voyageur Bus Lines.*

By rail: Both *Canadian National* and *Canadian Pacific Rail* operate into Québec. C.P. Rail comes in from Montréal and C.N. comes from the Maritimes as well as Montréal and all points west. (Note: please check U.S. train connections.)

By boat: From Lévis by ferry; from Montréal by the St. Lawrence.

ACCOMMODATIONS. Québec City has a happy choice of accommodations for visitors. Price categories for double occupancy are as follows: *Deluxe,* $90 or more; *Expensive,* $75–90; *Moderate,* $55–75; *Inexpensive,* $55 and under. CP—Canadian Pacific Hotel.

Most places accept the following major credit cards: American Express, MasterCard, and Visa; others may also be honored. Not all establishments accept credit cards, therefore we suggest you call for information.

Deluxe

Auberge des Gouverneurs. 690 St. Cyrille E. 647–1717. 379 rooms, free parking, sauna, outdoor pool.

Château Frontenac (CP). 1 des Carrières 692–3861. 523 expensive to deluxe rooms. One of the oldest hotels in Canada, built on an historic site overlooking the St. Lawrence River and Old Town. Parking, sauna, air conditioning. Beautiful old furniture in public rooms; great restaurants. Well worth seeing.

Concorde Hôtel (Loews). 1225 Place Montcalm. 647–2222. 413 rooms; constructed on historical site; parking, indoor and outdoor pools, sauna. Great restaurants, including *L'Astral,* very good cuisine in rotating rooftop dining room, and excellent service.

Québec Hilton. 3 Place Québec. 647–2411. 564 rooms, parking, indoor and outdoor pools, sauna. Modern, well decorated. Very fine restaurants.

Expensive

Auberge Quality Inn. Ste. Foy. 658–5120. 204 moderate to expensive rooms, free parking, indoor and outdoor pools. Some rooms with kitchenettes.

Le Château (Auberge des Gouverneurs). Mont Ste.-Anne. 827–5211. 258 rooms. All facilities.

Holiday Inn. 395 de la Couronne. 647–2611. 233 rooms, free parking, indoor pool, sauna.

Holiday Inn. Ste. Foy. 653–4901. 348 rooms, free parking, outdoor pool.

Moderate

Château Bonne-Entente. Chemin Ste.-Foy, Ste.-Foy. 653–5221. 102 rooms.

Hôtel Universel. Chemin Ste.-Foy, Ste.-Foy. 653–5250. 133 rooms.

Le Voyageur Laurentien. 2250 Ste.-Anne. 661–7701. 62 rooms, free parking, indoor and outdoor pools.

Ramada Inn. Blvd. Laurier, Ste.-Foy. 651–2440. 100 rooms.

Inexpensive

Hôtel Château Laurier. 695 Grande-Allée. 522–8108. 54 rooms, free parking. Very good food.

Hôtel Clarendon. 57 Ste.-Anne. 692–2480. 99 rooms, free parking, good food.

Hôtel Le Homestead. 20 Ste.-Anne. 694–1876. 23 rooms. Near Château Frontenac. Has one of Québec's good restaurants.

Hôtel Manoir D'Auteuil. 49 Auteuil. 694–1173. 16 rooms, free parking, some a/c.

TELEPHONES. The telephone area code for Québec is 418.

HOW TO GET AROUND. By bus: Fares are $1.00 (four quarters required; no bills accepted) for adults. *Gray Lines* operate tours from Place d'Armes as does *Maple Leaf Tours* and *Old Québec Tours.* Call (418) 872–9226.

By taxi: Drop fare is $1.20 plus 70¢ a km.

By boat: Cruising the St. Lawrence from Cap Rouge to Montmorency Falls and Île d'Orléans from Chouinard Wharf can be arranged in season.

By carriage: Calèches are available from rue d'Auteuil year round.

TOURIST INFORMATION SERVICES. Contact the Tourism and Convention Bureau of the Québec City Region, 60 rue d'Auteuil, tel. (418) 692–2471. Or write Québec Department of Tourism, 150 est. boul. Saint-Cyrille, Québec, GIR 4Y3. Or visit the Department's reception center at 12 Ste.-Anne Street, tel. (418) 643–2280, 7 days a week, 9 A.M. to 5 P.M.

INDUSTRIAL TOURS. For tour arrangements, call the Quebec Urban Community Industrial Promotion Office, tel. 529–8771, local 250.

CHILDREN'S ACTIVITIES. In addition to summer and winter sports activities for children of all ages, both the Aquarium, 1675 Avenue du Parc, Sainte-Foy (adults $2; young people 50¢; free for monitored groups) and the Québec Zoological Garden, Laurentien Blvd., Orsainville (admission: adults $2.50; young people 50¢) are open year round.

PARTICIPANT SPORTS. The entire province is big ski country and the city and its surrounding suburbs have a good number of slopes. But it is at Mont Ste.-Anne Park, 40 kms. (25 miles) to the east of Québec City that one finds the most prestigious ski center in eastern Canada. Opened to the public in the late 1960's, this world cup complex has 29 slopes and 11 ski lifts, including the famous gondola lift (the only one east of the Rockies), permitting *skiing* from mid-November to early May. (The park site is now being converted into an all-season recreation complex, with a golf course and cycling trails.)

Visitors to the city may also participate in *snowshoeing, tobogganing,* and *skating* on the Saint-Charles River between Samson and Marie-de-l'Incarnation bridges, a short distance away.

For further information on winter sports in accessible areas, see sections in *Practical Information for Québec Province* at the end of this chapter.

 SPECTATOR SPORTS. *Auto racing* at the Québec Autodrome (May to September), *baseball* at the Municipal stadium in Victoria Park, *professional hockey*—Québec Nordiques of the National Hockey League—at the Québec Coliseum, and *harness racing* at the Québec Hippodrome in Exposition Park are among the main possibilities. A unique sporting event that takes place during the Québec Winter Carnival in February is *motorcycle racing* on ice at the Parc de l'Exposition de Québec.

 MUSEUMS. *Augustine Monastery Museum.* 260 Langelier Blvd. (Hôpital Général). Free, by appointment only. 529–0931, local 228.

Chevalier House. Place Champlain, near Place Royale. 643–9689. Free. Displays evolution of Québec-style furniture.

Fornel House. Place Royale. 643–6631. Free. Displays objects found in archeological searches at Place Royale.

Historical Museum of the Augustine Order of Hôtel-Dieu. 32 Charlevoix St. 692–2492. Free. Holds treasures of the Augustine Order from the 17th and 18th centuries.

Historical Wax Museum. 22 Ste.-Anne St. 692–2289. Historical figures projected in wax. Adults $2.00; senior citizens $1.50; students $1.00; children 75¢.

Huron Village Museum. Village-des-Hurons. Free, by appointment only. 842-4308. Artifacts, dating from early Huron life, and Indian handicrafts displayed in the church sacristy.

Marie de l'Incarnation Centre. 12 Donnacona St. 694–0694. Treasures of the Ursuline Order of nuns. The skull of Montcalm rests here. Admission $1.00.

Musée du Fort. 10 Ste.-Anne St. 692–2175. Re-enactment of Québec's military history. Adults $2.50; children under 18 $1.25; under 6, free.

Québec Museum. On the Plains of Abraham. 643–2150. Displays Québec art and handicrafts. Free admission.

Royal 22nd Regiment Museum. Located in the Québec Citadel. 694–3563. Military history. Adults $2.25; children $1.00.

Séminaire de Québec Museum. Université St. 692–2843. Display of Canadian works of art. Open 11 A.M. to 5 P.M.; closed Tuesdays. Adults $2.00; children $1.00.

 THEATERS AND CONCERT HALLS. All of the following theaters offer a variety of plays, in English and/or in French, on a year-round or seasonal basis. Be sure to call for program information or check the local papers.

Institut Canadien. 37 rue Sainte-Angèle. 692–2135.

Le Grand Théâtre de Québec. 269 St. Cyrille St. E. 643–6967.

Le Palais Montcalm. Place d'Youville. 694–6219.

Le Théâtre du Trident. 350 St.-Cyrille St. E. 643–5873.

The Québec Conservatory of Dramatic Arts. 30 St.-Denis St. 643–2139.

Théâtre d'été la Fenière. 1500 rue de la Fenière, Ancienne-Lorette. 872–1424, 651–3218.

Théâtre de l'Île. 342 rue du Galandor, Île d'Orléans (paroisse Saint-Pierre). 828–9530.

DINING OUT. Québec City is the home of good French cooking in the Americas—perhaps with Montréal the only place in the world where you can eat as well as in France—and for a smaller price. Price ranges per person do not include wine, sales tax or gratuities: *Deluxe,* over $30; *Expensive,* $20–30; *Moderate,* $10–20; *Inexpensive,* under $10.

Most places accept the following major credit cards: American Express, MasterCard, and Visa; others may also be honored. Not all establishments accept credit cards, therefore we suggest you call for information.

Deluxe

L'Astral. Loew's Le Concorde Hotel. 647–2222. Revolving rooftop restaurant with magnificent view. French/continental.

Le Bonaparte. 680 Grande-Allée E. 522–4704. French classic dishes in beautiful old house.

Le Champlain. Château Frontenac Hotel. 692–3861. French specialties; chamber music.

Manoir St.-Castin. Lac Beauport. 849–4461. French.

Serge Bruyère (à la table de). 694–0618. 1200 St-Jean St. French, new and already considered one of the best in all Québec.

Expensive

Aux Anciens Canadiens. 34 St.-Louis St. 692–1627. Québec cuisine in elegant historic house.

Café de la Paix. 44 des Jardins. 692–1430. French/Italian.

Café d'Europe. 27 Ste.-Angèle. 692–3835. French.

Chez Guido. 73 Ste.-Anne St. 692–3856. Italian/French.

Chez Rabelais. 2 Petit-Champlain, 692–1503. French.

Continental. 26 St.-Louis St. 694–9995. Classical décor and fine French/American food with an elaborate wine list.

Jardin d'Italie. 925 St.-Jean St. 692–0373. Italian/French.

Kyoto. 560 Grande-Allée E. 529–6141. Japanese steakhouse.

La Caravelle. 68½ St.-Louis St. 694–9022. Seafood, excellent Spanish dishes, good service.

La Ripaille. 9 Buade St. 692–2450. French.

Le Deauville. 3000 Laurier Blvd. 658–3644. Seafood and steakhouse. Excellent.

Salle Charles Baillargé. At the Clarendon Hotel. 692–2480. French and Québec cuisine.

Le Marie-Clarisse. At the foot of the cliffside cable car. 692–0857. French.

Le Vignoble. Auberge des Gouverneurs. 690 St.-Cyrille E. 647–1717. Seafood and continental.

Moderate

Le Chalet Suisse. 32 Ste.-Anne St. 694–1320. Seafood and fondues.

Café Canadien. Château Frontenac. 692–3861. French.

Cafe de Paris. 66 St.-Louis St. 694-9626. French/Italian.

La Potinière. Hilton Hotel. 647–2411. Canadian.

Le Chambord. Holiday Inn, downtown. 647–2611. Canadian/French.

Le Saint-Amour. 48 Ste.-Ursule St., in old Québec. 694–0667. Small place, but good. French.

Cafe Buade. 31 Rue Buade. Canadian-style cooking.

Le Laurentien. 785 Rue Des Glacis. Wholesome Canadian cooking.

Le Paysan. 2480 Chemin Sainte-Foy. Steaks and chicken.

NIGHT LIFE. Québec City is not really a club city. Discos and night clubs are few and far between. The main hotels are your best bet for night life.

Disco Le Cabaret. Hôtel Le Concorde, 1225 Place Montcalm. 647–2222.

Disco L'Eden. Québec Hilton, 3 Place Québec. 647–2411.

There is also a commendable disco, *La Cousinière,* on Place Laurier in Sainte-Foy.

No cover charge required at any; drinks come to about $2.50 each.

EXPLORING QUÉBEC PROVINCE

The Laurentians

No matter when you discover the Laurentians, you will find an explosion of beauty. Just one hour away by car from the busy center of Montréal, this vast playground of the North delights skiers, water bugs, and nature lovers—depending on the season—in more than 50 specialized areas.

The Laurentians can be divided into three main regions—west, central, and east—each with a unique personality. The central part of the Laurentians has successfully fulfilled the early prophecy of one of its colorful forefathers, Curé Labelle, who dreamed of opening up the north and the west to colonization and who became known as the "king of the North." The first settlers here, over a century ago, were hardy French-Canadians who preferred to carve farms out of their own wilderness rather than emigrate to New England mill towns. Today, the region is world famous for its vast network of fashionable year-round resorts, offering accommodations and cuisine at their finest.

Access is very easy via the high-speed Laurentian Autoroute (toll) and Highway 117. The latter route, although slower, is the more picturesque, going by way of peaceful towns such as: Rosemère, Sainte-Thérèse, Saint-Janvier, Saint-Antoine, Blainville, and Saint-Jérôme, and passing directly through many of the major resort towns.

The country is mountainous but softened by numerous valleys. All the localities between Saint-Jérôme and Mont-Tremblant offer one or more popular winter resorts. Following Shawbridge and Piedmont there is a worthwhile stop at the town of Sainte-Adèle where the enchanting colonial Village de Séraphin is located.

Val-David, a colony for both the fine arts and the performing arts, is alive with shows in fascinating places, such as Butte à Mathieu, oldest boîte à chanson in the country. The July Marché des Artisans (Craftsmen's Market) features paintings, sculptures and ceramics.

Sainte-Agathe-des-Monts is the oldest tourist center in the region and has earned its outstanding reputation as the metropolis of the Laurentians. It offers summer theater, sparkling lac des Sables, campgrounds, and a municipal picnic area.

Saint-Faustin, the location of a government fish hatchery, is the point where Highway 117 gives way to a secondary road leading directly to famous Mont-Tremblant Park. Huge bodies of water skirt the mountain heights of the region offering the outdoor sportsman wildlife, fish of various species, camping, canoeing, picnic spots, cross-country skiing, snowshoeing, and snowmobiling.

Mont Tremblant is rapidly developing into a vast, well-integrated complex of winter facilities. A computer-programmed system of artificial snow increases the ski season and new ski lifts accommodate the crowds. A crop of new hotels and good restaurants has sprung up around, making it one of the new "in" places for winter fun.

Land of Lakes

Highway 125 takes you from Montréal to Saint-Donat, a distance of 113 kms. (70 miles). From central Montréal this route is reached by Sherbrooke Street east to Pie XI Boulevard, with a left turn on the latter, which is the city end of Highway 125. This highway now crosses Île Jésus and heads towards Terrebonne, which freely translated means "good earth." The term is appropriate, since this region offers a rich yield of pulp, tobacco, and truck gardening. The highway then continues north through Mascouche, with many old stone houses from the 17th century. Also encountered are Saint-Esprit and Sainte-Julienne, both farming communities. You will then approach Rawdon, just four miles from Highway 125—a charming resort area encircled by the Rouge and Ouareau Rivers. The surrounding area glistens with some 34 lakes.

Among the nearby towns and villages are: Chertsey, Notre-Dame-de-la-Merci and Saint-Donat, extending as far as the eastern entry to Mont-Tremblant Park. Population here swells during the summer with vacationing families enjoying nature at its best. The northern extremity of Highway 125 leads across two huge lakes, Ouareau and Archambault, in a regal setting of mountain peaks.

Garden Country

Highway 344 leads from Montréal to Saint-Michel-des-Saints, a distance of some 154 kms. (96 miles) northeast of the Laurentians. From Montréal, continue as far as Charlemagne Street where Highway 344 begins; then take Sherbrooke Street east and Le Gardeur Bridge. Following Charlemagne Street, the route crosses Saint-Paul-l'Ermite and L'Assomption, lined with ancient dwellings. Joliette, the most prosperous village in this particular region, is noted for its tobacco harvest. A stop at any of the many antique shops could turn up something of interest. Then on to Saint-Félix-de-Valois and from here a rewarding turn may be made to Saint-Gabriel-de-Brandon, a smart resort area nestled along the shores of Lake Maskinongé.

At Saint-Jean-de-Matha, the birthplace of Louis Cyr, famed Québec strongman, Highway 344 continues into a region where mountains and lakes begin to take shape in earnest, with distant panoramas quite unlike those found elsewhere in the Laurentians. A little farther on is the beginning of real wilderness and, for those with a spirit of adventure, it is a 20th-century explorer's dream come true.

Southern Québec

Motoring along the south shore of the St. Lawrence, from Montréal to Sorel, 64 kms. (40 miles), will lead you to the Richelieu River, a modern-day haven for sailing and yachting. Rue Université and the Bonaventure Autoroute lead to the Champlain Bridge from the heart of Montréal. Exit at Marie-Victorin on Highway 132, heading east. It passes by way of 17th-century seigniories, now cities, suburbs, or small industrial centers, such as Saint-Lambert, Longueuil, Boucherville, Varennes and Verchères. At Verchères, a monument has been erected in honor of Madeleine de Verchères, a 14-year-old girl who, in 1692, assumed command of the post there and successfully defended it for eight days against the Iroquois. An old windmill dating to 1708 may be found a short distance past the village on Highway 132.

Sorel, founded in 1642, is the fourth-oldest city in Canada. French-Canadian seafood is a specialty here and, during the summer, cruises are available to visitors.

From Sorel, Highway 133 skirts the Richelieu River, to Saint-Jean and Iberville, covering some 88 kms. (55 miles). The route is lined with towns and villages dating back to colonial times and events that shaped the nation. Saint-Ours, oldest church in the region (1650) is to be found here. The stately Manoir de Saint-Ours, 1792, is one of the most elegant historic mansions in the country and one of the few remaining from the 18th century.

Across the river is a colony of artists at Saint-Marc, just a ferry ride from Saint-Charles. The road continues on through Mont-Saint-Hilaire (a village in a region of orchards and vineyards), and on through Otterburn Park, Saint-Mathias, Richelieu, and Chambly (the site of a famous old fort, which still stands). Then come the larger centers of Saint-Jean and Iberville. Cantic is the last village before the American border, where Trans-Canada Highway 15 heads directly for Montréal.

Chemin du Roy (King's Road)

Between Montréal and Trois-Rivières (Three Rivers) and between Cap-de-la-Madeleine and Québec City, Highway 138 generally follows the route of Canada's first carriageway, the Chemin du Roy, or King's Road. The highway was opened in 1734 to link the stumps of road built on the seigniories at the beginning of the colonial era.

Highway 138 goes through the old seigniories. Manors and old churches, richly decorated by famous craftsmen of the day, still stand proudly, side by side, with modern buildings. Historic landmarks abound. And always throughout the region, the river is in view.

Worth a visit while passing through the Cap-de-la-Madeleine is the huge sanctuary of Notre-Dame-du-Cap. Honoring the Virgin Mary, it receives hundreds of thousands of worshippers a year. Beautiful gardens surround the basilica, one of the largest in Canada. Main pilgrimage date: August 15.

The Gaspé Peninsula

A trip to the Province of Québec is incomplete unless you tour the Gaspé Peninsula. Reaching out into the Gulf of the St. Lawrence at the southeastern extremity of the province, the Gaspé Peninsula, called Gespeg or "land's end" by the Indians, is a thick tongue of land measuring some 280 kms. (175 miles) from the Matapédia Valley to Cap Gaspé and from 112–144 kms. (70–90 miles) at its widest point between the St. Lawrence River and Baie des Chaleurs.

At times, the Gaspé's northern slope drops off sharply into the sea; at most points, however, it edges the 640 km. (400 miles) strip or terrace along which Highway 132 runs. The profile of the wooded slope, which the Micmacs called Chic-Chocs (Sigsoog, rocky mountains, or steep rocks) is one of long plateaus and jagged peaks rearing toward the sky, bringing to mind France's Brittany Coast or Cornwall in England. Some peaks are the highest in Eastern Canada. Here, at this altitude, lives the woodland caribou, a species threatened with extinction. And there are unusual alpine flora, including 12-foot-high firs that are centuries old. Lakes full of speckled trout feed the rivers in which the Atlantic salmon have been swimming upstream for thousands of years.

Geologically, the peninsula is hundreds of millions of years old—one of the oldest lands on earth—although one of the most recently populated.

This incredibly beautiful landscape features four major park areas: Port Daniel, Forillon, Causapscal, and de la Gaspésie (Gaspesian Park), which is the largest—so vast that it has two names, Gaspesian and Matane. All four combined cover an area of 2,292 sq. kms. (885 square miles).

Crossing the bridge at Québec City onto Route 132 on the south side of the St. Lawrence, you travel along the south shore of the St. Lawrence known as the Lower St. Lawrence with its historic towns and villages. This stretch hugs the shoreline from Lévis, opposite Québec City, to Ste.-Flavie where the Gaspé tour beings.

Following the coast all around the peninsula, Route 132 ends at Matapédia where it cuts across the peninsula back to the south shore of the St. Lawrence.

Starting at Ste.-Flavie, the coastline is dotted with small villages mixing farming and fishing for a livelihood. A few have old covered bridges—keep a lookout for them.

Traveling east you pass through the city of Matane, a former port which is now a lumbering and fishing community. Pushing on through Les Méchins, Cap-Chat, and Ste.-Anne-des-Monts, you finally arrive in Gaspesian Park, a rugged area of deep valleys and high peaks that are part of the Appalachian Chain.

As you continue along Route 132, you pass through many lovely towns until you arrive at Gaspé—a fishing port located on a bay that empties into three salmon rivers—Dartmouth, York, and St.-Jean. It was here that Jacques Cartier, on his first voyage to the New World, planted a wooden cross, embellished it with three fleurs de lys, and took possession of Canada in the name of the King of France.

From here, Route 132 heads south around the tip of the Gaspé Peninsula to world famous Percé, home of the Percé "rock," one of the natural wonders of the world.

Percé is now a well-appointed tourist and resort center, renowned for its gastronomy. With a landscape fashioned by the cataclysmic encounters between land and sea, it is surrounded by a semi-circle of mountains, opening onto two bays separated by two capes and Percé Rock, formerly linked to firm ground. It is behind this Rock that Jacques Cartier anchored his three small ships in July 1534.

Now, heading west on Route 132 toward Matapédia, you pass through Pabos, Newport, Port-Daniel with its beautiful beach, and New Carlisle, an old Loyalists' stronghold. Finally, you arrive at Matapédia where Route 132 turns north across the peninsula and joins itself just west of Matane.

QUÉBEC'S TOURISTIC REGIONS

A recent development in tourism in Québec has been the division of the territory into eighteen touristic regions. Each features a good information service through a permanent Regional Touristic Association and offers a number of budget-minded, all-inclusive tours. The system is coordinated through a central government agency, Information Tourisme Québec. Toll-free information is available by calling 1–800–361–5405, or by writing to Tourisme Québec, Case postale 20 000, Québec G1K 7X2, Canada.

Magdalen Islands *(Îles-de-la-Madeleine).* In the middle of the St. Lawrence Gulf, these islands are paradise for nature lovers. Life is slow and simple, and no one seems to mind it when the fog stops all activity at the airport. Life centers around two villages, Havre-aux-Maisons and Cap-aux-Meules. Tours leaving either from Québec City or from Dorval Airport offer transportation by boat or by air and accommodations at the Bellevue or Boudreau Motels.

For more information: Commission de développement touristique, Case postale 238, Lavernière, Îles-de-la-Madeleine, Québec G0B 1L0, (418) 986-4259.

The Gaspè Peninsula *(Gaspésie).* A long-time favorite of the Québec visitor, the Gaspé Peninsula (described earlier) offers an ever-changing panorama of life along a seacoast. An excellent road allows for a complete circuit, first going down the St. Lawrence River to Gaspé Point, then coming back by the Matapédia Valley. All along there are good, moderately priced inns and pensions and ample seafood: the delicate Matane shrimps, fresh cod tongues, clams, and the celebrated lobster. The Gaspé tour is mostly done by car, but there are tours, from one to four nights, leaving from Québec City and Montréal.

For more information: Association touristique de la Gaspésie, 942 route 132, Case postale 810, Carleton, Québec G0C 1J0, 1-800-463-0829.

Lower St. Lawrence *(Bas Saint-Laurent).* This region on the south shore of the St. Lawrence River stretches from Lévis (in front of Québec City) to the Gaspé region. Populated by three-centuries-old villages with names like Kamouraska, Témiscouata, Rimouski, Cacouna, it offers a variety of sights and interests that include a lot of open-air activities as in the nature center of Pohénégamook, where two-night weekend stays are available.

For more information: Association touristique du Bas Saint-Laurent, 506 rue Lafontaine, Rivière-du-Loup, Québec G5R 3C4, (418) 867-1272.

Québec City Region *(Région de Québec).* This interesting, centuries-old region is more largely described earlier. But note that there are special tours leaving from Montréal, including a four-night trout fishing excursion (price on request) and a six-night "Romantic Rendez-vous" in a deluxe apartment or private lodge with open fire at Mont Sainte-Anne, complete with the use of a car for 7 days (1,500 kms. free) and a "millionnaire's day" with a chauffeured limousine for shopping or touring and a gastronomic dinner with dance in a discothèque at the end of the day.

For more information: Quebec Urban Community Tourism and Convention Bureau, 399 rue St. Joseph est, Québec, Qué., G1K 8E2, 418-529-8771.

Charlevoix: Charlevoix is that mountainous region standing immediately east of the Québec region and on the north shore of the St. Lawrence. It offers a mixture of sea and sharply rising mountains dented into a series of capes of awe-inspiring beauty. It also features the famed Île-aux-Coudres, an island celebrated both by painters and nature lovers. The region is easily accessible by car from Québec City—the ride itself is worth the trip—but there are tours leaving from Montréal or Québec City.

For more information: Association touristique de Charlevoix, 136 Boulevard de Comporté, La Malbaie, Québec G0T 1J0, (418) 665-3811.

Maple Country *(Pays de l'Érable).* This region, rich in scenery, beautiful forests and quiet villages, forms a triangle between the Appalachians, Beauce County, and the St. Lawrence River. An easy ride from Québec City, it offers pleasures in all seasons: the green in summer and visits to such places as St.-Jean-Port-Joli, where the most famous Québec sculptors live: the Bourgaults; rich colors and small game hunting in the autumn; cross-country skiing and snowmobile trails in winter; and in the spring, of course, all the delicious products of the maple tree. All year round there is a two-day weekend tour leaving Québec City.

For more information: Association touristique du Pays de l'Érable, 800 Autoroute 20, Berniere, Québec G0S 1C0, 1-800-463-3381

The St. Maurice Valley *(Maurice, Bois-Francs, Centre du Québec):* This region spreads along the St. Maurice Valley, midway between Montréal and Québec City. Also known as "the Heart of Québec," it boasts Trois-Rivières as its capital. This region features a number of annual events which attract visitors by the thousands: the St. Maurice canoe race, the Lac Saint-Jean swim, the Trois-Rivières Auto Grand Prix, and duck hunting season. There is also the famed Notre-Dame-du-Cap sanctuary in Cap-de-la-Madeleine, right across Trois-Rivières. A two-night tour leaving from Montréal or Québec City in the summer months, will help you discover most of the charms of this region.

For more information: Association touristique du Coeur du Québec, rue Bonaventure, Trois Rivières, Québec G9N 5M4, 819–567-8646.

Eastern Townships *(Estrie).* Estrie is the Québec name for the Eastern Townships, a group of towns bordering the United States of which the main city is Sherbrooke. They also house the most important concentration of popular arts in Québec. Song, music, and popular festivals are held all year long in Bromont, Mount Orford and numerous other localities. Summer and winter sports are plentiful. A one-hour ride from Montréal or Québec City will get you there. So will a number of one- or two-night tours leaving from either city.

For more information: Association touristique de l'Estrie, 91 rue Carillon, Sherbrooke, Québec J1J 2K9, 1-800-567-6076.

The Richelieu Valley *(Richelieu/Rive Sud).* Rich in history, this region lies north of the American border and spreads on both sides of the Richelieu Valley. The scene of memorable battles, it lives in its glorious past through old manors, forts, and monuments well preserved. The north end of this region borders the St. Lawrence River and includes the Sorel Islands, a compact group of islands particularly well suited for boating and hunting. Recommended is an auto ride along route 132, between Contrecoeur and Valleyfield. Main events of the year are the International Regatta at Valleyfield, the Apple Festival at Rougemont, and the summer plays on the theater-boat anchored at Saint-Marc. Also to see are the Safari Park in Hemmingford and the craftsmen's village in Sainte-Martine. One-or two-night tours are available from Montréal or Québec City.

For more information: Association touristique Richelieu/Rive Sud, 1575 rue Bourgogne, Chambly, Quebec J3L 1Y7, 1-800-361-3614.

The Joliette Region *(De Lanaudière).* The name comes from Marie-Charlotte de Lanaudière, wife of Barthélemy Joliette, a member of the family of the famed explorer. Barthélemy himself founded the city of Joliette, capital of this region which starts right from the east end of Montréal Island and spreads in a northwest direction in a region famed for its natural beauties. It features such resorts as Rawdon, Saint-Michel-des-Saints, and Saint-Charles de Mandeville, and countless falls created by the swift rivers that abound in this natural paradise. Six- and nine-night canoe-camping safaris are available from Saint-Michel-des-Saints. Transport from Montréal can be arranged.

For more information: Association touristique de Lanaudière, 446 rue Queen, Rawdon, Québec J0K1TO, 1-800-363-2788.

The Laurentians *(Laurentides)*. This region encompasses the mountainous north of Montréal and its features are outlined in a preceding section.

For more information: Association touristique des Laurentides, 1000 rue Labelle, Bureau 200, Saint-Jérôme, Québec J7Z 5N6, 1-800-363-2573.

Montréal: See "Exploring Montréal."

The Ottawa Valley *(Outaouais Québécois)*. This region covers the Québec part of the Ottawa Valley. A hunting and fishing paradise, it offers 20,000 lakes, 24 rivers, and more than 100 purveyors centers. The Gatineau Park is rapidly developing its skiing facilities, but remains at all times a favorite destination for a car ride. Then there are the cities of Hull (in Québec) and Ottawa (in Ontario), the nation's capital, with its Parliament buildings and its beautiful Rideau Park. Ottawa is only 200 kms. (120 miles) from Montréal. Tours of Ottawa and of Gatineau Park are available from Montréal or Québec City, with tariffs on request depending on the accommodation required.

For more information: Société d'aménagement de l'Outaouais, 25 rue Laurier, Case postale 2000, Hull, Quebec J8X 3Z2, 1-800-567-9651.

North West Quebec *(Abitibi-Témiscamingue)*. Bordering Ontario and stretching in a north-south direction west of Montréal, this region is an ideal destination for outdoors fans. Fishing, hunting, canoe-camping—some excursions can go on for as many as 800 kms. (500 miles)—await the visitor who has no taste for the crowds. There is also a fairly wide selection of camping grounds for those who want to explore on their own. Two four-night tours are also available from Montréal.

For more information: Association touristique Abitibi-Témiscamingue, 212 Avenue du Lac, Rouyn, Québec J9X 4N7, (819) 762–8181.

The Saguenay River *(Saguenay/Lac Saint-Jean/Chibougamau):* This is the land of the powerful Saguenay River, a land of early explorers and pioneers. It offers both nature and industry and endless discoveries, from the cities of Jonquière, Tadoussac, Chicoutimi, and Alma to the vast expanse of Lac Saint-Jean and the close forests of the toundra. This is also the home of Maria Chapdeleine, the principal character of the powerful novel by Louis Hémon that still lives hard in memory, and of the Saint-Félicien zoo, one of the most interesting in Canada, and of ghost-town Val Jalbert. A number of tours, from one to five nights, leave from Montréal or Québec City and give a wide choice of interests.

For more information: Association touristique Saguenay/Lac Saint-Jean/Chibougamau, 198 est rue Racine, Bureau 107, Chicoutimi, Québec G7H 1R9, 1-800-463-9651.

The North Shore-Manicouagan *(Manicouagan-Côte Nord):* Manicouagan, the western part of the North Shore touristic region, is a country of giants: gigantic hydroelectric developments, giant rivers, giant forests. The region runs down the powerful St. Lawrence River from Tadoussac to the salmon breeding grounds of Baie-Trinité. The road along the river passes through charming, historic villages such as Les Escoumins, Sault-au-Mouton, Forestville (named for its rich forest industry). Then there are the industrial cities of Baie Comeau and

Hauterive and, between the two, "Energy Road," the 200-km. way to the gigantic Daniel-Johnson Barrage whose main vault would lodge the entire Place Ville Marie complex in Montréal. Tours available are jointly covered in the next region.

For more information: Association touristique Manicouagan, Case postale 366, Hauterive, Québec G5C 2T1, 1-800-463-8531.

The North Shore-Duplessis *(Duplessis/Côte Nord).* This is the eastern part of the North Shore, extending from Baie-Trinité to Labrador and the Atlantic Ocean. A country for the adventurous, but where everything is accessible by car, by rail, by boat, by plane. It features beautiful Anticosti Island where the salmon and the deer thrive, and the Mingan Islands. It boasts small but powerful little cities such as Havre-Saint-Pierre, Port-Cartier, and Sept-Îles, cradles of the iron ore mining developments. And it offers unsurpassed hunting, fishing, and canoeing. Tours covering either part of the North Shore are offered from Montréal or Québec City, from two to five nights, the last one covering from Sept-Îles to Labrador City and a visit to Mount Wright.

For more information: Association touristique régionale de Duplessis, 801 boulevard Laure, Sept-Îles, Québec G4R 2X2, 1-800-463-1755.

New Québec–James Bay *(Nouveau Québec–Baie James).* This is the last—and the largest—of the touristic regions of Québec, with 51 percent of the whole Québec territory to itself. It is the land of the Cree and the Inuit, of the midnight sun, of the tundra, of the northern lights, of 15-pound Arctic chars, and of over 250,000 caribou. This new northern frontier is also the site of the gigantic hydroelectric project of James Bay. The plane is the only way to get there, but once there the great North opens. There is a choice of tours, from one-day visits to the James Bay project to four-night fishing or hunting trips to glorious fifteen- or nineteen-night trekking and canoeing trips across the Baffin Land or along the white-water George River, complete with professional guides and all camping material.

For more information: Direction du développement, Ministère de l'industrie, du commerce et du tourisme, 710 Place d'Youville, 3ieme etage, Québec, Qué. G1R 4Y4, 1-800-361-5405.

PRACTICAL INFORMATION FOR

QUÉBEC PROVINCE

ACCOMMODATIONS. An interesting new development in the Québec tourist industry are the bed-and-breakfasts. A guide to rural homes that offer such accommodations has just been compiled by the ministère du Loisir, de la Chasse et de la Pêche (Leisure, Hunting and Fishing Department) in cooperation with the Fédération des agricotours du Québec (Rural Tours Federation). The guide offers a choice of over 40 locations, covering the eastern part of Québec, where you can find food and shelter in a congenial atmosphere and at very inexpensive rates, uniformly fixed for all the participant homes. Some of the homes even offer laundry service. *Additional information*

and reservations: Fédération des agricotours du Québec, 525 avenue Viger, Montréal, Québec H2L 2P1, (514) 288–8121 or toll-free 1–800–361–6196.

Price categories for accommodations throughout the province are for double occupancy as follows: *Deluxe,* $80 and up; *Expensive,* $65–80; *Moderate,* $55–65; *Inexpensive,* $55 and under. CP indicates Canadian Pacific hotels.

Most places accept the following major credit cards: American Express, MasterCard, and Visa; others may also be honored. Not all establishments accept credit cards, therefore we suggest you call for information.

BAIE-DES-SABLES. *Inexpensive:* **Motel Martinet Sur Mer Enr.** 10 rooms, dining facilities, free parking, telephone, TV. Near the lake. (1–418–772–6841.)

CAP-CHÂT. *Inexpensive:* **Lindya Motel.** 13 rooms, dining facilities, free parking, telephone, color TV. Near lake. (1–418–786–5564.)

CHICOUTIMI. *Expensive:* **Hôtel Chicoutimi.** 127 rooms. Free parking, TV. Exceptional cuisine. (1–418–549–7111.)

CLORIDORME. *Inexpensive:* **Motel La Sapinière.** 10 rooms, good food, TV, free parking. Near historical site. Near lake. (1–418–395–2990.)

GASPÉ. *Moderate:* **Adams Motel-Hôtel.** 66 rooms, TV, free parking. (1–418–368–2244.)

GRANBY. *Moderate:* **Le Castel Hôtel.** 138 rooms, free parking, outdoor pool, kitchenettes, color TV. (1–514–378–9071.)

GRANDE-RIVIÈRE. *Inexpensive:* **Motel Ross Enr.** 20 rooms, dining facilities, free parking, telephone and TV. Near lake. (1–418–385–2221.)
Hôtel Motel Lagacé. 11 rooms, dining facilities, free parking; telephone, color TV. Near lake. (1–418–385–2224.)

HULL. *Deluxe:* **Auberge de la Chaudière.** 244 rooms. Free parking, air conditioning, color TV. 2 Montcalm St. (1–819–778–3880.)
Expensive: **Hôtel-Auberge Sheraton Le Marquis.** 133 rooms, free parking, air conditioning, some kitchenettes, color TV (1–819–770–8550.)

LONGUEUIL. *Expensive:* **Holiday Inn.** 215 rooms, free parking, outdoor pool, color TV, nice restaurant. (1–514–670–3030.)
Moderate: **Motel La Barre 500.** 100 rooms. Free parking, color TV, nice restaurant. (1–514–677–9101.)

MATANE. *Moderate:* **Auberge des Gouverneurs.** 48 rooms, very good food, banquet facilities, free parking, air conditioning, telephone, color TV. Near the lake. (1–418–566–2651.)
Inexpensive: **Motel Belle-Plage.** Open seasonally, 43 rooms, exceptional cuisine, free parking, telephone, color TV. Nearby historical site; near lake. (1–418–562–2323.)

MATAPÉDIA. *Inexpensive:* **Hôtel-Motel Le Martin-Pêcheur.** 9 rooms, dining facilities, free parking, TV. Near lake. (1–418–865–2921.)
Hôtel-Motel Restigouche. 38 rooms, good food, banquet facilities, free parking, telephone, color TV. Near lake. (1–418–865–2155.)

LES MÉCHINS. *Inexpensive.* **Hôtel-Motel Méchins-sur-Mer.** 16 rooms. Free parking, TV. (1–418–729–8295.)

Motel Robi. Not open year-round. 14 rooms, free parking, outdoor pool, TV. (1–418–729–8292.)

MONTEBELLO. *Deluxe:* **Château Montebello.** 200 rooms, private grounds, free parking, air conditioning, indoor and outdoor pools, cross-country skiing, tennis, and good food. Beautiful private grounds; ideal for walking; bikes available. On the Ottawa River. (1–819–423–6341.)

MONT-TREMBLANT. *Deluxe:* **Cuttle's Tremblant Club.** 70 rooms. (1–819–425–2731.)

Gray Rocks Inn. 161 rooms, free parking; on the lake; skiing; tennis. (1–819–425–2771.)

Mont-Tremblant Lodge. 131 rooms. Free parking, outdoor activities. (1–819–861–6165.)

Moderate: **Auberge Chauvignon,** (1–819–425–2658.) **Château Beauvallon,** (1–819–425–7275.) **Châlet des Chutes.** (1–819–425–2738.) All three are commendable.

MURDOCHVILLE. *Moderate:* **Copper Mountain Hôtel Inc.** 25 rooms, dining and banquet facilities, free parking, telephone, TV, nearby golf course, fishing, boating, skiing facilities. (1–418–784–2512.)

NEWPORT. *Inexpensive:* **Motel Newport.** Open seasonally, 12 rooms, free parking, TV, dining facilities; near lake. (1–418–777–2683.)

NEW RICHMOND. *Inexpensive.* **Mackenzies Honeymoon Motel.** 5 rooms, open seasonally, free parking, kitchenettes. (1–418–392–5566.)

Motel Francis. 23 rooms, good food, free parking, telephone, TV. Near lake. (1–418–392–4485.)

PERCÉ. *Expensive:* **Hôtel Le Bonaventure.** Not open year-round. 83 rooms, very good food and facilities, free parking, telephone, color TV. Close to lake; near historical site. (1–418–782–2166.)

Hôtel-Motel La Côte Surprise. 51 rooms. (1–418–782–2261.)

Moderate: **L'Auberge du Gargantua.** Not open year-round, 13 rooms, excellent food, free parking; near historical site. (1–418–782–2852.)

Inexpensive: **Hôtel-Motel Manoir Percé.** Open year-round, 42 rooms, good food, free parking, telephone, TV. (1–418–782–2022.)

PIEDMONT. *Moderate:* **Motel Le Nomade,** 21 rooms. (1–514–227–5181.) **Motel Le Totem.** 48 rooms, some with kitchenettes. (1–514–222–2618.) **Motel Piedmont.** 23 rooms. (1–514–227–2833.)

PORT-DANIEL. *Inexpensive:* **Bay View Motel.** Open year-round, 33 rooms, dining facilities, some kitchenettes, free parking, TV. (1–418–396–9902.)

SAINT-EUSTACHE. *Moderate:* **Hôtel 640.** 63 rooms, free parking, air conditioning, color TV, sauna, outdoor pool. (1–514–472–2640.)

SAINT-JOVITE. *Inexpensive–Expensive:* **Le St. Jovite Hôtel et Motel.** 59 rooms, free parking, outdoor pool, TV; good food; nice location; near lake. (1–819–425–2751.)

VAL DAVID. *Deluxe.* **Hôtel La Sapinière.** 67 rooms, free parking, air conditioning, outdoor pool, skiing, tennis, color TV, great food. On the water. (1–514 –866–8262.)

 PARKS. Québec's government parks and reserves, as well as the Duchesnay Forestry Station near Quebec City, provide some 500 kms. (312 miles) of trails for snowshoeing, cross-country skiing in winter; hunting, fishing, camping, canoeing in warmer weather. Some have camping units, housekeeping facilities, and other amenities. Anyone can use these facilities— and they are free.

Mont-Tremblant Park is 155 kms. (97 miles) north of Montréal via Hwys. 15 and 117.

Saint-Donat, on Hwys. 15 and 329, is 122 kms. (76 miles) from Montréal.

Paul Sauvé Park, reached via Hwys. 15, 640, and 344, is 48 kms. (30 miles) from Montréal.

Mont-Saint-Bruno, reached via Hwy. 116, is 20 kms. (12 miles) from Montréal.

Des Voltigeurs Park, 100 kms. (62 miles) from Montréal is reached via Hwy. 20.

Mont-Orford Park, 125 kms. (78 miles) from Montréal, is reached via Hwy. 10 from Montréal.

Sherbrooke is reached via Hwys. 20, 143 and 10 from Quebec City, 240 kms. (150 miles) away.

Laurentides Park, 55 kms. (34 miles) north of Québec City is reached via Hwys. 73 and 175. The Forestry Station at Duchesnay is 42 kms. (26 miles) from Québec via Hwys. 440 and 367.

Mont Sainte-Anne Park is 40 kms. (25 miles) from Québec City on Hwy. 138. Portneuf Park, 120 kms. (75 miles) from Québec, is reached via Hwys. 138, 365 and 367. And Port-Daniel is 730 kms. (456 miles) from Québec City via Hwy. 132.

Outdoor enthusiasts will find numerous on-site services at these places: reception areas, snack bars, waxing rooms, heated relay stations, trail maps, ski patrols and, at the major spots, equipment rental and repair shops.

For additional information on Québec's parks as well as reservations, and a *Calendar of Events,* communicate with the Department of Trade, Commerce and Tourism, 150 est. Boul. Saint-Cyrille, Québec, G1R 4Y3, or from one of these reception centers: 12, rue Sainte-Anne, Québec; 2, Place Ville Marie, Montréal; Mirabel International Airport; Notre-Dame-du-Portage, Hwy. 20; Rivière-Beaudette, Hwy. 20; De la Vérendrye Park, Hwy. 117; Saint-Bernard-de-Lacolle, Hwy. 15.

 WINTER SPORTS. Québec is tremendous ski country with an average annual snowfall of 130 inches, providing perfect ski conditions more than five months a year. For downhill skiers, its nine mountainous regions have 120 alpine ski centers, more than 900 slopes, and over 350 mechanical lifts. While there is good skiing throughout the province, there are four major ski regions:

The *Laurentians,* north of Montréal, provide one of North America's leading year-round outdoor recreation areas, with some 40 ski centers located in or near about 20 towns and villages. Here one finds the largest concentration of inns and resort hotels in Québec, most with a reputation for fine cuisine.

The *Eastern Townships* stretch to the southeast of Montréal, touching the American border. This region holds 20 well-developed ski centers, including Mount Orford, which lies in the provincial park that bears the same name.

The *Ottawa Valley* (L'Outaouais) lies to the north of the city of Hull and opposite Canada's capital, Ottawa. Although this region's ski centers are still not numerous, all are well planned. But the most superb of all ski centers in Eastern Québec is in *Mont Sainte-Anne Park,* only 40 kms. (25 miles) from Québec City. It's 815-meter altitude, combined with the contrasting weather conditions on its north and south slopes, permit skiing from mid-November to early May. There are 29 slopes and 12 ski lifts, including its famous gondola lift. Located only 40 kms. (25 miles) from Québec City, this park is being turned into an all-season recreation complex, with a golf course and cycling trails.

Three major autoroutes provide easy access to these leading ski regions: the Laurentian Autoroute (Montréal-Sainte-Adèle, Hwy. 15), the Eastern Townships Autoroute (Montréal-Sherbrooke, Hwy. 10), and the Trans-Canada Hwy. (Montréal-Québec, Hwy. 20).

The more out-of-the-way areas—Saguenay-Lac Saint-Jean, Matapédia, la Mauricie, and Abitibi—also offer excellent skiing and welcome visitors from across the province and everywhere else.

There are also more than 1,000 trails (a total of 5,000 kilometers or 3,125 miles) for **cross-country skiers** and some 150 trails especially set up for **snowshoers**—all with modern advantages and services. These two ancient modes of transportation, one stemming from the Scandinavians and the other from the early Indians, now attract thousands of tourists and sportsmen every season.

The Laurentian region alone, north of Montréal, has some 50 centers for cross-country skiing and snowshoeing. A map of the Laurentian trail system has been released recently and is available at gas stations, ski areas, and hotels, or by writing to the association Touristique des Laurentides, 1000 rue Labelle, Suite 200, Saint-Jérôme, Québec, J7Z 5N6, Canada. Southern Québec offers 45 centers, while the Lower Saint-Laurent region has 23. The Québec City region and La Mauricie have 16 each. The Abitibi-Témiscamingue and the Saguenay-Lac Saint-Jean regions have a dozen each, while the Montréal, Outaouais, Charlevoix, and North Shore areas share the remainder.

Endurance events. For experts in cross-country skiing, challenging expeditions are available. The Lachute-Hull Canadian marathon, held in February, for example, is one of the world's longest (160 kms., 2 days) and attracts thousands of participants year after year. There is also the Valcartier Adventure (24 kms., 1 day) which takes place in the picturesque valley of the Jacques-Cartier River, near Québec City. Or, in the Lower Saint-Laurent region, the Pohenegamook Adventure takes cross-country buffs over a 28 km. course in magnificent countryside.

Ski week packages. Dozens of hotels and ski resorts in Québec offer a variety of ski week packages that usually include hotel rooms, full meals or breakfast only, ski lessons, lift tickets, and various other activities.

Further information: The Department of Trade, Commerce and Tourism, will supply you with all the information you may need to plan your winter holiday. Write to Tourisme Québec, 150 est, Blvd. Saint-Cyrille, 15th floor, Québec G1R 4Y3, or visit one of the department's seven year-round reception centers: 12, rue Sainte-Anne, Québec; 2, Place Ville Marie, Montréal; Mirabel International Airport; Notre-Dame-du-Portage, Hwy. 20; Parc de la Vérendrye, Hwy. 117; Rivière-Beaudette, Hwy. 20; Saint-Bernard-de-Lacolle, Hwy. 15.

DRINKING LAWS. Cocktail lounges and cabarets stay open until 2 A.M. and 3 A.M., respectively in Montréal. The legal drinking age is 18.

DINING OUT. Many of the Québec dishes are variations of old French dishes. Onion soup and Habitant pea soup are among the best known. Maple syrup is a distinctive flavoring in many preparations. Price ranges are per person and do not include drinks, tax, or tip. *Deluxe,* $25 and over; *Expensive,* $15–25; *Moderate,* $10–15; *Inexpensive,* under $10.

Most places accept the following major credit cards: American Express, MasterCard, and Visa; others may also be honored. Not all establishments accept credit cards, therefore we suggest you call for information.

CHICOUTIMI. *Expensive:* **Hôtel Chicoutimi.** French/Canadian. 127 rooms. Highly rated cuisine. (1–418–549–7111.)

GASPÉ. *Expensive:* **Adams Motel-Hôtel.** French. (1–418–368–2244.)

HULL. *Expensive:* **Auberge Le Marquis.** French. (1–819–770–8550.)

PERCÉ. *Expensive:* **Auberge du Gargantua.** French. (1–418–782–2852.)

RIMOUSKI. *Expensive:* **Hôtel St. Louis.** French. (1–418–723–1170.)

RIVIÈRE-DU-LOUP. *Deluxe:* **Hôtel St. Louis.** French. (1–418–862–3591.)

SAINTE-ADÈLE. *Expensive:* **La Bonne Bouffe à Pepi.** Steaks. (1–514–229–5377.)
La Clé des Champs. French. (1–514–229–2857.)
Le St. Trop. On rue Morin. New and already acclaimed as one of Québec's best restaurants. (1–514–229–3298.)
Lòs qui Fume. French. (1–514–229–4357.)
Moderate: **Le Chateau Boisé.** Sensational buffet. (1–514–229–2953.)

SAINT-HYACINTHE. *Expensive.* **L'Auberge des Seigneurs.** Seafoods, steaks. (1–514–774–3810.)

SAINT-JÉRÔME. *Moderate:* **La Maison Millaire.** Canadian and French. (1–514–436–7810.)

ST. JOVITE. *Expensive:* **La Table Enchantée.** On Hwy. 117. French and Québecois. (1–819–425–7113.)
Le Trou Normand. Fondues. (1–819–425–5594.)

SAINT-MARC-SUR-RICHELIEU. *Deluxe:* **Les Trois Tilleuls.** French. (1–514–584–2231.)
Moderate: **Auberge Handfield Inn.** French. (1–514–584–2226.)

SAINTE-MARGUERITE STATION. *Expensive:* **The Alpine Inn.** French. (1–514–229–3516.)

SAINT-SAUVEUR. *Moderate.* **Gilby's.** French. (1–514–227–5275.)

La Maison de l'Entrecôte. Steaks. (1–514–227–4585.)
La Vieille Ferme de 1900. French. (1–514–227–3083.)

SHERBROOKE. *Deluxe:* **Hotel King George.** French/Canadian. (1–819–569–2581.)

SOREL. *Moderate:* **Auberge de la Rive.** French. (1–514–742–5691.)

VAL DAVID. *Deluxe:* **Hôtel La Sapinière.** Prize-winning French cuisine. Menu changes daily. (1–819–322–2020.)

NEW BRUNSWICK

Natural Habitat for Sportsmen

by
COLLEEN THOMPSON

Author of New Brunswick Inside Out, *a native New Brunswicker's view of the province, travel writer Colleen Thompson has journeyed extensively throughout the Atlantic provinces. She is a regular contributor to various U.S. and Canadian magazines and newspapers, a travel columnist for the* Saint John Telegraph-Journal *and a regular commentator on CBC radio.*

New Brunswick is where the great Canadian forest, cut in vast swaths by sweeping river valleys and modern superhighways, meets the sea. It is an old place in North American terms, and the remains of a turbulent past exist in delightfully quiet nooks.

Some 1,400 miles (2,240 km.) of coast surround more than half the province. The violent Bay of Fundy, which has the highest tides in the world, sweeps up the coast of Maine, around the enchanting Fundy Isles at the southern tip of New Brunswick and on up the province's rough and intriguing southern coast. To the north and east, home of

222

the province's French Acadian heritage, it's the gentle Gulf of St. Lawrence that washes up on quiet beaches.

For all that, New Brunswick is also a province of inland attractions. Its land mass and its human side are dominated by the Saint John River Valley—a strip of gentle farmland with sweeping views, and genteel communities with a captivating heritage. The capital, Fredericton, is built on the river's banks and it enters the sea at Saint John, the province's main industrial city.

Although the winter is usually severe with lots of snow, the province is alive with winter sports from late November to late March with skiing leading the list. The province has extensive skiing facilities, both cross-country and downhill, with many annual competitions and championships.

Spring is a glorious time—the greening of the land begins in April. Summer is hot, more so in the inland cities such as Fredericton, where the average temperature of 21°C (70°F) can easily soar to 35°C. (95°F.). In the fall, especially October, the whole countryside is ablaze with some of the most magnificent color in all of North America.

Certain foods and seasons are often well paired in this Maritime province. In the spring, the tourist must sample New Brunswick's delicacy, the fiddlehead, picked fresh alongside the rivers and streams. Eaten as a vegetable (boiled with butter, salt, and pepper), it is delicious. Also in spring, the bony fish, shad and gaspereaux, are popular. Salmon, once the spring staple, is a special treat now that the price is high. Lobster is the Maritimer's favorite dish, eaten on the shore, not at the table. Indeed, all shellfish coming from the Bay of Fundy and Gulf of St. Lawrence waters are especially tasty. Look for oysters, scallops, clams, and crab. And don't overlook dulse, a salty seaweed eaten like potato chips. Wash down these hearty native dishes with rich Moosehead beer, brewed in Saint John (a strictly local brew for decades, it is now a well-known export beer), and you'll have feasted "New Brunswick" style.

A Quiet History

While the red-bearded Vikings may have been familiar with the shores of New Brunswick's Fundy Isles in the Passamaquoddy Bay, history records the first white explorer as Jacques Cartier who traded with the Micmac Indians on New Brunswick's northern shore in 1534 on his way to explore the St. Lawrence River. Some 70 years later, when Samuel de Champlain and Sieur de Monts landed at the mouth of the St. John River they were casually greeted by an elderly Indian chieftain, the same Chief Membertou who had met Cartier on his first North American adventure.

Throughout their exploration of New Brunswick (then part of the area known as Acadia—embracing Nova Scotia, Cape Breton, and Prince Edward Island), the French maintained good relationships with both the Micmacs and the Maliceets who inhabited the St. John River Valley. Hoping to pre-empt the land before the English, they encouraged French settlers, opening up the rich fur trade to them. Their strategy deteriorated, however, when many of the French fought

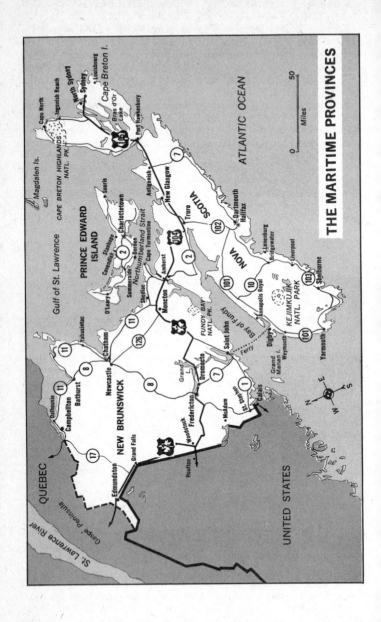

THE MARITIME PROVINCES

among themselves, a situation that allowed the English to launch successful attacks from Maine and establish their own settlements.

Finally, in 1713, the Treaty of Utrecht ceded Acadia to England. By 1755 there were estimated to be 10,000 Acadians still living in Nova Scotia (the area of New Brunswick and Nova Scotia). Of these, at least 7,000 were expelled by the English, who were concerned about the loyalties of this ever-increasing body should another war break out between France and England. Of the remainder, many were forced to flee to Québec and faraway places, such as Louisiana where the name Acadian has been corrupted to "Cajun." Yet, within 20 years many had returned, settling along the shores, especially in the New Brunswick communities of Cocagne, Shippagan, and Caraquet. Today one third of New Brunswick's population is made up of Acadians and the province is officially bilingual although attempts have only recently been made to familiarize residents with both languages.

The close of the Revolutionary War brought the Loyalists, 50,000 of them, loyal to Great Britain in deed or spirit. Because of the influx, the area known as Nova Scotia was divided into two colonies, and in 1784, the province of New Brunswick came into being.

Three thousand Loyalists arrived at the mouth of the Saint John River on May 11, 1783 . . . a large percentage of them gentlefolk, unaccustomed to deprivation. Here they were forced to seek shelter in tents and hastily constructed shacks, enduring hardships with amazing fortitude. Aged and infirm, women and children suffered deeply and many died of cold and exposure.

In time, settlers spread over the entire country away from the coast though a large number remained at the mouth of the Saint John River, founding the city which now bears that name. The hardy Loyalist spirit and the French persistence have made the New Brunswicker what he is today . . . stubborn, resourceful, fun-loving, sometimes rowdy . . . and fiercely independent.

The Great Outdoors

A province of great geographical variety, New Brunswick claims 1,400 miles of seacoast, including the hauntingly beautiful Fundy Isles, acres of rolling agricultural land along its rivers, and a rugged highland interior—forests, secluded lakes and mountains.

Crisscrossed with rivers, the province is a fisherman's heaven, offering Atlantic silver salmon, speckled trout, and black and striped bass. Especially the latter. New Brunswick offers pretty well the best bass fishing in North America. The season starts in mid-May with the Big Bass Tournament at Mactaquac, upriver from Fredericton. The Miramichi, the Restigouche, and the Nashwaak Rivers are prized by sport fishermen the world over.

Deep-sea fishing is also available for the avid sportsman. Canoeing, hiking, bird-watching—and more recently, whale-watching and windsurfing—are popular summer pastimes.

New Brunswick is still largely unsettled—88 percent of the province is forested lands. Inhabitants have chosen the easily accessible area around rivers, ocean, and lakes, leaving most of the interior to the pulp companies. In fact, the view from a plane will make you think that New Brunswick is still an unspoiled wilderness with little sign of civilization.

How New Brunswick Makes a Living

Lumbering, a major source of income since the days of pit props and ships' masts, has taken a back seat to the mineral industry in recent times. Zinc, lead, and potash are the major minerals. Fishing remains the major occupation along the shores while the rich agricultural lands of the upper Saint John Valley turn out profitable potato crops each year. Saint John is a major port and industrial city. The largest oil refinery in Canada is located there. Tourism also generates considerable economic activity. Manufacturing is mostly done on the small scale, and it is diverse.

Madawaska

As you cross the Québec border into New Brunswick (a large, new tourist information center has been built here, with displays, audio-visual presentations, etc.), you'll find yourself in the mythical Republic of Madawaska. As we delve into its history, we learn that in the early 1800's the narrow wedge of land which makes up most of Madawaska County was coveted by Québec on one side and New Brunswick on the other. On top of that, the U.S. claimed it as well. Seeking to retain it for New Brunswick, Governor Sir Thomas Carleton found it easy to settle with Québec. He rolled dice all night with the Governor of North America at Québec, who happened to be his brother. Sir Thomas won at dawn . . . by one point. Settling with the Americans was more difficult. The border had always been disputed; even the lumbermen engaged in combat, brandishing peavies as weapons and otherwise harassing each other from both sides of the border. Finally, with the Treaty of Webster–Ashburton, in 1842, the British flag was hoisted over Madawaska county. It is said that one old-timer, tired of being asked which country he belonged to, replied: "I am a citizen of the Republic of Madawaska." So Madawaska exists to this day with its own flag (an independent eagle on a field of white) and coat-of-arms. To be a member of the Republic is a singular honor indeed.

Edmundston, Capital of Madawaska

Edmundston has always depended on the wealth of the deep forest land surrounding it; even today the Fraser Company's paper mill provides the major source of employment. It was in these woods that the legend of Paul Bunyan was born, and the feats of a strong young Madawaskan embroidered. Tales were spread to Maine and even to the west coast. Other lands, other people have tried to claim him for their own . . . but Paul Bunyan was born and raised in the forests and lumber camps of Madawaska County.

Formerly called Petit Sault because of the small rapids which existed here, the town was renamed Edmundston after a visit by Sir Edmund Head, one-time Lieutenant Governor of the province.

Not really an Acadian town, most of the French population has come from neighboring Québec. The first French settlers arrived here in the 19th century, followed closely by the British, especially the Scots. That combination gives this happy, thriving city a unique background. The main language is French, but most people are bilingual, not to mention exuberant. The French from Madawaska are often called "Brayons." The annual midsummer Foire Brayonne festival (lumberjack competitions, folk dancing, handcraft exhibits, and other events) is one of the most popular festivals in New Brunswick. It is held annually during the last week of July.

Examine the two churches which dominate the skyline. The Roman Catholic Cathedral of the Immaculate Conception is regarded as one of the better examples of its particular style of architecture in eastern Canada, and the Church of Our Lady of Sorrows contains some beautiful woodcarvings, notably those of the Fourteen Stations of the Cross created by noted New Brunswick artist Claude Roussel.

At the College of Saint Louis-Maillet, the religious paintings of another native son, Claude Picard, decorate the walls. On the campus too, the Galerie Colline displays touring art exhibitions.

About 20 miles out of Edmundston on Route 120 is a very popular recreation area, the Lac Baker Provincial Park.

For other diversions, skiing is popular on the slopes of nearby Mount Farlagne, the 18-hole golf course is well recommended by residents, and you'll enjoy the old car museum on the grounds of Les Jardins Provincial Park. The new Madawaska Regional Museum has displays on regional history and sports an art gallery.

The Saint John River Valley

The Saint John River Valley is a scenic delight. Rolling hills of rich agricultural land and the blue sweep of the winding Saint John make the drive excellent viewing. From St. Leonard to Woodstock lies New Brunswick's famed potato belt. Note the endless fields of potatoes and the squat, half-underground potato storage houses. Though Grand Falls is itself largely French speaking, from there on down the river, the French tongue is replaced by English everywhere.

At Grand Falls, site of a large and beautiful cataract, you may want to inspect the wells in the rocks, deep holes worn by the action of the water, some with a diameter of 16 feet and a depth of 30 feet. One of the town's interesting features is its wide main street, formerly a military parade ground. As the residents built their homes around it to view the proceedings, it gradually became the center of town.

The legend of Malabeam, part of the town's history, is the story of a young Indian maiden who led her Iroquois captors to their deaths over the falls rather than take them to her village. In memory of her courage, old boats filled with flowers are occasionally sent over the falls during the town's annual celebration of the Potato Festival. Local history is depicted at the Grand Falls Historical Museum.

The Fundy Coastal Region

Route 1, leading along the Bay of Fundy from St. Stephen to Saint John, is one of New Brunswick's most interesting drives. St. Stephen (a small border town named for a surveyor, not a saint) has always enjoyed such good relations with its neighboring American town of Calais that during the war of 1812, while the rest of Canada and the United States were in conflict, St. Stephen obligingly lent gunpowder to Calais for its Fourth of July celebration. Each summer there is an international festival held jointly in the two towns. The Charlotte County Historical Society Museum, describing the area's Loyalist ancestry, is located here.

At Oak Bay, outside St. Stephen, you'll find a little provincial park complete with beach, shaded camping grounds, and barbecue pits stocked with plenty of wood.

Take the jog off Route 1 to St. Andrews, a town every visitor to New Brunswick should see. Long the summer resort of the affluent (mansions ring the town), it's also a fisherman's town. Little has changed in the last two centuries. Of the town's 550 buildings, 280 were erected before 1880. Of these, 14 have survived from the 1700's. Indeed, some ingenious Loyalists who settled here brought their homes with them, piece by piece, from Castine, Maine, across the Passamaquoddy Bay. The Old English character of the town is preserved and enhanced by many of the town's businesses.

A walking-tour map is available from the tourist information center on Water St. . . . follow it to some of the town's most interesting buildings. One of these, Greenoch Church, is an architect's delight. Stuart Trueman called it "the church that was born of an insult" in his book *The Fascinating World of New Brunswick*. The church was the result of a remark passed at an 1822 dinner party regarding the inability of the "poor" Presbyterians to have a church of their own. Presbyterian Captain Christopher Scott took exception to the slur. Sparing no expense, he erected an admirable building with a green oak tree carved on its tower in honor of his birthplace, Greenoch, England. The new Ross Memorial Museum on Montague Street features one of the finest antique collections in eastern Canada.

A drive up Joe's Point Road takes you to the Huntsman Marine Aquarium, an offshoot of the Federal Fisheries Research and Biological Station nearby. You'll see the shells of the two giant lobsters, Bonnie and Clyde, and be intrigued by the tank holding many varieties of marine life under a sign which says "Please Touch." Playful seals love to entertain the small fry and the film on current off-shore research is thoroughly engrossing.

The blockhouse on the shore is a restoration of one of five built in the area during the War of 1812. It's only 68 miles from St. Andrews to Saint John so take advantage of the route by taking some side trips to the numerous little coastal villages along the way. St. George, for instance, has one of the oldest Protestant graveyards in Canada as well as a fish ladder running up the side of the dam across the Magaguadavic River which flows through the town. And in nearby Lake Utopia (a scenic recreation area) lives the fabled Lake Utopian monster. He's been seen for generations . . . a rival for Scotland's Loch Ness monster.

Black's Harbour boasts the largest sardine cannery in the British Commonwealth. Nearby Pennfield the landing site of the British aviator Mollison, when he made the first nonstop, east-west crossing of the Atlantic.

The Fundy Isles

New Brunswick's Fundy Isles are true escapist retreats. It's hard to beat their windswept hospitable charm. Grand Manan, largest of the three, is the farthest away. It's a two-hour ferry ride from Black's Harbour, but you might see spouting whales, sunning porpoises, or a rare puffin on the trip out. It will be immediately apparent that the island's main preoccupation is fishing. The circular herring weirs dot the coastal waters and fish sheds and smokehouses appear along the shores. Names like Swallowtail, Southern Head, Seven Days Work, and Dark Harbour are as romantic as the island air, and the friendly folk speak with an accent all their own.

Grand Manan

About 20 miles of road lead from Southern Head to Northern Head, each Head with its own lighthouse perched high on jagged cliffs above the rocky surf. The famous American author Willa Cather spent her summers here and some of her novels were written on Grand Manan.

You'll want to visit Dark Harbour where no sun shines until late morning when it finally rises over the high hill that shades the harbor. The home of New Brunswick's dulse industry, it is here that dulse harvesters gather the purple seaweed from rocks left dry at low tide. They dry it in the sun on a natural rocky breakwater, and send it to mainland stores where it is purchased by New Brunswickers who enjoy the salty goodness of dried seaweed. The natives eat it like candy, but the visitor needs a little time to acquire the taste.

At Red Point, you'll find two different geological phenomena. Because of a long ago underwater upheaval, you will stand in one spot and note, on one side, 16-million-year-old volcanic material and on the other, the 6-billion-year-old sedimentary rock of the continental mass.

Welcome bird watchers! The island is known as an ornithologist's wonderland. Even John James Audubon came here in 1831 to study the various species; in fact, the rare puffin is the symbol of Grand Manan. If you'd like a close look at puffins, take a boat trip to Machias Seal Island, about 2 hours away by boat. Bird-watching tour packages are available to Grand Manan throughout the summer months. Contact Tourism New Brunswick for information. Whale-watching expeditions are also available through the Marathon Inn.

Anchorage Provincial Park on Grand Manan offers picnic, camping and hiking facilities. Hiking on Grand Manan generally is a very popular activity for tourists.

At the Grand Manan Museum, formerly the dwelling of Moses Gerrish, one of the first three settlers on the island, you'll be able to see many stuffed specimens of the island's birds as well as a large collection of artifacts from the oceans's bottom—the only residue of vessels wrecked in the waters of the Fundy Isles.

Campobello and Deer Islands

Neatly manicured, preening itself in the Bay, Campobello Island has always had a special appeal to the wealthy and the famous. It was here that the Roosevelt family spent its summers. The home of Franklin Delano Roosevelt, former president of the United States, is now maintained as a lovely museum in his honor. Located in the center of Roosevelt International Park, a joint project of the Canadian and American governments, President Roosevelt's home was the setting for the movie *Sunrise at Campobello.* A few miles away, a gracious mansion known as the Owens home is open to the public, and for overnight guests. Built by Captain William Owens in 1767, it has 21 rooms and nine fireplaces.

Herring Cove Provincial Park has camping facilities and a 9-hole golf course.

Connected to Lubec, Maine, by an international bridge, Campobello may still be approached from the other side by toll ferry from Deer Island.

An easy 20-minute free ferry ride from Letete near St. George brings you to Deer Island for a relaxing visit. You'll enjoy exploring the fishing wharves like those at Chocolate Cove. You'll find the world's largest lobster pound at Northern Harbour (owned by Conley's), and you'll want to walk through an interesting park at Deer Point, where you catch a toll ferry to nearby Campobello. If you listen carefully you may be able to hear the sighing and snorting of "the Old Sow," the second largest whirlpool in the world. If you can't hear it, you'll be able to see it, just a few feet off shore.

Exploring the island takes only a few hours. . . . it's 7½ miles long, varying in width from 3 miles to a few hundred feet at some points. If you decide to spend the night you might be interested to know that Deer Island is located exactly on the 45th parallel and one of the motels at Fairhaven is named just that.

Fredericton, Provincial Capital

The seat of government for New Brunswick's 710,900 residents has been the inland city of Fredericton on the St. John River since 1785. Loyalist to the core and named for Frederick, second son of George III, the city is the pride of the province. Tree-lined, resting sedately on the bank of the river, it was never a true frontier town. From the first town plan, the wealthy and scholarly Loyalists set out to create a gracious and beautiful place.

Its predecessor was the early French settlement of Ste.-Anne's Point established in 1642 during the reign of the French governor, Villebon, who made his headquarters at the junction of the Nashwaak and the Saint John. From Fort Nashwaak—now only a memorial cairn—he launched many successful raids into Maine, which caused great resentment among the English. Villebon left Fort Nashwaak in 1698, but the memory of the English was long and some forty years later a raiding party known as Hazen's Massachusetts Rangers burned the small village to the ground, killed most of the men, and carried the women and children off to Boston. The city of Fredericton rose from the ruins of this small French village.

EXPLORING FREDERICTON

Called the City of Stately Elms, Fredericton became an elegant British garrison town starting in 1825 when the military quarters were established there. A look at the military compound (including officer's quarters, enlisted men's barracks, guardhouse, and parade ground) is a must for any visitor interested in the city's past. Now designated a federal historic site, the military compound has been restored. Although the inside houses government offices, some parts, such as the guardhouse, are open to the public.

At present, the officer's quarters houses the York–Sunbury Historical Museum (largest community museum in the province, displaying many mementos of the past including replicas of 19th-century Fredericton homes), reconstructed with authentic furnishings of the period. You'll also find there the remains of one of Fredericton's legends. Staring at you from its glass case at the top of a staircase is the famous Coleman Frog, allegedly discovered in nearby Killarney Lake by hotelier Fred Coleman. Weighing 42 pounds, it was dispatched to an untimely death by a dynamite charge set by some disgruntled fishermen. Coleman had the frog stuffed; for forty years it sat in the lobby of his hotel on Queen Street where visitors were held spellbound by the stories of how it used to thrive on a diet of buttermilk, June bugs, fireflies, and whiskey fed to it by Fred and his friends. Resurrected from someone's garage after the old Barker House closed, it now holds a place of honor in the museum; and, of course, with a slight smile on its froggy face it never reveals its secret . . . which only Fred Coleman knew. Hoax or miracle? You'll have to decide for yourself.

Because of the gifts showered upon it by former New Brunswicker Lord Beaverbrook, multimillionaire, British peer, and newspaper baron, Fredericton has many fine buildings. On lower Queen Street, just two blocks from the Military Compound, you'll see the Playhouse, a gift of the Beaverbrook and the Dunn Foundation (former New Brunswicker Sir James Dunn, steel magnate and also Beaverbrook's close friend). The Playhouse (home of Theatre New Brunswick), built in 1964, provides year-round professional theater to city and province.

The Beaverbrook Art Gallery across the street will delight you with the wealth of its collection, including works by many of New Brunswick's noted artists as well as Salvador Dali's giant canvas *Santiago el Grande* (a huge painting bought especially for the Gallery's opening in 1959 by Sir James Dunn), canvasses by Reynolds, Turner, Hogarth, Gainsborough, the Canadian Group of Seven, and even works by Sir Winston Churchill. The Gallery houses a large collection of Graham

Sutherland (47), and the largest collection in any institution of the works of Cornelius Krieghoff, famed Canadian landscape painter, known for his portrayals of Canadian life in the early 1800's.

The Provincial Legislature, built in 1880, is across the street from the Gallery. Open to the public, it offers guided tours at no cost, except when the Legislature is in session. When the House is in session, the public may view the proceedings from the public gallery, where you must also examine Sir Joshua Reynolds' portraits of George III and Queen Charlotte which flank the Throne.

In the back room of the Legislature, near the handsome spiral staircase, is the Legislative Library which contains two interesting and rare items. The first is a copy of the *Domesday Book,* the first census ever written, commissioned by William of Normandy in 1087. (This edition was printed in 1783.) Then turn to the four-volume set of the rare king-size Audubon bird books, more than three feet high, containing 435 hand-colored pictures (1834).

At the triangle of Queen, Church, and Brunswick Streets, about a block from the Legislative Building, you'll find the Christ Church Cathedral, Fredericton's pride. Completed in 1853, it is a beautiful building, one of the best examples of decorated Gothic architecture in North America and the first new cathedral foundation built on British soil since the Norman Conquest. Inside you'll find a clock known as "Big Ben's little brother" designed by Lord Grimthorpe, probably as the test-run for London's famous timepiece. While there, watch out for the ghost of Mrs. Medley, wife of the first bishop, John Medley. She's often seen crossing the lawn to enter the Cathedral by the west door.

The University of New Brunswick (located at the end of University Avenue on a hill overlooking the city), is ancient by Canadian standards. Established in 1783, when it was called the College of New Brunswick, it later became known as Kings College until 1859, when it became the University of New Brunswick. Today the campus also includes St. Thomas University, a small but steadily growing institution. Site of many firsts, the University of New Brunswick campus had the first astronomical observatory (the Brydon Jack Observatory) in Canada. The building is now used as the headquarters of a noted literary publication, *The Fiddlehead.* The university initiated the first engineering school in Canada and the second forestry school. With an active enrollment in the sciences and arts as well, the university has come a long way since the first two B.A. degrees were awarded in 1828. Enrollment today is approximately 6,000.

On Woodstock Road, surrounded by spacious lawns, you'll find Old Government House, built in 1828 as a residence for the province's lieutenant governors. The classic old Georgian building has housed many famous guests, for example, the Prince of Wales (later Edward VII) who stayed here in 1860 when he visited New Brunswick as a young man of 19. Dancing all night at one of the city's gaiest balls, he won the hearts of all the women. Unfortunately, now that Government House is headquarters for the RCMP, it is not generally open to the public.

John James Audubon stayed here two years later as the guest of the Governor and painted his famous Pine Finch on the grounds. (You can view it at the Legislative Library.)

A walking tour of Fredericton's historic homes is available at bookstores.

But for a true understanding of New Brunswick's background and history, visit Kings Landing, located about 23 miles west of Fredericton on the Trans-Canada Highway. Challenging the imagination of visitors, this reconstructed village—55 buildings including homes, inn, forge, store, church, school, and working farm—is designed to illustrate life in the central Saint John River Valley between 1790 and 1870. The winding country lanes, creaking wagons, old houses, and the smell of freshly baked bread will pull you back a century or more to when the sound of the motor car was unknown. The costumed staff will answer your questions, and the Kings Head Inn is a friendly spot to rest your feet and quench your thirst with a draft of cold beer or a sip of wine. The restaurant upstairs serves old-fashioned traveler's fare such as cold cuts and hot meat pie. Just around the corner in a barn, the King's Theatre offers some of the funniest "mellerdrama" you've ever witnessed.

PRACTICAL INFORMATION FOR FREDERICTON

HOW TO GET THERE. By air: Both *Air Canada* and *Eastern Provincial Airways* service Fredericton airport at Lincoln (5 miles from Fredericton), with connecting flights from most major airlines.

By car: Follow the Trans-Canada Hwy. from Québec; U.S. 95 and Trans-Canada Hwy. from Houlton, Maine; Hwy. 3 and Trans-Canada Hwy. from Calais, Maine; Trans-Canada from Nova Scotia.

By train: *Via Rail* has daily rail liner service to and from Halifax through Saint John and Moncton. At Moncton it makes connections with the *Ocean Limited* train which travels Halifax–Montréal.

By bus: *SMT* bus service within the province provides regional transportation. Most major bus companies in USA and Canada connect with SMT.

ACCOMMODATIONS. Hotels and motels in and around Fredericton are not luxurious but are adequate with friendly service. A 10% sales tax will be added to your bill. Rates are based on double occupancy as follows: *Expensive,* over $43; *Moderate,* $30–43; *Inexpensive,* under $30.

Most places accept the following major credit cards: American Express, MasterCard, and Visa; others may also be honored. Not all establishments accept credit cards, therefore we suggest you call for information.

The Diplomat Motor Hotel. *Expensive:* Pleasant rooms, many with balconies overlooking pool, good dining room, intimate indoor bar and popular pool bar. Often patronized by Fredericton residents. Outdoor jazz café in summer. Phone 454-5584. Major credit cards.

Howard Johnson's Motor Lodge. *Expensive:* Rte. 2, Trans-Canada Hwy. Pleasant rooms, good dining area. Indoor court with pool and bar. Phone 472-0480. Major credit cards.

Keddy's Motor Inn. *Expensive:* Forest Hill at end of Princess Margaret Bridge. Pleasant rooms, lively lounge bar, dining room, pool, close to university. Phone 454-4461. Major credit cards.

The Lord Beaverbrook Hotel. *Expensive:* Popular pool bar, good main dining room and steakhouse. River Room bar draws civil servants, politicians, visiting VIPs at lunch and happy hour. Phone 455-3371. Major credit cards.

The Wandlyn Inn. *Expensive:* Prospect St. Pleasant rooms, good dining room, small cozy bar. Close to three major shopping malls, many restaurants, and two theaters. Heated pool. Phone 455-8937. Major credit cards.

The Condor Motel. *Moderate–Expensive:* Woodstock Rd. W. Adequate rooms, small dining room, heated pool. Phone 455-5537. Major credit cards.

The Fort Nashwaak Motel. *Moderate–Expensive.* Homey motel with adequate rooms, small restaurant, three minutes from city center. Also has indoor pool. Phone 472-4411. Major credit cards.

The Fredericton Inn. *Moderate.* Regent St. at the Trans-Canada Hwy. Phone 455-1430. Major credit cards. Excellent value. Nice rooms, good dining room, pleasant décor.

The Sequoia Motel. *Moderate.* Regent St. Better than average rooms, good small dining room, bar, pool, and sauna. Close to shopping centers, restaurants, and theater. Phone 455-9900. Major credit cards.

Fredericton Skyline Motel. *Inexpensive.* 502 Forest Hill Rd. 40 units, licensed dining room. Phone 455-6683.

Norfolk Motel. *Inexpensive.* On Rte. 2 just out of town. 20 units, a quiet and friendly place. Phone 472-3278

HOW TO GET AROUND. By bus: Fare in city, 60¢. *Fredericton Transit* buses travel across the river to Nashwaaksis, Marysville, Barker's Point and New Maryland. Catch a Fredericton Transit bus by the Military Compound on Queen St. for Silverwood. (An Edmundston bus from the SMT terminal on Regent will take you there too as well as to Oromoco and Lincoln.)

By taxi: As many taxis do not have meters, you could end up sharing a cab with other people. Some meter cabs are available, however.

From the airport: A limousine service is provided to the Lord Beaverbrook Hotel.

TOURIST INFORMATION. Tourist Office, City of Fredericton, telephone 472–1907. Municipal Tourist Information Centre, on Trans-Canada Hwy., open June to September, tel. 455–3092.

Province: Department of Tourism, 7th floor, Brunswick Place, corner Carleton and Kings Sts., P.O. Box 12345, Fredericton. U.S. residents call toll-free, 1–800–343–0812; Canadian residents call toll-free, 1–800–561–0213.

RECOMMENDED READING. Fredericton was the home of the late Alden Nowlan, the award-winning poet and novelist. *Bread, Wine and Salt, Between Tears and Laughter,* and *I'm A Stranger Here Myself* are collections of his poems; his book of stories, *Miracle at Indian River,* and his novel *Various Persons Named Kevin O'Brien* offer the most penetrating view available of rural life in the Maritimes. Fredericton has always been a center for writers, from the early Loyalist poet Jonathan O'Dell to contemporary novelist Kent Thompson *(The Tenants Were Corrie & Tennie)* and a group of poets centered around UNB and *Fiddlehead* magazine. New Brunswick has been more given to poetry and less to fiction than Nova Scotia, but younger writers like David Adam Richards *(Blood Ties, The Coming of Winter)* and Raymond Fraser *(The Black Horse Tavern)* may be changing that fact. A well-beloved writer of nonfiction is Stuart Trueman *(An Intimate History of New Brunswick, The Fascinating World of New Brunswick).* W.S. MacNutt has written histories of New Brunswick and of the Atlantic provinces generally. *History of Fredericton —the Last 200 Years* by W. Austin Squires gives a readable "human" history of the capital city. Another historian of note is A.F. Bailey *(Culture and Nationality)* who is also a poet *(Thanks for a Drowned Island).* *New Brunswick Inside Out* by Colleen Thompson is an invaluable handbook for visitors to the province and to Fredericton.

 CITY PARKS. Three hundred acres of wooded land at *Odell Park* off Waggoner's La. Nature trails, picnic tables with barbecue pits and wood, play equipment, duck pond, and deer enclosure. *Wilmot Park* on Woodstock Rd.—picnic tables, wading pool, playground, free tennis courts.

 THE ARTS. Fredericton is a small city (population about 46,000) and its cultural facilities are not extensive, although they are of nationally recognized quality.

The Beaverbrook Art Gallery, in fact, is internationally known, with a collection of works by Turner, Krieghoff, Gainsborough, Dali, the Group of Seven, plus several rotating exhibits.

The Playhouse is the home of *Theatre New Brunswick,* which brings professional live theater to the city. TNB also tours the province.

The *York Sunbury Historical Museum and Officers Square* is the city's main museum. It is part of a downtown historical restoration and features local and military history.

 SHOPPING. New Brunswick is famous for crafts, and Fredericton has many studios and artisans' sales rooms. *Aitkens Pewter,* 680 Charlotte St., and *Pewtercraft,* 582 Brunswick St., offer beautiful pewter holloware, goblets, belt buckles, jewelry and authentic reproductions of ancient folk dishes. *Shades of Light Studio and Gift Shop* on Regent St. features stained glass and other local crafts. *The Parlour Gallery,* 856 George St., designer Judy Thorpes soft sculptures, hand-painted animals, unique crafts.

The Regent Craft Gallery, 71 Regent St.; wide variety of quality handcrafts of local artists.

The *Boyce Country Market* on George St. operates every Saturday morning offering everything from crafts to home baked doughnuts and breakfast at Goofy Roofy's. An outdoor café, operating out of the market in the summer (in winter it goes indoors), it is an incredible experience as politicians, scholars, actors, musicians and writers come in to partake of Roofy's special omelets.

An elaborate booklet describing crafts in New Brunswick and listing all craftspeople is available from various tourist bureaus and offices.

 DINING OUT. Restaurants in Fredericton have improved a lot in recent years. A few are very good. Price categories are as follows: *Expensive,* over $16; *Moderate,* $11–16; *Inexpensive,* under $11. A 10% provincial tax will be added. Drinks and tip are not included.

Most places accept the following major credit cards: American Express, MasterCard, and Visa; others may also be honored. Not all establishments accept credit cards, therefore we suggest you call for information.

The Coffeemill. *Expensive.* Located in Fredericton shopping mall on Prospect St. Good seafood and generally good food. Phone 454-6376. Major credit cards.

Eighty-Eight Ferry. *Expensive.* 88 Ferry St. Charming old home decor. Excellent food. Friendly owners; drinks served in the garden. Highly recommended. Phone 472-1988. Major credit cards.

The Maverick Room. *Expensive.* Located in basement of Lord Beaverbrook Hotel and open only at night (from 6 P.M.), specializes in steak. The spareribs are excellent, the atmosphere dim, and the wines marked up. Phone 455-3371. Major credit cards.

The Terrace Room, Lord Beaverbrook Hotel. *Expensive.* Specializes in New Brunswick's own foods, like salmon, fiddleheads (New Brunswick's vegetable specialty), and shellfish including Buctouche oysters. Phone 455-3371. Major credit cards.

Victoria and Albert. *Expensive.* Seafood and steaks in Victorian England décor. Phone 455–2524. Major credit cards.

Mei's Chinese Restaurant, *Moderate.* 74 Regent St., 454-2177; Excellent varieties of Chinese food, moderate prices, understated, comfortable decor. Small.

Country Fair Café. *Moderate.* Daytime café under arches of Officer's Quarters in historical Officer's Square. Wonderful home-baking. Summers only.

Creme Café. *Moderate.* Gathering place for any hour of the day or night. Salads, sandwiches, fresh croissants, exotic coffees, desserts. Charming owners.

Pat's Gourmet. *Moderate.* Lower St. Mary's. Excellent Asian food of all persuasions. Phone 472-0992. Major credit cards.

Bar B Q Barn. *Inexpensive.* 540 Queen St. Ribs, fish and chips, and fried scallops. A family spot.

The Luna Steak House. *Inexpensive.* (Soon to be re-named but still to be located on premises of Luna Pizza.) 168 Dundonald St., 455–4020. Leans to Greek style cuisine; brochettes of chicken especially good; great garlic bread.

Ming Restaurant. *Inexpensive.* 1185 Smythe St., good variety of Chinese and Canadian food, excellent for family eating, moderate, pleasant.

NIGHTLIFE. In Fredericton, the most popular spots are the *River Room* at the Lord Beaverbrook Hotel where they feature folksingers; private clubs and discos such as *The Cosmo,* where you have to be signed in at the door. *The Chestnut Inn* has dining and live bands. The *Poacher's Lounge* at the Diplomat Motel on Woodstock Rd. is popular. So is *Hilltop* on Prospect St., a publike spot. The *Riverview Arms,* Lincoln Rd., and the *Rolling Keg* on King St. are taverns serving steaks and featuring loud music.

The Saint John River Valley

At Woodstock, the alternate route to Fredericton (Route 105 on the other side of the Saint John River) takes you through typical small communities over an uncrowded road. It's easy to cross back to the Trans-Canada Highway at Mactaquac where the road leads over the dam. Since the building of the hydroelectric dam over the river, the valley has changed even as far away as Woodstock. While many of the Saint John River islands have disappeared, the area of the headpond has become quite lovely. A provincial park has been established at

Mactaquac, probably the most comprehensive in all of New Brunswick. Visitors can enjoy everything from golfing on the 18-hole professional course to swimming, hiking and sailing. The campground is so popular that cars line up, sometimes all night, to claim the first empty camp lot in the morning. Your best bet is to get there early. There are 300 campsites, supervised recreation, two beaches, two marinas, as well as a licensed lodge with dining room. There's an Antique Arms Museum featuring antique firearms, trout fishing pond, and horseback riding nearby. If Mactaquac campsites are full, there are several other good campgrounds in the area.

Load your camera for Hartland. Here you'll find the longest covered bridge in the world—1,282 feet in length. Many of New Brunswick's covered bridges have been destroyed in recent years but the Department of Highways is now seeking to protect the 78 or so that still exist.

Woodstock, population 5,068, named for a novel by Sir Walter Scott, is also called the "hospitality town." It was an axiom in the old days that "no traveller, known or unknown, shall pass through the community without sharing its hospitality." That tradition remains strong today. You'll experience it especially at the annual Old Home Week celebrations in July when most of the Saint John River Valley residents participate.

There is a 9-hole golf course and during the summer months a farmers' market is held on Fridays at the Stewart parking lot where homemade foods may be purchased. Harness racing takes place at Connell Park.

The Old Courthouse (c. 1833) has been carefully restored by an interested community . . . it's been a coaching stop, a social hall, a political meeting place, and the seat of justice for the area. The guides have many tales to tell of famous trials held here.

Just below Woodstock at Meductic, young John Gyles, 9-year-old son of a New England judge, was held captive by the Maliceets for 6 years. His diary, reconstructed by New Brunswick writer Stuart Trueman, makes interesting historical reading.

There are two roads from Fredericton to Saint John. Route 7 is straight and dull for its 68 miles. The other, Route 102, leads along the Saint John River through some of the province's loveliest country. At Oromocto, the site of Canadian Armed Forces Base Camp Gagetown, largest military base in Canada, there's a reconstruction of Fort Hughes, an 1871 blockhouse which stands on the bank of the Oromocto River, and a fine military museum. You'll also find there a shopping mall and a beautifully laid out town, often called Canada's model town.

Along the river you'll notice small car ferries—from Jemseg to Upper Gagetown, Crystal Beach to Westfield, Clifton to Gondola Point, Gagetown to Lower Jemseg, Evandale to Hatfield Point, and Hampstead to Wickham. These cable-ferries are free, will take trailers and pickup campers, and provide you with a little respite from driving or a chance to look at the country on the other side. Grand Lake, for instance, offers camping in a provincial park, with freshwater swimming off sandy beaches.

At Jemseg, the Country Kitchen offers 24-hour service and specializes in good plain country cooking . . . all you can eat.

Closer to Saint John, the Evandale ferry takes you to Belleisle Bay and the Kingston Peninsula—a lovely landscape. At Gagetown, the Steamers Stop Inn provides pleasant dining over the river and rents six rooms.

At Gagetown, stop and have a look at the Queens County Museum, the former home of Sir Leonard Tilley, one of the Fathers of Confederation. While there, stop in at the Loomcrofters, one of Canada's better suppliers of handwoven goods. It's located in a 200-year-old blockhouse. The area is known for its many craftsmen.

Canada's Oldest City

Saint John is old . . . the oldest incorporated city in Canada, with the special weatherbeaten quality of any port city. When Champlain and de Monts landed here in 1604 on St. John the Baptist Day, it must have appeared a primitive spot. But not so primitive as it seemed to the three thousand Loyalists who poured off a ship one May morning in 1785 to find nothing but rocks and forests for shelter. Babies were born in windswept tents that first chill winter as their parents fought to stay alive. But they were a tenacious lot and, by the following year, most had built snug little homes, oddly furnished perhaps, with silver and crystal, damask cloths and lean-to beds. From those beginnings Saint John has emerged as a thriving industrial and port city, a tribute to its hardy Loyalist forebears. A recent face-lift and a new harborfront development have improved its appearance, and its history is fascinating.

Fiercely loyal to the British Crown, the early residents even laid out King Square in the design of the old Union Jack. Each year in July, a reenactment of the Landing of the Loyalists is held during the Loyalist Day celebrations. A costumed city joins in a colorful event that is the envy of many other communities.

Saint John (the spelling is never abbreviated) has the advantage of a year-round harbor. Ships from all over the world dock here, continually stimulating the economy. Among the outstanding enterprises are those run by the Irving family, descendants of a New Brunswick industrialist, K.C. Irving, who established the Irving pulp mill, the Irving Oil refinery, and a steel and drydock industry.

EXPLORING SAINT JOHN

Urban renewal is on the scene and the old face of Saint John is changing. The Saint John Harbour Bridge is the most conspicuous of the new developments as it spirals into the city in a modern way. But a walk along its historic streets (maps available at the Tourist Bureau on Sydney Street) guarantees you a charming picture of the old city.

Start at the Old Courthouse (1830) and inspect its famous spiral staircase. Built of 100 tons of unsupported stone ascending for three storeys, it is of special interest to architects and engineers.

Walk around the corner, then cross the street and walk down through the old Burying Ground where the first Loyalist settlers are buried. At adjacent King Square, you'll find a strange mass which looks like a piece of meteorite. It is actually a great lump of melted stock from a hardware store across the street which was demolished in Saint John's Great Fire of 1877, when 115 buildings were destroyed.

Just a few blocks along Charlotte Street, you'll come to the low stone walls of Trinity Church, dating back to 1877 when it was rebuilt after the fire. Inside the building over its west door, note the coat-of-arms, a symbol rescued from the council chamber of the Colony at Massachusetts Bay. The coat-of-arms was deemed a worthy relic and set in its place of honor in the church.

Walk down toward the harbor by way of Princess Street, site of an extensive restoration of historic buildings, and you'll come to a most intriguing building. Located on the corner of Princess and Prince William, it's commonly called Chubb's Corner. All around the cornices of the building you'll see carved stone heads grinning at you. They seem to represent an objection to the city council of the day. George Chubb, who commissioned them, had the carver, Mr. McAvity, portray Mr. Chubb, the mayor and members of the Common Council of 1878 in this way. Along the lower part of the building he has delicately carved flowers, fruits, vines, and the faces of the Chubb children. One could stand here fascinated for hours.

Amble down the street, past Market Slip where the Loyalists landed, to Barbour's General Store. This fully stocked 19th-century store was presented to the city as a Centennial project by the Barbour Company of Saint John. Its interior is redolent of smells of the past: tobacco, pickles, smoked fish, peppermint sticks and, on the floor, a big bag of dulse, that tangy edible seaweed New Brunswickers love to chew. No admission charge and the dulse is free. Next to Barbour's is the Little Red School House, a restoration of an 1800's school. Stroll along the boardwalk, visit the pub in the ship, and inspect the posh boutiques in Market Square; then walk up Union Street. At the corner of Union and Germain stands a lovely old Loyalist house. Built in 1810 by Daniel David Merritt, a wealthy Loyalist merchant, the house retains all its past beauty with authentic period furniture and eight fireplaces. Five generations of Merritts have lived there.

But visitors most enjoy the Old City Market. Built in 1876, it runs the full block from Germain to Charlotte. Here's where you'll find red, fresh-cooked lobster, great cheeses, more dulse and the friendly chatter of the marketplace.

Try to visit the New Brunswick Museum—the first in Canada and still recognized as one of the best of its size. You'll see the figurehead from the bad luck ship built in Saint John's famous shipyards—a ship which is said to have killed a man on every voyage.

Along with native animals displayed in natural surroundings, there are costumes, artifacts, even a collection of dolls, and an impressive art gallery to keep you interested for at least an afternoon.

Not far away, you'll note the Martello Tower, high on a hill, built in 1812 as a precaution against American attack. Costumed guides show you its walls 8 feet thick, and pose willingly for pictures. The view from the top of the tower is magnificent as is the one from Fort Howe, a reconstructed fortress on a cliff overlooking the harbor. Reached via a winding road, it is originally the site of Fort LaTour, a French stronghold resolutely defended by Madame LaTour from her absent husband's fur-trading rival. Finally surrendering on the condition that the lives of her men would be spared, the unfortunate woman was betrayed and forced to watch them all put to death. She died shortly thereafter—of a broken heart, it is said . . . a fate befitting her former profession as star of the Paris stage.

The celebrated Reversing Falls Rapids, now somewhat tarnished by the effluent of a pulp mill on its banks, are actually a series of rapids and whirlpools at which, twice a day, the Fundy Tides attempt to push the river water back upstream. When the tide flow weakens and ebbs, the river once again pours out over the rock ledges, and the rapids appear to reverse themselves. Downstream from the rapids is the Wharf Museum featuring marine exhibits.

Saint John also has a small zoo, located at Rockwood Park and year-round harness racing, golf, tennis, and several beaches in the area.

There are a number of side trips from Saint John. One of them along the coastal Route 111 takes you to St. Martins, a delightful seaside village featuring a colony of tame beavers nearby who come up from their pond to take food from the fingers of the local family that has befriended them. This performance is best seen in the late afternoon or dusk.

Following Route 1 NE from Saint John, you pass the engaging dairy town of Sussex, through rolling countryside to Penobsquis, where you may turn off to Fundy National Park, 80 square miles of sea-conditioned playground skirting the Bay of Fundy.

The coast road up to Moncton takes you over covered bridges and along rocky coasts. At Hopewell Cape, you'll find the famous giant flowerpot, one of many rock formations carved by the action of the Fundy tides.

New River Beach Provincial Park is located right on the southern Fundy shore where rolling breakers come roaring in. New Brunswickers swim in it but—a word to the wise—the Fundy water is usually chilly.

The peaceful hideaway fishing villages of Maces Bay, Dipper Harbour, and Chance Harbour are still much the same as they have been for centuries but residents fear a change since the advent of the nuclear reactor plant at nearby Point Lepreau. If you drive into the area, you'll find a great little tea room, The Fundy Haven, right on the cliffs overlooking the bay. Marvelous, inexpensive seafood!

PRACTICAL INFORMATION FOR SAINT JOHN

HOW TO GET THERE. By air: Both *Air Canada* and *Eastern Provincial Airways* make connections with most major airlines. Airport 10 miles east of city.

By car: From Nova Scotia by ferry from Digby; by road from Nova Scotia through Moncton via Rte. 1, from Fredericton via Rte. 7, from Calais, Me. via Rte. 1.

By train: *Via Rail* has service daily to Fredericton, Moncton, and Halifax. Connections for Montréal can be made at Moncton.

By bus: SMT bus service within the province provides regional transportation. Most major bus companies in USA and Canada connect with SMT.

ACCOMMODATIONS. In the summer, tourist accommodations tend to be at a premium in Saint John so it is best to reserve ahead to ensure a place to stay. Price categories are the same as for Fredericton. Rates are based on double-occupancy as follows: *Expensive,* over $43; *Moderate,* $30–43; *Inexpensive,* under $30.

Most places accept the following major credit cards: American Express, MasterCard, and Visa; others may also be honored. Not all establishments accept credit cards, therefore we suggest you call for information.

The Delta Brunswick Inn. *Expensive.* New downtown hotel atop Brunswick Sq. Dining, bar, banquet and convention facilities. Phone 648–1981. Major credit cards.

Hilton. *Expensive.* Newest part of Market Square overlooking harbor. Mammoth convention facilities, including a Medieval Great Hall. Adjoining shops, restaurants, bars, library. Phone 1–800–361–6140.

Holiday Inn. *Expensive.* Haymarket Sq. Dining room, heated pool. Phone 657–3610. Major credit cards.

Howard Johnson Motor Lodge. *Expensive.* At Chesley Pl. Caters to families. Has special facilities for children. Phone 642–2622. Major credit cards.

Keddy's Motor Inn. *Expensive.* Corner Portland and Main Sts. Heated pool, nice rooms, bar, dining room, and steakhouse. Phone 657–7320. Major credit cards.

Wandlyn Motor Hotel. *Moderate–Expensive.* Rothesay Ave. Probably not as modern as some other places in the city, but clean and comfortable. Nice little dining room, bar. Phone 696–4100. Major credit cards.

Bonanza Motel. *Inexpensive.* 594 Rothesay Ave. Adequate rooms, no dining facilities. Phone 696–2310. MasterCard only.

Fundy View Guest Home. *Inexpensive.* 968 Manawaqonish Rd., in Saint John.

Watt's Tourist Home. *Inexpensive.* 765 Manawagonish Rd., in Saint John West. 2 rooms. No dining facilities. Phone 672–2327.

HOW TO GET AROUND. Airport limousine: Between airport and Delta or Hilton Holiday Inn. $5.
Taxi: individual fares.
Bus: Good community service.
City Guide: Available at Tourist Info. Center, Reversing Falls and at Sydney St. Tourist Bureau.

TOURIST INFORMATION. City: Tourist Bureau, Sydney Street, telephone 657-2815. Reversing Falls, telephone 672–6990. Municipal Tourist Information Centre, 24 Sydney St., open 9 A.M.–9 P.M. year-round, telephone 658–2855.

SPECIAL INTEREST TOURS. Tours of the University of New Brunswick, Saint John, Moosehead, and Olands Breweries can be arranged. Inquire at Tourist Bureau.

CITY PARKS. *Rockwood Park,* within the city limits, is an excellent place for kids and adults alike. It surrounds several lakes, has a "children's farm" as well as Atlantic Canada's only exotic zoo, which includes many animals on the endangered species list. Also golf, swimming, and other facilities.

MUSEUMS. Saint John has a new art gallery and a number of interesting museums.

The *New Brunswick Museum* is the province's largest and also Canada's first established museum. Its galleries of Canadiana, marine display, Loyalist era artifacts, and other exhibits truly evoke early New Brunswick.

Loyalist House, a museum built in 1810, is still in operation.

The *Wharf Museum* has a collection of early tools, machinery, household items, and other pieces depicting the pioneer era.

The *Carlton Martello Tower,* built for the War of 1812, displays weapons, uniforms, and historical objects.

SHOPPING. As in the rest of the province, it's the little antique stores and craftshops that provide the best shopping. You'll find them sprinkled around the downtown area. Brunswick Square and Market Square in new harbourfront development offer airy shopping with many top quality boutiques.

DINING OUT. Several good, new restaurants of gourmet caliber have popped up in recent years. Try the ones specializing in seafood. Price categories per person are as follows: *Expensive,* over $16; *Moderate,* $11–16; *Inexpensive,* under $11. Drinks, tax, and tip are not included.

Most places accept the following major credit cards: American Express, MasterCard, and Visa; others may also be honored. Not all establishments accept credit cards, therefore we suggest you call for information.

Captain's Quarters. *Expensive.* The best seafood and most elegant atmosphere in the city. Fish bought fresh daily. Phone 642–2974. Major credit cards.

The House of Chan. *Moderate–Expensive.* Hilyard Place (near Keddy's and Howard Johnson's). Great luncheon buffet. Good Chinese and Canadian dishes. Lobster and steak specialties. Major credit cards. Phone 693–7777.

Pier I. *Moderate–Expensive.* Excellent and unusual seafood in a nautical setting. Phone 642–2562. Major credit cards.

Top of the Town. *Moderate–Expensive.* The steakhouse at the top of the new Keddy's Motor Inn has a warm atmosphere and a fabulous view of the city. Good steak and service. Phone 657–7320. Major credit cards.

The Continental. *Moderate.* Level III, Historical Properties, Market Square. European cuisine with pizzazz, served on china and silver. Major credit cards. Phone 642–1157.

Nick's Restaurant. *Inexpensive.* 451 Main. Plain-food restaurant.

Grannan's. *Inexpensive.* Market Square. Spills out over sidewalk in summer. Terrific desserts. Nice bar.

NIGHT LIFE. There are no nightclubs in Saint John but a few places offer entertainment or dancing. *The Mediterranean,* located on Rothesay Ave., is a place where you can dine, dance and drink, usually to hard rock.

The Image at the Holiday Inn is a mirrored discothèque with dancing, sometimes country folksingers.

Sullivan's, in the Delta Hotel, is a piano lounge.

The Squire's Tap, Holiday Inn, quiet friendly bar sometimes featuring singers.

Grannan's, Market Square, Good gathering place in nautical atmosphere.

Tugboat Ocean Hawk II, for oysters, drinks, and socializing. Market Square.

1880 Club, in a restored 19th-century building. Features dancing, dining, and a games room.

EXPLORING THE ACADIAN SHORE

From the Nova Scotian border at Aulac, along New Brunswick's northern shore, across the top of the province to Charlo, the Acadians settled on what is now known as the Acadian region.

Moncton

The city of Moncton has become the unofficial capital of Acadia and much of its history is interwoven with that of the Acadian people. Moncton, settled by Dutch and German families from Pennsylvania, was originally called Petitcodiac by the Indians, meaning the "river that bends like a bow." When the deeply religious Acadians came along they built a chapel and for a while the area was known as La Chapelle. Later it became Le Coude or The Elbow because the river bends so sharply here. Even to this day, one sometimes hears it called "The Bend."

In 1755, Lt. Colonel Robert Monckton finally captured nearby Fort Beausejour, bringing to an end the French occupation of the area. Moncton took his name, dropping the "K" over the years. After the Expulsion, a number of Acadians returned to areas around Moncton, settling most noticeably in Cocagne, Shediac and Grand Digue. Today in Moncton names like Belliveau, Blanchard, and Gaudet are mixed with Steeves (formerly Stief), Trites (Trietz), and Lutes (Lutz).

Once famous for shipbuilding, Moncton gradually became the province's main railway center and is now known as the "hub of the Maritimes" because all railroads seem to lead there. It is a natural center for sales and distribution throughout the Maritimes. A commercial town, its skyline has changed in recent years as economic activity increased.

The population is almost evenly divided between Catholics and Protestants, and churches dot the landscape. It is unfortunate that few historic buildings remain to tell the tale of Moncton's early days. The New Brunswick telephone tower is now the most striking edifice on the horizon and the eleven-storey "Assumption Place" with its adjoining Beausejour Hotel is the newest and most impressive addition to the skyline.

Built on the flat, marshy land on the banks of the muddy Petitcodiac, Moncton was built by railroadmen, sturdy, solid and enduring, but hardly of architectural consequence.

Walk out King Street and around to Mountain Road and you'll find, on Stedman Street, the oldest building in Moncton, a delightful little hall called the Free Meeting House, founded in 1821 by a group who believed in a common place of worship for the residents. Even the little graveyard beside it has been preserved. It has been the home of every denomination in the city, including Protestant, Roman Catholic, and Jewish.

Don't be startled by what you see next! The square modern building across the street has a strange old-fashioned entrance, completely out of keeping with the local architecture. But it happens to be the façade of the original town hall and it has been incorporated into the design of the new Moncton Civic Museum. Once inside the museum, railway enthusiasts and history buffs will delight in the steam engine mementos. And the curator will let you ring the huge cast iron bell. The museum has taken a forward step toward preserving some of the area's past.

One of Moncton's special attractions is the famous Tidal Bore. Viewed best from Boreview Park on Main Street, this low wall of water, which comes in right on time as befits any railroad town, is caused by the tide surging through the narrow entrance of the Petitcodiac River. As it rolls up the river it fills the wide muddy trench from bank to bank.

Moncton's Magnetic Hill—a rare optical illusion—must be seen to be believed. Drive down the hill to the white post. Turn off your motor, but put the car in neutral. As you gaze in astonishment at the steep hill behind you, your car will back up in such a hurry that you may be tempted to use your brake.

At Centennial Park, once more the steam engine reigns supreme. Crawl right up into the cab of the locomotive which is permanently on display there, and pretend your name is Casey Jones.

A drive through the spacious and modern campus of the University of Moncton will take you to the door of the Acadian Museum where you'll find artifacts and historical displays which present a clear picture of what life was all about in the days of the early Acadian settler. The ancient tools and primitive utensils are there along with the interiors of barns, schools and houses, all lovingly and beautifully reproduced.

Following the shore roads from Aulac to Moncton, you'll also follow the Trans-Canada Highway. On the way you'll pass the site of Fort Beausejour, a national historic site. Built by the French in 1751, and captured by the English in 1755, it was originally known as Fort Cumberland—the scene of the final battle for English supremacy in this region.

Sackville, a small university town, with the only harness shop in North America still producing handmade horse collars (and visitors welcome), is worth a short detour to the southeast from Moncton. Home of Mount Allison University, an arts oriented institution, Sackville is reminiscent of many old English villages. Don't miss the Owens Art Gallery on campus. It's open to the public.

Shediac

From Moncton it's only 20 miles to the town of Shediac, home of King Lobster, where each July the Shediac Lobster Festival takes place. The beaches, especially at the provincial park, are long, fine-sanded, and shallow, with water warmer than anywhere else on the coast.

Fishing is the major industry and you can find fresh lobster, cooked or uncooked, at Paturel's Fish Processing Plant; the nearby *Shore House,* run by Paturel's, offers fresh seafood. At Shediac, you can also find excellent and reasonably priced seafood at the *Fishermen's Paradise* just outside town at the Hotel Shediac, and fine dining at *Chez Francoise* in the old Tait Mansion. There are also several very good beaches in the area.

Traveling up the shore towards Bathurst you'll pass through the fishing villages of Cocagne, scene of international hydroplane races in the summer and the Acadian Bazaar, usually in August; Buctouche, noted for the quality of its oysters; Richibucto and Rexton (the latter the birthplace of Andrew Bonar Law, first and only prime minister of Britain to be born outside the British Isles). At Richibucto there's a new museum of local history covering the storied Richibucto River and Kent County.

Kouchibouquac National Park, recently developed, has camping facilities and a marvelous beach, with long miles of sandbar washed by the warm waters of the Northumberland Strait. It also has excellent recreational facilities: canoeing, hiking, and others. Check with the park superintendent about local lobster suppers.

In 1959, 35 fishermen were drowned in a sudden squall off Point Escuminac in one of New Brunswick's worst fishing disasters. A monument created by Claude Roussel, one of the province's foremost artists, has been erected on the shore. It depicts three fishermen starkly outlined against the sea behind them.

Chatham and Newcastle

Chatham and Newcastle, both early lumbering towns, are the exceptions on this Acadian coast, largely retaining the characteristics of the Irish, Scottish, and English immigrants who settled there. Anyone who lives along the Miramichi River is known as a "Miramichier" and proud of it. It's a region of folklore and superstition, of ballads and boisterousness, nourished by pride of ancestry. The hospitality is renowned and the friendly people still wave as you drive by.

Chatham, once a great shipbuilding area, was the home of Joseph and Henry Cunard, who came from Nova Scotia to build wooden ships. At one time the Cunards employed almost everybody, if not in the shipyards, then in the forests, cutting masts for the great ships. Joseph Cunard, flamboyant and wealthy, drove a coach-and-four, ordered peacocks for his lawns, and sent riders ahead to spread the word of his coming whenever he returned from his frequent visits to England. When the coming of the steam engine ruined his business, the area took a long time to regain its former prosperity. The building of a jet training school and air base in the region infused new life into the economy and today Chatham is thriving once again. The history of the area is related through exhibits at the Miramichi Natural History Museum. Loggie House is a late Victorian, Second Empire-style home furnished in antiques from the period. It functions as a cultural center in winter and is open to visitors in summer.

Max Aitken, the son of a poor Presbyterian minister, and later Lord Beaverbrook (a name he took from a brook running near his home), lived his boyhood years in Newcastle. Eventually a multimillionaire, owner of the London *Daily Express,* confidante of kings and politicians, and at one time minister of aircraft production in Churchill's wartime cabinet, Beaverbrook traveled a long way from his early beginnings in New Brunswick. One of his many bequests to Newcastle was his childhood home, the Old Manse, now a functioning library. He encouraged its custodian, the late Dr. Louise Manny, to record the hundreds of folksongs and "come all ye's" of the area and helped her set up an annual folksinging festival which takes place in July every year. His ashes are held in the bottom of his statue in the middle of the town square.

Outside Chatham on Route 11 is the MacDonald Farm, a major restoration of an 1830's working farm.

Three miles west of Newcastle is the Enclosure, the site of the graves of the first settlers, part of a lovely provincial park, largely donated to the province by Lord Beaverbrook.

The shortest route from Newcastle to Bathurst is the inland Route 8 but this route has little of interest.

The road along the shore is more rewarding. You'll pass through small communities with intriguing names such as Burnt Church, named for an ancient English raid; and Tracadie, once a leper colony. The Tracadie Museum, located in the Town Hall, commemorates this part of Tracadie's past. There is a new museum of local history at Tabusintac and a new marine museum at Shippagan, which is a major provincial facility. It depicts the history of the fishing industry and portrays the lives of the area's fishermen. Shippagan, typical of the north shore fishing villages, offers superb opportunities for photographers. This entire shore has fine beaches. You might want to take the free ferry to Miscou Island, where you can beachcomb along deserted beaches. Accommodations there consist of campgrounds and cabins.

Caraquet

Caraquet, a lively Acadian town, is prosperous and busy. You'll find a wooden shipbuilding factory, fish and crab packing plants, and a market on the wharf peddling fish and shellfish fresh from the boats at very good prices.

Down by the Fisheries School, the Acadian Museum perched over the water offers an interesting and informative encounter with area history. You'll even find a small handicraft shop tucked in one corner where you can pick up a hooked rug or a woven napkin for a reasonable price.

West of Caraquet is the Acadian Village, a restoration of 30 buildings, which depicts the Acadian lifestyle in New Brunswick between 1780 and 1880. Also, if you're in Caraquet around mid-August, it's worth staying for the Acadian Festival, a cultural event featuring the Blessing of the Fleet, Acadian folksinging, L'Acadie en fête, and various other unique celebrations. Caraquet is also the province's most popular port for deepsea sport fishing, especially for the bluefin tuna.

From Caraquet to Bathurst the seacoast reminds one of France's Brittany coast, and the design of the occasional house or barn along the way heightens that impression. As you drive along Route 11, the rocky shores of the Gaspé across the Chaleur Bay are clearly visible; at Pokeshaw, notice the curious flat-topped rock. Its dead trees are usually covered with birds, giving it the name "Bird Island."

Bathurst to Dalhousie

Bathurst (population 17,000) has recently found its wealth in mining. Nearby discoveries of iron, lead, and zinc have stimulated industries of all kinds. Always a happy town, it pleased both Jacques Cartier when he visited here in 1534 and also Champlain when he bartered for clothes right off the Indians' backs during his business trip. A century later another tourist from France, Nicholas Denys, liked it so well he settled at the mouth of the Nipisiquit River on Bathurst Bay where he ran a fish and fur-trading business as well as a mill. Bathurst has been a busy town ever since.

In colonial days, the area was known as St. Peters, but religion evidently yielded to politics when, in 1826, the town became Bathurst, after the Earl of Bathurst who was then Colonial Secretary.

As friendly and hospitable a town as it is busy, Bathurst has a special charm. Perhaps it comes from a happy blending of French and English, although the population breakdown always depends on the background of the person asked—English-speaking people say it's 60/40 English and the French say it's 60/40 French. Bathurst also has a war museum operated by the Royal Canadian Legion.

The beach at Youghall, where you'll find a provincial park and camp grounds, winds all the way around Bathurst Bay and the water in summer is warm. That's why Cartier named it *Baie de Chaleur* (Bay of Warmth).

One of the most popular pasttimes in the area is eating lobster on the beach. On a clear night, as you stare out to sea, you might see the phantom ship. All along the Bay of Chaleur from Bathurst to Campbellton, the ship has been sighted. No satisfactory explanation for this phenomenon has been given but descriptions have been pretty much the same: a burning sailing ship, sometimes with sailors scurrying about the flaming rigging; finally the ship disappears, still aglow, beneath the waves. Some say it's the ghost of a French ship lost in the Battle of the Restigouche; others claim it's a reflection of heat waves. Whatever it is, many have sighted it during the years—even a Sunday school teacher and his whole class. So keep your eyes on the Bay of Chaleur. You, too, might see the phantom ship!

Just west of Bathurst on Route 11, there's an Acadian crafts center attached to La Fine Grobe restaurant. At Belledune there's a huge smelter which processes the ores from the mineral fields and looks startlingly futuristic. You'll travel along Jacquet River, where a charming provincial park is situated right on the shore. At Eel River Crossing, you can join right in with your shovel to dig some of the finest clams in the world. Just across the long stretch of sand bar, the local Indians run a small handcraft shop.

In Dalhousie and Campbellton, Scottish and Irish settlers mingled with the Acadians to settle the area. Just as in the Newcastle/Chatham district, it's sometimes hard to pick out the accent. Is it French or Irish?

Dalhousie, a year-round port, is also the home of one of the province's largest industries, the newsprint mill of the New Brunswick International Paper Company. Large ocean-going ships stop here on their way to Europe. The Chaleur History Museum on Adelaide Street features local history of the area.

Campbellton

Campbellton (population about 10,422) retains the charm of a pioneer town. Nestling at the foot of Sugarloaf, a perfectly rounded mountain, it is reminiscent of lumbermen, river drives, and seagoing vessels. Still the headquarters for fishing outfitters for the famous salmon rivers of the region, the town is fast forging ahead into modernity. The new Restigouche Gallery is a major provincial exhibition center. The theater in the modern high school/trade school complex presents plays of professional quality. Theatre New Brunswick also brings its touring productions here where they are always well received.

The all-season Sugarloaf Provincial Park has an excellent ski hill and lodge. Newest winter sport wrinkle is an Alpine slide. Just across the river in Québec, Federal archeologists have been using a diving bell to bring up artifacts from the Battle of the Restigouche, the last naval engagement of the Seven Years' War fought off Campbellton in 1760. A summer salmon festival is held here from late June to early July.

Route 17, known locally as the Stuart Highway, cuts through the central forest where communities are sparse. The road, though narrow, is good, cutting across hills and valleys for 100 miles to the small town of St. Leonard.

PRACTICAL INFORMATION FOR

NEW BRUNSWICK

HOW TO GET THERE. By air: Airports serviced by *Eastern Provincial Airlines* and *Air Canada* at Moncton, Fredericton, and Saint John; EPA also flies to Charlo, near Dalhousie, from Moncton, Chatham and Montréal.

By car: By car ferry from Prince Edward Island, Trans-Canada Hwy. from Nova Scotia, Trans-Canada Hwy. from Québec, Interstate 95 to Houlton, Me., U.S. 1 to Calais, Me.

By train: Regular *Via Rail* passenger service from Moncton to Montréal and Halifax, with links via ferry to Prince Edward Island and Newfoundland. Also from Moncton, daily service to Saint John and Fredericton.

By bus: *SMT* within the province connecting with most major bus lines.

 ACCOMMODATIONS. New Brunswick has a number of officially designated "Heritage Inns"—places built mostly in the last century and having some local historic significance. They have either antique china or furniture or some other quaint touch and they provide accommodations that vary from homey to elegant, sometimes in the inexpensive category. They are noted as Heritage Inns in the following listing.

Price categories are based on double-occupancy. *Expensive,* over $40; *Moderate,* $30–40; *Inexpensive,* under $30.

Most places accept the following major credit cards. American Express, MasterCard and Visa; others may also be honored. Not all establishments accept credit cards, therefore we suggest you call for information.

BATHURST. *Expensive:* **Keddy's Motor Inn.** Central. Dining room, bar, coffeeshop. Phone 546–6691.

Expensive: **Atlantic Host Hotel.** Swimming pool, dining room. Phone 548-3335.

Moderate: **Danny's Motor Inn.** Comfortable and friendly. Good dining room and coffeeshop. Tennis courts on premises; beach nearby. Phone 546–6621.

Fundy Line Motel. Former seminary, now done up in sexy reds and shag rugs. Dining room. Phone 548–8803.

BUCTOUCHE. *Inexpensive:* **Hilltop Motel.** Rte. 11. Small but adequate. Phone 743–2455.

CAMPBELLTON. *Expensive:* **Howard Johnson Motor Lodge.** Rte. 11. Comfortable and friendly. Dining room. Phone 753–5063.

Moderate–Expensive: **Wandlyn Motor Inn.** Comfortable units. Good dining room and coffeeshop. Small bar. Phone 753-7606.

Moderate: **Fundy Line Motel.** Adequate units, excellent dining room (open only certain hours for breakfast and dinner). Phone 753-3395.

CAMPOBELLO. *Moderate:* **Friar's Bay Motor Lodge.** 10 units, licensed dining room, near the sea. Phone 752-2056.

The Owen House. *Moderate.* Historic old home. Five rooms. Charming bed-and-breakfast. Open June–Oct. Phone 752-2977.

Inexpensive: **Ponderosa Motel and Restaurant.** Beach swimming. Dining room. Phone 752-2100.

CARAQUET. *Moderate:* **The Motel Savoie.** Comfortable and modern. Restaurant on premises. Phone 727–3485.

Motel du Village. Dining room and bar. Phone 732–2982.

Inexpensive: **Hotel Paulin.** A Heritage Inn. Old hotel, est. 1887, no pretensions, undergoing renovations, charming in off-beat other-century way. Dining room has a reputation for good, low-cost seafood. Phone 727–9981.

DALHOUSIE. *Moderate:* **Cedar Lodge Motel.** About 12 miles from Campbellton. Pleasant rooms, some of which overlook the Bay so you can watch for the ghost ship. Excellent dining room, small bar, and dance floor with band. Phone 684–3363.

DEER ISLAND. *Inexpensive:* **The 45th Parallel Motel and Tourist Home.** Restaurant open summer only. Phone 747–2231.

Hartford's Guest Home. Seasonal, 3 units. Situated at Leonardville. Phone 747–2284.

EDMUNDSTON. *Expensive:* **The Wandlyn Motor Inn.** Pool, good dining room, coffeeshop, bar. Phone 735–5525.

Moderate-Expensive: **Howard Johnson Motor Lodge.** Restaurant, licensed dining room, indoor pool. Phone 739–7321.

Moderate: **The Lynn Motel.** Central, coffeeshop. Phone 735–8851.

FUNDY NATIONAL PARK. *Moderate.* **Alpine Chalets.** Seasonal. Phone 887–2848.

Fundy Park Chalets. Seasonal. Good location within park. Phone 887–2808.

Fundy View Motel. Within park. Seasonal. Phone 887–2880.

Many accommodations available at Alma, at gates of Fundy National Park.

GAGETOWN. *Moderate:* **Steamer's Stop Inn.** A Heritage Inn. Seven rooms with a lovely view over the Saint John River. Decorated with steamboat antiques and memorabilia. Good dining room. Phone 488–2903.

GRAND FALLS. *Moderate–Expensive:* **The Pres-du-Lac.** Pleasant rooms, dining room; small bar, heated pool. Phone 473–1300.

GRAND MANAN. Grand Manan Island is a small and very personal place. Expect accommodations to be likewise. A government liquor store operates on the island.

Expensive: **The Marathon.** A Heritage Inn. Hundred-year-old hotel overlooking the ferry landing. Built by a sea captain. Rooms furnished with antique furniture. Heated pool, tennis. Headquarters for whale watching expeditions. Rates include breakfast and dinner. Phone 662–8144.

Moderate: **The Shore Crest Lodge.** A Heritage Inn. An old house by the sea. Homey inn, meals, heated pool and games room. Phone 662–3216.

Surfside Motel. With 25 units, the largest motel on the island. Phone 662–8156.

Inexpensive: **The Compass Rose.** A Heritage Inn. Charming old house by the sea, near ferry landing. Rates include breakfast. Phone 662–8570.

MONCTON. *Expensive:* **Hotel Beausejour.** Main St. The hotel is decorated in old Acadian theme with thick, luxurious carpeting on the floor, plenty of comfortable and attractive furniture. Pleasant bar off lobby, coffeeshop, two dining rooms, pool. Phone 854–4344. Major credit cards.

Howard Johnson's Motor Lodge. Trans-Canada Hwy. Really lives up to the slogan "Your home away from home." Friendly, comfortable, dining room, nice bar, gorgeous pool. Great place for children. Phone 384–1050.

Keddy's Brunswick Hotel. Highfield and Main Sts. Newly renovated. Dining room, lounge/bar, central. Phone 854-6340.

The Park House Inn. Boreview Park. 434 Main St. New part preferred. Great view of bore; good, moderately priced breakfasts. Pool. Phone 382–1664.

Wandlyn Motor Inn. Near Magnetic Hill off Trans-Canada Hwy. Rooms plain but comfortable; pool, good dining room, small bar. Phone 384–3554.

Moderate: **Magnetic Hill Mini Motel.** Magnetic Hill. Coffeeshop, restaurant. Phone 384–3541.

Inexpensive–Moderate: **Hotel Canadiana.** A Heritage Inn in downtown Moncton. Has a fine antique collection, homey atmosphere. Phone 382–1054.

NEWCASTLE. *Expensive:* **The Wandlyn Motor Inn.** Pleasant dining room, sometimes fresh homemade doughnuts for breakfast. Phone 622–3870.

Wharf Inn. Restaurant and licensed dining room. Phone 622–0302.

Moderate: **Riverview Motel.** Overlooks Miramichi River. Phone 662–1727.

OROMOCTO. *Moderate–Expensive:* **The Oromocto Hotel.** Nice bar, good dining room. Phone 357–8424.

SACKVILLE. *Moderate:* **The Marshlands Inn.** A Heritage Inn with an impressive collection of 19th-century furniture. You'll enjoy a Marshlands special-breakfast. Make reservations well in advance. Phone 536–0170.

Inexpensive. **A Different Drummer.** Bed and breakfast, charming proprietors, friendly atmosphere. Phone 536–1291.

SHEDIAC. *Moderate.* **Chez Francoise.** Rooms in old mansion. Some with balconies. Excellent restaurant. *Inexpensive:* **Hotel Shediac.** A Heritage Inn. Grand old hotel of yesterday. Near the finest beaches in New Brunswick. Good seafood restaurant. Phone 532–4405.

SHIPPAGAN. *Moderate:* **Motel Shippagan.** Licensed dining room. Modern surroundings. Phone 336–2276.

ST. ANDREWS. *Expensive:* **Algonquin.** A venerable hotel and a local landmark, 193 rooms, pool, dining room, pub, dance hall, tennis courts. Modified American plan. Phone 529–8823.

The Rossmount Inn. A Heritage Inn. Huge old home, excellent dining room, pool, and lots of crystal and antiques. Phone 529–3351.

Moderate–Expensive: **Tara Manor.** A Heritage Inn. Early American and French Provincial décor. Former home of Canadian politician C.D. Howe. Putting green, lavish bedrooms, coffeeshop. Specify inn or motel. Excellent dining room. Phone 529–3304.

Moderate: **Shiretown Inn.** A Heritage Inn. One of the oldest operating inns in Canada. Large, old, high-ceilinged rooms, dining room, bar, coffeeshop. Old English pub. Homemade bread. Phone 529–8877.

ST. STEPHEN. *Expensive:* **Wandlyn Motor Inn.** Comfortable, good dining room. Phone 446–1814.

Inexpensive: **Haun's Holiday Farm.** Farm vacation home. Run by young German-Canadian family. About 7 miles from St. Stephen. Help with farmwork or just relax, ride the horses, take a picnic lunch and hike. Phone 466–4938.

WOODSTOCK. *Expensive:* **The Wandlyn Motor Inn.** Good dining room, pool. Phone 328–8876.

Inexpensive: **Cosy Cabins.** In town, dining room, pool, beach, studio of Woodstock Weavers. Phone 328–3344.

John Gyles Motor Inn. Trans-Canada Hwy. east. Great view of valley; restaurant, new units. Phone 328–2698.

Shirlee's Tourist Home. Three units, seasonal. Phone 328–6386.

Stiles Motel. In town, good food in tea room. Phone 328–6671.

HOSTELS. Hostels are located in Saint John, Fredericton, Moncton, Shediac, Tracadie, Caraquet, Bathurst, Campbellton, and Edmundston. All operate from 6 P.M. to 9 or 10 A.M., doors closing for the night around midnight—except in Moncton (11 P.M.), Shediac (11:30 P.M.), and Saint John (1 A.M.). Costs less than $5 a night except in Moncton, Fredericton and Saint John, where it is slightly higher. Meals are extra—breakfast, about $1, and some serve dinner early in the evening for under $2. Hostel provides bunk and foam mattress, usually dormstyle. Most have travel information. For details, write New Brunswick Hostel Association, R.R. 4, Douglas, New Brunswick. Telephone: (506) 453–4869 (9–5 P.M.), 472–1597 (evenings and weekends).

TELEPHONES. The telephone area code for all of New Brunswick is 506.

TOURIST INFORMATION. *Municipal Information Centres:* Bathurst, tel. 548–3844; Belledune, on Route 11; Bertrand, 727–2126; Buctouche, 743–5361; Campobello, park information desk, Roosevelt Park; Caraquet, 727–2575; Chatham, 773–9679; Dalhousie, CN Building, William St.; Depuis Corner, Route 15; Dieppe, Champlain Pl.; Fredericton, 455–3092; Grand Anse, on Route 11; Grand Falls, 473–4225; Hartland, 375–4658 (at end of covered bridge); Hillsborough, 734–2172; Moncton, 388–1510; McAdam, 784–2251; Oromocto, 357–9028; Riverview, at Coverdale Road and Wedgewood Ave.; Saint John, 658–2855; Shediac, 532–5447; Shippagan, at corner Rtes. 11 and 113; St. Andrews, 529–3909; St. George, 755–3142; St. Quentin, 235–2010; Sussex, on Main St. at O'Connell Park; Tracadie, 395–5932; Woodstock, 328–6892.

Provincial Tourist Bureaus: At Aulac on the Trans-Canada Highway, 536–0928; Campbellton at Sugarloaf Park, 735–5413; Edmundston on the Trans-Canada, 735–6103; Houlton Rd. on Rte. 95, 328–3419; Lutes Mountain on Trans-Canada, 382–8608; Newcastle at 454 King George Hwy., 622–2991; Penobsquis on Trans-Canada, 433–4326; Reversing Falls in Saint John, 672–6990; St. Leonard on Trans-Canada Hwy., 423–6324; St. Stephen on Rte. 3, 466–1139; Waweig on Route 1, 466–4858.

Or write for information to: *Tourism New Brunswick,* P.O. Box 12345, Fredericton, New Brunswick, Canada E3B 5C3. Telephone: (506) 453–2377; Telex: 014–46181.

TIME ZONE. The province is on Atlantic Time—one hour in advance of Eastern Time.

SEASONAL EVENTS. Food festivals abound all summer, celebrating the harvests of scallops, salmon, lobsters, oysters, clams, and important vegetables like potatoes and Brussels sprouts. Other festivals celebrate heritage, music, crafts, athletics, and old home weeks. For dates and locations, contact *Tourism New Brunswick.* Likewise for schedules of Atlantic Symphony Orchestra performances and art gallery exhibitions.

SPECIAL INTEREST TOURS. At Brunswick Mining and Smelting you can visit "the underground city," almost 3,000 feet down in a mine which produces zinc, lead, silver, and copper.

Boat Tours: Fundy Isles Marine Enterprises, 529–3688. Shediac—Romeo's Marine, 532–6444. Point-du-Chene—Moyak Marine, 532–4098. Dalhousie—Chaleur Phantom, 684–4219. In the Caraquet area there are numerous boat tour operators. Ask for information locally, or from Tourism New Brunswick.

Bird-watching is a special attraction on Grand Manan Island. There are over 240 species of sea birds that nest there. It's also a paradise for rockhounds, painters, nature photographers, and hikers—not to mention whale watchers! Bicyclists contact Carl White, 408 Princess Drive, Bathurst, New Brunswick, for information regarding special bicycle tours. Tours for all of these activities can be arranged by telephoning 662-8144 or contacting Tourism New Brunswick.

PARKS AND CAMPING. New Brunswick has two national parks. *Fundy National Park* fronts the Bay of Fundy—about 13 km. (8 mi.) of shore with an inland area of tall timber, lakes, and streams. There is a motel and chalets inside the park. It opens when the fishing season does—the third weekend in May.

Kouchibougouac National Park stretches 25 km. (15 mi.) along the Gulf of St. Lawrence shore. It's a panorama of forest, marshes, tidal lagoons, meandering rivers, sand dunes, and—especially—a vast and sweeping beach along much of its length. Canoes, bicycles, and boats may be rented on site.

Mactaquac, north of Fredericton, is the major provincial park. It has extensive camping facilities, golf, and other summer and winter sports facilities. *Sugarloaf* in the north is a year-round facility with the accent on skiing and other winter activities while *Mount Carleton* offers much wilderness and primitive camping facilities. There are smaller provincial parks throughout New Brunswick.

Miscou Island has camping facilities and cabins. Contact Miscou Island Campground and Cabins, Miscou Centre. Phone 344-8352.

Camping fees in provincial and national parks are generally between $4.50 and $6.00, depending on services. Private campgrounds may charge a bit more. The province's accommodations guide lists them all. The Avis Rent-a-Car company also rents tents and camping kits along with cars throughout the Maritime provinces.

FARM VACATIONS. About two dozen farms in the province take on people who wish to experience a farm vacation. Most cater to families, but some will take children alone. Contact *Tourism New Brunswick.*

SPORTS. Golf: New Brunswick has 31 golf courses, most with pro shops and rentals, as well as restaurants and shower facilities. Most are uncrowded.

Fishing and hunting: Charters for deepsea fishing are mostly concentrated in the Caraquet area, where angling for the bluefin tuna is a glamour activity. New Brunswick is also known internationally for its salmon and bass fishing, although its multitude of lakes abound in other freshwater species as well.

Hunting for deer, bear, and small game can be arranged. You will need a licensed guide and a nonresident hunting license for yourself. One outfit (Trius Tours Ltd., 455–8400) organizes bear-hunting expeditions.

Tourism New Brunswick has a fishing and hunting guidebook listing outfitters and other relevant information.

Winter sports: New Brunswick is a growing destination for winter vacationers. It has dependable deep snow and is abuzz all winter with skiing, snowmobiling, ice-fishing, and other activities over great open spaces. Canada East Tours (548-3447) in Bathurst organizes snowmobiling holidays.

Sailing: For the yachting enthusiast, there are the extensive and gorgeous waters of the lower Saint John River and Grand Lake. Yachts can be rented at Maritime Bareboat Charters Ltd. at Grand Bay (454-3525). Houseboat rentals are available from Houseboat Vacations, P.O. Box 2088, Sussex, N.B. E0E 1P0, or phone 433-4801 or 433-1609. Fredericton Rowing Club, Aquatic Centre, holds clinics and regattas for rowers.

For details on any of the above, contact Tourism New Brunswick, P.O. Box 12345, Fredericton, New Brunswick E3B 5C3, or phone 453-2377.

MUSEUMS. The province has a couple of dozen museums apart from the major ones found in Saint John and Fredericton. In particular there's the *Acadian Historical Village* and the *Acadian Museum* in **Caraquet,** plus the *Acadian Museum* at the University of Moncton campus in **Moncton**— all depicting the history of the Acadian people. *Eglise St.-Henri* at **Barachois** is an old wooden church converted to a museum also on the Acadian theme. Most small museums are on local history, but some have specific themes. For example, *Miramichi Salmon Museum,* **Doaktown** the *Central New Brunswick Woodsmen's Museum* at **Boiestown,** the *Automobile Museum* at **Edmundston,** and the *Fundy Antique Car Museum* at **Hopewell Cape,** Hillsborough-Salem Railway operates 1-hour steam locomotive trips in summer the *Antique Arms Museum* at **Mactaquac,** the *Marine Museum* at **Shippagan,** and the *Sportsman's Museum* at **Shediac.** The *Grand Manan Museum* has an interesting collection of birds and geological exhibits. The *Tracadie Historical Museum* pays tribute to those who dedicated their lives to a leper colony that once existed there. The *Moncton Museum* is another fairly large museum of provincial scale.

New Brunswick also has some 9,000 homes designated as "historic." Some can only be viewed from the outside, but some have exhibits and are open to the public. Check the Tourism New Brunswick publication *Historic Faces.*

SHOPPING. Bathurst's one unique store, *Frank's Furs,* specializes in designing and making fur coats in larger sizes.

In **Edmundston,** *Chiasson's Furs* offers stunning furs designed with the French flair. *Henri Nadeau* on the Trans-Canada for handcrafts or *Les Artisinat Handicraft* in nearby St. Basile, specializing in a variety of local works.

Moncton's shopping is some of the best in New Brunswick—five spacious malls and numerous pockets of shops in downtown Moncton. Among the crafts to look for are the yarn portraits of La Sagouine, "the old sage" of Buctouche. The sayings of an old Acadian woman as she goes about her daily chores were made famous in Antonine Maillet's novel *La Sagouine.*

St. Andrews has great English and New Brunswick woolens, lots of English bone china, and marvelous wool yarn at *The Sea Captain's Loft, Cottage Craft,* and *Saint Andrews Woollens.* Rare and out-of-print books, antiques, etc. at the

Pansy Patch, a stunning old home across from the Algonquin Hotel. Quality crafts are at *La Baleine* on Water St.

Fredericton's artist's studios and craftpeople are noted for their work.

At **St. Leonard,** be sure to visit the studio/store of the *Madawaska Weavers,* whose handwoven items are known the world over. Handsome skirts, stoles, and enchanting ties are some of the items for sale.

At **St. Stephen,** *Quartermain's Ltd.,* a long-standing business where you can browse for hours among quality Canadian and British goods.

In the studio of *Peter Hummel-Newell,* you'll find exquisite pieces of jewelry made from real New Brunswick wildflowers.

The *Directory of New Brunswick Craftsmen & Craft Shops,* available from the Department of Youth, Culture, and Recreation, Handcrafts Branch, Box 6000, Fredericton, N.B. or from tourist bureaus, will direct you to potters, weavers, glass-blowers, jewelers and carvers all over the province.

In summer, handcraft courses are offered at various locations throughout the province.

Shopping hours. Downtown shopping runs from 9 A.M. to 5 or 6 P.M. Monday–Saturday, and up to 9 P.M. on Fridays. The shopping malls are open 10 A.M. to 10 P.M. every day, except in Moncton where they close at 6 P.M. Saturday nights.

Holiday closings during the summer season occur on Victoria Day (3rd Monday in May), Canada Day (July 1), New Brunswick Day (1st Monday in August), Labor Day, Thanksgiving (2nd Monday in October), and Remembrance Day (November 11).

DRINKING LAWS. The minimum legal drinking age in New Brunswick is 19.

 DINING OUT. Expect surprisingly good dining in some places in rural New Brunswick, in others just average. Price categories: *Expensive,* over $15; *Moderate,* $10–15; *Inexpensive,* under $10. A 10% provincial tax will be added to your bill.

Most places accept the following major credit cards: American Express, MasterCard, and Visa; others may also be honored. Not all establishments accept credit cards, therefore we suggest you call for information.

ATHOLVILLE. *Moderate:* **Landry's Steak House.** Good steak.

BATHURST. *Expensive:* **La Fine Grobe.** Located at Nigadoo, near Bathurst. French and traditional Acadian cuisine at its best. Fine buffet; special drink of the house—old Acadian recipe from Prohibition times called Le Caribou. Art and craft gallery with folksingers.

Moderate: **Danny's Restaurant.** Good food, plainly served. Generous lobster cocktails, friendly service in serene dining room.

CAMPBELLTON. *Moderate:* **Fundy Line Motel Dining Room.** Good, plain food. Excellent steak and salmon.

Wandlyn Dining Room. Good food, pleasant surroundings.

CARAQUET. *Moderate:* **Hotel Paulin.** Excellent seafood and home-cooked Acadian dishes.

Le Poirier. A new restaurant with a good initial reputation. Seafoods a specialty.

CHATHAM. *Moderate.* **La Portage.** Good steak.

DALHOUSIE. *Moderate:* **The Cedar Lodge Dining Room.** Excellent food. The apple pie is highly recommended.

EDMUNDSTON. *Expensive:* **Le Baron.** Excellent food; pâté à la maison, crêpe Suzettes flamed at your table.
The Wandlyn. Good food, comparable to Le Baron. Piano bar, dancing.

FORT BEAUSEJOUR. *Moderate:* **Drury Lane Steakhouse.** In Aulac, near Fort Beausejour. Steak, clam chowder with home-baked rolls, steamed clams—all excellent.

GRAND MANAN. *Moderate:* **The Compass Rose.** Seafood in home-cooked style. Afternoon tea.
The Marathon. Dinner at six. Set menu. Bread baked fresh daily. Good food. Homey and friendly.

MONCTON. *Expensive:* **Chez Jean Pierre.** Features Provençal cuisine (stuffed baby pig, quail in raisin sauce, and others). Phone 382–0332. Major credit cards.
The Windjammer. The most elegant dining room in the Beausejour Hotel. Private booths and portholes with real fish swimming around in them. Although expensive, service is slick and food is good. Châteaubriand recommended. Phone 854–4344. Major credit cards.
Moderate–Expensive: **Cy's.** Main St. Noted seafood restaurant which richly deserves its reputation. The seafood platter, one of the specialties, will amaze you with its quality and quantity. Lobster a specialty, of course, and a great view of the tidal bore from a window table. Phone 382–0032. Major credit cards.
Papa Joe's. Fair food. Fiddleheads available, steaks are good; try some of the flaming coffees. Phone 854–2490. Major credit cards.
Moderate: **Ming Garden Restaurant.** Interesting Cantonese-Canadian food, the best in the Maritimes. One dish, chunks of fresh lobster, wrapped in thin slices of chicken, deep fried and served with oyster sauce should be tried. Open till 2 A.M. weeknights, 3 A.M. weekends. Phone 855–5433. Major credit cards.
Vito's. Mountain Rd. Good Italian food, popular. Phone 855-5000. Major credit cards.
Moderate–Inexpensive: **Le Cave à Pape.** Excellent French and Acadian cuisine. Phone 855–0581. Major credit cards.

NEWCASTLE. *Moderate:* **The Wandlyn Dining Room.** Small, cozy, good.

PERTH-ANDOVER. *Moderate:* **York's Dining Room.** Deserves special mention. A uniquely New Brunswick establishment, York's serves gargantuan helpings of excellent home-cooked foods in an unassuming dining room.

SACKVILLE. *Expensive–moderate.* **Marshlands Inn.** Fine old inn serving traditional English and New Brunswick foods such as steak and kidney pie, seafood, fiddleheads, in mahogany panelled dining room with antique lined walls.

SHEDIAC. *Expensive–Moderate.* **Chez Francoise.** Glowing old-fashioned dining rooms in old mansion. Cuisine *a la francais* with accent on fresh seafood of the region.

Moderate: **Paturel's Shore House.** At Cape Bimet a few miles east of Shediac. Lobster and seafood.

Shediac's Fisherman's Paradise. Good seafood in the heart of lobster country.

ST. ANDREWS. *Expensive:* **The Algonquin.** Excellent lobster dinners on weekends. Open dances in the Casino on some Saturday nights.

Conley's Shore House. Good fresh lobster in all forms, boiled, stewed or on rolls.

The Rossmount. Elegant décor, reservations suggested. Excellent food. House specialties—lobster and Bay of Fundy fish.

Moderate to Expensive. **Tara Manor.** Good dining room with friendly service.

Moderate: **The Shiretown.** Fairly good food. Lunchtime buffet interesting and hearty, local area food. Licensed. English inn atmosphere.

Smugglers' Wharf Restaurant. Seafare with a view over St. Andrews Harbour. Licensed.

ST. STEPHEN-MILLTOWN. *Moderate.* **Wandlyn.** Small, cheerful dining room with good average fare.

WOODSTOCK. *Expensive:* **The Wandlyn Dining Room.** Large pleasant room, good food.

Inexpensive–Moderate: **Stiles Home Town Tea Room.** Home cooking.

 NIGHT LIFE. In **Edmundston,** some of the hotels that offer live entertainment are *Charlies Bar* at the Wandlyn Motel, *Rita's Motel* bar, *The Riverside* and the *New Royal* (the last two have been known to offer strip shows), or the bars at the *Praga* tavern atmosphere with canned music.

In **Moncton** for dressed-up stepping out, the hottest spot is the *Cosmopolitan Club* in the old courthouse on Main St. *The Beaus and Belles* lounge in the Beausejour Hotel is an attractive spot decorated in Gay Nineties style where you can have a snack with your drink. *The Coach Room Lounge,* Keddy's Motel, dark, quaint and quiet. Perfect spot for a quiet tête-à-tête. *Lamplighter Room* in the Howard Johnson's Motor Inn, pleasant, congenial, and quiet.

In **St. Andrews,** two swinging bars in the Algonquin Hotel offer nightly entertainment. Quiet drinking in the *Shiretown Inn,* Water St., like a small English pub.

PRINCE EDWARD ISLAND

Garden of the Gulf

by
ALAN FREEMAN, RALPH SURETTE,
and
COLLEEN THOMPSON

Ralph Surette is a freelance journalist living near Dartmouth N.S. He writes for a number of Canadian magazines and is a regular commentator on Canadian Broadcasting Corporation Radio.

In the Gulf of St. Lawrence, off the coasts of New Brunswick and Nova Scotia, Prince Edward Island is Canada's smallest province, but in many ways its most captivating. The Micmac Indians, the island's original inhabitants (still represented here on four reservations), called the Island *Abegweit,* meaning "cradled on the waves." French explorer Jacques Cartier, sighting the island in 1534, described it as "the fairest land 'tis possible to see." More than two centuries later, the British were sufficiently enchanted to name the island after Edward, Duke of Kent, father of Queen Victoria. Today, tourist brochures refer to it as "the Garden of the Gulf," a tribute to the wide variety of fresh fruits and vegetables brought daily to the table from the Island's farms.

Red Cliffs—Green Fields

Prince Edward Island is characterized by an abundance of natural beauty. The southern coastline is a harmonious blend of red sandstone cliffs topped by rich green fields and trees. Summer visitors arriving by ferry across the Northumberland Strait will get their first impressions of the island from this shore.

The north shore, on the other hand, is famous for its white, silky sand. Inland, immaculate communities form a part of the gently rolling landscape.

That the island has been able to retain its popular appeal over the centuries is a tribute not only to its enduring attractiveness, but also to the friendly, hardy residents (many of them descendants of the early settlers), who live and work harmoniously while maintaining their individual heritages. Although a scant 140 miles long and from 4 to 40 miles wide at any given point, Prince Edward Island is the permanent home of 123,000 Islanders.

The island appeals to its inhabitants, who serenely weather the sometimes bitter winters, in much the same way as it attracts visitors, offering lovely land, a low-key style of living, clean environment, and a satisfying range of diversions. Throughout the island, the people have industriously developed the agricultural and coastal resources, and built good schools that do much to encourage succeeding generations to remain on the island. At the same time, they have retained an almost stubborn pride in their heritage—British, French, Scot, and Micmac Indian. You will find evidence of this in the many local museums that dot the island and in a number of cultural festivals held throughout the summer.

Agriculture

Prince Edward Island has been described as two huge beaches separated by potato fields. An oversimplification, of course, but not entirely inaccurate. Agriculture is the island's most important industry, and about 60,000 acres of potatoes, the major crop, are planted each year. Waving fields of barley, oats, wheat, and other grains provide a feast for the eye with their summer hues of brown, yellow, and green. Although potatoes are more profitable, more acreage is planted in grain, some of which is exported. Tobacco is a relatively new crop and is internationally known for its high quality. Many vegetables as well as strawberries, blueberries, apples, and raspberries are among the other crops under cultivation. The island has a healthy livestock population, too.

Tourism Is Number 2

As a source of revenue, tourism follows agriculture. Facilities accommodate more than half a million visitors annually. The Island is readily accessible via ferry service from New Brunswick, Nova Scotia, and the Magdalen Islands, and by plane from nearby major cities of the mainland. The tourist season is generally compressed into the summer months, owing to the island's North Atlantic locale; the accommodations are numerous, if modest. The range of vacation activities is broad: from fishing, boating and other watersports on both inland and coastal waters to golf (ten courses), horseback riding, professional sulky races, festivals, repertory theater, and an informal but frequently lively night life. Add to this good sightseeing at museums, art galleries, historic homes, and, for the children, a surprising number of amusement parks, animal enclaves, wildlife centers and youth-appeal museums within minutes of most major crossroads.

What the visitor will find distinctive, however, are the historic and personal elements: the enduring French Acadian influence; the vestiges of Micmac, English, and Scottish settlements; vacation farms that are a unique and refreshing experience for visitors who want to share the accommodations—and chores—of their farm family hosts; home/studios of local craftsmen (and there are many) where travelers can stop awhile and talk with the artists and, of course, buy their works; the serenity of the low inland hills, rarely more than a few miles away but seemingly far from the main routes; and, above all, an essentially rural island personality that sets this locale apart from similar but more commercial holiday destinations.

The sense of remoteness, in fact, is one of the island's most charming features; as a result many of the facilities here are oriented to the natural environment. Despite the island's minute size, it encompasses 3,700 miles of paved road that make all communities easily accessible. Camping and trailer sites are numerous in the official provincial as well as privately operated parks scattered along the coast and inland. Prince Edward Island, in effect, begs to be explored.

To facilitate sightseeing, there are three scenic motor routings, each marked with distinctive symbols, called Lady Slipper Drive, Blue Heron Drive, and Kings Byway. Each follows the coastline of the island's three major land divisions, which are naturally sectioned by indentations of bays and rivers. These divisions are also the approximate boundaries of the province's three counties, Prince, Queens, and Kings.

Local officials encourage visitors to allot at least one day for each drive, and point out that side trips should be the rule rather than the exception since distances between attractions are short and almost every side road eventually leads to a major highway. Each drive features access to beaches, parks, camping grounds, scenic lookouts, towns, villages with notable historic or special attractions, and places where you may buy fresh seafood and vegetables.

Although Prince Edward Island is very much part of the modern world, the province has retained a good deal of the slow pace and human qualities of an earlier age. Islanders are not only friendly but thoroughly hospitable, preferring unpretentious comfort, homey accommodations and plain, traditional food from land and sea. Food should be a treat, as a mainstay of the dinner table is the lobster, brought in daily from the deep waters off the coast when the season permits. The lobster supper, a Prince Edward Island tradition, is a unique dining experience and should be sought out when touring along the North Shore. Other popular local foods (in season) are oysters from the famed farming beds in Malpeque Bay, strawberries, cranberries, and blueberries, which thrive on the island's sandy soil, apples and cherries from native trees, and the plenteous home-grown farm vegetables that invariably surprise the visitor because of the island's limited size and growing season.

Fishing is P.E.I.'s third industry, with lobsters the most profitable of the more than 30 varieties of fish yielded up by the waters surrounding and crisscrossing the island.

History Is Sparsely Recorded

Except for scattered monuments, restorations, re-created villages (some frankly commercial), gravestones and the like, there are few visible reminders on Prince Edward Island of the earliest European settlements. But the island did experience a history of quarrelsome confrontations between those early rivals France and England in the race to exploit and colonize North America. The heritage of both remains.

The French came first but took their time in settling here. Jacques Cartier discovered Prince Edward Island in 1534, but the French did not establish an outpost on the Île St. Jean, as they named it, until 1663. A more complete settlement came along in 1720 when Compte St. Pierre and a band of 300 established Port La Joie, across the harbor from what is now Charlottetown, the capital. (Today, the site of Port La Joie is part of Fort Amherst National Historic Park.) France hoped that the new settlement would draw from the Acadian (French) settlements in what is now Nova Scotia, but there was little migration until the French were forced to leave, following the fall of Louisburg on Cape Breton Island to the English.

Capitalizing on this maritime foothold, the English continued to rout the French when Lord Rollo brought four ships and 500 men to take possession of the island. Following the British takeover in 1763, the name was Anglicized to the Island of Saint John. In 1799 it was changed again—this time to Prince Edward Island in honor of Prince Edward (later the Duke of Kent). In 1769 the island was separated from Nova Scotia.

Micmac Means "Allies"

There is little indication of any major strife here between the early French settlers and the Island's Micmac Indians. The tribe, made up of small groups, each with its own chief, did not live in permanent villages, preferring instead to move from place to place as hunters and fishermen. Today, about 400 Micmac Indians remain on the island's four reservations where they have found it difficult to maintain their native culture. By comparison, descendants of some of the early Acadians also remain on the island but retain their identity in a number of ways, notably in their food, their music, and their language. The Acadians are often considered to speak a debased form of French. They do not. Though many English words have crept into their speech over the years, their language is still basically good 18th-century provincial French, just as the distinctive accents of Newfoundland often prove to be pure 18th-century Devon or Dorset.

The population of the island grew during the American Revolution, particularly at its end when British Loyalists were forced to leave the newly established United States and flee to Canada. It was during this period that the island officially became a Crown Colony and was re-named Prince Edward Island. One of the more durable settlements was established by Scotland's Lord Selkirk, who arrived in 1803 with three ships of pioneers from the Scots Highlands. Restored log cabins and other shelters, as well as the group's church built in 1824, may be seen in the Belfast district of the island, where there are also a number of descendants of the original settlers.

For most visitors, the island's development in the first half of the 19th century has a more visible significance since a number of the homes, churches, government structures, monuments, and sites of his-toric or colorful interest can actually be seen and visited. Province House, in Charlottetown, is probably the most revered of these, having been the site of the 1864 conference of Confederation planners. Their deliberations led, three years later, to the union of all the British North American colonies into a united Canada, although P.E.I. did not join the Confederation until 1873. The imposing structure still serves as the province's legislature and still dominates the architecture of downtown Charlottetown.

A more contemporary symbol is Green Gables House, which served as the setting for Lucy Maud Montgomery's well-known novel *Anne of Green Gables*. Situated at Cavendish, in the center of the island's North Shore, the house should be visited by devotees of the book and other works by the author, although in other respects it is an unremarkable island farmhouse. Nearby, Green Gables Post Office is the island's most popular center for stamps and postmarks during the summer.

Other sites associated with Mrs. Montgomery and her works are Rainbow Valley, an amusement center which features, among other things, three-dimensional reproductions of the author and her fictional characters; Mrs. Montgomery's birthplace in New London; heroine Anne's House of Dreams, furnished in the style of the early 1900's, at French River; and Silver Bush Museum in Park Corner, where Mrs. Montgomery was married in 1911.

EXPLORING CHARLOTTETOWN

The provincial capital and Prince Edward Island's only city, Char-lottetown, reflects its Loyalist heritage even in its name (after Char-lotte, stylish consort of England's George III). It is often referred to as "the cradle of Confederation," a reference to the conference held here in 1864 that led to Canada's unification.

Essentially a small city (population 15,300), Charlottetown has no smokestack industry in the traditional sense. Its main activities center around government, tourism, and private commerce, and in these capacities it functions as a service center for the surrounding districts. Although new suburbs are springing up, the core of Charlottetown remains virtually unchanged. In fact, the waterfront is being restored to recapture the tempo and appearance of another era.

In addition, the façades of the old red brick buildings and the ginger-bread architecture of the wood houses lining its side streets are pleasant reminders of the past. The Prince Edward Island Museum and Heritage Foundation has strengthened this image by restoring an entire block of row housing on Great George Street across from St. Dunstan's Basilica.

The exceptionally handsome and modern Confederation Centre of the Arts, opened in 1964, as Canada's national memorial to the Fathers of Confederation, houses an art gallery, art workshops, a museum library, Children's Theatre, memorial hall, and the 1,100-seat Charlottetown Theatre. During July and August, the Confederation Centre's Summer Festival offers excellent professional entertainment, including the annual world-famous musical version of *Anne of Green Gables.*

Across the street from the Centre is the old Hughes Drug Store, officially designated a national historic site as Canada's first drugstore. Much of the original interior is still in place, including its elaborately carved woodwork. Protruding from the sidewalk in front of the store is a cannon barrel, now used only as a flower receptacle.

Two nearby churches are particularly noteworthy. St. Paul's Anglican Church, east of Province House, is the oldest (1747) Protestant church on the island. Its baptismal register includes the name of Margaret Gordon, sweetheart of author Thomas Carlyle and heroine of his masterpiece, *Sartor Resartus.*

St. James Presbyterian Church, better known as "the kirk," has impressive stained-glass windows and ancient relics from the island of Iona, one of the earliest sites of Christianity in Scotland. A block of granite resting on a marble slab embedded in the north wall of the kirk, in fact, came from St. Mary's Cathedral on Iona. It also has an intriguing legend. On the day in 1853 when the ship *Fairy Queen* went down in Northumberland Strait, the kirk was empty, but the kirk's bell, so the story goes, was heard to toll many times. A townsman who heard it claimed to have seen three women, bareheaded and barefoot, disappear through the locked doors of the kirk. Later it was learned that three female members of the congregation were lost in the wreck.

South of Province House, on Great George Street, stands St. Dunstan's Basilica, seat of the Roman Catholic Diocese in the province. It is not only one of the largest edifices of its kind in eastern Canada, but contains an impressive altar along with many beautifully executed Italian carvings.

St. Peter's Cathedral, in the northwest corner of Rockford Square, was erected in 1879 and consecrated by the Lord Bishop of Nova Scotia. The church chapel (1888) was designed by W.C. Harris, with murals by his famous brother, Islander Robert Harris.

Victoria Park, overlooking the expanse of water in Charlottetown Harbor at the southernmost tip of the city, is the setting for several notable buildings. Located on a hill between white birches is the old

Government House, a mansion built in 1835 as the official residence for the province's lieutenant governors. Next to the mansion stands Beaconsfield, a house designed by W. C. Harris, brother of artist Robert Harris, and an excellent example of Victorian architecture. Built in 1877 and named Beaconsfield for a nearby lake, the house is now the headquarters of the Prince Edward Island Museum and Heritage Foundation. Island artifacts are on display, and the interior design of this gracious old home is worth a visit.

Also in Victoria Park and overlooking the harbor is Fort Edward, built in 1805. It is one of a series of fortifications constructed along the Charlottetown Harbor entrance, and has a six-gun battery. From here one can look across the harbor mouth to Fort Amherst, now a National Historic Site.

The University of Prince Edward Island is located in the capital and is a popular gathering place for young Canadians throughout the summer months.

Exploring Routes Near Charlottetown

For a rewarding coastal drive, take Route 1 out of Charlottetown and Route 19 around Fort Amherst National Park, site of the old French fort. On the way, you'll drive through Cornwall, a spot where the locals swear a mermaid came ashore one day. Described "as big as a small girl," she talked to no one and allowed no one too close. After about an hour in the July sun, she slipped back into the ocean.

At New Haven on Route 1, Fairyland is one of P.E.I.'s many attractions that cater especially to children.

At Hampton, watch for Route 116, which takes you to the shore and to Victoria Provincial Park. No matter where you travel in this section, the scenery is delightful. Nearby Victoria is a quaint old English community. When you're here, take a drive around Augustine's Cove.

EXPLORING PRINCE EDWARD ISLAND

The best way to see all three sections of the island is via the Scenic Drives. These comprehensive routings are described in the brochure *Prince Edward Island Scenic Drives Tour Guide,* and outlined in the P.E.I. tourist map. Both are available from tourist information offices in Charlottetown and other locations throughout the Island and also at some car-rental agencies. Each Drive is color-coded in the literature, and easy to follow on the road because of the frequently posted symbols. Each is more or less a continuous circle, so the driver may start or stop at any point or travel in either direction. All together, the Drives tour the entire coast of Prince Edward Island and also provide easy access to inland areas and communities. Most highways are paved, with some short stretches of smooth red clay; with few exceptions, all roads are evenly surfaced and well maintained, for comfortable drives.

Blue Heron Drive

Circling Prince Edward Island's center segment, Blue Heron is the shortest of the three Drives, and in many ways a cross-section of the entire island. Highlights along the routing are the North Shore beaches, Anne of Green Gables country, scenic rural areas, the red sandstone seascapes along the southern shore, and a number of historic sites. It takes its name from the stately blue herons which you're likely to see along the route. The guide marker is a white square with blue border and blue heron in the center. Here is a suggested routing:

Driving north from Charlottetown in a counterclockwise direction, follow Route 15 to Brackley Beach, a pivotal intersection for access to the roughly 40 kms. (25 miles) of North Shore beaches that comprise the National Park. Symbols on the road map will advise you of available facilities (campsites, beaches, day-use parks, fishing).

Lobster Suppers

This is also the region where you must sample the island's distinctive lobster supper. Popular places for lobster suppers are Howe's Hall at Brackley Beach (you will also have a great breakfast here), New London, New Glasgow, St. Ann's Church in Hope River, Fisherman's Wharf in North Rustico, and Stanhope Beach Lodge.

At Brackley Beach, Blue Heron Drive turns left and follows Route 6 across Oyster Bed Bridge to South Rustico with its historic Farmer's Bank, chartered in 1864. Farmers and fishermen were its directors, and it prospered for 30 years by providing cheap credit to help the people of this predominantly Acadian community gain economic independence. Rustico, in fact, took its name from one of its early French settlers, René Rassicot, who came from Normandy. Townsfolk claim that the world's first automobile was driven in this community in 1866 when Father Belcourt drove around in a "strange, noisy contraption."

South Rustico is also the home of Jumpin' Jack's (admission $1.00, children under 12 free), an authentic old country store that dates back to the 1800's and features cracker barrels, fish barrels, egg crates, a checkerboard, potbellied stove, and countless other old items purchased and used by the residents' forefathers.

"Anne of Green Gables" Country

Farther along Route 6 is Cavendish and the farmhouse which served as the setting for Lucy Montgomery's *Anne of Green Gables*. Situated on the edge of the challenging 18-hole Green Gables Golf Course, the house is open to the public (admission is free) and offers bilingual guide service. The Green Gables Post Office, located on Route 6, offers all current postage stamp issues, including first-day covers, mint sets, plates, corner blocks, and sheets. Lucy Montgomery is buried in the Cavendish Cemetery, where you'll also find the graves of 21 American sailors who drowned when their ship, *Yankee Star,* sank many years ago off the Cavendish coast.

Blue Heron Drive continues along Route 6 for about 11 kms. (7 miles) to New London (you may want to see the white cottage where Lucy Montgomery was born) and then turns north onto Route 20. For an interesting side trip, turn off the Drive at Springbrook and turn left on Route 234 for the short drive to Long River. Here, look for the Old Mill Museum, containing amusing antique items such as a 100-year-old hand-pumped organ, an 80-year-old carriage, and a dog-powered butter churn. Built in 1820, the mill also houses a collection of old bottles, some the size of a thimble.

Returning to Springbrook, resume the drive north along Route 20 to the French River district near New London Harbor, where there are two pioneer-era cemeteries, Yankee Hill and Sims, located within 300 yards of each other. They contain inscribed tombstones of a number of residents who died between 1816 and 1843. Farther along the highway is Park Corner, where those who have read the stories of Pat of Silverbush (more of Lucy Maud Montgomery) might enjoy a visit to the Anne of Green Gables Museum at Silverbush. Lucy Maud was married here and many personal effects are on display.

Historic Malpeque

Crossing over from Queens to Prince County you come to Malpeque, one of the truly historic corners of Prince Edward Island. The French settled in this area in the early 1700's; before them, the wandering Micmac Indians camped here. Traces of their weapons and implements can still be found in Malpeque. In 1765, when the English sent Captain Samuel Holland to survey the new colony, he recommended that "Princetown," as he called the settlement, be made capital of Prince County (although it subsequently reverted to the Indian name). Five years later came the first sizable migration of Scots; many of their descendants live here today. The famous Malpeque oysters farmed in adjacent Malpeque Bay are shipped from here to seafood distribution centers throughout North America.

From Malpeque, follow the route to the southern coast and watch carefully for the Blue Heron Drive signs since the highway route numbers change several times. At Cape Traverse, east of Borden, you'll find a monument to the ice boat—the only way to travel to the mainland in the winter before 1917. Still farther east is Augustine Cove, an exceptionally attractive inlet, and beyond that Victoria, a quaint Old English community. Across the harbor is Victoria Provincial Park, a scenic setting for camping and picnicking.

Just beyond is DeSable and from here there are two major routings back to Charlottetown. The Blue Heron Drive continues along the red sandstone coastline to the end of the peninsula that faces Charlottetown south of its harbor. Just before this point is Fort Amherst National Historic Park, site of Port La Joie, the first French settlement and, later, of Fort Amherst (English), built in 1758. Today only the earthworks of the fort remain, but the Visitor Centre provides a social, political, and military history of the area.

At the tip of the peninsula is Rocky Point and the Micmac Indian Village. Displays at the village include birchbark wigwams and canoes, handmade hunting and fishing implements, and life-size sculptures of Indians and animals. Of special interest is the museum, which holds actual tools and weapons used by the first inhabitants of the island.

The final leg of Blue Heron Drive backtracks a short way down the north side of the peninsula, then crosses the West River, and continues to Cornwall, where it connects with the Trans-Canada Highway back to Charlottetown.

The alternate return from DeSable is more or less an inland drive along National Route 1 (Trans-Canada Highway) and is generally more entertaining as well as scenic. At Bonshaw, just beyond DeSable, is the Car Life Museum, with a collection of vintage gas pumps, handsomely restored autos from the Roaring Twenties era, and old farm equipment. Farther along the highway is Strathgartney Park, a scenic area for tenting with a stunning view of the surrounding countryside. Route 1 continues through New Haven and Fairyland, an attraction for children; then it rejoins the Blue Heron Drive at Cornwall for the last several miles into Charlottetown.

Lady Slipper Drive

The region encircled by Prince County's Lady Slipper Drive is considered one of the less developed areas of the island for tourism purposes. It is made up of small and very old villages (with the exception of Summerside, the largest P.E.I. community designated as a town, and second in size to Charlottetown), still adhering to a more traditional way of life. The area is also the home of the Island's Acadians, descendants of the original French settlers.

The Drive might be likened to a misshapen figure-eight, and is named for the lady slipper orchid that blooms in late spring and is the official Provincial Flower. The Drive marker, appropriately enough, is a white square with a red border and a red orchid in the center. In addition to the Acadian presence, Indians, farms, Irish moss and oysters are pronounced influences in the region.

At Summerside

Again, there is no official starting point for Lady Slipper Drive, but a logical place to begin is Summerside. An annual event here is the eight-day Summerside Lobster Carnival in mid-July. The Carnival is actually a combination fair and festival, with exhibits of livestock, agriculture, and handicrafts as well as parades, beauty contests, harness racing, a midway and, of course, lobster suppers (chicken too). Specific dates of the Carnival are available from the Island's Visitor Information Centres or from the Summerside Area Tourist Association.

From Summerside follow the Lady Slipper Drive signs on Route 1A to St. Eleanor's; then turn west on Route 2 to Miscouche. Here, the Acadian Museum has a collection of artifacts dating from before the 1800's which relate to Acadian lifestyles over the years. There are household and farm implements as well as other domestic items. The red stone monument behind the museum stands over a collective Acadian grave transferred from River Platte in 1839.

Following the northern route of the Drive, proceed up Route 12 to Rosehill, then turn right onto Route 123, and continue along the road that curves around the cape—jutting into Malpeque Bay, center of the island's oyster-farming industry. The road rejoins Route 12, which then winds along the western shore of the Bay, across rivers and harbor inlets and through small and large ports serving as harvest centers for other catches of the Island's important fishing industry.

Green Park, a Provincial Historic Park at Port Hill, merits a visit. There is a mansion here that was the onetime home of a shipbuilding family named Yeo, and the park area is now a permanent museum. The mansion, built in 1865, has been restored and refurnished. An interpretive center houses displays and artifacts from those early wooden ships, and there is also a shipyard with a display of a wooden vessel under construction. Guided tours are available at no charge and the park has campgrounds.

Much farther north is Alberton, one of several major deep-sea charter fishing ports along Lady Slipper Drive (others included are Skinner's Pond and Conway Harbor Inlet). Deep-sea fishing outings can be a family affair and all you need are warm clothing and a lunch. Most trips last four hours, with cod, mackerel, halibut, herring, and hake the usual catches. Cost is $10 per person or more. The cost for tuna chartering is usually $200 per 8-hour day for upwards of six persons, and there are often special rates for children. The boat captain will supply all the tackle and bait and you don't need a license.

Leavitt's Maple Tree Craft Shop in Alberton specializes in turned Bird's-eye maplewood products. The craftspeople here are always ready to talk with visitors, and Bird's-eye maple blanks can be purchased for home lathes. There is also a variety of finished wood products. Also in Alberton, the Alberton Museum features local and provincial artifacts and relics, housed in an old renovated barn. It focuses on the silver fox industry, which thrived here in the early part of this century, but also has Indian relics, farm and trade implements, glass, china, books and other artifacts.

At nearby Northport is Sea Rescue Park overlooking Northport Harbour. The park is the site of the restored lifeboat station from which Northport seamen performed a daring rescue of survivors from a floundering sailing vessel during a storm in the fall of 1906. There are picnic tables, washrooms, water tap, and a children's playground.

North Cape

Lady Slipper Drive continues past Cape Kildare, where French explorer Cartier reportedly first took a close look at the island, then proceeds to the northwesternmost tip of the island named, appropriately, North Cape. Motoring down the western coastline you will drive through Skinner's Pond and, a bit farther south, Miminegash at the head of the river of the same name, considered one of the better inland fishing areas in the western part of Prince Edward Island.

The next 48 kms. (30 miles) or so of Lady Slipper Drive follow the quietly attractive western and southern coastline. For a more sightworthy routing, leave the Drive at Campbellton and take Route 145 to

Route 2, turning right at Bloomfield to St. Anthony, and right again on Route 143 to Howlan, where there is a blacksmith shop. From Howlan, Route 148 takes you to the farming community of O'Leary, which has a museum.

At Coleman, you are again on Lady Slipper Drive and should take the southern routing back to Summerside in order to visit the Acadian Pioneer Village at Mount Carmel. The restoration includes a church, priest's house, blacksmith shop, homes, barn, and store. The buildings are furnished with artifacts and restored items relating to the life of the French settlers of the early 19th century. To enjoy Acadian food, visit the restaurant on the site and try Acadian soup or a potato dish. Prices are reasonable.

Kings Byway Drive

The Kings Byway takes visitors through some of the oldest and most interesting areas of Prince Edward Island. Many of the attractions recall early days of the island and the pioneering spirit which the settlers brought with them. There are also red-banked as well as white sand beaches, highly photogenic lighthouse points, tobacco farmlands, fisheries, and the "Tuna Capital of the World" at North Lake. This is also a considerably longer routing than the other two Drives and visitors wishing to enjoy it at a leisurely pace should think of making one or two overnight stays along the route. The Kings Byway symbol is a white square bordered in royal purple with a crown in the center.

There are many major sights and attractions along the way, beginning at Charlottetown and heading south. The agricultural heritage of the island's rural communities is highlighted at Orwell Corner, an officially designated Historic Site near Orwell. A living farm museum, the site contains a combined store, post office, school, church, farmhouse, and barns. Farming methods are those of former years, and there are old-fashioned musical evenings and hayrides. Farm life of the early inhabitants is also highlighted at Macphail Provincial Park at nearby Orwell. The home of Sir Andrew Macphail, a noted Prince Edward Island physician and author, is surrounded by picnic grounds open to the public.

Still another village tribute to the past, and one of the island's most historic, is the Lord Selkirk Settlement at Eldon. A memorial to the Scottish settlers who arrived here in 1803, it features several reproductions of shelters and cabins that served as the first homes of these pioneers. Farther along the route is Flat River, where the Flat River Crafts Studio specializes in good pottery. Visitors may chat with the craftsmen as they watch them at work.

Continuing along the coast, Kings Byway circles Murray Head peninsula, the southeasternmost tip of the Island, and passes through a number of special communities lining the large Murray Harbour inlet. At the community of Murray Harbour is the Log Cabin Museum depicting the lifestyle of the island during the last century, with many well-preserved implements and household necessities of both local and European manufacture. The building itself is made of logs and finished with hand-split island shingles. In Murray River, the Handcraft Co-op

Association shop on Main Street is one of the largest and most complete handcraft retail outlets on the island. And at Murray Harbour North, at the upper corner of the bay, wildlife fanciers may want to seek out Johnston's Centennial Campground from which to view a natural seal colony just offshore.

Just beyond the crossing at Sturgeon River, which happens to be a popular waterway for rainbow trout, Route 317 will take you to Milltown Cross and two of the island's more unique wildlife attractions. At Buffaloland Provincial Park, there is a small herd of North American buffalo, an imported species here, which grazes on a 100-acre enclosure. Nearby is Moore's Migratory Bird Sanctuary, a refuge for thousands of wildfowl, including black duck, American widgeon, blue-wing and green-wing teals, ringneck duck and, of course, Canada goose. Although privately operated, the sanctuary is free.

Rejoin Kings Byway by taking Route 4 from Milltown Cross north to Montague, where the Garden of the Gulf Museum features an interesting collection of old firearms, along with displays of farm tools and household items. Waterways cut deep into this eastern coast of Prince Edward Island north of Montague, forming a number of unusual seascape peninsulas. One of the more popular views is bordered by the Brudenell and Cardigan Rivers, the site of the 1,400-acre Brudenell Provincial Resort.

Since the Byway follows the heavily indented coastline north, duplicating scenery and sights, you may want to bypass part of this by taking Route 4 north to Dingwells Mills, then turning right on Route 2, which rejoins the Byway at Rollo Bay West. Moving more directly up the coast, you should not overlook the Basin Head Fisheries Museum, established in 1973 to preserve the heritage of the island's fisheries, notably that of the inshore fishermen. Displays and photographs illustrate how the small boats were used and the types of fish they caught. Replicas of the fish shacks have been constructed, and an old lobster canning plant by the water adds to the authenticity. There are excellent sandy beaches in this area.

Tuna Fishing

The Byway now proceeds to the tip of the island, East Point, then around to North Lake, major port for the island's big-game fishermen who battle the giant bluefin tuna. Some of the giants run to almost 1,200 pounds and can fight for hours before being brought to gaff. The North Lake Tuna Charter Association at North Lake has a number of properly equipped tuna boats which charter for about $200 per day for a maximum party of six. Most charters leave at 10 A.M. If you want to try standby, show up early at the wharf and you may be able to join a party for a share of the cost. Take a lunch and warm clothing; if a tuna is on the line, you may be out long past the normal 6 P.M. returning time. The tuna is the property of the boat captain. The angler gets a photograph of himself and the fish after the weigh-in as his trophy.

If has been said that the railroad on Prince Edward Island was built and paid for by the mile, wandering along for many miles without getting very far. Although the passenger service no longer operates, there is a railway museum which preserves the memories. A gift of Canadian National Railways, the Elmira Railway Station dating from 1911 has been refurbished and features photographic displays and railroading artifacts. Elmira is a short side trip south of North Lake, on Route 16A.

The Kings Byway routing back to Charlottetown follows the North Shore of Kings County, crossing the Morell River (good salmon fishing), and crossing back into Queens County at St. Andrews. If you're in a hurry, you can skip a portion of the Byway by remaining on Route 2, rejoining the Byway at Dunstaffnage. For antique car buffs, the Spoke Wheel Museum here has a 1916 Buick believed to be the only one in existence. This private collection also includes many models and vintages.

On the final leg of the Byway, flower fanciers may want to turn off at Rte. 25 for a very short detour to Jewell's Country Gardens, at the village of York. Specialties at these formal gardens are begonias and fuchsias; there is also an antique glass museum, old country store, and a children's playground.

PRACTICAL INFORMATION FOR
PRINCE EDWARD ISLAND

HOW TO GET THERE. By air: *Eastern Provincial Airways (EPA)* has direct flights to Charlottetown Airport from Toronto, Montréal and Halifax daily. *Air Canada* has one-stop (Ottawa) service from Toronto and also from Boston and New York, stopping at Halifax where you change to EPA for the short flight to the island. Schedules and other information are available from both airways. Many of the larger hotels and resorts in Prince Edward Island will meet guests at the airport if prior arrangements are made. A "limo service" will take passengers from the airport to major motels in Summerside.

By car ferry: Two ferry systems link Prince Edward Island with the mainland, providing service from New Brunswick via Borden and from Nova Scotia via Wood Islands to Charlottetown. Each ferry has a snack bar and newsstand. Ferry service also connects with the Magdalen Islands via Souris.

By rail: Transports passengers by bus to the train in Moncton, N.B. from Charlottetown and Summerside.

ACCOMMODATIONS. Double-occupancy rates in Prince Edward Island are categorized as follows: *Expensive*, $43 or more; *Moderate*, $33–43; *Inexpensive*, under $33. The 10% provincial sales tax is applied to all accommodation rates. Reservations should be made in advance through any P.E.I. tourist bureau. A listing of all accommodations, including the many comfortable guest homes and cottages on the island, can be obtained from P.E.I. Visitor Services Division, P.O. Box 940, Charlottetown, P.E.I., Canada C1A 7M5. You can make reservations by calling toll-free (1–800–565–7421) from Nova Scotia or New Brunswick from mid-May to mid-September.

Most places accept the following major credit cards: American Express. MasterCard and Visa; others may also be honored. Not all establishments accept credit cards, therefore we suggest you call for information.

ALBERTON. *Moderate:* **Westerner Motel.** Plain, comfortable accommodations. Housekeeping cottages and motel units. large play area; trout fishing. Open year-round. Off-season rates September 30 to June 1. Pets allowed. Phone 853–2215. Major credit cards.

BRACKLEY BEACH. *Moderate:* **Shady Spruce Tourist Home & Cottages.** 8 housekeeping cottages (one and two bedrooms) three miles from the beach. Phone 672–2264. No credit cards accepted.

Centennial Cottages. 9 two-bedroom cottages; housekeeping; nearly 6 kms. (3½ miles) from beach; surrounded by active farm with animals; 8 kms. (5 miles) to 18-hole golf course. Lobster suppers nearby. Phone 672–2729. Major credit cards.

Inexpensive: **Bayview Farm Apartments and Cottages.** On Rte. 15, 2 km. (1 mile) from National Park. Seven housekeeping cottages. Clam digging, picnic tables, swings and barbecues on premises. No credit cards.

Mac's Farm Tourist Home. On Rte. 15. 200 acres mixed farming. Ocean beach, golfing, and lobster suppers nearby. Phone 672-2545. No credit cards accepted.

BRUDENELL. *Inexpensive–Moderate:* **Fraser's Deluxe Housekeeping Cottages** River beach on the property. Open June 1 to October 31. Pets permitted. 10 housekeeping units. Phone 838–2453.

CARLETON. *Inexpensive:* **Carleton Motel.** Housekeeping cottages and motel rooms, weekly rates, near beach. Pets permitted. Coffeeshop serves breakfast and lunch. Open year-round. Phone 855–2644. Visa only.

Jenny's Cottages. Spartan; babysitting; near ocean beach. Pets permitted. Phone 855–2341. No credit cards accepted.

CAVENDISH. *Expensive:* **Bay Vista Motor Inn.** Social gathering spot, overnight and housekeeping units, lounge, pool, 3 miles to beach and golf course, excellent restaurant. Live lobster and shellfish pound on premises. Babysitting. Phone 963–2225. Major credit cards.

Cavendish Motel. Pool, babysitting, housekeeping accommodations. Phone 963–2244. Major credit cards.

White Eagle By the Sea. 22 two-bedroom housekeeping cottages, ocean view, near 18-hole golf course. Also, 4-bedroom house for rent, nearby. Phone 963–2361.

Moderate–Expensive: **Green Gables Bungalow Court.** Adjacent to golf course; tennis courts, babysitting arranged. Housekeeping bungalows from bedsitting rooms to 3 bedrooms. Pets on leashes. Phone 963–2722. No credit cards accepted.

Inexpensive: **Marco Polo Inn.** Farm home with 6 rooms, babysitting services, large campground. Pets permitted. Phone 963–2351. Major credit cards.

CHARLOTTETOWN. *Expensive:* **Charlottetown Hotel.** Central; babysitting arranged, indoor pool and sauna, newly redecorated. Pets on leash permitted. Phone 894–7371. Major credit cards.

Confederation Inn. At the junction of Rtes. 1 and 2 in West Royalty. Heated outdoor pool. Lounge. Some housekeeping units. Pets permitted. Phone 894–2481. Major credit cards.

The Inn on the Hill. Babysitting arranged; trained pets permitted. Phone 894–8572. Major credit cards.

The Kirkwood Motor Hotel. Nice units; indoor pool. Pets permitted. Phone 892–4206. Major credit cards.

The Rodd Royalty Inn. Excellent accommodations, pool, games room, babysitting arranged; pets in motel only. Phone 894–8566. Major credit cards.

Wandlyn Inn. Babysitting arranged. French cuisine. Outdoor pool. Pets on leashes. Phone 892–1201. Major credit cards.

Dundee Arms Motel. Babysitting arranged. Near golf course, harness racing, theater, historic sites, and ocean beach. Good dining room, Swiss food. Phone 892–2496. Major credit cards.

MacLauchlan's Motel. Bridal suite; babysitting arranged, sauna, indoor swimming pool, beauty lounge, barbershop. Pets on leashes permitted. Phone 892–2461. Major credit cards.

Moderate: **Caroma Lodge.** 9 units near downtown. 2 kitchens for use of guests, laundry facilities. Major credit cards. Phone 894–9039.

Inexpensive: **Auld's Overnight Guests.** One room. Located near theater and shopping. Phone 892–2730. No credit cards accepted.

Gateway House. 3 rooms; near harness racing. Small pets only. Phone 894–9761. No credit cards accepted.

KENSINGTON. *Inexpensive:* **Duggan's Bed & Breakfast.** 4 rooms, kitchen privileges, complimentary coffee, 13 kms. (8 miles) to ocean beach, 18 kms. (11 miles) to golf course. Phone 836–3444. No credit cards accepted.

KINGSBORO. *Moderate–Expensive:* **Seabreeze Motel.** Well-maintained and comfortable. Has a view over Basin Head Harbour, near the Fisheries Museum. White sandy ocean beach nearby. Motel will arrange deep-sea fishing charters. Dining room is good and features home-style cooking with fish as the specialty. Open year-round. Phone 357–2371. Major credit cards.

MONTAGUE. *Moderate:* **Lobster Shanty North.** One of the better places to eat and stay on the King's Byway. Features good dining with seafood specialties in a rustic licensed dining room which extends into the lounge bar overlooking the Montague River, 27 kms. (17 miles) to ocean beach and 11 kms. (7 miles) to Brudenell golf course. Deep-sea fishing charters can be arranged for guests. Open year-round. Quiet pets permitted. Phone 838–2463. Major credit cards.

Inexpensive: **Lane's Tourist Court.** 9 housekeeping units. Near center of Montague. Quiet, scenic atmosphere. Children's playground. Phone 838–2433. Major credit cards.

NORTH LAKE. *Moderate:* **Bluefin Motel.** Clean, comfortable accommodation near the North Lake tuna fishing area. Ocean beach 152 meters (500 feet) from the motel. Open July 1 to mid-Oct. Small pets permitted. Phone 357–2599.

NORTH RUSTICO. *Moderate:* **St. Lawrence Motel.** Weekly or nightly rates, babysitting arranged, games room, barbecues, golf range, bicycle rentals, supervised ocean beach. Tuna fishing arranged at waterside. Pets permitted. Phone 963–2053.

POOLES CORNER. *Moderate:* **Kingsway Motel.** Small, modern motel. Licensed dining room, good food, home cooked variety; cozy lounge bar. The river beach and golf course at Brudenell Resort are 5 kms (3 miles) away. Open year-round. Leashed pets. Phone 838–2112. Major credit cards.

RUSTICOVILLE. *Expensive.* **Pines Motel.** 8 overnight and 3 housekeeping units, babysitting arranged; dining room. Open May 1 to Oct. 14. Phone 963–2029.

SOURIS. *Inexpensive:* **Souris West Motel & Cottages.** Small, comfortable motel and cottages overlooking Colville Bay. On parle français ici. Open Apr. 1 to Jan. 1. Pets okay. Off-season rates before June and after Sept. 15. Phone 687–2676. No credit cards accepted.

SUMMERSIDE. *Expensive:* **Garden of the Gulf Motel/Quality Inn.** Heated outdoor pool, 9-hole golf course and bay beach on property. Babysitting arranged. Adjacent restaurant, poolside lounge and disco. Open year-round. Off-season rates Oct. 5 to June 20. Leashed pets okay. Phone 436–2295. Major credit cards.

Expensive: **The Linkletter Motel.** Downtown area. Babysitting arranged. Tuna and deep-sea fishing charters, car rental agency, and travel agency. Coffeeshop and dining room. Open year-round. Off-season rates Jan. 1 to May 31. Phone 436–2157. Major credit cards.

Inexpensive: **Cairns' Motel.** Babysitting available. Open year-round. Golf, riding academy, drive-in theatre nearby. Phone 436–5841.

Gallant Tourist Home. Small place with friendly hosts. Complimentary coffee and cookies for guests. Adults only, non-smokers only. Breakfast provided on request. Open May 1 to Sept. 30. Phone 436–3897. No credit cards accepted.

MacQuarrie's Lighthouse Motel. Housekeeping and overnight units. Near shopping, golf, beaches; playground on property. Phone 436–2992. Major credit cards.

Sunny Isle Motel. Babysitting arranged. Miniature golf nearby. Open May 1 to Nov. 1. Off-season rates before June 25 and after Sept. 15. Phone 436–5665.

TIGNISH. *Inexpensive:* **Murphy's Tourist Home & Cottages.** Housekeeping and overnight units. Breakfast served on request. Spacious playground. Pets on leash. Visa accepted. Phone 882–2667.

UIGG. *Inexpensive–Moderate:* **Dunvegan Farm Motel.** Noted for the friendly hospitality of owners Dorothy and Harold MacLeod. On a working farm with cows, horses, poultry, and pets. Motel equipped for housekeeping. Rooms available in farm home. Home-cooked meals and free horseback riding for guests. Open May 15 to October 15. Phone 651–2833. No credit cards accepted.

VICTORIA. *Moderate:* **Robertson's Folly.** Two apartments with private entrances; housekeeping accommodations. No pets. Ocean beach. Open June 1 to September 30. Phone 658–2977.

WOOD ISLANDS. *Moderate:* **Meadow Lodge Motel.** Clean, comfortable accommodation. Near picnic area and ocean beach at Wood Islands Provincial Park. Open May 15 to October 10. Small leashed pets okay. Phone 962–2022. Major credit cards.

YORK. *Inexpensive:* **Vessey's Housekeeping Units.** Quiet place only 8 km. (5 miles) from Charlottetown. 3 overnight units, one housekeeping apartment. No dogs allowed. No credit cards.

HOSTELS. *Canadian Hostelling Association's* main hostel is at 151 Mt. Edward Rd., Charlottetown. Showers, kitchen facilities. $5 for members, $6 for non-members. Open June 1 to Sept. 1. Phone 894–9696.

TELEPHONES. The Island has one long-distance telephone area code throughout (902).

HOW TO GET AROUND. By bus: Double-decker London-style buses tour Charlottetown and visit the North Shore daily, with departures from Confederation Centre.

By limousine: Service is available by reservation to South Shore points of interest, with departure from Charlottetown Hotel.

By taxi: City tours are $12 per hour or 80¢ per mile.

On foot: In Charlottetown, most attractions are within walking distance of one another. A booklet entitled *Walks in Charlotte Town* is a useful guide. It's available in many bookstores or at the P.E.I. Heritage Foundation.

By car: As tour operations in Prince Edward Island are not extensive, visitors arriving by air in Charlottetown might best tour the province by rented car. Rental agencies such as *Avis, Budget, Hertz,* and *Tilden* are located at the Charlottetown Airport. Some car-rental agencies maintain small branches in Summerside. During the summer months, it is advisable to book your car rental in advance through a travel agency or the local branch of the rental agency.

How to Reach the Blue Heron Drive. *By car:* From Charlottetown (following the blue heron sign), continue in a counterclockwise direction on Rte. 19, or take 15 north to Rte. 6 at Cavendish.

How to Reach Lady Slipper Drive. *By car:* From Charlottetown, take Rte. 2 to Summerside. Rte. 2 intersects Lady Slipper Drive at the tiny village of Traveller's Rest. Follow the red signs showing the silhouette of a lady slipper plant.

By ferry: The ferry service from Cape Tormentine, New Brunswick, docks at Borden, P.E.I., about 27 kms. (17 miles) from Lady Slipper Drive. From the ferry, turn west onto Rte. 10 to join the drive at Reads Corner. For ferry information, contact CN Marine, Borden, P.E.I. The service from Cape Tormentine takes 45 minutes. During July and Aug., there are hourly crossings from 6:30 A.M. to 8:30 P.M. then every 1½ hours to 1 A.M. with additional crossings as necessary during the day. Reduced crossings the remainder of the year. Reservations are not required. Tickets may be purchased at drive-through kiosks entering the ferry terminal area.

By bus: *Island Transit Co-Operative Ltd.* operates a bus service from Charlottetown to Tignish, a distance of 141 kms. (88 miles), daily except Sunday.

How to Reach Kings Byway Drive. *By car:* From Charlottetown, take Rte. 1 [the Trans-Canada Hwy.] east across Hillsborough Bridge and follow the purple crown Kings Byway signs. From Cavendish and the National Park area, take Rte. 6 east and go around Kings Byway drive in a clockwise direction. The ferry from Caribou, Nova Scotia, to Wood Islands, Prince Edward Island, lands visitors about 1½ kms. (1 mile) from Kings Byway. Turn east or west at Wood Islands. For ferry information, contact Northumberland Ferries Limited, 54 Queen St., Charlottetown, P.E.I., C1A 7L3. During the summer season—June to September—the ferry crossings run from 6 A.M. to 9:55 P.M., with reduced hours until service terminates in December. Reservations are not required.

FACTS AND FIGURES: Prince Edward Island is by far the smallest of all the Canadian provinces, covering only 2,184 square miles. The capital of P.E.I. is Charlottetown. The province has a population of about 123,000.

TOURIST INFORMATION SERVICES. The Charlottetown Visitor Information Centre is located at the Royalty Mall on University Avenue. Call 900–892–2457 long distance, or just 892–2457 locally. Or write to Visitor Services Division, P.O. Box 940, Charlottetown, P.E.I. C1A 7M5. The Visitor Information Centre at the Borden ferry terminal is open from May to Oct. Lady Slipper Visitor Information Centre at Summerside operates from June to September and the Alberton Centre from June to mid-Sept. There are also Visitor Information Centres at Brackley, Aulac, Cavendish, Kensington, Souris, Stanhope, and the Wood Islands Ferry Terminal (open May to Oct.). The Kings Byway Visitor Information Centre is open from June to October at Pooles Corner, almost 5 kms. (3 miles) north of Montague.

Dial-the-Island reservations and information system: This arrangement makes it easy for you to call ahead to plan your trip, secure any information you may need and to make reservations. Just call the central reservations office while en route to the Island. From New Brunswick or Nova Scotia, dial toll-free 1–800–565–7421. Once on the Island, a network of two-way radios at Visitor Information Centres gives you valuable assistance with reservations and other travel needs day by day.

RECOMMENDED READING. Prince Edward Island is the home of Atlantic Canada's most famous and successful author, the late Lucy Maud Montgomery, whose *Anne of Green Gables* and its successors are worldwide favorite books for girls. Montgomery's life and work are the basis of a small sub-branch of the tourist industry in P.E.I.

Réshard Gool, who teaches at the Island's university, is a poet, novelist *(Price)* and essayist *(Portraits and Gastroscopes,* with Frank Ledwell) and publisher. His Square Deal Press publishes many Island poets and playwrights; it has also published Christopher Gledhill's *Folklore of PEI* and the reminiscences of a folksy former premier, Walter Shaw's *Tell Me the Tales.* A recent comic novel is Jeffrey Holmes' *The Highjacking of the PEI Ferry.* A worthwhile memento of an Island visit is *Prince Edward Island Photographs,* by Wayne Barrett and Edith Robinson.

TIME ZONE. Prince Edward Island is on Atlantic Time (one hour ahead of Eastern Time).

FESTIVALS AND EVENTS. Alberton. The *Prince County Exhibition* takes place in late August.

Cardigan: the *King's County Craft Fair* is held in early July.

Charlottetown: The *Charlottetown Summer Festival,* one of Canada's summer highlights, takes place each year from June to September, presenting a series of plays in the Confederation Centre of the Arts. Two full-scale musicals play in repertory six nights a week, Monday to Saturday along with that perennial musical favorite, *Anne of Green Gables,* are among the performances. Special exhibitions of art are presented in the Art Gallery. For information on the summer season, write to: Confederation Centre for the Arts, P.O. Box 848, Charlottetown, Prince Edward Island, C1A 7L9.

May to October is harness racing season. Details available from local tourist bureaus.

Natal Day, a three-day festival, takes place in mid-June.

In July and August, at noon hours, there is *The Lunchtime Theatre* in the David McKenzie Building, with lunch available.

Country Days and Old Home Week is held in early August.

Eldon: *Highland Games and Gathering of the Clans* take place in early August.

Montague: The *Garden of the Gulf Fiddle Festival* is held in early July at the Iceland Arena.

O'Leary: The *Prince Edward Island Potato Blossom Festival* takes place in late July.

Orwell: Orwell Corner hosts the *Strawberry Fair* in early July.

Oyster Bed Bridge: Drag racing is popular on weekends. Admission is adults $6, children 8–14 $3.

Summerside: The *Cape Egmont Yacht Race* is held in June.

In late July the *Lobster Carnival and Livestock Exhibition* takes place.

Tyne Valley: The *Oyster Festival* occurs in early August.

Exact dates of festivals and events change yearly. Check dates and details in *1985 Events,* a free brochure available on request from P.E.I. tourist information centers.

TOURS. *Abegweit Sightseeing Tours* offer a *Charlottetown Tour* of the old and new capital city on a double-decker London-style bus; 6 one-hour tours daily, including Sunday; adults, $3.75, children under 12, $1.00. They also offer a *South Shore Tour* by limousine (reservations required) and a daily *North Shore Tour* by bus leaving the Charlottetown Hotel at 10:30 A.M. and returning in late afternoon. Adults, $15; children under 12, $7.50. Price includes all admissions.

PROVINCIAL PARKS. Along the Kings Byway, a small herd of North American bison is the feature attraction at the 100 acre *Buffaloland Provincial Park* on Rte 4, 6 kms. (4 miles) south of Montague. There is also a small picnic area.

Fantasyland Provincial Park on Rte. 348, near Murray River, has a nice picnic area, swimming, clam-digging, and boating facilities. For the children, there are giant replicas of fairytale characters and a playground.

The *Lord Selkirk Provincial Park,* on Rte. 1, east of Eldon, has a campground, picnic area, swimming, posted hiking trails, and clam-digging flats.

An excellent beach with supervised swimming is available, at the *Panmure Island Provincial Park* on Rte. 347, off Rte. 17 on the south side of Cardigan Bay. This recreation park also has campsites, picnic area, clam-digging flats, and a laundromat. Good for small-boating.

Sir Andrew MacPhail Provincial Park at Orwell is a day-use park on Rte. 1, 32 kms. (20 miles) from Charlottetown. The 143 acres of natural woodland has nature trails, fishing in the pond, a picnic area.

Near the Wood Islands Ferry Terminal is the *Wood Islands Provincial Park.* A day-use park, it overlooks the ocean and has a picnic area and a children's playground.

The *Marie Provincial Park* is another day-use park on the bank of the Marie River 3 kms. (2 miles) east of Morell on Rte. 2. Picnic and small recreational areas along the green riverbank.

Red Point Provincial Park and *Campbell's Cove Provincial Park*, both on Rte. 16, offer tenting sites and swimming for visitors to King County. Supervised beach.

The *Northumberland Provincial Park* is a complete camping and day-use park with supervised swimming and bathing houses with showers on the sheltered salt water beach. There are picnic areas, a children's playground, a laundromat, recreation hall, and clam-digging flats. On Rte. 4, 3 kms. (2 miles) east of Wood Islands Ferry Terminal.

In the Island's rugged North Cape along Lady Slipper Drive, the *Anglo Provincial Park*, a day-use park, has a good beach and playground for children. Rte. 12, just north of Tignish.

Another day-use park with a playground is *Bloomfield Provincial Park* on Rte. 2 near St. Anthony. Picnic area, washroom, and shower facilities.

A great picnic site with a view is *Campbellton Provincial Park* on the high cliffs overlooking Northumberland Strait, 2½ kms. (1½ miles) south of the junction of Rtes. 14 and 145 at the village of Campbellton.

Cedar Dunes Provincial Park, 18 kms. (11 miles) south of O'Leary on Rte. 14 at West Point, has a long sandy beach, playground, evergreen groves, tenting and trailer sites.

Jacques Cartier Provincial Park honors the French explorer who landed here in 1534. On Rte. 12, 8 kms. (5 miles) north of Alberton. Facilities include campground and beach, with a clam-digging and trout fishing area nearby.

Green Park Provincial Park in Port Hill near Tyne Valley has a interpretive center and a shipbuilding museum. Also a campground with shower and washroom facilities.

Cabot Provincial Park on Rte. 20 has a sandy beach, campground, 24-hour supervision and laundromat on the premises.

Along Blue Heron Drive, *Victoria Provincial Park* on Victoria Harbour, Rte. 10, has a good picnic area. There is swimming here and also at *Argyle Shore Provincial Park*.

Bonshaw Provincial Park on Rte. 1 offers a 32-km. (20-mile) hiking trail. Beginning at West River Bridge near St. Catherine, it goes on to Victoria, winding through large woodlots, fields, and country roads. Never far from roadways, the trail may be hiked in sections. *Strathgartney Provincial Park*, nearby, offers picnic and tenting facilities, as well as a 9-hole golf course.

The *Devil's Punch Bowl Provincial Park* near Granville, on Rte. 254, is a day-use park with a short hiking trail which leads to the spring from which the park got its name.

Scales Pond Provincial Park, Rte. 109, is the site of the Island's largest hydroelectric operation which began in 1798 and closed in 1963.

The Prince Edward Island Visitor Information Centres supply information, locations, opening and closing dates for other smaller day-use and camping provincial parks with picnic, beach, swimming, and other attractions.

 GARDENS. Good red earth has made the entire province a garden spot during summer months. *Jewell's Gardens and Pioneer Village* at **York,** off Kings Byway on Rte. 25, specialize in begonias and fuchsias. An antique glass museum, an old country store, and a children's playground are nearby. Open June 14 to October 11, Monday–Saturday, 9 A.M. to 5 P.M. Open until dusk during July and August. Admission: adults $3.50, children under 12 $1.50. pre-schoolers free.

Malpeque Gardens on Rte. 20 features brilliant varieties of dahlias and dozens of floral arrangements. An old-fashioned windmill irrigates the gardens. Open June 25 to August 31, daily 9 A.M. to dusk. 9 A.M.–5 P.M. during September. Admission: adults $2; children under 14, $1; preschoolers free.

FARM VACATIONS AND FARM TOURIST HOMES.

For visitors seeking less commercial accommodations, farm vacation and tourist homes offer both an economical way to spend a holiday and an opportunity to meet the people of an area and live among them for a time. Farm tourist and vacation homes take guests on a daily or weekly basis. Some of the homes are on working farms; others are in rural areas. Guests stay in spare rooms, share meals, activities, and even chores with the host family.

Daily rates, ranging from about $15 to $20 per day for two people, may include home-cooked country meals and a snack before bed. Most farm homes have special rates for children.

In general, farm pets do not welcome visiting pets. Check before you come. Bring old clothes and shoes or boots for everyone, especially the children. Farm families usually go to bed early and rise early. Pay for your farm holiday in advance—it's easier to do business before you've become friends.

The P.E.I. Visitors Information Centres have complete listings of farm vacation and tourist homes with rates. Make reservations well in advance directly with the farm family hosts, especially for an extended stay.

RESORTS. *Very Expensive:* **Dalvay-by-the-Sea** at Grand Tracadie north of Charlottetown by the P.E.I. National Park. 25 rooms in manor surrounded by rolling green lawns, 2 cottages. American plan with American and French cuisine in dining room. Babysitting arranged. Two tennis courts, bowling greens, ping pong, driving range, canoeing and trout fishing on premises. Ocean beach 200 yards. Open mid-June to mid-September. Phone 672–2048. Major credit cards.

Expensive: **Brudenell Resort** at Roseneath on the east end of the Island. Probably the best known resort in P.E.I. and an excellent family holiday location. All chalets, most with housekeeping facilities. The complex has been developed on spacious grounds overlooking the Brudenell River. Supervised heated outdoor pool, trail riding, lawn bowling, river beach, 18-hole championship golf course, volley ball and tennis courts, shuffleboard and giant checkers. Supervised children's playground. Gift shop. Deep-sea fishing charters arranged for guests. Open June 1 to the second Monday of October (Canadian Thanksgiving). Phone 652–2332. Major credit cards.

CHILDREN'S ACTIVITIES.

Beaches, playgrounds, and parks throughout the province offer excellent activities and facilities for children. Other points of interest include:

Burlington near Kensington: *Woodleigh Replicas,* displays scale models of famous castles and cathedrals, including the Tower of London. Some are large enough to enter and walk around in.

Bonshaw: *Bonshaw 500* has karting for all members of the family. Children drive their own karts. Picnic tables; playground.

Cavendish: *The Royal Atlantic Wax Museum* has life size wax figures of famous people from Josephine Tussaud.

Green Gables House is the famous farm home in Lucy Maude Montgomery's *Anne of Green Gables.*

Rainbow Valley as described in L.M. Montgomery's *Rainbow Valley,* has a Children's Farm, a playground, Fantasy Area, Flying Saucer, and boating lakes.

DeSable: *House of Dolls* exhibits miniature dolls of famous people from many nations. Also, children's corner.

Harrington: *Pinehills Playground* has large play area with long slide, maze, haunted cave, swings, Indian area, and prehistoric animals.

North Rustico: *The Wildlife Park,* complete with picnic area, has fine collection of native animals and wild birds.

Rocky Point: *Micmac Indian Village* has Indian Trail and authentic Indian Village.

Stanley Bridge: *Marineland Aquarium and Manor of Birds* has fine collection of mounted birds; fish tanks; seal pool, butterflies.

Also check under *Festivals and Events, Provincial Parks,* and *Camping* in this section.

SPORTS. P.E.I. is sports-oriented. On an island of **golf** courses, one of the best known in Atlantic Canada is the championship Brudenell Golf Course, located in the resort complex at *Roseneath.* The Belvedere course in *Charlottetown,* the Mill River championship course on Lady Slipper Drive, and the Summerside Golf Club Course (all are 18-hole courses) are also among the best.

The Green Gables Course, part of the National Park, surrounds the home of the storybook character Anne of Green Gables, in the *Cavendish* area.

The *Rustico* Golf Course is flanked by trees and waterholes overlooking Rustico Bay. An 18 holer, it is near recreational activities of all kinds.

The *Stanhope* Golf and Country Club is situated near Prince Edward Island National Park.

A 9-hole course, the Glen Afton, is located on the south coast near the historic *Fort Amherst* site. Another 9-hole course, Forest Hills Golf Course, is located on Rte. 6 in *Cavendish.*

The *Strathgartney* links offer a par three, nine-hole course.

Bicycling. Its small size and veinwork of quiet country roads make P.E.I. a natural attraction for the cyclist. Bicycles can be rented at MacQueen's Bike Shop, 430 Queen St., *Charlottetown* (892-9843) or at Summerside Advance Rental, 133 Water St., *Summerside* (436-3867); cost: about $12 daily, $30 weekly at both places.

Canoeing is also growing in popularity in the province's many meandering tidal estuaries—a delight of rolling sandbars and quiet havens. Visitor information bureaus can tell you where to rent canoes.

Hiking and cross-country skiing are a pleasure on the low rolling terrain of Prince Edward Island. There are hiking trails and numerous nature walks.

Devil's Punch Bowl Trail—one mile long, located between the Rattenbury Rd., Rte. 254, and South Granville—down an old horse and carriage road through hardwood forests. Easy enough for children.

Bonshaw Hills Trail—20 miles long, from West River Bridge (near St. Catherines) to Victoria, not far from Borden.

P.E.I.'s national park has several trails. And in winter there are four loop-style cross-country ski trails.

Information on hiking and cross-country ski trails is available from the P.E.I. Department of Tourism.

Fishing. The Island has some of the best salt- and freshwater fishing in eastern Canada. *Freshwater fishing* for brook trout and white perch is usually no more than a few minutes' walk across a field. The trout season runs from mid-April to September 30, with a limit of 20 trout a day. Non-resident fishing licenses cost $10, obtainable from the Fish and Wildlife Division in Charlottetown or any other license vendor; guides are not required. All the inland fisheries are fine places to catch brook trout. For rainbow trout, fish the Dunk, Cardigan, and Sturgeon Rivers and two inland lakes—Glenfinnan and O'Keefe.

Saltwater or deep-sea fishing can be a family outing. Most trips last 4 hours and most fishing ports have boats available for charter. Cost is $8 for adults and $4 for children. The boat captain supplies all tackle and bait. Boats listed by the Visitor Information Centres have passed rigorous safety standards set by the federal government. Reservations can be made in advance by phone. A boat list is available at the nearest Visitors Information Centre or at a wharf displaying the deep-sea fishing sign.

Tuna fishing is serious sport in P.E.I. The North Lake area on the Kings Byway is still the giant bluefin capital of the island. On the Blue Heron Drive, North Rustico, and Malpeque Harbour are tuna fishing ports. On King's Byway there are two other tuna ports: Morell Harbour and Savage Harbour. Tuna charters are roughly $200 (max. 6 persons). Further information on tuna charters and other deep-sea fishing arrangements is available from any P.E.I. Visitors Information Centre. Or write Tourism Services Division, P.O. Box 940, Charlottetown, P.E.I., C1A 7M5. The Fish and Wildlife Division, P.O. Box 2000, Charlottetown, P.E.I., Canada C1A 7N8 will also have any additional information you need.

Along with golf and fishing, another top sport is **harness racing.** Many residents race their own horses at the small racetracks throughout the province. Two major tracks—at Charlottetown and Summerside—feature competitions from all over Canada and the U.S.

Other popular sports are tennis, swimming, boating, and horseback riding, available at a good number of resorts, campgrounds, and at the national park.

 CAMPING. For a small island, P.E.I. has a good number of private and provincially operated campgrounds for tenting, trailering, and camping. Check open dates for each campground. Unless stated otherwise, reservations may be made directly with the camping area.

Along the Kings Byway, at Roseneath, near Brudenell Resort, is the *Brudenell River Provincial Park*, on Rte. 3 between Pooles Corner and Georgetown. The 90-acre park has 94 unserviced sites and 12 two-way hookups. Campers can use the 18-hole Brudenell golf course and the fresh water beach on the Brudenell River. Open mid-May to mid-October. Reservations not accepted.

For campers who prefer saltwater beaches, *Johnston's Centennial Campground* at Murray Harbour North has a saltwater beach on the premises and another ocean beach just a short distance away. Located 16 kms. (10 miles) from Murray River via Rtes. 4 and 17, the 25-acre campground has 17 unserviced sites, 25 two-way hookups, and 60 three-way hookups. Open June 1 to Oct. 15.

For the camper with an interest in history, the *Lord Selkirk Provincial Park* commemorates the Scottish settlers who broke the land here in 1803. Located 1½ kms. (1 mile) east of Eldon, just off the Trans-Canada Hwy., the 50-acre camping portion of the park has 52 unserviced sites and 20 two-way hookups. Among other amenities is the nearby reconstructed Lord Selkirk Settlement, saltwater beach, picnic sites, marked hiking trails, and clam-digging flats within the park. Open from the beginning of June to September 6. Reservations not accepted.

MacInnis Cove Tent and Trailer Park is on Rte. 16, 24 kms. (15 miles) east of Souris at Lakeville. This 8-acre campground has 20 unserviced sites and 20 two-way hookups. Ocean beach on the premises. Open June 1 to late August.

Jacques Cartier Provincial Park has 24 unserviced sites and 12 two-way hookups on 22 acres. Located 6 kms. (4 miles) from Alberton off Rte. 2 at Kildare Capes. Ocean beach on premises. Reservations not accepted. Open June to Labor Day.

One of the best ocean beaches is at *Cedar Dunes Provincial Park,* 24 kms. (15 miles) from O'Leary. The 100-acre park has 36 unserviced sites and 10 two-way hookups. Reservations not accepted.

Green Provincial Park, which includes a wooden shipbuilding museum and restoration, is 32 kms. (20 miles) west of Summerside, on Rte. 12. There are 66 unserviced sites and 24 three-way hookups with an ocean beach on the premises. Reservations not accepted. June to Labor Day.

About 6½ kms. (4 miles) west of Summerside on Rte. 11, *Linkletter Provincial Park* has 52 unserviced sites and 32 two-way hookups. Saltwater beach on the premises. Reservations not accepted. Open mid-May to mid-September.

Along Blue Heron Drive, beach camping is excellent in the campsites of Cavendish, Brackley, and Stanhope, all part of the National Park. The privately owned Cavendish Sunset Campground has a swimming pool, tennis courts, ocean beach, and a miniature golf course. Reservations accepted.

At *Blythwood Trailer Park,* Cavendish, pets permitted on leash, mini-bikes not permitted; ocean beach, and 18-hole golf course.

At *Rustico Island Campground,* a section of the national park, 5 kms. (3 miles) west of Rte. 15 on Gulf Shore Rd., you'll find 113 developed acres and 148 unserviced sites. There's an interpretative program, outdoor theater, ocean beach, and 18-hole golf course. Reservations not accepted.

The *Prince Edward Island National Park* runs 25 miles along the coastline and beaches of the North Shore. Excellent beaches, campgrounds, and sporting facilities.

Another section of the national park at Stanhope on Gulf Shore Rd. has 5 developed acres with 103 unserviced sites and 14 three-way hookups. An interpretive program, ocean beach, and 18-hole golf course are available. Washing machines on site. Reservations not accepted.

Camping fees range from $5.50 to $8.50 daily, depending on the type of site. Private trailer park daily rates are $4 and up depending on services and location.

Note: Camping on Prince Edward Island is restricted to organized camping grounds. It is against the law to camp on a beach or on property not designated as a camping area.

The P.E.I. Visitors Information Centres have listings of campgrounds with rates at their bureaus.

MUSEUMS AND HISTORIC SITES. P.E.I. Tourism's brochure *Visitor's Guide* describes and illustrates museums and historic sites by County, and is available by request, at no charge from the provincial tourism department. Some highlights—In **Charlottetown,** historically important *Province House* now houses the province's legislature; *Beaconsfield* is headquarters for the Prince Edward Island Museum and Heritage Foundation; and *Old Charlottetown* houses a wide variety of old shops, museums, stores, craft centers, restaurants, churches, and homes.

The Kings Byway Dr. will take you through many attractions that recall the early days of the Island and the early settlers' pioneering spirit. (See *Kings Byway Drive* section earlier in this chapter for additional Museums and Historic Sites.)

The agricultural heritage of rural P.E.I. is re-captured at Orwell Corner, near **Orwell.** Open June 26 to September 6 daily, 10 A.M. to 6 P.M. Admission: adults $1; children under 12, free.

The Lord Selkirk Settlement at **Eldon** features reproductions of settlers' shelters and cabins. Open 9 A.M. to 7 P.M., July and August; 9 A.M. to 4 P.M., June 19 to September 11. Admission $2.25 per adult, children under 16, $1.00. The *Polly Gift Shop* is on the premises.

The Log Cabin Museum at **Murray Harbour** depicts the Island's 19th-century lifestyle. Open July 1 to Labor Day, 9 A.M. to 7 P.M. daily. Admission: adults, 75¢, children 25¢, under 6 free.

An interesting collection of old firearms is one of the features at the *Garden of the Gulf Museum* in **Montague.** Open June 27 to September 16, 9:30 A.M. to 5 P.M., Monday–Saturday, 1 to 5 P.M., Sundays. Admission: adults, about $1.00; children under 12, 50¢. Displays and photographs in the *Fisheries Museum at Basin Head* show how small boats were used by early fishermen.

Antique car buffs might visit the *Spoke Wheel Car Museum* at **Dunstaffnage.** Open June 1 to September 30, 9 A.M. to 8 P.M., during July and August; 10 A.M. to 6 P.M., the remainder of the season. Admission: adults $2.50; children 1 to 6, $1.00; pre-schoolers, free.

Along Lady Slipper Drive, *Green Park Provincial Park* at **Port Hill** commemorates a 19th-century shipping complex. Admission: adults $1.00, children under 12 free. Open daily 10 A.M. to 6 P.M. June 25 to September 6. Check for hours after September 6. A campground is also part of the park.

At **Northport,** *Sea Rescue Park* has picnic tables, washrooms, water tap, and a children's playground. Sea Rescue Park is open from June 1 to October 31, from 9 A.M. to 10 P.M. daily. Free.

The *Acadian Museum* at **Miscouche** has an impressive collection of 17th- and 18th-century household, farm, and other domestic implements portraying the Acadian lifestyle over the years. Open from June 24 to September 6, Sundays 1:00–5:30 P.M. and rest of week, 10 A.M.–6 P.M. Adults $1.50; children 75¢; under 12, free.

(See *Lady Slipper Drive* section earlier in this chapter for additional information.)

Blue Heron Drive passes the historic *"Farmers' Bank"* (chartered in 1864) at **South Rustico.**

At **Long River,** Rte. 234 off Rt. 20, the *Old Mill Museum* contains antiques and a collection of bottles. Adults $1.50, children 75¢. Hours: 10 A.M.–5:30 P.M.

The **French River District** has two pioneer era cemeteries, *Yankee Hill* and *Sims.*

At **Bonshaw** just beyond DeSable is an interesting *Car Life Museum.* Open May 24 to October 1; July and August, 9 A.M. to 9 P.M. daily, May, June and Sept. 10 A.M. to 6 P.M. Admission: adults, $2.50, children 6–14, $1.25, pre-schoolers, free.

At **Rocky Point** across the harbor from Charlottetown, the earthworks of the historic *Fort Amherst* (formerly Port La Joie, 1720) are a reminder of 18th-century occupation.

One mile east on Rte. 19, a *Micmac Village* has been re-created . . . birchbark canoes, wigwams, and an Indian craftshop.

ART GALLERIES. *The Confederation Centre Art Gallery and Museum* at the Confederation Centre in Charlottetown, is one of Canada's premier art museums. It is dedicated to the work of Canadian artists and hosts major exhibits from Canada, the U.S. and overseas. Its permanent collection includes the country's largest collection of paintings by Robert Harris (1849–1919), Canada's foremost portrait artist. Admission is $1, family $2. Open 10 A.M. to 8 P.M. July and August; 10 A.M. to 5 P.M. (and closed Mondays), September to June.

The Great George Street Gallery at 88 Great George St., Charlottetown, is a nonprofit gallery run by artists and supported by the national and provincial governments. It provides a program of exhibitions by local and regional artists, plus some special events. Admission free.

THEATER. During July and August, the **Charlottetown** Festival at the Confederation Centre for the Arts includes that P.E.I. perennial, *Anne of Green Gables,* plus a number of other, usually musical, productions. Feature plays are staged six nights a week in the 1,100-seat *Main Stage Theatre.* International concert artists are featured Sunday evenings on Main Stage. The adjacent *Cameo Theatre* cabaret productions of Canadian musicals six nights a week.

The King's Playhouse at **Georgetown** on Rte. 3, 30 miles (50 km.) east of Charlottetown, provides professional summer theater. Three plays in repertory plus variety concerts. Open daily, July 5–August 28.

The Governor's Feast at *The Barn* restaurant on Rte. 1 near **Charlottetown** is light dinner theater featuring the governor of 1842 and retinue. Similarly, there's *The Prohibition Feast,* bouncing 1930's stuff, at *The Brothers Two* restaurant on Rte. 1A near **Summerside.**

SHOPPING. Since colonial times, handcrafted items have been valued by P.E.I. inhabitants and craftspeople excel at jewelry making, wood carving, pottery, enameling, leather work, quilting, and weaving—just a few of the crafts executed with great skill. The P.E.I. Craftsmen's Council, Inc., P.O. Box 1573, Charlottetown, P.E.I. C1A 7N3 (tel. 892–5152), or the P.E.I. Visitors Information Centre can supply full information on outlets and types of crafts available.

Along Lady Slipper Drive, look for turned Bird's-eye maple wood products at the Leavitts' Maple Tree Craft Shop in **Alberton.** Open year-round, 8 A.M. to 5 P.M., Monday–Saturday.

Lennox Island Indian Arts and Crafts on **Lennox Island,** Rte. 163, has MicMac beadwork, moccasins, masks, turtle rattles and other crafts.

One major stop is the Acadian Pioneer Village at **Mont Carmel,** a restored early 19th-century community. Also visit the restaurant on the site and try an Acadian soup or potato dish. The restaurant is open from 10 A.M. to 11 P.M. daily. Prices are reasonable. The museum village is open from mid-June to mid-Sept., 10 A.M. to 7 P.M. daily.

For good pottery, visit the Flat River Crafts Studio on Kings Byway Drive. Open year-round, daily, 9 A.M. to 9 P.M.

One of the largest and most complete handcraft shops in P.E.I. is the Wood Islands Handcraft Co-Op on Main St. in **Murray River.** All the Island crafts are represented in this retail outlet on Kings Byway, which is open from June to Sept.

In **Charlottetown,** there's the Island Craft Shop located at 146 Richmond St. This shop contains a wide selection of island crafts. Open year-round from Monday to Saturday, 9 A.M. to 5 P.M. In July and August it's Monday to Saturday, 9 A.M. to 8 P.M.

Shopping malls are open 10 A.M. to 10 P.M., Monday to Saturday. Other stores throughout the province generally open at 9 A.M. and close at 5 or 5:30 P.M. On Friday evenings, most stores stay open until 9 P.M. Country stores generally open earlier and close later.

Holiday closings: Good Friday, Easter Monday, Victoria Day (in mid-May), July 1 (Canada Day), Labor Day (September 3), Thanksgiving (October 8), and Remembrance Day (November 11).

DRINKING LAWS. The legal drinking age is 18. Liquor stores are open six days a week for about 12 hours a day.

DINING OUT. The Island offers plenty of plain, wholesome, home-cooked food with friendly (often slow) service in an informal setting. In Charlottetown, however, good formal dining can be had in at least half a dozen restaurants.

Restaurants are categorized on the basis of full course dinners; drinks, tax, and tip are excluded. *Expensive,* over $15; *Moderate,* $10–$15; *Inexpensive,* under $10. A 10% provincial tax will be added to all meals over $2.00.

Most places accept the following major credit cards: American Express, MasterCard and Visa; others may also be honored. Not all establishments accept credit cards, therefore we suggest you call for information.

CAVENDISH. *Moderate:* **Chez Yvonne.** Good food, all home cooking; has its own garden, fresh vegetables. Phone 963–2070.

Fiddles & Vittles. Fresh shellfish, chowder, and steak. Open 4–9 P.M.; licensed. Phone 963–2225.

Marco Polo Inn. Well-known; good food. Phone 963–2351. Major credit cards.

Inexpensive–Moderate: **Cavendish Arms.** Steak and seafood, licensed; Irish and modern music; dancing. Phone 963–2732.

CHARLOTTETOWN. *Expensive:* **The Confederation Dining Room,** Charlottetown Hotel. Elegant surroundings, pleasant food. Phone 894-7371. Major credit cards.

Griffin Dining Room in the Dundee Arms Inn. Situated in a Victorian home. Checked tablecloths, fireplace, good food. Licensed. Swiss-French cuisine. House specializes in fondue Bourguignonne and has a special knack with locally caught fish. One of the best. Phone 892-2496. Major credit cards.

Minnie's. Seafood specialties—scampi, sole, excellent scallops wrapped in bacon, lobster. Homemade cheesecake and strawberry crêpes. True gourmet dining. Many people call Minnie's the best restaurant on the island. Call for reservations. Phone 894–7232. Major credit cards.

Moderate–Expensive: **Hidden Harbour.** A cozy place on the harborfront specializing in steaks and seafood. Phone 892–4733. Major credit cards.

The Smugglers Gallery at the Confederation Inn. Good but not ritzy. Phone 892–2481. Major credit cards.

Moderate: **Caesar's Italy.** Italian foods plus local steaks and seafoods. A casual place with a salad and soup bar. Phone 892–9201. Major credit cards.

The Dispensary. Early Canadian atmosphere. Located in historic building. Fondues a specialty. Has a good reputation. Phone 892–5195. Major credit cards.

MacLauchlan's Motel. Scottish atmosphere. Home-style cooking. It has gained popularity in recent years for its accent on traditional island dishes. Phone 892–2461. Major credit cards.

The Rodd Royalty Inn. An uncomplicated but fairly attractive menu of steaks and seafoods. Phone 894–8566. Major credit cards.

The Showboat Dining Room. Home-style cooking. Accent on seafood. Live entertainment, large dance floor. Phone 892–7998.

Inexpensive: **Casa Mia.** Situated in old home. Quiet. Italian and Canadian food. Phone 892–8888. Major credit cards.

CORNWALL. *Moderate:* **Bonnie Brae.** Good family restaurant. Phone 675–2241.

GRAND TRACADIE. *Expensive:* **Dalvay-By-The-Sea Hotel.** Located 3½ miles off Rte. 25 (near Stanhope). One of the Island's most elite eating places. Built as a summer home for a wealthy American who later sold it to his coachman (in lieu of 7 years' wages, according to locals), it has a large staircase and elegant interior. Excellent seafood. Reservations preferred but not always necessary. Phone 672–2048. Major credit cards.

KENSINGTON. *Moderate:* **Recreation Center.** Homemade food; not elegant but good.

KINGSBORO. *Moderate:* **Seabreeze Motel.** Good dining room, licensed; features home cooking with seafood specialties. Open year-round. Phone 357–2371.

MONTAGUE. *Moderate–Expensive:* **Lobster Shanty North.** One of the best places to eat on the Kings Byway. Dining room has rustic décor that extends into the lounge bar overlooking the Montague River. Licensed, and features seafood, particularly lobster. Open year-round. Phone 838–2463.

MONT CARMEL. *Moderate:* **Étoile de Mer** in the Acadian Pioneer Village. Specializes in Acadian dishes—rapure and meat pies. Try Acadian soup or a potato dish. Open mid-June to mid-September, 10 A.M. to 11 P.M. daily.

MORELL. *Moderate:* **Village Diner.** Only restaurant between Charlottetown and Souris on Rte. 2. Features home-cooked meals and specials every day. Overlook the rough atmosphere and enjoy the food. Licensed with adjacent lounge bar. Open year-round.

POOLES CORNER. *Moderate:* **Kingsway Motel.** Licensed dining room, good food and a cozy lounge. Open year-round. During off-season—dancing. Phone 838–2112. Major credit cards.

ROSENEATH. *Expensive:* **Brudenell Resort Restaurant.** Usually good service and good food in the resort complex. Licensed. Two lounge bars adjacent. Open June 1 to September 30. Phone 652–2332. Major credit cards.

RUSTICO. *Moderate–Expensive:* **Fisherman's Wharf Restaurant.** Open mid-May to October. 7 A.M.–10 P.M. daily. Seafood and special mussel chowder. Phone 963–2669.

SOURIS. *Moderate:* **Bluefin Restaurant.** Plain food in unpretentious surroundings. Licensed with adjacent lounge bar featuring entertainment. Open year-round. Phone 687–3271.

SOUTHPORT. *Moderate–Expensive:* **The Barn.** Features beef and seafood. Rustic atmosphere. Phone 569–2228.

SUMMERSIDE. *Moderate–Expensive:* **Brothers Two.** Steaks and seafood, scallops a specialty. Open and airy atmosphere, pleasant service. Licensed. Dancing. Also "Prohibition feast," specializing in Island seafood served by a cast of talented performers who dine, dance and perform during feast. 6 P.M. to 9 P.M., Monday to Saturday. Phone 436-9654.

Moderate: **Linkletter Motel.** Licensed; specialty is good buffet at noon weekdays & on Friday evenings. Phone 436–2157. Major credit cards.

Papa David's. Seafood, mostly in a cozy waterfront setting. Phone 436–4606. Major credit cards.

LOBSTER SUPPERS: You must sample the lobster suppers; usually served in church halls or community centers, they are an Island tradition.

Brackley Beach Lobster Suppers, open June 21–September 6, daily, noon–9 P.M., phone 672–2352 or 672–2718, on Rte. 15 in Brackley Beach at Howe's Hall, manager, Gordon MacCallum.

New Glasgow Lobster Suppers, open June 4–Oct. 23, daily 4 P.M.–8:30 P.M., phone 964–2870, New Glasgow on Rte. 224, manager, Ralph Dickieson.

New London Lion's Club Lobster Suppers, open June 5–Oct. 3, daily 4 P.M.–8:30 P.M., phone 886–2599, New London on Rte. 6, manager, Nelson Roberts.

St. Ann's Church Suppers (licensed), open June 20–September 10, daily 4 P.M.–9 P.M., phone 964–2351 or 964–2385, Hope River on Rte. 224, manager, Rev. E. Van De Ven.

Stanhope Beach Lodge, Lobster plus smorgasbord. Also rolls, salads . . . all you can eat for about $17. June 30 to September 5.

Fisherman's Wharf Lobster Suppers, North Rustico, 963–2669.

NIGHTCLUBS, BARS, LOUNGES. A lounge in P.E.I. is a fully licensed bar which usually has some live entertainment part or all of the week. Some lounges also have a limited food menu during certain hours of the day. All are closed on Sundays.

Charlottetown: *The Tudor Lounge,* Charlottetown Hotel, is quiet, popular on Friday evenings. *The Smuggler's Jug,* Confederation Inn. Rustic beams, quiet background music. *Page One,* Rodd Inn. Cozy, dim and attractive, small lounge. *The Gallows Lounge,* small, built on Gallows Hill with rather macabre gallows décor; daily happy hours. *Prince Edward Lounge* and *WR's Place.* Often feature local entertainers who have now achieved national recognition—Anne Murray, Stompin' Tom Connors, John Allen Cameron, Ryan's Fancy. *Showboat Dining Lounge.* Nightclub-like atmosphere, big dance floor, entertainment, popular and rock music. *The Tackroom.* Small bar, great drinks. *Mrs. K's,* Kirkwood Motor Hotel. 1920's decor, lively crowd. *Sea Shell Lounge* (large and plush) and *Crossed Keys Bar* (small and intimate), both in Prince Edward Hilton hotel.

Summerside: *Regent Lounge.* Disco to 2 A.M. weekends, 1 A.M. weeknights. *Scrooge's Lounge* above Clovie's Restaurant, closes at 1 A.M. *Papa David's Lobster Trap Lounge,* disco to 2 A.M. weekends, 1 A.M. weekdays. *Friday's Lounge* and *Capt. Grady's Pub* are both in Brothers Two restaurant.

NOVA SCOTIA

Old Legends—New Attractions

By
ALAN FREEMAN and RALPH SURETTE

Alan Freeman is a travel writer based in Nova Scotia and New Brunswick.

Nova Scotia! The name itself—Latin for "New Scotland"—evokes the magic rhythms of the sea. Sometimes serene, sometimes violent, the sea encircles all but the narrow isthmus which attaches the province to New Brunswick and the Canadian mainland. The coast, unspoiled and accessible almost everywhere, is one of grand rocky sweeps and intimate coves, clifftop views, and gentle beaches. The sea winds its way, too, through the province's economy, its long history—and its legends.

The Vikings may have seen its shores around A.D. 1000. One of the oldest European settlements in North America was established at Port Royal, on the Bay of Fundy, in 1605. And the area was of pivotal importance during the French-English wars of the 17th and 18th centuries that determined the future of Canada. The French fortress at Louisbourg, Cape Breton, one of the most ambitious historical reconstructions ever undertaken in Canada, and the Citadel which dominates downtown Halifax are but two of the many fortified remains of that period. It was an epoch, too, that gave rise to a rich lore of ghost ships, buried treasure and other pirate tales that form a constant theme in the province's many museums.

But Nova Scotia is more than a coastline encompassing history and legend. Its inland parts are also compelling—from the apple orchards and farmland of the Annapolis Valley to the beautiful highlands of Cape Breton and through all the lakes, streams, fields, and forests in-between and beyond.

Despite the attractiveness of field and shore, it is the capital, Halifax, that provides one of the province's most intriguing sides. The modern pressures of development have marked it, yet Halifax has preserved the essentials of its architecture and traditions. Its mix of old and new, history and modernity, is considered among the best in North America.

The Tides of History

As early as 1518 and again in 1523, French expeditions tried—with no success—to establish permanent settlements in the area. The first Europeans to colonize the region were French explorers de Monts and Champlain who secured their "Habitation" in 1605 near present day Port Royal and called it Acadia. Eight years earlier, British navigators John and Sebastian Cabot had stopped briefly on the northern tip of Cape Breton, claimed the entire continent for England, and then moved on. It was not until 1621, when King James I of England and VI of Scotland granted the province to Sir William Alexander, that the British made their first attempt to settle in Nova Scotia, the first British colony to possess its own flag. Derived from the original arms presented by King James, it is made up of the blue cross of St. Andrew with a shield depicting the red lion of Scotland. A new order of knighthood—the Baronets of Nova Scotia—was created and each knight was awarded a grant in the new territory. Although the scheme to colonize the area failed after a few years, the Order still exists.

The French were more successful at colonization but less so at retaining their territory. The entire region was the scene of continuing French/British conflict for supremacy over all of Canada in the 17th and early 18th centuries until the Treaty of Utrecht transferred Nova Scotia to British rule in 1713. Cape Breton Island (a separate province until 1820) remained French for a short time thereafter.

Although the French struggled to preserve their beachheads in the British part of the province, disaster struck in 1755 when they were driven from the province by British troops who questioned their loyalty. Some journeyed to Quebec, Prince Edward Island, or Cape Breton Island; others set out for Louisiana where their descendants are known today as "Cajuns," a corruption of "Acadians." Henry Wadsworth Longfellow, 19th-century American poet, immortalized the tragedy of the forced evacuation in *Evangeline:* "Waste all those pleasant farms and the farmers forever departed!" In return Acadians immortalized both Longfellow and *Evangeline.* There are stone monuments to the poet and his creation in the Grand Pré National Historic Park, although according to historians Longfellow never set foot in Nova Scotia.

The Acadians' lands were quickly settled with thousands of New England "planters," who were British Empire Loyalists escaping the American Revolution. The Acadians who managed to return to their former holdings found them occupied. Moving further down the Nova Scotia coast, they settled the area between Yarmouth and Digby—where the Acadian language and traditions are maintained to this day.

The Treaty of 1763 gave Britain permanent possession of Nova Scotia and most of what is now eastern Canada; France relinquished all claims, including Cape Breton Island, except for the tiny islands of St. Pierre and Miquelon which remain French Departments to this day.

Until 1784, Nova Scotia included what is now the province of New Brunswick. Following the influx of tens of thousands of United Empire Loyalists to the enlarged Nova Scotia, the separation of the New Brunswick portion was accomplished.

Early in 1800, the Highland Scots began to arrive; within 30 years more than 50,000 had settled in Cape Breton, and Pictou and Antigonish counties. Present-day Scots have maintained their Highland tradition, taking a fierce pride in the Gaelic language, the kilt, bagpipes, and traditional dances. Today, no parade in Nova Scotia is complete without a pipe band, (bagpipe, that is), and throughout the summer there are numerous Highland Games, gatherings, and concerts.

After the American Revolution, about 25,000 American colonists, with strong ties of allegiance to England, migrated to Nova Scotia where they founded Shelburne. In the war of 1812, Nova Scotia was the leading British base in North America.

The colony became the first one in British North America to achieve representative government—government elected by the people. That happened in 1758. In 1848 it became the first part of Canada to achieve "responsible" government—in which the cabinet was chosen from the elected members rather than appointed by the crown.

Today, Nova Scotia has become a stable meld of the various peoples and nationalities who made up the original settlements. Various areas remain Acadian; in the Lunenburg area, the people are Dutch or German; the Scots are dominant in the eastern part of the province. Indeed, it is said that there are more clans represented in Nova Scotia than in Scotland itself. And 5,400 of the original people, the Micmac Indians, still live on a number of reserves around the province.

Industry in Nova Scotia

Nova Scotia has a highly diversified economy. Manufacturing takes many forms—from electronics to textiles to steel—in both large and small plants. Fishing is obviously a major activity, but so are forestry, agriculture, and even tourism. One interesting note with regard to forestry is that the county of Lunenburg is considered the Christmas tree capital of North America. Hundreds of thousands of cultivated firs are shipped from there every autumn. Manufacturing is dominated by the French multinational company, Michelin Tires Ltd., which has three tire-making plants in the province. Another dominating installation is the steel mill at Sydney, which employs several thousand people. Sydney is the only other city in the province apart from Halifax and Dartmouth, which form one metropolitan area. Shipbuilding and ship repair are also important throughout the province, while Halifax, of course, is a major Canadian port and naval base.

Mining has been an up and down affair over the decades. There was a short-lived gold rush in the late 1800's, then a decline, and now there's a revival in mining generally. Around the turn of the century, Nova Scotia was a major gold producer. Today there is evidence of this prosperity in heaps of mine tailings and abandoned pits on remote back roads in areas such as Moose River Gold Mines off Highway 7, or at The Ovens, near Lunenburg, where there's a local museum on gold mining.

Coal mining has had a checkered history in Nova Scotia, bringing vast fortunes to a few industrialists and little more than bitter memories to the miners early in the 20th century. As oil became more common, the collieries declined, and in 1969, the Canadian government set up the Cape Breton Development Corporation to wind down the mines and transfer the miners to other work. After the rapid rise in oil prices since 1973, coal has again become a valued resource. Several new mines have been opened in the Cape Breton coalfield, employing thousands of miners.

Tourists may take mine tours in Springhill, a town built above the deepest coal mines in Canada, and in Cape Breton at Glace Bay and Sydney Mines. The Miners' Museum at Glace Bay has an excellent layout and display area, including reproductions of typical early buildings from the mining towns.

History Preserved and Polished

The province abounds in historic homes, building sites, and other attractions that have been maintained or restored by the provincial and federal governments. There are eight specially designated tourist routes that cover most of the areas of interest. These follow mostly the old trunk highways that wind their way through the villages and towns. Traffic is usually light on these roads, since the province also has a network of modern superhighways for through traffic.

The South Shore (Lighthouse Route) between Halifax and Yarmouth is often called the quintessential Nova Scotia. It features intriguing fishing villages and small towns nestled in a sometimes rugged, sometimes gentle coastline loaded with seafaring tradition. Near Mahone Bay, for instance, there's the famous Oak Island money pit—an ingeniously designed pit believed to have held pirate treasure but which defies sure explanation to this day. Peggy's Cove—the province's showpiece fishing village—is on this route. So is Lunenburg, site of the Fishermen's Museum, a small town which is pretty well the Canadian capital of the fishing tradition.

The Annapolis Valley route (Evangeline Trail) takes you past Annapolis Royal, the site of Samuel de Champlain's 1605 settlement; the entire downtown has recently received an historic facelift with numerous old buildings being restored. Nearby is North America's first tidal power plant on the Annapolis River. The valley is also a very scenic drive.

The Fundy Shore (Glooscap Trail) runs along the site of the world's highest tides, where ships rest on the bottom and fishermen collect their catch on foot at low tide. The cliffs contain a wealth of fossils, especially near Joggins. And Cape Blomidon Provincial Park located here is as lovely a spot as you'll find anywhere.

The Eastern Shore (Marine Drive) follows the ever-captivating Atlantic coast from Halifax to Cape Breton, with a high point at Sherbrooke Village, the province's main 19th-century reconstructed historic village.

The Northumberland Shore (Sunrise Trail) has plenty of beach and warm water for swimming—the only part of the province that has it.

Cape Breton has three trails. There's the Cabot Trail with its breathtaking views—one of the most gripping marine drives on the continent. The Fleur-de-Lis Trail goes to the reconstructed fortress at Louisbourg and some Acadian parts of Cape Breton, while the Ceilidh (pronounced *kay-lee*) Trail takes you to places like St. Ann's, Baddeck, and other centers of the province's rich Scottish-Gaelic heritage.

The Climate

Weather in Nova Scotia depends on the area. Inland, the temperatures tend to be more extreme, roughly −10 to −1°C. in January and 11 to 29°C. in summer (13–30°F. in January and 52–75°F. in summer), than temperatures along the coast. Along the coast, weather tends to be more variable, particularly in winter, changing as much as 23°C. (45°F.) over an eight-hour period. Precipitation may be snow inland and rain along the coast. While the ocean causes variable weather, it also warms the land, keeping the province relatively warm in winter and cooler in the summer.

Each season brings its own pleasures. In the spring (mid-April to the end of May), days are mild, nights are cool. A season of crocuses, tulips, and budding trees. Average temperatures: 7 to 14°C. (45–58°F.).

Summer (June, July, August) is time for fun in the sun. Even the hottest summer day is cooled in the evenings by soft ocean breezes. Be prepared for the occasional summer shower and, for comfort, take a light sweater for evening. Temperatures range from 18 to 32°C. (65–90°F.).

No part of Nova Scotia—54,390 sq. kms. (21,000 square miles)—is more than 56 kms. (35 miles) from the sea. During July, August, and even into early September the many sandy beaches are well used. For comfort, saltwater swimming should be restricted to the Northumberland Strait coast where water temperature will reach up to 21°C. (70°F.). On the other coasts the water temperature is distinctly cool, and so cold in the Bay of Fundy as to be dangerous to swimmers. A number of beach areas on all coasts have been developed by the provincial government and several have supervised swimming areas. These vary from year to year. Check with the Department of Tourism for an up-to-date list.

Indian Summer (September) is one of the favorite times of year for travelers to Nova Scotia. Days are warm, but not hot; evenings crisp, but not cold. Expect temperatures from 18 to 23°C. (65–75°F.), cooling to 15°C. (60°F.) at night.

Autumn (October) brings on Nova Scotia's most colorful season. Leaves turn first in the inland areas; then, in a predictable 2-week period, the vibrant colors spread to the coast. Temperatures hover between 13 and 18°C. (55–65°F.), cooling at night.

Autumn travel has become more popular in recent years. During July and August, accommodations and the better service facilities are usually taxed to the limit, and charge high season rates. After September 1, the traffic flow dwindles considerably and travel operations become less crowded.

Particularly in the Cabot Trail region of Cape Breton and certain sections of the Annapolis Valley, the brilliant autumn leaves combined with clear, crisp weather bring out native Nova Scotians as well as visitors. The best fall colors can usually be seen during the first two weeks of October, depending on the preceding weather.

In winter, November days are blustery and snowfalls begin in time for a white Christmas. Snows are intermittent and rarely predictable from December through March.

Cape Breton/Cabot Trail

With dramatic seascapes, rugged highlands, and lovely, old fishing villages, Cape Breton, the island part of Nova Scotia, is the province's most popular tourist area. The Cabot Trail, some 278 kms. (172 miles) of mountain and sea on a circular loop, is one of the most spectacular day drives in North America in any season. The controversy that rages as to whether one should drive the trail in a clockwise or counterclockwise direction is usually settled in favor of the clockwise direction. This puts the sun to the side of the car or behind it, and allows driving on the "inside"—next to the mountain rather than the cliff, so that the steepest grades are descended rather than climbed. Part of the Cabot Trail lies within the Cape Breton Highlands National Park, but no entrance fee is required unless specific Park facilities are to be used.

The Bras d'Or Lakes form a large inland salt lake which has become popular with yachting enthusiasts. Most of them headquarter at the Baddeck Yacht Club and spend days cruising the sheltered inland sea.

Cape Breton has a history of chronic unemployment due to the unsteady fortunes of the coal and steel industries. As a result, much of the Sydney–Glace Bay industrial area and environs have acquired a permanently depressed appearance. Yet the people are friendly and the place has its own rough charm. The traditions of steelworking and coalmining are cherished despite the hard times they evoke.

The Scottish tradition is still very strong in Cape Breton, particularly around the Baddeck-Iona region. Many people still speak Gaelic and the Gaelic College in St. Ann's is unique on this continent with its summer courses in piping, highland dancing, and Gaelic language.

Say "Hello" and Find a Friend

Nova Scotians, like most Atlantic Canadians, are quiet people who appear to have a touch of shyness. Often it is the visitor who must say the first "hello" or ask for help. But once the ice is broken, the visitor has a new friend—ready to give directions, lead the way, offer advice, or explain the fine points of a local attraction. Meeting Nova Scotians will be one of the greatest pleasures of your visit.

EXPLORING HALIFAX/DARTMOUTH

Founded in 1749 by Lord Cornwallis, Halifax—capital of Nova Scotia, largest city in the Atlantic Provinces, and one of the oldest cities in Canada—today combines the best of the colonial heritage with contemporary life.

Originally a military and naval base designed to defend the British colonies and also to counteract the defenses raised by the French at Cape Breton Island at Louisbourg, Halifax—built on a small peninsula —protected its harbor by a series of fortifications including the Citadel, which became the mightiest fortress in British North America and is now an historic site.

A Spectacular Harbor

Enjoying the benefits of one of the finest harbors in the world, Halifax is joined to the city of Dartmouth to the northeast by two suspension bridges. The "old bridge," the Angus L. Macdonald Bridge, was opened in 1955 and is some 1597 meters (5,239 feet) long. The "new bridge," the A. Murray McKay Bridge, was opened in 1970. The toll on both bridges starts at 25¢ for cars in either direction. The tollbooths are on the Dartmouth side of the bridges.

At the foot of both cities is the harbor where the shipping of the world ties up. The busy container port often operates around-the-clock. While one ship may be loading grain for eastern Europe, another is off-loading automobiles from the Orient at the Autoport.

Halifax/Dartmouth is the home of the Canadian Forces Maritime Command (Atlantic), and the sleek gray warships are a common sight under the two massive suspension bridges spanning the harbor.

Together, Halifax and Dartmouth form the largest metropolitan area east of Montréal. With a population of some 280,000 people, they are the major urban center for almost half of Nova Scotia as well as the business, financial, educational (also medical; most of the major hospitals are located here), and shopping center for Atlantic Canada. The area is also the seat of provincial government and headquarters for most government offices, both federal and provincial.

"Historic Properties"

The combination of old and new in Halifax is nowhere more apparent than in and around the area known as *Historic Properties*. Only one block away is the ultramodern Scotia Square, a shopping-office-apartment-hotel complex. High-rise office and apartment buildings spear the skyline in downtown Halifax, yet Historic Properties is only a few steps away. A joint development of the City of Halifax, Historic Properties Ltd., a Halifax company, and the federal department of Indian and Northern Affairs, the area has 12 buildings, of which several date back to the early 1800's.

When the area was originally built in the 1800's, it was the center of business for the young city. The Privateer's Warehouse was a stone building which housed the cargoes captured by Nova Scotia schooners serving as privateers until the captured ships and cargoes could be auctioned off by the Admiralty.

Collins Bank was the headquarters of Nova Scotia entrepreneur Enos Collins. When Collins died in 1871, he was reported to be the richest man in British North America.

The block of North American Renaissance buildings on Granville Street, between Duke and Buckingham, was constructed after the great Halifax fire of 1859, which razed the area. Designed by William Thomas, architect, of Toronto, the buildings were not all built at the same time but all exhibit a common theme and exterior format. Some of the storefronts which still remain were fabricated of cast iron and were probably designed by Bogardus. The only way to tell if they are metal is to test with a magnet. While many of the details of the architectural extravagances of the 1870's have been obliterated by time, the original elegance may still be seen in the tall windows and storefront designs. That part of Granville Street is now a strictly pedestrian area.

Between June and October in Historic Properties you can hear the town crier, take water tours, walking and bus tours, *Bluenose II* tours, and enjoy numerous special events.

Saved by the People

Early in the 1960's, the Historic Properties area was slated for demolition to make way for a superhighway along the waterfront. A successful campaign by civic groups saved the area from the wrecker's ball and the City of Halifax, which owns most of the property, called for redevelopment plans to restore the buildings to their original appearance on the exterior, while retaining commercially usable interiors.

The buildings have nooks and crannies in interesting locations, arches and odd-shaped windows, stucco and wooden beams—all of those beautiful "useless" architectural appendages which modern designers seem to eliminate in their functional steel and glass buildings.

The buildings of Historic Properties once again hear the footsteps of Haligonians (inhabitants of Halifax) and visitors alike walking the old cobblestone streets and shopping for wares in shops featuring handmade articles—leather, wood, glass, and ceramic. There are law offices,

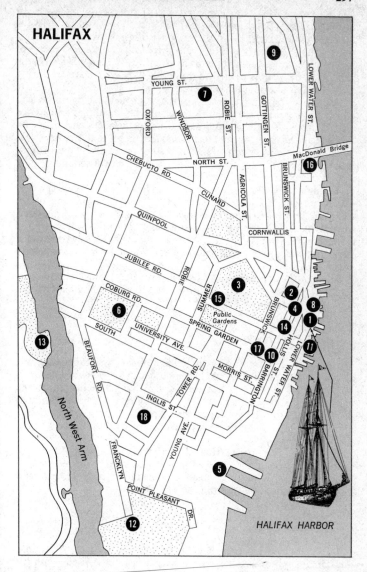

HALIFAX

Halifax—Points of Interest
1) Bluenose II Wharf
2) Chateau Halifax
3) Citadel
4) City Hall
5) Container Port
6) Dalhousie University
7) Exhibition Grounds
8) Fisherman's Market
9) Fort Needham
10) Government House
11) Maritime Museum
12) Martello Tower
13) Memorial Tower
14) Neptune Theater
15) Nova Scotia Museum
16) Old Dutch Church
17) St. Mary's Basilica
18) St. Mary's University

federal and provincial government offices, the campus of the Nova Scotia College of Art and Design, and restaurants and pubs. Nova Scotia's floating ambassador, the schooner *Bluenose II*, docks at Privateer's Wharf, just as vessels tied up there 200 years ago. Instead of loading the exotic plunder of faraway countries, *Bluenose II* lowers the gangplank for visitors to enjoy a cruise out in Halifax Harbour during summer afternoons and evenings.

One block up from Historic Properties is the new Barrington Hotel, which continues the tradition of revitalizing old buildings. Its exterior was rebuilt with the original granite from the façade of an entire city block, but the interior contains a modern hotel and two levels of boutiques, craftshops, restaurants, and some of the city's finest stores. It is also linked to Scotia Square, the main downtown shopping, hotel and office complex.

A couple of blocks to the south along Upper Water Street is a new waterfront development that includes the Maritime Museum of the Atlantic. Displays that describe Nova Scotia's golden age of sail, when the province's flag was seen in ports around the world, dominate. The main display is docked outside, however. It's a 900-ton hydrographic ship, the *Acadia,* which charted the Labrador and Arctic coasts early in this century.

Between the museum and Historic Properties, the Halifax–Dartmouth ferries chug in and out of a new terminal. It's a cheap (35¢) sightseeing tour in itself.

Plenty of Open Space

With such development in the middle of the downtown core, one might assume that the Halifax/Dartmouth metro area is not an entirely relaxing place in which to live and work. Although there is the hustle and bustle associated with any city, both cities are blessed with hundreds of acres of open green park and recreation space as well as salt- and freshwater recreation areas which can be used by the area's residents.

The North West Arm, Halifax Harbour, and Bedford Basin are dotted with pleasure boats of all shapes and sizes during the season which runs from spring to "frostbite" time in November. Dartmouth has no less than 22 lakes within the city limits.

No Longer Drab

Halifax was once appropriately known as the "gray city." Its dour and somber appearance has been replaced since the mid-60's with the establishment of new business and shopping centers, a night life which is interesting, and the vibrant atmosphere associated with a growing city.

Part of the drab reputation that once tagged the city comes from its long history as a military port. Here, roaming press gangs kidnapped unsuspecting young men from the streets and forced them into service aboard British naval ships.

Fort Needham, a long hill in the north end of Halifax, has been developed as a memorial park and offers a panoramic view of the area devastated in the Great Halifax Explosion on December 6, 1917. The explosion, the largest single man-made blast prior to the atomic bomb, was caused when a munitions ship collided with another vessel in the harbor. Two thousand fatalities were recorded, 10,000 more suffered serious injuries, 25,000 were left homeless, and the shockwave was felt in the town of Truro, more than 60 miles away.

One of the most pleasant spots in summertime Halifax is the Public Gardens on Spring Garden Road. Preserving much of the original landscape design (1753), the 18 acres have formal gardens, a large pond for ducks, geese and swans, lawns, a wide variety of exotic plants and trees, fountains, and plenty of park benches for quiet enjoyment.

Most visitors to Halifax take one of the excellent water tours. The famous *Bluenose II* sailing schooner takes passengers on harbor cruises from Privateer's Wharf, as does a company called Halifax Water Tours. Harbour Island Tours leaves from the new Marine Museum of the Atlantic and takes passengers to historic and mysterious McNab's Island at the harbor mouth for a two-hour walking tour.

The best view of the city is from the ring-road around the top of the Citadel, the old fort which dominates the Halifax skyline near the waterfront.

Fairview, a suburb of Halifax, has its own recollections. It was here that recovered victims of the *Titanic* disaster (1912) were buried.

Halifax in Sun and Rain

Summer evenings bring out locals and visitors along the pathways of the Commons in the center of Halifax to enjoy amateur sports or just to walk about.

Halifax is a quiet, clean, and pleasant city but a couple of cautions are in order. Food and accommodations can be expensive and parking is a problem in the downtown area of Halifax. The best bet is to head for either the Scotia Square Parking Garages which usually have some space, or the Historic Properties parking area on the waterfront.

In the rain, take refuge in the provincial pioneer and military museums inside the Citadel and the Nova Scotia Museum on Summer Street; the latter features natural history and has supervised programs, mainly for children. The new Marine Museum of the Atlantic on Lower Water Street displays the seagoing tradition of the east coast. The Dartmouth Heritage Museum exhibits early history, while the suburban Cole Harbour Heritage Farm features agricultural history. Art galleries at St. Mary's, Dalhousie, and Mount St. Vincent universities, as well as the New Art Gallery of Nova Scotia, have regular exhibitions.

One can even don rainwear on damp days and walk to Point Pleasant Park's Black Rock to watch ships come and go only a few hundred yards away. Ship watching is equally pleasant in fine weather. Be sure to look for some of the Scottish heather here—apparently the only location in North America where the plant grows wild. The seeds came from mattresses shaken out by British sailors many decades ago.

Halifax is a city to explore. The old and new stand side by side in a fine blend. The only shots to be fired from the Citadel are the cannon announcing the arrival of noon each day—a custom which is still preserved, much to the shock of unwary passersby.

PRACTICAL INFORMATION FOR HALIFAX/DARTMOUTH

HOW TO GET THERE. By air: *Air Canada* operates flights into the Halifax International Airport from all major and some minor points in the Atlantic Provinces and the rest of Canada; also from Boston and London, England. *CP Air* flies Montréal–Halifax and Halifax–Amsterdam. *Eastern Provincial Airways* flies from Toronto and most airports in the Atlantic Provinces.

By car: Most highways in Nova Scotia lead to Halifax/Dartmouth. Hwys. 3/103, 7, 2/102 and 1/101 terminate in the twin cities. Hwy. 104, the Trans-Canada Hwy. from Amherst at the New Brunswick border joins Rtes. 2/102 at Truro.

By bus: Within Nova Scotia, Halifax is served by *Acadian Lines Limited;* along the South Shore only, service is operated by *MacKenzie Bus Lines.* Through interconnecting lines, most major North American bus lines serve Nova Scotia.

By train: *Via Rail* passenger services serve Halifax from most major Canadian centers. From the United States, *Amtrak* connections may be made in Montréal.

ACCOMMODATIONS. Accommodation in Halifax/ Dartmouth is generally comfortable and reservations are a necessity any time of year. Reservations can be made by calling the toll-free numbers listed in the *Tourist Information* section. Hotel/motel rates in Halifax/Dartmouth, based on double occupancy, are categorized as follows: *Expensive,* $44 or more; *Moderate,* $33 to $44; *Inexpensive,* less than $33.

The 10% provincial sales tax is added to all hotel/motel rates.

Most places accept the following major credit cards: American Express, MasterCard and Visa; others may also be honored. Not all establishments accept credit cards, therefore we suggest you call for information.

HALIFAX. *Expensive:* **Barrington Inn.** Barrington at Granville Sts. Part of a shopping and convention complex incorporating the reconstructed façade of an entire historic city block. No charge for children under 18 sharing parents' room. Phone 429–7410. All major credit cards.

Chateau Halifax. 1990 Barrington St. in Scotia Square. A CP Hotel with 305 rooms. Rooms are better than average but corridors are dark and narrow. Heated indoor-outdoor pool, sauna, dining room, pub and lounges. The best part of this hotel is that it is part of the big Scotia Square shopping-office complex. Phone 425–6700. All major credit cards.

Citadel Inn. 1960 Brunswick St. 189 rooms, quiet lounge and dining room. Rooms are excellent; patronized by businessmen and sales personnel. Phone 422–1391. All major credit cards.

Dresden Arms Motor Hotel. 5530 Artillery Pl. 94 rooms in pleasant surroundings off the main street but still downtown. Dining room usually good. Pool, sauna, whirlpool and exercise area. Phone 422–1625. Major credit cards.

Holiday Inn. 1980 Robie St. at the Willow Tree. Better than average Holiday Inn with 237 rooms, indoor pool, sauna, rooms for the handicapped, dining room, lounge and pub. Phone 423–1161. All major credit cards.

Hotel Nova Scotian. 1181 Hollis St. at the railway station. A local landmark. Facilities for the handicapped. No charge for children sharing parents' room. Phone: 423–7231. Major credit cards.

The Lord Nelson Hotel. 1515 S. Park St. opposite the Public Gardens. A local landmark. 320 rooms. Phone 423–6331. Major credit cards.

Wandlyn Motor Inn. No. 2 Hwy. at Fairview. About 15 minutes from downtown. Water-view rooms have a good view over Bedford Basin. 74 rooms, coffee bar, licensed dining room. Off-season rates January to June, October to January. Pets permitted. Phone 443–0416. All major credit cards.

Moderate: **Carleton Hotel.** 1685 Argyle St. 68 rooms, 40 with bath. Licensed lounge and dining room; free parking. Phone 423–7111. Major credit cards.

Keddy's Motor Inn. 20 St. Margaret's Bay Rd., Armsdale. About 15 minutes from downtown. Part of a chain. 132 rooms (7 efficiency) of adequate quality; pool and sauna. Off-season rates November to May. Phone 477–5611. All major credit cards.

Inexpensive: **YMCA.** 1565 S. Park St. 68 pleasant rooms for men with full use of Y facilities: sauna, pool, gym, and squash. Downtown location. Phone 422–6437. Visa only.

YWCA. 1239 Barrington St. 12 pleasant rooms for women, with use of Y facilities. Phone 423–6162. No credit cards accepted.

DARTMOUTH. *Expensive:* **The Atlantic Inn.** 739 Windmill Rd. 92 units near Dartmouth Industrial Park. Coffee shop, licensed dining and lounge. Off season rates October to April. Phone 469–0810. All major credit cards.

Holiday Inn. 99 Wyse Rd. at MacDonald Bridge. 120 rooms with no surprises; dining room with less than adequate food and lounge. Outdoor pool. Off-season rates October to May. Phone 463–1100. All major credit cards.

Keddy's Dartmouth Inn. Mic Mac Rotary. One of the better mmebers of this chain with 82 rooms and 36 motel units. Efficiency units available. Licensed dining and lounge. Phone 477–5611. All major credit cards.

HOW TO GET AROUND. Walking is a good way to get around many areas of downtown Halifax and Dartmouth. In downtown Halifax, in particular, parking may be a problem during the business day.

By taxi: Taxi rates start at $1.20 and meter up based on mileage and time combined. A crosstown trip should cost about $4.00 to $5.00, depending on traffic. Hailing taxis on the street is often difficult. Call a stand and have the taxi pick you up.

By bus: The *Metropolitan Transit Commission* operates a bus system covering the entire metropolitan area. Basic fare is 60¢, and exact change is needed. Call 426–6600 for information.

By ferry: The *Dartmouth Ferry Commission* operates two passenger ferries from the George Street terminal in Halifax to the Portland Street terminal in Dartmouth. Ferries operate from 6 A.M. to midnight on half-hour and hourly schedules. Fare for a single crossing is 35¢. Call 466–2215 for schedules and information.

TOURIST INFORMATION. *For Nova Scotia.* Write Nova Scotia Department of Tourism, P.O. Box 130, Halifax, Nova Scotia, Canada, B3J 2M7. Phone: (902) 423–5464.

Call-toll free: in continental U.S.A. (except Alaska and Maine), 1–800–341–6096; in Maine, 1–800–492–0643; Canada-wide, 1–800–565–7166; in the Maritime Provinces, 1–800–565–7105; in Newfoundland and Québec, 1–800–565–7180; in Ontario, 1–800–565–7140; in British Columbia, 112–800–565–7166. You can also make hotel and motel reservations through these numbers.

Tourist information desks are located on the ferries to Nova Scotia from Port-aux-Basques and Argentia, Nfld. At Bar Harbour and Portland, Me., tourist-information desks are inside the ferry terminals. These ferries go to Yarmouth on a daily basis. And the N.S. Department of Tourism operates a tourist information center at Port Hastings on the Cape Breton side of the Canso Causeway (625–1717), and at Pictou, a few miles from the landing of the Wood Island Ferry from P.E.I.

You will find provincially operated tourist bureaus at Yarmouth and Digby near the ferry wharves; at Antigonish on the Trans-Canada Hwy.; near the Halifax International Airport; at Amherst near the New Brunswick border; and at the Pictou Rotary a few miles from the ferry landing from Prince Edward Island. Most are open from 8 A.M. to 8 P.M. from mid-May to the end of October, and at the Red Store, Historic Properties, Halifax, year-round. You're generally no more than 15 miles from a tourist bureau anywhere in the province.

For Cape Breton: Write The Cape Breton Tourist Association, 20 Keltic Dr., Sydney River, N.S., Canada B1S 1P5. Telephone (902) 539–9876.

From June to September the Tourist Association distributes a free monthly guide to events and places called *What's Happening,* which you'll find in restaurants, motels, and tourist bureaus.

Park information centers are located at both the Ingonish and Cheticamp entrances to Cape Breton Highlands National Park.

*The Red Store, Historic Properties, Halifax—*The *City of Halifax,* the *National Parks Department* and the *Nova Scotia Department of Tourism* all operate information centers in the Red Store. For city information, call 426-6448; for provincial information call 424-4247; for national parks information call 426-9211. Offices open year-round. Also, there's a year-round information center at Halifax International Airport.

The City of Dartmouth operates a tourist bureau on Thistle St. from mid-May to mid-October. Call 466-2728 during the open season, and 469–7848 off-season.

Throughout the province there are some 40 tourist information bureaus run by local municipalities and boards of trade.

RECOMMENDED READING. The novels of Thomas Raddall (and, to some extent, Will R. Bird) give a vital and colorful account of the province's rich history. Raddall's *Halifax: Warden of the North* has been called a model of local history. The speeches, essays and poems of Joseph Howe are compiled in several anthologies; Howe was the greatest political and intellectual leader in 19th century Nova Scotia. Thomas Chandler Haliburton's *The Clockmaker* set out to scourge the Bluenoses for their want of thrift and industry; it became the first Canadian book to achieve international fame. Haliburton learned his satiric trade in part from Thomas McCulloch, a pioneer clergyman, satirist and educator (among other things, he was the first president of Dalhousie University), whose sharp satiric portrait of Pictou, *The Stepsure Letters*, is still in print and still funny.

The fiction of Ernest Buckler (particularly *The Mountain and the Valley* and *Oxbells and Fireflies*) and of Charles Bruce *(The Channel Shore)* are meditative, beautifully written portrayals of the traditional Nova Scotian lifestyle. Helen Creighton's *Bluenose Magic* and *Bluenose Ghosts* reveal the depth of folklore in the province.

Recent Nova Scotia fiction includes Chipman Hall's *Lightly,* Alistair Mac-Leod's *The Lost Salt Gift of Blood,* and Susan Kerslake's *Middlewatch.* Recent nonfiction may be represented by Harry Bruce's *Lifeline,* the story of the Maritime ferry system, and by Silver Donald Cameron's account of the great fishing strike of 1970/71, *The Education of Everett Richardson.* Jim and Pat Lotz have written a comprehensive volume, *Cape Breton Island. Nova Scotia in Your Pocket* by John Prince is a good general guide.

BUSINESS HOURS. Most stores are open between 9 or 10 A.M. until 9 P.M., Wednesdays, Thursdays, and Fridays. From Monday to Saturday, they close at 6 P.M.

Banks are open 10 A.M. to 3 P.M. generally; most stay open until 4 P.M. Thursdays and Fridays, while some stay open until 5. A few banks in the shopping centers keep shopping center hours.

SEASONAL EVENTS. Every year the N.S. Department of Tourism publishes a *Calendar of Events,* free on request, which describes provincial festivals and events. Some highlights:

May: Antique Show & Sale, Halifax May 12–13. Late May: Apple Blossom festival, Kentville area (one of the major Nova Scotia festivals: it includes dances, parade, sports, entertainment).

June: Mid-June: Annual Summer Antique Sale, Halifax.

July: In Dartmouth, the Festival of Piping; later in the month, Halifax Natal Day (road races, rock concerts, band concerts, parade in the morning, children's program, barbecue, sports events, rock dance, fireworks).

August: Early August—Sing Summer, choral concerts; Dartmouth Natal Day. Mid-August—Nova Scotia Festival of the Arts, in Halifax.

September: Late September: The Joseph Howe Festival (oratorical contest, pony express ride, pancake breakfasts, open-air and craft markets, dances, concerts, beer fests, parade, whaler races, bazaar, multicultural concert, and town crier championships).

October: Antique Show and Sale, with paintings by maritime artists, Halifax.

FREE EVENTS. The programs listed in the *Childrens' Activities* section are free. So is entry to all the city's museums and other public cultural facilities. Participation in the various cultural festivals is without charge. And the Sunday-afternoon band concerts at the Public Gardens are free as well.

TOURS. Both the *Metropolitan Transit Commission* and *Gray Line* (operated by Acadian Bus Lines) have coach tours of Halifax, each lasting about two hours.

The Gray Line tour may be boarded at the Acadian Lines terminal on Almon Street, and at most major hotels. For times and information call 454-9321. *Halifax Transit* tours may be boarded at Historic Properties. Call 426-6600 for full information. Cost of both tours is about $4.00 ($1.50 for children).

Halifax Water Tours operates an excellent 2-hour boat tour of Halifax Harbour and the Northwest Arm leaving from Privateers Wharf four times daily, June 16–September 9, with fewer tours daily starting May 26 and lasting to Oct. 8. The tour boat is comfortable and licensed; commentary by the hostesses is very good. For information and times call 423–7783 or 425–7414. The cost is about $6.00 per person ($2.00 for children).

During most of July, August, and September, visitors may enjoy a sail on a Halifax Harbour cruise aboard *Bluenose II*, the 143-foot replica of the famous Nova Scotia sailing schooner. A 2-hour sail costs about $9.00 per person ($4.00 for children, $4.50 for senior citizens) and the vessel leaves from her wharf at Historic Properties. For information on sailing times, call 424-4247.

One unique package involves a sail to McNab's Island, at the mouth of Halifax Harbour, for a 2-hour walking tour. The name of the company is *Harbour Island Tours,* and it leaves twice daily through most of the summer from near the Maritime Museum of the Atlantic. Phone 422–9523.

Further information on day charters, boat rentals and cruises can be obtained from the Nova Scotia Department of Tourism's publication, *Sports and Activities,* P.O. Box 456, Halifax, N.S. B3J 2R5.

The Halifax, Dartmouth, or Provincial tourist bureaus have details of a number of well-organized self-drive tours of the area. Walking tours of historic sites in downtown Halifax and Dartmouth are available.

A non-guided tour of Halifax Harbour is as simple as taking a trip on the Dartmouth Ferry on a bright, sunny day. The round trip costs 50¢ and takes 45 minutes to an hour. Passengers can sit outside on the top of the ferry.

A Cyclist's Guide to Nova Scotia is available from N.S. Tourism and local sports stores. Halifax is an easy city to explore by bike.

PARKS. *Point Pleasant Park* covers the entire tip of the peninsula of the City of Halifax. As it is a natural woodland park, automobile traffic is banned. Surrounded on three sides by saltwater, there are trails, picnic areas, a swimming beach, and a number of partially ruined fortifications.

Fort Needham, a hill in the north end of Halifax, has been developed as a small park.

Fleming Park on the North West Arm is known locally as "The Dingle." The area was donated to the city by Sir Sandford Fleming, a railroad builder who also invented Standard Time. The tall tower was built to commemorate the first elective assembly held in the British colonies. The view from the top of the tower overlooking the Arm and the City makes the many steps well worth your while.

The Citadel as well as *Horseshoe Island Park* in Halifax are also pleasant.

Many of the 22 lakes in Dartmouth have small parks, beaches, and picnic areas along the shores.

The Halifax Commons is a large area in the center of the city with children's playground, wading pool, ball fields, tennis courts lighted for night play, and lots of grassy area.

GARDENS. The *Halifax Public Gardens,* 18 acres of color in the heart of the City, is a favorite spot for relaxation for visitors and Haligonians. Landscaped originally in 1753, these gardens are among the oldest on the continent. In addition to trees and shrubs from every corner of the globe, there are fountains, a bandstand, and a large pond with various waterbirds. One corner has been set aside as a children's area.

The gardens are open mid-May to mid-November, 8 A.M. to sundown daily. No admission charge.

CHILDREN'S ACTIVITIES. During July and August, the Halifax and Dartmouth Recreation Departments operate summer programs at *school playgrounds,* the *Halifax Commons,* and at the *Dartmouth Lakes.* The playground facilities, including swings and other equipment, wading pool and playground fields at the Halifax Commons may be used without charge.

Dartmouth and Halifax have supervised swimming at many of the lakes and Halifax has supervised salt water swimming at *Point Pleasant* and *Flemming Parks.*

The Nova Scotia Museum on Summer Street in Halifax has special children's programs throughout the year. Call 429–4610 for information.

For children of all ages, fishing from a waterfront wharf or breakwater on the incoming tide usually yields some small but interesting specimens of salt water fish.

For complete information, call Halifax Recreation at 426–6426; or Dartmouth Recreation at 469–9211.

SPORTS. Halifax is the home of the American Hockey League *Nova Scotia Voyageurs,* a farm team of the Montréal Canadiens. The team plays more than 20 home games from November to April against international competition. For information on game dates and tickets, call 453-4015.

College-level sports events take place throughout the school year. For full information, contact the Halifax Tourist Bureau.

Hard surface *tennis* courts, lighted for night play, are available at the Halifax Commons. For *sailing* enthusiasts there are five yacht clubs in Halifax/Dartmouth. *Canoeing* is a popular sport in Dartmouth and is centered on Lake Banook and Micmac Lake.

Bicycle tours available from Bicycle Nova Scotia, 5516 Spring Garden Road, P.O. Box 3010 Halifax, N.S. B3J3G6 Phone: 425–5450.

For full information on all sports in the Halifax/Dartmouth area, contact the tourist bureau in either city.

HISTORIC SITES. Halifax has three surviving military installations, all of British origin, which once served as essential elements of the defense against the French threat at Louisbourg. The *Citadel,* a star-shaped fort, was begun in 1749. A third version, completed in 1828, now has an excellent military museum and a commanding view of the Nova Scotia capital. Open year-round. Other installations, built in the late 1700's, include the *Prince of Wales Martello Tower* and the *York Redoubt,* which was modified and used throughout the 19th century as part of the harbor defense. Open June 1 to September 30. Telephone: 426–5080. There are also ruins of other fortifications in Point Pleasant Park.

The *Naval Dockyard* on North Barrington St. was begun in 1757 and is still in operation.

Charles Dickens called *Province House* "a gem of Georgian architecture." The building is still used as the province's legislature and has an excellent library. It is the oldest existing legislative building in Canada.

A number of Halifax churches are historically significant. *St. Matthew's Church* on Barrington St. is very old and has a fine interior. One of the earliest ministers was the great-grandfather of U.S. president Grover Cleveland. *St. George's Round Church* on Brunswick St. was built in 1800 and is a rare example of circular ecclesiastical architecture. *St. Mary's Basilica* on Spring Garden Rd. is a fine granite structure, reputed to have the highest granite spire in the world. *St. Paul's Church* on Barrington St., built in 1749, is the oldest Protestant church in Canada. The *Old Dutch Church* on Brunswick St., built in 1756, was the first Lutheran Church in Canada.

Admission is free to all historic sites.

MUSEUMS AND GALLERIES. Museums: The *Halifax Citadel National Historic Park* is a hilltop fortress built in 1828 on the site of earlier fortifications dating back to the city's founding in 1749. Dominating the city and offering excellent views, The Citadel houses the Army Museum, depicting the history of colonial warfare. Kilted soldiers drill and there is a unique gift shop. On the fortress grounds is the Old Town Clock, originally built in 1803, and now the unofficial symbol of the city. Parking outside the fortress is limited. Open 9 A.M. to 8 P.M., June to October; 10 A.M. to 5 P.M., the rest of the year.

The *Marine Museum of the Atlantic,* 1675 Lower Water St. The seagoing tradition, housed in a restored chandlery and dockside warehouse. It includes, docked outside, the hydrographic ship *Acadia,* which was used to chart the coasts of Labrador and the Arctic earlier in this century.

The *Maritime Command Museum,* Admiralty House, CFB Stadacona, on Gottigen at Almon St., has military artifacts; open year-round.

The *Nova Scotia Museum* on Summer Street in Halifax features both permanent exhibits on *Man and His Environment* and general and natural history exhibits of Nova Scotia. Many parts of the museum feature "touch and feel" sections and there are special areas for children's activities. Open daily; call 429-4610 for opening and closing times.

The *Dartmouth Heritage Museum and Art Gallery* on Wyse Rd. features displays on early life in Dartmouth and the surrounding area. The art gallery features permanent and traveling exhibits. Open daily; call 463-3183 for opening and closing times.

Other museums include *Province House,* the seat of the Nova Scotia government and the oldest legislative building in any Canadian province; *Prince of Wales Martello Tower; York Redoubt National Historic Park;* and the *Public Archives of Nova Scotia* at the corner of Robie St. and University Ave.

Galleries: The *Art Gallery of Nova Scotia,* on Coburg Rd., is the main non-commercial gallery. Others are located at the *Dartmouth Heritage Museum, Mount Saint Vincent University, Dalhousie University* and *St. Mary's University.*

Of the several commercial galleries in Halifax, the best are *Manuge Galleries* on Hollis St. near Sackville; *Zwicker's Gallery* on Doyle St. near Brunswick; *Gallery 1667* in the Promenade Block from the Potomac Bldg., Historic Properties; and *Atlantic Art Gallery* at Hollis and Duke Sts. *Three Oaks Corporation,* 3 Albert St. in Dartmouth is owned and operated by Tom Forrestall, a popular Canadian realist, and his works are featured in this pleasant gallery.

Admission to any of the private or public museums or galleries is free.

MUSIC AND THEATER. The *Rebecca Cohn Auditorium* (sometimes referred to as the *Dalhousie Arts Centre*) is one of Halifax's centers for live concerts and musical presentations featuring international artists, year round. Call 424-2298 for box-office information and bookings.

Major musical presentations in Halifax take place at the *Metro Centre*, a new sports and cultural complex located downtown. For up to date information on what's playing where, check with the Halifax Tourist Bureau.

Neptune Theatre is Nova Scotia's only professional live theater group. Most of their presentations are given at *Neptune Theatre* on Sackville St. Most of the plays are in repertory and offer comedy and drama, both modern and traditional. For box office and information call 429–7300.

A better-than-average amateur group known as the *Kipawo Showboat Company* performs at the new amateur playhouse at Historic Properties. Members perform mostly musicals. What they lack in professional polish they make up in enthusiasm, offering an evening of theater that is fun.

 SHOPPING. There are several specialty shopping areas in Halifax. The Spring Garden Rd. area is the older one with more traditional goods, particularly British imports. The newer and more exquisite area is actually in the oldest part of Halifax—*Historic Properties* and the *Barrington Inn* complex —where you can find fine crafts in such stores as the Pewter House, Nova Pine, and The Eskimo Gallery, as well as top line manufactured goods. A block away, in the *Scotia Square* complex, is the city's main downtown mall for day-to-day shopping. The principal suburban shopping centers are *Micmac Mall* in Dartmouth and the *Halifax Shopping Center*, the *Maritime Mall*, and *Bayer's Road Shopping Center* in Halifax.

 DINING OUT. Dining out in Halifax/Dartmouth is usually good to excellent in the better restaurants. The surroundings are usually excellent too. Many restaurants are set in refurbished historic homes or other restored quarters.

Service is generally good in the better restaurants, although it can be slow, especially if the place is busy. Your waiter or waitress can usually suggest the best items on the daily menu or the specials of the day.

Restaurants are categorized on the basis of full course dinner, with drinks, tax and tips excluded: *Expensive*, over $17; *Moderate*, $12–$17; *Inexpensive*, under $12. A 10% provincial tax will be added to all meals over $3.00.

Most places accept the following major credit cards: American Express, MasterCard and Visa; others may also be honored. Not all establishments accept credit cards, therefore we suggest you call for information.

HALIFAX. *Expensive:* **Cameo.** 5511 Spring Garden Rd. Food well prepared and service efficient. Menu ranges from steaks to seafood. Phone 423–8887. Major credit cards.

Clipper Cay. Historic Properties. Restaurant with the best location, overlooking Privateer's Wharf and Halifax Harbour. Ask for window table with a harbor view. The *Cay Side*, downstairs, has lunch outdoors on the wharf during summer months. Phone: (Clipper Cay) 423–6818, (Cay Side) 429–5639. All major credit cards (both restaurants).

Fat Frank's. 5411 Spring Garden Rd. Edwardian atmosphere, gourmet dining (Fat Frank's boasts it can prepare any known dish on demand). Lunch and dinner. Seats only 55, so reservations, especially in summer, are recommended. Phone 423–6618. Major credit cards.

The Henry House/Little Stone Jug. 1222 Barrington St. Dining room and pub-style restaurant in historic granite building. Food is excellent and the atmosphere classic Georgian. Call for reservations. Dress casual, but no dungarees. Phone 423–1309. All major credit cards.

Les Deux Amies. 1522 Birmingham St. An elegant restaurant in old Victorian townhouse with French gourmet cooking. Phone 425–5222. All major credit cards.

Moderate–Expensive: **Old Man Morias.** 1150 Barrington St. Open year-round. Hellenic cuisine (spitted lamb, moussaka, etc.) served in renovated townhouse. Licensed. Phone 422–7960. Major credit cards.

Moderate: **DA's.** Dresden Arms Motor Hotel, 5530 Artillery Pl. Good food in pleasant dining room. Try the Maid's Brunch at lunchtime. Call for reservations. Phone 422–1625. All major credit cards.

The Gondola Restaurant. 5175 South St. Known locally as "Pino's." Features authentic Italian cuisine in trattoria-style surroundings; terrace dining during summer. Start with appetizer of spaghetti and continue from there. Call for reservations. Phone 423–8719. Major credit cards.

The Hermitage. South Park St. at Inglis St. Swiss and French décor and cuisine. Phone 423–7638. Major credit cards.

The News Room. Carleton Hotel, Argyle and Sackville Sts. Old brick and glassed-in courtyard. Seafood and prime rib are specialties. Phone 423–0624. Major credit cards.

Pepe's. 5680 Spring Garden Rd. Superb surroundings and food to match. A bright and cheerful restaurant. Phone 429–7321. Major credit cards.

Sanford's Second Story. Hollis and Duke Sts. Sanford's offers natural foods, crêpes and quiche. Phone 423–4560. American Express and Visa only.

Other fine moderate restaurants are **The Pacific Station,** Barrington St.; **Five Fishermen,** Argyle St.; **Thackery's,** Spring Garden Rd.; **Lawrence of Oregano's,** Argyle St.; **My Apartment,** Argyle St.; and an excellent little café called **Quelque Chose,** serving quiche, salads, light dinners and mouthwatering desserts, Hollis St.

Inexpensive: **The Boardroom.** Lower Mall, Scotia Square. Lunch spot for young executives from 11:30 to 2:30. Then it becomes a piano bar where the same types gather. Specials are chowder and thick sandwich with beer or wine. Phone 422–3553. All major credit cards.

Privateer's Warehouse. Historic Properties, Lower Deck and Middle Deck for lunch. 11:30 to 2:30. Sandwiches, chowder, sauerkraut, and sausage with beer are the specials. Informal atmosphere popular with young professionals, secretaries, and students. The Upper Deck dining room is in the *Inexpensive* category for lunch and the *Moderate* category for dinner, but the average quality of the food does not make up for the lack of atmosphere. Phone 422–1289. Major credit cards.

 NIGHTCLUBS AND BARS. Night life in the area tends to be centered in downtown Halifax with a variety of clubs and bars offering entertainment, food, and congenial surroundings.

The most popular nightspot with the young professionals in Halifax is *Privateers Wharf* in Historic Properties. The Lower Deck on the ground floor is a tavern with beer only and accordion music. The Middle Deck on the second floor is a bar with light jazz music. Both Decks are usually packed on weekends so get there early. Cover charge on weekends.

The second most popular nightspot for young Halifax/Dartmouth people is the *Jury Room* in the Carleton Hotel on Argyle St. Although the hotel is somewhat down at the heels, new owners have revitalized the bar. Packed on weekends; full house during the week.

The Palace, across from the Halifax Citadel, and the *Misty Moon,* 3700 Kempt Rd. in the city's north end, are the two largest nightclubs. They carry rock, blues, and other popular recording genres.

For a quiet drinking place, try the *Victory Lounge* in the Lord Nelson Hotel on South Park and Spring Garden Rd. The *Wyse Owl Tavern* on Wyse Rd. in Dartmouth is a workingman's tavern with a rough interior which offers the best blues and country blues music in the area.

The Split Crow, corner Duke and Granville, a decorous pub popular with young professionals.

PRACTICAL INFORMATION FOR CAPE BRETON

HOW TO GET THERE. By air: *Air Canada* has direct flights to Sydney from Halifax, Toronto, Montréal, and Québec City with connections to international flights. *Eastern Provincial Airways* has flights to Sydney from Montréal, Newfoundland, New Brunswick, and Prince Edward Island. Sydney is also the connecting airport for flights to the French islands of St. Pierre and Miquelon which lie off the south coast of Newfoundland. *Air St. Pierre* (with Eastern Provincial Airways) operates a year-round schedule of flights to France's last North American possessions.

By boat: Regular ferry service connects North Sydney with Port-aux-Basques, Newfoundland. A summer service is operated to Argentia, Newfoundland. For information and reservations, contact any *CN Marine* ticket office in Canada or your travel agent.

By bus: Daily bus service to Cape Breton from Halifax is operated by *Acadian Lines Limited* which connects with other bus lines throughout the country.

By car: The automobile (camper, motorcycle, or other recreational vehicle) must cross the Canso Causeway if approaching Cape Breton from mainland Nova Scotia. The toll is $1.50 per vehicle, payable only when entering Cape Breton.

By train: *Canadian National* operates train service to Sydney and intermediate points from Halifax and Truro. For information and reservations, contact any *Via Rail* ticket office.

ACCOMMODATIONS. Accommodations in Cape Breton are generally comfortable with at least one excellent seasonal hotel. Hotel/motel rates in Cape Breton, based on double-occupancy, are categorized as follows: *Expensive,* $39 or more; *Moderate,* $30 to $39; *Inexpensive,* under $30. Reservations for accommodations throughout Cape Breton and Nova Scotia can be made by dialing the toll-free numbers listed under "Tourist Information" in the "Exploring Halifax-Dartmouth" section.

The 10% provincial sales tax is added to all hotel/motel rates.

Most places accept the following major credit cards: American Express, MasterCard and Visa; others may also be honored. Not all establishments accept credit cards, therefore we suggest you call for information.

BADDECK. *Expensive:* **Inverary Inn.** One of the best places to stay in Cape Breton. Motel units, efficiency units, and cottages. Dining room is licensed. Private beach and children's playground. Open May 1 to November 1. Off-season rates before May 15 and after October 15. Phone 295-2674. Major credit cards.

Silver Dart Motel. Good view over Bras d'Or. Licensed dining room. Open mid-May to mid-October. Off-season rates before June 15. Efficiency units available; pets permitted. Phone 295-2340. Major credit cards.

Moderate: **Telegraph House.** Traditional place to stay. Dining room. Open year round. Phone 295-9988.

CHETICAMP. *Moderate:* **Acadian Motel.** Licensed lounge and dining room. Open year-round. Off-season rates October 30 to May 15. Phone 224-2640. Major credit cards.

Laurie's Motel. Breakfast and dinner available to registered guests. Open year-round, except closed weekends from mid-October to mid-May. Off-season rates mid-October to mid-June. Pets permitted. Phone 224–2400. Major credit cards.

IONA. *Expensive:* **Highland Heights Inn.** Comfortable and friendly hosts. Licensed dining room with good food. Open May 1 to October 31. Off-season rates before July 1 and after September 15. Croquet, hiking, birdwatching. Phone 622-2360. Major credit cards.

MARGAREE HARBOUR. *Moderate:* **Duck Cove Inn.** Licensed dining room, canoe rentals, deep-sea fishing, horse shoes, giant checkers; river salmon and trout fishing, guides available. Open June 1 to October 31. Off-season rates are in effect before June 15 and after October 15. Phone 235-2658. Major credit cards.

Whale Cove Summer Village. Modern deluxe housekeeping and overnight cottages. Laundry facilities, store, playground, deep-sea and freshwater fishing nearby. Open mid-June to mid-October. Phone 235-2202. Major credit cards.

ST. PETER'S. *Inexpensive:* **Macdonald's Hotel.** Fifteen rooms in renovated house; pets permitted; open year-round. Licensed dining room. Phone 535-2997. Major credit cards.

SYDNEY. *Expensive:* **Cape Bretoner Motel.** King's Road. 51 units. Licensed dining room. Phone 539-8101. Major credit cards.

Isle Royal Motel. Dining room, lounge and gift shop. Do not confuse with Isle Royal Hotel downtown. The motel, in the suburbs, offers comfortable accommodations. Phone 564-8101. Major credit cards.

Keddy's Motor Inn. Licensed dining room. Part of a chain noted for inconsistent quality, particularly in food service. Off-season rates November 1 to April 30. Phone 539-1140. Major credit cards.

Wandlyn Motor Inn. Coffeeshop, licensed dining room, games room. Part of chain offering clean but usually plain accommodations. In converted nursing institution which is adequate for the purpose but its architecture is odd. Pets permitted with permission from manager. Phone 539-3700. Major credit cards.

Holiday Inn of Sydney. Typical Holiday Inn located a bit away from downtown area. Coffee bar and dining room are both of minimum quality and service; pool, cocktail lounge and bar, one with live entertainment; open year-round. Off season rates October 1 to May 31. Phone 539-6750. Major credit cards.

Moderate: **Vista Motel.** Comfortable, plain accommodations. Off-season rates October 15 to June 1. Phone 539-6550. Major credit cards.

Inexpensive: **Paul's Hotel.** On the corner of Pitt and Esplanade Sts., handy to shops. 24 rooms, 5 with bath; coffee bar. Cape Breton working people use Paul's in Sydney. Phone 562-5747.

HOSTELS. Canadian Hostelling Assoc. (Nova Scotia office is located in the Trail Shop Cooperative, 6260 Quinpool Rd., Halifax; 423-8736/423-4438) have information on hostels in Halifax, Chester, Liverpool, Shelburne, Yarmouth, Annapolis-Royal, Canning, Wentworth, Amherst, New Glasgow, Antigonish, and Sheet Harbour, N.S., and Point Cross, Sydney Mines, and Seal Island, Cape Breton.

BED-AND-BREAKFAST. More than 50 Cape Breton families participate in the bed-and-breakfast program. Rates for private bedroom in the family home are about $16 a night for one, $18 per night for two, including full breakfast the following morning. For visitors on a budget or wanting to meet some very hospitable people, this is an excellent program.

Participating families display a distinctive bed-and-breakfast sign. For reservations or listings of bed-and-breakfast locations, contact the Cape Breton Tourist Information Bureau, 20 Keltic Dr., Sydney River, Nova Scotia; the Cape Breton Development Corporation, P.O. Box 1330, Sydney, Nova Scotia, or the Nova Scotia Department of Tourism.

HOW TO GET AROUND. From the airport: Transportation from Sydney airport is operated by *Briands Cabs.* A one-way trip is about $3.00 to downtown hotels. Briand's Cabs and *Bill's Yellow Cabs* operate scheduled tours of the Cabot Trail and to the Fortress of Louisbourg.

Car rental: Rent-a-car agencies are located at the airport and most also have downtown offices. Cars should be reserved in advance, particularly during the summer season.

By bus: Several small bus companies operate local service to communities in Cape Breton from Sydney. For up-to-date schedules, contact the Cape Breton Tourist Board.

By car: Using your own transportation is still the best way to get around Cape Breton. Most highways are paved and in good condition, although secondary roads may be winding and hilly. The local people know the roads and will drive faster than most visitors. Pull over and let them pass if they seem to be tailgating—it makes everyone happier and a lot safer.

By ferry: Two car ferries operate on route 223—one at Little Narrows and another at Grand Narrows. Both operate 24 hours a day on a 10- to 15-minute schedule. Fare for each passage is about 50¢ per vehicle.

TOURIST INFORMATION. The Department of Tourism operates a tourist information center at Port Hastings (625–1717) at the entry point to Cape Breton by highway. The Cape Breton Tourist Board has one at Sydney River (539–9876). Otherwise, all Nova Scotia tourist bureaus have information on Cape Breton. Or write: Nova Scotia Department of Tourism, P.O. Box 130, Halifax, Nova Scotia B3J 2M7.

For information on seasonal events, camping parks and national parks, regional theater, and other bits of practical information for Cape Breton see the *Practical Information for Nova Scotia* section.

TOURS. Tours by passenger car to Louisbourg, Miner's Museum, Bell Museum, and the Cabot Trail are operated by *Cape Breton Tours,* 263 Esplanade, Sydney; call 564-6200 or 564-6151. Operates from mid-May to September 20. *Yellow Cabs Ltd.* operates tours to the same Cape Breton destinations from May 15 to October 15. Address is 10 Pitt St., Sydney; call 564-4481 or 564-8161. Contact operators for rates, duration, and departure times.

Cape Breton is part of many coach tours operating from points in the United States and Canada. For information, contact a travel agent or the Nova Scotia Department of Tourism.

RESORTS. The Keltic Lodge at Ingonish Beach is one of the province's most elaborate resorts. It has 32 rooms in the main lodge, 40 motel rooms, and 24 cottages. It has convention space, sitting rooms with fireplaces, and there's evening entertainment in a licensed lounge. It operates year-round and features a wide array of indoor and outdoor activities—golf, skiing, fishing, tennis, swimming and so on. European Plan and Modified American Plan (dinner and breakfast included). Two-, three-, five- and seven-day packages available. Phone 285-2880. Major credit cards.

The **Dundee Golf Course and Cottages** at Dundee, overlooking the Bras D'Or lakes, is more modest. It has 39 fully equipped housekeeping cottages, swimming pool, marina, tennis, 9-hole golf course, pro-shop, licensed dining room and lounge. Phone 345-2649. Major credit cards.

SPORTS. Several Cape Breton waters, ranging from quiet rivers to expert white water runs, are highly regarded by **canoeing** enthusiasts. The Cape Breton Tourist Association has several good publications and maps. For canoe route information, contact Sport Nova Scotia, P.O. Box 3010 South, Halifax, N.S. (425–5450), or the Nova Scotia Bookstore, 1597 Hollis St., Halifax, N.S.

Golf courses come in various sizes and ratings from several good nine hole courses like the professionally designed lakeside course at Dundee (off Rte. 4) to the championship 18 hole Cape Breton Highlands in the National Park. **Tennis** is also a popular sport; a number of communities have outdoor courts open to the public.

Scuba divers find Louisbourg Harbour and waters off southern Cape Breton excellent for wreck hunting. Contact Jim Wilson at Dive Cape Breton Ltd., P.O. Box 130, Louisbourg, or call 733-2877 for information on underwater tours of 1–5 days.

Hikers will find a variety of trails in the national park. There's a booklet on hiking called *Walk Cape Breton* available at tourist bureaus. **Anglers** may seek Atlantic salmon and trout in streams and rivers. Angling regulations are available from the Nova Scotia Department of Tourism.

Yacht rentals for **sailing** the 450 square mile Bras d'Or Lakes are available from: Baddeck Marine & Sports (sloop daysailers & charters), 295-2434; Bras d'Or Charter (all types of sailboats), 295-2756; Anchors Aweigh (paddleboats, canoes, tours) in Baddeck, 295-2713 and on *The Balaema,* a 32-ft. diesel schooner out of Margaree Harbour, 235-2943. Cruises to Bird Islands ($6 a person) by Boularderie Cruises in Big Bras d'Or, 674-2384.

For those who bring their own boat, launching ramps are located at a number of sites along the Bras d'Or. Check with the tourist information bureau for the closest one.

The Nova Scotia Department of Recreation operates supervised **swimming** at Port Hood Beach, Inverness Beach, Dominion Beach, and East Bay Beach.

For **skiing** during the winter months, the Cape Smokey Ski Centre at Ingonish on the Cabot Trail operates three major runs of about one mile each. The biggest drop is about 1,000 feet. Snow from December to mid-April. Double chairlift and pony. Call 285-2588 for snow conditions.

For specific information, contact the Cape Breton Tourist Board or the Nova Scotia Department of Tourism.

 MUSEUMS AND HISTORIC SITES. Cape Breton has a number of local history museums and several very unique museum complexes which will appeal to visitors.

Mining coal has long been a way of life in Cape Breton. The first recorded mining operation was by the French who, in 1720, dug into an exposed coal seam at Port Morien. The site of this mine and other 19th-century operations is the first stop on the *Three Mine Tour* in the Glace Bay area. Two hundred million year old fossils can be seen in the coal face at the walk-in mine. Open from noon to 8 P.M. during July and Aug.

The second stop is at the *Miners Museum* in Glace Bay which displays a 200-year history of mining in the area. Visitors can walk into the Ocean Deeps Colliery with a veteran miner accompanying each group. The Men of the Deeps, an internationally known miners' choral group, sing weekly in summer evening concerts. Check with museum for times. The mining area has a very low roof in places and, although quite safe, is definitely not for claustrophobics. Helmets and protective shawls are provided. The adjoining *Miner's Village* has a replica of the company store and company housing. The Miner's Village Restaurant is licensed and serves seafood prepared by local women—nice surroundings with coal oil lamps. The museum, located at Quarry Point in Glace Bay, is open daily, mid-June to mid-September, from 9 A.M. to 8:30 P.M., and the rest of the year on Wednesday from 9 A.M. to 9 P.M., and Thursdays to Sundays from 9 A.M. to 5 P.M. The restaurant is open 9 A.M. to 9 P.M. daily, year-round (Reservations: 849–9344). Tour costs about $1.75 for adults and 75¢ for children, $1.00 for students. Museum free.

The third mine is the *Princess Colliery* in *Sydney Mines* where visitors descend 682 feet to the pit bottom before being hoisted back to the surface in coal boxes on the mine railway. Protective clothing is provided. Quite safe but not for the claustrophobic or the faint of heart. Open during July and August from 11 A.M. to 7 P.M. Admission is about $2.00 for adults.

The *S&L Railway Museum* in Louisbourg is in a restored 1895 railway station. Open June 1 to Labor Day, daily. Free. Special tours, by appointment.

The *Old Sydney Museum* in the St. Patrick's Church Building is open June 1–July 4, daily 1–6 P.M.; July 5–August 15, daily 1–9 P.M.; August 16–October 9, daily 1–6 P.M. Free.

The Garrison Church, circa 1784, in Sydney, Charlotte at Nepean St., allegedly the oldest parish in Cape Breton, was built with stones from the wrecked buildings of Louisbourg.

In Sydney, *Cossitt House,* is the restored residence of Rev. Ranna Cossitt, the oldest house in Sydney, built around 1787. Open May 15 to October 15.

In Baddeck, the *Alexander Graham Bell Museum* has excellent displays of the works of the inventor of the telephone and the first airplane to fly in the British Empire. A replica of Bell's schooner-sized Hydrofoil, along with the dismembered original are on display. Free admission. Open May 20 to October 15 from 9 A.M. to 9 P.M. and October 15 to May 15 from 9 A.M. to 5 P.M., except holidays. Tel. 295-2069.

Victoria County Archives & Museum in Baddeck offers well-organized archives of local history. Free. Open summer months to the public.

Fortress Louisbourg, at Louisbourg, is the most ambitious restoration project ever undertaken in Canada. The original fortress, constructed by the French 1720–45, was the major French fortification in Acadia and a focal point of struggle between the French and English until its total destruction by the English in 1760. Restored homes are "inhabited," and the lifestyle is that of 1750, complete with town "characters." A new interpretive center was opened in 1976 and provides a long range view of the fortress, looking much as it did in 1750. If you are a history, architecture, or restoration buff, plan to spend at least a half day there. A park bus takes visitors from the interpretive center to the Fortress proper. 733–2280. Bus fare is included in the fee which is about $2.00 for adults and about 50¢ for children. A maximum family rate of about $4.00 gets everybody in.

The *Nova Scotia Highland Village* on Rte. 233 at Iona is a collection of refurbished and reconstructed buildings—a carding mill, forge, country store, school and cabin—recalling the early Scottish settlers to the area. Open June 15 to Oct. 15, 10 A.M. to 5 P.M. daily. Admission is about 50¢ for adults and 25¢ for children. The *Acadian Museum* in Cheticamp is more of a handcraft shop and village center. Local women demonstrate Acadian-style rug hooking, weaving, and spinning. Snack bar.

The *Margaree Salmon Museum* at North East Margaree has a collection of fishing paraphenalia used on the famous Margaree River in search of the fighting Atlantic salmon. Open 9 A.M. to 5 P.M. daily, mid-June to mid-October. Admission for adults is about 25¢, children 10¢.

In Margaree, the *Museum of Cape Breton Heritage* has a collection of Scottish, Acadian and Indian household items, and arts and crafts. Free. Closed Sundays.

The *Gaelic College of Celtic Folk Arts and Highland Crafts* at St. Ann's on the Cabot Trail welcomes visitors to the daily concerts and the grounds. Bagpipes and drums only. Small charge for the evening concerts; afternoon practice sessions are free. For information, call 295–2877.

St. Ann's has the *Giant MacAskill Highland Pioneers Museum.* Free. Open May 24–October 15 from 9 A.M. to 5 P.M.

South Cape Breton. In Arichat, the *Le Noir Forge* (off Rte. 4 on 320), a restored 18th-century stone blacksmith shop with working forge. Adults, 25¢, children 10¢. Open July and August on Sundays from 1 to 5 P.M. and Monday to Saturday from 9 A.M. to 12 P.M.

The Nicholas Denys Museum in St. Peter's (Rte. 4) has implements and artifacts from as far back as 1638. Adults 25¢, children 10¢. Open June 1 to September 30 from 9 A.M. to 5 P.M.

The *Marble Mountain Museum & Library* in Marble Mountain (off Rte. 105 or Rte. 4 at Cleveland) shows the history of limestone quarries and the business of Marble Mountain. Free. Open in summer months only.

MUSIC. Much of the music of Cape Breton takes a traditional form—bagpipes, fiddle, guitar, and piano with voices singing folk style songs in English, French, or Gaelic. Throughout the summer visitors will find Scottish concerts at places such as *Broad Cove* and traditional Scottish Ceilidh's (kay'lees) in various Cape Breton communities.

The *Gaelic College* at St. Ann's has daily concerts by students. Afternoon session, from about 2 to 3 P.M.; evening session, from about 7 to 8 P.M. most days during July and August. For exact times, contact the Cape Breton Tourist Association at 20 Keltic Dr., Sydney River, or the nearest local tourist bureau.

The *Gaelic Mod* at St. Ann's in early August and *Iona Highland Village Day*, usually the first weekend in August, are excellent showcases for Scottish and other Cape Breton talent in dance, piping, and traditional music.

Every second year in early July, the village of Glendale (in Inverness County just off Rte. 105) hosts a weekend festival of Cape Breton fiddling and stepdancing, with fiddlers returning to Cape Breton from all over the continent. *The* music event of the year in Cape Breton when it's held. Look for Scottish concerts in Frenchvale, Cheticamp, Mabou, St. Ann's and summer festivals in Marion Bridge, St. Joseph du Moine, Wycocomagh, Margaree, Petit de Grat, and Louisbourg—and for Cape North's *Blueberry Festival: Action Week & Highland Games* in Sydney; the *Community Bazaar* in Arichat; *Highland Dancing* festival in St. Peter's (Rte. 4); the *Richmond Exhibition* in Louisdale (off Rte. 4); and the *Festival of the Strait,* a week-long celebration in Port Hawkesbury. N.S. Department of Tourism's *Calendar of Events,* or local newspaper supplements, will give you exact dates and times.

The *Men of the Deeps* is a male choir made up of coalminers from the Cape Breton area. They have toured many North American centers and have also toured China. Tourist information bureaus have schedule.

DINING OUT. Dining out in Cape Breton can be something of an adventure in the specialty restaurants and a taste delight (French cuisine) in the island's best dining room.

Ask your waiter or waitress to suggest the best items on the daily menu or the specials of the day.

Most places accept the following major credit cards: American Express, MasterCard and Visa; others may also be honored. Not all establishments accept credit cards, therefore we suggest you call for information.

Restaurants are categorized on the basis of a full-course dinner, with drinks, tax, and tips excluded: *Expensive,* over $15; *Moderate,* $10–15; *Inexpensive,* under $10.

LOUISBOURG. *Expensive:* **Épée Royalle.** 18th-century French dining with 18th-century animation. Open June to September from 11 A.M. to 8 P.M. daily. Licensed. Phone 733–2280. Major credit cards.

L'Hotel de la Marine. Part of the Fortress Louisbourg restoration, the dining room has been recreated to portray the lifestyle of Louisbourg of the 1740's. Food is prepared from authentic 18th-century French recipes and served in that informal style. Atmosphere is excellent; food is wholesome and interesting. Open from about 11 A.M. to 8 P.M. from June to Sept. Phone 733–2280. Major credit cards.

Moderate: **Grubstake Restaurant.** Pleasant surroundings, good food. Phone 733–2308. Credit cards.

Inexpensive: **Lobster Kettle,** Seafood by the wharf. Phone 733–2877. Visa only.

INGONISH BEACH. *Expensive:* **Keltic Lodge Dining Room.** International cuisine and an excellent choice of menu—all for the one table d'hôte price. Good wine selection. Strict atmosphere of resort luxury: Jackets for men; women requested not to wear casual attire at dinner (e.g., no daytime pant suits, jeans, etc.). Open mid-June to mid-October. Reservations necessary. The Lodge's

Coffee Shop, open 8 A.M. to 10 P.M., is moderately priced. Phone 285–2880. Major credit cards.

IONA. *Moderate:* **Highland Heights Inn.** Scottish home-style cooking, with fresh fish in season. Atmosphere of a Scottish inn with huge stone fireplace in dining room, overlooking the Bras d'Or at Grand Narrows. Licensed. Phone 622–2360. Major credit cards.

MARGAREE HARBOUR. *Moderate:* **Schooner Restaurant "Marian Elizabeth."** Aboard a former fishing schooner built in Nova Scotia in 1918; now permanently beached in Margaree Harbour. Licensed with seafood specialties. The chowder is usually excellent; the atmosphere is an experience. Open mid-May to mid-October. Call for reservations. Phone 235-2317.

CHETICAMP. *Moderate.* **Acadian Museum** serves delicious old Acadian food in tiny restaurant.

ST. PETER'S. *Moderate–Expensive:* **Macdonald's Hotel.** Home-style and French cuisine; children's plates half price; open year-round. Licensed. Good food, nice people. Attached to a 13-room inn in an old Richmond County Home on Rte. 4. Phone 535-2997. Major credit cards.

SYDNEY. *Expensive:* **Petit Jean.** Tries to be French; succeeds moderately well. Lunch on Monday to Friday only from noon–2 P.M.; dinner daily 6 P.M. to 10 P.M. Call for reservations. Phone 539-4671.
　Moderate: **Jasper's.** Open 24 hours with plain, tasty food. Beer and wine license. Phone 564–6181.
　Joe's Warehouse. Good food. Cabaret on lower floor called *Smooth Herman's.* A fun place. Phone 539–6686.
　Inexpensive: **Venice Pizzeria.** On Welton St. Try their Mexican food. Phone 539-4973.

SYDNEY MINES. *Moderate:* **The Cauldron.** Located at the Princess Tourist Mine. Open daily May to September. Home-cooked-style food with daily specials. Phone 736-6823.

WHYCOCOMAGH. *Moderate:* **Village Inn.** Home-cooked meals in tiny country inn. Old-style friendly service and delicious food. Licensed. Make reservations, 756–2002. Major credit cards.

PRACTICAL INFORMATION FOR NOVA SCOTIA

HOW TO GET THERE. By car: The Trans-Canada Hwy. eastbound will deliver you to Nova Scotia by the overland route through New Brunswick, entering the province at Amherst.

　By ferry: Visitors may also reach Nova Scotia by one of the six-car ferry connections from Maine, New Brunswick, Prince Edward Island, and Newfoundland.

　Passenger and vehicle ferry service is operated between Yarmouth, Nova Scotia, and Portland, Maine, by *CN Marine* and by *Prince of Fundy Cruises.* A one-way trip takes between 10 and 12 hours. Cabins, dining facilities, entertainment, and recreation are available on both ferries. Advance reservations must be made for both vessels, especially during the summer season. Contact Prince of Fundy Cruises at the International Terminal in Portland. Call (207) 775-5611. CN Marine may be booked through any CN ticket office in Canada or by calling toll-free in Maine (800) 432-7344 or toll-free (800) 341-7981 in mid-Northeastern United States. Or contact a travel agent for bookings. There is also a CN Marine passenger and vehicle ferry service between Yarmouth and Bar Harbour, Me. Crossing time: six hours. Same telephone information as for Portland ferry.

CN Marine also operates frequent vehicle and passenger service between Saint John, New Brunswick, and Digby, Nova Scotia. The 40-mile crossing takes about 2½ hours. Make reservations in advance, especially for summer months. Book through any CN ticket office in Canada or by calling toll-free in Maine (800) 432-7344 or toll free in mid-Northeastern United States or book through a travel agent.

The ferry service between North Sydney, Nova Scotia, and the Newfoundland ports of Argentia (summer service) and Port-aux-Basques (year-round service) is also operated by CN Marine. The crossing to Port-aux-Basques takes about 6 hours; to Argentia about 18 hours. Cabins, dining, entertainment, and recreation facilities are available on the vessels. Bookings may be made at the above CN Marine numbers or through a travel agent. Make reservations for Argentia, especially during the summer season, and on the Port-aux-Basques night service. Reservations are not accepted on the Port-aux-Basques day service.

Passenger and vehicle service between Wood Islands, Prince Edward Island, and Caribou [near Pictou], Nova Scotia, is operated from May to late December by *Northumberland Ferries Limited*. The 14-mile crossing takes about an hour. Lunch-counter facilities are available but there are no cabins. Reservations are not accepted and the line-ups may take several hours during the summer season. It is best to cross early [first ferry leaves at 6 A.M. in summer] or late in the evening. For information, contact Northumberland Ferries, P.O. Box 634, Charlottetown, P.E.I., or call (902) 894–3473. In Caribou, Nova Scotia (902) 485–9015.

By train: *Via Rail* provides train service to Nova Scotia from major centers across Canada. *Amtrak* from New York makes connections with CN in Montréal.

By bus: Service to most Nova Scotia areas is provided by *Acadian Lines* and other bus companies. Connections are made at Amherst, Nova Scotia, and with the ferries at Yarmouth, Digby, Caribou and North Sydney, Nova Scotia.

By air: *Eastern Provincial Airways* flies to Halifax and Sydney, Nova Scotia, from centers within Atlantic Canada and from Toronto. *Air Canada* also flies into Halifax, Yarmouth, and Sydney from Atlantic centers—Montréal, Québec, and Toronto. *CP Air* flies from Montréal. *CP Air* and *Air Canada* have extensive national and international connections.

ACCOMMODATIONS. Accommodations are generally good and friendly throughout the province. Reservations can be made by calling the toll-free numbers listed under "Tourist Information" in the "Practical Information for Halifax/Dartmouth" section. Rates based on double-occupancy. *Expensive,* over $39; *Moderate,* $30–39; *Inexpensive,* under $30.

A 10% provincial tax will be added to your bill.

Most places accept the following major credit cards: American Express, MasterCard and Visa; others may also be honored. Not all establishments accept credit cards, therefore we suggest you call for information.

AMHERST. *Expensive:* **Wandlyn Motor Inn.** 60 units outside of the town beside the highway. Clean, comfortable accommodations with large fields for children. Two miles from New Brunswick–Nova Scotia border. Coffeeshop, licensed dining and lounge, heated outdoor pool. Off-season rates October to June. Pets with permission. Phone 667–3331. Major credit cards.

ANNAPOLIS ROYAL. *Moderate:* **Royal Anne Motel.** 20 units with licensed restaurant, gardens, and open lawns. Pleasant surroundings near most historical sites in the area. Off-season rates mid-September to mid-June. Pets allowed with permission. Phone 532–2323. Credit card: Visa only.

AULD COVE. *Moderate:* **The Cove Motel.** Secluded, on peninsula; licensed dining room overlooking the Strait of Canso, near the Canso Causeway; 31 units including 12 chalets; pets permitted. Phone 747–2700. Major credit cards.

BRIDGETOWN. *Expensive:* **Bridgetown Motor Hotel.** 33 units, comfortable accommodation, licensed dining, and lounge with bar shaped like distillery barrel. Sauna, pool, table tennis. Off-season rates mid-September to June. Attended pets permitted. Phone 665–4491. Major credit cards.

BRIDGEWATER. *Expensive.* **Wandlyn Motor Inn.** Clean, comfortable accommodations. Coffeeshop, licensed dining and lounge, indoor pool, sauna. Gift shop. Off-season rates October to June. Pets with permission. Phone 543–7131. Major credit cards.

DIGBY. *Expensive.* **The Pines.** Elegant resort. Excellent golf. Tennis, pool, fine service and gracious dining. Phone 245–2511.
Moderate–Expensive. **Admiral Digby Inn.** 40 units, licensed dining room and lounge. Indoor pool. Phone 245–2531. Major credit cards.
Moderate. **Mountain Gap Inn.** Large motel. Some cottages with one to two bedrooms. Pool, tennis, beach, bar, dining room. Phone 245–2277.

KENTVILLE. *Expensive:* **Wandlyn Motor Inn.** 75 rooms, clean, comfortable accommodations. Coffeeshop, licensed dining and lounge, pool, playground, golf green, horseshoe pit, games room, pool table; pets with permission. Off-season rates October to June. Phone 678–8311. Major credit cards.

LUNENBURG. *Inexpensive:* **Bluenose Lodge.** 9 rooms with bath; licensed dining room; deepsea fishing excursions arranged; displays local crafts. Phone 634-8851. Major credit cards.

NEW GLASGOW. *Expensive:* **Heather Motor Inn.** 76 units, clean and comfortable, licensed dining room (good seafood) and lounge. Open year-round; pets permitted. Phone 752–8401. Major credit cards.
Moderate. **Peter Pan Motel.** 390 Marsh St. Good buy. Bar, dining room, pool. Phone 752–8327.

SHEET HARBOUR. *Moderate:* **Marquis of Dufferin Hotel.** 14 units overlooking the Atlantic. Adjacent restaurant; pets permitted. Off-season rates, October to May. Phone 654–2696. Major credit cards.

TRURO. *Moderate:* **Tidal Bore Inn.** 24 rooms. Clean and comfortable; in the viewing area for the tidal bore rapids. Licensed restaurant. Open mid-May to mid-October. Off-season rates before mid-June. Phone 895–9241. Major credit cards.

WESTERN SHORE–OAK ISLAND CHANNEL. *Expensive:* **Oak Island Inn.** 71 rooms, comfortable and well-appointed. Ocean view overlooks the marina and Oak Island treasure island. Licensed dining and lounge. Pool, marina, sailboat rentals, deep sea fishing charters. Open year-round. Phone 627–2600. Major credit cards.

WOLFVILLE. *Expensive:* **Old Orchard Inn.** 74 rooms and 30 chalets with 10 efficiency units; comfortable with a spectacular view over the Annapolis Valley from the main building. Licensed dining and lounge, with nightly entertainment; coffeeshop. Pool, sauna, tennis, nature trails, playground. Motel open year-round; chalets open May to October. Phone 542–5751. Major credit cards.

YARMOUTH. *Expensive:* **Rodd's Grand Hotel.** 138 rooms, clean and comfortable, near the ferries from Portland and Bar Harbor, Maine. Licensed dining and two lounges. Pets permitted. Phone 742–2446. Major credit cards.
Manor Inn. On Hwy. 1, Colonial mansion with rose garden, estate, and lakefront; 29 rooms, licensed dining and lounge with entertainment; pets permitted. Open mid-June to October. Phone 742–7841. Major credit cards.

BED AND BREAKFAST. Nova Scotia also has a well-developed bed-and-breakfast program. Private homes that take overnight guests for as little as $15 to $22 a night. In the towns they go by the name of "guest homes." The provincial accommodations guide, available at tourist bureaus, lists them all.

TELEPHONE. The long-distance area code for the entire province (plus neighboring Prince Edward Island) is 902.

HOW TO GET AROUND. By car: Major highways in Nova Scotia are good to excellent. The routes tend to follow the coastline and the three-digit routings [e.g. 104] are the faster, but less scenic, roads. Most of the 10 routes are paralleled by the older and more scenic highways. During the summer months, Nova Scotia's unpaved highways are usually in very good condition and, aside from raising some dust, make for quiet and scenic drives.

As in the rest of Canada, summer is "highway repair time" and motorists are cautioned to be alert for the flag-people with warnings of road works ahead.

Car-rental agencies are located at both the Halifax International and Sydney airports, all Nova Scotia entry points, and in the cities of Halifax and Sydney. Reservations are necessary during the summer months and may be made through local agency offices or a travel agency.

By train: *Via Rail* serves many major centers in Nova Scotia and Via Rail operates a daily service from Halifax to Digby. For the traveler, train service in Nova Scotia is inconvenient at best. The tracks usually run through the least interesting scenery and service is not frequent. Bookings may be made at any CN ticket office in Canada or through a travel agency.

By bus: *Acadian Lines Ltd., MacKenzie Bus Line Ltd.,* and *Zinck's Bus Company Ltd.* operate daily service to all parts of Nova Scotia. Information and bookings may be made through a travel agent or by contacting Acadian Lines Limited, 6040 Almon Street, Halifax, Nova Scotia, (902) 454-9321, or an Acadian Lines office.

By air: Both *Air Canada* and *Eastern Provincial Airways* have flights between Sydney and Halifax several times daily. In Halifax, contact Air Canada at 429-7111 and EPA at 861-3860. In Sydney, call Air Canada at 539-6600 and EPA at 564-4545. Bookings may be made through any travel agency. The flight between the two cities takes about 40 minutes.

TIME ZONE. Nova Scotia is on Atlantic Time (1 hour in advance of Eastern Time).

SEASONAL EVENTS. The **winter** season in Nova Scotia is a time of performances by Neptune Theatre and the Atlantic Symphony in *Halifax* and on tour. **Winter** carnivals are held at the major universities in *Halifax, Wolfville,* and at *Antigonish* as well as at larger centers with service club sponsorship.

During **March** and **April** (maple sugar weather) the *Glooscap* Maple Sugar Festival invites visitors to the sugar bush for pancake suppers and maple candy.

As **May** turns into **June,** the Apple Blossom Festival is celebrated in the Annapolis Valley towns of *Kentville, Wolfville,* and *New Minas.* In May and June the Blessing of the Fleet is held in many French villages—*Meteghan, Main-á-Dieu, Petit de Grat*—before the boats begin the inshore and offshore fishing season. Scottish Concert and Dance, with performers from around the Maritimes, is held annually in *Pictou.* Rhododendron Sunday in *Kentville* in mid-June brings out the flower lovers. The landing of explorer John Cabot in 1497 is remembered in late June at *Cape North* in an annual pageant.

Festivals and events ranging from week-long galas to community suppers are held throughout the summer months in all parts of Nova Scotia. The Department of Tourism can provide complete lists with dates. Many of the festivals have an ethnic background—Scottish or Acadian—or feature local fishery or agricultural fairs and exhibitions. Some events have special foods—such as lobster carnivals and steer barbecues—which provide excellent informal dining at minimal costs.

July 1, as well as being Dominion Day, is also the Gathering of the Clans in *Pugwash* and the beginning of the multi-cultural festival known as the Festival of the Strait in *Port Hawkesbury.* The first week sees the Annual Lobster Supper Weekend in *St. Peter's.* The *Sydney* Highland Games take place in early July, as do the Maritime Old Time Fiddling Contest in *Dartmouth,* the *Pictou* Lobster Carnival, the *Antigonish* Highland Games, and the Acadian Festival of *Clare* held at Meteghan River. In *Kingston,* two steers are barbecued in mid-July.

The *Margaree* Summer Festival is held in late July. The fictional clock salesman, Sam Slick, is remembered in the home town of his creator during Sam Slick Days and Regatta in *Windsor* at that time, and the Acadian Day Festival in *L'Ardoise* and the East Pictou Annual Fair in Thorburn are held in late July.

Once again in a Scottish vein, the Gaelic Mod is the attraction at the Gaelic College in *St. Ann's* early in **August** when the South Shore Exhibition in *Bridgewater* begins the series of agricultural fairs and exhibitions throughout the province. In *New Glasgow* early in August kilts swirl at the Festival of the Tartans and at Highland Village Day in *Iona.* The Piper's Picnic in *Earltown* is the scene for pipe bands, highland dancing and a gathering of the clans. In mid-August rockhounds from many parts of North America congregate in the *Parrsboro* area for the annual Rockhound Round-up. The *Canso* Regatta, the traditional *Johnstown* Milling Frolic, the Highland Summer Festival in *Inverness,* and Scallop Day in *Digby* are other local events in mid-August.

Throughout July and August there are Scottish concerts and many communities have a Ceilidh (kay-lee) with piping and fiddling and Gaelic folk singing.

During early **September** the blueberry is king in the *Amherst* area during the Blueberry Festival, while in *Lunenburg* the Nova Scotia Fisheries Exhibition celebrates the harvest from the sea.

TOURS. *Nova Tours Ltd.* operates several bus tours per season through Nova Scotia. For departure dates and rates, telephone 429-3702. Other operators offering bus tours through Nova Scotia and other Maritime Provinces are *Evangeline Tours,* Wolfville (542-9109); and *Atlantic Tours,* Saint John, New Brunswick (657-6386). Also *Bridges Tours,* Halifax (422-8462), and *Village Bus Tours,* P.O. Box 35, Cornwallis, Nova Scotia B05 1H0.

The Nova Scotia Department of Tourism can provide complete information on guided and self-guiding tours of the province.

SPECIAL INTEREST SIGHTSEEING. The Canada Department of Agriculture Research Station in Kentville conducts poultry and horticultural research on its 650-acre site. Open Monday to Friday from 8:30 A.M. to 5 P.M.

Wildlife parks with native animals and birds in natural open settings are operated by the province at Shubenacadie, about 48 kms. (30 miles) from Halifax on Rte. 102, at Upper Clements on Rte. 1 between Annapolis Royal and Digby, and near Marion Bridge, about 20 miles from Sydney. Open May 1 to end of October from 8:30 A.M. to 7:30 P.M. daily. Wear walking shoes and take a camera. A good way to entertain children.

NATIONAL PARKS. The two national parks in Nova Scotia offer you great contrasts. Cape Breton Highlands National Park is high and forested with sheer cliffs dropping off into the sea. Kejimkujik National Park is inland —a hilly forested area with many lakes.

Cape Breton Highlands is partially ringed by the spectacular Cabot Trail. The interior of the Park is wilderness and inaccessible by normal means. The 950 sq. kms. (367 square miles) area has numerous rivers which provide good fishing and the forest is home to many animals. Facilities in the park are available for fishing (provincial regulations apply), excellent hiking with nature trails starting at the highway, canoeing, and camping including a trailer park. There are also an interpretive center and a very good 18-hole championship golf course. Rates for golf are about $5 per day and about $25 weekly. A number of saltwater beaches on the eastern coast offer excellent swimming.

Cape Breton Highlands is both a summer and winter park, with extensive skiing facilities and other winter activities. For more information, contact the Superintendent, Cape Breton Highlands National Park, Ingonish Beach, Cape Breton, Nova Scotia B0C 1L0.

Kejimkujik (ke-jim-kú-gik) National Park is in the western part of the province and is reached by Hwy. 8 between Liverpool and Annapolis Royal. A former Micmac Indian reservation, the park was named for the largest lake.

The 381-sq.-km. (238-square mile) park has a relatively mild winter climate combined with many lakes inhabited by a wide range of reptiles and amphibians. Essentially a wilderness, Kejimkujik has well marked canoe routes into the interior with primitive campsites.

There are park facilities for camping, boating and boat rentals, hiking (nature trails), fishing (under provincial regulations), and freshwater swimming. There is also an interpretive center. Many animals live in the park and in the adjoining Tobeatic Game Sanctuary. Deer are often seen.

Kejimkujik has one minor problem—dog ticks, introduced into the area by the hunting dogs used by United States hunters earlier in the century. Although the ticks do not carry disease and are easily removed from the skin, tight-fitting clothing and a thorough examination after being in the woods are necessary. During midsummer, the pest declines in numbers and is virtually gone by autumn. Visitors with dogs and other domestic animals must be careful to avoid a tick infestation on the pet. Visitors who avoid the heavy woods are not likely to have any problem.

For additional information on Kejimkujik National Park, contact the Superintendent, P.O. Box 36, Maitland Bridge, Annapolis County, Nova Scotia B0T 1N0.

Both national parks have a user fee of about $1.00 per vehicle per day, $2.00 for a 4-day pass, and $10.00 for an annual pass valid for all Canadian national parks. There is no charge for vehicles passing through Cape Breton National Park on the Cabot Trail.

Camping fees in both parks range from about $4.50 to about $8.00 per day depending on the facilities.

PROVINCIAL CAMPING PARKS. Provincial campgrounds are located throughout the province. All have well-managed facilities and all except Beaver Mountain have picnic sites.

Battery. 114 acres, almost 2 kms. (one mile) north of St. Peter's on Rte. 4. Features hiking trails.

Beaver Mountain. 329 acres off Rte. 104 at Beaver Mountain Road between New Glasgow and Antigonish.

Blomidon. 1667 acres, 16 kms. (10 miles) north of Canning on Rte. 1. Has a spectacular lookout over the Bay of Fundy with the world's highest tides.

Boylston. 225 acres, 6½ kms. (4 miles) north of Guysborough on Rte. 16.

Caribou. 78 acres, 8 kms. (5 miles) north of Pictou on Rte. 106 near the ferry from Prince Edward Island. Has hiking and swimming area.

Ellenwood Lake. 281 acres, 19 kms. (12 miles) northeast of Yarmouth on Rte. 340. Has hiking trails and a boat-launch ramp. Lake swimming.

Five Islands. 1020 acres, 24 kms. (15 miles) east of Parrsboro on Rte. 2 along the Bay of Fundy coast. Has hiking trails and unique scenery.

Graves Island. 123 acres, 3 kms. (2 miles) east of Chester on Rte. 3.

Laurie. 71 acres, 40 kms. (25 miles) north of Halifax on Rte. 2. Has hiking trails and boat launch ramp.

Mira River. 216 acres, 24 kms. (15 miles) south east of Sydney on Rte. 22. Has boat launch ramp and hiking trails along the river.

Porter's Lake. 216 acres, 19 kms. (12 miles) east of Dartmouth on Rte. 7. Has hiking trails and boat launch ramp on the lake.

Risser's Beach. 18 acres, 27 kms. (16 miles) south of Bridgewater on Rte. 331. Has an interpretive center and one of the best beaches in Nova Scotia, but the water is cool at the best of times.

Salsman, 26 acres, 13 kms. (8 miles) south of Goshen off Rte. 316; *Saltsprings,* 76 acres, 24 kms. (15 miles) west of New Glasgow; and *Valleyview,* 134 acres, 5 kms. (3 miles) north of Bridgetown off Rte. 1, have no facilities except for camping and picnics, although *Valleyview* does have an excellent view over the lower Annapolis Valley farming country.

Smiley's. 100 acres, 13 kms. (8 miles) east of Windsor on Rte. 14; and *Wentworth,* 243 acres at Wentworth Centre on Rte. 104, have hiking trails.

The Islands. 62 acres, 5 kms. (3 miles) west of Shelburne, on Rte. 3; and *Whycocomagh,* 503 acres, east of the community of Whycocomagh on Rte. 105, have hiking trails and boat launch ramps.

These provincial recreation areas are open from mid-May to mid-October. Most have water, toilet facilities, fireplaces, and firewood or some of these; many have sewage disposal stations. Camping fees at most recreation areas begin at about $5 per day depending on the facilities.

A number of provincial camping parks and day-use parks (without camping areas) are spotted around the province overlooking scenic views or by the water.

BEACHES. The Nova Scotia Department of Recreation operates supervised beaches in the following areas: on the Northumberland Strait coast at Heather Beach, Caribou Beach, Melmerby Beach; on the Nova Scotia Atlantic coast at Summerville Beach, Rissers Beach, Queensland Beach, Crystal Crescent Beach, Lawrencetown Beach, Martinique Beach, Clam Harbour Beach and Taylor Head Beach. There is a supervised swimming area in Kejimkujik National Park with freshwater swimming. There is also supervised freshwater swimming at Ellenwood Lake Beach and both fresh and saltwater beaches in the Cape Breton National Highland Park.

In addition, there are dozens of unsupervised beaches ranging from small strips to huge sandy beaches such as Mavililette Beach at Cape St. Mary about 24 kms. (15 miles) north of Yarmouth. On the Northumberland Strait coast, the summer water temperature is in the 18–21°C. (65–70°F.) range, quite pleasant for swimming. The Atlantic coast water temperatures range from distinctly cool to dangerously cold.

FARM AND COUNTRY VACATIONS. More than 40 Nova Scotia families are members of the farm and country vacation program. This includes farmers, fishermen, and rural people who have opened their homes to guests on a year-round or seasonal basis.

Country vacation guests live, eat, and become part of the host family for a few days or weeks. Guests may take part in the farm activities or go fishing with the host. Many country vacation homes have swimming, fishing, and hiking facilities on or near their property.

Guests are advised to take along old clothes and extra shoes and boots. Paying for the vacation is more easily done on arrival. Ask before bringing along the family pet.

Costs range from about $85 to $125 per person per week; children under twelve from about $50 to $60 per week. Includes three home-cooked, home-grown meals plus snacks each day. Reservations should be made early and directly with the country family chosen. Information and listings of families in the program may be obtained from the Nova Scotia Department of Tourism or at individual tourist bureaus.

RESORTS. *Expensive:* **Liscombe Lodge.** At Liscombe Mills, on Hwy. 7 (Marine Dr. 35 units, including cottages and chalets. Tennis, boat, and canoe rentals, lawn games, deep-sea and freshwater fishing, marina. Phone 779–2307 (in winter, 424–3258). Major credit cards.

The Pines Resort Hotel. At Digby. 90 bedrooms in main lodge, 60 more in deluxe cottages. Licensed dining room with dress regulations in effect. Live entertainment, outdoor swimming pool, floodlit tennis courts, 18-hole golf course, other activities. Modified American Plan optional (breakfast and dinner). Phone 245-2511. Major credit cards.

Moderate: **The Mountain Gap Inn.** At Smith's Cove near Digby. 100 motel units and 12 cottages. Licensed lounge and dining room. 25 acres of landscaped ground with tidal-beach frontage. Swimming pool, tennis courts, conference and convention facilities. Phone 865–9356. Major credit cards.

White Point Beach Lodge. At Hunt's Point, near Liverpool. 300-acre beach resort with ocean beach, freshwater lake, heated pool, golf course, tennis courts, boating facilities. 24 rooms in lodges and 40 cottages with one to three bedrooms. Phone 354-3177. Major credit cards.

 CHILDREN'S ACTIVITIES. With many picnic and recreation areas, the main highways tend to follow the coast where children can safely explore beaches and rocks.

The wildlife parks at Shubenacadie, near Halifax/Dartmouth, in Upper Clements near Digby and at Marion Bridge, near Sydney, are good for a half day each. No admission fee.

Many of the provincial parks have special areas for kids, and many of the commercial camping parks have playgrounds. At Cabotland, Cape Breton, at the junction of Rte. 105 and the Cabot Trail, there is a children's farm with pettable animals, pony rides and other attractions.

Fishing can provide hours of enjoyment. Saltwater fishing requires no license and in most places youngsters can fish from the local wharf with some hope of a catch.

Bryce and Sylvia Milne, Grand Pré, Nova Scotia, have a large farm with riding horses and lots of pets. The Milnes are members of the farm and country vacation program, but they take only children—up to three at a time. Cost is about $125 per week per child, which includes everything. Address: P.O. Box 31, Grand Pré, N.S. 3OP 1M0; 542-3054.

 SUMMER SPORTS. Boating: During the summer Nova Scotians take to the water. Nova Scotia's most famous ship, the *Bluenose II*—a reproduction of the original race champion fishing schooner, *Bluenose I*— sails daily except Mondays from the Privateer's Wharf in Halifax for 2-hour harbor cruises. Call 424-4247 for information. Halifax Water Tours offers tours of Halifax Harbour and environs, starting from Historic Properties. Phone 423-7783. Guided walking tours of the islands of Halifax Harbour take place May 15 to September 25. Boat leaves from near the Maritime Museum of the Atlantic. Call 422-9523. Along the *South Shore,* the Oak Island Inn Marina at Western Shore, Lunenburg County (627-2600) gives tours of the Mahone Bay area and charters large and small sailboats. In Dayspring, R.R. No. 3, Bridgewater, in Lunenburg County, Brian Stokes has a 34-foot ketch, two lasers, and 18-foot keel sloops available, with or without crew; he also gives sailing lessons. 543-3658. In Chester, Lunenburg County, you can take 2½-hour cruises on the *Buccaneer Lady,* a 50-foot cabin cruiser, sailing from the Buccaneer Lodge in Chester (275-3505). In Mahone Bay, Whitehouse Marine Ltd. (627-2641 in-season, 861-3418 off-season) charters a crewed boat, sailing out of Oak Island Marina. Marriotts Cove Charter (275-4886) has bare boat or skippered charters in the Mahone Bay–St. Margaret's Bay area aboard the 25-foot diesel auxiliary ketch *Ailsa III.* In Lunenburg, *Timberwind,* an authentic 35-foot gaff-rigged sailing schooner, sails daily, June to late September, from the Lunenburg Fisheries Museum four times a day. $8.50 per person. Charters also available. Phone 634-4400. Along the *Northumberland Shore,* contact the Tatamagouche Tourist Bureau in Tatamagouche, Nova Scotia, for information.

The Nova Scotia Dept. of Tourism's brochure *Sail Nova Scotia* has additional information on marinas, charters and rentals.

Canoe route information is available from the Nova Scotia Government Bookstore, 1597 Hollis St., Halifax, and the Canadian Hostelling Assoc., 5516 Spring Garden Rd., Halifax. The publication *Canoe Cape Breton* is available for $1.00 from the Cape Breton Development Corporation, Sydney, Nova Scotia.

Golf: Nova Scotia and Cape Breton have 38 golf courses as well as driving ranges and miniature golf courses, all described in *Golf Nova Scotia,* available, free, from the N.S. Dept. of Tourism.

Tennis is popular and many private clubs have excellent courts. For a list of public courts, contact the Nova Scotia Department of Tourism.

Bicycling: Information prepared by *Bicycle Nova Scotia* is available from the Nova Scotia Dept. of Tourism, P.O. Box 130, Halifax, Nova Scotia B3J 2M7.

Other Sports: The Tourism Department will also supply complete information on other popular activities such as *hiking, bicycle touring, golf* courses and fees, *scuba diving, fishing* in both fresh- and salt-water, and *hunting.*

CAMPING OUT. Nova Scotia has a large number of private and provincial (government) campgrounds throughout the province. The provincial recreation areas listed in the previous section all have camping facilities, as have the two national parks.

Private campgrounds are inspected by the provincial department of tourism and licensed if they pass inspection. The better campgrounds display the "Approved Campground" sign issued by the Department of Tourism. The awarding of the approval sign is based on an operation displaying a high degree of cleanliness, comfort, and hospitality over and above the necessary minimum for licensing.

Minimum charge at most private campgrounds is about $5.00; the maximum is dependent on the services provided. Provincial recreation area campground charges begin at about $4.00; and, in the national parks, at about $3.50. The national parks also have a user permit of about $1 per vehicle per day, $2 for a four day pass, and $10 for an annual pass valid at all Canadian national parks.

Camping in Nova Scotia is allowed only at designated camping areas. No camping is allowed in picnic areas, day use parks, or along public highways.

WINTER SPORTS. Skiing, particularly cross-country, is becoming more popular in Nova Scotia but the province does not have the heavy and consistent snowfall necessary to make it a great ski area. January, February, and March usually provide the best snow, but it is not unusual for snow to be wiped out by a warm rain early in the season.

Other sports: *Ice skating, ice boating,* and *snowshoeing* are also popular winter sports.

Contact the Nova Scotia Department of Tourism for information.

HISTORIC SITES. The first permanent European settlement north of the Gulf of Mexico was at Port Royal in what is now Nova Scotia. Here, in 1605, the French explorers Champlain and de Monts established their *Habitation,* or trading post, which stood until Virginian raiders scattered the French and leveled the buildings in 1613.

To reach the Habitation compound, now rebuilt, follow Rte. 1 toward Annapolis Royal and turn off to the right (if approaching Annapolis Royal from the east) just before crossing the Annapolis Causeway.

Fort Anne National Historic Park in Annapolis Royal documents part of the two-century French-English struggle for North America. Check open hours; call 532–5197.

Longfellow's poetic story of Evangeline and Gabriel, two Acadians driven apart by the French-English struggles, has its memorial at *Grand Pré National Historic Site* near Wolfville. The interpretive center has displays and artifacts. Call 542–3631.

Fort Edward, in the town of Windsor, has the oldest surviving blockhouse in Canada. Call 426–5080.

With the exception of Fortress Louisbourg (see *Practical Information for Cape Breton*) there is no admission charge to any National Historic Sites which are usually open from mid-May to mid-October, 9 A.M. to 8 P.M., though times may vary with the site. For material on any of the sites, write to Parks Canada—Atlantic Region, 5161 George Street, Halifax, Nova Scotia B3J 1M7, (902) 426–3405.

MUSEUMS AND SITES. Nova Scotia has a well developed series of museums, living museums, and historic homes and buildings. Most towns have a small local museum which depicts the history of the area.

The Nova Scotia Museum operates the following sites in the province:

Perkins House in **Liverpool** is a fine restored New England-style example of the Nova Scotia lifestyle prior to the American Revolution. In **Shelburne,** the *Ross-Thompson House* has been restored with trade items of the day.

Uniacke House, at **Mount Uniacke** near Halifax, presents one of the finest examples of the architecture and furnishings of the early 1800's to be found in North America. Thomas Chandler Haliburton, creator of the famous Sam Slick stories, completed his home in **Windsor** in 1836. *Haliburton House.* *"Clifton,"* is now open to the public. *Lawrence House* in **Maitland** was the home of the builder of Nova Scotia's largest wooden ship. The gracious Georgian brick house of Charles Prescott was completed about 1814 at **Starr's Point** near Wolfville. The early 19th-century home of *Thomas McCulloch* in **Pictou** has fine examples of carved interior woodwork.

The Museum also operates three historic mills in Nova Scotia. The *Wile Carding Mill* in **Bridgewater,** water-wheel driven, is unchanged since the days of the mid-1800's. The *Woolen Mill* in **Barrington** shows how the wool was woven into bolts of twills and flannels, blankets and suitings. The *Balmoral Grist Mill* at **Balmoral Mills** is one of the oldest operating mills in the province, dating from 1860. Visitors may purchase sample bags of stone ground flours and meals. A pleasant picnic ground overlooks the mill pond and falls.

The historic homes and mills are open from mid-May to mid-October, 9:30 A.M. to 5:30 P.M. daily. No admission charge.

Sherbrooke Village on Rte. 7 is a living village museum—a restoration of a 19th-century lumbering and gold-mining community. The inhabitants of the village still live in their homes within the "museum" and all of the buildings are staffed by costumed residents "working" at their trades. Wear walking shoes and try the excellent home-made soup or other fare at Bright House or What-Cheer-House. Open May 15 to October 15, 9:30 A.M. to 5:30 P.M. daily. Adult admission is $1.50; children enter free.

Ross Farm Museum, on Rte. 12 about 19 kms. (12 miles) north of Chester Basin, is a living museum which illustrates advances in farming from 1600 to 1925. Wear comfortable shoes or boots and old clothes. Adult admission is $1.50, children under 14 about 25¢. Family admissions are about $3.50. Open mid-May to mid-October, 9:30 to 5:30 daily. Open by appointment only the remainder of the year; 389–2210.

Museums on the Tourist Trails: On the **Evangeline Trail** (reached by Hwys. 1 and 101). In Yarmouth, the *County Historical Society Museum & Research Library* displays ship models and paintings, and the *Firefighters Museum* which illustrates the history of firefighting in the province; in Clementsport, the *Old St. Edwards Church Museum* (1797) is built like a ship of hand-hewn timbers; *North Hills Museum* at Granville Ferry has English furniture and bric-à-brac from the Georgian (1714–1830) period; in Annapolis Royal, the already-mentioned historical sites and the *O'Dell Inn & Tavern* and *The McNamara House* are restored buildings from the 19th and 18th centuries; in Middleton, the *Phinney Clock Collection* at the *Annapolis Valley MacDonald Museum,* an exhibit of 115 clocks and 52 watches, most of them brought to Nova Scotia by original settlers; in Wolfville, the *Historical Museum* features historical material from the New England Planters and Loyalists; in Hantsport, the *Churchill House and Maritime Museum* (1860) has a collection of shipbuilding tools, nautical instruments, old ships' logs and pictures.

Lighthouse Route (reached by Hwys. 3 and 103). The *Acadian Museum,* West Pubnico, tells of local history; *The Old Meeting House,* which is the oldest nonconformist church building in Canada (1766), and the *Cape Sable Historical Society Archives,* both in Barrington; in Lockeport, the *Little School Museum* is a restoration project housing a local history collection; in Bridgewater, the *Des Brisay Museum and Park,* which is the oldest municipally owned museum collection in Nova Scotia; the *Fort Point Museum* in La Have, a former lighthouse keeper's house; in Parkdale, the *Parkdale-Maplewood Museum* which emphasizes the German heritage of the area; in Blockhouse, the *Roaring 20's Museum* houses Nathern Joudrey's private collection of antique cars; in Lunenburg the *Lunenburg Fisheries Museum* and the *Aquarium* which is aboard two former fishing vessels and a one-time rumrunner; and via Rte. 332 from Lunenburg is the site of an old-time goldrush with monuments, caverns and a museum at the *Riverport-Ovens Natural Park.*

Glooscap Trail (reached by Hwys. 2 and 215). In Minudie, the *Amos Seaman School Museum,* which is housed in a restored one-room schoolhouse; the *Geological Museum* in Parrsboro has minerals and semiprecious stones from the region; in Springhill, visitors can go down into an actual mine and dig coal from the face at the *Miners' Museum;* in Truro, the *Colchester Historical Society Museum;* in Walton, the *Walton Museum* of local history; and on Rte. 14 the *South Rawdon Museum* has a small collection reflecting the former local temperance movement in a one-time Sons of Temperance Hall.

Sunrise Trail (reached by Hwy. 6). The *Sunrise Trail Museum* in Tatamagouche features memorabilia of the local-born giantess Anna Swann; in Pictou, the *Micmac Museum* is located next to a 17th-century Micmac burial ground and is the largest archeological discovery of its kind in Eastern Canada; in New Glasgow, the *Pictou County Historical Museum* which features "Samson", the first steam locomotive used in Canada; and in nearby Stellarton, the *Mining Museum & Library;* in MacPherson Mills, *MacPherson's Mill & Farmstead* has a water-powered grist mill and restored farm buildings.

Marine Drive Trail (reached by Hwys. 7, 316, 16 and 344). In Musquodoboit Harbour, the *Railway Museum* is housed in a 1917 CNR station and features two restored railway cars; in Jeddore Oyster Pond, the *Fisherman's House & Museum* illustrates the life of the inshore fisherman from 1890–1920; in Sheet Harbour the *Marine Gallery Museum* has local history collected; and in Sherbrooke, the whole center of the village has been restored as a living museum; in Guysborough town, the *Old Court House* (1843) and in Canso town, the *Canso Museum* features a special marine exhibit and a widow's-walk.

MUSIC. With the vast Scottish heritage, bagpipe music and Gaelic songs are an important part of Nova Scotia culture. Although Gaelic is spoken only by a small minority, the skirl of the pipes has been adopted by Nova Scotians of every background. Scottish concerts are held throughout the summer months in a number of communities. If you find an announcement for a ceilidh (pronounced kay-lee), that means a Scottish concert. Check *"Seasonal Events"* section earlier in this chapter, the newspaper events supplements, and Nova Scotia Tourism's *Calendar of Events.*

REGIONAL THEATER. Live amateur theater is alive and well in Nova Scotia. The *Kipawo Show Boat Company* in Wolfville (542–3500 or 3542) is the best-known, but the *Mulgrave Road Co-op Company* in Mulgrave, *Mermaid Theatre* in Wolfville, *Theatre Antigonish* in Antigonish, the *Deaf-Gypsy Mime Company* in Centreville, *Savoy Theatre* in Glace Bay, and *Mermaid Theatre* in Dartmouth also are making themselves known. Some of these companies tour the province, putting on two or three productions a year. Also the puppet theater, *Canadian Puppet Festivals* in Chester (275–3171 or 3430), has drawn critical acclaim. The department of tourism or the department of culture can tell you more.

SHOPPING. Nova Scotia's shopping centers tend to be uninspiring, not much different from anything you might find anywhere else in North America. The exciting shopping and fascinating browsing is found in the shops of craftspeople all over the province—where you'll find everything from blacksmiths in East Dover, silversmiths in Waverley, to leaded glass hanging ornaments in Purcells Cove, to wooden toys in Middleton, pewter in Wolfville, pottery in Arichat, apple dolls in Halifax. Beware the junky lobster ashtrays on the tourist trails. The N.S. Dept. of Culture, Recreation and Fitness (P.O. Box 864, Halifax, N.S. B3J 2V2, 424-4061) or the Dept. of Tourism will send you the Handcraft Directory, an excellent guide to the craftspeople of Nova Scotia.

Antique stores proliferate all over Nova Scotia and Cape Breton. One of the better—and more genuine—ones is *Dana Sweeny Antiques* in Mahone Bay.

Another source of unique shopping and browsing experiences (and, likely, good stories from the shopkeepers) are the hundreds of tiny, rural general stores in villages all over the province. In these you might find anything from yard-goods to harnesses, sou'westers to weird ointments—well worth poking around in these stores.

The largest shopping center in the province is MicMac Mall in Dartmouth off the A. Murray Mackay Bridge. It is also the largest east of Montréal. Next is Scotia Square in Halifax, which has dozens of chain stores as well as dozens of specialty shops; the next largest is the Woolco shopping center in Sydney, on the highway as you go in on Rte. 4. Here, you'll be able to get recordings of local but well-known musicians like Lee Cremo or the Men of the Deeps, The Steel City Players, "Rise & Follies of Cape Breton" or the Glendale Concert albums.

 DRINKING LAWS. The legal drinking age in Nova Scotia is 19 years. Bottled alcoholic beverages are sold only in Nova Scotia Liquor Commission (NSLC) retail stores, located in most major communities. NSLC hours vary from place to place, but they are usually open from 10 A.M. to 5 P.M. weekdays and Saturdays, and to 9 P.M. on Friday evenings, and all are closed on Sundays.

Beer and alcoholic beverages by the glass are sold in licensed restaurants (food must also be ordered) and in licensed lounges (cocktail lounge, a bar with entertainment, only the name is changed). Beer by the bottle and draught beer by the glass are sold in taverns and beverage rooms, which often offer surprisingly good snacks and light meals. Open hours average from 10 A.M. to midnight. Licensed lounges average from 11 A.M. to 2 A.M.

There are no restrictions on women entering taverns in Nova Scotia, although the atmosphere in many taverns tends to be a bit rough.

A few "dry" areas still remain in Nova Scotia, but barriers are falling rapidly and the "wets" are prevailing. For a list of dry districts, contact the Nova Scotia Department of Tourism.

 DINING OUT. The food in most Nova Scotia restaurants in well prepared—especially the seafood. In the past few years the standard of cuisine and its presentation have improved greatly.

Service is generally good in the better restaurants although it can be slow, especially if the place is busy.

Restaurants are categorized on the basis of a full-course dinner, with drinks, tips and tax excluded. *Expensive,* over $15; *Moderate,* $10 to $15; *Inexpensive,* under $10.

A 10% provincial tax will be added to all meals over $3.

Most places accept the following major credit cards: American Express, MasterCard and Visa; others may also be honored. Not all establishments accept credit cards, therefore we suggest you call for information.

ANTIGONISH. *Moderate–Expensive:* **Lobster Treat Restaurant.** On the Trans Canada Hwy. Undistinguished-looking on the outside, a pleasant surprise inside. Seafood specialties. Licensed. Phone: 863–5465.

BRIDGETOWN. *Moderate:* **Continental Kitchen.** Spotlessly clean, excellent food prepared in a country style, huge portions. Licensed. Be sure to make reservations early in the day. Phone 665–2287.

CHESTER. *Expensive:* **Rope Loft.** One of the best views in the province. Food usually excellent. Licensed. Bring a camera. Open summer season only. Open noon to 10 P.M. Reservations recommended. Seafood specialty. Phone 275-3430.

The Captain's House. Restored to its early 1800's elegance. Specializes in fine Maritime recipes. An experience. Phone 275-3501. Major credit cards.

DIGBY. *Expensive:* **The Pines Resort Hotel Dining Room.** Usually good food served in large dining room of older resort hotel. Pleasant grounds overlooking Digby harbor. Specialty is Digby scallops. Call for reservations. Dancing. Phone 245-2511. Major credit cards.

LISCOMBE MILLS. *Expensive:* **Liscombe Lodge Dining Room.** A good dining room in this resort overlooking the Liscombe River. Licensed with stone fireplace, often lit for dinner. Specialty is fresh salmon caught in river nearby. Call for meal hours and reservations. Open June to mid-Oct. Phone 779-2307. Major credit cards.

NEW GLASGOW. *Expensive:* **Heather Motel Dining Room.** Clean, comfortable place, licensed, with friendly service and usually good food. Call for reservations. Phone 752-8401. Major credit cards.

SHERBROOKE VILLAGE. *Moderate:* **The Bright House.** A licensed dining room on Main Street serving lunch and dinner, specializing in roast beef. Phone 522-2691.

Inexpensive: **What Cheer House.** In historic Sherbrooke Village living museum. Turn of the century village inn with hearty seafood chowder, beef stew, home-baked beans & bread. Not licensed. Lunch & tea only.

TRURO. *Expensive:* **The Palliser Restaurant.** Excellent family restaurant overlooking tidal bore river. Open 8 A.M. to 8:30 P.M. mid-May to mid-Oct. Call for reservations. Phone 893-3895. Major credit cards.

Glengarry Motel Dining Room. 138 Willow St. Features home cooking in large dining room. Phone 895-5388. Major credit cards.

YARMOUTH. *Expensive:* **Harris' Seafood Restaurant.** (Restaurant on the right side of the highway is run by the same people but is a short order place.) Possibly the best seafood in Nova Scotia. Lobster is a specialty. Call for reservations.

Manor Inn. Good food in pleasant surroundings. Beer garden, dining room in manor with folk singers. Licensed. Steak and lobster especially good. Call for reservations.

Moderate: **Grand Hotel Dining Room.** Ordinary hotel dining room except for Hot Lobster Sandwich—big chunks of creamed lobster served on toast. Live entertainment & dancing except on Sundays. Phone 742-2446. Major credit cards.

NEWFOUNDLAND AND LABRADOR

An Early European Beachhead

by
ALAN FREEMAN, RALPH SURETTE
and
COLLEEN THOMPSON

Perhaps the legendary Leif Ericson was among the Viking crew and passengers of the Norse longship that came ashore, sometime about A.D. 1000, on a point of land that is now thought to be Newfoundland. Perhaps not. At least we know that the half-barbarian, half-literate adventurers were the first discoverers of Newfoundland—and possibly the first Europeans who landed on North American shores. While the Norsemen made several voyages to this area during the next 100 years, it was not until 1497 that John Cabot, sailing from Bristol on the west coast of England, found the almost invisible niche in the rock leading into a protected harbor. Legend has it that he arrived on St. John's Day, and thus named the port St. John's.

Nearly a hundred years passed and the "new found land" remained unknown in Europe except to a handful of Bristol merchants and the fishermen employed by them. For a century, these westcountry men carried back the rich harvest from the Newfoundland fishing banks, even establishing seasonal colonies from which to support the fishery. Yet little is known of this early period of exploration. For years, the West of England fishermen sought to conceal their profitable voyages from the scrutiny of a tyrannical Crown in order to avoid payment of oppressive taxes. But the trade became too large and too prosperous to be hidden for long; in 1583 Sir Humphrey Gilbert claimed the land for Elizabeth I. To reinforce his claim, he set up a trading stall on what is now the St. John's waterfront, and opened it up for business. Sir Humphrey also distinguished himself by bringing from England the first professional dancers and musicians to play in the New World; these were the "hobby horses and Morris dancers and many like conceits" who performed on shore at St. John's on August 5, 1583.

Hard Times for Settlers

Gilbert's claim for Britain ended the laissez-faire days of international fishing off the coast of Newfoundland by 30,000 fishermen from half a dozen nations who operated in relative peace and security. It began the infamous era of the Fishing Admiral which was to last for another century. The Fishing Admiral was the first captain to sail into any Newfoundland harbor each year. This distinction allowed the fortunate skipper to set himself up as a total despot for the season, thereby creating unceasing turmoil between permanent settlers and English adventurers.

It was also the time of bitter dispute between the merchant overlords in Devon and the English west country and the would-be colonists. Settlement in Newfoundland was against the law and anyone who tried colonization was laying his life on the line. The colonists could see the rich future in settlement and pursuit of the rich inshore fishery. The merchants could see the colonists rapidly wresting control of the rich trade in salt fish away from the motherland.

In 1711, the colony was placed under the rule of Naval Governors and the fishing admirals' empire was dissolved. Although harsh legislation had been enacted, settlement had continued during the reign of the admirals. Around the bays and inlets were tiny settlements and individual families. Most could be reached only by boat and signs of habitation were usually well hidden from outsiders. Sometimes known as "the lost men," these tiny communities were enlarged by further groups of settlers, some successful, some doomed.

Though harsh anti-colonization laws were passed and repealed from time to time at the whim of the British monarchy, Newfoundland settlements became a fact. Some credit for their survival may go to the New England colonies who aided and abetted a settlement policy for many years.

Dominion to Colony to Province

In 1811 the British government legalized permanently the granting of land and the building of houses in the colony. By 1855, Newfoundland had become a self-governing Dominion within the British Commonwealth.

By 1934, having weathered the growing pains of a new country, a world war, and the first years of the Great Depression, Newfoundland was bankrupt. There was no alternative but to become a British colony once again with a commission government to administer its affairs. With the advent of World War II, however, Newfoundland found itself in the middle of supply lines from North America to Europe, and the Allies poured money and men into Newfoundland to spur on the effort of building bases where only wilderness had existed before. The problem was no longer to find money, but to find men to do the work.

Prosperous throughout the war and the post war period, Newfoundland again considered its future. To join the nation of Canada, with Newfoundland on its front doorstep, seemed the logical choice to many Newfoundlanders. Finally, after a bitter and stormy campaign and referendum, Newfoundland joined Confederation on March 31, 1949, becoming Canada's tenth province. Since that time, it has developed its natural resources and, in some part, rearranged the once isolated outport society which made up most of Newfoundland.

Settlement in the larger communities, university and trades education, and modernization of the fishing, forestry, and mining industries characterize the contemporary directions of the province. Yet, despite the encroachments of 20th-century living, Newfoundland and Newfoundlanders have managed to retain their special personality and their culture, a combination that makes Canada's newest province a most unique acquisition.

The Newfoundland flag—a new one proclaimed in 1980—has two triangles (representing Labrador and the Island of Newfoundland) and stylized ornamentations representing the Christian, and Beothuk and Naskapi Indian backgrounds of the province. The colors are blue (the sea) and red (human endeavor) on a background of white (snow). It replaces the Union Jack which had served as the provincial flag before. The provincial coat of arms—developed in 1637, lost, rediscovered, then finally adopted officially in 1928—is a red shield quartered by the white cross of Saint George. The quarters contain the white unicorns of England and gold lions of Scotland.

A Craggy Isle

Newfoundland, an island off the coast of northeast North America and situated between the Gulf of St. Lawrence and the Atlantic Ocean, is separated from the mainland by the Strait of Belle Isle on the North and Cabot Strait on the southwest. Labrador, the northeast corner of the continent, is the province's mainland section. To neglect to mention the massive land area of this province is to leave the unsuspecting traveler unprepared for his journey. In terms of the United States, only Alaska, Texas, and California are greater in size.

Largest of the four Canadian Atlantic provinces, Newfoundland has a total area of 404,520 sq. kms. (156,185 square miles). Most of the province's population of 582,900 is concentrated on the island—in the cities of St. John's, the capital, and Corner Brook, and in the towns of Gander and Grand Falls. The Labrador towns of Goose Bay/Happy Valley, Wabush, and Labrador City are also on the upswing.

Visitors flying overhead have commented that the province seems to be made up of bodies of water surrounded by bits of land. Indeed, about 10 percent of the province is lakes and streams—thousands of them!

Labrador is mountainous, dotted with lakes, and cut by rivers. The mountains are ancient, ground blunt by the passage of glaciers eons ago. Most of the slopes are forest covered up to the tree line with a hardy, slow-growing spruce, suited to endure severely cold winters and short summers.

The island of Newfoundland is also mountainous and lake-strewn. On the west coast, the flat, forested mountains form an escarpment some 2,000 feet high which plunges sharply into the sea at the coast. In the central region, the mountains give way to low land and boggy forests and more ranges of hills and mountains. Along the east coast, the mountains again drop off into the sea, although the cliffs are not as steep as on the opposite coast.

It was this forbidding landscape which made the fishery the chief economic mainstay of Newfoundland for 450 years. With the riches of the Grand Banks there for the taking and an inshore fishery which yielded vast quantities of cod and other fish, there was no need to look inland. Even today, agriculture tends to be concentrated in smaller operations and in areas such as the Codroy Valley in the west coast.

The inland riches of Newfoundland now lie in the forests and under the barren rock and in the tumbling water. Forestry, mining and the production of hydroelectricity are major industries. Newfoundland has generally the highest unemployment rate of Canada and is considered its poorest province. But the discovery of huge oilfields on the Continental Shelf may change all that.

Newfoundland is in a unique time zone, one-half hour later than Atlantic Canada. The weather varies widely as the province extends more than 1200 kms. (750 miles) north to south. In St. John's, average summer temperatures range from 21°C (70°F) to roughly 13°C (55°F) at night. In the north, the summer temperatures follow about the same range, although the season is shorter. Winter temperatures in St. John's are about 0°C (32°F) by day, dipping to about −7°C (20°F) at night. On the west coast of the island and in Labrador, winter temperatures can fall to −45°C (−50°F).

Another unique geographical fact is that the island part of the province has no skunks, snakes, or ragweed pollen.

Words . . .

The visitor to Newfoundland is charmed by the unique speech of the outport people, the originality of their idiom, and the dialects that one hears only in this province. The St. John's accent has an Irish quality (the name of the city is pronounced "sin jahns," with the accent at the end); accents in places like Harbour Main, Ferryland and Placentia are similar. In the north, one listens to a Dorset or Devon dialect of three centuries ago complete with words and idioms long forgotten in England. Then there are the traditional figures of speech that have been retained through four centuries of settlement. Words like "ballycater" —ice formed on the shore by spray or little cakes of sea ice; "cuddy"—a covered space in the bow of a boat, and "kingcorn"—a person's Adam's apple. "Sparbles" are bits of grit or gravel, and a "yaffle" is an armful of dried fish—the word used as a unit of measure—a yaffle of fish.

In 1811, immigration to Newfoundland became legal. The isolated settlers kept the words of their own times, and passed them on to succeeding generations. Absence of books and formal literacy helped preserve the old words. Terms relating to the sea and the fishery were kept to the forefront and if a suitable word did not exist, one was made up "right off the bat."

. . . and Music

Newfoundland seems to have more folk songs than any other part of Canada, most of them with an Irish flavor. Many old folk songs were brought from Britain with the settlers through 300 years of illegal and legal settlement. Another group of songs originated in Newfoundland —songs of the sea, of love affairs, the eternal triangle, and the loss of a lovelorn man or maiden.

One of the most prolific of later-day Newfoundland folk song writers was Johnny Burke whose home was a gathering place for many of the finest singers in Newfoundland. Born in 1851, he lived here with his sister until his death in 1930. Burke's most popular piece was *The Kelligrew's Soiree,* the story of an all-out party in the community of Kelligrews, just outside St. John's.

Dancing is part of Newfoundland musical heritage. Local square dances are full of movement, rhythm, and grace. When no one is available to play on a fiddle or jew's-harp, somebody has to furnish "chin-music."

A Modern City

But Newfoundland is not all mountains and folk music. St. John's, its capital, is a flourishing, contemporary city, symbolizing new directions of the province (and the country). It is a pleasure to visit.

EXPLORING ST. JOHN'S

A Strategic Location

St. John's is situated on the eastern coast of the Avalon Peninsula, an "H"-shaped promontory jutting out by a spindly isthmus from the southeast corner of the Island of Newfoundland. Because of its strategic location almost halfway between Montreal and Europe, St. John's has long been connected with shipping across the North Atlantic. Lying almost on top of one of the world's richest fishing banks, the old city has been a second home to European fishermen for more than four centuries. A walk along St. John's waterfront, even today, reveals a polyglot culture that adds great vitality to the life of the city.

John Cabot, as noted earlier, arrived in 1497, naming the harbor St. John's and the whole island New Founde Isle before sailing off to the Canadian mainland.

Six years later, the British Bristol Company tried, without success, to plant a colony on Cabot's new found harbor in the New World. But more hardy people were to follow. In 1583, Sir Humphry Gilbert proclaimed the land for Elizabeth I, announcing that anyone daring to disobey the rule of Her Majesty would have his ears cut off. By this time St. John's was a prosperous town—the rocky walls of the harbor sheltering the fishing fleets of many nations. Well-established merchants did a thriving business and the town was ruled by the law of the Fishing Admiral.

Despite the harsh winters and a forbidding landscape, St. John's was coveted by several European nations over the centuries including the Dutch, Portuguese, Spanish, French and British. Thus, the city was periodically besieged by contending nations as well as attacked several times by freelancing pirates. The final shots of the Seven Years' War between the French and English were fired in St. John's in 1762.

Under strong British rule, St. John's settled into a comparatively quiet and stable way of life. The merchants traded and prospered. The fishermen struggled and barely made a living. The cosmopolitan character of the city broadened and international history continued to be played out around the old port. The "townee" of St. John's (as distinguished from the "bayman" who lived outside the town) cast a curious eye at these events, but refused to become overly excited. So he took it in stride when Guglielmo Marconi received the first wireless signal from across the ocean at his receiver atop Signal Hill in St. John's in 1901; and few well-wishers cheered Alcock and Brown when they took off from Lester's Field to complete the first trans-Atlantic flight in 1919. And it seemed only natural to the "townee" that Roosevelt and Churchill should choose to meet on the quiet waters of nearby Placentia Bay to draft the terms of the Atlantic Charter.

Two world wars brought successive waves of uniformed "mainlanders" from Canada as well as seafaring men of a dozen nations to walk the steep cobblestone streets along the waterfront, waiting to board convoy ships for Europe. Many young men and women joined the much-decorated Newfoundland fighting units and merchant marine, and died in defense of the countries which had given life to their city centuries before.

St. John's was probably closer to the wars than most North American cities. During World War II, German U-boats constantly cruised the waters off Newfoundland in search of allied shipping and convoys, torpedoing ships only a few miles outside St. John's harbor.

After the signing of the Lend-Lease agreements, St. John's became familiar with the uniform and accents of United States military personnel as Britain exchanged leases on territory in return for American shipping and hardware with which to continue the war. The complex by the shores of Quidi Vidi (pronounced *Kiddy-Viddy*) Lake was built by the United States and known as Pepperell Air Force Base. It has since been returned to the city, and renamed Pleasantville, and is now office space for various government agencies, a hospital, and other institutions.

Following the last war, a new era began for Newfoundland and for St. John's, which was named capital of North America's oldest territory and Canada's youngest province. This change (which some Newfoundlanders still regard, with good humor, as the time when Canada joined Newfoundland) was to have a dramatic effect on the new province and especially on St. John's.

Old City, New Life

The old city—one of the oldest in the New World—rapidly became the showplace of the province. As it took its place as Newfoundland's leading retail, wholesale, and service center, a major ocean port, and a focus of transportation, its citizens benefited economically. With expansion of its shipbuilding, fish processing, and manufacturing industries, a new and more contemporary lifestyle began to emerge.

The townie took the changes, both good and bad, with a philosophical attitude. Mainlanders arrived by the boatload and "tried to teach us their way." But the city simply sighed, and made room for them, and proceeded to turn them into Newfoundlanders.

The sprawling campus of Memorial University is a far cry from the tiny college-school of only a few years ago. New housing and high-rise buildings have changed the skyline. The discovery of oil offshore has changed the economic base; but attitudes have remained traditional in many ways and the citizenry retains its unique character. Though friendly and hospitable to all visitors, the people are hardy to the point of stubbornness. How else to account for their unbounded resilience in the face of extreme hardship and a succession of tragedies over the years? The original settlers were mostly fishermen from the villages of Devon, Cork, Dorset, Somerset, and Waterford. Their descendants survived England's harsh policy toward permanent settlement only to watch their city captured and plundered four times and finally leveled by fire in 1817. Indeed, St. John's was the first North American city to have been totally destroyed by fire. Fire struck again in 1846 and, for the third time, in 1892 when 13,000 people were left homeless. Yet today, St. John's is alive and well, as cosmopolitan as London or Montréal and as English as Victoria.

Tea is still the favorite nonalcoholic drink, with rum in first place for those who like something a bit stronger. English biscuits are still preferred over mainland cookies and many offices still close for lunch between 12:30 and 1:30. Living is still leisurely and everyone celebrates all the provincial and federal holidays with a few extra of their own, such as St. Patrick's Day and Orangemen's Day. One special nonholiday event is Bonfire Night—Guy Fawkes Night—on November 5th. Gambling is a Newfoundland passion—bingo, wheels of fortune, and raffles for live turkeys and pigs at Christmas are well attended. Every townie is expected to go trouting, or angling, and he enjoys his leisure, extending hospitality to any who will enjoy it with him.

Water Street, running quite naturally along the waterfront, is probably the oldest street in North America. In the shops and stores one can purchase everything from an anchor to a needle. Secretaries in the latest fashions mingle with fishermen in rubber boots and school children in English-style uniforms. Even if you do not buy, it is interesting to walk the length of the street. Stop at the Speakeasy in newly-restored, historic Murray Premises and enjoy your tea with the locals.

A number of walking and self-drive tours have been developed for St. John's and the surrounding area. The best way to see St. John's is on foot even though the hilly streets, as the natives say, go in only two directions—up and down. A heritage foundation has restored many of the quaint clapboard houses in the downtown core.

A publication entitled *Everyman's Complete St. John's Guide* costs about $3.00 and offers several detailed walking and self-drive tours. And remember—when you journey outside the city, take your camera or your sketch book! (For further information, see *"Special Interest Tours"* under Practical Information for St. John's.)

No matter what time of year you visit St. John's and whatever historic sites you choose to see, your most enduring memory will be of the people. St. John's has an accent all its own—mainly Irish and a bit English, with unusual idioms spicing the conversation. The accent is soft and expressive, tumbling off the tongue; most visitors will come to adopt it during their stay, even in spite of themselves.

Find any excuse to start a conversation with a total stranger. Your new friend will accompany you, just to keep you on track, pointing out all the sights along the way. And if you ask a few questions about the old city, you may have found a friend for your entire visit to St. John's.

PRACTICAL INFORMATION FOR ST. JOHN'S

HOW TO GET THERE. By air: *Eastern Provincial Airways* and *Air Canada* operate regularly scheduled flights to St. John's from points throughout Canada, the U.S., and within Newfoundland.

By car: St. John's is the eastern terminus of the Trans-Canada Hwy. (Hwy. 1) from Port-aux-Basques and the car ferry from North Sydney, Nova Scotia. Visitors taking the other ferry from North Sydney to Argentia, Newfoundland, follow highway 100 to the intersection of the Trans-Canada Hwy. (TCH). Turn east toward St. John's.

By train/bus: Passenger train service in Newfoundland has been discontinued. Motorcoaches operated by *Terra Transport* (737–5916) carry passengers from the ferry terminals to St. John's. For tickets and information, contact any *Via Rail* ticket office (agents for *Terra Transport*) in Canada; see also the "How to Get There" section in Practical Information for Newfoundland and Labrador.

ACCOMMODATIONS. St. John's is changing rapidly since oil was discovered off the shores of Newfoundland. Accommodations can be hard to come by at times. Make reservations. Most St. John's hotels are on the expensive side. There are some "Hospitality Homes," however, that provide inexpensive accommodation. Double-occupancy rates are as follows: *Expensive,* $46 or more; *Moderate,* $35–45; *Inexpensive,* under $35.

A 12% provincial tax will be added to your bill.

Most places accept the following major credit cards: American Express, MasterCard and Visa; others may also be honored. Not all establishments accept credit cards, therefore we suggest you call for information.

Airport Inn. *Expensive.* Plain, comfortable accommodations near airport. Dining room and cocktail lounge. Phone 753–3500. Major credit cards.

The Battery Inn. *Expensive.* Top place to stay in St. John's. Located about half way up Signal Hill with harbor rooms offering a great view of the city. Dining room and coffeeshop (good food), cocktail lounge, sauna, and pool. Phone 726–0040. Major credit cards.

Château Park. *Expensive.* Mt. Pearl St. Excellent dining and lounge facilities. Phone 364–7725. Major credit cards.

Holiday Inn. *Expensive.* Portugal Cove Rd. Typical Holiday Inn; dining room and coffeeshop with indifferent cooking; cocktail lounge and outdoor pool. Phone 722–0506. Major credit cards.

Hotel Newfoundland. *Expensive.* Cavendish Sq. downtown location. In the process of being replaced by a new 350-room hotel located behind the old hotel. Phone 726–4980. Major credit cards.

Kenmount Motel. *Expensive.* Elizabeth Ave. Comfortable; dining room and cocktail lounge. Phone 726–0092. Major credit cards.

Lester Hotel. *Expensive.* Blackmarsh Rd. Dining room, cocktail lounge. Phone 579–2141. Major credit cards.

Hotel St. John's. *Expensive.* Dining room, cocktail lounge. Phone 722–9330. Major credit cards.

Skyline Motel. *Moderate.* Plain, comfortable accommodations. Restaurant featuring Chinese food; cocktail lounge. Phone 722–5400. Major credit cards.

Sea Flow Tourist Home. *Inexpensive.* 5 rooms, kitchen facilities. Phone 753–2425.

Bonaventure House. *Inexpensive.* 4 units with room service and a nice little dining room. Phone 753–3359.

TELEPHONE. The area code for St. John's and all Newfoundland, including Labrador, is the same: 709.

HOW TO GET AROUND. From the airport: *Gulliver's Taxi* operates a taxi/limo service from the St. John's Airport to downtown hotels. Cost is about $3.50 per person. **Car rental:** Major car rental agencies have desks at the St. John's airport and in some hotel lobbies. Advance booking recommended through a travel agent or the local office of the rental agency. Most agencies will deliver cars to St. John's hotels.

By bus: The *Metrobus* system operates throughout St. John's and into the outlying areas. Routes start operating between 6:45 and 8:00 A.M. and stop running between 6:00 P.M. and 12:30 A.M. depending on the route. For information, call 722–9400. Single adult fares are 50¢. Persons using the Metrobus must have exact fare as drivers do not carry change. Fares outside the city limits are higher. Fare to Mount Pearl is about 70¢. A number of small bus operators run services to other regions of the Avalon Peninsula. Contact the nearest tourist information office for routes and timetables or call the St. John's tourism office.

By taxi: Taxis do not generally "cruise" in St. John's. It is usually necessary to call one of the stands and have the cab meet you. The meter starts at about $1.50 and runs up to about $2.40 for the first mile and about 90¢ per mile thereafter, depending on traffic.

TOURIST INFORMATION SERVICES. St. John's Tourist Chalet, Trans-Canada Hwy. Call 368–5900. St. John's Tourist Commission, City Hall, New Gower St. Call 722–7080. Tourist Information Desk, Colonial Building, Military Rd. at Bannerman Rd. Call 753–9380. Tourist Information Desk, Confederation Building, Confederation Parkway. Call 737–3630. Tourist Information Desk, Newfoundland Museum, Duckworth St. Call 737–2461. Provincial Department of Development, Tourism Branch, Atlantic Place, Water St. Call 737–2830.

RECOMMENDED READING. The indispensable book for tourists in Newfoundland is Harold Horwood's *Newfoundland,* a superb account of the people, traditions, resources, and places of the province. Horwood is the greatest Newfoundland writer, a novelist *(Tomorrow Will Be Sunday, White Eskimo)* and biographer *(Bartlett: The Great Canadian Explorer)* and natural historian *(The Foxes of Beachy Cove,* a minor masterpiece). Ray Guy is a brilliant humorist, whose mordant wit is collected in *You May Know Them As Sea Urchins, Ma'am,* and the award-winning *That Far Greater Bay.* Guy has been known to shake Newfoundland governments. Other contemporary novels are Percy Janes' *House of Hate* and Gordon Pinsent's *The Rowdyman.*

Poet Al Pittman's *Down by Jim Long's Stage* and the plays of Michael Cook are published by Newfoundland's own Breakwater Books, a venture which has achieved remarkable national stature despite its youth and distance from major markets. Former premier Joey Smallwood compiled *The Book of Newfoundland,* and his memoirs *I Chose Canada* include a lively account of the campaign which brought Newfoundland into Confederation in 1949. Cassie Brown specializes in marine disasters; her *Death on the Ice,* about a catastrophe at the famous (or infamous) seal hunt in 1914, was an international success. Paul O'Neill's *The Oldest City* is a detailed history of St. John's.

TIME ZONE. St. John's is on Newfoundland Time, as is the rest of the island—that is, ½ hour in advance of Atlantic Time and 1½ hours ahead of Eastern Time.

SEASONAL EVENTS. In **February** and **March** there are winter carnivals in many Newfoundland towns and villages. In **February,** the Kiwanis Music Festival; at the end of **March,** the Provincial Drama Festival. In **May,** the Newfoundland Kennel Club All-Breed Championships, and the Lion's Trade Fair. **May to October,** sailing races around St. John's, including the annual Regatta, said to be the oldest continuous sporting event in North America. In **June,** the Newfoundland Kite Festival is held in the strong ocean breezes on Signal Hill. During **July** and **August** the Summer Festival of the Arts is held, as well as civic festivals throughout the island; and from mid-July to the end of August, the Newfoundland Militia perform a colorful military tatoo on Signal Hill on Tuesdays, Thursdays, Saturdays and Sundays at 3 and 7 P.M., weather permitting. Musket and cannon fire, military drill, and the red uniforms of the militiamen make this an exciting performance. In **September,** the Newfoundland Amateur Golf Championship.

TOURS. *Overland Tours* (722–6990), the *St. John's Transportation Commission* (722–4771), *Newfoundland Historic Trust* (753–9262), *Gulliver's Tours* (753–1989), *Fleetline Tours* (722–2608) and *Chalet Tours* (368–6027) have bus tours of the city and environs. *Harbour Charters* (754–1672) and *Lucky Strike Boat Charters* (753–3940) take passengers sightseeing and fishing in the harbor and beyond.

SPECIAL INTEREST TOURS. A number of **walking/ driving tours** of St. John's are available at the tourist information desks or by mail from the St. John's Tourist Commission, City Hall, New Gower St., St. John's. **Self-guided driving tours** to outlying areas of the city and environs include tours to Marine Drive/Pouch Cove, Portugal Cove/St. Phillips, and Petty Harbour/ Maddox Cove. All these drives offer dramatic seacoast scenery and take you to fishing villages and inland forested regions.

A well-marked **nature trail** starts at King George V Park and leads walkers for some distance along the river and ponds to an area outside the city. Inquire at the travel information desk for the best place to begin the trail.

For bicyclers, a **cycle path** begins at Kent's Pond, just west of the junction of Portugal Cove Rd. and Confederation Pkwy., leading through the woods and coming out on Higgin's Line.

Eight-day **nature excursions** to make "human contact" with the whales, porpoises and dolphins that abound off eastern Newfoundland are offered by *Ocean Contact Ltd.* Reservations needed well in advance. Write Box 10, Trinity, Trinity Bay, Newfoundland AOC 2S0.

Newfoundland has three important **seabird sanctuaries**—one on Gull Island in Witless Bay, 30 km. (19 mi.) south of St. John's on Rte. 10; one at Cape St. Mary's, approximately 193 km. (120 mi.) southeast of St. John's; and one on the Funk Island, 50 mi. off the northeast coast of Newfoundland.

The best time to go to Gull Island is June 15–July 15 and the best way to reach the island three miles offshore is by making arrangements with local fishermen. The best time for Cape St. Mary's is June 15–August 15. A rough 16 km. (10-mile) road branches off Rte. 100 about 3.2 km (2 mi.) past St. Bride's and leads to Cape St. Mary's. The bird colonies at Cape St. Mary's are viewed from a spectacular clifftop lookout. A trip to Funk Island is a major expedition. Further information from the Department of Development, Tourism Branch, Recreation and Culture.

PARKS. *C. A. Pippy Park*—4,000 acres on the city's northern boundary—is St. John's favorite open-air recreation spot, and a marvelous place to take children. There are extensive woodlands with nature trails, picnic areas, campgrounds, golf course, a small botanical and wildlife reserve, playground, children's farm, and others. The Memorial University campus, the Confederation Building, and several other noteworthy buildings are within the park's confines.

Another favorite relaxation spot for residents and visitors is *Bowring Park,* in the west end. It has a year-round playground with wooded areas, open fields, swimming pools in summer and skating rink in winter. *Bannerman Park* on Bannerman Rd. behind the Colonial Building has an outdoor pool and playground. *Quidi Vidi Picnic Ground* on the north shore of Quidi Vidi Lake has tables and fireplaces for picnics. *Cochrane Pond* and *Butterpot Provincial Parks* are within easy driving distance of St. John's on the Trans-Canada Hwy. With the exception of the provincial parks, there is no entrance fee to any St. John's park.

CHILDREN'S ACTIVITIES. St. John's is an outdoor city with lots of open space and walking areas along the waterfront and seacoast. See the sections on "Parks," "Special Interest Tours," and "Sports" for activities for younger people.

PARTICIPANT SPORTS. For **golf,** the *Bally Hally Golf and Country Club* is a private club but visitors can play. Call 753–6090. Also in St. John's is the *Halliday Farms Golf Club* in C. A. Pippy Park; 753–7110. Stephenville, Gander, Corner Brook and Grand Falls also have courses, with summer tournaments.

Ice skating during the winter and **roller skating** during the summer at the half-dozen arenas and rinks in town. **Bicycling** is becoming popular. The *St. John's Club* has tours Wednesdays and Sundays. All invited.

For **swimmers,** there are outdoor summer pools at *Bowring Park,* Waterford Bridge Rd., call 364–3880; *Bannerman Park,* Bannerman Rd., call 753–4655; *Victoria Park,* Water St., call 726–8181. Indoor year-round pools are located at the *Torbay Recreation Centre* at St. John's Airport, call 737–2792; *Downtown Boys and Girls Club,* Water St., call 753–7080; *Mount Pearl Swimming Pool,* Park Ave., call 368–0128, and *Wedgewood Park Pool,* 45 Gleneyre, call 753–0570. Also the new *Aquarena,* call 754–1977.

SPECTATOR SPORTS. *Regatta Day* on Quidi Vidi Lake is St. John's big holiday of the year. Called for the first Wednesday in August, or the first fine day following, it is the oldest (1826) sporting event in North America still being held. It is probably the only civic holiday that is decided at 7 A.M. on the morning of the holiday. Townies listen to their radios for the magic phrase "The races are on!" which signals the holiday. Thousands crowd the lakeshore to watch the events as teams of oarsmen and oarswomen in racing shells compete up and down the lake, and to gamble on the games of chance at the booths set up throughout the area.

The *Avalon Raceway* at Gould's, 16 km. from St. John's, has **harness horse racing** Wednesdays, Sundays and holidays, spring to fall, on a variable schedule. Usually at 7:45 P.M., but better check for times.

HISTORIC SITES AND SIGHTS. *Signal Hill National Historic Park* is probably the focal point in St. John's. At the top, the *Cabot Tower,* near where (the precise spot is marked by a plaque) Marconi received the first overseas wireless message, has become a symbol of the city. The bleak and rocky headland was the site of early forts as well as the last battle of the Seven Years' War in North America. Here you will have a breathtaking view of St. John's and the harbor as well as the last landfall before Europe. In spring, large white and turquoise Arctic icebergs, known as "growlers," can sometimes be sighted. *Gibbet Hill* near Deadman's Pond was the site of the old gallows. The *Interpretive Centre* halfway up Signal Hill offers another great view of the city and the harbor; it also has a number of interesting displays and artifacts that document the city's history. There are interpretive walks and lookouts in the park. Obtain information from the Interpretive Centre—open 9 A.M. to late evening in summer.

The *Sir Humphrey Gilbert Memorial* is a plaque set below the National War Memorial on Water St., and marks the spot where Sir Humphrey planted the Royal Standard of Elizabeth I in 1583 and claimed Newfoundland for England; the *National War Memorial,* whose figures represent freedom, was unveiled on July 1st, 1924. The *Queen's Battery,* overlooking the harbor entrance just below the crest of Signal Hill, dates back to the 18th Century when France and England were still struggling for possession of Newfoundland, to the time of the last battle on Signal Hill in 1762 when the English took St. John's. *Chain Rock Battery* was located at the narrowest part of the harbor entrance, and in the late 1700's a large chain was put between Chain and Pancake Rocks so that two capstans were used to raise it to obstruct enemy vessels, and during World War I a chain boom was used to protect ships in the harbor, then in World War II the place was used for an anti-submarine net.

The Anglican *Cathedral of St. John The Baptist,* a fine example of North American church Gothic architecture, was started in 1816, destroyed by fire in 1842 and again in 1892, then the present building was restored in 1905. The clergy is pleased to provide information. The *Basilica of St. John The Baptist,* started in 1841 and finished in 1850, is made of limestone and Irish granite, built in the shape of a cross, with 138-foot towers, and holds 2,000 people.

MUSEUMS. *Newfoundland Museum* on Duckworth St. opposite Cathedral St. has a number of artifacts from shipwrecked vessels, displays of early settlements in Newfoundland, as well as the only known relics of the Beothuk Indians, a vanished race that once roamed the island. Open days seven days a week plus Thursday evenings until 9 P.M. Admission free.

The Newfoundland Museum at the Murray Premises, a downtown branch of the main museum, has displays of the province's sea-going history, plus a collection of military firearms, equipment, uniforms and other exhibits. The hours are the same as those of the main branch.

Presentation Sisters Museum at their convent on Cathedral Square has artifacts and photos about this third oldest English speaking order of nuns in North America. Appointment is required. The *Anglican Cathedral* (with a small museum) on the corner of Gower St. and Church Hill, is rated one of the finest examples of ecclesiastical architecture in North America. Its museum is located behind the small organ screen to right of altar. Usually open when cathedral is open.

Commissariat House, a provincial historic site, is a former military residence and rectory restored to the style of the 1830's. The small restoration of Quidi

Vidi Battery on Quidi Vidi Rd. has a small museum of military objects. Open June 1–Sept. 15.

ART GALLERIES: The *Memorial University Art Gallery* at the Arts and Culture Centre has lectures, films, and other presentations, in addition to art exhibits. The Gallery, 284 Duckworth St., deals in Canadian paintings, prints and sculpture. *Studio 131,* at 131 LeMarchant Rd., presents changing exhibits of local artists' work. *Atlantic Arts Ltd., Fine Arts Gallery,* sells a variety of works.

THEATER AND MUSIC. Live theater in St. John's is not necessarily abundant, but it is lively. *CODCO* and the *Newfoundland Mummers Troupe* are two groups that have caught national attention with their own material. They play in various places. More formal theater, including Shakespearean presentations, are staged at the auditorium of the *Arts and Culture Centre* at Memorial University, and also at the *Little Theatre* at the university. *The Arts and Culture Centre* is the city's main stage and also hosts symphony orchestras, jazz concerts, and the like. Phone 737-3900 for information.

SHOPPING. Newfoundland handcrafts have an international reputation. It is the home of such exotica as Grenfell parkas, Labradorite jewelry, and so on. St. John's abounds in craftshops—most of them being concentrated in the commercial area along Duckworth St. Restored Murray Premises has excellent quality shops. The Newfoundland and Labrador Crafts Development Association, 77 Bond St., has a complete list of craft shops, products, and information on prices. The Tourism Division, Department of Development, Atlantic Place, Water St., also has booklets listing crafts and outlets. The *Avalon Mall* is the main downtown shopping mall. Malls are mostly open Monday–Saturday, 10 A.M.–9 P.M. Other shopping areas open Monday–Saturday, 9 A.M.–5 P.M., except Friday night when they stay open to 9 P.M. Most stores are closed Victoria Day (late May), Memorial Day (late June), Labor Day, and Thanksgiving. Some stores may be closed St. George's Day (late April), Discovery Day in mid-June, Orangemen's Day in early July, and Remembrance Day (November 11).

DINING OUT. Restaurants are categorized on the basis of full-course dinners; drinks, tax and tips excluded: *Expensive,* over $16; *Moderate,* $10–$16; *Inexpensive,* less than $10.

A 12% provincial sales tax will be added to your bill.

Most places accept the following major credit cards: American Express, MasterCard and Visa; others may also be honored. Not all establishments accept credit cards, therefore we suggest you call for information.

Dining out in St. John's can be a pleasant experience if one samples the various Newfoundland dishes and chooses wisely from the menu. Seafoods tend to be the best choice. Expect them to be prepared in a fairly traditional manner —wholesome but not too exciting. Most of the better restaurants can provide small side orders of traditional food such as cod tongues, scrunchions (bits of fat pork, crisply fried), fish and brewis, or seal flipper.

Service is generally good in the better restaurants although it can be slow, especially if the place is busy. Strike up a conversation with your waiter who can often provide you with an enjoyable meal and friendly humor.

The ACT III Restaurant. *Moderate-Expensive.* At the Arts and Culture Centre. Quality dining in a relaxed atmosphere. Phone 754–0790. Major credit cards.

The Fishing Admiral. *Moderate-Expensive.* Live lobster, seafood, Newfoundland dishes. Phone 753–6203. Major credit cards.

Battery Motel Dining Room. *Moderate.* On Signal Hill. One of the best places in St. John's. Ask for a window table overlooking St. John's at night. North American menu with Newfoundland specialties. Organ music most nights during dining. Phone 726–0040. Major credit cards.

Captain's Table. *Moderate.* Dining room at the Hotel Newfoundland. General menu is limited and food uninspired, but the Sunday buffet is good and good value. Plenty of choices of hot and cold food with some interesting desserts. Reservations. Phone 726–4980. Major credit cards.

Colonial Inn. *Moderate.* In community of Topsail on Hwy. 3 just outside St. John's. Good but limited menu; décor should be seen only in dim light. Fireplace, nice, little bar, cozy. Reservations. Phone 722–6933. Major credit cards.

Starboard Quarter. *Moderate.* Royal Trust Building on Water St. Has good view of waterfront and ships. Service sometimes slow but friendly. Nice atmosphere for lunch or dinner. Reservations. Phone 753–9510. Major credit cards.

Captain's Cabin. *Inexpensive.* Cafeteria in Bowring's Department Store on Water St. has nice view of harbor and waterfront. Specialties—Newfoundland dishes and Irish coffee. Phone 726–3280.

NIGHTCLUBS AND BARS. A St. John's pub crawl is a cultural experience in itself. It's a city that expresses itself, rather in an Irish way, in its multitudes of ebullient lounges, taverns, and bars. The minimum legal drinking age in Newfoundland is 19.

Club Max, 130 Water St., a lively disco club with psychedelic interior.

The *Brand E Saloon,* 379 Duckworth St., has soft pop and western music (live) and a small but cozy dance floor.

The Speakeasy, Murray Premises. Basically a wine bar, but everything available. Live entertainment weekends. Nice spot for a drink in restored historic premises.

The *Ship Inn,* 265 Duckworth St. Tinkling piano entertainment, roomy bar, good pub snacks. A very popular spot with the locals.

Christian's, 23 George St., specializes in coffees and wines.

The *Captain's Quarters* at the Holiday Inn is heavy on the distinquished nautical atmosphere.

The *Cock 'n' Bull,* 223 Duckworth St., and *Upstairs-Downstairs* are English-style pubs.

Other interesting spots include *Rob Roy's Pub,* with Scottish setting, *Bridgett's,* a popular neighborhood pub at 29 Cookstown Rd., The *Station Lounge,* the *Silver Knight Lounge,* and *Schoeder's Piano Bar.*

EXPLORING NEWFOUNDLAND'S WEST COAST

The west coast begins at the ferry terminal and fishing town of Port-aux-Basques, a name that reveals the Basque past of this part of Newfoundland.

On Table Mountain, just a few miles north of Port-aux-Basques on the Trans-Canada Highway (Highway 1), is a big yellow and black wind-warning sign: "Notice. Dangerous winds up to 120 miles per hour known to occur next 10 miles." The sign explains that if drivers have difficulty handling their cars they should wait or turn back "as high winds [are] known to blow trains from rails, and overturn motor vehicles." In characteristic Newfoundland style, no punches are pulled in wording the sign. The wind, funneled by the Long Range Mountains on one side and the open sea on the other, can blow a terrific gale across the plateau. The ground-hugging bushes and stunted, twisted trees quietly attest to the might of the wind.

Safely across Table Mountain, the mountains rise forested and quiet, one after another toward the horizon. Cottages nestle beside the lakes here and there. Privacy is the rule—there are enough lakes to go around.

The town of Stephenville was one of those created by World War II. Under the lend-lease agreement between Britain and the United States, land for an air base was turned over to the U.S. military. The complex was named Harmon Field and thousands of American military people at one time or another set foot in Newfoundland. The field and buildings were eventually turned back to the Newfoundland government and are used today as a commercial airport. A liner board mill was opened here during the 1960's, went bankrupt in the 1970's, but now has opened again as a paper mill. Forestry is the town's main industry.

Corner Brook, the "western capital," is the center of Newfoundland's west coast. At the mouth of the Humber River, the city is a major pulp and paper producer and retail distribution center for half of Newfoundland. Corner Brook is on the Humber River, which teems with salmon during the season. Journeying north past Deer Lake, one must stop to enjoy the grandeur of Bonne Bay and Gros Morne National Park. The *Practical Information* section on national parks toward the end of this chapter gives more detailed information.

To reach the park, one must turn off the Trans-Canada to Highway 430. Highways in the park region are maintained by the Parks Department and although some of the routes are gravel surfaced, they are usually in excellent condition.

North from Gros Morne Park, Highway 430 follows the coast for nearly 640 kms. (400 miles) to St. Anthony. Although the highway is well maintained, this is not a journey for the faint-hearted in the winter. During the summer it is a trip to be long remembered. The road passes through tiny villages at the foot of forested mountains beside the sea. The country is wild and if the interior looks uninhabited, that is because it is the domain of moose, bear, and other animals. If the drive gets tiring, a night at Cow Head or Hawke's Bay, is a good idea.

At Port au Choix, the National Historic Park is dedicated to the ancestors of Indians and Inuit who lived here 4,000 years ago. The Viking ruins at L'Anse-aux-Meadows National Historic Park, recently placed on the World Heritage list by UNESCO, have been preserved and housed for viewing. Standing on the barren headland, one can imagine the high-prowed longship bringing the Norsemen across the sea from Greenland as they sought the legendary Vinland.

At St. Barbe, a small ferry takes cars across the Strait of Belle Isle to the coast of Labrador at Blanc Sablon. A 48-km. (30-mile) drive brings one to the Pinware River Provincial Park for fishing and a view of one of the world's last frontiers. Check with a Newfoundland tourist center for ferry times and fishing regulations.

In general, the west coast has rather different weather from the central and east. Temperatures on the west coast tend to drop lower in winter and rise higher in summer, and areas such as the Marble Mountain Ski area may have more than 150 inches of snow on the ground at the end of the season.

EXPLORING CENTRAL AND EASTERN NEWFOUNDLAND

Looking at a map of Newfoundland, one sees that the interior of the province is marked by an absence of roads and that communities along several hundred miles of the south coast have no roads, in or out. With Newfoundland entering confederation as late as 1949, it might be said that highway development had some catching up to do. The highway across the island, now known as Highway 1 (the Trans-Canada Highway), was for many years gravel surfaced and paved only in sections. To cross the province was something of an adventure. By the mid-1960's, the paving was completed and work has been directed at improving the remainder of the trunk roads. Most communities are now serviced by paved roads.

The paving of the TCH linked the east and west coasts and has assisted in opening up the central portion of the island. West from Deer Lake, the highway runs through what seems to be deserted country—forests of spruce, occasional bogs, and mountains in the background. Most of the exits turn to the seacoast. Pick an exit, find yourself a tiny community with a name like Sop's Arm or Harry's Harbour, and stop a while.

The twin towns of Windsor and Grand Falls straddle the TCH halfway across the province. Both are paper towns and retail centers for the surrounding area. The Mary March Museum in Grand Falls has displays of logging and natural history of the region. Mary March was the Christian name given to Shananditti, a young Beothuk Indian woman captured by John Peyton, Jr., near Grand Falls. Shananditti died in 1829 at the age of twenty-two, the last survivor of a tribe that may have numbered more than 50,000.

The town of Botwood at the mouth of the Exploits River might have become a world aviation capital. Prior to World War II, the aviation industry was undecided as to the merits of flying boats versus land-based aircraft. With the outbreak of war, the superiority of the wheeled airplane became evident and Botwood, which had been scheduled to become a major flying boat base, became the victim of technology. The town of Gander, only 91 kms. (57 miles) away and at the time just a small air station, was expanded as the airbase for the trans-Atlantic air ferry service and the first North American landfall when passenger crossings were being made by propeller-driven aircraft. A small museum in the Gander airport portrays the long history of trans-Atlantic aviation in Newfoundland and displays models of many of the early aircraft.

One of the best drives on Newfoundland's east coast is along the Eastport Peninsula. Take Highway 310 at Glovertown, follow the partly graveled road to the community of Salvage, and stop at the tiny local history museum. The museum was created by purchasing a house and all of the furnishings, fixtures and fittings from a retired fisherman and his wife. The couple was given a new completely furnished home nearby. Beaches, a shipyard, and even a community called Happy Adventure are there for the tourist's pleasure.

EXPLORING LABRADOR

Labrador, one of the last North American frontiers, has been called "the land that God gave Cain." Icy and desolate in winter, it has an austere charm in summer. It has few people but is rich in minerals, water, wildlife, and forests. Still relatively unexplored, Labrador is a land of mystery and power. Its land mass constitutes the larger part of the province of Newfoundland.

Goose Bay and the adjacent community of Happy Valley were once bustling and busy. Goose Bay was built as a ferry station for aircraft during World War II. The United States obtained the base under the lend-lease arrangement and the British and Canadian forces also owned portions of the base. Recently, the U.S. has cut back on the use of the base so that the future of the communities is now uncertain. The commercial airport uses part of the base facility and the community is a service center for the various outposts up and down the Labrador coast. "Goose" is also the jumping off point for anglers and hunters taking bush planes into private lakes and rivers. Visitors can reach Goose Bay only by plane or by CN Marine coastal boat.

Wabush and Labrador City are twin mining towns on the Labrador–Québec border which produce about 50% of Canada's iron ore. They are pleasant company towns with relatively few facilities for tourists except the Smokey Mountain Ski Club which attracts the hardier cross-country skiers. The area boasts one of the world's best cross-country ski ranges, at which international competitions are held occasionally.

Labrador's main appeal for tourists is fishing and a limited amount of hunting. Salmon, Arctic char, trout, and northern-pike are fished. See *Practical Information* section on "Fishing" and other related sections at end of this chapter for further details.

PRACTICAL INFORMATION FOR
NEWFOUNDLAND AND LABRADOR

HOW TO GET THERE. By air: *Eastern Provincial Airways* operates scheduled jet services to a number of Newfoundland centers including St. John's, Gander, Corner Brook, Goose Bay, Churchill Falls, and Wabush, from Toronto, Montréal and other eastern Canadian points. *Air Canada* operates scheduled jet flights from Toronto, Montréal and eastern Canadian points to St. John's and Stephenville. *Quebecair* operates scheduled jet flights from Montréal to Wabush.

By car: With the exception of some 50 miles of highway from Blanc Sablon to Red Bay and local roads in Goose Bay and Wabush/Labrador City, Labrador has no roads. The island of Newfoundland has about 9,654 km. (6,000 miles) of highway, including the 906-km. (565-mile) Trans-Canada Hwy. from Port-aux-Basques to St. John's. Most main roads, including the Trans-Canada, are paved; however, the secondary highways are usually gravel surfaced.

From North Sydney, Nova Scotia, to Port-aux-Basques, Newfoundland, there is a daily year-round car/ferry service (with up to five crossings per day in summer). A crossing takes about six hours. During the summer season, it is best to travel early in the day and early in the week. Cabins, restaurants, bars, cinema and a tourist bureau are available during the summer. Reservations are required on all crossings and must be picked up at the ferry terminal 1½ hours before sailing.

CN Marine also operates a summer service from North Sydney, Nova Scotia, to Argentia, Newfoundland—an 18-hour mini-cruise for visitors with some room for cars. The service runs from mid-June to mid-September, three days per week. Cabins, a restaurant and bar, cinema, and tourist bureau are available. Reservations are required and must be picked up 1½ hours before sailing at the ferry terminal. For information and reservations, contact CN Marine, Reservations Bureau, P.O. Box 250, North Sydney, Nova Scotia B2A 3M3.

By train: Train service to Newfoundland is operated by *Via Rail* through the ferry crossings from North Sydney, Nova Scotia, to Port-aux-Basques, Newfoundland. Connections may be made to Via Rail by *Amtrak* from New York. Since Newfoundland had operated under the British rail system, all trains in the province ran on narrow-gauge tracks. The alternative to replacement of all track and antiquated rolling stock was to discontinue passenger service by rail during the 1960's and institute an efficient service by motor coaches (known in Newfoundland as "road cruisers"). Road cruisers reach most major communities in Newfoundland adjacent to the Trans-Canada Hwy.

CN Marine provides a toll-free telephone service from eastern Canada and the northeast U.S. From the latter (except Maine) call 1–800–341–7981; from Maine, 800–432–7344. From Nova Scotia, P.E.I. and New Brunswick call 1–800–565–9470; from Québec and Ontario, 1–800–565–9411. Via Rail offices in eastern Canada also have information. Or see your travel agent.

By bus: Most major bus lines throughout North America connect with *Acadian Lines* in Nova Scotia to take visitors to the ferry in North Sydney, Nova Scotia. For information, see your local bus line agent or your travel agent.

ACCOMMODATIONS. Visitors to Newfoundland will find traditional, comfortable accommodation throughout the province. In the larger centers, the motels may appear more modern, but they cannot exceed the hospitality of the smaller properties. Most lodgings are small and have a dining room and/or bar as part of the business. Some of the older properties may not have private bathrooms in all units; you must specify if you wish a private bath. Usually, the owners live on the property and welcome guests personally.

Double occupancy rates in Newfoundland are categorized as follows: *Expensive,* $40 or more; *Moderate,* $30–40; *Inexpensive,* under $30.

The 12% provincial sales tax will be applied to all accommodation rates.

Most places accept the following major credit cards: American Express, MasterCard and Visa; others may also be honored. Not all establishments accept credit cards, therefore we suggest you call for information.

BURGEO. *Moderate–Expensive:* **Sou'Wester Inn.** Accommodations by the sea. Lots of atmosphere. Adequate dining room. Phone 886–3309.

CLARENVILLE. *Expensive:* **Holiday Inn.** Typical Holiday Inn. Coffeeshop, dining room, cocktail lounge. Outdoor pool. Phone 466–7911. Major credit cards.

CORNER BROOK. *Expensive.* **Glymill Inn.** Lots of atmosphere; main dining room is baronial. Phone 634–5181. Major credit cards.

Holiday Inn. No surprises. Typical of the chain. Adequate dining room. Phone 634–5381. Major credit cards.

Mamateek Motor Inn. Good accommodations. Restaurant and coffeeshop. Phone 639–8901. Major credit cards.

DEER LAKE. *Expensive:* **Deer Lake Motel.** Basic accommodations. Coffeeshop and licensed dining room. Phone 635–2108. Major credit cards.

DUNVILLE. *Moderate:* **Northeast Arm Motel.** 8 rooms in a quiet setting. Restaurant and dining room. Phone 227–3560. Major credit cards.

EASTPORT. *Moderate:* **Eastport Motel.** Motel units and housekeeping cabins. Children stay free. Restaurant and cocktail lounge. Saturday-night dancing. Phone 667–2458.

White Sails Inn and Cabins. Rooms in lodge and housekeeping units. Meals available. Open May 24 to October 15. Phone 677–3400.

FORTUNE. *Moderate:* **Sea View Motel.** Basic accommodation with restaurant and cocktail lounge. Phone 832–1411.

GANDER. *Expensive:* **Albatross Motel.** Excellent seafood dining room—specialty: the Albatross seafood platters. Cocktail lounge, beauty salon. Base for Eastern Provincial Airways stewardesses and pilots. Phone 256–3956. Major credit cards.

Holiday Inn. Typical Holiday Inn. Nice, cozy cocktail lounge. Coffeeshop and dining room are merely adequate. Outdoor pool. Phone 256–3981. Major credit cards.

GLOVERTOWN. *Inexpensive:* **Ackerman's Hospitality Home.** Friendly hosts. Breakfast available. Phone 533–2811.

GRAND BANK. *Moderate:* **Granny Motor Inn.** 10 rooms, lounge and dining room. Intimate little place. Phone 832–2180. Major credit cards.

GRAND FALLS. *Expensive:* **Mount Peyton Motel.** Good place to stay; dining room is excellent. Cocktail lounge. Children under 12 free, if in room with parents. Open year round. Phone 489–2251. Major credit cards.
Moderate: **Highliner Inn.** All housekeeping units; pleasant and comfortable. Cocktail lounge. Phone 489–5639. Major credit cards.
Inexpensive: **Town and Country Inn.** Lounge, functional dining room, Continental breakfast. Phone 489–9602.

HARBOUR GRACE. *Inexpensive–Moderate:* **Pike's Motel & Hotel.** 14 motel and 7 hotel rooms; adequate restaurant, separate dining room plus cocktail lounge. Phone 596–5072.

HAWKE'S BAY. *Moderate–Expensive:* **Maynard's.** Motel and housekeeping units. Specify if you wish motel unit with private bath. Dining room and cocktail lounge. Phone 248–3131. Major credit cards.

LEWISPORTE. *Moderate–Expensive:* **Brittany Inn.** Hospitable staff; good service. Dining room and cocktail lounge. Phone 535–2533. Major credit cards.

PLACENTIA. *Inexpensive–Moderate:* **Harold Hotel.** Basic accommodations in older hotel. Specify if you wish room with private bath. Restaurant and cocktail lounge. Phone 227–2107. Major credit cards.

PORT-AUX-BASQUES. *Expensive:* **Hotel Port-aux-Basques.** Basic accommodations in old-style ferry landing hotel. Major credit cards. Phone 695–2171.

PORT UNION. *Moderate:* **Seaport Inn.** Older hotel; toilet and basin in room; shared bath. Good food in dining room; licensed. Phone 469–2257.

ST. ANTHONY. *Expensive:* **Vinland Motel.** Basic motel accommodations. Dining room, coffeeshop and cocktail lounge. Phone 454–8843. Major credit cards.
Moderate: **St. Anthony Motel.** Basic motel accommodations. Dining room and cocktail lounge. Phone 454–3200. Major credit cards.

STEPHENVILLE. *Expensive:* **Island Inn.** 75 West St. Comfortable; food is good in the dining room. Phone 643–5616. Major credit cards.

TRAYTOWN. *Inexpensive:* **Lewdrews Housekeeping Cabins.** Lovely spot, especially for families. Phone 533–2553.
Traytown Tourist Cabins. All housekeeping cabins. Clean and comfortable. Grassy fields for children; boats available. Open May to mid-October. Phone 533–2246.

TRINITY. *Inexpensive:* **Trinity Cabins.** All housekeeping cabins. $2 for each child under 12. Groceries, gift shop, beverage room, swimming pool. Drive-in and travel-trailer park. Open May to September 30. Phone 464–3657.

WOODY POINT. *Moderate:* **Stornoway Lodge.** Small clean motel with dining room and tea room. Phone 453–2282.

HOW TO GET AROUND. By car: With the exception of a few miles of highway from Blanc Sablon to Red Bay and local roads in Goose Bay and Wabush/Labrador City, the Labrador area of Newfoundland has no roads suitable for normal vehicles. The island has about 9,654 km. (6,000 miles) of highway, including the 906-km. (565-mile). Trans-Canada Hwy. (signposted throughout Newfoundland as "TCH") from Port-aux-Basques to St. John's. Secondary roads are generally paved; some gravel-surfaced roads remain, but they are usually in good condition in summer.

By train: Since Newfoundland operated under the British rail system, the trains in the province ran on narrow-gauge track. Passenger service by rail was discontinued during the 1960's and a bus service is operated by *Terra Transport.* Known as "roadcruisers," the buses reach most major communities in Newfoundland adjacent to the Trans-Canada Hwy. For information, contact *Via Rail* (see information for trains in "How to Get There" section), call Terra Transport (737–5916) in St. John's or a travel agent.

By air: *Eastern Provincial Airways* operates jet passenger flights connecting St. John's, Gander, Corner Brook (via Deer Lake and Stephenville airports), Goose Bay, Churchill Falls, and Wabush/Labrador City. An unscheduled charter service by float- and ski-equipped bush aircraft is operated from Goose Bay by *Labrador Airways* to major settlements on the Labrador coast and into the bush. Write Labrador Airways, Box 219, Goose Bay, Labrador. Call (709) 896–3387.

By boat: One of the most interesting ways to see Newfoundland and Labrador is by one of the *CN Marine* coastal boats. The south coast service has sailings from Argentia to Port-aux-Basques, calling in at a number of tiny ports along the way. Many of these ports are not connected to the highway system and the boat brings in the mail, freight and passengers. Operates year-round.

The North Coast and Labrador CN boats service many tiny isolated communities on the Labrador coast from St. John's and Lewisport as starting points. Sailings from spring thaw (mid-May to mid-June) until mid-November.

A round trip on one of the Labrador boats can take up to a week, covering some 1,600 nautical miles and calling at up to 40 communities.

The coastal steamer service operated by CN Marine provides passenger and freight connections to the many settlements in Newfoundland and Labrador not reached by road or railway. Trips on these boats offer extremely interesting vacation travel, passing through numerous picturesque coastal villages. Reservations on this service can only be made from within the Province of Newfoundland by contacting CN Marine Reservations Bureau, P.O. Box 520, Port-aux-Basques, Newfoundland AOM 1C0. Phone 1–800–563–7381.

TOURIST INFORMATION. Travel information on Newfoundland may be obtained from Tourism Branch, Department of Development, P.O. Box 2016, St. John's, Newfoundland A1C 5R8. For information while in St. John's, call 737–2830.

Tourist Information Chalets are conveniently located along the Trans-Canada Hwy. (Hwy. 1). They are: Port-aux-Basques, 695–2262; Corner Brook, 639–9792; Deer Lake, 639–9792; Springvale, 673–3110; Grand Falls, 489–6332; Gander, 651–3860; Clarenville, 466–3100; Marystown, 279–3830; Dunville, 227–5602; Notre Dame Junction, 535–8547; Twillingate, 629–7207; Whitbourne Junction, 759–2170; Stephenville, 647–9208.

Tourist desks are also located on the ferries sailing from North Sydney, Nova Scotia, to Port-aux-Basques and Argentia and at the ferry terminal at North Sydney.

TELEPHONE. The telephone area code for all Newfoundland is 709.

TIME ZONE. Newfoundland has its own unique time zone—Newfoundland Time. It's ½ hour in advance of Atlantic Time and 1½ hours ahead of Eastern Time. Some parts of Labrador, however, are on Atlantic Time and some are on Eastern.

 SEASONAL EVENTS. January is winter carnival time in many Newfoundland towns and villages. The biggest carnivals are held in Corner Brook and Labrador City. Parades, snow sculpture, skiing, and other outdoor events and lots of parties are featured. In mid-**March,** the Wabush Winter Carnival.

From spring to fall there are weekly harness horse racing cards at Goulds near St. John's. Also at Meadows Raceway near Corner Brook.

In the 1920's the late Johnny Burke wrote a song about the Kelligrews Soiree, a party to end all parties. In **July,** the village of Kelligrews on Conception Bay relives the soiree and the town of Placentia holds an annual regatta for the surrounding area.

July is also the month for the Harbour Grace Regatta and the towns of Carbonear and Botwood celebrate a civic holiday with picnics, entertainment and special events.

August features a number of civic festival days in various Newfoundland towns including Channel-Port-aux-Basques, Fortune, Gander, Windsor, and Grand Bank, and the Lion's Fair in Lewisporte.

During **September** and **October,** regional agricultural exhibitions and fairs are held throughout Newfoundland.

All-Breed Dog Championship Shows are held at St. John's in **May,** at Corner Brook in **July,** and in Harbour Grace on the Labor Day weekend.

 TOURS. Newfoundland's tourist industry is greatly geared to the traveler—especially the adventurous one —who wishes to fly in and experience the coast or the interior. There are boat tours and charters available in a half dozen places; there are organized canoe tours and "safaris" to the province's gripping interior; there's a "Trap Line Tour" by dogsled in Labrador; and there's wilderness sightseeing by air available. There's also whale-watching and bird-watching tours. And, of course, there are a half dozen companies offering bus tours to various parts of the province.

The Tourism Branch, Department of Development, will supply brochures on request, or you may pick them up at tourist bureaus. The major agency handling tours of various kinds is *Newfoundland Nature Tours and Travel,* Box 1734, St. John's, Newfoundland A1C 5PS. Phone 754–2052.

NATIONAL PARKS. Newfoundland is a wild, rugged, and beautiful land of mountains, lakes, forests, and wild-life—a description that is also appropriate for the province's two provincial parks.

Gros Morne National Park covers 1942 sq. kms. (750 sq. miles) of seacoast and mountain about 120 kms. (75 miles) north of Corner Brook. The mountains of the area drop sharply into the sea; the escarpment is sometimes 610 meters (2,000 feet) high. A tiny ferry carries cars across Bonne Bay from Woody Point to Norris Point at the foot of flat, gray, bald Gros Morne which rises 806 meters (2,644 feet) above the village.

Gros Morne National Park was the home region for a number of peoples including Archaic Indians (4,500 years ago), Eskimos about 1,000 years ago and, more recently, the Beothuk Indians until the time of their extinction in 1829.

The park will be in process of development until some time in the 1980's with some upgrading of facilities each year. Now the park has 159 unserviced camping sites, heated washrooms and showers, kitchen facilities, picnic areas, swimming, hiking, boat facilities, fishing and wilderness backpacking as well as a sewage disposal station. The maximum stay permitted in a campground is two weeks.

The Park Information Centre near Rocky Harbour has a large facilities and activities map for easy reference, with staff to answer questions. During the summer, a free interpretive program is offered by the park naturalist staff which includes conducted hikes and illustrated talks.

Activities in the park include hiking in the summer and snow shoeing and cross-country skiing in the winter. The well-marked hiking trail to the top of Gros Morne offers a commanding view of Bonne Bay and the Long Range Mountains. Fishing for salmon and brook trout are popular in the lakes and streams while mackerel and cod may be taken in the salt water. Fishing regulations are available from park officials and local merchants in the villages.

For swimmers, a large sandy beach at Shallow Bay offers saltwater bathing in water which can reach 21°C (70°F) during July and August. The mouth of Western Brook is also suitable for swimming and has a small sand beach.

Camping fees start at $3 for unserviced sites and rise from there. For additional information, write The Superintendent, Gros Morne National Park, Rocky Harbour, Newfoundland.

Terra Nova National Park is Canada's most easterly national park, covering 396 sq. kms. (153 square miles) of forested hills and lakes on Bonavista Bay. The park is about 232 kms. (145 miles) northwest of St. John's and 79 kms. (48 miles) southwest of Gander, on the Trans-Canada Hwy.

The surface of Terra Nova Park was scoured and gouged by the glaciers of the Ice Age; from convenient lookouts visitors can see six or more lakes; all at different altitudes, on the sides of the surrounding hills. In the park's bogs are a variety of wild flowers including the province's official flower, the pitcher plant. This unique plant is a carnivore that traps, drowns, and digests insects. Arctic char can be caught by patient anglers and brook trout are common in the streams. Whales and seals frequent the ocean shore. The park is home to numerous sea and land birds as well as animals of all sizes from moose to mink.

Park naturalists have developed an extensive interpretive program which includes guided hikes, boat tours and illustrated talks. During the summer, swimming, canoeing, boating, hiking, and fishing are popular. Winter activities include cross-country skiing, winter camping, and snowshoeing.

Serviced campsites are available at Newman Sound and Malady Head on a "first come" basis. Open year-round. Motel and restaurant facilities are available at Charlottetown and Newman Sound, at villages within the Park, or at various villages just outside the Park boundaries during the summer months.

Except for through highway traffic, an entrance fee to Terra Nova Park will be charged. Daily permit is about $1; $2 for a four-day permit and $10 for the season. Camping rates are $5.25–$5.75 per day. The overnight boat docking fee is from $3 to $9 depending on the length of boat.

Staff at the Park Information Centre, located at the headquarters area just off the Trans-Canada Hwy., can direct visitors to facilities and special events. For additional information, write The Superintendent, Terra Nova National Park, Glovertown, Newfoundland A0G 2L0.

 PROVINCIAL PARKS. One good way to enjoy the great outdoors in Newfoundland is to use the network of provincial parks—43 camping parks, 15 day-use parks and 19 "Natural Scenic Attractions" parks. All 77 parks have picnic areas; most have swimming facilities and well marked trails for hiking or strolling.

From mid-July to mid-August, the fresh water lakes and salt water ponds on the shore are at their best for swimming, usually between 16–20°C (60–70°F). Open salt water can be uncomfortably cold.

Three types of parks have been designated in Newfoundland: (1) Camping parks, which have both camping and day use facilities. The maximum stay is 24 consecutive days and requires a camping permit costing $5 per day; plus you will have to buy a $10 vehicle-entry permit, which is valid for all provincial parks throughout the season. The vehicle permit fee for one day is $2. No reservations for camping are accepted. (2) Day-use parks have no camping facilities. (3) Natural Scenic Attractions are parks with special scenic qualities or natural significance. They have ample parking and walking trails, and some have interpretation centers. Anyone 65 years or over is admitted free to all provincial parks upon proof of age. Angling is permitted in all parks and is subject to the provincial regulations. For licensing information, see park staff. No hunting is allowed in the parks.

Although the parks offer outdoor living at its best, there are some drawbacks such as black flies, mosquitos, and various other pests. The underbrush has been cleared as much as possible, however, to allow freer circulation of air. When picking a picnic site, try for one with a good breeze. A commercial insect repellent is often helpful.

The following provincial parks offer a good sample of Newfoundland outdoors:

Aspen Brook. Day-use only with small pool for swimming. Highway 1 at Aspen Brook, 11 kms. (7 miles) west of Windsor.

Backside Pond. Near Whiteway on Hwy. 80; 51 campsites, picnic area, swimming, hiking trail, trout and saltwater fishing. The Atlantic Cable Museum at nearby Heart's Content tells the story of trans-Atlantic communication.

· *Barachois Pond.* On Hwy. 1 about 64 kms. (40 miles) south of Corner Brook, there is one of the largest parks in the system. Swimming, boating, angling for salmon and trout, and water skiing on lake. Guided walks and evening programs by park naturalist; 158 campsites with dumping station. Hiking on Erin Mountain Hiking Trail for spectacular views.

Bellevue Beach. Hwy. 201 at Bellevue on Isthmus of Avalon. Picnic area, swimming, and boating in a protected barachois pond. Angling for trout and saltwater fish; 77 campsites.

Beothuk. Rte. 1 at Rushy Pond, just west of Windsor; 64 campsites, picnic and swimming, boating and trout fishing on Rushy Pond. Reconstructed logging camp open June 1 to September 6, 10 A.M. to 8 P.M. Admission included in permit fee.

Blow Me Down. At Lark Harbour on Hwy. 450, about 48 kms. (30 miles) west of Corner Brook; 27 campsites, picnic areas. Hiking trail to lookout over Bay of Islands. Saltwater angling.

Blue Ponds. Hwy. 1 about 24 kms. (15 miles) south of Corner Brook. Twin limestone lakes for swimming, hiking, picnic area; 37 campsites and trout streams.

Butter Pot. Probably Newfoundland's most popular park, on Hwy 1, about 32 kms. (20 miles) from St. John's. Freshwater beach, hiking trails to two spectacular lookouts, guided nature walks, interpretive center, picnic areas, 177 campsites, dumping station, and trout fishing.

Catamaran. Hwy. 1, about 48 kms. (30 miles) west of Windsor, on Joe's Lake; 55 campsites, picnic area, swimming, and boat launch. Trout fishing.

Chance Cove. On Hwy. 10 near Cape Race. Camping park with picnic area, 25 campsites, swimming, trout and saltwater fishing. Bay seals live along the shallows during certain seasons.

Cheeseman. Hwy. 1 just north of Port-aux-Basques and the CN ferry to Nova Scotia; 103 campsites, picnic area, swimming, trout and saltwater angling. Try beachcombing on the Cape Ray Sands.

Cochrane Pond. Hwy. 1 about 16 kms. (10 miles) south of St. John's. Day-use park with picnic areas, swimming, and trout angling in pond.

Crabbes River. Hwy. 1 near intersection of Hwy. 405; 32 campsites, picnic area. Good salmon and trout fishing.

Dildo Run. Highway 340 on New World Island. Take highway from Trans-Canada toward Lewisporte and continue toward Twillingate; 31 campsites, picnic sites, swimming, and saltwater fishing.

Duley Lake. Labrador City, Labrador; 100 campsites, sandy beach on lake with swimming, boating, and trout fishing.

Father Duffy's Well. Hwy. 90 about 24 kms. (15 miles) south of Holyrood. Day use only. Shrine dedicated to 19th century Irish priest.

Fitzgerald's Pond. Hwy. 100, about 32 kms. (20 miles) east of Argentia. Near CN ferry to Nova Scotia and Castle Hill National Historic Park; 24 campsites, picnic, swimming, and hiking. Angling for salmon and trout.

Flatwater Pond. Hwy. 410 to Baie Verte, about 40 kms. (25 miles) north from the Trans-Canada Hwy.; 25 campsites, picnic area, freshwater swimming, boat launching, trout angling.

Frenchman's Cove. Near Garnish on Hwy. 213. Burin Peninsula. Salt- and freshwater swimming, picnic sites, 81 campsites, trout and saltwater fishing, bird-watching.

Freshwater Pond. Hwy. 220 near Burin. Sandy beaches and freshwater swimming, 30 campsites, picnic areas, boat launch, salmon and trout fishing.

Glenwood. A day-use park on Hwy. 1, just west of Gander. Picnics, trout fishing, and fresh water swimming.

Grand Codroy. Hwy. 406, off Hwy. 1, about 40 kms. (25 miles) north of Port-aux-Basques; 25 campsites, picnic area, and freshwater swimming. Canoeing, salmon and trout angling.

Gushues Pond. Hwy. 1 about 48 kms. (30 miles) from St. John's. Two ponds for swimming; trout fishing and boating; 117 campsites.

Holyrood Pond. Hwy. 90 on St. Mary's Bay, more than 96 kms. (60 miles) south of the village of Holyrood. Long, narrow saltwater pond for warm salt water bathing, boating, trout and saltwater fishing; 15 campsites and picnic area.

Indian River. Hwy. 1 near Springdale. Canoeing on river, swimming, hiking, salmon and trout fishing, picnic area; 49 campsites.

Jack's Pond. Hwy. 1 near Arnold's Cove on Avalon Isthmus. Freshwater boating, swimming, trout fishing, picnic area; 74 campsites.

Jonathan's Pond. Hwy. 330 about 16 kms. (10 miles) north of Gander. Birch forest, boating, swimming, 96 campsites and picnic area.

LaManche Valley. Hwy. 10, about 48 kms. (30 miles) south of St. John's; 51 campsites, picnic area, hiking, swimming, trout and saltwater fishing. Waterfall and bird-watching.

Lockston Path. Hwy. 236 on the Bonavista Peninsula; 20 sheltered campsites, fresh water beach, picnic area, swimming, boat launch.

Mary March. On Hwy. 370 to Buchans. Named after Mary March, the last known Beothuk Indian, who was captured nearby. Red Indian Lake provides good swimming, trout fishing and swimming. Picnic sites and boating; 26 campsites.

Mummichog. Hwy. 1, about 24 kms. (15 miles) north of Port-aux-Basques. Named after a small fish found in the brackish waters of the lagoon; 38 campsites, picnic area, swimming, boat launch, and hiking trails. Salmon and trout fishing in stream.

Northern Bay Sands. Hwy. 70, about 24 kms. (15 miles) north of Carbonear. Fresh and saltwater swimming; 42 campsites, picnic area, and saltwater fishing.

Notre Dame. Hwy. 1, about 32 kms. (20 miles) east of Bishops Falls. Swimming, picnic area, and 100 campsites with dumping station.

Otter Bay. Hwy. 1, about 24 kms. (15 miles) east of Port-aux-Basques; 5 campsites, picnic area, swimming, trout and saltwater fishing.

Piccadilly Head. Hwy. 463 on the Port au Port Peninsula; 50 campsites, picnic area, hiking, swimming on a long sandy beach, and saltwater fishing.

Pinware River. Take the ferry from Flowers Cove on Hwy. 430 to the Labrador coast and follow Hwy. 510 toward Red Bay for about 48 kms. (30 miles). Camping park at the mouth of a good salmon river. 15 campsites. Trout and saltwater fishing, too.

Pipers Hole River. Camping park on Hwy. 210 near Swift Current. 30 campsites. Picnic area, scheduled salmon river, hiking trail. No swimming.

Pistolet Bay. Hwy. 437 near St. Anthony. Canoeing country with 27 campsites, picnic area, swimming, salmon and trout fishing; near L'Anse au Meadows Viking settlement and historic park.

River of Ponds. Hwy. 430 near the village River of Ponds; 40 campsites, picnic area, swimming, boat launch, salmon and trout angling; exhibit of whale bones.

Sandbanks. At the community of Burgeo. Accessible only by boat; 8 campsites, picnic area, and swimming at sandy beaches; trout and saltwater fishing.

Smallwood. Hwy. 320 north of Gambo; 27 campsites, picnic area, fine salmon angling; working model of a watermill.

Squires Memorial. Hwy. 422 near Deer Lake. One of the larger provincial parks; 159 campsites, picnic area, good salmon fishing, boat rental facility. Reserve the night before. Cost about $6 per day.

Square Pond. Hwy. 1 near Gambo; 93 campsites, picnic area, swimming, boat launch, hiking, salmon, trout and Arctic char angling.

Sop's Arm. Hwy. 420 near the village of Sop's Arm on White Bay; 25 campsites, picnic area, salmon, trout and saltwater fishing.

Windmill Bight. Hwy. 330 near Cape Freels on Bonavista Bay; 29 campsites, picnic area, fresh- and saltwater swimming, salmon, trout and saltwater fishing. Good place to watch for icebergs.

Natural Scenic Attraction parks, a Newfoundland specialty, are especially worthwhile. There are 19. Here are a few:

The Arches. North of Gros Morne National Park on Rte. 430. Natural rock archway created by tidal action.

Cataracts. Hwy. 91, 100 kms. (60 mi.) southwest of St. John's. A deep river gorge with two waterfalls. Stairs and walkways.

Deadman's Bay. Hwy. 330. Grand coastline; spot to watch for in early summer.

Dungeon. Rte. 238 near Bonavista. Features a sea cave with a natural archway carved by tidal action. A restored 19th-century lighthouse nearby.

Eastport North Beach. Hwy. 310. Excellent beach and scenery on Eastport Bay. Terra Nova National Park and craft shops nearby.

French Islands. Hwy. 220 south from Grand Bank. Excellent view of St. Pierre and Miquelon islands, owned by France.

Maberly. Rte. 238 near Bonavista. A sea bird colony nesting on an off-shore island is visible from the jagged shore.

Northeast Arm. Hwy. 310 off Glovertown. Spectacular ocean view overlooking Terra Nova National Park from across the water.

Point La Haye. Hwy. 90 about 150 kms. (90 mi.) southwest of St. John's. Historic beach utilized by Basque fishermen in centuries past for drying their catch.

CHILDREN'S ACTIVITIES. Keeping children occupied in Newfoundland should present little problem, but do not look for amusement parks or fully equipped playgrounds except in the larger centers. Concentrate on the network of provincial and national parks.

Obtain a fishing license for the family and pack a couple of rods and reels for hours of entertainment. Sturdy footwear and clothing make hiking and walking easier in the parks.

A trip to a fishing village in mid- to late afternoon should put visitors at the wharf in time to see local fishermen cleaning their catch and carting away the fish. Nature walks and lectures at the parks will hold the attention of older children and a camera may keep a child involved for the entire trip.

SUMMER SPORTS. Sports in Newfoundland tend to be the outdoors variety. **Water sports** such as water skiing, canoeing, power boating, and sailing are popular activities. There are **harness horse racing** cards at the Avalon Raceway in Goulds, near St. John's, from spring to fall every Sunday and Wednesday evening and at other unscheduled times. There is also great interest in **golf, tennis, bowling, roller skating,** and **rowing** in centers where facilities are available.

Golf courses include the Grand Falls Golf and Country Club and the Blomidon Golf and Country Club in Corner Brook. Nine hole courses are located at

Stephenville and Labrador City. Check with local tourist information centers for rules on visitors at each course.

Newfoundland is a **canoeists'** paradise. The tourism department offers a list of about twenty routes, ranging in length from 12 to 336 kms., and they should be consulted about current restrictions on forest travel in the fire season. Canoe tours to the deep interior are arranged by some outfitters. Canoes can be rented at numerous places. Check with the tourist bureaus.

See sections on "Fishing" and "Hunting" for information on these sports.

FISHING. Newfoundland is one of the best fishing areas in North America. Brook trout can be found in most streams and salmon populate many of the larger rivers. In saltwater, codfish can be jigged and sea trout, flounder, tuna, mackerel and caplin can be caught. Deep-sea tuna fishing is also available.

Nonresidents must have a valid fishing license. For salmon fishing they must be accompanied by a licensed guide. Inland fishing licenses are available from most service stations, sporting goods stores, hardware stores, and department stores. Nonresident salmon fishng licenses cost about $40 for the season. Family salmon licenses are about $60 for the season. Salmon may be taken by artificial fly only during the season from June 20 to August 31 on the Island of Newfoundland and from June 20 to Sept. 15 in Labrador.

Nonresident trout licenses cost $10 for individuals for the season and $15 for a family. The license covers all rivers except those indicated as scheduled rivers. These are usually well marked. Salmon licenses are required for these waters. Special licenses from park officials are required for fishing in Terra Nova National Park. The open season for rainbow trout is June 1 to September 15. The season for all other trout is January 15 to September 15.

Licensed guides are required for all fishing in Labrador where the fishing waters are usually located far from habitation and are reached by bush plane. The season for Arctic char, northern pike, and trout other than rainbow trout is January 15 to September 15 in unscheduled rivers in Labrador.

The bag limit for trout in Newfoundland and Labrador is 24 per day per license, or the number of trout totaling 10 pounds in weight plus one trout, whichever is the lesser. The limit for lake trout is four per day; northern pike, 24 per day; Arctic char, 4 per day.

Several dozen outfitters in both Newfoundland and Labrador operate special fishing cabins for the more serious sportsmen. They are listed in the *Newfoundland Outdoor Guide,* obtainable from any tourist bureau or by writing Tourism Branch, Department of Development, Province of Newfoundland, P.O. Box 2016, St. John's, Newfoundland. This kind of fishing is expensive; expect to pay $1,000 a week or more.

HUNTING. The *Newfoundland Outdoor Guide* describes hunting opportunities (see "Fishing" section). Basically, Newfoundland is famous for its moose hunting. This, however, is for the serious hunter. You will need a licensed guide who also functions as an outfitter.

CAMPING OUT. Complete information on camping in Newfoundland Provincial Parks may be found in the "Provincial Parks" section.

Sixteen private campgrounds-trailer parks are in operation in Newfoundland.

Complete information on camping in Newfoundland's two national parks is in the *National Parks* section.

WINTER SPORTS. The west coast of Newfoundland averages 152 inches of snow per year with average temperatures in the −12 to −4°C. range (10 to 25°F). **Ski** runs over a mile long with drops of at least 213 meters (700 feet) make Marble Mountain Ski Resort one of the best ski areas in eastern Canada. The resort is about 24 kms. (15 miles) from Corner Brook on Hwy. 1.

The Smokey Mountain Ski Club in Labrador City can be reached only by air to Wabush/Labrador City. The hill has 5 trails and one open slope. The longest run is 299 meters (4,500 ft.) with a 1,372-meter (980 foot) vertical drop. Three of the trails are lit for night skiing.

Although many Newfoundland communities have indoor arenas or outdoor rinks for **ice skating,** ponds and lakes are excellent for outdoor skating in most areas.

Curling is a growing sport in Newfoundland and local and regional bonspiels are held throughout the winter months. Major curling clubs are located in St. John's, Gander, Grand Falls, Corner Brook, Labrador City and Stephenville. **Snowmobiling** is also a popular sport in winter. In Labrador, snowmobiles have been used as a prime source of winter transportation for some years now, replacing the traditional dog teams in the remote sections of the province.

HISTORIC SITES. *Cape Spear* is the closest North American point to Europe and the site of one of Canada's oldest surviving lighthouses, built in 1836. During World War II, a coastal battery was constructed here. Crashing waves and the sight of so much open sea make this 8-km. (5-mile) drive south from St. John's worthwhile.

The remains of both French and British fortifications may still be seen at the *Castle Hill National Historic Park* at Placentia. Originally built by the French to protect their colony, the fortifications were taken over by the British in 1713. An interpretive center contains displays and artifacts. Guided tours are available from June to September.

Prior to the 1960's, scholars had long sought tangible evidence of *Viking settlements* in North America. Helge and Anne Stine Ingstad, over a seven-year period, excavated the area near L'Anse aux Meadows on the tip of Newfoundland's Great Northern Peninsula where they thought the Vikings had landed. Their patience was rewarded with positive evidence of Viking settlement at least 1,000 years ago. The dig site can be viewed by visitors. A reception center and museum are at the site.

The *Port au Choix National Historic Park* is located on an important Maritime Archaic Indian (and later Dorset Eskimo) burial ground. The interpretive center portrays the lifestyle of the people who lived here 4,000 years ago. Port au Choix is on Hwy. 430, about 8 kms. (5 miles) north of the community of Port Saunders.

Quidi Vidi Battery just outside St. John's is a small restoration of the original fortification which formed part of the St. John's harbor defenses. Inside the palisade is a small military museum. Open June 1 to mid-September.

MUSEUMS. There are many—for history buffs and fishermen: *Ferryland Museum.* General history museum in one of the oldest settlements in province. Open during summer months in courthouse. *Hibb's Cove Fishermen's Museum.* Fishing artifacts in typical Newfoundland fishing village combined with arts and music center. Open summer months. *Heart's Content.* History of the trans-Atlantic communications cable which first came ashore here. Open summer months. *Trinity Museum and Archives.* Local artifacts and papers. Open summer months. *Bonavista Museum.* Local history. Open summer; winters by appointment. *Salvage Museum.* Local history in fisherman's house. *Greenspond Museum.* Local history displayed in courthouse. Open summer months. *Durrell Museum.* Local history; open summer months. *Twillingate Museum.* Local history in old Anglican Rectory. Open summer months. *Cow Head Museum.* Local history; open year round. *Grand Falls, Mary March Regional Museum.* Local history of the logging industry and natural history. Named after Shananditti (named Mary March by her captors), the last known Beothuk Indian who was captured in the region. Open year-round. Grand Bank. *Southern Newfoundland Seamen's Museum.* Displays relating to the fishery on the south coast. Open year-round. *Gander Airport Aviation Exhibit.* Displays and history of pioneer aviation, trans-Atlantic and domestic, located in airport terminal building. Open year-round. The *Conception Bay Museum National Exhibition Centre* at Harbour Grace which is located in the old Court House displays traveling exhibits along with its own permanent collection, and it is open year-round. In Wesleyville, you can explore local history in the *Wesleyville Museum,* and the *Durrell Museum* in Durrel has local history and also artifacts from World War I. The *Fishermen's Museum* in Musgrave Harbour is also a local history museum, as is the *Placentia Area Museum* in Placentia.

MUSIC. Newfoundland has its own indigenous rhythms, mostly of Scottish and Irish derivation, and you'll find them everywhere—in local festivals, in nightclubs, bars and taverns, and at local concerts.

SHOPPING. For the most part, goods and services tend to be slightly more expensive in Newfoundland than elsewhere in Canada. The same general range of merchandise is available as on the mainland.

Newfoundland handcrafts, such as knitted goods, woven items, and clothing are usually good purchases because of the quality of the product.

Other unique Newfoundland items include: Labradorite jewelry (Labradorite is a quartz-like rock which takes a high polish), earrings of codfish ear bones (quite attractive), seal skin products, and Eskimo and Indian carvings.

Store hours are roughly the same as for St. John's, except that some stores outside St. John's may be closed on Mondays. Holidays closings are roughly the same, except for local civic holidays. See the "Shopping" section in *Practical Information for St. John's.*

DRINKING LAWS. The legal drinking age is 19.

DINING OUT. In general, the best places to dine in Newfoundland (outside of St. John's) are the hotels and motels which usually combine accommodation, a cocktail lounge, and dining room or restaurant.

At best, dining out in Newfoundland is something of an adventure. Visitors should sample home-cooked food and specialties of the area and the season. Fish and salt meat dishes are the best bets everywhere—expect it to be wholesome and hearty, rather than delicate and gourmet-style. Restaurants are categorized on the basis of full-course dinners, drinks, tips and tax excluded: *Expensive,* over $13; *Moderate,* $8–$13; *Inexpensive,* less than $8.

The 12% provincial sales tax will be added to your bill.

Most places accept the following major credit cards: American Express, MasterCard and Visa; others may also be honored. Not all establishments accept credit cards, therefore we suggest you call for information.

CORNER BROOK. *Expensive:* **The Carriage Room.** In the Glynmill Inn. Newfoundland dishes and all types of fish. Licensed.
The Wine Cellar. On Cobb Lane. Steaks and Italian food. Licensed.

GANDER. *Moderate:* **Albatross Motel.** Seafood platters. Licensed.
Sinbad's. Canadian food. Licensed.

GRAND FALLS. *Expensive:* **Mount Peyton Hotel.** Canadian food. Licensed.

WESTERN CANADA

MANITOBA

Home of Hudson's Bay Co.

by
ROGER NEWMAN

Roger Newman, proprietor of Western News Service, Winnipeg, has written extensively for a number of Canadian and U.S. periodicals.

Manitoba, the most easterly of Canada's three prairie provinces, was founded in 1870. But the white man is a Johnny-come-lately compared with the earlier inhabitants. The ancestors of Manitoba's Indian people came to the region from Asia between 15,000 and 25,000 years ago, say the historians.

By 1600, four distinct Indian tribes lived in the 251,000-square-mile territory that was to become Manitoba. In the north, the Chipewyans made their homes on the rugged tundra around Hudson's Bay. Farther south, bands of Cree and Salteaux roamed the great forests of the Canadian shield; while the famous buffalo hunters, the Assiniboines, ranged the broad plains to the southwest, along the present Canada–U.S. border.

The first known white man to set foot in Manitoba was the English-man Captain Thomas Button, who wintered two ships at Port Nelson on Hudson Bay in 1612. He, and other European explorers, chanced upon the Hudson Bay area in their search for a northern sea trade route to the Orient. Instead of a sea route to the riches of the East, they discovered a land with an abundance of animals and game—and the lucrative fur trade began. Soon, the lakes and rivers of Northern Manitoba were being explored by a host of adventurers from across the world—the Radissons, the Grosselliers, the Kelseys, and the LaVerendryes.

The real seeds for Manitoba's future development were planted in 1670 when King Charles of England granted exclusive possession of all lands draining into Hudson Bay to an English fur-trading syndicate, the Hudson's Bay Co. Faced with ever-increasing food import costs, officials of the company decided in 1811 to establish a permanent agricultural settlement at the junction of the Red and Assiniboine Rivers in the southern half of the company's territory.

The original idea was to supply sustenance to Hudson's Bay fur traders at cheaper cost, thereby gaining a competitive edge over rival trading firms. But development of the settlement—which was christened the Red River Colony—actually signaled the start of the agricultural industry in western Canada.

The Red River Colony

Soon, land suitable for farming rapidly eclipsed the fur trade as the bonanza that attracted immigrants to the prairies. The Red River Colony—the first prairie agricultural service center in Canada—eventually became Winnipeg, Manitoba's capital city which today has a population of about 600,000. In 1870, however, there were only 12,000 settlers in the Red River Colony.

At that time, the Hudson's Bay Company relinquished control of all its western Canadian land for a payment of 300,000 pounds sterling by the Canadian government. Three years earlier—in 1867—Canada had come into being through a confederation of four eastern provinces. Federal officials then proposed that Manitoba join Canada as the fifth province; this was vigorously opposed by the Métis, a people of white and Indian blood, mostly French-speaking, who were led by Louis Riel. There followed the famous Riel Rebellion, pitting the adherents of the Métis leader against Canadian authorities. The uprising, one of the few major battles in western Canada's otherwise peaceful history, was put down. Louis Riel was hanged.

As a result, Manitoba became a Canadian province on July 15, 1870. Over the years, the status of Louis Riel has changed from villain to that of provincial hero; a statue of the Métis leader has been in recent years one of the principal attractions on the grounds of the Manitoba Legislative Building in Winnipeg.

The Railroad Arrives

Manitoba's development got going in earnest in 1882 when the first transcontinental railroad started operating across Canada. The arrival of the railroad, coupled with a program of land grants to homesteaders,

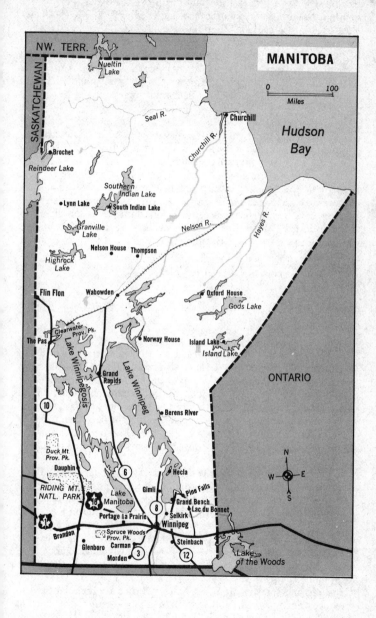

MANITOBA

0   100
Miles

NW. TERR.

SASKATCHEWAN

Nueltin Lake

Seal R.

Churchill

Hudson Bay

Churchill R.

Brochet

Reindeer Lake

Southern Indian Lake

Lynn Lake •   • South Indian Lake

Granville Lake

Nelson R.

Hayes R.

Nelson House •   • Thompson

Highrock Lake

Flin Flon   Wabowden

Oxford House

Gods Lake

Clearwater Prov. Pk.

The Pas

Lake Winnipegosis

Norway House

Island Lake

Island Lake

ONTARIO

Grand Rapids

Lake Winnipeg

(10)

Berens River

Duck Mt. Prov. Pk.

Dauphin

(6)

Hecla

RIDING MT. NATL. PARK

(16)

Lake Manitoba

Gimli

Pine Falls

Grand Beach

Lac du Bonnet

Portage la Prairie

(8)

Selkirk

Winnipeg

Brandon

Spruce Woods Prov. Pk.

Steinbach

Glenboro   Carman

(3)

Morden

(12)

Lake of the Woods

N
W   E
S

set off a flood of immigration into the province. By the turn of the century, Manitoba's population had increased to 255,000; wheat production had reached 50,000 bushels annually.

Since 1900, the province has maintained a slow but steady rate of economic growth. Today, Manitoba has slightly more than a million citizens, more than 50 percent of them living in Winnipeg. Agriculture remains the foundation for the province's prosperity and it thrived especially from 1972 to 1976, when grain prices hit unprecedented levels.

Over the years the province has diversified its economy, adding a wide range of secondary industries. Just about all types of manufacturing and processing are represented in Manitoba, with the sole exception of the automobile manufacturing industry.

The province's principal industries are garments, furniture-making, construction, electronics, tourism and machinery manufacturing. Agriculture is at the base of Manitoba's economy, but the province's 25,000 farmers have been suffering because of low grain prices and high production costs. The worldwide recession in 1982 halted Manitoba's pattern of modest growth. But the province started to recover in the first half of 1983 and has seen a gradual improvement in business conditions.

Rich in Resources

While not as rich in natural resources as neighboring Alberta and Saskatchewan, Manitoba does have significant mineral deposits in its northern section. Major nickel, copper, and zinc mines are operated by INCO Ltd. at Thompson, by Hudson's Bay Mining and Smelting Co. Ltd. at Flin Flon, and by Sherrit-Gordon Mines Ltd., at Ruttan Lake. Unfortunately, these mines have been operating at less than capacity because world mineral prices are sluggish. Uranium has also been discovered in the province's northwest corner, raising hopes for future development.

Northern Manitoba is also the site of the billion-dollar Nelson River power development which Manitoba Hydro, the province's publicly owned power utility, is building. By 1985, Hydro had intended to develop a chain of six large power plants along the Nelson River, the province's last harnessable waterway, but with three plants completed, further construction has been postponed until excess electrical generating capacity is utilized. However, the project may resume soon because of new export sales and plans for aluminum and potash developments in Manitoba.

Fishing and forestry are other industries that are dominant in the province's north. And in southwestern Manitoba—centered around the town of Virden—a small oil industry has flourished for 25 years and is currently the scene of renewed exploration and development, with more than 240 new wells drilled last year.

A Melting Pot

Manitoba offers a rich, cosmopolitan flavor. The province's first great influx of settlers was largely English-speaking from eastern Canada. Then, in 1874, the first Mennonites arrived from Russia. They were followed in 1875 by numerous Icelanders and French-speaking families from Québec and France. By 1881, there had also been substantial migration from Britain; the province's population had jumped to 70,-000 from 30,000 in 1876. The ethnic flavor was further enhanced in 1891 by the arrival of the vanguard of substantial numbers of Ukrainians.

Today, Manitoba's population figure is about 1,051,000, with almost 700,000 of these people being of British origin. Other principal ethnic groups in the province are: German, Ukrainian, French, North American Indian and Eskimo, Polish, Dutch, Italian, and other groups in that order. In recent years, large numbers of Asian, Philippine, Vietnamese, and South American immigrants have added to the cosmopolitan flavor of the province.

For almost 25 years following World War II, Manitobans elected traditional, free enterprise-supporting Liberal and Conservative governments for the province. There was a big change in 1969 when the New Democratic (Socialist) party squeezed into power, ousting an 11-year-old Conservative administration. At the time, the New Democratic victory caused quite a stir. This was the first time that a Socialist party had been elected in the province—and only the second occasion that a government of this stripe had held power anywhere in North America. The New Democrats, led by Premier Ed Schreyer, who is of German stock, were re-elected in 1973. In October 1977, however, a Conservative government led by Sterling Lyon was again elected to power, returning provincial administration to a more traditional posture. Due to a slumping economy, the Conservatives, in turn, were ousted in November 1981, with the New Democrats regaining power this time under the leadership of Howard Pawley. The premier, Mr. Pawley, is a lawyer from the rural town of Selkirk. The former New Democratic leader, Mr. Schreyer, is now Canada's ambassador to Australia.

Manitoba is as culturally and industrially advanced as any North American province or state, although the relatively small population means that things are on a smaller scale. The Universities of Manitoba and Winnipeg, both in the capital city—plus the University of Brandon, 125 miles west of Winnipeg—provide for the province's higher-education needs. In other centers throughout Manitoba, community colleges and technical schools all have full enrollments.

EXPLORING WINNIPEG

In just over 110 years, Winnipeg has developed from a tiny, fur-trading outpost into one of Canada's most sophisticated urban communities. Its population totals about 600,000.

As water transportation was the most convenient method of getting their goods to market from that region in the 1870's, the fur companies logically set up their trading posts at the junction of the Red and Assiniboine Rivers. From this spot Winnipeg has spread out in all directions to become today's great city.

The city was the scene of one of Canada's first major competitive business struggles, involving the Hudson's Bay Company fur operation and its keen rival, the Northwest Company. The Hudson's Bay firm, established more than 300 years ago in England, won that battle and went on to set up a chain of more than 200 department stores across Canada. Today, the Hudson's Bay Company is one of Canada's major retailers and it ranks as the oldest commercial enterprise in North America.

Red River Ox Carts

Winnipeg, however, was only a tiny village in 1870 when the Canadian Government created the province of Manitoba. At that time there were only 215 inhabitants and 18 business establishments. By 1874 Winnipeg had 1,879 citizens, 100 businesses, and 27 manufacturing enterprises. This rapid growth prompted civic leaders that year to incorporate Winnipeg, an event that was commemorated with extensive centennial celebrations in 1974.

Since its inception, Winnipeg has been the primary warehousing and distribution center for western Canada. In the early days goods stored in the city were hauled by Red River ox carts to surrounding farms, villages and hamlets. These carts were also used as early as 1850 on the first regular trade route linking Winnipeg with St. Paul, Minnesota. The carts were subsequently outmoded by Red River paddlewheel steamers; these in turn were replaced by a Winnipeg–Minneapolis railroad in 1878.

In 1882, Winnipeg became a mainline point on the first east-west Canadian railroad. Rapid development was occurring at this time, and the city blossomed as the leading financial, industrial and retail center for the territory stretching from Lake Superior to the Rocky Mountains.

A Place of "Ethnic Diversity"

At about the same time agriculture started to make a major impact on Winnipeg's economy. Following the first shipment of wheat from Manitoba in 1876, numerous grain trading businesses began springing up in the city as traders realized that the prairies were destined to become one of the world's major grain producing areas. The Winnipeg Grain Exchange—now the Winnipeg Commodity Exchange—was established in 1887 and its busy trading floor is still one of the main tourist attractions in the city.

Winnipeg's greatest burst of expansion took place between 1901 and 1914. Population increased by 100,000 as European and American immigrants flocked to the prairies attracted by the success stories that were flowing back from the western Canadian frontier. This wave of immigration brought substantial numbers of Ukrainians, French-Canadians, Germans, Poles, and Scandinavians, creating an ethnic diversity that remains as one of the city's principal characteristics. Instead of being forced into the "melting pot" mold, the various ethnic groups were encouraged to maintain their traditions and languages. Consequently, Winnipeg each year is the scene of a large number of ethnic festivals, including the *Festival du Voyageur* held in February, and *Folklorama,* an Expo-type of celebration by all of the city's ethnic groups, staged in August.

A New Building Boom

The 1900–14 period was also the era when the majority of Winnipeg's downtown buildings were erected. The arrival of so many immigrants at the turn of the century created an enormous demand in the city for residential accommodation, office buildings, and manufacturing space. Winnipeg became the home of numerous construction firms, as well as for companies supplying lumber, steel, brick, stone, and building supplies of all kinds.

Winnipeg experienced another building boom in the early 1970s. This was precipitated by the need to replace original downtown buildings that have decayed with age. The burst of construction started in 1969 when the city enacted a development plan that offered special incentives to developers undertaking projects in the central core. Also in the same year, James Richardson and Sons Ltd., the prominent Winnipeg investment and grain dealers, erected the 34-story Richardson Building at Portage and Main, the city's key downtown intersection.

The development plan and the trail-blazing Richardson Building were the catalysts for a resurgence of downtown construction. More than two dozen new high rises have been built in the central district since 1969, giving Winnipeg a completely new skyline. Most recently the 32-story Trizec Tower was completed at Portage and Main, providing, among other things, a new, computerized trading floor for the Winnipeg Commodity Exchange. In recent years, however, the building boom has diminished as economic recession has hit Winnipeg. However, government officials hope to bring new life to the downtown cove by undertaking a $400 million redevelopment program that will include a mixture of private and public projects.

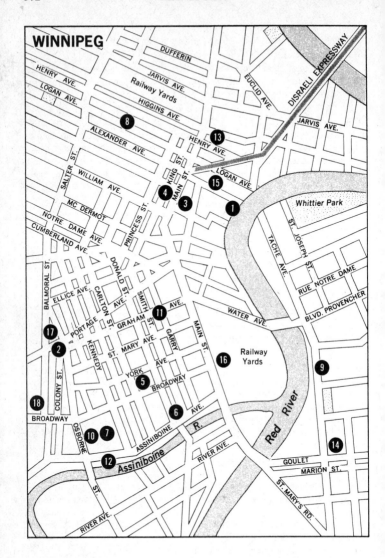

WINNIPEG

Whittier Park

Railway Yards

Red River

Assiniboine R.

Winnipeg—Points of Interest
1) Alexander Dock
2) Art Gallery
3) Centennial Center (Museum of Man and Nature-Concert Hall-Planetarium)
4) City Hall
5) Convention Center
6) Dalnavert-MacDonald House
7) Federal Building
8) Ivan Franko Museum
9) La Verendrye Monument
10) Legislative Building
11) Post Office
12) Riel Monument
13) Ross House-first Post Office
14) St. Boniface Cathedral and Museum
15) Ukrainian Cultural Center
16) Union Station
17) University of Winnipeg
18) Winnipeg Stadium

The Canal and Winnipeg

Winnipeg suffered a severe economic blow in 1914 when the Panama Canal was opened. Prior to that, the city was the main warehousing and distribution center for goods moving to all parts of western Canada. To the detriment of Winnipeg, the canal proved to be a cheaper route for shipping to British Columbia and Alberta.

Offsetting this blow to some extent, Winnipeg has slowly but surely developed into the major manufacturing center for the prairie region. The city has large secondary industries that make clothing, furniture, food products, farm machinery, machine tools, electronic parts, and a host of other goods. This diversity and balance give Winnipeg a measure of economic stability often not present in communities dependent on one or two key industries.

A Major Performing Arts Center

On a cultural and recreational level, Winnipeg is proud of facilities that rank with most large cities in North America. The beaches of Lake Winnipeg—one of the world's largest freshwater lakes—are within 50 miles of the city. The city itself has more than 50 parks and golf courses, and the Birds Hill provincial park and beach is just outside Winnipeg's boundaries.

Downtown, nightlife has improved considerably in recent years, partly because the postwar "baby boom" generation has grown up and is looking for some "action." The city has more than 100 hotels within its limits; it also possesses a $25 million convention center with several restaurants and can host gatherings of 8,000 delegates.

As far as the performing arts are concerned, Winnipeg is unique for a community of its relatively small size. The city is the home of six professional performing arts companies that regularly present everything from drama and ballet to symphony and opera. Some of these companies, such as the Royal Winnipeg Ballet and the Manitoba Theatre Centre, have won international reputations for the quality of their presentations.

The professional companies, together with the city's numerous amateur theatrical groups, have made Winnipeg the major performing arts center on the prairies.

The city's other cultural attractions include the Winnipeg Art Gallery and the Manitoba Museum of Man and Nature and the adjacent planetarium. A multimillion dollar downtown civic library was completed in 1976.

PRACTICAL INFORMATION FOR WINNIPEG

HOW TO GET THERE. By air: Airlines serving the Winnipeg International Airport include *Air Canada, CP Air, Nordair, Frontier, Northwest Airlines* and *Pacific Western.* Charter and regional companies provide connections to the province's other major centers and *Perimeter Airlines* has scheduled flights to Dauphin, the Lake Winnipeg communities, Yorkton, Sask., and Red Lake, Ont.

By car: Trans-Canada Hwy. 1 passes through Winnipeg on its east-west route. Hwy. 75 runs south to connect with main highways in North and South Dakota and Minnesota, and intersects Hwy. 1 in the south end of the city.

By train: *Via Rail,* Canada's government-subsidized rail passenger service, serves Winnipeg providing daily east-west runs from its station at Broadway and Main.

By bus: There is *Greyhound* bus service from as far away as New York City. Other lines running to Winnipeg include *Beaver, Grey Goose* and *Eagle.* The Greyhound/Grey Goose terminal is at 487 Portage Ave.

ACCOMMODATIONS in Winnipeg still include some well-preserved establishments that couple modern conveniences with traditional service. Many new hotels and motels have been built in recent years, especially in the downtown area. Plans for several more downtown hotels are on the drawing boards, and a new Sheraton Hotel will open in early 1985.

Accommodations are listed according to the following price categories, based on double-occupancy: *Deluxe,* $60–$80; *Expensive,* $50 to $60; *Moderate,* $35 to $50; *Inexpensive,* under $35.

Most places accept the following major credit cards: American Express, MasterCard, and Visa; others may also be honored. Not all establishments accept credit cards, therefore we suggest you call for information.

Deluxe

Birchwood Inn. 2520 Portage Ave. Licensed dining room, cocktail lounge and coffeeshop. Indoor swimming pool, sauna. Easy access to airport. Major credit cards.

Hotel Fort Garry. 222 Broadway. Elegant old hotel. Personal service and plush, dignified surroundings. Excellent cuisine. Cocktail lounge, guest parking. Major credit cards.

Holiday Inn–South. 1200 Pembina Highway. Satellite Television is the main attraction at this recently opened hotel. Major credit cards.

International Inn. 1808 Wellington Ave. Convenient for airport. Cabaret, indoor swimming pool, restaurant, color TV. Major credit cards.

Marlborough Inn. 331 Smith St. Three licensed dining rooms, a cocktail lounge with entertainment. Convention and banquet facilities, free parking for registered guests. Major credit cards.

North Star Inn. Portage at Smith St. Centrally located. Licensed dining room, cocktail lounge, beverage room, indoor swimming pool. Indoor walk-through to the T. Eaton Co., theaters (2), babysitting. Major credit cards.

Winnipeg Holiday Inn. St. Mary's and Carlton. Popular with conventioneers. Connected by a walkway to the Convention Centre. Cabaret, cocktail lounge, licensed dining room, convention and banquet facilities, indoor pool, sauna and recreational area. Courtesy limousine service. Major credit cards.

The Westin Hotel. Two Lombard Pl. Modern highrise in the heart of the business district. Connected underground to the Lombard Concourse. Several restaurants and bar. Enclosed guest parking, year-round swimming pool. Major credit cards.

Expensive

The Brittany Inn. Carlton and Ellice. Convenient location. Banquet facilities, meeting rooms. Licensed dining room, cocktail lounge, entertainment, guest parking. Major credit cards.

Charterhouse. 330 York Ave. Centrally located with dining room, lounge, coffeeshop and outdoor pool. Major credit cards.

Niakwa TraveLodge. Trans-Canada Hwy. E. at St. Anne's Rd. Dining room, cocktail lounge, beverage room, beer vendor, coffeeshop, entertainment. Bowling alley, golf course across the street. Guest parking. Major credit cards.

Polo Park Inn. 1405 St. Matthews. Modern new motel, convenient for shopping, airport and sports. Dining and drinking facilities. Recreation center for bowling, billiards, swimming and sauna. Major credit cards.

Viscount Gort Motor Hotel. 1670 Portage Ave. Sauna, lounge, licensed dining room and color TV. Major credit cards.

Moderate

Assiniboine Hotel. 1975 Portage Ave. Licensed dining room, cocktail lounge, beverage room, site of some of the best jazz in the city on Saturday afternoons. Visa.

Curtis Gordon Motor Hotel. 1011 Henderson Hwy. Licensed restaurant, beverage room, beer vendor, entertainment, dancing, guest parking. Visa.

Downs Motor Inn. 3740 Portage Ave. Modern facilities convenient to shopping and racetrack. Dining room, lounge, and beverage room. Country/Western entertainment. Major credit cards.

Grant Motor Inn. 635 Pembina Hwy. Beverage room, cocktail lounge, entertainment, licensed dining room, guest parking. Major credit cards.

St. Regis Flag Inn. 285 Smith St. Dining room, coffeeshop, beverage room. Major credit cards.

Inexpensive

Aberdeen Hotel. 230 Carlton St. Good downtown location, comfortable rooms, poor service.

Chalet Gordon Hotel. 611 Archibald St. An out-of-the-way hotel frequented by colorful cattlebuyers and cowboys.

Norwood Hotel. 112 Marion St. Fine place to eat, drink, and listen to good music. Visa.

Osborne Village Motor Inn. 160 Osborne. Located in a quaint remodeled shopping and restaurant area and within walking distance of downtown.

St. Boniface Hotel. 171 Dumoulin St. Located in the French district of town.

HOW TO GET AROUND. By bus: Maps of the bus system are available at the Lombard Place concourse under Portage and Main, and at gas stations. *D.A.S.H. bus service:* from 11:00 A.M. to 3:00 P.M., Monday to Friday. Buses travel a continuous route through the downtown and into the warehouse area and charge no fare. Regular city transit runs from 6:00 A.M. to 1:30 A.M. Monday to Saturday and from 7:00 A.M. to midnight on Sunday. Fares are 30¢ for children and 75¢ for adults, exact change required.

By taxi: There is metered taxi service, and also a limousine service from the airport to all major downtown hotels.

TOURIST INFORMATION. Travel Manitoba Visitor Reception Centre at the Legislative Building, downtown. Telephone 944–3777.

TOURS. Visitors may tour the *Legislative Building* at Broadway and Osborne. Made of native Tyndall stone, the building contains the legislative chambers, offices of the premier and cabinet ministers and some departments of government. Atop the 240-foot-high dome of the Legislative Buildings is the Golden Boy, one of the best known symbols of Manitoba.

The Centennial Centre on Main St. N., comprising the Concert Hall and the Planetarium, schedules tours of the concert hall (phone 956–1360) and arranges tours for the planetarium as well. The Concert Hall and Planetarium portions of the centre were completed during 1967, Canada's Centennial Year.

City Hall tours can be arranged by phoning the mayor's office at 946–0196. *Winnipeg Commodity Exchange,* Portage Ave. and Main St.—one of the largest in the world—is open to visitors Monday through Friday. Guides are available. *Winnipeg Art Gallery,* 300 Memorial Blvd., offers tours some evenings and weekends. Phone 786–6641. Exhibits are changed regularly and feature collections of traditional and contemporary Canadian, American, and European art. The *Winnipeg Mint,* said to be the most modern in the world, has been designed so that the public can see how money is made. Tours weekdays.

Paddlewheel Riverboat Cruises along the Red River operate each summer, taking excursions to Lower Fort Garry. In conjunction, double-decker London buses conduct daily tours of the city, departing from major downtown hotels.

The *River Rouge Pleasure Ship* offers afternoon and evening cruises along the Red and Assiniboine rivers, while the 1,500—ton *Lord Selkirk* plies the Red north of Redwood Bridge.

SPECIAL INTEREST TOURS. The *Zoological Museum* in the Duff Roblin Building, U. of Man., is open by appointment. Others include: *Crafts Guild of Manitoba,* 183 Kennedy St.; *Uvan Historical Museum,* 203–456 Main St. *The Living Prairie Museum,* on Ness Ave. and the Fort Whyte Nature Centre, 2505 McGillivary Blvd., conducts guided nature walks throughout the summer.

INDUSTRIAL TOURS. Tours are offered by the *Winnipeg Free Press,* the city's daily newspaper. *Manitoba Sugar Co.,* a sugar beet refinery at 555 Hervo in Fort Garry, schedules tours by appointment, Wednesday and Friday, usually from October to January. Other industrial tours are offered by *Winnipeg radio* and *television stations, Palliser Furniture Ltd., United Grain Growers Ltd.,* and *Great-West Life Assurance Company* and *Versatile Farm Equipment Co.*

CITY PARKS. The 362 acres of *Assiniboine Park* include an English Garden, a conservatory, miniature railroad, a zoo, and a refreshment pavilion. *Kildonan Park,* popular for tobogganing and ice skating, also features the *Rainbow Stage,* Canada's only active semi-outdoor theater.

CHILDREN'S ACTIVITIES. Children always enjoy a trip to the zoo, and Winnipeg has one of the finest in Canada—the *Assiniboine Park Zoo. The Planetarium* in the Centennial Centre offers exciting programs that are both educational and fun. *The Manitoba Museum of Man and Nature,* also in the Centennial Centre, features displays explaining the history and prehistory of man. June through September, the *Prairie Dog Central* makes a one-hour steam train excursion to Headingly from Charleswood. The train departs from Ridgewood Ave. and Elmhurst Rd., Sunday. Or maybe your children would like to board one of Winnipeg's cruise ships and enjoy the sights along the Red and

Assiniboine Rivers. *Fun Mountain Water Slide Park* has four twister slides that will plummet you into a large heated swimming pool. *The City of Winnipeg Library Department* holds story hours, films, and puppet shows in library branches. A telephone call to the Centennial Library will steer you to the nearest and most convenient.

SPORTS. Spectator. You'll see all your favorite sports in Winnipeg, starting in summer when the Winnipeg Blue Bombers take on the opposition football teams at the Winnipeg Stadium. The Winnipeg Jets play in the National Hockey League and draw big crowds. Professional wrestling and boxing and college basketball, hockey and volleyball are also popular in the city. Thoroughbred horse racing and exciting harness races thrill crowds year-round at Assiniboia Downs. **Participant.** Those who like to get into the action find an excellent selection of golf courses and tennis courts in all areas of the city. The city operates three indoor and numerous outdoor swimming pools for the aquatic crowd. The Pan Am Pool on Grant Ave. houses an aquatic museum. The Winnipeg Roller Rink at Portage Ave. and Langside St. also offers an evening of active entertainment, as do the Hamelin St. roller rink in Fort Garry, the McPhillips St. rink in the north end and the Transcona roller rink. Curling clubs provide interesting winter spectator sport. The Tourist and Convention Association can give you further information on these.

HISTORIC SITES. Milestones of Winnipeg's past are traced through historic sites in all parts of the city. Nothing speaks for the city's early years as eloquently as its many beautiful old churches.

Grant's Old Mill, overlooking Portage Ave. near the Grace Hospital, is a watermill built on the site of the Red River Settlement's first mill. Stone-ground flour made at the mill is available for purchase. Open daily June 1 to September 1, and weekends in May, September, and October.

Knox United Church on Edmonton at Qu'Apelle St. in downtown Winnipeg is one of the city's oldest churches, yet retains a modern look. Construction of the church was begun in 1914, but because of World War I, the building was not completed until 1917. Knox welcomes visitors to its Sunday services. Open to the public daily at 8 A.M.

Kildonan Presbyterian Church, John Black Ave., the first church of that denomination in western Canada, was completed in 1854 under the direction of the Rev. John Black, the first resident Presbyterian minister in that region.

St. Boniface Basilica, Tache Ave., is the oldest cathedral in western Canada. Its exterior has survived several fires and the interior has been rebuilt as a modern chapel. On the grounds are the graves of Father Provencher and Louis Riel.

A monument to the memory of *Thomas Simpson* who, with *Peter Warren Dease,* between 1837–39, carried out important explorations in the Arctic regions, stands at Main St. and St. John's Ave.

In *Kildonan Park* a plaque commemorates the first steam-powered vessel to reach Fort Garry via the Red River from the south. The *S.S. Anson Northup* arrived at the settlement June 10, 1859.

In a park adjacent to 100 Main St., a tablet commemorates four fur-trade forts once built on this site at the forks of the Red and Assiniboine Rivers. They were Fort Rouge, Fort Gilbraltar, and the first and second Fort Garry. The north gate of the latter still stands.

Opposite the CPR Station on Higgins Ave., a cairn marks the site of the Hudson's Bay Company's *Fort Douglas,* built to protect the Red River Settlement.

Ross House, 176 Higgins Ave., is the first post office in the Red River Settlement.

A small stone shaft on north Main St., in West Kildonan commemorates the *Battle of Seven Oaks* in which Governor Robert Semple of the Hudson's Bay Company and 20 Selkirk settlers were killed by rival traders of the North West Company.

On Tache Ave., opposite St. Boniface Hospital, the *La Verendrye Monument* honors Pierre Gautier de La Verendrye, the first white man to travel west by the Great Lakes chain to reach the forks of the Red and Assiniboine Rivers.

Dalnavert-MacDonald House, the restored Victorian home of Sir Hugh John MacDonald, former premier of Manitoba, is located at 61 Carlton St. Open throughout the year. Guided tours.

 LIBRARIES. The *University of Manitoba* and the *University of Winnipeg* both have their own libraries. *Dafoe Library,* the main library at the U. of Man., contains 4,000 volumes of rare books and manuscripts, including the manuscripts of Fredrick Philip Grove, the well known Canadian novelist. It also houses the papers of John Dafoe, the prominent Winnipeg editor for whom the library is named. *The Ukrainian Arts and Crafts Museum,* 1175 Main St., also has a rare book section, the majority of which deal with 17th-century literature and folklore written in the Ukrainian language. An excellent collection of volumes concerning art history and fine arts is at the *Winnipeg Art Gallery,* 300 Memorial Blvd., along with a large number of periodicals and reports. The *Winnipeg Public Library,* on Graham Ave., has an extensive Canadian section, including early writings on Manitoba's history. The *Ukrainian Cultural and Educational Centre,* 184 Alexander Ave. E., contains one of the largest Ukrainian-related libraries in North America.

 MUSEUMS AND GALLERIES. The varied ethnic backgrounds of Winnipeg's population, and the history of Manitoba, are reflected in the city's museums and galleries.

Museums. Largest and most well known of these is the *Manitoba Museum of Man and Nature,* 190 Rupert Ave. It is a unique and interpretive center that uses graphics, specimens, reconstructions, and audiovisual presentations of the human and natural history of the province. There are also galleries depicting the beginnings of earth and the universe, the history and prehistory of man's existence, and Winnipeg's environment, past, present, and future. Open daily.

Mineral and geological specimens are on exhibit in the *Minerology Museum* at the Geology Building, U. of Manitoba.

Ivan Franko Museum, 603 Pritchard Ave., displays memorabilia of the Ukrainian author and poet, Ivan Franko.

The Aquatic Hall of Fame and Museum of Canada at the Pan-Am Pool, 25 Poseidon Bay, features the Cutty Sark Club Collection and aquatic mementos, on display during regular hours of the Pan-Am Pool.

The Historical Museum of St. James-Assiniboia, 3180 Portage Ave., contains pioneer material relating to the history of the area. Daily April 1 to September, Sunday October 1 to March 31.

The *St. Boniface Museum,* 494 Tache, is housed in Winnipeg's oldest building, with displays and artifacts depicting the history of Manitoba's French minority. Year-round.

Galleries. Canada's third-largest art gallery, the *Winnipeg Art Gallery,* 300 Memorial Blvd., is housed in one of the most up-to-date structures in North America. It contains a permanent collection, gallery shop, art rental and sales gallery, library, restaurant, education and exhibitions program. Open six days a week.

The Medea, in Winnipeg's popular Osborne Street Village, is the city's first cooperative gallery. Browsing encouraged.

FILM. The National Film Board of Canada screens top-notch Canadian films at its new cinema on Main Street. Admittance is free. Information about the time, date, and subject of each screening can be obtained from the NFB at 949–2815.

In addition there are numerous privately owned cinemas in Winnipeg. They include: Capital 1 and 2 (942–6020), Cinema 3 (783–1097), Cinema Gallery (786–7811), Cine-Plex 1, 2, 3, 4, 5, 6 and 7 (943–6149), Colony (942–3019), Convention Centre (947–0783), Epic (943–8261), Festival Cinema (772–7779), Garden City 1 and 2 (338–8747), Garrick 1, 2, 3 and 4 (942–2034), Grant (453–4084), Kings (888–1344), Northstar 1 and 2 (943–0089), Metropolitan (942–7710), Odeon (943–4743), Park (452–3118), Polo Park (786–3100) and Towne Cinema 1, 2, 3, 4, 5, 6, 7 and 8 (942–3336).

Movies are rated by a censorship board. "General" movies are recommended for family viewing. "Mature" movies are designed for adult entertainment but anyone may see them. Movies rated "Adult Parental Guidance" may be viewed by minors only if a parent is in accompaniment. "Restricted Adult" movies are just that—restricted to adult viewing only.

Monthly, from September to June, travelogs are screened at the *Centennial Concert Hall* by the CBO (786–3811—ask for CBO) and the Rotary Club (942–6654).

PERFORMING ARTS. Winnipeg has earned its reputation as a cultural center, encouraging the development of ballet, theater and other cultural activities.

Dance. *The Royal Winnipeg Ballet,* Canada's first ballet company was established in 1938, and has since become a professional company, winning two gold medals at the International Dance Festival in Paris. In addition to performances from October to April, the company stages a series of free, outdoor summer concerts in Assiniboine Park, called Dancing in the Park. *Winnipeg's Contemporary Dancers* was founded in 1964 by Rachel Browne. It became a fully professional company in 1970. Its performances, dedicated to bringing the best in modern dance entertainment to North America, are scheduled from October to April at the Playhouse Theatre.

Music. *Winnipeg Symphony Orchestra* holds a season of concerts, from Sept. to April in the Manitoba Centennial Concert Hall. It gives an occasional concert in Assiniboine Park—usually on July 1. *The Manitoba Opera Association* gives a season of three operas at the Centennial Concert Hall. Other ethnic and cultural groups perform regularly during the summer in Assiniboine and Kildonan parks. *University of Manitoba's School of Music* gives free concerts throughout the year. The *Manitoba Chamber Orchestra* holds a series of concerts during the winter at Westminster Church.

Stage. *The Manitoba Theatre Centre* is one of the leading regional theaters in North America. From October through April, it presents a series of outstanding plays featuring a full professional staff, including Canada's leading actors. *Prairie Theatre Exchange* stages performances at its own theater, 166 Princess St. The new *Gas Station Theatre* in Osborne Village is always busy with professional and amateur companies. They are listed in the local telephone directory. *Rainbow Stage,* western Canada's only semi-outdoor theater, presents musicals during July and August. A special event at the end of March is the *Theatre for Children* at the Winnipeg Art Gallery.

 SHOPPING. In addition to nationally known department stores such as *Eatons, Sears,* and *The Bay,* there are a variety of interesting shops and boutiques. *Townsite,* at 283 Bannatyne Ave., is being reopened as a boutique shopping centre after experiencing hard times during the recession. *Osborne Village* is a street crammed with stores and workshops selling treasures you would probably have difficulty finding anywhere else. Everything from weaving yarn to necklaces of New Mexican silver to western Canadian contemporary art is sold here. In the heart of Winnipeg, it's the perfect place for afternoon browsing. *The Unicity Mall* on Portage Ave. in West Winnipeg is one of the city's newest and most comfortable enclosed shopping mall. *Polo Park* is also a conveniently located enclosed shopping center. Both locations sport a wide selection of specialty and general goods stores. The *St. Vital Shopping Centre* on St. Mary's Road at Bishop Grandin Blvd. is the city's largest. Smaller shopping areas are located throughout the city. From mid-May to mid-September *Old Market Square,* near city hall, holds an open-air market on Saturdays, with fresh produce and other goodies. The *Winnipeg Convention Centre* also has a host of boutiques and specialty shops on its second level, as does *Winnipeg Square* beneath the Portage and Main concourse.

 DINING OUT. In Winnipeg is an opportunity to experience the cuisine of the many and diverse cultures that typify this city. The atmosphere in most Winnipeg restaurants is one of casual informality. Restaurants are categorized on the basis of their own medium-priced full-course dinners per person; drinks and tips excluded. *Deluxe,* $30 and higher; *Expensive,* $20–30; *Moderate,* $15–20; *Inexpensive,* under $15.

Most places accept the following major credit cards: American Express, MasterCard, and Visa; others may also be honored. Not all establishments accept credit cards, therefore we suggest you call for information.

American and Canadian

Moderate

Haynes' Chicken Shack. 275 Lulu. Authentic Southern fried chicken, mouthwatering BBQ spareribs, and deep-fried shrimp. No credit cards.

Teepee. 236 Edmonton. Native Indian specialties include pemmican, buffalo, partridge, and rabbit. Continental dishes available. Major credit cards.

Austrian
Moderate

Engl's. 159 Osborne St. A simple but appealing décor. Specializing in veal, especially Wienerschnitzel. Open for lunch and dinner. Can be expensive. Major credit cards.

Chinese
Moderate

Mandarin. 613 Sargent Ave. Pleasant atmosphere. Northern Chinese cuisine.

Ming Court. 209 Broadway. Northern Chinese chow mein is the house specialty. Licensed.

Inexpensive

Kum Koon Garden. 426 Main. Extensive selection of dim sum dishes. Recommended by the Chinese residents of Winnipeg. Visa.

Mandarin. 613 Sargent. Northern Chinese and Szechuan dishes. No credit cards.

Continental
Deluxe

Dubrovnik. 390 Assiniboine Ave. Continental-Yugoslavian. An elegant dining spot located in a renovated, stately old Winnipeg residence. The food is consistently excellent and the service prompt and cheerful. An extensive menu, with stuffed veal or pork the chef's specialty. Major credit cards.

La Vieille Gare. Provencher Ave. and Des Meurons St. Boniface. Continental French food is the specialty of this restaurant. Fashioned from an old railway station, the décor is attractive and luxurious. Flamed pepper steak and veal sweetbreads are two popular entrées. The restaurant also has a wide selection of wines. Major credit cards.

Old Swiss Inn. 207 Edmonton St. One of Winnipeg's best and most reliable restaurants. It is small and inviting, with a menu that offers several fish dishes, and the chef's special, shrimp sautéed in butter at the table. The steak is excellent. Major credit cards.

Oliver's Old Bailey Restaurant. 185 Lombard Ave. A luxurious restaurant decorated with antique furnishings and fixtures. Specialties are scampi, Australian lobster tail, and grilled steak. Desserts include good cheesecake and very good sabayon Marsala. Major credit cards.

The Royal Rib Room. Charterhouse Hotel, Hargrave St. and York Ave. Specialties include onion soup and prime ribs of roast beef. The roast beef is always tender and good-tasting. Extensive wine list. Major credit cards.

Victor's. Elegant dining in the Osborne Village boutique district. Executive Chef Heinz Kaltenfeld offers a menu that features bouillabaisse, veal dishes, and rack of lamb. Joanna's Happy Cake is a favorite dessert. 454 River Ave. A sister restaurant, Pantages on Portage Ave., is also tops. Major credit cards.

Westin Hotel. 2 Lombard Pl. A complete dinner section of the menu offers Cornish game hen, prime roast beef, and river trout with shrimp. Includes soup, salad, and dessert. Two-star entrées are fresh lobster from the restaurant's tanks and an excellent rack of lamb. Major credit cards.

Expensive

Churchill's. Marlborough Inn, 331 Smith St. Posh dining room for the romantically inclined. Food adequate. Major credit cards.

Hy's. 216 Kennedy St. A veteran eating establishment but still one of the best in town. This is the place for steak, beef, lamb and ribs. Cheese bread and toast is a specialty. Can be expensive. Major credit cards.

Moderate

Zorba's. 704 Sargent Ave. Good quality at reasonable prices. American as well as Greek food. Licensed.

Danish

Moderate

Bistro Dansk. 63 Sherbrook St. Charming, small and casual. Homemade soups, bread and pastries. All authentic Danish meals, including frikadeller (Danish meat patties). No credit cards.

Inexpensive

Kronborg. 1875 Pembina. Small family restaurant with delicious home-cooking and 64 varieties of open-faced sandwiches. Visa.

East Indian

Inexpensive

Ardjuna. 457 Notre Dame Ave., specializes in Indonesian pork sate, lumpia egg rolls, marinated chicken, and Dutch croquettes. Wine and beer licence.

French

Deluxe

Bertram's. 940 Corydon Ave. Some of the best food in town. Wine bar and terrace. Closed Sundays. Licensed. Downtown counterpart under same ownership, *Bottles,* 177 Lombard Ave.

Expensive

La Grenouillère. 150 Provencher Blvd., St. Boniface. Cozy restaurant. Emphasis on Winnipeg's French-Canadian contribution to cuisine. Best of the specialties include smoked ham in maple syrup, baked beans *de l'habitant,* and frogs' legs. No credit cards.

German

Expensive

Happy Vineyard. 715 Ellice Ave. European atmosphere. Extensive menu includes a dozen German specialties such as Wienerschnitzel, sausage dishes, and Sauerbraten. The wine list is one of the largest in Winnipeg. The noon special is a popular and pleasant buffet. Major credit cards.

Greek

Moderate

Homer's. 520 Ellice Ave. A Greek restaurant with a pleasant atmosphere and good food that caters to Winnipeg's television crowd. Major credit cards.

Hungarian
Moderate

Hungarian Village Restaurant. 174 Isabel St. Comfortable atmosphere. Try the veal meatball dish served with noodles, the goulash or the breaded rabbit and half-pheasant. Cosmopolitan wine list.

Italian
Moderate

Da Mamma Mia Pizzeria. 631 Corydon Ave. Best Italian pizza in town. Major credit cards.

Paradise. 789 Portage Ave. First-class Italian food. Liquor license.

Japanese
Moderate

Tokyo Joe's. 132 Pioneer. Korean/Japanese. Specialties include steak tartar and pickled cabbage. Pleasant atmosphere. Wine license. Major credit cards.

Yamato. 667B Stafford. Excellent Japanese food. Liquor license.

Caribbean
Moderate

Sabrina's. 1134 Main St. Premises are modest but food is tasty. Wine licence.

Mexican
Moderate

Casa de Sol. 2991 Pembina Hwy. Tasty food. Licensed for wine.

Chilean
Moderate

La Pena. 359 Johnston St. Wines. Entertainment on weekends.

Lunch and Light Specialty Dinners
Moderate

Garden Crêperie. 349 York Avenue. Casual, easy and light dining with rolled crêpes the specialty. Fully licensed. Major credit cards.

Tony Roma's, 203 Kennedy. Good barbecued ribs at acceptable prices. Licenced.

Inexpensive

Basil's. 117 Osborne St. in the Osborne Village. Open-faced European sandwiches, cheese plates and variety of specialty coffees. Excellent pastries. Wine license. Visa only.

 NIGHTCLUBS AND BARS. Winnipeg's entertainment scene is as vibrant as the city itself, catering to a variety of moods and preferences. For a night of dancing, *Uncle's* in the Holiday Inn is a popular spot. Dress is casual, but jeans are not allowed. Those who like dancing, live entertainment and interesting décor flock to the *Ramada Inn* on Pembina Highway; *Georgie's,* 3321

Portage Ave.; *Benjamin's,* 294 Kennedy St.; and *Broadway's,* in the Fort Garry Hotel. A favorite night spot for dinner theater featuring Hollywood stars is *Stage West,* 317 Kennedy St. Again, dress is casual. Situated in the midst of Winnipeg's business district, the *Old Bailey,* 185 Lombard Ave., attracts the office crowd for drinks after five. Also in the same neighborhood, the *Lock, Stock and Barrell,* 171 McDermot, caters to the after-work and after-theater crowd at its Cheaters' Bar. For quiet, undisturbed conversation, the cocktail lounge in the Hotel Fort Garry, 222 Broadway, is a popular meeting place. *Club Morocco,* 575 Portage Ave., is the oldest and busiest late night spot in the city. For lovers of jazz and blues, the *Norwood Hotel,* on Sunday nights, *The Avenue,* 1133 Portage Ave., and the *Blue Note,* 220 Main St. The *Assiniboine Hotel* offers live entertainment. In addition, *The Hollow Mug* in the International Inn presents musical revues followed by dance music. *Bogard's,* 139 Albert St., a dining room with stand-up and sit-down bars, soft rock music and light show, is popular with the swinging singles, as is *Brandy's* on Princess St.

EXPLORING MANITOBA

The history of Manitoba is interwoven with the era of exploration in North America and the development of the fur trade. As a fur-trading center, the region was involved in the imperial struggle between France and England. Since those days, the province has attracted immigrants from all over the world, and today it is noted for its diverse cultural strains. The influence of still strong ethnic roots has uniquely shaped its towns and influenced its countryside.

A Water Highway

The Red River was the main transportation route and the focal point for settlers in the 18th and 19th centuries. Today, the river offers a beautiful scenic drive and a journey into Manitoba's pioneering past.

From Winnipeg's Perimeter Highway 101, take Metro Route 52 (Highway 9) and drive northeast. There is an interesting side trip on Highway 410 (St. Andrews Road), three quarters of a mile east to River Road. There you will see the lovely St. Andrews Church, built in the early 1880's. Some original furnishings remain, including kneeling benches covered in buffalo hide. Nearby, the Red River House Museum contains artifacts of a former Hudson's Bay Company fur trader and explorer.

To see a re-enactment of pioneer life as it was more than 100 years ago in the environs of Lower Fort Garry, continue northeast on River Road back to Hwy. 9, then go north. The approach to the fort is impressive—huge stone walls and cannons pointing menacingly across the Red River.

One of the oldest stone-built, fur-trading forts in North America, its history is preserved within the original buildings which are stocked with period furniture and mementos of the early days. Members of the fort's staff, dressed in the fashions of the old days, play their roles of early residents of the fort. There's even a blacksmith who has forging tools and horseshoes in his smithy.

Continuing north on Highway 9, you will reach Selkirk, a haven for pleasure craft, fishing fleets, and freighters. There is a popular marine museum in the town. A reminder of the early settlers is the huge replica in the municipal park of a Red River cart. The town is famous for its Highland Gathering in July.

The Western Shore

Lake Winnipeg is a large and shallow lake with a variety of beaches. Winnipeg Beach is a popular vacation area; it has a wide beach and a wayside park that provide picnic and boating facilities.

North again on Highway 9 brings you to Gimli. The town was founded in 1875 and is the second largest Icelandic community outside of Iceland. This fishing town has even more to offer than its harbors and beaches. Its annual Islendingadagurinn festival is held the first week in August. To further explore the town's origins, don't miss the Gimli Historical Museum and the giant Viking Statue in town.

Hecla Provincial Natural Park is the site of another Icelandic settlement. Its large Gull Harbour Resort reflects the early Icelandic architectural styles. From Gimli the route to the island is via Highways 8, 234 and 233. The rugged shoreline scenery resembles that of the Maritimes and the marshy areas have a profusion of wildlife and flora. On the island there is plenty for the visitor to do: a rich history to be studied, camping and sports facilities to be enjoyed and teeming wildlife to be observed.

Lake, River, and Falls

Hecla-Hole River Ferry is an enjoyable way to reach more fine beaches and interesting tour spots. It leaves from Gull Harbour during the summer months and crosses the lake to Wanipigow (Hole or Hollow Water). Here you can join up with Highway 304 heading south and turn northwest on Highway 11 to reach Pine Falls where the 82,000-kilowatt generating station is open to visitors. You can also see over the Abitibi-Price paper plant; tours are provided by appointment.

You have a choice of continuing north on Highway 11 for a taste of more expansive beaches, or you can go south on that highway to view more of Hydro Power's power plants. The stations at Winnipeg River and Seven Sisters offer tours. The mining town of Lac du Bonnet is a good center for sportsfishermen; angling equipment is also available. A side trip along Highway 211, west, will give the opportunity to take in the atomic energy plant at Piniwa.

The main leg of this tour continues south on Highway 11. Turn west on Highway 307 to reach Seven Sisters, the largest of the six power stations on the Winnipeg River; it is open to visitors. This road will take you into Whiteshell Provincial Park where recreational and camping facilities blend into a scenic, pre-Cambrian setting of sparkling lakes and jackpine forests. At the junction of Highway 1 and Highway 44, turn west for West Hawk Lake. Some 365 feet deep, this deepest lake in Manitoba is believed to have been formed by a meteor about 150 million years ago. Follow Highway 301 out of the park, but do take time to explore Falcon Lake.

Heritage Odyssey

Southern Manitoba is full of ethnic variety and historic interest. To explore this area, take Highway 1 from Winnipeg until you reach Highway 12, then go south to Steinbach. This town's Mennonite Village Museum is located about 1½ miles north of the town on Highway 12; here you can see the sights and hear the sounds of a Mennonite village of 1874. You can even taste the sort of foods the villagers ate in those days by visiting the Big Red Restaurant. In early August, the village holds its Pioneer Days Festival to honor its Mennonite forefathers who emigrated from Russia in the 1870's.

To visit St. Pierre, home of the Frog Follies in early August, drive west on Highway 52, then north on Highway 59. The typical French-Canadian town of St. Mâlo can be reached farther south on Highway 59. Displays illustrating the history of this predominantly French-Canadian district can be seen at the Pioneer Museum. The St. Mâlo recreation area includes beach, picnic, and camping facilities.

To visit Morris, home of the Manitoba Stampede, go north on Highway 59, then head west on Highway 23. Traveling from Winnipeg, Morris is 30 miles south on Highway 75. Direct from Calgary's Stampede, this well-known event features rodeos, chuckwagon races, and an exhibition in mid-July.

Western Manitoba

See the longest swinging footbridge in Canada at Souris, 20 miles south of Brandon. It is 582 suspense-filled feet of faltering footsteps. Also at Souris is a quarry where you can collect rock agates and petrified wood for a small fee. And there is first-class swimming and boating at Killarney.

PRACTICAL INFORMATION FOR MANITOBA

HOW TO GET THERE. By air: Manitoba's largest airport is in Winnipeg. It is served by *Air Canada, CP Air, Nordair,* and *Pacific Western Airlines.* Additionally, *Northwest Airlines* and *Frontier Airlines* fly in from Minneapolis and Denver respectively.

By car: A circle highway route, originating in the United States, is linked to the Manitoba highway system. In the southeast, Hwy. 75 runs to Winnipeg from the U.S. border and connects with Trans-Canada Hwy. 1. To the southeast, Hwy. 10 runs from the border, passing through Brandon and continuing north to Dauphin, The Pas, and Flin Flon.

By train: The main lines of the *Canadian Pacific* and *Canadian National* railroad systems serve Winnipeg, Portage La Prairie, and Brandon. Canadian National also provides services from Winnipeg to the northern regions of the province through Dauphin, The Pas to Thompson and Churchill on Hudson

Bay. But passenger service has been transferred to *Via Rail,* a government agency.

By bus: Service is provided by two mainline bus companies, *Grey Goose* and *Greyhound,* and several local companies.

 ACCOMMODATIONS in Manitoba range from the deluxe to inexpensive, but in the smaller towns it is sometimes difficult to find anything but the most basic accommodation. The price categories in this section are based on double occupancy. *Deluxe,* over $40; *Expensive,* $26 to $39; *Moderate,* $18 to $25; *Inexpensive,* below $18. All have dining facilities.

Most places accept the following major credit cards: American Express, MasterCard, and Visa; others may also be honored. Not all establishments accept credit cards, therefore we suggest you call for information.

BRANDON. *Deluxe.* **Royal Oak Inn.** Indoor solarium, pool, and sauna. Excellent dining room. Lounge, tavern and entertainment. Major credit cards.

Rodeway Inn. Saunas and game room are two special features of this motel. Major credit cards.

Victoria Inn. Pool, sauna, cocktail lounge, and licensed dining room. Major credit cards.

Expensive: **Canadian Inn.** Indoor pool, licensed dining room, coffee shop, cocktail lounge. Major credit cards.

CARMAN. *Moderate.* **Carman Motor Hotel.** Well known for its open steak pit, where you cook your own steak.

DAUPHIN. *Expensive:* **Rodeway Inn Motel.** Indoor pool, sauna whirlpool. Color TV. Self-serve breakfast nook. Major credit cards.

FLIN FLON. *Deluxe:* **Kelsey Trail Motor Inn.** Full range of comforts and conveniences. Indoor pool, licensed dining room, and beverage room. Major credit cards.

GIMLI. *Moderate:* **Viking Motor Hotel.** Licensed dining room, sauna, cocktail lounge and beverage room. Color TV, air conditioning. Major credit cards.

HECLA PROVINCIAL NATURAL PARK *Deluxe:* **Gull Harbour Resort Hotel.** Lounge, adult games room, indoor pool, sauna, deck and play area, gymnasium, 18-hole golf course, lake swimming facilities, snowshoe and cross-country ski trails. Amphitheater, marina. Major credit cards.

LAC DU BONNET. *Moderate:* **Lakeview Motor Hotel.** Licensed restaurant and beverage room. Major credit cards.

LA RIVIÈRE. *Moderate:* **Chalet Motel.** Convenient to ski hills. Air-conditioned, color TV, cocktail lounge and licensed dining room. Fishing licenses can be bought here. No credit cards.

MINNEDOSA. *Expensive:* **Valley Motor Hotel.** Licensed dining room, beverage room, cocktail lounge, and coffeeshop. Indoor pool, color TV. Major credit cards.

MORDEN. *Expensive:* **Morden Motor Inn.** Licensed restaurant and dining room, cocktail lounge, sauna, and color TV. Major credit cards.

PINAWA. *Expensive:* **Pinawa Motor Inn.** Licensed dining room, coffeeshop, and beverage room. Major credit cards.

PORTAGE LA PRAIRIE. *Expensive:* **Best Western Manitoba Inn.** All facilities, including swimming pool. Major credit cards.

Westgate Flag Inn. Color cable TV. Choice of waterbeds, queen-sized beds. Kitchenettes in some units. Major credit cards.

Westward Village Inn. Across from major shopping center. Dining and lounge facilities; newly opened.

Moderate: **Midtown Motor Hotel.** Licensed restaurant, dining room, and beverage room. All major credit cards accepted.

RIDING MOUNTAIN NATIONAL PARK. *Expensive:* **Elkhorn Ranch.** Indoor pool, licensed dining room, and cocktail lounge. Major credit cards.

STEINBACH. *Expensive:* **Frantz Motor Inn.** Licensed dining room, cocktail lounge, and beverage room. Visa only.

THE PAS. *Expensive:* **La Verendrye.** Dining room, lounge. Color TV. Major credit cards.

Wescana Inn. Dining room, cocktail lounge and beverage room. Major credit cards.

THOMPSON. *Expensive:* **Burntwood Motor Hotel.** Choice of dining and drinking facilities. Major credit cards.

Mystery Lake Motor Hotel. Large hotel with choices in dining and drinking facilities. Limousine service to airport. Major credit cards.

WHITESHELL PROVINCIAL NATURAL PARK. *Expensive:* **Rennie Hotel.** Tiny hotel with beverage room, cocktail lounge, and color TV. No credit cards or personal checks.

HOW TO GET AROUND. By air: *Pacific Western,* a major interprovincial airline, serves centers throughout Manitoba, Saskatchewan, and Alberta. *Nordair* provides regional service to Thunder Bay, Sault Ste. Marie, and Toronto, all in Ontario. Other regional and charter companies offer flights to areas in the province.

Car rental: Car rental companies such as *Avis, Budget, Hertz, Host,* and *Tilden* have facilities in all major centers, as well as a number of the smaller centers.

MANITOBA FACTS AND FIGURES. Manitoba's name originated with the Indian words Manitou bau—Strait of the God—describing the Lake Manitoba Narrows. It is often called Friendly Manitoba. Its floral emblem is the crocus; the Coat-of-Arms, "Vert on a rock a buffalo stantant proper, on a Chief Argent the Cross of St. George"; the provincial flag, a red ensign bearing Manitoba's coat-of-arms.

Winnipeg, population 600,000, is the provincial capital. The population of Manitoba is 1,051,000.

TOURIST INFORMATION. Tourist Information, Travel Manitoba is ready to answer any questions you might have. You will find them at the Legislative Building, Broadway and Osborne, Winnipeg, Manitoba R3C 0V8.

Seasonal Reception Centres are in operation from mid-May to September at six border and highway locations.

Camping, fishing, canoeing, hunting, winter recreation, and complete tourism information can be obtained by writing to: Travel Manitoba, Dept. 4001, Winnipeg, Manitoba, R3C 0V8.

The *Manitoba Vacation Guide* is available free of charge at all government information centers. It includes information on hotel and motel facilities, campgrounds, points of interest, historic sites, museums, recreational and sport facilities, and so on.

SEASONAL EVENTS. January: *Snowmobile races* start off the year in a number of Manitoba communities. Curling fans enjoy the *Manitoba Curling Association Bonspiel*—the world's largest bonspiel—usually held the last week of January. *Ukrainian Week,* an ethnic celebration of music, song, dance, crafts and native food is staged in Winnipeg at the end of January.

February: The *Canadian Power Toboggan Championship Races,* featuring top racers from Canada and the U.S., are hosted in Beausejour. Held in conjunction with the races, the *Beausejour Winter Farewell* is highlighted by the crowning of Miss Power Toboggan. The *Festival du Voyageur* in St. Boniface features a costume ball, ice sculpture, and many other winter activities. In The Pas, tourists and residents alike enjoy the *Northern Manitoba Trappers' Festival.*

Both the University of Manitoba and Winnipeg present winter festivals around a theme chosen as current and of particular interest to the students and the community.

March: The *Manitoba Music Competition Festival,* Canada's largest music festival, is held in Winnipeg.

April: The *Royal Manitoba Winter Fair,* including livestock judging and horse shows, is staged in Brandon at the beginning of the month. Also in Brandon, the *Brandon Music Festival* is held at the West Man Auditorium. Annually on Easter Sunday, the *Aurora Snow Festival* in Churchill heads into a week of dog team and snowmobile races.

May: The *Shrine Circus* comes to the Winnipeg Arena at the beginning of May. Racing enthusiasts enjoy stockcar racing at *Winnipeg Speedway,* starting in mid-May and continuing to September.

June: The rural French-speaking community celebrates St. Jean Baptiste Day during *Fête Franco-Manitobaine,* in La Broquerie. In Winnipeg, the *Red River Exhibition* features carnival attractions and stage shows at the end of June. The International Peace Gardens on the Manitoba/North Dakota border, hosts the *International Music Camp* featuring jazz concerts, drama and workshops.

July: The *Winnipeg Folk Festival* presents three days of music in Birds Hill Park, In July and Aug., *Rainbow Stage,* the only outdoor theater in western Canada, presents musicals in Winnipeg's Kildonan Park. Dancing, drumming and piping are presented at the *Manitoba Highland Gathering.* At Assiniboia Downs in Winnipeg, horse lovers gather for the *Manitoba Derby.*

This is the month for Manitoba's famous rodeos and festivals. There's the *Manitoba Stampede* in Morris, the *Threshermen's Reunion* in Austin, the *Annual Manitoba Sunflower Festival* in Altona, *Thompson Nickel Days* in the northern mining community of Thompson, and *Steinbach Pioneer Days,* an ethnic Mennonite celebration, in Steinbach. Workshops in painting and music are scheduled for the *Holiday Festival of the Arts* in Neepawa. Three days of rodeo and exhibits are featured at the *Northwest Round-up and Agricultural Fair* in Swan River at the end of July. The football season, starring the *Winnipeg Blue Bombers,* starts in July and continues to November.

August: Gimli presents the *Icelandic Festival of Manitoba* early in the month. *Harness racing* gets under way at Winnipeg's Assiniboia Downs. Winnipeg's cultural mosaic is well represented at *Folklorama,* a week of music, dancing and foods from many lands at pavilions located throughout the city. Morden's *Corn and Apple Festival* continues Manitoba's festival tradition during the last days of the month. In Dauphin, it's the *Canada's National Ukrainian Festival,* and in Boissevain, the *Canadian Turtle Derby.*

October: *Hockey,* featuring the *Winnipeg Jets,* starts at the Winnipeg Arena and continues through March. The Royal Winnipeg Ballet and the Manitoba Theatre Centre begin performances.

November: Brandon stages the *Brandon Agricultural Exhibition* at Keystone Centre. And, for the pleasure of both children and adults, there is the Santa Claus Parade, held near the end of the month in Winnipeg.

December: The Winnipeg Symphony celebrates the Christmas season with its annual *Christmas Fantasy* presentation and the Royal Winnipeg Ballet also has its special Christmas season.

 TOURS. Tours are available in Winnipeg and surrounding areas and also to Manitoba's northland. *Via Rail's Hudson Bay Explorer Tours*—a five-day, combined train and plane tour to sub-Arctic Churchill, and the Arctic Islands. Contact your travel agent or the Via Rail Passenger Sales Office for information and reservations.

Grayline Bus Tours, 285 Eniskillen, Winnipeg, as well as around the city, has package tours, including paddlewheel riverboat cruises on the Assiniboine and Red Rivers.

River Rouge Ltd., Nairn Ave., arranges tours on its *River Rouge* and *Lady Winnipeg* river cruise ships, as well as on its three double-decker buses. And, if you want to sail around on your own yacht, call M.S. *Black Hawk Charter Cruise* in Selkirk. *FunShip Cruise Lines* offers cruises on the 1,500-ton *Lord Selkirk* north on the Red River from Redwood Dock (284–3031).

 INDUSTRIAL TOURS. *Whiteshell Nuclear Research Establishment* has general tours of the plant during summer, including a portion of the reactor building and laboratories, 10 A.M. and 2 P.M. daily, except Sundays. Expectant mothers and children under 12 are not allowed to make the tour, but they may see films and displays in the information center.

Abitibi-Price Paper Co., Pine Falls, on the Winnipeg River is open for tours Monday to Friday, providing advance notice is given. Camp and picnic grounds are located across the river from the town. Visitor tours are available at several of Manitoba Hydro's power plants—Pine Falls, Seven Sisters, and Pointe du Boise. All stations are accessible by road.

NATIONAL PARKS. *Riding Mountain National Park,* a 1,150-square-mile parkland area in western Manitoba, includes both evergreen and hardwood forests, prairies, rolling hills, valleys, lakes and streams. Plateaus rise to heights of 2,480 feet above sea level and tower 1,100 feet above the surrounding countryside. Black bear, white-tailed deer, moose and elk, and numerous other smaller animals roam the park. Beaver are to be found in streams in many places in the area. A carefully controlled herd of buffalo grazes in a 1,314-acre enclosure and provides an ever-popular attraction for visitors. A special observation area affords a good view of these animals in their natural habitat.

Lakes and streams offer good fishing. Northern pike (a prime species in the region), walleye, whitefish, and lake trout flourish in cold waters such as Clear Lake, while rainbow and brook trout are among those found in Lake Katherine and Deep Lake. Clear Lake, the largest in the park, also offers opportunities for sailing and waterskiing.

The resort town of Wasagaming is the focal point of vacation activity in the park. In the town, visitors have a choice of theater, bowling, tennis, a natural history museum, and formal gardens. There is also an 18-hole golf course in the locality. A variety of good accommodation is available. Wasagaming and several of the lake areas in the park have campgrounds for both tents and trailers.

The park is bisected by Hwy. 10 and it can also be reached using Hwy. 5.

PROVINCIAL PARKS. Plenty of opportunity here for relaxation or adventure among the forests, lakes, streams, and rolling hills. Hiking, picnicking, canoeing, camping—whether you like to stray from the beaten path and rough it, or make use of the excellent facilities in Manitoba's provincial parks, you'll find what you are looking for regardless of season.

Recreation areas are provided with facilities for winter sports, including ski slopes and tows, motels and other types of accommodation. Groups of more than 40 persons are advised to make reservations at least a week in advance.

Provincial parks include:

Agassiz Provincial Forest, 50 miles east of Winnipeg, is reached by Hwys. 44 and 15. There are several picnic sites along the highways crossing the area.

Asessippi Provincial Park covers 5,000 acres beside the lake formed behind the Shellmouth Dam at the junction of the Shell and Assiniboine Rivers near the Saskatchewan border. It is reached by Hwy. 83 and is designed for water vacation activities.

Belair Provincial Forest has 164,920 acres of timberland. North Star Trail, the main route, begins just north of Stead off Provincial Rd. 219 and exits on Hwy. 59 near Grand Beach Provincial Park. The forest may also be entered a little farther north on Hwy. 59. This trail exits on Hwy. 11. Trails are being improved for public use and are accessible by most vehicles.

Birds Hill Provincial Park, 14 miles north of downtown Winnipeg on Hwy. 59, comprises 8,300 acres. The park includes an 80-acre man-made lake dotted with small islands and is suitable for swimming. A large tenting and trailer campground with modern facilities is provided. A commercial riding stable is also located in the park. Throughout the winter, group hay rides may be booked and for cross-country skiing enthusiasts, equipment may also be hired through the stable.

Clearwater Provincial Park, north of The Pas on Hwy. 10, is a 147,000-acre area surrounding Clearwater Lake—said to be one of the three true bluewater lakes in the world. (There are two modern campgrounds.)

Cormorant Provincial Forest, located 30 miles northeast of The Pas along the Hudson Bay railroad, adjoins Clearwater Provincial Park. It includes a fishing and hunting lodge.

Duck Mountain Provincial Park, comprises a 492-square-mile area in the Duck Mountain Provincial Forest northwest of Dauphin. Its 73 lakes have good fishing and it has excellent camping facilities.

Grand Beach Provincial Park covers over 59,000 acres, and is located 57 miles north of Winnipeg via Hwys. 59 and 12. Private cottages, a motor hotel, and camping facilities are available.

Grass River Provincial Park is the ultimate for wilderness camping. It consists of 565,000 acres of roadless terrain. The park is entered from Hwy. 10 at Cranberry Portage or from Provincial Rd. 231 along its southern boundary.

Hecla Provincial Park is only a few hours' drive north of Winnipeg via Hwy. 8 and Provincial Rds. 234 and 233. The park includes the Lake Winnipeg islands of Hecla, Black, Deer, and several smaller islands as well as the lake area in the vicinity. Hecla Island is joined to the mainland by a causeway. Golfing, resort accommodation complete with indoor pool, tennis courts, and convention facilities.

Porcupine Provincial Forest, north of Swan River adjoining the Saskatchewan boundary, is reached by Hwy. 10 and forestry roads. The lakes and rivers provide good sport for fishermen; facilities for picnicking and tenting are available.

Sandilands Provincial Forest is located between the southern boundary of Agassiz Forest and the United States border. Main access is by Hwy. 12 and the Trans-Canada Hwy. E. Picnic sites are situated within the area.

Spruce Woods Provincial Park, thirty miles east of Brandon and between the Trans-Canada Hwy. W. and Hwy. 2, covers 90 square miles. One of the newest provincial parks, it provides modern campground and picnic facilities. This is the eastern segment of the Spruce Woods Provincial Forest, and its 57,000 acres are well wooded with aspen and spruce trees. Spruce Woods Provincial Forest itself is 25 miles east of Brandon between Hwys. 1 and 2. The park and forest may be reached from the communities of Glenboro on Hwy. 2 or through Carberry on the Trans-Canada Hwy. from the north.

Turtle Mountain Provincial Park, one of the smaller provincial parks, covers 47,000 acres of rolling, forested hills and fertile valleys along the International border in the southwest corner of the province. One of its main attractions is the world's largest garden dedicated to peace: the International Peace Garden. The park has a total of 29 lakes.

Whiteshell Provincial Park, a 1,065-square-mile park, comprises the major vacation area of the eastern region. Lakes, rivers, and streams in the area provide ample opportunity for fishing, hunting, camping, and other outdoor activities. The park includes one of Canada's most modern recreational townsite developments at Falcon Lake, with tennis, an 18-hole golf course and a ski resort. Falcon Lake resort is 90 miles east of Winnipeg on the Trans-Canada Hwy. Two other resort areas are on Falcon Lake, a popular spot for waterskiing, sailing, and fishing. The Whiteshell has numerous campgrounds and picnic sites, plus modern accommodation in lodges and motels.

GARDENS. *The International Peace Gardens,* at the junction of Hwy. 10 and North Dakota 3, cover an area of 2,300 acres in the Turtle Mountains Provincial Park. Dedicated to international peace and goodwill, the formal gardens surround ornamental spillways originating from a series of lakes. The Centennial Pavilion in the garden commemorates Canada's 100th birthday.

Named for Errick F. Willis, it was built as a memorial to the former Lieutenant-Governor of Manitoba. A permanent feature of the garden is the nondenominational Chapel of Peace financed by the General Order of the Eastern Star. The Chapel stands astride the international border, overlooking the panels of the formal gardens. No charge for admission to the gardens.

Morden's *Experimental Station* opens its gates each summer during its open house. Tours of the exotic, beautiful and/or agricultural facilities yield botanical oddities and hardy farm plantings.

FARM VACATIONS AND GUEST RANCHES. Manitoba offers hospitality on more than 50 host farms, many of which accommodate visitors both in winter and summer. Activities range from helping with the chores to just plain relaxing. Many farms offer all the traditional holiday activities of fishing, golfing, swimming and boating, with the additional bonuses of old-fashioned hayrides and country-style barbecues. A vacationer can either "live in" with meals supplied or camp on the property with meals on request. Some host farms prefer children only, senior citizens, convalescents, or adults only, while others accommodate one-day touring groups, trailers, or a family holiday lasting a week or more.

For further information, contact Travel Manitoba, Dept. 4001, Legislative Building, Winnipeg, Manitoba R3C 0V8, or the Manitoba Farm Vacations Association, 437 Assiniboine Ave., Winnipeg, Manitoba R3C 0Y5 (tel. 943–8361).

The Hostelling Association of Manitoba offers accommodation in Winnipeg, Brandon, Glenboro, and at the Lilac Motel, 25 miles east of Winnipeg on Hwy. 1. To make arrangements, telephone: (204)786–5641. The Bed-and-Breakfast Association also offers hospitality to visitors in members' homes. For information, write the association at 35 Pontiac Bay, Winnipeg R3K 0S6.

CHILDREN'S ACTIVITIES. Ride on the *Prairie Dog Central,* hitched on to an old-time steam locomotive. It runs from Winnipeg to Grosse Isle. Kids love the four wooden coaches and the caboose. Adults will enjoy this glimpse of the past. Refreshments and souvenirs aboard.

Rockhounding is a favorite family activity in **Souris** and buckets of rare agate and fossils are yours to collect for a small fee.

Take a closer look at Manitoba's wildlife. *Alf Hole Goose Sanctuary,* near **Rennie,** Hwy. 4, for a close range look at Canada geese. *The Delta Marsh* near **Portage La Prairie** is one of the largest and best-known waterfowl staging marshes in North America, and it is closely rivaled by the *Netley Marshes* near **Petersfield. Flin Flon,** where the 25-acre park is home to many species of wildlife. The zoo at **Winnipeg,** one of the world's finest, with more than 100 animal species. Many monkeys. See *Aunt Sally's Farm* there for the young animals. Zoo is open year round; Aunt Sally's Farm open during summer months.

For three to five weeks each summer, beginning in late June, the *strawberries* are ripe for the plucking. U-Pick signs mark the location of farms which allow families to pick their own sweet berries for nominal charge. For further information call: Citizen's Inquiry 1–800–292–8920 toll-free.

SUMMER SPORTS. Sports enthusiasts will find every type of summer sport in Manitoba, for both spectators and participants.

Fishing: The 90,000 lakes in the province offer ample opportunity for good sport. There are more than a dozen varieties of gamefish native to Manitoba's waters, including northern pike, walleye, and smallmouth bass.

Hunting: There is an abundance of wildlife ranging from white-tailed deer and elk to black bear and all types of game.

Hiking: The province has many exciting trails to explore. The *Amisk* trail in Whiteshell Provincial Park, one of the more challenging trails, runs through pre-Cambrian country and is bridged over a moss swamp. Those more interested in geology and plantlife should explore the interpretive trails. A printed pamphlet explaining the vegetation and wildlife along the way is available at the start of the trail.

Watersports: Manitoba's rivers and lakes are excellent for canoeing, swimming, sailing, and other watersports. For the sea lovers, the 3-mile stretch at *Grand Beach* is one of the finest sandy beaches in North America.

Golf: Golfers will find numerous, challenging courses in all parts of the province, including *Falcon Beach Golf Course,* and the *Sandy Hook Golf Course, Riding Mountain* and the *Hecla Provincial Course.*

Riding and racing: Horse lovers can either go riding at one of the many fine stables in the province, or head for *Assiniboine Downs,* Winnipeg, for the thoroughbred and harness racing. The *Manitoba Derby* is run mid-July.

CAMPING OUT. Private and government-operated campgrounds abound throughout the province with facilities for both tents and trailers. There are more than 5,000 private and 5,000 public campsites ranging from simple to fully serviced facilities; some are complete with restaurants, laundromats, stores and other features. For further information about camping facilities, contact Travel Manitoba, Dept. 4001, Legislative Building, Winnipeg, Manitoba R3C 0V8.

WINTER SPORTS. Every region in the province provides excellent facilities for active participation in winter sports. The number of ski resorts in Manitoba has grown considerably since it was begun by a handful of Winnipeggers 40 years ago. Some of them, with facilities including modern chalets and high powered snow-making equipment, are among the best in Canada. *The Falcon Lake Ski Resort* has always been popular with beginners and intermediate skiers. Located 96 miles east of Winnipeg, the resort offers equipment rentals, a ski shop, and certified ski instruction. In Manitoba's central region, *Birch Ski Resort, Holiday Mountain Ski Resort, Snow Valley Resort,* and *Stony Mountain Ski Park* are favored ski areas. In the west, the major ski centers are *Mount Agassiz, Mount Glenorchy,* and *Mark Valley Ski Resort,* and in Manitoba's north, *Mystery Mountain* and the *Ptarmigan Ski Club* offer a wide range of facilities. (Some of the resorts also have tobogganing, skating, and snowmobile rentals.)

Many of Manitoba's parks are catering to the growing enthusiasm for cross-country skiing, and numerous trails have been developed. In Winnipeg and other centers, ice hockey and wrestling are among the main sports attractions.

HISTORIC SITES. Arnes: *Stefansson Memorial Park* honors the Arctic explorer—one of the first to report to the Canadians on climatic conditions in the Northwest Territories.

Betula Lake: Near Betula Lake in *Whiteshell Provincial Park* are large stone figures arranged on the base rock in the shapes of turtles, snakes, fish, and birds. These ancient mosaics were used by the Ojibwa Indians in ceremonies associated with their Medicine Society.

Emerson: *Fort Dufferin,* 2 mi. N of Emerson. From this fort, in 1874, the newly-organized North West Mounted Police began their historic trek to bring law and order to the western plains. The site is marked by a cairn.

Gardenton: The first Ukrainian Greek Orthodox church to be erected in North America is located 5 mi. E of Hwy. 59. The first Ukrainians on the continent settled here.

Gimli: The first permanent Icelandic settlement was established at *Gimli,* October 1875. The townsite was named for the home of the gods in Norse mythology.

Lockport: *St. Andrew's Church,* Provincial Rd. 410 and River Rd., was built in the early 1800s and is the oldest stone church in western Canada still used for worship.

Morris: The *Morris River,* known as the Scratching River in 1801, was the site of North West and XY companies, fur-trading posts. Settlement began here in 1874, where the trail from Pembina crossed the river.

Pilot Mound: On Hwy. 3, *Old Mound,* is the site of prehistoric burial grounds. Later, it was used as a signal hill by the Assiniboine Indians. It was also a prominent landmark for explorers and settlers traveling through southern Manitoba.

Poplar Point: *Ste. Anne's Church* (1864) on Hwy. 26, is one of the oldest log churches in continuous use in western Canada.

Portage La Prairie: Marked by a cairn, *Fort La Reine* was built by La Verendrye as a base from which he left the rivers and ventured onto the plains, seeking the "white" Indians near what are now Bismark and Mandan, North Dakota.

Selkirk: *Lower Fort Garry* is one of the oldest stone-built fur trading posts in North America. Built in the 1830's by the Hudson's Bay Company, it was once a center for the western fur trade and for exploration to the Northwest Territories. It later became a training base for the Royal Canadian Mounted Police.

Souris: *Souris River Fur Trade Post*—seven of these were built between 1785 and 1832 by the North West, Hudson's Bay and XY companies. A cairn marks the site.

Steinbach: In 1873, eight townships were set aside in the Steinbach vicinity for the exclusive use of *Mennonite* settlers from Russia. More than 50 villages were founded by 1923.

Swan River: From 1787, when the first trading post was built near Swan River, until 1821, the *Swan River Valley* was the scene of intense rivalry and competition between the North West and the Hudson's Bay companies.

Winnipeg Area: *La Barriere,* a half mile south of St. Norbert, Hwy. 75, where the Metis followers of Louis Riel turned back emissaries of William McDougall, first Lieutenant-Governor of Manitoba. On the Trans-Canada Hwy., 13 mi. W of Winnipeg, near Headingly, marks the *Principal Meridian.* The land survey system for all of western Canada started from this point. Both sites are marked by cairns.

MUSEUMS AND GALLERIES Brandon: *Brandon Allied Arts Council,* 1036 Louise Ave., has yearly programs of changing exhibits, paintings, prints and handicrafts. Lovers of wildlife and conservation will find plenty to enthuse over at the *B. J. Hale Museum of Natural History* in the Arts and Library Building at Brandon University. A special feature is the collection of 400 mounted birds representing 250 species, and the mammal collection that includes northern animals in a setting of ice and snow. Open daily except holidays.

Carman: For the car buff, *Heaman Antique Autorama,* near Carman, houses autos dating to 1902.

Churchill: At the *Eskimo Museum* you will see Eskimo artifacts and survival tools in stone, bone, ivory and metal, as well as wildlife exhibits. Open year-round, no charge.

Cook's Creek: For a look at Slavic pioneer materials, there's the *Cook's Creek Museum* on Hwy. 212. Religious objects and an outdoor display of farm machinery also included.

Dugald: The town is planning to build a permanent home for its famous *Dugald Fashion Collection,* one of the country's most extensive and beautiful costume collections, with clothing dating back to Western Canada's earliest history.

Elkhorn: *Manitoba Automobile Museum* has 80 antique cars, plus pioneer objects.

Emerson: Two restored buildings at *Gateway Stopping Place Museum* display articles of the North West Mounted Police and the plains Indians.

Gardenton: The focus is on Ukrainian domestic and agricultural aspects at the *Ukrainian Museum and Village.*

Gimli: *Gimli Historical Museum* also displays Ukrainian and Icelandic pioneer materials.

Grandview: *Crossley Museum* shows pioneer relics in an old log school. A separate building has Indian artifacts, wood carvings, and cut and polished rocks. Open Tuesday to Sunday by appointment.

Hadashville: *Conservation Training Museum* features an outdoor museum of animal and natural history exhibits. Guided tours July and August.

Killarney: *J.A. Victor David Museum* features articles of Indian and pioneer life and natural history.

Leaf Rapids: *Leaf Rapids National Exhibition Centre* focuses on traveling art and photographic exhibits. Local displays and native handicrafts on sale.

Melita: Prehistoric pottery and Indian wares are exhibited at the *Antler River Historical Society Museum.* Open June 1 to Labor Day, afternoons or by request.

Miami: *Miami Pioneer Museum* houses pioneer artifacts as does the *Minnedosa and District Cooperative Museum* in **Minnedosa.**

Morden: *Morden and District Museum* offers a varied display of prehistoric fossils and specimens going back as far as 70 million years, Piggot papers, and antique furniture.

Neepawa: *Beautiful Plains* features pioneer and Indian exhibits. Open July to September.

Pilot Mound: Both the *Pilot Mound Centennial Museum* and *Marringhurst Pioneer Park* specialize in pioneer material pertaining to that district.

Portage La Prairie: Hundreds of items illustrating Manitoba's history are in the *Fort la Reine Museum and Pioneer Village.* The complex embraces a fort, log home, school, church, and two major display buildings.

Rapid City: *Rapid City Museum Cultural Centre,* the *Historical Museum,* **Reston,** and the *Chapman Museum,* **Rivers,** all have pioneer farming and domestic material exhibits.

Roblin: *Keystone Pioneer Museum* has agricultural machinery exhibits in working order, and pioneer domestic articles.

Selkirk: Plenty of history at the *Lower Fort Garry National Historic Park Museum,* once a central provisions and supply depot for the fur trade in Northwest Canada. Built in the 1830's. Restored buildings and contemporary facilities open mid-May to mid-October.

Shilo: *The Royal Regiment of Canadian Artillery Museum,* Canadian Forces Base, portrays the regiment's history with a display of guns, ammunition, uniforms, medals and historical documents. Tours arranged by written request.

St. Andrews: At *Red River House Museum* you can get a glimpse into the life of Arctic explorer Captain William Kennedy.

St. Claude: The French influence on the province can be seen in the display of artifacts in the *St. Claude Museum.*

Steinbach: A replica of a Mennonite village with historic, competely furnished buildings is located in Steinbach. The *Mennonite Village Museum* includes an original log house, windmill, blacksmith's shop, general store, antiques and manuscripts.

Teulon: The *Sam Waller Little Northern Museum* displays Northern Indian and pioneer material.

Virden: *The Pioneer Home Museum of Virden and Districts* is a large brick house depicting life in the Victorian era. Year-round tours by appointment.

Winkler: *Pembina Threshermen's Museum* shows how it was, with steam threshing equipment in working order and pioneer antiques and artifacts.

 MUSIC. *The Winnipeg Symphony* gives over a dozen concerts in the Centennial Concert Hall between October and May, in addition to an occasional open-air concert in Winnipeg's Assiniboine Park.

The annual *Winnipeg Folk Festival* attracts top folk artists from across the continent who gather at Birds Hill Provincial Natural Park for three days of workshops and entertainment each July.

At the *International Peace Gardens,* an annual music camp and workshop is held featuring a round of summer activities including jazz concerts and drama.

 SHOPPING. Major stores in Winnipeg, such as the *Hudson's Bay Co.,* and *Eatons,* offer the vacation shopper everything from the smallest necessities to fine china, British woolens, silverware, and jewelry. Branches of these stores will be found in the *Polo Park Shopping Centre,* the *Unicity Shopping Center, St. Vital, Garden City,* and similar centers throughout Manitoba.

The city and provincial centers have a variety of unusual shops and boutiques. Just north of *The Pas* is an Indian handicraft shop where the visitor can watch Indian women making moccasins, mukluks, jackets, other clothing and jewelry. For that special souvenir, you may find what you are looking for at the *Rock Shop.* Here you can choose from a fine line of costume jewelry made from the rock from a local quarry. Also, you can buy an inexpensive permit to collect your own rock.

DRINKING LAWS. The legal drinking age in Manitoba is 18. Liquor may be purchased by the bottle or the case from Government Liquor Commission stores and beer from government-approved vendors. Wines are generally cheaper in Manitoba than in other provinces.

 DINING OUT. Rural Manitoba offers a wide choice of restaurants ranging from ultra-expensive to moderately-priced with good home-cooked food.

Most of the best restaurants outside Winnipeg are located in hotels and motels. Brandon, the province's second largest city, has an excellent selection of restaurants, as does Portage La Prairie, halfway between Winnipeg and Brandon. There are also a number of first-class eating places catering to tourists in the Whiteshell, Lake Winnipeg and Clear Lake resort areas. Generally, price ranges per person for a meal are: *Expensive,* $20 and up; *Moderate,* $15–20; *Inexpensive,* under $15.

Most places accept the following major credit cards: American Express, MasterCard and Visa; others may also be honored. Not all establishments accept credit cards, therefore we suggest you call for information.

Southern Manitoba

BRANDON. *Expensive:* **North Hill Inn.** 10th and Braecrest Dr. Phone 727–4455. Dining room sits atop a hill and overlooks the lights of the city. Dancing and entertainment are featured. There is also a lounge and a nine-hole golf course.

Royal Oak Inn. 3130 Victoria Ave. Phone 728–5775. First-class selection of dining, lounge, and café facilities.

Suburban Restaurant. 2604 Victoria Ave. Phone 728–3031. Long established top-grade restaurant offering a varied menu.

Victoria Inn. 3650 Victoria Ave. Phone 725–1532. Features dining room, lounge, and tropical café overlooking the swimming pool.

Inexpensive: **Smitty's Restaurant.** Brandon Shopper's Mall, 18th St. Phone 728–0690. Caters to families. Major credit cards accepted.

CLEAR LAKE. *Expensive:* **Elk Horn Ranch Resort Hotel.** Mooswa Dr. Phone 848–2802. Open year-round, featuring fully-licensed dining room and cocktail lounge with wheelchair service.

DAUPHIN. *Inexpensive:* **Becky's Family Restaurant.** 8 Seventh Ave. E. Phone 638–3012. Licensed dining room offering take-out service. Pizza, ribs, and steak are house specialties.

Dauphin Community Inn. 104 Main N. Phone 638–4311. Licensed restaurant and beverage room.

King's Hotel. 204 Main N. Phone 638–6090. Light snacks to full course meals in the dining room and adjoining cocktail lounge.

LAKE WINNIPEG AREA. *Moderate:* **Falcon Restaurant.** 72 First Ave., Gimli. Phone 642–8868. Features varied menu. Entertainment on weekends in this pretty Lake Winnipeg town.

Sandy Hook Village Inn. Lot 15, Sandy Hook. Phone 389–5473. Great home cooking, open Tuesday to Sunday, fully licensed and air-conditioned.

Inexpensive: **Viking Motor Hotel.** N.W. 7th and Centre, Gimli, Phone 642–5181. Cocktail lounge and dining room facilities.

MINNEDOSA. *Moderate:* **Valley Motor Lodge.** 28 Main N., Phone 867–2741. Fully licensed restaurant adjoining indoor pool and sauna.

PORTAGE LA PRAIRIE. *Expensive:* **Manitobah Inn.** Highway No. 1 and Yellowquill Trail. Phone 857–9791. A Best Western Hotel with dining room, lounge, enclosed pool and recreation area.

Moderate: **Midtown Motor Inn.** 177 Saskatchewan Ave. W. Phone 857–6881. Good dining facilities in the heart of the downtown district.

Inexpensive: **Consumers Co-op Restaurant.** Highway 1A. Phone 857–8701. Cafeteria-style eating for the whole family.

Northern Manitoba

FLIN FLON. *Expensive:* **Bakers Narrows Lodge.** Bakers Narrows near Flin Flon. Good accommodation and lodging catering to hunters and fishermen.

Kelsey Trail Motor Inn. No. 10 Highway. Phone 687–7555. Dining and beverage rooms, indoor pool, sauna.

SWAN RIVER. *Moderate:* **Valley Hotel.** 703 Main E. Phone 734–3497. Beverage room and licensed restaurant.

Westwood Inn. Highway 10 N. Phone 734–4548. Restaurant, cocktail lounge, convention facilities, indoor pool.

THE PAS. *Moderate:* **Wescana Inn.** 439 Fischer. Phone 1–800–442–0400. Full dining and beverage facilities in a modern hotel.

THOMPSON. *Expensive:* **Mystery Lake Motor Hotel.** Cree and Selkirk. Phone 778–8331. Licensed dining room, lounge, and beverage room.

Moderate: **Burntwood Motor Hotel.** Selkirk Ave. Phone 677–4551. Licensed dining room and lounge, beer vendor.

Eastern Manitoba

FALCON LAKE. *Expensive:* **Falcon Lake Resort and Club.** Lake Blvd. Phone 349–8212. Open year-round, offers first-class dining and imbibing facilities to summer campers and winter cross-country skiers.

GRAND BEACH. *Moderate:* **Grand Beach Inn.** Grand Beach Rd. Phone 754–2554. Dining and beverage room at popular Lake Winnipeg resort.

LAC DU BONNET. *Inexpensive:* **Lakeview Motor Hotel.** 57 Park N. Phone 345–9301. Beverage room and licensed restaurant on the shore of the Winnipeg River.

PINAWA. *Moderate:* **Pinawa Motor Inn.** Lot 147. Phone 753–2443. Beverage and dining room, licensed and airconditioned.

PINE FALLS. *Inexpensive:* **Papertown Motel.** Highway 304, St. George. Phone 367–2261. Licensed dining room and cocktail lounge.

SASKATCHEWAN

The Land of Outdoor Fun

by
BARBARA LEWIS and ROGER NEWMAN

Barbara Lewis is a freelance travel writer contributing to newspapers, magazines and business publications. She was born and raised in Alberta.

To the vacationer, angler, camper, and outdoor enthusiast—in fact, to everyone who visits the Province of Saskatchewan—it is the "Land of Outdoor Fun."

The visitor will find that true throughout the province, from the Badlands of the southeast or Cypress Hills in the southwest, where elevation is over 3,000 feet above sea level, through the flat grain lands to the northern country of lakes and forests. There are more than 400 campgrounds, 17 provincial parks, 99 regional parks, and the Prince Albert National Park. Most have provisions for camping, nature trails, swimming, boating, golf, tennis, riding, and children's playgrounds. In winter, skiing, skating, hockey, and iceboating take over.

With lakes and rivers covering almost 15 percent of Saskatchewan's total area, fishing here has gained international fame. Northern fly-in fishing trips are readily available to those who wish to fish virgin lakes.

Geography and All That

The Province of Saskatchewan is the center of the three Prairie Provinces of Canada, bounded by Manitoba on the east, Alberta on the west, the Northwest Territories to the north. Its southern boundary extends along the states of Montana and North Dakota. The total area is 251,700 square miles.

Saskatchewan's climate is dry, helping to alleviate temperature extremes. Blue skies and memorable sunsets in the summer, and sunshine and less than 50 inches of snow in the winter, characterize the weather, which varies from 100° Fahrenheit in summer to –50°F degrees in winter. The average frost-free period varies from 135 days in the south to less than 105 days in the northern part of the plains area. Total precipitation varies from 11 to 15 inches on the open plains.

Eleven cities dot the province. Regina, the largest with a population of 172,700, is its capital. It is also the training center for the Royal Canadian Mounted Police. Saskatoon, the second largest (164,304 people), is the home of the University of Saskatchewan. Other cities are Moose Jaw, Prince Albert, Swift Current, Yorkton, North Battleford, Estevan, Weyburn, Lloydminster, and Melville. Population is divided almost evenly between urban and rural regions, with racial origins stemming mainly from the British Isles, Germany, the Ukraine, Scandinavian countries, France, the Netherlands, Poland, and native people.

Agriculture is Saskatchewan's largest single industry—accounting for half the value of goods produced in the province and about half of Canada's total grain production. Increased diversification and mechanization have altered the Saskatchewan farm picture during the past two decades: average farm size has increased, rural population has stabilized, and farm homes have all the amenities of their city counterparts. Farmers are also encouraged to participate in food processing more fully.

Saskatchewan is also a major mineral producer. It is the major producer of potash in Canada, pumps oil from numerous fields and has rich uranium deposits. And Canada's only known natural supply of sodium sulfate, used in paper, detergent, and glassmaking industries, is located here.

By far Saskatchewan's largest natural resource, however, is her forests, not only for the lumber and pulp and paper industries, but also as a people pleaser—hunters, canoeists, hikers, naturalists, and fishermen all derive direct pleasure from this unspoiled habitat in the northern half of the province.

Teepee Rings and Rock Carvings

The first inhabitants of Saskatchewan, some 20,000 to 30,000 years ago, were Paleo-Indians who crossed from Asia to North America to

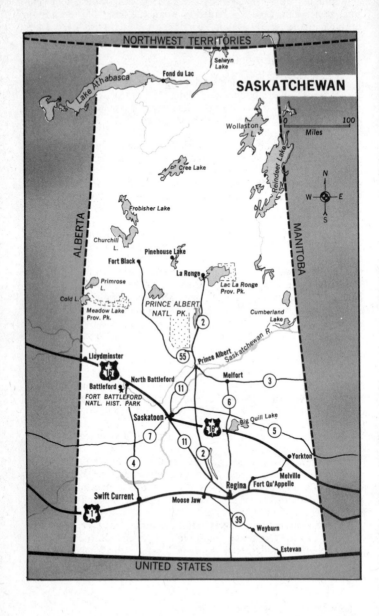

hunt and forage. When the first white man, Henry Kelsey, arrived, almost 300 years ago, he found Saskatchewan occupied by various tribes of Indians—Chippewa in the north, Blackfoot in the central parklands, and Assiniboines in the south. Although actual historical evidence of these tribes is limited to a few teepee rings and rock carvings, their presence is remembered by the lyrical names they gave Saskatchewan rivers, lakes, hills, and settlements. Pick up a map of Saskatchewan and you'll find them—Pasquia Hills, Katepwa, Nipew Lake, Wataman River. In fact, the name Saskatchewan comes from the Cree word *Kisiskatchewan,* which means "the river that flows swiftly."

The Fur Adventure

On the heels of the explorers came fur traders in search of both fur and adventure. Competition was fierce, and to protect their assets, the fur companies were forced to establish trading posts inland. The first post built in Saskatchewan was Cumberland House in 1774 by Samuel Hearne for the Hudson's Bay Co. The North West Company was not far behind, however, and as the fur trade flourished more forts were established by the two rival companies, usually a short distance from each other and in direct competition. Finally, in 1821, these two companies joined under the name Hudson's Bay Co. and held a monopoly on the fur trade until the 1870's, when the trade era ended. These trading posts became the beginnings of many present-day cities, and their overland routes, roads by which settlers reached new homesteads.

Provincial Status

The first permanent settlers were Métis of mixed Indian and European blood from the Manitoba Red River Valley. However, in 1872, when the Canadian government offered free land to all who wanted it, a flood of settlers from all over the world began to move into the empty plains. The construction of the Canadian Pacific Railway and the establishment of the Northwest Mounted Police, forerunner of the Royal Canadian Mounted Police, brought even more. Settlements were formed, local governments set up, and in 1905, Saskatchewan and its 250,000 people became a province of the Dominion of Canada. The first Saskatchewan legislature was opened at Regina, March 29, 1906. From 1972 to 1982, the province was governed by a New Democratic (Socialist) government led by Premier Allan Blakeneny. However, the NDP was defeated by the Conservatives under the leadership of Grant Devine, a University of Saskatchewan agricultural economics professor, in a mid-1982 election.

The Last Canadian Conflict

Any historical sketch of Saskatchewan would be incomplete without mention of the famous Riel Rebellion. The seeds of this rebellion were sown in Manitoba's Red River Valley in 1812, when the Métis living there learned that land did not necessarily belong to the men born and living on it. More and more settlers arrived, and in 1869, when surveyors ran lines across the Métis strip farms, the Métis rebelled and formed a provisional government under Louis Riel. The Canadian government moved quickly, making Manitoba a province and setting aside 1,400,-000 acres for Métis settlement. Riel was exiled, and when the government offered scrip—entitling each holder to 240 acres of land—the leaderless Métis, not understanding its value, did not collect it or sold it for a fraction of its worth. Further demoralized by the loss of freighting jobs because of the cessation of steamboat operations, the Métis headed for the South Saskatchewan River Valley in Saskatchewan.

They survived here for almost 15 years on mediocre farmland. They petitioned to the government for land rights but were ignored, and finally, in 1884, they sent for Louis Riel. Riel's moderate reform program garnered no sympathy from Ottawa, and so, knowing of an impending solar eclipse, he told the Métis and Indians that if God were on their side, He would blot out the sun on March 16. Of course, the divine sign occurred, and three days later Riel formed a provisional government with Gabriel Dumont as his commander-in-chief. The first clash occurred at Duck Lake on March 26, 1885, between a Métis Indian band and a 100-member force of police and volunteers. Militia units were organized in Ontario and Québec, and 850 men led by Major General Frederick Middleton went west by Canadian Pacific Railway. With several impressive victories to his credit, Dumont wanted to harass Middleton's forces, but Riel convinced him to stand and defend Batoche.

Middleton and his main force arrived at Batoche on May 8, and for three days the Métis Indians held the edge in the battle. On the fourth day, Middleton's troops attacked, using the new multibarreled Gatling gun, and in two hours Batoche was taken. The Métis' attacks against the Gatling gun with muzzle-loaders using nails and gravel as ammunition were hopeless. Riel escaped but surrendered a few days later. He was tried for treason and hanged at Regina. Dumont fled to the United States, where he joined Buffalo Bill's Wild West Show. He returned to Batoche after being granted amnesty and died there in 1906.

The Riel Rebellion was the last armed revolt in Canada. Batoche is a national historic site undergoing a facelift for the rebellion's 100th anniversary.

EXPLORING REGINA

Although situated on the treeless prairie, Regina is full of trees. The city's heart is a 2,500-acre park called Wascana Centre, the Indian name for Regina.

Founded in 1882, Regina was originally called Pile of Bones from the Indian practice of piling the bones of buffalo in the belief that this would ensure that they would always come back to be hunted for food. It was officially renamed Regina (the formal Latin title of the Queen) by Princess Louise in honor of her mother, Queen Victoria. The surrounding area is world-famous for the production of high-quality bread wheat. However, the city no longer depends to such a large extent on the grain industry; its economic base has widened to include secondary industries resulting from potash and oil reserves as well as manufacturing establishments, including the largest steel mill (IPSCO) in Western Canada, and agricultural-related production plants.

Little Chapel on the Square

Regina has always been in the midst of Canadian history. From 1882 to 1905 it was the capital of the Northwest Territories. In 1903 it was incorporated as a city, and two years later became the capital of the newly formed Province of Saskatchewan. Also during this period it was the headquarters for the Royal Canadian Mounted Police, known then as the Northwest Mounted Police. In 1920 the force's head office was moved to Ottawa, but Regina continued as a training center, and today 1,000 recruits a year are taught law enforcement and investigation techniques.

The R.C.M.P. depot division contains barracks, sport facilities and classrooms, a scientific laboratory, a museum, and a chapel. This "Little Chapel on the Square" is well worth a visit. Built in 1883 as a mess hall and converted to a chapel fourteen years later, it gives the visitor a glimpse back into the past. The stained glass windows depict Northwest Mounted Police members—one sounding reveille; one standing, head bowed, rifle upside down in mourning position. The flags on either side of the chapel flew over Fort Walsh from 1875 to 1880. The baptismal font is in memory of a Mountie who died at Cutknife Hill, one of the battles of the Riel Rebellion.

The museum furnishes a chronological history of the Royal Canadian Mounted Police. There is a uniform worn by Superintendent J. M. Walsh, the man who negotiated with Sitting Bull when the Sioux fled to Canada following the Battle of the Little Big Horn. There are displays depicting the hunt for "the mad trapper of Rat River" and the crucifix that Louis Riel, the Métis leader of the Northwest Rebellion, carried to the hanging scaffold on November 6, 1885.

In Barracks Square a monument commemorates the first voyage through the Northwest Passage by the R.C.M.P. patrol boat *St. Roch,* a tablet honoring Mounties killed in the line of duty, and 2 sevenpounder muzzle-loading cannons dating back to 1808. Beyond the square is a cemetery almost as old as the force.

History buffs visiting Regina in July and August can see a reenactment of Louis Riel's trial for treason, in Saskatchewan House, once the residence of lieutenant governors. A life-size statue of Riel by John Nugent may be seen near the Legislative Buildings in Wascana Centre.

You might also be drawn to IPSCO Zoo, a short distance north of Regina, and if you are a football enthusiast, Regina's Taylor Field is the home of the Saskatchewan Roughriders of the Canadian Football League.

A Unique Agribition

If you enjoy getting close to the land, don't miss the Canadian Western Agribition. It is held in Regina in late fall every year and, besides the traditional livestock shows and sales, features a "Mexabition" of equipment, inventions, gadgets, house and garden amenities and products, and do-it-yourself ideas, to mention a few. A championship rodeo is also held, and if you miss this rodeo, visit Saskatchewan in August when Buffalo Days are held in Regina, a pioneer celebration with ten days of horse races, band concerts, midway and grandstand entertainment.

Parks and Museums

A visit to Regina would not be complete without exploring the parks within the city: Wascana Park, in the southern portion of the city situated on the banks of Wascana Lake (formed by damming Wascana Creek); Victoria Park in the center of the city, where a monument commemorates the inauguration ceremony for the Province of Saskatchewan on September 4, 1905; and King's Park, which has a golf course and is located a short distance out of the city proper.

Wascana Park, containing over 2,500 acres, has an impressive list of things to see and do. Here rests Diefenbaker Homestead, the boyhood home of John G. Diefenbaker, Canada's thirteenth prime minister; the Legislative Buildings, built between 1908 and 1912 of Tyndall stone and some 34 kinds of marble, the Saskatchewan Archives with memorabilia of the early history of the province and the Northwest Territories; the Saskatchewan Center of Arts for live-theatergoers. Also picnic and barbecue areas, band shells, swimming and boating facilities, and a bird sanctuary on Willow Island in Lake Wascana which can be reached by ferry from Wascana Park. The Museum of Natural History is dedicated to the pioneers of the Province. Graphic displays and habitat groups show Saskatchewan's varied landscape, plant and wildlife.

A Trip to History

An interesting side trip out of the confines of Regina itself can be taken to Last Mountain House Historical Park simply by driving on Highways 11 and 20 five miles past Craven, a distance of 26 miles. Here you can see the house built by Issac Cowie in 1869, as well as the men's house, ice cellar, and other buildings.

PRACTICAL INFORMATION FOR REGINA

HOW TO GET THERE. By air: *Air Canada, Pacific Western, Frontier Airlines,* and *Norcanair* service Regina.

    By car: Access to Regina from eastern and western Canada is on the Yellowhead and Trans-Canada Hwys. From the United States Hwys. 6, 47, and 39 provide access.

By bus: *STC* and *Greyhound* serve Regina.

By train: *Via Rail* through Regina on an east/west axis.

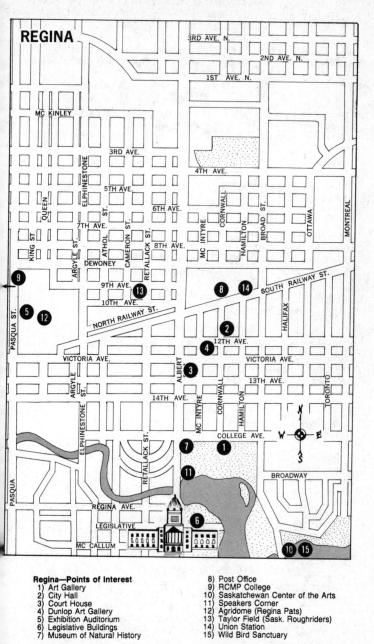

Regina—Points of Interest
1) Art Gallery
2) City Hall
3) Court House
4) Dunlop Art Gallery
5) Exhibition Auditorium
6) Legislative Buildings
7) Museum of Natural History
8) Post Office
9) RCMP College
10) Saskatchewan Center of the Arts
11) Speakers Corner
12) Agridome (Regina Pats)
13) Taylor Field (Sask. Roughriders)
14) Union Station
15) Wild Bird Sanctuary

ACCOMMODATIONS. Based on double-occupancy, without meals, price categories are as follows: *Expensive,* $50–80; *Moderate,* $40–60; *Inexpensive,* under $40.

Most places accept the following major credit cards: American Express, MasterCard and Visa; others may also be honored. Not all establishments accept credit cards, therefore we suggest you call for information.

Expensive

Chelton Inn. 11th Ave. and Rose St. Extra-large rooms, fully licensed restaurant, refrigerators and bar sinks in each room.

Hotel Saskatchewan. Victoria Ave. and Scarth St. Old atmosphere, restaurant and dining room, lounge, entertainment.

Regina Inn. Victoria Ave. and Broad St. Restaurant and dining room, lounge, entertainment, confectionery.

Sheraton Centre. Broad and Victoria. Lounge, dining room, indoor resort complex and meeting rooms.

Moderate

Imperial 400 Motel. 4256 Albert St. Indoor pool, whirlpool, sauna, dining room and lounge.

Landmark Inn. 4150 Albert St. Two restaurants; extra-large rooms.

Vagabond Motor Inn. 4177 Albert St. Beverage and cocktail rooms, dining room, entertainment, pets permitted.

Westwater Inn. Victoria Ave. and Broad St. Dining room, coffee shop, cocktail lounge with entertainment.

Inexpensive

Plains Motor Hotel. Albert St. and Victoria Ave. Beverage and dining rooms.

Prairie Inn Motel. 1020 Albert St. Modern rooms, restaurant.

Relax Inn. 1110 Victoria Ave. E. 190 modern rooms, limited food service.

HOW TO GET AROUND. Maps of bus routes are available from the *Transit Department,* and tours by *Sightseeing Tours* are also regularly scheduled. Regina also offers commercial taxi services.

Saskatchewan Transportation offers regular service to nearly every place in the province.

TOURIST INFORMATION. *Tourism Saskatchewan,* a branch of the Department of Tourism and Small Business, is located at 2103 11th Ave., Regina, S4S 5W6. The *Regina Chamber of Commerce* at 2145 Albert St. will also provide information.

TOURS. Sightseeing and industrial tours are available in Regina. Ask *Tourism Saskatchewan* for further information. Among the 28 auto tours listed by *Tourism Saskatchewan,* several include Regina. Bus tours are scheduled daily during June-September. Custom group tours and special-interest tours may also be arranged. *Saskatchewan Transportation,* the province's largest bus company, offers a number of tours.

CITY PARKS. *Wascana Centre,* some 2,500 acres of parkland in southern Regina, has an impressive list of things to do and see—picnic and barbecue areas, band shells, swimming and boating facilities in Wascana Lake, a bird sanctuary on Willow Island. Within the Centre's boundaries are many features significant in the past, present and future of Saskatchewan. The seat of the provincial government, in the stately Legislative Building, is set in 167 acres of government grounds, the largest in the world. The University of Regina is located on a 330-acre site in the center. There are also a number of historical sites located in this park area—bus tours are available. Information on the Centre may be obtained on site at the Information Guide office.

Victoria Park: a small daytime park for relaxing and taking walks into the heart of downtown.

SPORTS. Regina is home of the *Saskatchewan Rough-riders* of the Canadian Football League. Their games are held at Taylor Field. In the winter the *Regina Pats Junior A* team plays a full schedule of games at the Agridome.

HISTORIC SITES. *Little Chapel on the Square*—located at R.C.M.P. depot, originally a mess hall converted to a chapel—has been preserved to give the visitor a glimpse of history. Also on the depot grounds can be found *Barracks Square* with a monument commemorating the maiden voyage through the Northwest Passage (by R.C.M.P. vessel *St. Roch*). Tours are conducted.

In Wascana Centre the *Diefenbaker Homestead,* boyhood home of Canada's thirteenth Prime Minister. This three-room frame house, built in 1906, was moved from Borden, Saskatchewan, in 1967. Open from May to September.

LIBRARIES. The Regina Public Library has branches conveniently located throughout the city. Films, discussion groups and lectures are regularly scheduled at the Central Library, 2311 12th Ave.

MUSEUMS AND GALLERIES. Regina is an interesting place for museums and art galleries. **Museums.** *The Museum of Natural History,* located on Albert St. and College Ave., built in 1955, is dedicated to the pioneers of Saskatchewan. Open all year. *The R.C.M.P. Museum,* located at depot, provides history of R.C.M.P. Open from June to Sept. *Saskatchewan Archives,* 3303 Hillsdale Ave., details Saskatchewan history. Open year-round. Also of interest are the *Plains Historical Museum,* 1801 Scarth St., and the *Saskatchewan Sports Hall of Fame,* 2205 Victoria Ave.

Galleries. *Dunlop Art Gallery,* located in the Regina Public Library, 12th Ave. and Lorne St., has displays of paintings, sculptures, and handicrafts by local artists. *The Norman Mackenzie Art Gallery,* located on the University campus, College Ave. at Scarth St., has collections of English, American, and Canadian painters, as well as early Egyptian, Chinese, and Greek sculpture. The *Susan Whitney Gallery,* 1627 Victoria Ave., features contemporary prairie and folk art.

PERFORMING ARTS. The *Regina Symphony Orchestra* regularly performs at the Saskatchewan Centre of the Arts, Regina's cultural and convention center. Ballet, opera, and visiting variety artists also appear regularly at the Centre. The *Globe Theatre's Adult Company* is the province's first professional drama group, performing in the 200-seat Globe Theatre as well as in other centers. *Regina Modern Dance Works* performs contemporary works in their theater on Osler St.

 SHOPPING. Several centers, including the *Golden Mile* Plaza on Albert St. S., comprised of 36 stores, and the *Midtown Centre,* offer visitors a wide selection of goods from which to choose, both imported and locally handcrafted. New *Cornwall Centre* in downtown area features *Eatons, Sears,* and two-floor enclosed mall with close to 100 stores.

 DINING OUT. Restaurant price categories are for hors d'oeuvres or soup, entrée and dessert. Not included are drinks, tax, and tips. Restaurants are classed as: *Deluxe,* $40 and up; *Expensive,* $30–40; *Moderate,* $20–$30; *Inexpensive,* under $20.

Most places accept the following major credit cards: American Express, MasterCard and Visa; others may also be honored. Not all establishments accept credit cards, therefore we suggest you call for information.

Expensive

Golf's Steak House. 1945 Victoria Ave. Service in this specialty steakhouse is good and efficient.

L'Habitant. 1711 Victoria Ave., adjoining the Westwater Inn. One of the best steakhouses in the province.

Hotel Saskatchewan. Victoria and Scarth. Eating facilities are varied, from the *Ranch Room* coffeeshop, where the menu offers a variety from coffee and toast to kippers, to its evening atmosphere, where a variety of hors d'oeuvres, soups, salads, and desserts complement the main entrée. Entertainment is featured on the weekends.

Regina Inn Restaurants. Broad and Victoria. Be prepared to choose from a large selection of foods, décor, and price range.

Upstairs, Downstairs. 2305 Smith St. Located in an old house; features fine food, jazz Muzak and good art on the walls.

Moderate

The Brother's Theatre Restaurant. 1867 Hamilton St. Features live dinner music and European and Chinese cuisine.

Cellar Dining Room. Sheraton Centre, 1818 Victoria Ave. Fully licensed, modern. Also try *Coffee Plaza,* a coffee shop in the same hotel.

The Copper Kettle. 1953 Scarth St. Open for lunch and evening dining. Lunchtime features pizza and smoked meats. Evening dining, in the steakhouse, features steak and lobster and specialty salads. It is renovated and friendly service is notable.

Geno's. 1515 Albert St. and in the Gordon Rd. Shopping Centre. Two locations with fine Italian food.

Keg Restaurants. Two locations at Albert St. and Hamilton St. A broad selection of seafood and beef cuts in a friendly "party" atmosphere.

Seven Oaks Motor Inn. 777 Albert St. In the *1887 Room* dining is quiet and relaxed with a view of the pool area. Service is excellent, menu varied, and the children's menu is a take-home circus mask. Free parking.

Lakeshore Inn Steakhouse. 350 23rd Ave. Good steak in the suburbs.

Landmark Inn. 4150 Albert St. *The Blade and Barrel* dining room has a relaxed atmosphere with an excellent assortment of cuisine.

Mieka's Kitchen. 1810 Smith St. Regina's only vegetarian restaurant, serving both lunches and suppers.

Inexpensive

Bartleby's Dining Emporium. 1920 Broad St. Antique décor and tops in atmosphere. No reservations necessary.

Elephant and Castle Restaurant. 2102 11th Ave., Cornwall Centre. Place to rest your feet in a major shopping center.

Plains Flag Inn. 1965 Albert St. Dining room features noon smorgasbord, evening buffet, and full menu.

 NIGHTCLUBS AND BARS. For an evening on the town Regina offers enough variety to accommodate everyone's taste, with a dozen night spots within walking distance of Broad and Victoria, the city's busiest section. *W. H. Shooters* on Broad St. draws western music lovers; **The Brother's Theatre Restaurant,** 1867 Hamilton St., features the Regina Jazz Society every second Friday night; *The French Quarter* in the Sheraton Centre, Broad St. and Victoria Ave., presents live brassy bands; and *The Gold,* 3970 Albert St., caters to the young at heart.

EXPLORING SASKATOON

Saskatoon, the "City of Bridges," with six bridges spanning the South Saskatchewan River, with a population of approximately 164,-000, is Saskatchewan's second largest city and a university center. It began in 1883 as a temperance colony . . . twenty years later its population was only 113 people. It would appear the early pioneers were not for abstinence!

Since Saskatoon's development has been mainly in the twentieth century, town planning has ensured wide, tree-lined streets and industrial development on the fringe. Saskatoon marks the ending of the prairie and the beginning of northern Saskatchewan's parklands.

Here, as in the Regina area, wheat production is an important activity; a 5.5-million-bushel grain elevator located in Saskatoon attests to this. It is a major distribution point, has a good industrial sector including foundries, machine shops, woodworking plants, sheet metal works, tanneries, creameries, potash-uranium, and petroleum-related industries, and one of the West's major meat-packing plants.

Parks, Museums, and Art Galleries

If you are interested in Saskatchewan history and Canadian artists, Saskatoon is a must on your stopping list. Memorial Art Gallery, just off 11th Street, has over 50 paintings on display by Canadian artists, including Homer Watson, John William Beatty, and James Henderson. This gallery is a war memorial.

Farther northeast, along the west bank of the South Saskatchewan River, is the Mendel Art Gallery and Conservatory. Sculptures, flowers, and a collection of works by Canadian artists, including Group of Seven artists, are displayed here.

Directly across the river from the Mendel Gallery is the University of Saskatchewan, founded in 1907, which now has an annual enrollment of about 20,000 students. A number of interesting displays are open to the public here: Marquis Hall Art Gallery; W. P. Herbarium, containing plants, mosses, liverworts, and lichens; Victoria School—Saskatoon's first school, built in 1887, containing replicas of original furniture and equipment. The university is also the site of the John G. Diefenbaker Centre, which displays mementos of the career of the Saskatchewan-based former Canadian Prime Minister.

Museums depicting Ukrainian history, crafts, and costumes as well as one of Canada's largest collections of antique automobiles and agricultural machinery, furniture, and artifacts are located in Saskatoon. The Western Development Museum has recreated a street with buildings, implements, and cars indicative of communities found in Saskatchewan in 1910. It is known as Main Street, Boom Town, Saskatchewan.

Saskatoon has its own symphony orchestra which performs regularly. Moreover, the city's Centennial Auditorium frequently offers Broadway plays, opera and Grand Ole Opry.

There are some 17 parks for the summer visitor, including Diefenbaker Park, Victoria Park, Gordon Howe Park Complex, and Lief Ericksen Park. All offer recreational facilities in close proximity to the South Saskatchewan River. There are also a number of golf clubs within the city.

Pioneer Days—And All the Fun!

Every July, for seven days, the city of Saskatoon celebrates Pioneer Days in conjunction with the Saskachimo Exposition, known as the biggest pioneer show in North America. There are history pageants, antique farm equipment demonstrations, antique car displays, threshing competitions, harness racing, and livestock and agriculture shows. This is all in addition to the midway and grandstand of the exposition.

A Man-Made Mountain?

Yes! truly, made by man—300 feet high and 700 feet at the base. This is Blackstrap Mountain, a ski resort 25 miles south of Saskatoon and well worth a visit. It was built in 1971 for the Canadian Winter Games, and its main ski run is 1,400 feet long.

PRACTICAL INFORMATION FOR SASKATOON

HOW TO GET THERE. By air: *Air Canada, Frontier Airlines, Norcanair,* and *Pacific Western* service Saskatoon.

By car: Access via the Yellowhead Hwy. and Trans-Canada Hwy. from the east and west and Hwy. 6 and 11 from the south.

By train: *Via Rail* has service from Regina into Saskatoon.

By bus: *STC* and *Greyhound* serve Saskatoon.

ACCOMMODATIONS. Based on double occupancy, price categories are as follows: *Expensive,* $50 and up; *Moderate,* $40 and up; *Inexpensive,* under $40.

Most places accept major credit cards; however, not all establishments accept credit cards, therefore we suggest you call for information.

Expensive

Bessborough Hotel. 601 Spadina Cres. Dining room, coffeeshop and lounge. Banquet facilities and swimming pool.

Holiday Inn. 90 22nd St. E. Restaurant and dining room, lounge, entertainment, indoor pool, and sauna.

Imperial "400" Motel. 610 Idylwyld Dr. N. Restaurant and dining room, lounge, indoor pool, sauna, and whirlpool. Limousine service from the airport.

Ramada Renaissance. Saskatoon's newest hotel brings a touch of international elegance. It features dining, entertainment, and a gigantic water slide.

Sheraton-Cavalier Motor Inn. 612 Spadina Cres. Restaurant and dining room, lounge, entertainment. Swimming pool, sauna.

Moderate

Capri Motor Hotel. 2nd Ave. and 20th St. 64 modern rooms with full dining facilities.

Park Town Motor Hotel. 924 Spadina Cres. Dining room, lounge, entertainment.

TraveLodge. 106 Circle Drive W. Restaurant and dining room, lounge; also motel units available.

Inexpensive

King George Motor Hotel. 157 2nd Ave. N. Restaurant and dining room, lounge, and entertainment.

Skybird Motel. 16 33rd St. E. 19 units and 11 light housekeeping; pets allowed.

Yellowhead Motor Inn. 1715 Idylwyld Dr. N. Saskatoon's newest budget motor inn; free local phone calls.

HOW TO GET AROUND. By bus: The *Saskatoon Transportation Co.* (STC) and *Sightseeing Tours* provide adequate access to the city proper.

TOURIST INFORMATION. *Tourism Saskatchewan* in Regina at 2103 11th Ave. has up-to-date information. The *Saskatoon Board of Trade* will also provide information.

TOURS. Auto tours of Saskatoon and the surrounding area have been mapped by *Tourism Saskatchewan.* Organized bus tours, group, and special-interest tours are also available. *Northcote River Cruises* offers cruises on the Saskatchewan River, boarding from behind the bandstand south of the Bessborough Hotel. Adults $4.00; children $1.00.

SPECIAL INTEREST TOUR. On the university campus a collection of Saskatchewan and Arctic plants can be found at the W. P. Herbarium.

PARKS. Saskatoon has a number of parks along the South Saskatchewan River system. Most have picnic facilities, benches to relax on, golf courses, and pools. *Forestry Farm Park,* located northeast of the city, has over 300 animals.

SPECTATOR SPORTS. For sports fans, the *Saskatoon Junior Blades* of the Western Hockey League and the University of Saskatchewan football and hockey teams play regularly during their respective seasons.

HISTORIC SITES. *Barr Colony Campsite:* a plaque marks the campsite of 1,500 colonists en route to Lloydminster led by Rev. Isaac M. Barr. *The Stone Victoria School,* built in 1887 as Saskatoon's first school, is located on the University campus.

LIBRARIES. One central library with 4 branches located throughout the city.

MUSEUMS AND GALLERIES. Galleries. *Mendel Art Gallery and Conservatory* features a permanent display of Canadian and European artwork set amidst flower arrangements. Open year-round. *Gallery One Studio Ltd.* shows well-known Canadian artists; *The Shoestring Gallery,* 306A 20th St. W., features work by local artists, with major changes each month. The *Photographers' Gallery,* also with monthly exhibit changes, features Canadian and local work. Open September to April.

Museums. *Museum of Anthropology and Archeology,* located in Arts Building on University campus, has displays showing man's evolution, prehistoric man in Saskatchewan, and settlement of the West. *Ukrainian Arts and Crafts Museum,* located in the Mohyla Institute, exhibits costumes, tapestries, and handicrafts of Ukrainian people. *Western Development Museum,* located close to Exhibition Grounds at 2610 Lorne Ave. S., displays the kind of community that grew up throughout Saskatchewan in pioneer days. One of largest collections of agricultural machinery and antique autos.

THEATER. *The 25th Street House,* Saskatoon's professional theater company, presents a season of main stage productions each winter.

SHOPPING. A variety of shopping opportunities are open to visitors to Saskatoon. *The Confederation Park Plaza* has 34 stores and the *Midtown Plaza* has a similar number. Saskatoon also has a good selection of handicraft and specialty shops.

DINING OUT. Restaurant price categories are for hors d'oeuvres or soup, entrée, and dessert. Not included are drinks, tax, and tips. *Deluxe,* $40 and up; *Expensive,* $30 and up; *Moderate,* $20–25; *Inexpensive,* under $30.

Most places accept the following major credit cards: American Express, MasterCard and Visa; others may also be honored. Not all establishments accept credit cards, therefore we suggest you call for information.

Expensive

The Bessborough. 601 Spadina Cres. Diversified dining with a coffeeshop. Breakfast, lunch, and dinner menus and *Aerial's Cove* for evening dinner. Fresh seafood flown in from the Maritimes is a feature of the menu.

Golf's Steak House. 317 21st St. E. Fine dining featuring steaks and seafood.

Hy's Steak House. Midtown Plaza. Quiet, relaxed atmosphere also featuring steaks and seafood.

Lucci's. 3rd Ave. French and European dishes; entertainment.

Smuggler's. 416 21st St. E. Menu features prime rib and salad bar in a nautical atmosphere.

Villy's. Sasktoon Square Penthouse. Extensive menu in comfortable surroundings and a magnificent view of the city and river.

Moderate

Artful Dodger. 119 4th Ave. S. Old English pub décor with a menu to match.

Bar K Ranch House. 22nd St. and Avenue Y. A licensed ranch house with country and western entertainment and western cuisine. The specialty of the house is beefsteak. Dancing after 9:00 P.M.

Cave. 8th St. Popular restaurant with good pizza.

Saskatoon TraveLodge. 106 Circle Dr. West. Located just off the main highway a few minutes from the airport and downtown Saskatoon. The fully licensed *Captain's Table* dining room features specialties and a children's menu.

Shaheen's Curry. 135 20th St., W. Award-winning Indian Restaurant.

Raffle's Family Restaurant. Eighth St. and Arlington Ave. Multi-ethnic cuisine, Ukranian dishes, reasonable prices.

Inexpensive

Imperial 400 Motel. 610 Idylwyld Dr. N. Rich Mediterranean décor of the motel dining room creates the setting for family dining.

NIGHTCLUBS AND BARS. For a night of dancing *Foxy's* on Eighth Street offer nightly live entertainment. *The Bar K Ranch House* at 22nd Street and Avenue Y has live country and western entertainment. *Fast Freddie's* in the Park Town Hotel, 924 Spadina Cres. E, attracts the young "swinging singles" crowd. The *Tiki Tiki Polynesian Restaurant,* 701 Cynthia St., offers dining, dancing, and two Polynesian floor shows nightly.

EXPLORING SASKATCHEWAN

Are you looking for an interesting and different vacation, especially for a family? You'll find it in Saskatchewan, on one of the many vacation farms. All you need are your old clothes, a camera, and an "I'm willing to try anything" attitude.

The Saskatchewan Farm Vacations Association has a list of 30 farm families willing to share and show you their farm. You will need reservations. Don't be afraid of getting lost on country roads—once in the province there are information centers to help you.

The whole family—including the children—will be able to help with the chores—gather eggs, feed the chickens, care for the small farm animals—and take in some of the surrounding scenery and fresh air. Have you ever smelled fresh mowed hay or watched a prairie sunset? You can on a Saskatchewan farm.

Another unique Saskatchewan vacation idea is a northern canoe or fishing trip. Water accounts for one-eighth of the province's area and the greater part of this water lies in the sparsely-populated northern half. If you're planning a canoe trip, be prepared to meet a varied wilderness environment. The country is forested, the water bodies vary from rock-bound lakes to tea-colored sloughs, shallow marshlands, and boiling rapids. Numerous islands dot the lakes, and an abundance of wildlife—deer, bear, moose, loons, grebes, ducks, muskrat, beaver, mink, and otter—inhabit the area. Even the rare bald eagle can be observed.

While canoeing, it is quite likely you will meet or see native Indians, as many Crees who live in frontier settlements and on reserves fish during the summer. Most speak some English, and they will certainly provide information.

Some 56 canoe trips have been mapped out giving starting and finishing points, number of portages, length of trip in days and miles, and features to note along the way. Detailed information is available from Saskatchewan Tourism or individual outfitters. Seven of these adventures are for canoeists not ready to tackle more difficult routes. All but two have starting points which can be reached by road; these two require fly-in by chartered aircraft.

Canoe trips are of two basic types: the loop, which returns the traveler to his starting point, and the circuit, which does not finish at its origin.

Angling is a major attraction to many canoeists. Northern waters abound with pike, pickerel, and perch, and farther north, with grayling and lake trout. However, if you are not a canoeist, there are some 200 drive-in and fly-in fishing camps. Arrangements for accommodations and transportation can be made by your travel agent or airline. Of course, you will need a license and a regulation guide, and these can be obtained from the fishing camp, sporting goods stores, or Saskatchewan Tourism.

Touring

There are a number of fascinating trips to take in Saskatchewan by vehicle, planned or otherwise. By planned, we mean that the Saskatchewan government has come up with 28 planned auto tours through the southern prairies, the central parklands, the wilderness north, as well as city tours of Regina and Saskatoon. The tours include vacation farms, industrial tours, museums, geological and historical attractions, and parks. A complete list of these tours can be found under the section *Practical Information for Saskatchewan*, but let's take one out of Regina, the province's capital: on Highway 10, White City at Mile 8 is the location of Dad's Cookies—stop and take a look. At Mile 16 Balgonie, a collection of old-time tractors is on display. Travel northeast on Highway 10 to Mile 45—view the fabulous Qu'Appelle Valley made famous by the poetess E. Pauline Johnson. The twin lakes of Pasqua and Echo are the setting for Echo Valley Provincial Park, where you can enjoy swimming, boating, and a host of other activities.

Traveling on the south side of Echo Lake, to your right, directly at the bottom of the hill, make a stop at the Fish Culture Station, open daily, to learn what's involved in caring for millions of fish from the time they hatch until they stock provincial waters. Continue driving on the south side of Echo Lake to the town of Fort Qu'Appelle, where the museum is open. A museum is joined to an original 1864 Hudson's Bay Company post and displays Indian artifacts and Hudson's Bay Company articles.

From Fort Qu'Appelle turn south on Highway 10 and then right just before the top of the hill and take a side trip to the vacation farm of Harman's Western Playground. It is easily spotted for its rodeo-style structure. Echo Valley Centre, also on the north side of the lake, is now the home of Saskatchewan Summer School of the Arts, and each weekend during the summer session, public concerts and displays of students' work are held. Travel north on Highway 35 to Mile 55—Huber's Manufacturing—where tours are offered of their operation in the manufacture of Christmas decorations, gardening tools, and other items.

With the lush valley of the Qu'Appelle behind, take Highway 22 west through typical farming country to Earl Grey at Mile 96. Here, the Centennial Museum displays old machinery, pioneer items, and turn-of-the-century books and catalogues. This museum is open evenings or by request. West on Highway 22 and west again on Highway 220 brings you to Mile 121—Rowan's Ravine Provincial Park, where the big thing is swimming at the long sandy shores of Last Mountain Lake. Four miles south is the Lakeside Museum with a collection of Indian and pioneer artifacts. Traveling east on Highway 220 and southeast on Highway 332, you will arrive at Mile 142, Last Mountain House Historic Park. Established in 1869 by the Hudson's Bay Company, the post was a major trading center for two years. The master's house has been rebuilt, and other buildings marked. Picnic facilities are on the site.

Traveling southeast take note of the market gardens in the Qu'Appelle Valley between Craven on Highway 20 and Lumsden on Highway

11; stop for some fresh produce. Return to Regina at Mile 164 via Highway 11.

If you do not like to follow a planned route, a good map and a willingness to camp are all you need. Saskatchewan has seventeen provincial parks with campsites and picnic areas as well as one national park, regional parks, and campgrounds scattered throughout the province. They are open from May to September; a few remain open year-round, but services are limited. The provincial parks have well-marked nature trails, slide presentations, talks on wilderness survival, swimming, canoeing, sailing, and fishing. If you do not wish to camp, there are some cabins for rent. Side trips from these provincial parks may be taken—"little England on the Prairies," better known as Cannington Manor, the site where Sitting Bull and 5,000 American Sioux Indians set up camp following their victory at the Battle of the Little Big Horn, or that geological oddity, the Cypress Hills. Museums, wheat fields, badlands, game farms, dams, Indian carvings, *roches moutonnées,* antique cars and machinery, early architecture, virgin wilderness, wildlife, freaks of nature are all within reach.

It becomes abundantly clear that Saskatchewan is a paradise for outdoor people, but there is something here for everyone. Cities and towns offer many activities—museums, live theater, sports activities, nightspots, art galleries, fine cuisine, exhibitions, fairs, rodeos, carnivals, natural history exhibits, and libraries.

PRACTICAL INFORMATION FOR
SASKATCHEWAN

HOW TO GET THERE. By air: Saskatoon and Regina have the major airports. *Air Canada, Frontier Airlines* and *Pacific Western,* serve the major cities, and *Norcanair,* a regional carrier, the smaller centers.

By car: East/west access to southern Saskatchewan on the Trans-Canada Hwy. through Moosomin to Regina from the east and Swift Current, Moose Jaw, and Regina from the west; to northern Saskatchewan on Hwy. 16 from the west through Lloydminster, North Battleford, Saskatoon, and Hwy. 16, from the east through Langenburg and Yorkton. Access from the United States into the eastern part of the province can be obtained through Port of Estevan/Noonan, North Dakota, on Hwys. 47 and 39, and North Portal/Portal, North Dakota, on Highway 39, both going through Estevan, Weyburn, Moose Jaw to bisect the Trans Canada; through Port of Regway/Raymond, Montana, on Hwy. 6 to Regina. Access into the western part of the province from the United States through Port of Climax/Turner, Montana, on Hwy. 37 and the Trans-Canada to Swift Current, Port of Monchy/Morgan, Montana, on Hwy. 4 to Swift Current. Altogether there are 13 ports of entry between the United States and Saskatchewan.

By train: Transcontinental passenger service of *Via Rail* crosses Saskatchewan daily, making connections with Regina, Moose Jaw, Swift Current.

By bus: Saskatchewan is well served with bus routes. Several companies, including *Greyhound Lines of Canada* and *Saskatchewan Transportation Com-*

pany (STC), maintain passenger service as well as express and charter service to all their points of call.

 ACCOMMODATIONS. Double-occupancy rates are categorized as follows: *Deluxe,* $40 and up; *Expensive,* $30–40; *Moderate,* $20–30; *Inexpensive,* under $20. These rates are subject to a 5% provincial sales tax. (There are accommodations in the smaller towns around Saskatchewan and although they have not been listed in this guide, they are basically adequate, with inexpensive rates.)

Most places accept the following credit cards: American Express, Master-Card and Visa; others may also be honored. Not all establishments accept credit cards, therefore we suggest you call for information.

ESTEVAN. *Moderate:* **Derrick Motor Hotel.** 125 4th St. Dining room, beverage room, and 70 rooms.
Fai's Motel. Hwy. 39 E. on South Service Rd. Newly renovated, adjoins service station.
Swank Motel. Hwy. 39 W. 21 modern housekeeping rooms.

FORT QU'APPELLE. *Moderate:* **Country Squire Motor Hotel.** Modern rooms, restaurant, and beverage room.
Valley Trails Motel Ltd. Old Hwy. 35. 11 rooms.

LLOYDMINSTER. *Moderate:* **Capri Motor Inn.** 5615 50th Ave. Beverage room, dining room, entertainment. 60 rooms.
Inexpensive: **Prince Charles Motor Inn.** 50th Ave. and 49th St. Beverage room, restaurant, cocktails, dining room, entertainment, pets allowed.

MOOSE JAW. *Expensive:* **Harwood's Moose Jaw Inn.** 24 Fairford E. Beverage room, restaurant and dining room, cocktails, entertainment, pets allowed, indoor swimming pool, and sauna. 100 rooms.
Thunderbird Motel. 5610 44th St. Courtesy coffee, 36 rooms, local calls free.
Moderate: **Park Lodge Motor Hotel.** Jct. Hwy. 1 and 2. Licensed dining room. Indoor pool and courtyard, whirlpool and sauna. Tastefully decorated in the Old English style of the Tudor reign. Also coffeeshop. 82 rooms, 10 light housekeeping.

NORTH BATTLEFORD. *Moderate:* **Beaver Brook Lodge.** Hwy. 16. Licensed steakhouse, electric heat, coffee shop.
Inexpensive: **Auditorium Hotel.** 1025 101 St. Crown Dining Room. Dancing, live entertainment in the medieval décor of the Black Knight. 30 modern, 10 semi-modern rooms.
Capri Motor Hotel. 992 101st St. Restaurant, beverage and coctail rooms. 91 rooms.
Park Motel. Hwy. 4 N. 26 rooms, cable TV.

PRINCE ALBERT. *Expensive:* **Sheraton Marlboro Motor Inn.** 67 13th St. E. Coctail and beverage rooms, restaurant and dining room. 114 rooms, indoor pool and sauna.
Moderate: **Coronet Motor Hotel.** 3551 2nd Ave. W. Beverage and cocktail rooms, restaurant and dining room, indoor pool, sauna and whirlpool, pets allowed. 101 rooms.

Prince Albert-Imperial 400 Motel. Hwy. 2 S. Enclosed pool, lounge and dining room. 139 rooms.

Inexpensive: **Porter's Motel.** 2½ mi. S. on Hwy. 2. Pets allowed. 12 units.

SWIFT CURRENT. *Moderate:* **Rodeway Inn Motel.** 1200 Begg St. E. Restaurant, sauna, whirlpool. 28 rooms, all wheelchair-accessible.

Best Western Swift Motel. Outdoor barbecues, picnic tables, heated pool, pets allowed. 55 units, 13 light housekeeping.

TraveLodge Motel. Hwy. 1 E. Outdoor barbecues, heated pool and sauna. 49 rooms.

WEYBURN. *Moderate:* **Weyburn Inn.** 5 Government Road. 2 dining rooms, 2 lounges and pool. 50 rooms.

Inexpensive: **Andy's Motel.** 3 2nd Ave. S.W. 24 rooms, dining nearby.

King George Hotel. 3rd St. and Railway Ave. Redecorated.

YORKTON. *Moderate:* **Corona Motor Hotel.** 345 Broadway W. Restaurant and dining room, beverage and cocktail rooms, entertainment, swimming pool. 85 rooms.

Flag Holiday Inn. 110 Broadway E. Restaurant and dining room, entertainment, cocktail room, pool, 92 rooms.

Imperial "400" Motel. Broadway and Dracup. Restaurant, indoor swimming pool. 99 rooms.

Inexpensive: **Yorkton Hotel.** 14 2nd Ave. N. Beverage room, restaurant, and pets allowed. 23 modern and 20 not-so-modern rooms.

HOW TO GET AROUND. By air: *Air Canada, Frontier Airlines,* and *Pacific Western* provide national service into the larger cities. *Norcanair* provides service into the smaller centers and also operates a charter service. It has offices in Cluff Lake, Fond du Lac, La Ronge, Prince Albert, Regina, Saskatoon, Stoney Rapids, Uranium City, and Wallaston.

By car: Saskatchewan has more miles of road than any other Canadian province. The southern part of the province is a gridiron of hard surface roads, and there are miles and miles of graveled and graded roads to the smaller towns and villages.

By train: Service is available to some major centers in Saskatchewan on an east/west axis. There is dayliner service between Regina and Saskatoon.

By bus: Bus service is good in Saskatchewan. The largest carrier in the province is *Saskatchewan Transportation Company* (STC). Its buses average 10,000 miles a day on 30 regular routes covering about one third of the provincial highway system. This company also offers a wide variety of tours.

FACTS AND FIGURES. Saskatchewan was derived from the Cree word *Kisiskatchewan,* meaning "the river that flows swiftly." Nicknamed "the wheat province" because of the great volume of cereal grains grown. The provincial flower is the western red lily (*lilium philadelphicum andium*), and the provincial bird is the prairie sharp-tailed grouse (*pedioecetes phasianellos campesetris*). Saskatchewan has one provincial motto: *Honi soit qui mal y pense,* "Evil be to him who evil thinks." Regina is the provincial capital, and the provincial population is one million. Saskatchewan has sunny cold winters with an average snowfall of 50 inches, and short warm summers.

TOURIST INFORMATION. *Tourism Saskatchewan,* 2103 11th Ave. in Regina, can supply up-to-date travel information on campsites, towns and cities, activities and attractions, tours, accommodations, fishing, and canoeing from June to September. The phone number is 565–2300 during regular office hours. There are toll-free lines for in-province calls—1–800–667–3674 is the number.

Information can also be obtained by writing *Department of Tourism and Small Business,* Regina, Saskatchewan S4P OJ6.

Also during the summer months (May to September) information centers are open throughout the province with travel counselors available to provide free information and travel planning services. These centers are located on the main access routes into Saskatchewan:—Trans-Canada Hwy. in various campgrounds: east approach—near Manitoba border at Fleming; west approach—Maple Creek Junction of Hwys. 1 and No. 21 and in the Maple Creek Campground; Yellowhead Hwy. (Hwy. 16): east approach—Langenburg; west approach—Lloydminster. From the United States, Hwy. 39: North Portal just beyond the Canadian Customs Office.

For tourists not traveling by car, air facilities maps can be purchased from the Central Survey & Mapping Division, Department of Highways, 1855 Victoria Ave., Regina, Saskatchewan.

Remember *Tourism Saskatchewan* of the Department of Tourism and Small Business, Regina, is the place to contact for any information you require on Saskatchewan, or you can go through your travel agent, carrier, auto club, or local chambers of commerce.

SEASONAL EVENTS. For up-to-the-minute information on annual events and special events, contact *Sask-Travel.*

January: The winter months are the time for curling bonspiels, winter carnivals, snowmobile racing, and winter sports such as downhill and cross-country skiing and snowshoeing. A three-day mid-January winter carnival with snow mobile races takes place at Humboldt.

February: Estevan, Fort Qu'Appelle, Lloydminster, Melfort, and Prince Albert all celebrate their winter carnivals during this month. Prince Albert's hoopla is highlighted by a championship dog derby, an event where 8-dogteams compete with each other in a 3-day, 48-mile race. "King Trapper" is also chosen, the winner of a marathon of log sawing, wood chopping, flour carrying, and bannock baking. Estevan holds International 250 Snowmobile Race from Regina to Minot.

March: Again this is a month for winter carnivals and curling bonspiels—Craik, Kelvinton, Kyle, Meadow Lake all celebrate this month.

April: An Easter-week Pee Wee Hockey Tournament at Weyburn, a music festival at the end of the month in North Battleford, and *carnivals* at Lloydminster and North Battleford round out this month.

May: Moose Jaw is the setting for an international band festival put on by the local Kinsmen. It is one of the continent's biggest band events and attracts over 70 bands and 5,000 musicians. Saskatoon's Vesna Festival is an annual spring multicultural festival patterned after Regina's Mosiac celebration, held the same month.

June: The summer months are swamped with shows and expositions. In North Battleford, a Those Were The Days Festival is an annual event. Pioneer machinery and tools are operated; the outdoor pioneer village and 40,000 square feet of indoor displays are there for browsing. It is held in late June and an exhibition, parade, and harness racing also take place. In Regina, a unique event takes place from mid-June to August—The Trial of Louis Riel, the leader of the Northwest Rebellion of 1885, is reenacted three times weekly at Saskatchewan House. Moose Jaw holds a biannual air show on the Canadian Forces base there.

July: In Saskatoon the week-long Pioneer Days, called the biggest pioneer show in North America, takes place with historical pageants, pioneer equipment and machinery demonstrations, antique displays, harness racing, and livestock and agricultural shows. Saskatchewan's biggest rodeo is also held this month in Swift Current with parades, street dancing, and a fair. The Saskatchewan Craft Festival in Battleford brings the best crafts people together.

August: The town of Craven's big rodeo and Regina's Buffalo Days Exhibition, ten days of pioneer celebration, horse racing, barbecues, picnics, band concerts, midway and grandstand entertainment make this a good month to visit Saskatchewan.

September: Visit the Harvest Festival in Swift Current put on by the Chamber of Commerce. Stop by the Moose Jaw Wild Animal Regional Park—300 acres with buffalo, elk, yak, deer, and antelope as well as a children's zoo. September–October Swift Current holds Western Canadian Olde Tyme Fiddling Contest. Thresherman's Show in Yorkton draws contestants from across the prairies.

October: The Tomahawk Rodeo at Cutknife is presided over by the world's largest tomahawk—54-foot, 6-ton fir handle and 2,500-pound fiberglass blade. A film festival at Yorkton, a turkey shoot at Unity, and the Pineland Mexpo at Prince Albert finish off this month.

November: The Mexabition in Saskatoon in November and in Regina in late November and early December is an annual event. In Regina it is held in conjunction with the Agribition, an international livestock show. Agricultural equipment, inventions, gadgets, house amenities and products, lawn and garden accessories, and equipment, as well as the livestock shows and sales, are featured.

December: This month is the time to visit the cities of Saskatchewan where Christmas events are happening. Bands, symphonies, choirs all present special concerts.

TOURS. There are 28 auto tours mapped out by *Tourism Saskatchewan.* They have been listed below, and if more detailed information is required, you can contact the above department. Rental accommodations, campgrounds, points of interest, and industrial tours are plotted on each tour.

Tour 1. Maple Creek, Cypress Hills Provincial Park, Fort Walsh Historic Park, Swift Current.

Tour 2. Maple Creek, Gull Lake, The Great Sand Hills.

Tour 3. Moose Jaw, Assiniboia, Wood Mountain Historic Park.

Tour 4. Buffalo Pound Provincial Park, Lake Diefenbaker recreation area.

Tour 5. Moose Jaw, Big Muddy Badlands, Wilcox

Tour 6. Regina, Fort Qu'Appelle, Rowan's Ravine and Echo Valley Provincial Parks, Last Mountain House Historic Park.

Tour 7. Swift Current, Saskatchewan Landing Provincial Park, Kindersley.

Tour 8. Saskatoon, Lake Diefenbaker recreation area, Mount Blackstrap, Manitou Beach.

Tour 9. North Battleford, Saskatoon, Rosetown.

Tour 10. Indian Head, Fort Qu'Appelle, Katepwa Provincial Park, Melville.

Tour 11. Lloydminster, Cut Knife, North Battleford.

Tour 12. Foam Lake, Touchwood Hills Historic Park, Rowan's Ravine Provincial Park, Lanigan.

Tour 13. Wynyard, Quill Lakes, Kinistino, Humboldt.

Tour 14. Lloydminster, Fort Pitt and Steele Narrows Historic Parks, St. Walburg, North Battleford

Tour 15. Moose Mountain Provincial Park, Weyburn, Estevan, Cannington Manor Historic Park.

Tour 16. Moose Mountain Provincial Park, Broadview, Esterhazy, Moosomin.

Tour 17. Duck Mountain and Good Spirit Provincial Parks, Yorkton, Esterhazy.

Tour 18. Duck Mountain Provincial Park, Porcupine Hills, Hudson Bay.

Tour 19. Greenwater Lake Provincial Park, Tisdale, Kelvington.

Tour 20. Greenwater Lake Provincial Park, Carrot River, Hudson Bay, Wildcat Hills Wilderness Area.

Tour 21. Saskatoon, Batoche, Duck Lake.

Tour 22. Prince Albert, Prince Albert National Park, MacDowall, Waskesiu Lake.

Tour 23. Prince Albert, Nipawin Provincial Park, Creighton, Denare Beach.

Tour 24. Prince Albert, La Ronge, Approximate Geographic Center of Saskatchewan.

Tour 25. Prince Albert, Nipawin, Cumberland House, Squaw Rapids Hydroelectric Station.

Tour 26. Prince Albert, Candle Lake, Nipawin Provincial Park.

Tour 27. City Tour of Saskatoon.

Tour 28. City Tour of Regina.

NATIONAL PARKS. *Prince Albert National Park,* located less than 100 miles north of the city of Prince Albert, is the only national park in Saskatchewan. The park covers 1,496 square miles; has one townsite, Waskesiu; and is home to one of Canada's biggest white pelican colonies. Elk, moose, caribou, black bear, wolf, coyote, beaver, birds of prey, waterfowl, and buffalo inhabit the park. A point of particular interest to many is the grave of Grey Owl, the famous conservationist, and the cabin where he lived the last seven years of his life located beside Ajawaan Lake.

PROVINCIAL PARKS. From the prairies, through the parklands, to the north, Saskatchewan has a provincial park to suit you—17 in all. There are also many regional parks and campgrounds. The park season is from Victoria Day to Labor Day. Some of the campgrounds stay open with limited services past this date. Up-to-the-minute information on camping may be obtained by calling *Tourism Saskatchewan at 565-2300.*

The parks have planned naturalist programs, but if you prefer not to plan your days, there are slide shows, campfire singsongs, team sports, tennis, golf, arts and crafts, swimming, fishing, boating, waterskiing, and hiking. Most parks offer complete amenities: laundry facilities, washrooms, showers, outdoor toilets, water standpipes, grocery stores, and cafeterias. There are cabins for rent at some of the provincial parks, and arrangements for accommodations can be made through the individual park superintendents.

Lac La Ronge: northeastern Saskatchewan, excellent for canoeing and fishing; 255 campsites, rental accommodations nearby, all amenities, swimming, fishing, and canoe outfitters.

Meadow Lake: 600 sq. miles of lake-studded forest; over 700 campsites, all amenities, swimming, nature trails, golf, rental accommodations, fishing and boat outfitters.

The Battlefords: west-central Saskatchewan; over 360 campsites, swimming, nature trails, 18-hole golf course, all amenities.

Greenwater Lake, Duck Mountain, Good Spirit: east-central; over 600 campsites; full facilities, swimming, boat rentals, nature trails, bicycle trails, tennis courts, golf course and cabin rentals.

Douglas, Daniel, and *Saskatchewan Landing:* created from building of Gardiner Dam, located around Lake Diefenbaker; over 260 campsites, amenities not complete, nature trails.

Pike Lake Provincial Park and *Blackstrap Recreational Area:* near Saskatoon; 60 campsites at Blackstrap but limited facilities, mainly a ski area; 250 campsites at Pike Lake, full amenities, swimming, nature trails, fishing, picnic areas, bicycle trails, tennis courts.

Buffalo Pound Park: 260 acres, 148 campsites, excellent services and facilities, ideal for water sports, swimming pool, nature trails, winter skiing at *White Track Ski Resort.*

Rowan's Ravine, Echo Valley, and *Katepwa:* in Qu'Appelle Valley; over 600 campsites, fishing, boating, waterskiing, swimming, playgrounds for kids, golf courses, picnic areas. Katepwa has no camping facilities.

Cypress Hills Provincial Park: southwestern Saskatchewan; geological freak of nature—see cactus, lodgepole pine, animal mutations such as white ants, and scorpions all alien to the prairie; excellent facilities. 466 campsites and rental lodging.

Moose Mountain: southeastern Saskatchewan; over 320 campsites, fully serviced; excellent recreational programs, fishing, hiking, riding, swimming, bicycle trails, lake cruises, golf.

FARM VACATIONS. The *Saskatchewan Farm Vacations Association,* Box 24, Bateman, Saskatchewan, (306) 648–3530, has more than 30 members willing to share their farms, and their chores, with you. Reservations are needed and can be obtained by contacting the individual farms or *Tourism Saskatchewan,* which also provides a list of the farms with a short description of each. Or contact Irene Lightbody, Box 24, Bateman, Sask., SOH OEO. Phone (306) 648–3530.

CHILDREN'S ACTIVITIES. Saskatchewan is a family province offering a variety of outdoor things to do for children as well as adults—provincial parks, zoos, fairgrounds, farm vacations, and fishing trips.

SPORTS. Summer: *Baseball* is a popular sport during the summer. Many towns have annual sports days with *hardball* and *softball* tournaments. Of course, the parks offer areas for *swimming, waterskiing, canoeing, fishing, hiking, golf,* and *tennis.* **Winter** activities include downhill and cross-country *skiing, snowshoeing, snowmobiling, hockey,* and *curling.* Almost every small town has at least one curling bonspiel a year.

CAMPING OUT. There are camping and tenting facilities located throughout the province. *Tourism Saskatchewan* can provide up-to-date information on the availability of sites in particular areas. Service is on a first-come, first-served basis in most areas.

The majority of campgrounds are open from Victoria Day to Labor Day only, but a few remain open offering limited service.

 HISTORIC SITES. Most of Saskatchewan's historic sites have been preserved through historic parks. There are 9 of them open throughout the summer from Victoria Day to Labor Day. *Tourism Saskatchewan* has up-to-date information on all historic parks as well as the many museums and art galleries throughout the province.

St. Victor Petroglyphs Historic Park: St. Victor, 16 miles southwest of Assiniboia, is the site of this park, so named for the Indian rock carvings, or petroglyphs, on top of a sandstone outcropping. A picnic area and steps leading up to the carvings are provided.

Battleford National Historic Park: On Hwy. 29, near junction with Hwy. 16. Four of the buildings once used by the Northwest Mounted Police are located with Fort Battleford's reconstructed palisade; guard room, Sick Horse stable, officer's quarters and commanding officer's residence.

Cumberland House Historic Park: 100 miles northeast of Carrot River on Hwy. 123, it was the Hudson's Bay Company's first inland fur trading post. At the park, plaques describing the complete history of this area are erected.

Fort Carlton Historic Park: about four miles northwest of Carlton and 45 miles northwest of Saskatoon. Fort Carlton was headquarters for the Hudson's Bay Company during the mid-1800's and a favorite stopping place for famous travelers.

Fort Pitt Historic Park: 14 miles west of Frenchman Butte, it was established in 1829 as a Hudson's Bay Company post and played a critical role in the fur trade and settlement of the west.

Fort Wash National Park: 23 miles west of Cypress Hill Provincial Park, Northwest Mounted Police fortified post in 1800's. In 1942 RCMP chose the location for a remount ranch, largely because of historical associations.

Touchwood Hills Historic Park: Located 5 miles southeast of Punnichy on Hwy. No. 15, it was a Hudson's Bay Post which served as a provision center on the Fort Qu'Appelle–Touchwood Hills Trail as well as being a fur trading fort. A cairn is erected to describe the post's history.

Last Mountain House Historic Park: Located 5 miles north of Craven on Hwy. 20. Built by Issac Cowie in 1869, this fort stood on the northern edge of the great plains area. By 1872 the post was closed, as the buffalo herds had retreated southwest. Today, on site, is the reconstructed Master's house, men's house, and ice cellar.

Wood Mountain Historic Park: Located 3 miles south of Wood Mountain village, this fort played an important part in North American history. In 1874 a North West Mounted Police depot was set up at Wood Mountain. By 1877, almost the entire Sioux Nation under Chief Sitting Bull, fresh from a victory at the Battle of the Little Big Horn south of the border, was camped near Wood Mountain. The Sioux remained for four years; then finally hard times forced them to return to reservation life in the United States.

Cannington Manor Historic Park: Located 8 miles north and two miles east of Manor, this is a unique site. Cannington Manor was Captain Edward Pierce's dream come true of establishing a colony in the New World, based on agriculture, where he and others like him could pursue the life of English gentlemen. The original church, a museum in an old schoolhouse, an old log house, the blacksmith's shop, and carpenter's house can all be seen.

Steele Narrows Historic Park: Located 6 miles west of Loon Lake, this was the site of the last battle of the Riel Rebellion of 1885, the last armed conflict on Canadian soil. Big Bear and his band of Crees, holding 30 prisoners, met Major Sam Steele of the North West Mounted Police, with about 60 troopers, in battle here on June 3, 1885. Major Steele was victorious, and the prisoners were released a few days later. Today there are markers indicating the battlefield and a plaque describing the battle.

MUSEUMS AND GALLERIES. Most of the larger cities, and any of the small towns, which shared in Saskatchewan's history, have museums and art galleries. The cities' museums and art galleries have regular hours. Most galleries and museums have no admission charge. In smaller towns, the museums will be opened by request of the private owners.

Major attractions are the province's four *Western Development Museums,* each of which depicts a different Saskatchewan historical theme through extensive exhibits. The various museums and their themes are: Moose Jaw, the story of transportation; North Battleford, the story of agriculture; Saskatoon, the integrated story of western development; and Yorkton, the story of the people.

SHOPPING. Saskatchewan has a number of small craft stores that offer original pottery, silkscreens, rock jewelry, potash clocks, embroidered leather, denim garments, purses, mitts, hats.

DRINKING LAWS. The drinking age is 19 years or older. Liquor is sold only in licensed liquor stores, licensed restaurants, cocktail lounges, dining rooms and beverage rooms, or by vendors. Retail liquor stores are operated throughout the province.

DINING OUT. The people of Saskatchewan come from many different racial backgrounds—European, African, Asian, Australian. Each race brings its own culture, molding it into the Saskatchewan way of life. Every ethnic group is represented in the food and restaurants of Saskatchewan: Ukrainian, French, English, German, Romanian, Italian. There is a restaurant to meet each taste.

The major hotels in Saskatchewan have eating facilities ranging from coffeeshops to dining rooms. There are several top-flight entertainment centers which offer quality meals and top performers. There are also home-style restaurants, places that specialize in good eating only. For the tourist on the go there are also take-out and fast-food establishments. Costs are per person for the medium priced meals on the menu: *Deluxe:* $30 and up, *Expensive,* $20–$30; *Moderate,* $15–20; *Inexpensive,* under $15. In most cases the prices include soup, entree, and dessert. Beverages are extra, and the 5% provincial tax and tips are not included.

Most places accept the following major credit cards: American Express, MasterCard and Visa; others may also be honored. Not all establishments accept credit cards, therefore we suggest you call for information.

ESTEVAN. *Inexpensive:* **The Old Homestead.** A pleasant relaxing atmosphere with background music. Varied menu and special children's menu. Located in the Estevan Shoppers Mall, lots of free parking.

LLOYDMINSTER. *Expensive:* **Wayside Inn.** Hwy. 16, just two blocks from Sask.-Alta. border. Fine dining room, poolside restaurant.

MOOSE JAW. *Expensive:* **Grayson Hall Restaurant.** 7–30 Stadcona St. W. Featuring a lounge and full dining facilities.

Hopkins Dining Parlour. 65 Athabasca W. Located in a 78-year-old mansion with extended hours of operation.

Grant Hall Inn. 24 Fair Ford St. E. Good dining in recently renovated hotel. New cocktail lounge.

PRINCE ALBERT. *Expensive:* **The Penn Night Club.** A Las Vegas atmosphere with dining and dancing. Specialty of the house is sirloin steak. Free parking. Located on Hwy. 2 south of Prince Albert.

Inexpensive: **Venice House Restaurant.** This is a family restaurant where courtesy and good, fast, friendly service are stressed. Has a varied menu. Free parking. Located in downtown Prince Albert.

SWIFT CURRENT. *Expensive:* **Wong's Kitchen.** South Service Rd. on Highway 1 East (Trans-Canada). Serving Oriental and Canadian dishes, Wong's enjoys a reputation throughout Saskatchewan. Features live entertainment daily.

Moderate: **DB's Steak House.** 730 Central Ave. N. Daily specials and a variety of steaks and burgers.

WEYBURN. *Moderate:* **El Rancho Pizza and Steak House.** 53 Government Rd. Feature steaks, seafood, and Italian dishes.

Whistler's Family Dining. Located downtown at 7 Souris Ave., featuring salad bar, daily smorgasbords, and homemade bread and soup. Also features steak and seafood.

YORKTON. *Moderate:* **Gladstone Inn.** Features German cuisine with a good wine list. Located at the corner of Broadway and Gladstone.

Inexpensive: **Yorkton Hotel.** Daily specials feature local ethnic dishes. Homemade desserts.

ALBERTA

Land of the Fearsome Blackfoot

by
JACK HERRMANN

Jack Herrmann, a freelance writer born and raised in Alberta, has been involved with tourism for over twenty years.

Despite the paucity of archeological knowledge of Alberta, it is known that there have been Albertans of one sort or another for thousands, perhaps tens of thousands of years. We do know that the early inhabitants were hunters and fishers. They migrated from more northerly regions, stayed awhile, then moved on—generally to the south, in search of a better life.

Their comings and goings are perhaps aptly summarized in the poetic words of Crowfoot, Chief of the Blackfoot Indians—the last native inhabitants to arrive in Alberta:

> What is life? It is as the flash of a firefly in the night.
> It is as the breath of a buffalo in the winter time.
> It is as the little shadow that runs across the grass
> and loses itself in the sunset . . .

The Blackfoot emerged from the scrub forests of the pre-Cambrian Shield and onto the Great Plains with a decisive impact. Of Algonkian linguistic stock and handsome appearance, the Blackfoot were comprised of three main and related nations—the Siksika, Piegan and Blood, plus a protected "little brother" tribe, the Athabaskan—speaking Sarcee. These were warriors, a people who admired courage above all.

Continually at war with the other Indian nations, the Blackfoot gained the reputation of being the most fearsome fighters on the North American flat lands. The Tigers of the Plains, as they were called, ultimately ended up containing the entire northern migratory area of the buffalo. From mid-Alberta to Yellowstone was Blackfoot country, and from this territory Blackfoot war expeditions marched to the Pacific and well into Mexico.

These were an ambitious and a ferocious people. They almost exterminated the Crow nation. They halted and frustrated the powerful Sioux. In admiration, and in hopes of an alliance that never came, they were called "Brother" by the colorful Cheyenne. They were feared and respected above all the other Indians by the few white traders, hunters, and adventurers in Alberta at that time. The Blackfoot tolerated the white intruders along the borders of their territory, but any effort by the whites to penetrate the Blackfoot lands was harshly dealt with. Yet, in the end, the Blackfoot capitulated before the threat of all-out war—and they delivered their lives and futures into the care of the white man.

La Verendrye and La Jonquière

Henry Kelsey came close to Alberta when he discovered the Canadian prairies in 1691. But the French explorer and voyageur La Verendrye was the first recorded white man to set foot on Alberta soil in his search for the illusory Northwest Passage to the Orient. It is thought that La Verendrye may have established Fort La Jonquière in 1751. The original site of that fort is unknown, but it is conjectured to be in the city center of Calgary.

The explorations by Anthony Henday and Samuel Hearne followed soon after. Both of those adventurers returned eastward with stories of the opportunities that existed in the west for founding a rich fur trade. Before the 18th century ended, the Hudson's Bay Company and the North-West Company were well established and engaged in a fierce trade battle. The companies had followed the North Saskatchewan River from the east into Alberta—leapfrogging each other with the construction of trading forts. Building those forts on the north shore in Cree Indian territory, the fur traders stayed close to their fur sources in the vast forests of central and northern Alberta—and wisely: across the wide river were the perilous lands of the Blackfoot Indians. The fur trade thrived throughout the 1800's, and both companies maintained trading posts well into the 1900's. Even today, trapping remains a source of livelihood for many Albertans.

Rev. Rundle: Integrity, Honesty

It has been said that wherever men of fortune wander, men of the cloth are close behind with their evangelism. So it was in Alberta.

At first the religious leaders just passed through, the Anglicans in 1836 and the Roman Catholics in 1838. Then the Wesleyans posted Rev. Rundle to Edmonton in 1839. He worked mainly among the Stoney Indians, a Siouian tribe occupying the foothill country on the eastern slopes of the Rocky Mountains, and he discovered that the Indians had no great need for his particular doctrine—they had their own religion and it had served their purposes well for centuries. However, they did respect him for his devotion to their well-being. Rundle was a man of integrity and of honesty. He realized that, as well as attending to their spiritual needs, it was vitally urgent to help them with their material needs. By doing so, Rundle set the pattern that was followed by later missionaries, resulting in a successful relationship with Alberta's native people. Most noteworthy were the self-sacrificing careers and accomplishments, reaching almost heroic proportions, of the Oblate priest, Father Albert Lacombe, and the Wesleyan, Rev. George McDougall.

The Mounties: Law and Order

The North West Mounted Police was founded in 1873 by an Act of Parliament of the Government of Canada. Initially it consisted of 300 men and was a military organization in everything but name. Originally called the North West Mounted Rifles, the change was made in view of the sensitive relations with the United States. As well as soothing any suspicious minds in the American government, it served other purposes. It made it easier for the Mounties to deal with the Indians and whites in a manner never done before—introducing law and order, strictly enforcing those laws fairly, and without prejudice to either group.

The Plains Indians hated anything resembling the U.S. Cavalry; the arrival of mounted policemen in British-type red tunics had a more soothing influence than if they had come as an out and out military force. They would be called police, Redcoats and Mounties—but they would never be referred to as soldiers or military. They were different; they made sure that they would be recognized as such.

The Fight Against Firewater

The Mounties had another important job to do—they had to get rid of the notorious Whiskey Forts.

With the decline of Hudson's Bay fur trading activities in Alberta, some of the traders had to look elsewhere for business opportunities. Such a group, based at Fort Benton, Montana, thought that there was a chance to make quick profits from trading with the Indians. Some two dozen forts were built for handling trade with the Blackfoot—and the principal commodity was whiskey.

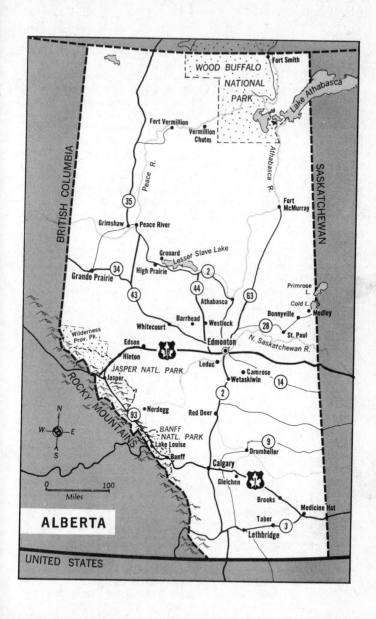

ALBERTA

Whiskey it was called, but a name like "Satan's liniment" would have been a more accurate description. It did contain alcohol, both the rubbing and the drinking kind; it was also fortified with red ink, Tabasco, red peppers, molasses, turpentine, and/or chewing tobacco. (Rumor at the time had it that the really good stuff was not complete without a pair of "Alf Hamilton's socks and Johnny Healy's last year's long underwear.")

Canadian officials really cared little what the concoctions contained —articles of clothing, false teeth, or gunpowder. Their chief worry was that American commercialism had made a successful entry into unguarded and unprotected western Canada.

Worse still, this fearsome brand of hooch was responsible for outbreaks of lawlessness and violence in the territory. Although the violence was first confined to the whiskey traders and the Indians, there was a danger that it would spread south of the border. This in turn could lead to preventive sorties by American Cavalry into Canadian territory, and the eventual construction of fortresses on Canadian soil —leading to an all-out Indian War involving a full native alliance (something the Sioux had tried many times to bring about). If left unchecked, the situation might lead to the loss of half of Canada to the United States.

Thus the Mounties had a real job to perform. This small company of men endured a forced march of 1,000 miles, closed down the whiskey trading operations, began construction of their first fort (Ft. Macleod), and gained control and respect of Chief Crowfoot and his Blackfoot nation—all in only four months.

Crowfoot and Treaty No. 7

Crowfoot, the tall and lean chief of the Blackfoot, played an important role in the subsequent development of the province. Crowfoot's contribution was not as a warrior (he certainly was that), but rather one of vision, of gentle philosophy, and of concern for the ultimate good of his people.

He watched the battles won and lost by Indian tribes south of the border—tribes he himself had fought. He saw the methods of the American "Longknives" and marveled at the seemingly endless numbers of them. He was deeply concerned about his own people—especially over the moral deterioration that had set in because of their craving for the cheap liquor. He looked carefully at the Mounties, and realized that a great change had come. The old ways were gone. The legend of the Mounties had already begun, born out of that force's determination, endurance, courage and fairness.

So, on September 22, 1877, at Blackfoot Crossing near Cluny, Alberta, Crowfoot signed Treaty No. 7 and said,

> While I speak, be kind and patient, I have to speak
> for my people who are numerous and rely upon me
> to follow that course which in the future will tend
> to their good. The plains are large and wide. It is
> our home, and the buffalo has been our food always. I hope you look upon the Blackfoot, Bloods

and Sarcee as your children now, and that you
might be indulgent and charitable to them. . . . I
am satisfied. I will sign the treaty.

Butchery of the Buffalo

With peace relatively assured, the wide short-grass land of Alberta
began to look more appealing to adventurous entrepreneurs from both
eastern Canada and the United States. The influx began.

Hide hunters were the first to take full advantage of the peaceful
conditions; by 1881 they had succeeded in devastating vast buffalo
herds. Millions of buffalo had previously thrived on the rolling landscape of Southern Alberta, but the slaughter was so extensive that the
species had practically disappeared, not only from Alberta, but from
the entire North American plains.

A few small herds survived, but the extinction of the buffalo appeared imminent. Canada is credited with taking the necessary action
that saved this animal for future generations. In 1906 Canada purchased a herd of about 700 from a rancher in Montana. These animals,
probably the last remaining large herd on the American continent,
were shipped to Alberta where they received care and attention. Today
Alberta has great herds in national parks throughout the province, as
well as small groups on Indian reserves and ranches.

Longhorns and Herefords

Immediately following the disappearance of the buffalo, the thought
came to some that where there had been buffalo, there possibly could
be cattle. The need was certainly there. So the cattlemen came—from
Montana and Texas with Longhorns, and from the east with Herefords.
The unsettled, unfenced and unbroken land was a strong attraction for
a new generation of settler. The cattle thrived—and so did the industry.

The CPR and Settlers

By 1883 the Canadian Pacific Railroad, snaking its long and arduous
journey across the country, had reached Calgary. With it came lucrative contracts for beef, desperately needed to feed the "navvies"—the
railroad construction workers. Back east, the government and the railroad had been impatient to use both this new transportation service and
these new lands in order to solve the railroad's financial problems. At
the same time, it would also firm up Canada's hold on the western
provinces. Special rates and deals designed to lure settlers to the west
received extensive advertising.

It worked beyond their wildest dreams. Settlers poured into Alberta,
coming not only from eastern Canada but Europe and the United
States. Although it was a rugged life, the settlers persisted in their
struggle.

Generally, their first shelter was simply a dugout in a cutbank that
enabled them to survive the first winter. In the spring, they progressed
to a "soddy," or sod hut. This was followed in time by a log structure
and eventually by a frame farm or a ranch home.

The settlers cleared the land, grew their crops, and began their first milling and processing plants. They were so industrious that when the rush for homesteads reached its peak in Alberta in the early 1890's, large areas of the province had already been settled.

Today, only a minute amount of homestead land (in the northern Peace River country of Alberta) remains. But: the total agricultural production of wheat, oats, barley, rye, rapeseed, and livestock exceeds $1 billion annually.

The Story of Kootenai Brown

Kootenai Brown wrinkled his nose at the odor, grit his teeth and forced himself to continue skimming off the brown, putrid ooze that floated on the surface of the slough. He admitted to himself that he had never been the cleanest galoot this southwestern Alberta country had known; yet, even for him, this filth was almost too much.

He had made himself what he considered to be a fairly good deal: he had purchased the slough from the Blood Indians for one horse. After skimming and stuffing this revolting mess into jugs he could sell it for a dollar a gallon. It made good engineering grease.

It's certainly no wonder it was good for engineering and mechanical use—it was crude oil. The time was the late 1890's and the location was near Carson Creek in what is now Waterton Lake. Although an oil company was formed at that time, no significant strikes were made until 1914 at Turner Valley. When Digman No. 1 blew in, it brought with it a period of excitement not seen in North America since the Klondike gold rush. For a few months nearby Calgary was converted into a full-fledged and furious boomtown. Stock manipulations, real estate trading and get-rich-quick schemes raged. It didn't last long; it was snuffed out with the first shot of World War I.

"Hell's Half Acre"

The Black Gold Fever was temporarily abated but it was far from dead. Following the war, exploration continued, and there was a huge discovery by Imperial Oil in 1924. The well blew in with 21 million cubic feet per day of gas, accompanied by 500 barrels of high-grade naphtha. It was a wild well; to get the oil out, the producers flared millions of cubic feet of waste gas. For years a bright red glow could be seen in the sky, and Turner Valley became known as Hell's Half Acre.

The excitement and the exploration continued. In 1936 Alberta's future was established once and for all with another major strike. The timing was perfect. The west was in the doldrums of the Great Depression and the 1936 well helped pull Alberta out of the "dust bowl and poverty" years.

Following World War II, in 1947, the vast Leduc oilfields were discovered. On the heels of this came a series of tremendous oil strikes that brought unparalleled prosperity and riches to Alberta. Alberta now is in an enviable situation with large resources of light crude oil plus its incalculable fields of oil-bearing sands that are, in themselves, equal to the world's entire known petroleum reserves.

Wealth of the "Princess Province"

In 1892, a railroad crew discovered natural gas while drilling for water near Medicine Hat. Within the next few years, it was discovered that Medicine Hat was located over an immense and natural gas field. So great and so spectacular was this reserve, that when the city flared a gas well in honor of Rudyard Kipling's visit, the colorful author dubbed Medicine Hat as "The City With All Hell For A Basement." Subsequently, vast reserves of natural gas were discovered scattered throughout most of the province.

Alberta has been blessed with a third source of natural energy—coal. Here again, the vastness of the reserves staggers the imagination. Primarily located in the valley of the Red Deer River at Drumheller, and in the southwestern portion of the province in the Crowsnest Pass, these coalbeds have provided a substantial economic contribution to the "Princess Province."

Alberta, with its wealth of petroleum, natural gas, and coal, plus its extensive agro-business, is the most fortunate of the Canadian provinces. Yet it remains ambitious. Realizing that its natural resources are nonrenewable, and therefore limited in their long term benefits to the economy, Alberta has embarked on a plan designed to revitalize some of its smaller agricultural communities by attracting industry and the professions to them. It began in 1974; great efforts have been made by the Alberta government toward formulating incentive programs to lure new industries to the province.

Alberta is an attractive province: one of the most beautiful in the country. Economically it is one of the most inviting in Canada. Alberta's growth rate has been the highest of all the provinces each year for the last decade. Alberta has no sales tax, no inheritance tax, and the lowest provincial income tax rate.

There has been a strong population movement to Alberta from the rest of Canada.

Alberta has become the important western Canadian center for banking, resource industries, commerce and economic decision-making.

EXPLORING CALGARY

Little is known about the earliest inhabitants of the area in which Calgary (over 700,000) stands today. Archeological probes at this prairie oasis of the Valley of the Bow at the confluence of the Bow and Elbow rivers show this site was inhabited about 10,000 years ago—probably by native American Indians.

The identity of the first white explorers to reach the area is also a matter of speculation. Recent evidence seems to indicate that Calgary possibly is the site for Fort Jonquière, built "somewhere" in western

Canada in May, 1751 by a group of Frenchmen, led by La Verendrye and sent by De Niverville from The Pas in Manitoba.

The early Indians told of men who had crossed the mountains from the west and had traded with their ancestors. The Russians traded with the natives of Alaska over 400 years ago. The Spanish in search of everything from gold to the fountain of youth may have found their way this far north and west; the Blackfoot once had acquired pieces of Spanish armor.

Seekers of Gold and Fortune

In October 1754 Anthony Henday crossed the Red Deer River north of Drumheller and marched a further three days westward. He was welcomed at a Blackfoot encampment of more than 300 lodges; from this camp he saw the Rocky Mountains. Peter Fidler, another explorer, may have passed a winter here, as did another Hudson's Bay Co. adventurer, David Thompson, in 1787.

From the mid 1800's on, the site of Calgary was very likely visited by mountainmen, trappers, and seekers of gold and fortune: Jim Bridger is said to have followed the Old North Trail (the ancient Indian trail extending north to south on the eastern slope of the Rocky Mountains); Lewis and Clarke, in their historic trip to the upper Missouri, were a mere few hundred miles south. Enterprising fortune seekers from Montana established whiskey forts in the Calgary vicinity. ("Liver Eatin' Johnson" had such a fort, but this was burned out just a few years prior to the coming of the Mounted Police.)

It was a warm summer's day in 1875 when a detachment of the North West Mounted Police arrived at the junction of the Bow and Elbow, crossed the rivers and made their camp; they then contracted the construction of a fort to the I.G. Baker company from Fort Benton, Montana. This outpost fort was built within a few months—it became the foundation of Calgary.

The Big Voice of Bulls Head

The fort was garrisoned by "F" Troop under the command of Inspector E.A. Brisebois, who promptly named the settlement after himself. Brisebois' action was not well received by his commandant, Col. J.F. Macleod (who at that time was stationed at Fort Macleod—a base similarly entitled).

He quickly sent a dispatch decrying the name "Brisebois" and offered his own suggestion: Calgary would be a far more suitable name for the new settlement. (He neglected to mention that his own birthplace, on the Isle of Mull in Scotland, was called Calgary.) So Calgary the settlement became—and Calgary it has remained.

The Mounties also remained. In the next few years the contingent of Redcoats dwindled to about a dozen. Their life sometimes was arduous, sometimes boring, and at other times downright hair-raising. The Sarcee Indian encampment was five miles to the southwest.

Bulls Head, the Sarcee chief, whose voice it was said could be heard at the fort when he was angry, decided one winter day to lay siege to the tiny Fort Calgary.

Defying the loud-mouthed threats of torture and death by Bulls Head, the garrison sent out a lone rider who managed to evade the Indians and to ride swiftly to Fort Macleod, one hundred miles to the south. The rider returned with Col. Macleod and a strong force of Mounted Police. Matching threat for threat, and loud voice with loud voice, Macleod herded the grumbling but cowed Bulls Head and his warriors back to their reserve.

The Fledgling Grows

The first of Calgary's many economic booms occurred eight years after the establishment of Fort Calgary. In 1883, the arrival of the Canadian Pacific Railway had an impact on the settlement that changed its character forever. There was the need to feed the railroad workers; this led naturally to many lucrative contracts for the supply of cattle and other items of food and necessities.

Ranching became a major business. And, as well as bringing in the settlers to till the soil and raise the crops needed by the fledgling Canadian nation, the railroads also offered a swift means of getting those products to the markets.

In the 1880's Calgary was a boisterous, rough-and-ready railroad town and cowtown. Those were exciting, romantic years. Although lacking the gun play of American frontier settlements (the law arrived before the big population expansion), Calgary nonetheless possessed the atmosphere and action necessary to inspire the imagination of adventurous souls around the world.

Immigrants poured in. Real estate prices rose. The sound of hammering and sawing of building construction blended with the sounds of horses hooves; the laughter, yells and curses of saloon patrons; the chug and hiss and lonesome wail of C.P.R. trains; the songs and giggles of the female community at Strawberry Flats; and the admonishing pleas of the shacktown preachers.

The "Sandstone City"

One Sunday morning, in 1886, Calgary's great fire occurred. It began in a log structure. It spread quickly to devastate the downtown area.

The event changed the course of Calgary's architectural development: a city edict made it mandatory that all future buildings constructed within the city be built of sandstone. Calgary became known as the "Sandstone City." Then, in 1914, the cry of black gold rose from the Turner Valley district to the southwest—and Calgary once again boomed.

Those were the beginnings. Richly endowed by nature, blessed with the good fortune of a series of economic windfalls, Calgary today enjoys the best of the Canadian world. Nestled in a valley of two rivers, with the magnificent Canadian Rockies in its front yard, with the fabulous wealth of golden grain fields and green ranchlands, surrounded by one

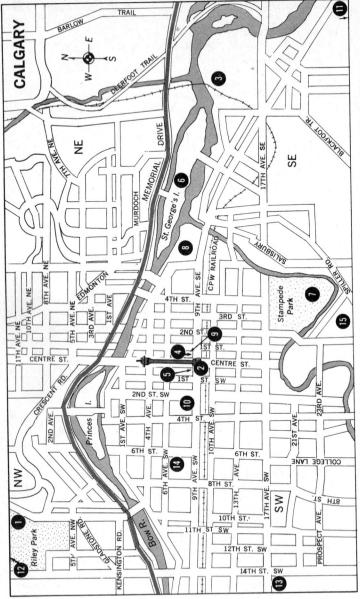

Calgary—Points of Interest
1) Burns Memorial Park
2) Calgary Tower
3) Sam Livingston Fish Hatchery
4) Convention Center
5) CPR Station
6) Dinosaur Park and Zoo
7) Exhibition and Stampede Grounds
8) Fort Calgary Site
9) Glenbow-Alberta Museum & Gallery
10) Devonian Gardens
11) Inglewood Bird Sanctuary
12) Jubilee Auditorium
13) Tourist Information
14) Planetarium
15) Reader Rock Garden

of the greatest deposits of petroleum the world has known, Calgary is a happy city.

The Blessed Chinook

As if all these gifts weren't enough for one city of over half a million people, Calgary enjoys yet another of nature's benefits—the Chinook.

The Chinook orginates in the Pacific as a prevailing westerly wind from a low-pressure area. As it progresses across British Columbia, it dumps most of its moisture. Jammed against the mountains, it is forced to rise, thereby gaining speed. Because of the pressures and friction, it increases in temperature. Skimming over the tops of the Rockies, it breathes its warmth on the Alberta plains, spreading out like a great fan from the Montana border to just north of Calgary.

The Chinook brings welcome relief and respite from winter's harsh prairie cold. Temperatures have been known to increase by 60 degrees within several hours in Calgary. In years when the Chinook runs hard, Calgary's winter is confined to a few short weeks in January.

Places Worth a Visit

Any tour of Calgary should start at the Calgary Tower, a 626-foot structure at the center of the city (9th Ave. S. and Center St.) This is Calgary's most distinctive landmark. From the observation deck there is an unchallenged view of 75 miles in every direction. For a more relaxing view of the panoramic mountains and prairie, take advantage of the Tower's lounge and revolving dining rooms. There is a $2 elevation charge.

The tower is part of a complex housing the Via Rail terminal, Palliser Hotel and a number of retail stores and boutiques; it is connected by an enclosed elevated pedestrian walkway with the Glenbow Museum, the Convention Center and the Four Seasons Hotel.

The Glenbow Museum has an amazing collection of Indian and Inuit art and historical western Canadian artifacts from the days of the fur trade through the time of the oil boom. The wide variety of exhibits include a military section with armor and guns; a stamp and coin collection; sculpture, paintings and prints.

One block south of Center St. is the 8th Ave. Mall, a lively pedestrian area ideal for people-watching, sunning and shopping. The mall covers 4 blocks between 3rd St. W. and 1st St. E. Continue north on 3rd St. W. to 7th Ave. and the Toronto Dominion Square. On the fourth level is the Devonian Gardens, a 2½-acre enclosed oasis with close to 1,600 subtropical plants, waterfalls, fountains and pools crisscrossed with bridges and paths. There are shops, snack bars, even a playground.

The Calgary Centennial Planetarium and Aerospace Museum is 8 blocks west at 7th Ave. and 11th St. The observatory, model rockets, vintage aircraft and weather station display complement the 255-seat theater.

From here it is a brisk 12-block walk northeast to Princes Island Park on the south side of the Bow River. Calgary has more than 11,000 acres of such public parkland. Princes Island is a good place, close to downtown, to let the kids run and work off steam. Several sculptures decorate the gardens. To get back to the center of town, walk south on 2nd or 4th St. W. to 9th Ave. S. and turn left to Center St.

If you are not in Calgary during the first two weeks of July, you can still see Stampede Park, a short ride south on the new light rail transit system (LRT),—where the famous Stampede takes place. (See below.) There is a long season for both harness and thoroughbred racing at the park. Eat at one of the park's several restaurants. Nearby Reader Rock Gardens at 26th Ave. and 2nd St. S.E. also warrant a visit.

East of the Calgary Tower is Fort Calgary (950 9th Ave. S.E.). Multi-screen audiovisual presentations will take you back to frontier days. Unfortunately, there is no significant trace of the original fort. Admission is free.

Continue on 9th Ave. to 12th St., then turn left to St. George's Island for both the Calgary Zoo and Dinosaur Park. The zoo is Canada's second largest, with 1,200 animals representing 400 species. There is also a children's zoo. The 8.2-acre Dinosaur Park boasts life-size replicas of dinosaurs that roamed Alberta in prehistoric times and an excellent collection of fossils housed in two buildings.

Retrace the route to 9th Ave., turn left and proceed to 20A St. S.E. and the Inglewood Bird Sanctuary, a unique river flats area that is a forested sanctuary for both migratory and resident birds. More than 217 species have been recorded. Admission is free.

Returning again to 9th Ave., travel west to the Blackfoot Trail, then south to Heritage Drive, and west to Heritage Park. The park is dedicated as "a living memorial to those who pioneered the early west." Two authentic town sites and 90 exhibits depict Alberta in the early part of this century and life as it was for early trappers, miners and settlers. It takes at least 3 hours to see the park fully. To get back downtown from here, retrace the route to Blackfoot Trail, then to 9th Ave. and head west to Center St.

The Stampede is B-I-G

The Calgary Stampede bills itself as The Greatest Dad-burned Show on Earth and, it just might be that. Held annually, generally within the first two weeks of July, the Calgary Stampede is ten days of superb western fun and games.

One hundred and fifty thousand dollars in prize money attracts the greatest rodeo competitors in the world. The daily chuckwagon races— a mad and frantic competition between four wagons and twenty men and thirty-two thoroughbreds—all try to beat the others around a standard race track. Dazzling stage shows, trade and livestock exhibitions, gambling casinos, colorful midways, dancing in the streets, downtown curbside breakfasts, cowboys, Indians, red-coated Mounted Police, and a million good-time-seeking dudes: these all add up to—if not the greatest—certainly one of the top fiestas in the world.

PRACTICAL INFORMATION FOR CALGARY

HOW TO GET THERE. By car: There is easy access by several interprovincial, state, and regional highways. **By train:** *Via Rail* serves Calgary. **By bus:** *Greyhound* is the major carrier. Its head office in Canada is in Calgary. **By air:** Calgary is served by *Air Canada, C.P. Air, Pacific Western, United, Wardair* and *Lufthansa.*

ACCOMMODATIONS. Calgary has a wide variety of hotels and motels ranging from luxurious to average. There is no provincial tax on accommodations, but some hotels and motels will charge for local phone calls. Price categories for double-occupancy are: *Deluxe,* $90 and up; *Expensive,* $60–90; *Moderate,* $40–60; *Inexpensive,* under $40.

During the first two weeks of July, the Calgary Stampede literally sells out the city. As a result, accommodation is at a premium and the cost of a room can jump 20 percent.

Most places accept the following major credit cards: American Express, MasterCard, and Visa; others may also be honored. Not all establishments accept credit cards, therefore we suggest you call for information.

Both the *YMCA* and *YWCA* have large facilities. Each offers complete Y-club amenities. YMCA, 332 6th Ave. S.E. YWCA, 320 5th Ave. S.W. Although the YWCA is for women only, they will accept children (boys under 7) on an overnight basis.

Deluxe

Delta Bow Valley Inn. 209 4th Ave. S.E. 400 rooms. This new property offers all the services and amenities of a deluxe hotel. Convenient location.

Four Seasons Hotel. 9 Ave. and Centre St. S. One of top hotels in town. Silver tableware. Rooms are all special. Hotel is adjacent to charming indoor garden.

International Hotel. 200 4th Ave. S.W. High rise hotel. All 255 rooms are suites. Cable T.V., sauna, and health club. Delightful piano bar. Executive suites available. No charge for children under 16 if occupying parents' room.

Westin Hotel Calgary. 4 Ave. and 3rd St. S.W. This 554-room property is perhaps the finest in Calgary. Its Owls Nest dining room is rated one of Canada's top 10 eating establishments.

Expensive

Calgary Center Inn. 202 4th Ave. S.W. Slight extra charge for water beds and 9-foot, heart-shaped playpens; air conditioning, bar, licensed dining, pool, and massive beer parlor.

Carriage House Motor Inn. 9030 Macleod Trail. The works. Air conditioning to wheelchair services. Cable TV, direct-dial phones, in-room movies, cabarets, saunas, nightclub.

Château Airport. 2001 Airport Rd. N.E. 300 rooms and suites. Adjoining Calgary International Airport. Weekend rates and family plan available. Some rooms may run more expensive.

Crossroads Motor Hotel. 2120 16th Ave. N.E. On Trans-Canada Hwy. at eastern entrance to city. 210 air-conditioned rooms. Western entertainment in its tavern. Suites available.

Holiday Inn. 4206 Macleod Trail S. New and up to International standards. No charge for children under 18 in same room as parents.

Palliser Hotel. 133 9th Ave. S.W. A. C.P. hotel. Luxurious lobby has been seen in movies. 350 rooms and suites have been redecorated, upgrading the entire operation to satisfy modern demands.

Westward Motor Inn. 119 12th Ave. S.W. Shrewd management and new, comfortable, well-equipped rooms make this establishment popular.

Moderate

Motel Village. Trans-Canada Hwy. and Crowchild Trail N.W. Not just one motel but an area of some two dozen, with a total of over 1,000 rooms. Most times, you have shopper's choice: during the popular season, you'll find some accommodations here. Some rooms are more expensive.

Hotel Empress. 219 6th Ave. S.W. An older "family" hotel; clean, bright rooms. Center of downtown.

Highlander Motor Hotel. 1818 16th Ave. N.W. Older but well-kept. Dining room is one of Calgary's best. Licensed coffeeshop, bar, tavern, beer parlor, and cabaret.

Port-O-Call Inn. 1935 McKnight Blvd. N.E. 156 units. Executive suites, steam room, raquetball courts, hot tubs and Jacuzzi tubs. Wheelchair facilities.

Westgate Motor Hotel. 1111 33rd St. S.W. Good clean operation and a good local watering hole. Big beer parlor, bar, and good dining lounge.

York Hotel. 7th Ave. and Centre St. S. 135 rooms; character beer parlor, but good family house, color TV, dial telephones, sauna. Some air-conditioned.

Inexpensive

Relax Inns (North and South). 2750 Sunridge and 9206 McLeod Trail. Reasonably priced, clean—qualities that are attracting more and more believers. Convenient to highway.

Plumtree Inn. 76 rooms. Reasonable and clean. TV, elevator. Corporate rates.

HOSTELS. Canadian Youth Hostels Association, 1414 Kensington Rd., N.W. Year-round accommodation in near downtown area. Members $5.00, non-members $7.00 per night single.

HOW TO GET AROUND. By car: The province has an extensive system of highways and roads—many leading in and out of Calgary. **By train:** *Via Rail* has good dayliner service between Calgary and Edmonton. **By transit and taxi:** Calgary has an excellent transit system. Fare is 95¢, exact change. Taxi fares tend to be high by North American standards. Airport limo to downtown is a good deal compared to bus if 3 or more people share.

TOURIST INFORMATION. Comprehensive information about attractions, accommodations, prices, and maps is available by writing to *Travel Alberta,* Capital Square, 14th Floor, 10065 Jasper Ave., Edmonton, Alberta, Canada, T5J 0H4, or from *Calgary Tourist and Convention Association,* Hospitality Centre, 1406th Ave., S.E., Calgary, T2G 0G2, 236–8510.

SEASONAL EVENTS. March: *Rodeo Royal, Agricultural Round-up.* **May:** *Calgary International Horse Show.* **July:** *Calgary Stampede* (rodeo). **September:** *Spruce Meadows Masters* (Equestrian). **December:** *Christmas Box Concert* and *Singing Christmas Tree.*

PARKS AND GARDENS. Calgary has over 11,000 acres of parkland within its boundaries. Some of the most important are Bowness, Confederation, Edworthy, Glenmore, and Patric Burns Memorial. Be sure to visit *Reader Rock Gardens, Aviary at Zoo, Brewery Gardens, Devonian Gardens* (Downtown) and *Garden Terrace* (Convention Centre).

CHILDREN'S ACTIVITIES. In addition to all participant sports available in and around Calgary, *St. George's Island Zoo* should be entertaining. *Calaway Park* is a 60-acre theme park with 50 rides, 3 miles west of Calgary on Hwy. 1. Admission: $9.95 per person; a variety of plans available. *Calgary Zoo* and *Dinosaur Park,* 9th Ave. and 12th St. Adults: $3.50; children under 12: $1.00; Seniors: free.

SPORTS. Participant Sports. *Skiing* is also highly popular with two slopes—Paskapoo and Shaganappi right in the city. The mountain runs of Fortress, Sunshine, Lake Louise, and Norquay offer skiing from November to May. Rentals of equipment are readily available in the city, and several bus packages provide economical and popular transportation packages. *Tennis, swimming, jogging,* and *hiking* facilities are numerous and free. There's lots of area for *cross-country skiing* in the winter. *Racquetball* and *health-exercise* facilities are numerous. And, of course, *horseback riding* is always available. Finally, Calgary has a city-wide *biking* trail that is widely used.

Spectator Sports. Aside from *rodeo,* Calgary is immensely proud of its Canadian *Football* League *Calgary Stampeders* and National Hockey League *Calgary Flames.* It has pro *soccer* and *baseball* and a host of semi-pro and amateur teams in a myriad of leagues.

CAMPING. For information, contact *K.O.A.* Box 10, Site 12 S.S. 1, Calgary; *Standard Kampgrounds of America* operation located on the Trans-Canada Hwy. west of the city; *Sunalta Trailer Parks, Ltd.* Box 6531, Station "D," Calgary.

MUSEUMS AND SITES. *The Glenbow/Alberta Institute* is located on 9th Ave. at 1st St., S.E. Covers a broad spectrum of Alberta history. Its displays include one of greatest collections of guns and coins in existence, war trophies and equipment, Eskimo art and Indian artifacts, plus a fine carriage collection. Adults: $2.; children: $1.

Heritage Park is a living, working museum. An entire town lives within its 60 acres. Buildings are authentic and were brought here from their original settings in various parts of Alberta. Majority of people who run the community, i.e., paddlewheeler steamboat, mining train, blacksmith shop, general store, bakery, newspaper, are all retired career persons who now enjoy carrying on their life's work here. Adults: $4.00; children: $2.00.

Centennial Planetarium, 11th St. and 7th Ave. S.W., is a unique mixture of entertainment, education, thrills, and facts. It offers star shows, an observatory, and an aerospace museum. Admission 50¢.

Ft. Calgary, 750 9th Ave. S.E. On 30 acres of prairie, the ruins of the 1875 North West Mounted Police fort are marked for your wandering around enjoyment. Exhibits of artifacts and suberb audio/visual/sensory presentation make a visit more than worthwhile. No admission charge.

Military Museum, on Canadian Forces Base Calgary at Richard Rd. and Crowchild Tr. S.W. Dedicated to the men of the two regiments who participated in Canada's wars and peacekeeping operations. Great for military buffs. It is necessary to make an appointment by telephoning (403) 246–7525.

Sam Livingstone Fish Hatchery. 1440 17A St. S.E. Displays showing species and explaining habitats, breeding, and location of fish found in Alberta. Free admission.

 PERFORMING ARTS. Music. *Calgary Philharmonic Orchestra* presents several series from classic to pop each season. *Mount Royal Woodwind Quintet,* performs regularly at the Leacock Theatre at Mount Royal College. *Music at Noon,* a noon time program offered September through April at the W.R. Castell Central Library. Further, Calgary is a recording center for all manner of contemporary groups and artists; consequently a full spectrum of entertainers may be heard at various locations throughout the year.

Choral. *Calgary Renaissance Singers and Players* is an unusual group performing at the University of Calgary Theatre. *Southern Alberta Opera Association* presents three operas a year at the Jubilee Auditorium. *Devonian Gardens* features regular entertainment from concerts to impromptu sessions.

Theater. *Alberta Theatre Projects,* at the Canmore Opera House in Heritage Park. Excellent group offering five plays per year. *Calgary Theatre Singers* present old-time favorites and musicals. *Loose Moose Theatre* offers innovative productions at the Pumphouse Theatre. *Lunchbox Theatre* performs irregularly in Bow Valley Square at noon hour. *Story Book Theatre* gives matinees every weekend at the Pumphouse Theatre. *Theatre Calgary* is a top professional organization with two series each season at the QM Centre.

Dance. *Alberta Ballet Company* is an excellent young company performing primarily at the Jubilee Auditorium.

SHOPPING. Try *The Calgary Cabin* and *Green's Lapidary* for special Albertan products.

 DINING OUT. Alberta is cattle country and Calgary is the absolute heart of it all. It doesn't really matter what kind of beef you order, just as long as it's steak! The melt-in-your-mouth smoothness and special taste of Alberta sweet-grass-fed-and-grain-finished steak should not be missed. Calgary is also loaded with ethnic restaurants and gourmet menus. Naturally the fast-food takeouts and franchises are also in abundance.

Restaurants are listed by price category as follows: *Deluxe,* $28 and over; *Expensive,* $19–28; *Moderate,* $13–19; *Inexpensive,* under $13. Prices include an appetizer or soup, entrée, and dessert. Drinks and tips are not included.

Most places accept the following major credit cards: American Express, MasterCard, and Visa; others may also be honored. Not all establishments accept credit cards, therefore we suggest you call for information.

Deluxe

The Owls Nest. Westin Calgary. 320 4th Ave. S.W. One of the top ten restaurants in the country. Gourmet cooking with interesting selections. Worth the cost.

Traders. In Four Seasons Hotel, Centre St. and 9th Ave. S.E. Exquisite service in the grand European tradition. Silver place settings, elegant atmosphere. Tops in Canada.

Blackbeards. 235–10th Ave. S.W. A steakhouse amid a central mast, rigging, bellaying pins and other paraphernalia of an authentic pirate ship.

Caesars. 512 4th Ave. S.W. A simple but elegantly decorated restaurant. Possibly the finest food in Calgary. Steaks, ribs, seafood, and chicken.

The Calgary Tower. 9th Ave. at Centre St. International cuisine with a revolving dining room close to 600 feet above street level.

Don Quijote Restaurant. 1220 Kensington Rd. Seventy-six-item menu specializes in cuisine native to southern Spain. Specialties include roast suckling pig.

The Dynasty. 703 6th Ave. S.W. Simple but attractive décor. Excellent Continental cuisine. Impressive menu.

Franzel's Gasthaus. 2417–4 Street S.W. The feeling of a Rhine castle, the sounds of an "oompah band," and exquisite Bavarian food.

Hy's. 316 4th Ave. S.W. This is the original Hy's and still his best. The steaks are unbeatable in Calgary; the seafood nearly as good.

The Mad Trappers. 602 11th Ave. S.W. Dinner and dancing. Menu includes buffalo, gamebirds, frogs' legs and rabbit. Steaks, fish, and ribs.

Moose Factory. 1213 1st St. S.W. Two dining areas—two décors (Art Nouveau to intimate Modern). Dress regulations. Excellent menu. Piano/vocalists.

Omi of Japan. 615 2nd St. S.W. In the tradition of Japanese restaurants where you sit at the stove. Elaborate Samurai steak ceremony, excellent food.

The Red Carpet. Elbow Dr. and Glenmore Trail. Standard menu of steak, seafood, and prime rib, but sensational quality.

The Stagedoor. 830 9th Ave. S.W. Located in the Theatre Calgary building and filled with mementos of the 20s, 30s, 40s, this charming restaurant features rack of lamb, curried shrimp, and prime rib of beef.

Three Greenhorns. 503 4th Ave. S.W. Good beef, carefully aged and prepared.

Tiki–Tiki. 718 8th Ave. S.W. Tropical, Polynesian, grass thatching—an enjoyable experience. Polynesian food and charcoal-broiled steaks.

Expensive

Becky's Bistro. 402 8th St. S.W. Small, intimate. Checkered tablecloths. Fine European food and wines.

Black Angus. 1818 16th Ave. N.W. in the Highlander Motor Hotel. Fine food and service.

Casa D'Italia. 2820 Centre St. N. Excellent Italian food. Small, but with tasteful atmosphere.

Dilettante. 3rd floor, Scotia Centre, 225 7th Ave. S.W. Sophisticated. Outstanding wine list. Frogs' legs, truffles, steak Maubeuge, and lobster Newburg.

Inn on the Lake. Acadia Drive and Lk. Bonavista Dr. S.W. On Lake Bonavista with fantastic view. Plush velvet trappings. Fine food.

La Chaumiere. 121 17th Ave. S.E. Refreshingly French. Meticulous quality and service. Flaming duck, brandied tomatoes, steak Diane and crêpes.

Pardon My Garden. 4th Ave. and 4th St. S.W. Décor after fine, old garden of Calgary mansion. Crêpes, seafood, and steaks.

Primos. 1116 1st St. S.W. Mexican food and wonderful entertainment with a south-of-the border atmosphere.

Sukiyaki House. 517 10th Ave. S.W. Total Japanese experience. Sit on floor. Intimate booths. If you like, cook your own sukiyaki.

Taj Mahal. 4816 Macleod Trail S. Finest authentic Indian cuisine and atmosphere. Exotic delicacies. Curry.

Wellington's Fine Restaurant. 10325 Bonaventure Dr. S.E. A promise of gourmet delights fulfilled.

Moderate

Greek Korner Ristorante. 1604 14th St. S.W. Fried squid and pickled octopus are among the varied dishes.

Greek Village. 1212 17th Ave. S.W. Best Greek feeling in town. Superb food. Authentic décor.

Long Bar. 8th Ave. and 1st St. S.W. Location of historic longest bar in the west. Refurbished of course. Now with superb buffet, 50-item à la carte dinner menu, and mature disco in evenings.

Mother Tucker's. 345 10th Ave. S.W. Informal homespun with truly great food, fresh bread, homemade desserts.

Inexpensive

Karouzo's. 2620 4th St. N.W. Listed primarily for the city's finest pizza experience.

Keg 'n Cleaver. 1101 5th St. S.W. Three of these in town, but the one addressed is tops. Steaks and prime rib are the specialties.

Old Spaghetti Factory. 628 9th Ave. S.W. Spaghetti and Italian foods served in a warehouse, redone in turn-of-the-century décor.

Phoenix Inn. 616 9th St. S.W. Best special is chop suey. Great Chinese smorgasbord.

 NIGHTCLUBS AND BARS. Calgary is an entertainment-loving city with hundreds of spots featuring professional talent. One notable completely in the Western character of Calgary is *Ranchman's* with two locations: 1117–1st St. S.W. and 9311 Macleod Tr. S. It features many popular artists along with drinking, dining, and dancing.

EXPLORING EDMONTON

In the late 1700's, the two great fur-trading companies—the Hudson's Bay and the North West—leap-frogged their rivalrous way west along the North Saskatchewan River. Soon after they had penetrated what is now Alberta, those companies built the first two in a series of forts: the Augustus (North West Company) and Edmonton (Hudson's Bay Company).

The first two forts were established near the Sturgeon River, close to the present Fort Saskatchewan. These were eventually abandoned and new ones were built within the present Edmonton city limits. Again called Edmonton and Augustus, they remained in use until they too were abandoned in 1810.

A third series of forts was built several miles downstream. One of the series was called Edmonton, and another was named Fort White Earth, or Terreblanche. These, too, met a similar fate, being abandoned in 1813. Two more forts were constructed at the present site of Edmonton's power house. In 1821 the two companies amalgamated under the name of the Hudson's Bay Company. Once again the forts were abandoned, this time because of floods. The Augustus fort was awash in

1825, and the Edmonton fort was flooded five years later. In the summer of 1830 the traders moved to higher ground and started work on the final Fort Edmonton, which was built on what is now the site of the Alberta Legislative Building.

Short-Lived Fort Sanspareil

Feeling that the original names of the forts—Edmonton and Augustus—had in some way a supernatural or negative effect on the enterprise, the Hudson's Bay employees tried to change the name: they dubbed the new post Fort Sanspareil. However, either wiser or more stubborn heads, undoubtedly possessed of greater "clout," restored the name Edmonton. This final fort lasted until well into the settlement era but was finally dismantled in 1915.

Alberta's north was commercially developed ahead of the south. The forts constructed along the North Saskatchewan River invariably were constructed on the north side of the river. The reason for the prior northern development and for the northshore construction of the forts was not just happenstance or force of habit. It was deadly practical: the entire land south of the North Saskatchewan River was Blackfoot Indian territory. These were the fearsome Tigers of the Plains who controlled the land from that point as far south as Yellowstone National Park in Wyoming. The Blackfoot were extraordinarily mean to white folks and notoriously adept at illustrating their dislike with imaginative forms of painful torture.

The Riel Rebellion

The land lying to the north of the North Saskatchewan River was Cree Indian territory. The Cree Indians were friendly and cooperative to the white traders with the natural result that the fur traders looked to the north. The Cree were enemies of the Blackfoot; although they spoke the same language, albeit with a different dialect, they waged constant war with each other. The objective of the struggle was possession of the grazing land of the great northern buffalo herds.

The cooperation between trader and Cree Indian continued harmoniously until the Riel Rebellion of 1885. In the spring of that year, the territory from Frog Lake 140 miles east northeast from Edmonton to the junction of the South Saskatchewan River was seething with unrest. The Métis—French-speaking progeny of fur traders and Indians—feared and hated the encroachment of white settlers. Their means of livelihood—the buffalo hunts and the fur trade—were declining. Their hope of building a new, free separate community of their own seemed to have become a shattered dream. Their small farms on the banks of the North Saskatchewan were being surrounded by English-speaking Protestant settlers. As sparse as that homesteading infringement was, it nevertheless was a disturbing and alarming situation for the Métis.

The Indians were unhappy as well. The free days of roaming and hunting were gone. Confinement to reserves meant frustrating attempts at farming—an occupation totally foreign to the nomadic spirit of

Indians. Additionally, a series of brutally hard winters had caused widespread starvation on the reserves. The ignorant and insensitive attitudes of government agents caused more hard feelings. Frustration led to regret, regret to anger, and anger to a stubborn resurgence of native pride.

On the morning of April 2, a band of Cree Indians under the leadership of Big Bear struck at the village at Frog Lake. They ransacked the Hudson's Bay Company store and entered the small church there. They killed nine men including two priests, the Indian agent and the farm instructor.

The North West Rebellion had begun in earnest. The Cree band that attacked Frog Lake proceeded on to Fort Pitt where they were successful in routing North West Mounted Police Inspector Francis Dickens (son of English novelist Charles Dickens) and his men. (Eventually, this Cree band was captured, but by then the all-out revolution was underway.)

The government of Canada had moved swiftly. On April 20, the Alberta field force of 150 mounted riflemen left Calgary, arriving at Fort Edmonton on May 1. After 18 days of mind-breaking tension, rest came a little easier to the people of that small settlement. With the forts Edmonton and Saskatchewan now suitably garrisoned, it became feasible to launch major sorties into the homeland of the rebels. Major General Strange began a strong movement from Edmonton toward the Métis community of Batoche.

Major General Sir Frederick Middleton had already set out from Fort Qu'Appelle in southern Saskatchewan; the pincer movement was on. On the fourth day of siege, the Métis capital of Batoche fell. Riel Rebellion was over almost before it had begun. Edmonton and the rest of Canada gave thanks and set out once again to fulfill their destiny.

A Stage Stop

Industry apart from the fur trade came to Edmonton in 1875 when the Hudson's Bay Company began operating a small sawmill. Disappointment came early, too. Great hopes were held by Edmontonians that the transcontinental railroad would pass through their settlement and on the West Coast via the Yellowhead pass, but this was not to be. The larger settlement to the south, Fort Calgary, was chosen by the Canadian Pacific Railway Co. Edmonton had to settle for a stage stop.

Thus were sown the seeds for the fierce rivalry between the two cities. Undaunted by the loss of the economic advantage offered by the railroad, the Edmontonians continued their vigorous industrial progress. By 1889 they had established the first bank west of Winnipeg. In 1891 they obtained an electric light plant. The community expanded from being a hamlet to the status of a town the following year; by 1884 the population numbered more than 1,000.

Edmonton fortunes, even in those early years, appeared to be to the north. Riverboat action on the waterways from Fort Smith to the mouth of the Mackenzie River increased the city's optimism. By 1897 Edmonton was maturing and gaining confidence. That year turned out to be quite a magic year.

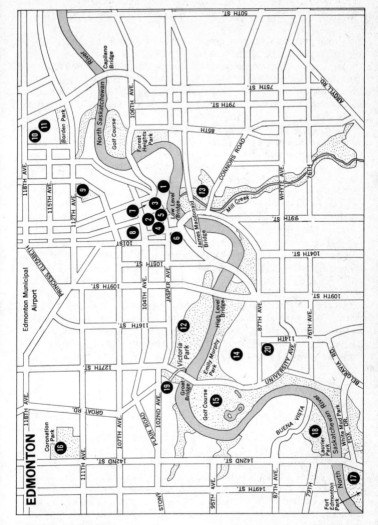

Points of Interest

1) Convention Center & Aviation Hall of Fame
2) Art Gallery
3) Citadel Theater
4) City Hall
5) Civic Center
6) Vista 33 Observation AGT Bldg.
7) Post Office
8) CN Tower (Via Rail station)
9) Commonwealth Stadium
10) Northlands Park
11) Edmonton Northlands
12) Legislature Building
13) Muttart Conservatory
14) University of Alberta
15) Hawrelak Park
16) Space Science Center
17) Fort Edmonton Park
18) Valley Zoo
19) Provincial Museum
20) Jubilee Auditorium

Plague of the Yellow Fever

In 1897 Edmonton experienced its gold rush. Specks of the glittering mineral were panned on the shores of the North Saskatchewan. Quickly, both banks of the river were thick with prospectors' claims. Gold fever was there in all its chaotic activity and enterprise, but the gold was scarce and was limited to mere traces. (Even today similar gold traces may be panned from the gravel of the North Saskatchewan River in the heart of Edmonton.)

Three weeks after the first news of gold in Edmonton came reports of the large Bonanza Creek find near the Klondike River in the Yukon. The yellow fever Edmonton had felt before was a mere symptom of the disease that ripped minds and hearts during the early days of the great Klondike Gold Rush that followed.

There was no easy overland way to the Klondike fields and most prospectors took the easier sea route from Seattle to Skagway and then overland to the Yukon. Some 1,500 gold seekers departed from Edmonton. Half of them went via the Mackenzie River. The other half decided on the tortuous land route through forest and muskeg.

Both were dismal failures. Of those who went by the river route, 565 arrived in the Yukon; of those who went overland, only 160 made it to the Yukon. They arrived at the goldfields long after the bloom was off the "Glory Hole"—and the last steamers were leaving Skagway with many of the disheartened and disillusioned prospectors.

That period of excitement, however, was a stimulus to the hopes and aspirations of Edmonton. In 1904 it became incorporated as a city. And in 1905 its fortunes changed radically when the Canadian National Railroad came to Edmonton.

Edmonton vs. Calgary

Edmonton is the geographical center of Alberta. In 1905 it was politically liberal and its rival to the south, Calgary, was conservative; thus it had a definite advantage in dealing with the federal government which was also liberal. Alberta was to become a province; part of its responsibility was to send representatives to Ottawa. Thus electoral constituencies had to be established, a situation which Edmonton saw as a golden opportunity to score over Calgary.

A capital had to be chosen. Red Deer, Calgary, Lethbridge, and Banff all felt that they would be the most suitable. The worthies (Edmontonians) manipulated the drawing up of the constituencies so that most radiated from Edmonton, thus insuring that that city would be the capital of the new province. The southern cities protested strongly, but Edmonton sat fat and happy, knowing that finally it had gained the upper hand over its chief competitor: Calgary.

Calgary was again mortified by the announcement that the new University of Alberta would be located—not in Calgary as expected—but in Strathcona, a newly incorporated city of 3,500 located adjacent to Edmonton on the south shore of the North Saskatchewan. Salt was rubbed further into Calgary's open wounds shortly after when Edmonton revealed that North America's last remaining buffalo, purchased from Montana by the Canadian Government, would be located at Elk Island, a short distance from Edmonton!

The rivalry between Calgary and Edmonton has continued unabated for more than 70 years. It is not so acrimonious as it was, and in recent years has been reduced to mere mutterings of "unfair," grumblings of "favoritism," and a suspicious and continuous eyeing of each other.

Gateway to the Arctic

The great oil find at Turner Valley in 1914 had much the same effect on Edmonton as it did on Calgary. Many Edmontonians headed immediately south to the oilfields. Within three days following the announcement of the Dingman No. 1 well, 100 new brokerage offices opened in Edmonton. The First World War curtailed Edmonton's commercial and industrial growth but after the war, optimism returned and in the 1920's Edmonton experienced a staggering industrial expansion.

Depression struck Edmonton hard in the '30s; by 1936 recovery was in sight. Air traffic to the north was established; this was the start of the colorful and adventurous era of the Canadian bush pilots. Edmonton's position as supplier of goods and services as a gateway to the Arctic was firmly established at this time.

In 1940 the defense plans of the United States included a new look at the old overland route to the Klondike. The threat of war convinced the U.S. government that a land route to Alaska was vital. A decision was made and an incredible accomplishment followed.

Work began on the Alaska Highway on March 9, 1942. It was completed just nine months later on November 22! In that short period, 1,523 miles of road had been built through some of the most formidable terrain on earth. And the jumping-off point for supplies and services to Alaska was Edmonton.

Edmonton: Vibrant, Modern, Clean

The final making of Edmonton as a modern industrial city was the discovery of the Leduc Oilfields in 1947; this was followed in quick succession by other massive petroleum finds at Woodbend and Red Water. The great Alberta oilfields now circled Edmonton. Further discoveries to the north and northeast ensured that Edmonton would be the headquarters for drilling contractors, service industries and refineries.

Including its adjoining communities, Edmonton currently has a population of well over 700,000. It is a vibrant, modern, and clean city. This, the most northerly major city in North America, offers entertainment and sightseeing activities on a par with almost every other Canadian city.

Sightseeing in Edmonton

Edmonton's most striking physical characteristic is the valley formed by the North Saskatchewan River, which flows right through the city. Seventeen miles of parks have been developed in the river valley, linked by hiking and bicycle trails. Pedestrian footbridges criss-cross the river.

It's easy to find your way around the city. Edmonton's road network is laid out on a grid system: avenues run east/west; streets run north/south. The center of town is the intersection of Jasper Ave. (101st Ave.) and 100th St.—marked on its southeast side by the venerable Hotel Macdonald (closed for refurbishing between mid-1983 and 1985).

Two blocks east is Edmonton's stunning new Convention Center, an $84 million complex sunk into the river bank and home of Canada's Aviation Hall of Fame. Proceed north from 100th St. to 102nd Ave. to find Sir Winston Churchill Square and the Civic Center. Surround-ing the square are a number of interesting buildings. At the southeast corner of 102nd Ave. and 100th St. is the Centennial Library, con-structed in 1967 to celebrate Canada's 100th birthday. The Citadel Theater is nearby. A startling blend of brick and glass, it is western Canada's center for the performing arts. The Edmonton Art Gallery is to the north at the intersection of 99th St. and 102A Ave.; next door is a striking inverted pyramid, the Law Courts Building. At the north end of the square is City Hall, and to the west is Edmonton Center, a climate-controlled complex of shops, restaurants, office towers and hotel. Immediately north of the square, behind City Hall, are the CN Tower, which houses the Via Rail station, and the Central Post Office.

A walk back to Jasper Ave. from Sir Winston Churchill Square and then west takes you past a variety of shops—try the Bay (the descen-dant of the Hudson's Bay Company) for Canadian sculpture and art. Some small galleries and the Canadiana Store are near 104th St.

The Alberta Legislature is located south of Jasper Ave. on 108th St. Built on the site of an early Fort Edmonton trading post, it was com-pleted in 1912. Tours of the building are available. The grounds, with manicured lawns, lovely gardens and a greenhouse, are open to the public and make for a delightful summer stop. If you walk down the hill through the grounds to 97th Ave. and cross the river on the James Macdonald Bridge, you'll come to the Muttart Conservatory, an imaginative botanical garden. Housed within five glass pyramids are tropical, desert, temperate and floral showcases. There is an excellent view of downtown from the reflecting pool at the base of the pyramids. (It is actually quite a long walk from the Legislature to the Muttart; a cab might be in order.)

Travel south of Jasper Ave. on 109th St. and cross the 160-ft. High Level Bridge (built in 1913). If you turn right onto 87th Ave., you'll reach the University of Alberta. Founded in 1908, this is Canada's third largest university, with more than 25,000 students. Buildings of interest are Rutherford House, 1153 Sask Dr., the former home of Alberta's first premier; the Hub Mall, a unique shopping center and residential complex, open to the public; the Geology Museum in the Agriculture Building; and the University Medical Complex.

One of the visitor highlights of Edmonton is Fort Edmonton, located on 158 acres of parkland on the south bank of the river, west of the University. A steam locomotive takes you from the parking lot to the early trading post, from which the city grew. The park also has restorations of streets from 1885, 1905, and 1920. Also worth a visit in the park is the John Janzen Nature Center.

As you leave Fort Edmonton, heading back toward the center of town, visit the Valley Zoo in Laurier Park—a must for children. The animal displays feature storybook characters and there are a miniature train, carousel and food concessions.

The drive from Laurier Park along 142nd St. to 102nd Ave. skirts three of Edmonton's most exclusive residential areas: Valleyview, Capital Heights and Old Glenora. Proceed right on 102nd Ave., east to the Provincial Museum at 128th St. Built in 1967, the museum displays artifacts of human and natural history in Alberta. One of the world's finest dinosaur exhibits, a superb collection of native crafts and remarkable geological section make this a rewarding stop. Also of interest is the beautiful old Lieutenant Governor's mansion. Admission is free. To get back downtown, proceed east on 102nd Ave., turn south at 124th St. to Jasper Ave., and then head back to 100th St.

PRACTICAL INFORMATION FOR EDMONTON

HOW TO GET THERE. By car: There is easy access by several interprovincial, state, and regional highways. **By train:** *Via Rail* serves Edmonton. **By bus:** *Greyhound* is the major carrier. **By air:** Edmonton is served by *Air Canada, C.P. Air, Pacific Western, Wardair, United, and Northwest Orient.*

ACCOMMODATIONS. Edmonton has a variety of hotel and motel accommodations. There is no provincial tax on accommodations, but most hotels and motels will charge for local phone calls. Price categories for double-occupancy are: *Deluxe,* $90 and up; *Expensive,* $60–90; *Moderate,* $40–60; *Inexpensive,* under $40.

Reservations are recommended at all times. Many hotels have toll-free numbers; or rooms can be booked through travel agents.

Most places accept the following major credit cards: American Express, MasterCard, and Visa; others may also be honored. Not all establishments accept credit cards, therefore we suggest you call for information.

YMCA, 10030 102A Ave., T5J 0G5. *YWCA,* 10305 100th Ave., T5J 0G5. Accommodation from $7.

University of Alberta, 44 Lister Hall, U. of A., T6G 2H6. Student residences are available from May through August only. (The residences involved are located at 87th Ave. and 116th St.)

Deluxe

The Edmonton Westin. 10135 100th St. 416 rooms and suites. Luxury accommodation with lobby bar, pool, Carvery Dining Room.

Four Seasons Hotel. One of the Four Seasons Group; 314 rooms, part of Edmonton Centre shopping/business complex. Best dining room in town, excellent coffee shop, good pub. Entertainment. Edmonton's best.

Expensive

Alberta Place. 10049 103rd St. 85 suites; kitchens. Excellent downtown location. A good buy.

Chateau Lacombe. 101th St. at Bellamy Hill. One of Canada's fine hotels with 320 rooms. A Canadian Pacific Hotel.

Convention Inn. Convenient southside location on Hwy. 2. 237 rooms, many in a new wing. Good dining room.

Edmonton Inn. Kingsway and 119th St. Interesting and well-managed hotel. 442 rooms. Edmonton's largest. Close to Municipal Airport.

Northwoods Inn. 10155 105th St. 102 newly renovated rooms. Pleasant public areas and restaurants.

Terrace Inn. 4440 Calgary Trail. On Hwy. 2. 228 rooms. Very attractive; good selection of restaurants and lounges; entertainment; pool.

Moderate

Capilano Motor Inn. 9125 50th St. Southeast location. 150 rooms. Air-conditioned, swimming pool, wheelchair facilities, licensed dining and cocktails.

Hillside Plaza Apartment Hotel. 9730 106th St. 100 3-room units with kitchenettes, color TV, telephones, private parking, sundeck. Convenient.

Renford Inn on Whyte. 10620 Whyte Ave. 90 rooms. Executive suites. Cable TV, sauna and health pool, dining and lounge. Convenient to university.

Mayfield Inn. Mayfield Rd. and 109th Ave. 250 rooms. Tennis courts, theater restaurant, licensed tavern, saunas. A fine complex, convenient to west end.

Sandman Inn. 17635 Stony Plain Rd. 150 clean, bright, air-conditioned rooms; swimming pool and all amenities.

Van Winkle Motor Lodge. 5116 103rd St. 196 units with TV, telephones, swimming pool, sauna and exercise rooms.

Inexpensive

Relax Inns. 2 locations: Southside: 10320 45th Ave. West End: 18320 Stony Plain Rd. Each has 227 units; reasonably priced, clean. Good hwy. locations. Good value.

HOSTELS. Edmonton Youth Hostel, 10422–91st St., T5H 1S6. Sleeping bag accommodation at $5.00 per night for CHA members or $7.50 per night for nonmembers.

HOW TO GET AROUND. By car: Hwy. 16 (the Yellowhead) is the major east/west route; Hwy. 2 the major north/south route. **By train:** *Via Rail* offers service to some major centers. **By transit and taxi:** Edmonton has an excellent transit system. Fare is 90¢ (exact change) on bus or rail transit. Cabs can be hailed or telephone ordered. Guided sightseeing tours are available from *Grayline* during the summer.

TOURIST INFORMATION. Comprehensive information about attractions, accommodations, prices and maps is available by writing to *Travel Alberta,* Capital Square, 14th Floor, 10065 Jasper Avenue, Edmonton, Alberta, Canada, T5J 0H4, or from *Edmonton Convention & Tourism Authority,* 500, 10123-99 St., Edmonton, T5J 3H1.

SEASONAL EVENTS. March: *Western Superrodeo.* **July:** *Klondike Days.* City-wide extravaganza during last 2 weeks that includes "Sourdough Raft Race" on first Sunday (essentially a flotilla of junk on the river); the "Promenade" later that same day (200,000 participants in Klondike-period clothing parading through the streets); lots of free entertainment. **August:** *Summerfest,* includes Jazz City, Folk Festival, Theater. **November:** Largest *rodeo (Canadian Finals)* of fall season.

CHILDREN'S ACTIVITIES. *Muttart Conservatory,* 98th Ave. and 96A St. Unique glass pyramids offering plant species representative of specific world climatic zones. Adults $2; Children $1.

John Janzen Nature Center; Whitemud Fwy. and Fox Dr., "hands-on" displays, films, special nature walks. Free.

Edmonton Space Science Center, 134th St. and 111th Ave. in Coronation Park. Multi-media productions of astral activities. Opening spring 1984.

Valley Zoo, Buena Vista Rd. and 134th St. Story-book fairytales form the theme for the exhibition of 500 birds and animals. Adults $2.25; children $1.

 SPORTS. Pride, joy and ecstasy could describe an Edmontonian's feeling for the three major professional teams, the *Eskimos* (CFL **football**), the *Oilers* (NHL **hockey**), and *Trappers* baseball. Yet, besides these clubs, there are hundreds of others, semi-pro and amateur, actively engaged in a myriad of competitive sports. Recreational participation in sports is a civic preoccupation. As a result, Edmonton is able to offer opportunities and facilities that are perhaps unequaled in Western Canada.

 CAMPING. *Shakers Acres,* Box 59, Winterburn, T0E 2N0 (on Hwy. 16, west at Winterburn overpass). 178 sites with food service, indoor pool, laundry and showers, groceries, and gameroom.

Glowing Embers, Hwy. 16 west and Hwy. 60, 273 sites, hook-ups, laundromat, store.

Klondike Valley, Box 2, Site 3, R.R. 1, Edmonton, T6E 0A6. 160 sites, laundry, groceries, showers, firewood.

 HISTORIC SITES. *McDougall Church* (at Ft. Edmonton Park) was the first Protestant church built in Edmonton. Today it is a museum.

John Walter Historic Site (southwest of 105 St. Bridge —location of the 1st home built on south side of the North Saskatchewan River in 1874. Also, site of first telegraph office (1879).

 MUSEUMS AND GALLERIES. Museums. *Geology Museum,* University of Alberta, 112 St. and Saskatchewan Drive. Free.

Fort Edmonton Park, Whitemud Fwy. and Fox Dr. (exit on south end of Quesnell Bridge). 178-acre site consisting of the reconstruction of an 1846 fort, a farm, and a "living" town featuring specific dated streets that trace Edmonton's history. Adults $4.00, youth $2.50, Senior Citizens and children (6 to 12) $2.00, preschoolers free.

Provincial Museum of Alberta, 12845 102nd Ave. Wildlife, Native history and culture, geology, fossils, dinosaurs, and Alberta's pioneer past. Free.

Strathcona Science Park, south of Hwy. 16 east on 17th St. A collection of displays which describe and interpret how Alberta's natural resources are put to use; plus the evidence of man's existence in prehistoric times featuring an actual "dig" for artifacts to 3000 B.C. Admission is free.

Ukrainian Museum of Canada, 10611 110th Ave. Costumes, Easter eggs, dolls, and tapestries are displayed. Free.

Galleries. *Beaver House,* 10158 103rd St., Alberta art. Free admission. *Edmonton Art Gallery,* 2 Sir Winston Churchill Sq., offers extras in the way of concerts, films, and theater. Free. *Ring House Gallery* at the University of Alberta (south of the Faculty Club off Saskatchewan Dr.). Free.

 PERFORMING ARTS. Music. The famous *Edmonton Symphony Orchestra* performs at the Jubilee Auditorium. *Edmonton Opera Society* features noted world stars within its numerous productions throughout the year. Music is very much a part of Edmonton's attitude and appetite, and the type of music played is as varied as the cultural background of the city.

Theater. *The Citadel Theatre,* with its most impressive facilities in uptown Edmonton, is close to being Canada's top-rated company. Its productions feature international name players. Additionally, Edmonton enjoys a healthy array of amateur companies that offer performances during various times of the year. One of the most successful dinner theaters in Canada is at the *Mayfield Inn.*

SHOPPING. Try *The Bay* for special Albertan products.

 DINING OUT. Edmonton is a highly cosmopolitan city. As a result, it likes to boast that it has ". . . an enchanting potpourri of cultures and tastes . . . you can eat in over twenty-four different languages.. . ." Discovering just how diversified is the Edmonton palate can be an exciting and satisfying part of your visit. You don't have to be afraid to try ethnic eateries here. They have to be good, for those who patronize know the difference between genuine and a hopeful imitation.

Restaurants are listed by price category as follows: *Deluxe,* $28 and over; *Expensive,* $19–28; *Moderate,* $13–19; *Inexpensive,* under $13. Prices include an appetizer or soup, entrée, and dessert. Drinks and tips are not included.

Most places accept the following major credit cards: American Express, MasterCard, and Visa; others may also be honored. Not all establishments accept credit cards, therefore we suggest you call for information.

Deluxe

Beans and Barley. 10309 81st Ave. A beautiful room. Specials usually pleasant. "4-B" soup is a must, the spinach salad outstanding.

Four Seasons Room. Four Seasons Hotel, 102nd Ave. & 101st St. A fine dining room with broad, imaginative menu. Worth the money.

Oliver's. 11730 Jasper Ave. A formal setting for some of the best beef in town. An ambitious menu with something for everyone.

Victor's. 10405 Jasper Ave. A private elevator lifts you to a candlelit dining room. Prompt service and Continental cuisine. A well-run establishment.

Waldens. 10245 104th St. Lush greenery and skylights. Beef, veal and fresh fish daily. Excellent vegetables.

Expensive

Between Friends. 8615 51st Ave. An inventive kitchen crew prepares beef, veal, pork and lamb. Leave room for dessert.

Bruno's. 8223 109th St. Italian food with the accent on northern dishes. Homemade paté, hearty minestrone. Scallopine Grand Duke is memorable.

Cosmos Greek Village. 10312 111th St. Greek all the way in food, service, and atmosphere.

The Crêperie. 10220 103rd St. (The Boardwalk). 16 different selections of crêpes offered in this delightful eatery in a renovated warehouse.

The Japanese Village. 10126 100th St. Japanese style flavored with "Teppan" adds a plus to a great restaurant.

Ling Nan. 10582 104th St. One of Edmonton's venerable Chinese restaurants. Personal attention, very large selection.

Tribes. 8006 103rd St. The cuisine of Canada's native peoples is showcased. Cree and Coastal Indian recipes are used. Buffalo, rabbit and whitefish.

Moderate

Bistro Praha. 10168 100A St. A bohemian gathering place. Large portions of hearty fare served in an air of informality.

Bones. 10201 104th St. Hickory-smoked ribs and chicken. Good burgers. Enthusiastic service.

The Courtyard. Four Seasons Hotel. This is the less formal of the hotel's two restaurants. An excellent variety of food, carefully prepared.

Cucci's. Sun Life Bldg. 99th St. and Jasper Ave. Reasonably priced continental fare. Pleasant surroundings and attentive service.

Dagwoods Deli. Melton Bldg., 10310 Jasper Ave. Hearty soups, smoked meat and all your old favorites.

Mongolian Food Experience. 100A St. and 101st Ave. The chef stir-fries vegetables and meat to your taste. Unique in Edmonton.

Red Diamond House. 7500 82 Ave. Not downtown but worth the trip. Reliable Cantonese cooking. Hot pots a specialty.

Steakboard. 10220 103rd St., located in the Boardwalk. Good steak and well-stocked salad bar. Steak sandwich is the best buy.

Trapper John's Trading Post. 10355–105 St. Western-town setting, with Campfire ribs, Goldmine Chicken and Fools' Gold. Good salad bar.

Inexpensive

High Level Diner. 109th St. and Sask Dr. A cheery place popular with the younger set. Inventive menu, desserts worth the anticipation.

Merryland. 7006 109th St. Basic Korean food and basic décor. Good food and value.

Strathcona Gasthaus. 8120 101st St. Hearty German fare and large portions. Excellent value in down-to-earth setting. Closes early. Unlicensed. No reservations, no credit cards.

 NIGHTCLUBS AND BARS. Edmonton takes a back seat to no city when it comes to night entertainment. Nightclubs, cabarets, taverns, lounges, and that infamous Alberta watering hole—the beer parlor—combine to provide a constant offering of local and international artists.

EXPLORING ALBERTA'S ROCKIES

In prehistoric times, this part of North America was a shallow sea. Violent geological changes then occurred and the sea bed was thrust upward to become a marshy, swampy lowland. About 70 million years ago, the cataclysmic forces that were shaping the earth brought tremendous rock movements to the Alberta/British Columbia region . . . movements that left the region with its present-day configuration.

The bedrock of the Rocky Mountains consists of ancient Paleozoic deposits of the Cambrian Age, their foothills being of Tertiary, a later geological deposit. The forces of wind, water and glacial action were at work all those millions of years, shaping the character of the mountains and valleys of Alberta's Rockies.

Four major and distinct regions have been established to protect and preserve the beauty and the wilderness of Alberta's mountain park regions: Waterton National Park in the south, Banff National Park in the center, Jasper National Park in the north, and the Rocky Mountain Forest Reserve to the east.

Three major east/west highways pass through this mountain terrain. In the north, the Yellowhead Highway leads from Edmonton to Jasper, and thence on to Kamloops in British Columbia. In the center, the Trans-Canada Highway from Calgary leads through Banff and Lake Louise to Golden in British Columbia. In the south the number 3, or Crowsnest Pass Highway, leads from Lethbridge through the Crowsnest to Cranbrook, B.C. Two routes travel north/south. The paved Icefield Parkway runs from Jasper to Lake Louise through the most beautiful portion of the Rockies. The mostly gravelled Adventure Highway winds a leisurely and spectacular path along the eastern slopes of the Rocky Mountains from Grande Prairie to Coleman.

Three Primary Zones

Using a criterion of distinguishing life zones through the variations of forest cover, botanists have identified several primary zones in the mountain parks. The treeless alpine tundra is the highest life zone and is found above the 7,200-foot level; it resembles the rolling tundra of the Arctic and supports only a growth of scrub, grasses and lichens. The growing season at this level is very short, and the winds gust at speeds far greater than those in the valleys below.

The mid-zone—the sub-alpine—supports heavy stands of spruce and alpine fir. It experiences less wind velocity and has an altogether more accommodating climate.

The Montana forest is found on southerly exposed slopes and in valley bottoms below 4,500 feet. In this region cottonwoods, poplars, birches, spruce, pine and fir form a relatively dense forest. Animals are in abundance too. Squirrels, chipmunks, beaver, muskrat, porcupine, bear (black and grizzly), elk, deer, moose, goats and sheep.

The Beginnings of National Parks

The Rocky Mountains were first sighted by white men in 1754 when Anthony Henday came within 100 miles of them. It wasn't until 1800 that the first known crossing of the main ranges by white men occurred when two Northwest voyageurs named Le Blanc and La Gassi crossed via Howse Pass near the Banff/Jasper National Park border. David Thompson (who has had a highway leading from Howse Pass to Rocky Mountain House named for him) crossed the mountains in 1807 by way of this pass and established the first fur-trading post in the Columbia River Valley.

In the first half of the 1800's the mountains were visited by innumerable fur traders, mountain men, explorers, gold seekers, settlers, even by artist Paul Kane, and a pair of British spies. In 1881 Major A.B.

Rogers, an American surveyor of Scots descent in the employ of the Canadian Pacific Railway, discovered the Rogers Pass through the formidable high Selkirks. As the railroad snaked through the Rockies, a number of rough-and-ready mining towns sprang into existence including Anthracite, Bankhead, and Silver City. Their lifespan was short; they had their moment of two-fisted excitement and glory, then withered and died as quickly as they had come to life.

In 1887 William Van Horne, the brains and driving force of the Canadian Pacific Railway, convinced Ottawa that a certain amount of land should be set aside for public enjoyment at a beautiful railroad encampment named Banff. The attraction here was not only the spectacular scenery, but also the hot mineral springs located at the base of Sulphur Mountain. This was the beginning of Canada's National Park system.

Not long after, the first 10 square miles of park preserve were increased to 260 square miles, and in 1892 a further 50-square-mile area was set aside at Lake Louise. In 1888, believing that the scenery and the hot mineral springs would attract visitors, the C.P.R. opened the Banff Springs Hotel for business.

Phillip Abbott gained a dubious niche in the history of Canada's National Parks by becoming the first alpinist to die in the attempt to ascend a mountain: the 11,230-foot Mount Lefroy near Lake Louise, one that over the years has claimed the lives of many adventurers.

It wasn't until 1907 that Jasper National Park (in anticipation of the trans-continental railway system that would run through Edmonton and utilize the Yellowhead Pass) was established. Today, Banff National Park takes in 2,564 square miles, Jasper National Park an additional 4,200 square miles, and Waterton Lakes National Park 203 square miles.

Banff National Park

After leaving Calgary, the Trans-Canada Highway begins to climb as it winds its way west. The ranchland foothills gain character and ruggedness with every passing mile. Some 55 miles west from Calgary, it meets Alberta's north-south "Adventure Highway."

The Trans-Canada Highway follows the Bow River and the Via Rail Services rail tracks past an excellent campground at Bow Valley Provincial Park. The eastern entrance to Banff National Park is located at Canmore which is dominated by the Three Sisters peaks.

Within the first four miles, two picnic areas are encountered: Carrot Creek and Valley View. From Valley View a fascinating look at the northeast side of Mount Rundle may be enjoyed. What is seen is the drop-off face of the mountain, the portion that was torn straight out of the earth and pushed upwards by incredible geological forces. Mount Rundle extends some 10 miles along the edge of the Bow Valley.

Tunnel Mountain junction intersects the Trans-Canada Highway and is a secondary route into Banff townsite. This road partially climbs Tunnel Mountain, passes by a stand of rock sentinels known as the Hoodoos—geological oddities that are the product of glacial action, erosion and time—and continues on through the 868-site Tunnel

Mountain campground goes past some excellent rental chalets and motels and winds back down Tunnel Mountain to enter Banff itself.

The junction leading to Lake Minnewanka is a loop drive well worth exploring. Only a little more than eight miles long, this drive leads to Two Jack Lake, Johnson Lake and Lake Minnewanka. The fishing is great here; boats are available for rental during the summer months.

This short drive continues on, eventually bisecting the ghost coal town of Bankhead. Bankhead closed its mines in 1922 when it was no longer profitable to work its mediocre seams. Today, Nature is creeping back and little of Bankhead remains.

This loop road rejoins the Trans-Canada Highway just two miles from where it first left. At this point, Cascade Mountain looms, with its near-perfect profile of rock. A cascade of water—from which the mountain derives its name—may be seen gushing from the center of this gigantic rock, crashing down the side in a misty cloud of spray.

A traffic circle here allows easy east-west access to the Trans-Canada Highway or direct access to the town of Banff. A small herd of plains buffalo are kept at the buffalo paddock on the way into Banff; a roadway winds through this enclosure enabling visitors to search out and see the animals at closer range.

Banff

The town of Banff has a population of 4,627 people. It lies nestled in the valley of the Bow River encircled by imposing mountains—Rundle, Cascade, Norquay, and Sulphur. Banff Avenue is the main street and it bisects nearly the entire town.

Banff is a year-round resort. In winter, the slopes of Mount Norquay are tremendously popular, attracting skiers from all over the world. A few miles away, Sunshine has the best snow conditions in the Canadian Rockies with an average of 400 inches per season. The ski season at Sunshine normally begins in November and can last to the end of May.

In the other than winter seasons, Banff is a playground. Most visitors come here to simply wander, see, and relax. The very atmosphere of Banff is soothing. Its days are warm and its evenings are cool.

Animals of the mountains and forest are in abundance. It is not unusual to see a black bear at the side of the road . . . or elk wandering through the grounds of a motel . . . or deer patroling the streets of Banff in the evening.

Never a Dull Moment

Many interesting shops are featured in Banff, selling Irish linen, British woolens, china and Canadian Native crafts. There are also retailers displaying the product of local artisans.

Recreation in the form of canoe trips on the river, horseback riding on forest and alpine trails, bicycling on footpaths, or hiking and climbing occupies a great deal of the vacationer's holiday. Rental of all necessary equipment is readily available and moderately priced. The tourist office of the Banff/Lake Louise Chamber of Commerce (located on Banff Avenue) is able to provide full information.

Several activities are on the "must" list for any visit to Banff. The time spent touring the Luxton Museum and the Natural History Museum is assuredly worth while. A game of golf on the incredible Banff Springs Hotel Golf Course is an experience that even non-golfers enjoy. A trip to the top of either Sulphur Mountain or Mount Norquay is a good idea. Gondolas gently hoist you to the summit of Sulphur Mountain, and the view from there is understated when using an adjective such as superb. A charming tea house adds to the pleasures. The same descriptions hold true for Norquay. Here, there is a choice of either gondola or chairlift. The faint of heart may decide to choose an enclosed gondola.

Hot Hot Springs

You should also experience a swim in the Upper Hot Springs pool near the Sulphur Mountain gondola lift. Banff first aroused interest because of its hot springs. The C.P.R. built the Banff Springs Hotel because (aside from the beauty of the area) they believed the public would come to sample the health-restoring attributes of the warm, sulphurous waters. So there is no reason why a visitor to Banff today should not enjoy a similar invigorating plunge into the Upper Hot Springs. A note of caution: enter the water slowly and carefully, allowing your body to become accustomed to the high temperature. Do not stay too long, for the bath does drain body energies.

Following the euphoric dip, the visitor's curiosity may be aroused enough to want to see the Cave and Basin Spring which is the actual birthplace of Canada's National Parks. This original spring was in use in the 1800's. Bathers then had to descend into the cave from a hole in the roof of the cave. Today, access is easier, by way of a tunnel bored into the inner chamber. The top temperature of these waters is generally 33°C (91°F), varying to a few degrees under that.

The road that passes by the Cave and Basin Pool continues on past marshes that are an overflow flat of the Bow River. The forest closes in once again and a little farther on is the entrance to Sundance Canyon and picnic area. A one and a half mile hiking trail, leading up along the tumbling waterfalls of Sundance Creek, is well worth taking.

There are many interesting drives to take in the Banff town area. The drive through the Banff Springs Golf Course, the School of Fine Arts/Tunnel Mountain drive and the Vermilion Lakes drive are all enjoyable trips amid beautiful scenery. Perhaps the best of all is the spectacular, switchback Mount Norquay drive. This begins at the Trans-Canada Highway at the west end of Banff and meanders up the mountain, climbing 1,000 feet to end at the base of the Norquay chairlift.

Thirty Beautiful Miles

Visitors to Banff, who have never explored deeper into the Canadian Rockies, may feel that nature simply could not be more beautiful. That would be a mistake. The scenery of the Rockies does become more beautiful. The Trans-Canada Highway leading west to Lake Louise is in itself a continuation of that beauty. There is also an alternate route—

the 1A Highway, which allows an even more leisurely and relaxing tour.

The distance from Banff to Lake Louise is 30 miles (via the 1A Highway) and access can be gained to it about 3½ miles west of Banff. This is an area populated by Bighorn sheep and mountain goat. It is not uncommon to see these animals calmly grazing by the roadside.

A few miles ahead on the 1A is an interesting picnic area called Muleshoe Lake. This spot is the home of a colony of gophers, or more correctly, Columbian ground squirrels. Here also is the entrance to a short—less than a mile—steep nature trail which leads through a montane-type forest to an excellent meadow for viewing the surrounding countryside. A further 2,000 feet above, in the rock wall of Mount Cory, you will see the black opening of the Hole-In-The-Wall cavern. The mountains here rise up to 10,000 feet.

One of the most popular hikes along the 1A is the trek into Johnston's Canyon. The trail begins at Johnston's Canyon Bungalow Camp and proceeds to the Lower Falls about ¾ of a mile distant. Most visitors end their tours here; however, if you are able, continue the hike a further mile to the Upper Falls and ultimately to the Ink Pots, two more miles beyond the Upper Falls. The canyon runs into a meadow beyond the Upper Falls and a group of cold water springs are located there. Two of the pools are of a turquoise green and murky hue. Apparently, their color is caused by the water percolating through quicksand, causing silt to remain in suspension.

Several miles beyond Johnston's Canyon, an open alpine meadow is all that remains of Silver City. Coming into life with the railroad in 1883, Silver City once had a population of 2,000 occupying themselves searching for copper and silver. Things not only didn't pan out, they didn't mine out either—and by 1886 Silver City had gone the way of many towns like it. From this area a magnificent view of Castle Mountain (known briefly as Mt. Eisenhower) can be seen.

From this point to the junction of Lake Louise, the highway passes through extensive stands of lodge pole pine. It is interesting to note that this particular tree proliferates generally only after a forest fire, for it takes heat in excess of 100°F to cause the cones to burst and release the seeds. Thousands of acres of forest were ravaged by fires during the construction of the Canadian Pacific railroad and the years when spark-throwing, steam locomotives were used.

Lake Louise

Tom Wilson, a member of a survey party of the C.P.R., was told of the Lake of the Little Fishes by Indians. It was the summer of 1882 and Wilson followed the Indians to the shore. He stood on the bank where, in later years, the great Château was erected. He looked upon that jewel of a scene that was to become known as one of the ten natural wonders of the world. He named it Emerald Lake. This was soon changed to Louise in honor of the wife of the Governor-General of Canada at that time.

It's a winding, climbing 1½ miles of good road from Lake Louise village to the lake. On any average summer's day the cold, green-blue water provides a perfect mirror image of the 11,365-foot Mount Victoria and its glacier. Two adjacent mountains—the Beehive on the right and Fairview Mountain on the left—complete the portrait by forming a "V" in the center of the pictorial wonder.

Lake Louise, as with most mountain lakes, is far too cold for swimming. However, you can rent canoes from a concession area near the Chateau Lake Louise. Here again, a number of fine hiking trails can provide hours of stimulating and inspiring recreation. From the Saddle-Back trail, leisurely hikers can reach a good viewpoint two and a half miles away. The Lakes in the Clouds trail proceeds on a steady climb that takes in Mirror Lake and Lake Agnes in the course of its 3½ miles. During the summer, visitors can stop at Agnes Tea House for refreshments and light meals. Another teahouse serves those who trek the Plain-of-the-Six Glaciers trail. This 4-mile trail follows the shore line of Lake Louise and proceeds beyond the gap to allow hikers a closer view of Victoria Glacier and Mount Lefroy.

There are many fascinating, short side trips in the Rockies that are missed by some visitors as they hurry through. The Valley of the Ten Peaks, with its exquisite Moraine Lake, is one such side trip. Just three quarters of a mile east of the Lake Louise road on the 1A highway, a smaller side road branches to the south and continues some eight miles to this lake. During the peak visitor season a lodge supplies accommodation and meals, as well as canoe rentals.

The Icefield Parkway

Perhaps the most stunning stretch of highway in Canada is this 144-mile ribbon of broad pavement connecting the Trans-Canada Highway with the town of Jasper to the north. Scaling two passes on its way—Bow Summit, 6,700 feet, and Sunwapta Pass, 6,700 feet, the parkway approaches the uppermost limits of timberline. Wildlife is in abundance the entire length and the grandeur of the panorama is beyond description.

Entrance is gained to the Icefield Parkway 1 mile west of the Lake Louise Village exit. The striking reddish rock at this juncture is some of the oldest to be found in the Rockies. Dating back some 600 million years, this rock was once part of an ocean floor.

To really savor all that this route offers, take your time. There are numerous picnic areas, viewpoints, lakes and trails that should be visited to gain the full enjoyment and impact of this alpine wonderland. For example, within the first 12 miles, travelers hurrying on their way could easily miss Herbert and Hector Lakes and the Hanging Valley point-of-interest. This would be a shame, for it is not true that once you have seen one lake you have seen them all. Although most have been carved by glacial action, each is unique and each offers its own surprises within its silent beauty.

Approximately 21 miles north is the Crowfoot Glacier viewpoint. Perched on the cliffs above the blue-green tranquility of Bow Lake, two great toes of the glacial foot are seen. About 70 years ago there was a third, lower toe dipping down into the forest. The ravages of time and the weather have taken their toll—or in this case, the toe. Trails lead away from this point, climbing to Helen and Katherine lakes and the Dolomite Pass. This is roughly a 12-mile walk.

In the early part of this century many guides and outfitters traveled along this highway. Before this area was a national park (and as such, a game preserve) hunting was a popular sport. Parties of the wealthy came from all parts of Europe to enjoy the hunt and the wilderness.

At the headwaters of the Bow River nestles one of the most beautiful lakes in the park, and certainly one of the two most magnificent waters along the Icefield Parkway. A range of peaks provide a glorious background for Bow Lake. Portions of glaciers bejewel the limestone cliffs and crevasses and all is mirrored in crystalline waters. Before the highway was built Num-ti-Jah Lodge was accessible only on horseback, via a winding trail from Lake Louise. Now, this lodge is open all year round; in the winter it caters to the cross-country skiers.

Streams Flow North and South

At Bow Summit (6,700 feet), streams, formed by glacial melt, separate—some flowing north and others flowing south. This is the beginning of the two immense, prairie drainage systems that become the North and South Saskatchewan Rivers. The South Saskatchewan joins the North in the province of Saskatchewan. The great river's journey continues eastward until ultimately it empties into the Hudson Bay.

A secondary road here leads to the Peyto Lake viewpoint, not quite a mile away. A short distance from the parking lot a dramatic viewing position can be reached. Eight hundred feet below lie the beautiful and serene Peyto Lake and the Mistaya Valley. This lake is also fed by the glacial runoff from the Peyto Glacier, which is visible to the southwest, as a tongue of the Wapta Icefield.

Two exploration trails lead off from this position. One travels downward to the edge of the lake. The other continues to climb, ending at the Bow Fire Lookout (1½ miles away). The second trail features meadows covered with wild flowers which bloom in July and August.

Once again, a reminder is in order, do not miss the many, thrilling viewpoints studding this highway. They are all well worth the time taken. If you are able to afford to spend even extra time, be sure to pursue the delights of the short hiking trails—for example, Mistaya Canyon Trail, a short section of which leads to the gorge of the Mistaya Canyon. Crossing the bridge, other trails may be taken to reach Sarbach Lookout about three miles away; and, for the serious adventurer, to Howse Pass 17 miles distant.

Just after the Saskatchewan River warden station, an interpretive trailer has been located during summer months for the last few years. This center offers interesting and factual information regarding the early and ongoing human history in this area, as well as its natural history. This point is also the junction of the David Thompson Highway, which leads eastward, following the North Saskatchewan River out of the mountains and on to the prairie of Alberta. It eventually terminates at Red Deer, 160 miles to the east. Also, from a viewpoint at this position Mount Wilson (10,500 feet) and Mount Murchison (nearly 11,000 feet) may be seen. This is certainly an area that one

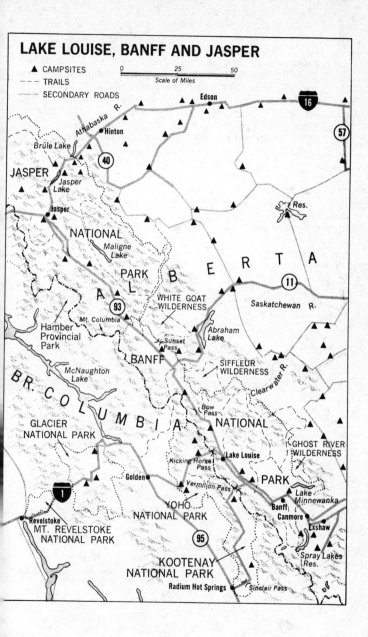

LAKE LOUISE, BANFF AND JASPER

▲ CAMPSITES
--- TRAILS
— SECONDARY ROADS

Scale of Miles
0   25   50

Athabaska R.

Edson

16

57

Hinton

Brûle Lake

40

JASPER

Jasper Lake

Jasper

NATIONAL

Maligne Lake

Res.

A L B E R T A

PARK

11

WHITE GOAT WILDERNESS

Saskatchewan R.

93

Mt. Columbia

Sunset Pass

Abraham Lake

Hamber Provincial Park

BANFF

SIFFLEUR WILDERNESS

McNaughton Lake

B R.   C O L U M B I A

Clearwater R.

Bow Pass

GLACIER NATIONAL PARK

NATIONAL

GHOST RIVER WILDERNESS

Kicking Horse Pass

Lake Louise

PARK

1

Golden

Vermilion Pass

Lake Minnewanka

Revelstoke

MT. REVELSTOKE NATIONAL PARK

YOHO NATIONAL PARK

Banff

Canmore

Exshaw

95

KOOTENAY NATIONAL PARK

Spray Lakes Res.

Radium Hot Springs

Sinclair Pass

should plan on exploring. The Parkway Lodge Saskatchewan River Crossing is open throughout the summer season with 68 units, a general store, gift shop and a variety of dining facilities.

Continuing on to Sunwapta Pass and the Columbia Icefields, the scenery gets even more impressive. Some of the more important viewpoints are: Marshlands (an excellent environment for moose); Weeping Wall (featuring water "flows" over limestone cliffs, and a fine opportunity to observe the results of incredible earth forces exerted on the solid rock in the ridges and mountains to the north); both north Saskatchewan Valleys (offering superb views of the Saskatchewan River Valley); and Panther Falls (with two waterfalls—Bridal Veil across the valley, and Panther).

The Parkers Ridge Trail offers ecologically minded travelers a chance to explore a seemingly rugged yet actually delicate environment. This trail ascends above the treeline to approximately 7,000 feet. Here the growing season is short—a few weeks annually—and in some years it is never entirely frost-free. Nature works slowly in locales like this. In the hospitable climes and atmosphere of sea level, the growth rate and replacement of various forms of landlife are considered in terms of seasons; but at this altitude it is considered in decades.

At Sunwapta Pass (6,600 feet) is the watershed divide of the North Saskatchewan system and the Athabasca system draining even further to the north. The Athabasca flows into the Mackenzie and eventually reaches the Arctic Ocean. This is also the boundary between Banff and Jasper National Parks.

Jasper National Park

Jasper National Park is rich in history. The effect of glacial activity is extensive and is seen everywhere. The passes, formed by great natural upheavals, and the valleys, carved by massive ice flows, were traversed by explorers and fur traders crossing the Rockies.

The park was named after Jasper House, established in 1811 at Brule Lake by the Northwest Company. Essentially a supply station for fur traders crossing the moutains, Jasper House was taken over by the Hudson's Bay Company during the 1820's. Its first factor was Jasper Hawes.

In 1846 Paul Kane—the artist whose paintings of northwestern United States and western Canada gave the world its first pictorial impressions of this magnificent wilderness—had this to say about Jasper House:

> Jasper's House consists of only three miserable log huts. The dwelling-house is composed of two rooms, of about 14 or 15 feet square each. One of them is used by all comers and goers: Indians, voyageurs, and traders, men, women and children being huddled together indiscriminately; the other room being devoted to the exclusive occupation of Colin (the chief Factor) and his family, consisting of a Cree squaw, and nine interesting half-breed children.

The more than 600 miles of hiking trails and profusion of alpine meadows and deep blue lakes make this park a paradise to those who enjoy hiking, photography, and fishing. The hiking trails consist of both the short-distance strolls and the longer, more rugged walks.

Most of the Park's larger lakes offer good boating and canoeing. Rentals . . . even cruises (on Maligne Lake) are available to those of more leisurely, relaxed tastes. In the meadows of high alpine ranges the snow is slow to melt in the spring; as a result, wildflowers do not bloom until mid-July. The warmth of summer comes earlier in the lush and tranquil mountain valleys, where flowers are a full month earlier in reaching their colorful glory.

It is not unusual for visitors traveling the Icefield Parkway to suffer a certain degree of weariness at this point. It seems that a personal involvement with so much grandeur has its effect. With every mile, every dip, every rise, every turn of the road, a startling new scene of grandeur attacks eyes and minds. Beauty piles on beauty. Magnificence upon magnificence. Inspiration is absorbed to such an extent that senses, emotions and intellectual capacity are overwhelmed.

Columbia Icefield

The Columbia Icefield is 60 miles south of Jasper townsite. This is the largest body of ice in the Rocky Mountains and it covers 150 square miles. Glaciers are formed by periods of intense snowfall. The layers of snow on the bottom are pulverized and pressurized into hard glacial ice. The advancement takes place in a direct ratio between the snowfall and the front end melt. At one time most of North America was covered by such vast bodies of ice. The Columbia Icefield actually feeds many glaciers (which are termed tongues) radiating from the central ice mass. The particular glacier here is called Athabasca.

The Athabasca Glacier is currently both advancing and retreating. The rate of melt at its toe is greater than its downward flow; thus it retreats at the rate of approximately 30 feet per year. As it retreats it leaves a glacial deposit. This is known as moraine. This moraine is for the most part rock debris, or small triangular pieces of rock showing signs of dragging and pulverization. It is interesting to note that the retreat of some glaciers in the world (specifically Siberia) has left behind the carcasses of whole animals, such as mammoths.

About nine miles past Columbia Icefields we come upon Stanley Falls. This point is easy to miss; however, you should keep a careful watch for it, for it is one of the more picturesque cascades along the highway. The old highway runs adjacent to the forest. At the mouth of Beauty Creek Canyon there is a gap in the road where an old bridge was sited. Stanley Falls is just a short distance above. The mountains gain in height, and at the Sunwapta River viewpoint Diadem Peak rises to more than 11,000 feet. In the distance the even taller Mount Kitchener can be seen.

Elk, Mountain Goat, and Bighorn

The Athabasca Valley viewpoint is an excellent locale from which to scan the broad Athabasca Valley. As for wildlife, this section of the highway from Mount Christie picnic area through to Goat viewpoint offers some of the best opportunities to see elk, mountain goat, and bighorn sheep.

It is a good idea to leave the Icefield Park Highway at its junction with Highway 93A. This is a 15-mile, alternate highway that takes a more scenic route. It rejoins the Icefield Parkway approximately five miles south of Jasper townsite.

Immediately after entering the 93A highway, Athabasca Falls is encountered. This is definitely one of the more spectacular and popular scenic diversions in the Rockies. These falls are a major point of interest and are characterized by the awesome power of water generated by the Athabasca River being forced through a narrow gap in the walls of the canyon.

At Athabasca Trail point-of-interest, raise a glass of crystal water and join the ghosts of early fur traders in drinking a toast in honor of the chiefs of the Hudson's Bay Company. This historical tradition was started by George Simpson who crossed the pass in 1824. David Thompson made the earliest recorded ford of this confluence of the Whirlpool and Athabasca rivers during the winter of 1810–11. This historical spot saw many voyageurs and explorers pass on their way to and from the settlement of Boat Encampment on the Columbia River, on the western side of the high Rockies.

Approximately 12 miles along this alternate roadway the intersection with Mount Edith Cavell Road is reached. This is a narrow, nine-mile-long road leading to the base of the 11,000-foot Mount Edith Cavell—the highest mountain in this section of the park. Once known as Montagne de la Grande Traverse to the early voyageurs (because it was their landmark to the Whirlpool Valley and the Athabasca Pass) this mountain was renamed after World War I to commemorate the heroism of the British nurse who was executed by the Germans. A trail from the parking lot leads to an exquisite and winding way to Angel Glacier. During peak tourist season this area is extremely popular and at times can become congested. Just before the alternate highway rejoins the Icefields Parkway, it reaches Marmot Basin. Marmot Basin is a ski area in wintertime.

Jasper

Although the Jasper townsite vicinity was a wilderness throughout the 1800's, there was a regular traffic of explorers, traders, Indians and missionaries traveling to and from the Columbia River in British Columbia. The park itself was created in 1907 by the Canadian government.

There had been one house (Henry's House) near the Jasper townsite since the early 1800's. This was another supply station for the trade traffic. The actual development of the town did not occur until the arrival of the Grand Trunk Pacific Railway in 1911. At that time the town was known as Fitzhugh; but it was changed to Jasper in 1913. The Canadian National railroad was completed in 1915 and this line eventually absorbed the Grand Trunk. By World War I, the first visitor facilities had been constructed on the shores of nearby Lac Beauvert. Jasper Park Lodge was not completed until early in the 1920's by the Canadian National Railway.

Today, Jasper is a town of 4,000 people whose main employers are the CN railroad and tourism industries. The townsite is pretty enough in itself; yet, its great advantage to visitors is its proximity to a number of magnificent scenic attractions.

The Pyramid Lake drive is a good example. It's a five-mile road northward from Jasper to a pair of lakes at the foot of Pyramid Mountain. This mountain is one of the best known landmarks near the town and a very popular picnicking spot. The two lakes are known as Pyramid Lake and Patricia Lake. At Pyramid Lake you can cross a foot-bridge to a tiny island.

Lake F-stop 11

Two miles east of Jasper, the Yellowhead Highway intersects with the Maligne Lake Road, which road runs for about 28 miles up the Maligne Valley, reaching one of the top five beauty spots in the Canadian Rockies. Maligne Canyon, 6 miles from the highway, is a spectacular gorge. Nature has sculptured the limestone to a depth of 180 feet and decorated it with deep turquoise pools, underground rivers and waterfalls cascading from all sides. The canyon features many bridges and viewpoints, all constructed to make full enjoyment easier. Maligne Lake stretches for nearly 14 miles through the mountains, at an elevation of 5,400 feet. The main parking areas are located at the northwest end of the lake and a tour boat office and chalet are in the general area. The tour is worthwhile. Make sure you get to photograph the lake's "Spirit Island" (recently rechristened "f11" because it is perhaps the most photographed vista in the Canadian Rockies).

Another interesting secondary trip out of Jasper is the Valley Lakes tour. You can reach this road by crossing the tracks at Hazel Avenue and Connaught Drive intersection. The road continues crossing the Yellowhead Highway and reaches a left-hand turnoff to Lac Beauvert and Old Fort Point (the site of Henry's House). Jasper Park Lodge is situated on Lac Beauvert. After following the lake and passing through the lodge grounds, this road continues northward to a right-hand branch which carries on to Annette and Edith Lakes. The road loops and you can return the way you came or continue on to Maligne Canyon—a short distance to the east.

If you feel like climbing a mountain the easy way, you might be interested in a visit to Whistler Mountain and the Jasper Sky Tram. To reach this aerial tramway, head south of Jasper and turn right at the Whistler Mountain road. The lower terminal offers good views of the Athabasca and Miette valleys, but, at an elevation of nearly 7,500 feet, the upper terminal offers a much more impressive panorama.

Five miles inside the park's east entrance gate, and 27 miles northeast of the Jasper townsite, is the Pocahantas turnoff. A further ten miles on Pocahantas brings travelers to the Miette Hot Springs resort area. The crystal-clear mineral waters, with temperatures up to 126°F, cooled to 98° for visitor comfort, have been advertised as being beneficial to those troubled with muscular ailments, rheumatism, arthritis, or circulatory disorders. The baths are stimulating, but it is the hiking, trailriding, fishing, climbing and photography that are the great attractors.

The Yellowhead Highway continues east from the National Park gates to the town of Hinton, some 45 miles from Jasper.

The Adventure Highway

From Hinton the incredible Adventure Highway runs south to the American border through the beauty of the eastern slopes of the Rockies. The road also extends 200 miles north from Hinton to Grande Prairie; but in this chapter the way south will be highlighted.

It is precisely what it has been named . . . an adventure highway. Much of its surface is gravel, so travelers should check out the weather conditions along its entirety. Portions of the road are sometimes be closed due to risk of forest fire. This is not a road that is suitable for towing large trailers; it leads into the backwoods. Although there are many Ranger Stations and exit roads leading you east to civilization, it should be remembered that this road travels south for more than 400 miles, and many services often taken for granted on ordinary highways are not available. It would be wise to carry at least minimal survival gear—sleeping bags, ground sheets, large axe, flashlight, extra batteries, waxed matches, fish line, and most important, a first aid kit. An ample supply of insect repellent will also help to always make life more comfortable.

Service stations in the forest areas are few and far between so make sure you have a full tank and a serviceable spare tire before setting out. As mentioned before, this road has a gravel surface and dust can be a hazard.

The region is a tremendous water shed storage area. It is estimated that about 90 percent of the water supply for the western prairies of Canada is stored here. The provincial forestry area covers 27,000 square miles, primarily of white spruce and lodge-pole pine. This huge wildland provides opportunities for extensive outdoor interests. The fishin' streams and the fishin' holes are all here in abundance. A myriad of hiking trails lead off west and east from the full length of this highway. More than 60 recreation areas have been established here by the Alberta Forest Service.

The road travels south through timber and coal leases. The town of Nordegg, once a thriving coal community, was closed down in the 1950's and became a modern-day ghost town. At Nordegg is the major junction with the David Thompson Highway. This highway leads to Red Deer in the east and to the Icefields Parkway in the west. Just south of Nordegg, Ram River Falls cascades over high rock ledges and provides a dramatic backdrop for picnics and camping.

Kananaskis Country

You will come to the junction of Highway 1A. Travel west on 1A to regain access to the newly paved Kananaskis Route 40. On this short, 17-mile, hard-surfaced detour you will find the historical McDougall Church on the Stoney Indian Reserve, the Indian Agency at Morley, and Stoney Indian Park, with its ruins of Piegan Post which was active in the fur-trading business in 1832.

Kananaskis Country is a 1,600 square-mile, multi-use recreational area developed by the provincial government. Spectacular scenery and new facilities for camping, boating, hiking, cycling, fishing and golf make this a marvelous region to explore. It will be the site of the Alpine events of the 1988 Winter Olympic Games.

Route 40 passes the Kananaskis Experimental Station—now a federal forestry research operation, but during the Second World War a camp for German prisoners—and Kananaskis Provincial Park (40 miles south of Highway 1A), a 508 square mile wilderness with magnificent valleys and high-altitude lakes.

60 miles south, the gravel resumes at Highwood Pass, the highest drivable pass in Canada (7,234 feet). From December 1 to June 15, the road south of the park and the pass are closed due to weather conditions and migrating elk.

The streams that this road traverses drain onto the prairies. In this area some of the world's most difficult white water is found; indeed, the authorities have labeled some of them as deadly to canoeists of any experience.

The road joins east/west Highway 3 at Coleman. This is the Crowsnest Pass country and not far from here is the location of the Frank Slide. It was four o'clock on the morning of April 29, 1903, that a section of Turtle Mountain tumbled and crashed into the valley. It partially destroyed the town of Frank and forced abandonment of the remainder. Ninety million tons of rock swept over a mile of the valley and completed its devastation within two minutes, killing 70. Near here is the site of Massacre Butte where 12 men, women and children in an immigrant train were massacred in 1867 by a party of Blood Indians. This train was a part of Captain Fiske's expedition from Minnesota to Oregon. It had left the main party in Montana, following a rumor that there was gold to the north.

Traveling east from Coleman on Highway 3, and south on Highway 6, you will reach Waterton National Park.

Waterton National Park

Waterton National Park adjoins the Glacier National Park in Montana. Together, they form what is known as the International Peace Park. Waterton is a jewel; small, only 203 square miles, it provides a maximum of scenery in a minimum of space. It's unique, too, in that visitors pass abruptly from rolling prairie into steep-walled mountain valleys. The theme of Waterton Lakes is "where the mountains meet the prairie."

Each national park has its own character and its own unique story as a living, outdoor museum.

The mountains in Waterton have been carved out of a series of layered sedimentary rocks more than a mile thick and they include some of the oldest known rocks in the Canadian mountains. Its highest peak is Mount Blakiston at 9,600 feet. Waterton is noteworthy for its sculptured geology, formed by glacial action, such as cirques (steepwalled basins), tarns (rock-basin lakes), U-shaped valleys, hanging valleys, and waterfalls.

Lt. Thomas Blakiston, of the Palliser expedition, discovered the lakes in 1858 and named them after Charles Waterton, a famed 18th-century naturalist. In 1886 traces of oil were found in Lineham Creek, and later, George "Kootenai" Brown became the first man to capitalize on Alberta's vast petroleum reserves. Brown lived most of his life in this area, became the park's first superintendent, and lies buried in a specially marked grave, between his two wives, on the shore of Lower Waterton Lake.

Established by order-in-council in 1895, Waterton Lakes encloses both short-grass prairie and alpine environment within its bounds. The park itself is open year-round; however, most visitor facilities are in service only during the summer season. Traditionally, summer season is from May 24 through September 1. The park offers more than 110 miles of back-country trails. Pike, whitefish, and a variety of trout are caught in its lakes and streams. Horses, canoes and rowboats may be rented. Motorboats are allowed on Waterton Lakes provided they meet federal safety and navigation regulations.

In winter, the park is open to those hardies who enjoy camping, snowshoeing, cross-country skiing, and snowmobiling. Park officials, however, require registration for most winter activities. There is a valid reason for this. It is a matter of safety, for in the winter the weather here can be extremely hazardous because of the swiftly changing conditions.

The geological turmoil that created Waterton also decorated it in a style that is both unique and colorful. Rock colors vary from purples and blue-greys through ochres to rust reds. An abundance of wild flowers blooms from late spring on the prairie to late summer in the alpine meadows. In late summer and early fall the grassland delivers a harvest of delicious wild berries, such as saskatoon and chokecherry. Most of the trees are evergreens of the fir, pine, and spruce varieties. The narrow band of foothills has some deciduous trees such as aspen, cottonwood, and maple.

A Zoological Who's Who

Waterton is a naturalist's dream world. A large number of different species of animals make the park their home, including grizzly bears, elk, pika, mule deer, black bears, beaver, cougar, marmot, fox, marten, weasel, mice, rabbits, skunk, badger and mink.

In the sky, hawks, falcons and eagles soar above innumerable songbirds, marsh birds, waders and swimmers, herons and gulls.

A series of four lakes form a chain that gives this park its name. Immediately after entering the park at its northeast entrance, we come upon the marsh lake of Maskinonge. Next in line is the Lower Waterton Lake, which is connected by a stream approximately one mile long to the mid-Waterton Lake. This in turn is connected to Upper Waterton Lake by a narrow channel known as Straits of Bosporus. Upper Waterton Lake is close to seven miles long, and nearly half of it is in the United States. All in all, there are some 40 lakes and ponds, plus twice that many streams, within the boundaries of the park.

The usual entrance to the park is from the northeast via Highway 6 from Calgary or Highway 5 from Lethbridge. There is another approach on Highway 17 leading northwest from Great Falls, Montana. Known as the Chief Mountain International Highway, it enters the park at the International Border. It then cuts across a timber stand belonging to the Blood Indians, and it re-enters the park boundary to join Highway 5 at Maskinonge Lake. The major road through the park extends from this junction to the town of Waterton and on to Cameron Lake in the southwestern corner. It is known as the Akamina Parkway.

A second scenic road extends from the intersection of the Akamina Parkway and Blackiston Creek. This road winds its way north westward to Red Rock Canyon. At its terminus, at Red Rock Canyon, a self-guiding trail is encountered. The trail is about 1½ circular miles in length. Its easy course leads by many interesting vistas. An explanatory pamphlet is available at the trailhead to aid in your enjoyment.

Trek the Tamarak

The hiking trails in the park range from easy walking tours, such as Red Rock Canyon, to difficult hikes. For example, the Linam Lakes Trail is 3½ miles long and for the most part is not too difficult. Yet a climbing permit is needed because of a 300-foot perpendicular cliff that must be scaled to reach the lakes. The lakes at 7,000 feet have excellent fishing, for not many anglers get there. If you are a climber, you may gain access to this trail at the point where Linam Creek crosses Akamina Parkway. Remember to take your fishing gear with you and remember, too, you must get permission from a park warden before attempting the hike.

No permission is required to trek the Tamarak Trail. It is wise though to obtain full information from a park warden as to the complexities that will be encountered. Tamarak Trail is a wilderness trail, and it is maintained that way. It is approximately 12½ miles long. It begins about one mile south of the Linam Lake Trail entrance. It leads beyond the Rowe Lakes and ascends the saddleback between Mount Linam and Mount Hawkins. The scenery is spectacular and the elevation at this point is about 8,000 feet. The trail then begins a descent to the headwaters of Blackiston Creek, and continues north to Lone Lake. Lone Lake has rough camping facilities and the fishing for cutthroat trout is good. From Lone Lake the trail becomes much better defined and leads for another two miles to the South Kootenay Pass Trail.

A really good trail for families who wish to stay overnight is the Krandle Lake Trail. It can be traversed in as little as one hour. Two campsites at Krandle Lake tempt and invite an extended stay. This trail also has the asset of being very close to town. Entrance can be gained from two points, either from the Akamina Parkway (just beyond the first parksite), or from the United Church camp on the Red Rock Parkway.

The scenic attractions of the Crypt Lake Trail make it a popular one. Depending on where you start—in the townsite, or at a small boat landing on the east side of Upper Waterton Lake—the trail can be either a 20 mile or 11 mile round trip. From the boat landing, the route leads past the fury of Hell Roaring Canyon and waterfall, and the delightful Twin Falls, via a tunnel which must be crawled through, to a spot where an underground stream gushes from the side of a mountain, then crashes 600 feet down a cliff face. Starting from the townsite, you will have to cross the Bosporous, either on horseback (and the horse will have to be a darned good mudder) or by renting a boat.

The trails of Waterton National Park were designed and established to meet the tastes of all types of visitors. Only a few of the trails are mentioned here, but you can get full information about all of them from the park information center. This center is located at the entrance to the townsite.

Also, the park wardens offer a free interpretive program of conducted walks, field trips, fireside talks, slide and film presentations to help visitors enjoy the park more. This service is available to any organized group provided they make arrangements in advance with the park superintendent. Individuals are encouraged to visit the park information centre and/or consult any of the uniformed park staff. Queries by mail should be directed to the Superintendent, Waterton Lakes National Park, Waterton Park, Alberta. T0K 2M0. Canada.

Ride a Trail Trike

The townsite of Waterton is small. Its permanent population is less than 2,000, but it offers all the essential services for visitors. Rentals of most equipment likely to be needed by vacationers are available, including a charming three-wheeled and canopied trail trike. Despite its name, it is not a machine suitable for use on the trails, but it does provide a pleasant means of pedaling leisurely through the streets and avenues of the town.

The mountain streams of Cameron Creek make a surprisingly violent entrance into Waterton at the Cameron Falls. But once over the falls, the creek runs more sedately through the town and its campground to flow into Upper Waterton Lake. A sightseeing cruise down the length of Upper Waterton Lake should be taken. The cruises go from Waterton townsite to the head of the lakes in Montana. The boats offer the pleasures of either open-air or glassed-in sightseeing. A round trip takes slightly more than 1½ hours and gives quite a different perspective of mountains, glaciers, caverns, waterfalls, and geological curiosities of Waterton Park.

In addition to its magnificent natural surroundings, Waterton offers the facilities of an 18-hole golf course, tennis courts, heated swimming, a buffalo pasture, gift and novelty shops, churches, a theatre, beaches, and a number of licensed lounges and dining rooms.

Waterton Lake National Park may well be termed as unknown in relation to Banff, and Jasper. It is a quiet place. It's a park for the lover of nature and the adventurer, or for those who seek deeply moving calmness amid enthralling beauty. Waterton Lakes National Park is a place to "take the time to visit."

EXPLORING ALBERTA

Like most Canadian provinces, Alberta is a vast tract of land. It stretches more than 700 miles, north to south, and at its widest point, east to west, it is more than 400 miles. It covers 248,800 square miles.

Alberta is a giant plateau 2,200 feet above sea level. It rises from this level in the east to more than 12,000 feet at the summit of Mount Columbia on the Icefields Parkway. The province has four major areas: rolling prairie, to a point about 200 miles north of the American border; a parkland region—extending from south of Red Deer to north of Edmonton; the great northern expanse of forests, lakes and streams that continues to the border of the North West Territories; and finally, the foothill/mountain portion that takes in the southern half of the Alberta/British Columbia border.

Within this area, the Canadian Government has established five National Parks comprising more than 24,000 square miles. Additionally, Alberta maintains another 150,000 square miles of public forest lands. This is joined by 58 provincial parks which provide further recreational opportunities for visitors. Thus, it is apparent that Alberta is an immense, scenic playground.

To streamline the administration, regulation and service of all aspects of the tourist industry, Alberta has regionalized the province into 14 tourist zones. For the visitor, this makes exploring immeasurably easier. Of even greater convenience is the location of free rest/picnic stops (one at least every 50 miles) on every major Alberta highway. Four of the tourist zones—Jasper, Banff, Calgary and Edmonton— have been described; the remaining ten are summarized below.

ZONE 1—CHINOOK COUNTRY

Zone 1 is an attractive prairie region in the southwestern corner of the province. Its major city is Lethbridge, which is Alberta's third largest city, with a population of 56,500.

Indeed, just seven miles south on Highway 5 at the confluence of the St. Mary and Belly rivers, the notorious Whiskey Fort Whoop-Up was located. This site has been established as a National Historic Site. A reconstruction of this fort is located within the boundaries of Lethbridge, on the west bank of the Old Man River. It is one of the attractions of Indian Battle Park . . . the locale of the last great Indian battle in Canada.

Fought between the Blackfoot and the Crees in the fall of 1870, the main fighting took place between the two parallel escarpments of the river. In that battle the Crees lost between two and three hundred men; while the Blackfoot lost just 40. The following year a formal peace treaty was made between the two Indian nations ending forever hostilities between them.

Lethbridge also possesses the strikingly beautiful Nikka Yuko Japanese Gardens. One of the largest authentic Japanese gardens in North America, the Nikka Yuko was created in 1967. It was a gift to the Canadian Centennial by Lethbridge district people of Japanese descent. These people were removed to this part of Canada from their original homes on the Pacific Coast during the early part of World War II.

Nine provincial parks lie within Zone 1 and one of the most fascinating is Writing-On-Stone, situated 20 miles east of Highway 4 on the Milk River. Thousands of eroded hoodoos form a classic badlands environment in the river valley. This was once a native, secret writing ground and pictographs are found inscribed on the rocks. At other times, it was the whiskey-smuggling passage from Montana to southern Alberta.

At Park Lake provincial park, a 15-minute drive north of Lethbridge on Highway 25, swimming and boating are featured. Some 30 miles east of Lethbridge, the town of Taber boasts a provincial park that has been termed a "bird watcher's paradise." West of Lethbridge on Highway 3, the town of Fort Macleod has reconstructed its namesake—the first North West Mounted Police fort in Alberta. This fort is open year-round and welcomes visitors to its extensive collection of Western memorabilia, at little charge.

Mormons and Hutterites

Directly south of Fort Macleod on Highway 2 is Cardston. The town is built on reserve land of the Blood Indians. It began with a wagon train of Mormon immigrants who had traveled northward from Utah. They paused here to spend the winter of 1878, were given a 100-year lease by the Indians and built their town. The focal point is a magnificent granite structure that is the temple of the Church of Jesus Christ of Latter Day Saints.

Adjacent to Cardston is a Hutterite Colony. The Hutterites are descendants and followers of the teachings of Jacob Hutter, and their lifestyles in many ways are similar to Quakers and Mennonites. Just 28 miles west of Cardston are the gates of Waterton National Park.

More directly west from Fort Macleod on Highway 3 is the colorful and adventurous area known as Crowsnest Pass. Portions of this area have been described previously in the Adventure Highway section; but it is interesting to note that in the hills north of Lundbreck Falls is the supposed location of the Lost Lemon Mine. The legend of the mine includes all the elements of high adventure . . . murder, madness, supernatural and frightening events . . . plus authentic assay records of some of the richest gold-bearing ore ever discovered. If you like, take time out and join the thousands who, over the years, have searched fruitlessly for the gold of Lost Lemon Mine. Even if you join the unlucky in your search, all will not be lost, for you will have spent a pleasant time in some of the most beautiful scenery in the world.

ZONE 2—"THE GATEWAY ZONE"

This zone takes in the extreme southeast corner of the province. Again, it is rich in history. Essentially flat lands that were formed from a shallow sea in prehistoric times, Zone 2 is made more interesting with its truly western panorama of cliffs, bluffs, rimrocks, dips, draws and coulees. Studded with prickly pear cactus and sagebrush, this rolling plainsland is almost treeless. The shores of a number of creeks and streams (that flow into the South Saskatchewan River), sloughs, small lakes, and numerous pockets where water gathers, do, however, support stands of cottonwoods and willows.

The pride of Zone 2 is a geological oddity known as the Cypress Hills. One of the very few places in Canada untouched by glacial action, the hills support an abundance of flora and fauna, not native to Canada, and which are generally found only in the southern United States. The hills rise from the prairie plateau 2,000 feet. They extend into Saskatchewan and are less than four miles wide. Now a provincial park, they have a definite montane/alpine atmosphere. There is a point just south of Elkwater Lake (a popular boating/swimming resort) where you can see across the entire southern boundary of Alberta. This is a distance of more than 175 miles, and standing here it is simple to understand the ease with which Blackfoot warriors could patrol their territory.

Within the Cypress Hills, and a mile and a half in the province of Saskatchewan, the North West Mounted Police garrison post of Fort Walsh lies nestled in a valley of Battle Creek. This was the terminus of the mounties' great trek across the Canadian plains in 1874. Not far from the fort is the site of the Chipewyan massacre by white "wolfers" from Montana. Adjacent to this site are the reconstructed remains of two small whiskey forts that were active in the 1870's.

Access to the Cypress Hills can be gained by using Montana State Highway 232 which becomes Alberta provincial Highway 48. This road bisects the Cypress Hills and connects with the Trans-Canada Highway 20 miles east of Medicine Hat—a place which has an intriguing legend.

Many years ago, so the story goes, a Cree warrior stole the woman he loved away from his tribal chief. The couple fled to the point where the South Saskatchewan River bends sharply north. The woman, knowing the vanity of Red Deer, the chief who was pursuing them, suggested that their lives might be saved if they presented him with an elaborate gift. The brash warrior captured a number of eagles. Selecting the finest tail feathers, the young Indian girl made a magnificent feathered bonnet. Eventually the chief caught up with the couple and was offered the bonnet. The change in him was so immediate and extreme that all who witnessed felt magic was involved. The war chief and his warriors went back to their encampment and the young couple were left to live their lives in happiness. From that time on, that spot at the great bend of the river has been known as the place of the Great Medicine Hat.

Modern Medicine Hat

An oasis on the plains, Medicine Hat was blessed with huge natural gas reserves that could be obtained by merely drilling for it in any part of town. Today, this city of 40,380 is one of the most rapidly growing communities in Alberta. Trees line and arch its streets, and one would never guess that these same streets once witnessed great cattle drives, bull trains, and the cowboys that herded them. Parks calm and beautify the banks of rivers that once knew the activities of sternwheel steamers hauling coal and goods to Lethbridge, Saskatoon, and Edmonton.

The oldest rodeo in Alberta is held here in late July. And in recent years, visitors have been making a regular habit of touring an industry that has become a community pride—the "Altaglass" glass-blowing plant. World-scale petrochemical plants dot the northern skyline, while an excellent museum and "Natural Exhibit Centre" record the area's history. This is a relaxed, friendly city. Its inhabitants seem always to be ready and able to spend a little time with you, teasing your imagination with tales tall and tales true of Rudyard Kipling's favorite North American settlement.

Sixty-five miles west of Medicine Hat the Trans-Canada Highway meets Highway 873 at Brooks. Turning north on 873, thirty miles of well signposted secondary roads bring you to Dinosaur Provincial Park. This consists of 22,000 acres of extraordinary country studded with the works of erosion run rampant. These badlands and weird rock formations cloak a natural museum. In reality, this museum is a 70-million-year-old graveyard of prehistoric reptiles such as brontosaurus, tyrannosaurus rex, and pterodactyls. Park authorities have produced many interesting displays of partially excavated dinosaur skeletons and exhibitions of fossils, relics, and other vestiges of the time when this land was a tropical home for monstrous reptiles.

Backtracking to the Trans-Canada Highway at Brooks, a visit (no charge) to the greenhouses of the horticultural research center, or the Alberta Wildlife Centre, is a worthwhile diversion. Twelve miles south of Brooks, on Highway 873, Kinbrook Island Provincial Park (east shore of Lake Newell) provides excellent swimming, boating, fishing and camping. If you prefer to continue west on the Trans-Canada, a stop at Cluny should be planned.

The Grave of Chief Crowfoot

Cluny lies about one mile south of the highway, and a few more miles south of town is Blackfoot Crossing. This bluff overlooks the site of the signing of Treaty No. 7, one hundred years ago. At that time the formidable Blackfoot nation agreed to give up its free and warlike way-of-life and retire to reserves. Here, too, is the location of Chief Crowfoot's last tipi—and of his grave.

West again from Cluny, and immediately past the town of Gleichen, visitors can see a "buffalo jump" on the south side of the highway. This is simply an escarpment of a plains plateau—a cutbank some 50 feet high. The Blackfoot would run entire herds of buffalo over the edge of this, killing or crippling them ready for butchering at the bottom. The buffalo disappeared from the plains in 1883, but prior to that, the herds numbered hundreds and thousands of animals. Indeed, early explorers reported seeing the prairies blackened with buffalo in herds extending from horizon to horizon. Herds of this magnitude would number in the millions.

The Gateway Zone is essentially a healthy dose of "prairie tonic." Although the prairies seem to be a flat and boring sight to many, in reality they offer fascinating possibilities for exploration. Teeming with stories and legends, this zone offers the perceptive and curious visitor experiences as numerous as the sagebrush that grows on it.

ZONE 3—THE BIG COUNTRY

Extending from its westward boundary between Calgary and Red Deer, the Big Country area offers travelers an opportunity to view the stark remains of pre-historic life on the continent and wander, at will, around semi-desert areas; deep, cool lakes; baked, sandstone landscapes; and heavily wooded forests.

Perhaps the best way is to direct yourself straight to the heart of the action—Drumheller (population 6,508). From Calgary, travel east on the Trans-Canada Highway about 29 kms. (18 miles) to a junction with Inter-provincial number 9 highway. Following Highway 9, it is 109 kms. (68 miles) through the finest wheat growing country in North America to Drumheller. The small town of Beiseker has produced many winners of the "World Wheat King" award. Near Beiseker is a colony of Hutterian Brethren, a religious sect, who follow the teachings of Joseph Hutter and live a communal life supported entirely by agricultural activity.

Near Drumheller is an incredible introduction to the pre-historic civilization of the Red Deer River Valley area. Stopping at the vantage point of Horseshoe Canyon, one finds evidence of a world 70 million years old at the bottom lands some 400 feet below. The sides of the hills reveal layers of the earth's strata—each created by rivers and flood plains of eons past.

The pastel shading and sculptured formations of Horseshoe Canyon are but a preview of the remarkable "Badland" scenery of the valley of the Red Deer River. The best perspective of this area is to be had by following the 45-km. (28-mile) Dinosaur Trail which begins in the downtown section of Drumheller.

Coal, subbituminous number 2, the finest heating coal in Canada, was first discovered in this area by Alexander Mackenzie in 1790. In 1911, Sam Drumheller began the first mining operation which launched the town as well as Alberta's great coal industry.

The Dinosaur Trail begins at the Dinosaur and Fossil Museum on 1st Street East, in the town center of Drumheller. Museum displays are designed to interpret the geology and paleontology of the area. Artifacts, dating back to the time of tropical swamp and rain forest, through submergence by an inland sea, past innundation by glacial advancement, to the recent prehistoric area of plains and nomadic people, are displayed. Major interest focuses on petrified skeletal remains of dinosaurs.

In the summer of 1884, Doctor J. B. Tyrrell discovered the head of a petrified monster. This touched off a series of expeditions that were to unearth a treasure house of remains never before seen by the paleological world. Today, skeletons and skulls from the Drumheller district are displayed in museums of New York, Chicago, London, and other major cities.

Museum of Contrasting Contrasts

The Dinosaur Trail advances from the museum, across the bridge on the number 9 highway and north a short distance. Then, with an abrupt left, it swings west to pass another interesting sight—the Homestead Antique Museum. This 8-acre development is a hodge-podge of artifacts ranging from coal-mining instruments and tools to military badges, medals and ribbons, from Indian relics to early automobiles and steam engines, from articles of pioneer times to one of the country's largest firearm collections. It is a museum of contrasts.

Farther on, the picturesque Little Church welcomes visitors to meditation. Unique in its badland setting, the Little Church accommodates 20,000 people a year—six at a time. The Golf and Country Club is across the road.

The Dinosaur Trail continues on through oilfields and wheatfields, through beds of petrified oysters (proof that this was once the bed of an inland sea), and across an antique car ferry; it circles around on its way back to Drumheller town. Not far from the Munson Ferry is the Dinosaur Burial Grounds and a rich fossil area. Travelers should know that it is illegal to remove or disturb any of the artifacts here.

Another very interesting drive from Drumheller is the number 10 highway which leads 21 kms. (13 miles) to East Coulee. This road leads through the old mining towns of Wayne and Rosedale and passes through the valley's famous "Hoodoos." On the south side of the Red Deer River in this area, you may keep any prehistoric treasures you find. Another attraction along this route is the Atlas Coal Mine which, in the summer, allows those who are interested to descend to the depths of a working coal mine and explore the heart of a bituminous seam.

South of East Coulee lie the beautiful Wintering Hills, an expanse of rolling ranchlands that are interesting to explore. East from East Coulee, the great Alberta prairie stretches out once again; here are the beginnings of Alberta's network of recreational lakes.

Other points of interest include, not far from Empress, the final meeting place of Sitting Bull and Crowfoot who decided (over 100 years ago) not to form a Blackfoot/Sioux military action against the white man. In the Youngstown area is the great breeding ranch for the Calgary Stampede. Farmers, ranchers, and villagers here are friendly and hospitable, ever ready with stories, legends and directions. Also in the Youngstown/Hanna/Oyen area is one of North America's finest Goose and Duck hunting locals. At Three Hills, the Prairie Bible Institute draws theological students from all over the world.

ZONE 4—LAND OF DAVID THOMPSON

The area around Red Deer (population 48,562), with its eastern boundary running between Calgary and Edmonton, extends west to the Rocky Mountains. The prairies come to an end here; instead there are forests, mountains, streams, and foothills.

David Thompson (1770–1857) was the last of the great North American explorers—perhaps the greatest of them all. A cartographer in the employ of the North West Fur Trading Co., Thompson discovered the Columbia River and mapped the area radiating north and south from the North Saskatchewan River. He spent 28 years in this country exploring more streams and passes than any dozen men before him. The accuracy with which he mapped and charted key points from the Hudson's Bay to the Pacific Ocean and from the Peace to the Missouri Rivers guaranteed his place in history. River, mountain, highway, and area carry his name as tributes to his accomplishments.

This is country for recreation, offering whitewater canoeing, stream fishing, and lake boating. Adventurers who seek challenging waterways will find the headwaters of the Red Deer and its tributaries all they can handle—some are even classified as life-threatening. The Clearwater River and North Saskatchewan yield more sensible adventure.

The streams that originate on the eastern slopes of the mountains and wind their way through this area teem with fish. Arctic grayling, mountain whitefish, and a half a dozen different types of trout offer fishermen good sport and good food.

Also to be enjoyed are the lakes—Sylvan, Pine, Gull, and Crimson, offering lake trout, pike, perch, goldeye for the fisherman and swimming, sailing, and motor boating for other outdoor buffs.

The David Thompson Highway

Extending west from the major number 2 north/south highway are four main wilderness access roads. One leads from the town of Olds, the second from Innisfail, a third from Carstairs, and a fourth from Red Deer. All but one terminate on the forestry trunk road. Highway 11 (the David Thompson) leading west from Red Deer cuts right through to the Icefields Parkway just south of Athabasca Glacier.

The David Thompson Highway cuts through the scenic part of this splendid area. Fourteen kms. (9 miles) from Red Deer, the highway skirts Jarvis Bay Provincial Park and Sylvan Lake as it slices through farmland, forest and streams to Rocky Mountain House 64 kms. (40 miles) away where there is excellent big game hunting in season.

Nearby to the southwest are the remains of early fur trading posts. Here a cairn is dedicated to David Thompson who, 182 years ago, explored the area. Fourteen kms. (9 miles) northwest of Rocky Mountain House is Crimson Lake Provincial Park offering swimming, fishing, and hiking. Challenging golf courses are located at Rocky Mountain House and Sylvan Lake.

At Rocky Mountain House, visitors may continue west on the David Thompson, through the modern ghost town of Nordegg, past the gigantic Big Horn Dam to the Icefields Parkway; or, at Nordegg, you can travel north or south on the Forestry Trunk Road. From Rocky Mountain House, you may take the north route, circling through beautiful wilderness areas and eventually come out on the Highway 2 or the number 16 (Yellowhead Highway). South from Rocky also offers fine wilderness drives; yet you are never too far away from civilization.

Use the urban center of Red Deer as the base for your explorations of this area. The city still maintains that appealing combination of urban amenities and rural friendliness. A full range of goods and services is available for convenience and its memorial center provides facilities for the performing arts. Red Deer's most interesting activity may be the International Folk Festival—a two-day event highlighting the songs, dances, and culture of many ethnic groups who form the Alberta character. The festivities include international food booths, cultural displays, ethnic entertainment and art, and authentic costumes.

ZONE 5—THE BATTLE RIVER

The Battle River area, extending on the west from the Saskatchewan border to the great bend of the North Saskatchewan River, starts roughly south of Edmonton and runs almost to Red Deer on its southern boundary. A blend of prime parkland and some prairie, it is "pastoral"—with dozens of small communities (population 100–600) serving as social and service locales for the area's agricultural and petroleum activities. Grain, ranching, and mixed farming remain as family operations rather than corporate endeavors.

Residents take pride in the fact that the extraordinary explorer Anthony Henday trekked through much of this area in his Alberta wanderings of 1754. The Battle River, meandering in a great bow through the land, gets its name not from one battle, but from many native skirmishes. This was part of the Blackfoot empire; however, a Cree reservation is located at Hobbema just south of Wetaskiwin on Highway 2A.

Ukrainians and Elk Island

Two major visitor attractions—Elk Island National Park (east on Highway 16) and Polar Park (east on Highway 14)—are located within 32 kms. (20 miles) of Edmonton.

Elk Island National Park (on Highway 16) is one of Canada's smallest parks—only 197 sq. kms. (76 square miles). It is located in Alberta's Beaver Hills which rise slightly above the surrounding farmland parkland. A gull's-eye-view would give you an impression of an island of rolling hills, heavily forested and spotted with lakes, ponds, and marshes.

Elk Island Park was originally homesteaded by many ethnic groups. The most populous were Ukrainians from the province of Glacia. Evidence of their occupation is still seen in the park's central region, and a replica of a Ukrainian pioneer home is maintained as a museum. The entire park is fenced in to contain its large animal population (especially elk and bison). The park has recorded over 200 species of birds, 30 species of mammals, and 240 varieties of plant life. Elk Island offers many miles of hiking trails (including two self-guiding nature trails), swimming, boating, fishing, and golf.

In 1957 zoologist Al Oeming found he had sufficient money saved from years of professional wrestling to enable him to build a sanctuary for wild animals—a lifelong dream. The Alberta Game Farm has recently evolved into Polar Park, a wildlife preserve specializing in animal species from the cold regions of the world. The animals are housed and bred in surroundings simulating their natural habitat. More than 1,000 animals—many of them rare, exotic creatures and many on the endangered lists—roam the 1,500-acre park.

Agriculture is not the only industry in this predominantly rural zone. Oil and gas exploration and production, forestry, coal and tourism are all important factors in its economy. Immense Brazeau Dam, accessible from Drayton Valley, at the western edge of the zone, supplies hydroelectric power.

The larger cities and towns offer all necessary services for visitors and a number provide considerable entertainment as well. Camrose (pop. 13,000) has stock car races, industrial tours, picnic and floral parks. There are also 648 oil wells within a 32-km. (20-mile) radius of the city. In Wetaskiwin, the Reynolds Museum has over 1,000 cars, trucks, steam engines, motorcycles, airplanes, fire engines, and carriages in its extensive antique automobile collection. Many towns also feature summer rodeos and seasonal sport days which are hotbeds of activity during the fall (game bird hunting) and the winter (skiing, curling, skating, and snowmobiling). Other major population centers include Wainwright, Stettler, Sherwood Park, Fort Saskatchewan, and Leduc. Each of these has unique attractions and/or fascinating historical backgrounds.

ZONE 6—THE LAKELAND

A piece of Alberta tourist promotion literature describes the Lakeland as "Big adventure! Big space! Big variety! Big fish! Big memories!" This is no overstatement. The lakeland area, which takes in nearly a quarter of the province, includes over half of Alberta's eastern boundary with Saskatchewan and also more than half its northern boundary with the Northwest Territories. Running south to Edmonton, it encompasses most of the east/west interprovincial Highway 16. Here, cities and towns alike demonstrate Alberta's "open-handed friendliness."

Within its boundaries is Canada's largest national park—Wood Buffalo National Park—an immense wilderness—44,807 sq. kms. (17,-300 square miles)—undeveloped for ordinary tourism. A place for adventurers, it cannot be reached by road or highway; only by air, or waterway via the Athabasca or Peace Rivers. True, there is a road, some 320 kms. (200 miles) long, that circles from Fort Smith through a small portion of the park. It is possible to get your vehicle to Fort Smith via the Mackenzie Highway to Hay River on Great Slave Lake, then down and around to Fort Smith—a journey of about 1360 kms.

(850 miles) from Edmonton. Far better is transportation by airplane or boat. Both can be chartered at Fort McMurray. Wilderness, yes; but not so primitive that you can't camp, boat or fish. This is a land where the last of the whooping cranes nest . . . where the haunting call of the loons echo across a thousand lakes . . . where Canada exemplifies its frontier character.

South of Wood Buffalo National Park lie the Great Canadian Oil Sands. These deposits of oil-bearing sands have been estimated to contain enough petroleum to supply all of North America for the next 60 years. Less conservative estimates claim that these deposits contain as much oil reserves as the world's known total. Fort McMurray is in the middle of it all.

At Lac La Biche there are over 50 large lakes within a 96-km. (60-mile) radius. So complex is the pattern of lakes that fishing trips take on the excitement of exploration sorties. These are trophy waters where the fish will bite at anything. Watch your thumbs!

The Northwest (Riel) Rebellion

East southeast of Lac La Biche is Cold Lake, possibly the finest commercial and sport fishing source of whitefish, an international delicacy. Grand Centre (slightly to the south) supplies the goods and services for this region and is another community that finds itself in the midst of large oil sands deposits—164 billion barrels of black gold.

Driving south on a secondary highway (897) for approximately 64 kms. (40 miles), travelers reach the historic Frog Lake massacre site. Here, on April 2nd, 1885, the first shots of the Northwest (Riel) Rebellion were fired. A band of Plains Cree, under Chief Big Bear, attacked the settlement and cut down nine men (including two priests and the Indian agent) as they rushed from the doors of their morning church services.

Looking back from Frog Lake to St. Paul, you will enjoy the peace and splendor of lake and forest countryside. St. Paul was originally established as a reservation for Metis settlement. It gradually welcomed a sizeable mixture of settlers of different ethnic origin. In 1967, when Canada celebrated its 100th birthday, St. Paul led the nation in centennial projects. Among them was a Flying Saucer Landing Pad (complete with a time vault to be opened June 3, 2067).

The town of Vegreville also gave itself an interesting centennial birthday present—a 30-foot Ukrainian Easter egg that is a geometrical and architectural wonder.

Lloydminster (population 9,000), a city with a split personality, is situated exactly on the Alberta/Saskatchewan border. This is complicated by the fact that Alberta has no sales tax, but Saskatchewan does—a situation that doesn't bother the citizens, for they shop on the Alberta side. But it creates hardship for the Saskatchewan tax collector.

Lloydminster, one of the great posts of the Hudson's Bay Company, was also involved in the Northwest Rebellion. It was here that British Barr colonists settled in 1903. Today, Lloydminster is recreation minded; its people invite visitors to participate in an array of sports from hockey and shooting to swimming and snowmobiling.

ZONE 7—THE EVERGREEN AREA

It is 368 kms. (230 miles) from Edmonton to Jasper, and that is the width of the Evergreen area. From the Brazeau Dam in the south to Grande Cache and the Berland River in the north, a vast playground of ecological beauty lies in wait for the nature lover, offering hundreds of hiking trails branching off from access arteries. Within its boundaries, the terrain varies from flat farmland near Edmonton through lightly wooded regions to heavy timber bursts in the foothills of the Rocky Mountains.

To understand the wilderness aspect of this area and northern parts of Alberta, be aware that this province encompasses over 660,450 sq. kms. (255,000 square miles). Of this area, only 18,130 sq. kms. (7,000 square miles) are fresh water. This large province is sparsely settled by 2.3 million people, of whom two-thirds live in Calgary and Edmonton. Endless opportunities to be alone in a state of nature!

Yet, with a bit of pre-planning you may enjoy a wilderness experience, but never be uncomfortably isolated from civilization. For example, the Yellowhead Highway (number 16) bisects this area, moving from Edmonton to Jasper. At the town of Hinton, the forestry trunk road leads south. At about the 128 km. (80 mile) mark, near the southern boundary of the area, secondary highway 620 leads back east past the Brazeau Dam to Drayton Valley in the center of the Great Pembina Oil Fields. Also, highways 40 and 47 form a short and interesting circle tour from the village of Entrance to the town of Edson. About 29 kms. (18 miles) east of Edson, an unnumbered graded road leads south to Wolf Lake and joins highway 620. These highways and roads allow easy access to this frontier land and the province has established safe and comfortable campgrounds at convenient locations along every one of them.

Of course, visitors traveling through the wilderness should always pre-plan, checking with the forest warden, mountain police post, or local townspeople about local conditions.

The Evergreen area has four provincial parks—Pembina River, Hasse Lake, William A. Switzer, and Wabamun Lake.

Opportunities for Summer Fun

Very convenient to reach, the Wabamun Lake provincial park is 64 kms. (40 miles) east on the Yellowhead Highway from Edmonton. At this popular resort center offering sunny stretches of sandy beaches you can rent a cabin, sail, swim, waterski, and fish. Other sun bathing and waterfun resorts include Alberta Beach on Lac Ste. Anne (on highway 33); Edmonton Beach (on the Yellowhead), and Lake Eden. Near the town of Onoway 56 kms. (35 miles) from Edmonton on highway 33, Lake Eden is a gem of a summer resort. It features a high standard of summer fun opportunities, and in winter turns into a ski or snowmobiling resort.

Among big game hunters, the regions radiating from the towns of Hinton (population 8,819) and Edson (population 6,291) are recognized as being among the most favorable in the world for the taking of moose, deer, elk, bear and mountain sheep. The hunting season starts in September or October and lasts well into December.

ZONE 8—THE LAND OF THE MIGHTY PEACE

One hundred years ago, only a handful of white men knew this land. Two hundred years ago, when Alexander Mackenzie made his epochal canoe journey through this northwestern section of Alberta, one of the understatements of all time was recorded. After days and days of paddling, seeing nothing ahead or on either side but forest, old Alex was heard to mutter, "There's room to grow in this land. . . . "

The area is named for the mighty Peace River which snakes its way from the lower southwest portion of the area, nearly bisecting it as it leaves to flow into Wood Buffalo National Park and on to Lake Athabasca, eventually contributing to the massive waters of Great Slave Lake. In this part of Alberta, the mighty Peace is the most important of the four major water lifelines; the other three are Hay River, Chinchaga, and Wabasca. These great rivers and their numerous tributaries form the drainage system of this vast tract of land. They also provide great challenge to the fearless canoeist.

Even though the north/south Mackenzie Highway (number 35) allows easy access to the heartland of the mighty Peace, this section is not for everyone. The Mackenzie Highway is hard-surfaced to the border of the North West Territories. Beyond this point, it is gravel—all the way to Yellowknife.

One of the "last frontiers," this area includes Caribou Mountains and Buffalo Head Hills; Dizzy Creek and Wolverine River. Names of the communities hint at their own histories—Bonanza and Eureka; Bear Canyon and Deadwood; Indian Cabins and Carcajou; Moonshine Lake and Beaverlodge. Much of it is rugged, wild, and untamed; yet fly-in charters can take you to an isolated lake for a day or a week for a once-in-a-lifetime camping or fishing experience. The highways thread their way through fertile farmlands, extensive gas and oilfields, lumber industry and flourishing modern towns. Further, traveling is made more convenient by Alberta's policy of establishing conveniently situated campsites. Numerous privately or municipally owned trailer parks, campgrounds, summer resorts and beaches will also enhance your enjoyment of a "wilderness" experience. Provincial Parks—Moonshine Lake 20 miles west of Spirit River and Queen Elizabeth Prov. Park near Grimshaw—are well worth seeing. As is the valley from Dunvegan Historic Site through the Shaftsbury Trail to the town of Peace River.

ZONE 9—JASPER (see earlier section)

ZONE 10—THE LIVIN' WEST (also see Calgary section)

Calgary is part of the western tourist area that extends from the eastern city limits of Calgary in a narrow band to the Banff Park gates. Within this strip of foothills country, speared by the Trans-Canada Highway, are several points of interest.

A secondary road number 22 leaves the Trans-Canada Highway on a southward course 32 kms. (20 miles) west of Calgary. This short road takes you to Bragg Creek provincial park. In this general area are Elbow Falls and the Ice Caves. The access route to the Ice Caves is a 6½-km. (4-mile) trek down a dry creek bed. Along the way, the escarpment of the creek contains layers of fossilized shellfish, deposited there when the land was the bottom of a shallow sea. Tourists wishing to visit the Ice Caves should seek advice and information at the warden's office at the Bragg Creek forestry station.

From Calgary leading west is an alternate route to Banff, Highway 1A. This road takes you through the small ranching town of Cochrane, the site of the first ranch to be established in Alberta. A highlight there is a drop-in call at Scotty McKay's Ice Cream Emporium. Scotty makes his own ice cream in over 60 flavors.

Continuing on the 1A, you pass by the Stoney Indian Reserve and Stoney Indian Park. The park offers picnicking, camping in teepees, buffalo, horseback riding, and an archeological excavation of the Old Bow Fort, established in 1832.

Nestled under the awesome Three Sisters peaks is the old coal town of Canmore. Here, the home of Canada's foremost potter, Stonecroft Studio, is always open to visitors. Coal was discovered at this spot in 1888 and today the company store provides a bit of economic history as you tour. Finally, there are several scenic hiking trails emanating from the town.

ZONE 11—EDMONTON (see earlier section)

ZONE 12—BANFF (see earlier section)

ZONE 13—GAME COUNTRY

Its name says it all. This is rugged, untamed country, flecked with some farmland along its southern borders (near Mayerthorpe on Highway 43), but largely a rich wilderness. From cougar to bear, and all sizes and shapes in between, the four footed population is unusually high. As the saying goes, the area here is "as thick as the stink from a frightened polecat."

Six roadways accommodate traffic in this area. From Whitecourt, Highway 43 (in the eastern portion) joins number 34 at Valleyview. This is the true beginning of the Alaska Highway. Number 34 moves laterally westward across the top of the Game Country to join with the north and south artery of Grande Prairie. The Highway 2 continues north and west from Grande Prairie, eventually reaching Dawson Creek. The forestry trunk road bisects the area and rural and unimproved number 666 works its way into some of the land's most inaccessible wilderness areas.

Among points of interest and places to visit here are four provincial parks—O'Brien, Saskatoon Island, Williamson, and Hommy. O'Brien provincial park is just 11 kms. (7 miles) south of Grande Prairie and provides a quick, beautiful setting for picnicking although it cannot accommodate overnight camping. Saskatoon Island, on the other hand, has a well-developed 250-acre campsite. Located 19 kms. (12 miles) west and about 3 kms. (2 miles) north of Grande Prairie, it offers boating, swimming, and a chance to view the nesting grounds of the rare Trumpeter Swan. Hommy is a very small park and again able to accommodate only day visits. It is located 8 kms. (5 miles) northwest of Beaver Lodge; its tranquility and setting make it popular with visitors. Twenty-four kms. (15 miles) west of Valleyview, Williamson Park on Sturgeon Lake attracts visitors with its sun bathing beaches and superb fishing waters for northern pike, walleye, and yellow perch.

The largest community in the Game Country Zone is Grande Prairie, a city of 24,000 people. Its industry is based on agriculture, supplemented by the economic benefits of heavy involvement in pulp and timber. A cultural center, Grande Prairie has its own symphony orchestra, a resident music conservatory, an exhibiting art gallery, and a full season of live theater.

At Grande Prairie's pioneer museum you will find not only a moose, but a white Albino moose—one of the mounted wildlife specimens displayed at this museum. A favorite spot for children is Bear Creek Centennial Park (102nd Street and 102nd Avenue). The park encompasses some 190 acres of developed recreational land and undeveloped natural flora. Its features excellent hiking trails.

Game Country is great wilderness fringed by civilization . . . an up-to-date hotel with a trap line outside . . . an 18-hole golf course with an elk nibbling on the 17th green . . . an oilpatch drill site with a call of the loon across the lake . . . an enjoyable area for adventuresome touring.

ZONE 14—THE LAND OF THE MIDNIGHT TWILIGHT

The middle-north of Alberta has a touch of everything Albertan—prairie, rolling hills, cool lakes, and roaring rivers. And it has history.

At the city of St. Albert, a short distance north of Edmonton, the crypt of Alberta's heroic religious figure, Father Lacombe, is located. The road that leads you north is Highway 2 (which was the beginning of the Klondike or the Trail of '98). Along this same path some 5,000 seekers of fortune began their long, arduous trek to the goldfields of the Klondike. It took a year of hardship to make the trip and only a handful ever reached Bonanza Creek.

To the northeast is the Alberta Wildlife Park, which houses more than 100 species of animals and has a petting zoo, campgrounds and picnic areas. The adjacent Red Barn is the largest barbecue restaurant and square dance hall in Canada.

Progressing on Highway 2, visitors bypass some of Alberta's richest farmland. The ethnic mixture here is French, Ukrainian, Scottish, and German. Make this a leisurely part of your trip; enjoying talking with residents of the farming communities.

In the early days of the fur trade, Athabasca Landing, near the town of Athabasca, was an important distribution point for traders continuing into the far north. A few miles east of Athabasca is Cross Lake provincial park, one of Alberta's quietest and most scenic parks. Boating and fishing are available here.

Highway 2 continues to circle through the Midnight Twilight area, eventually hugging the southern shores of Lesser Slave Lake. Despite its name, Lesser Slave is one of Alberta's larger lakes and its crowning glory is the longest white sand beach in Canada. The entire lake lies within the provincial park which also contains three large campgrounds: North Shore, Lilly Creek, and Martin River. An interesting side trip is a visit to Grouard on the west end of Lesser Slave Lake—the oldest community in the area and, at one time, a serious contender for the capital of the province. It had sidewalks in 1902. Girouxville, 9 miles north of Donnelly Corner, boasts a history museum detailing the lives of the Indians, missionaries and pioneers who opened the area.

Winagami Lake provincial park, 40 kms. (25 miles) north of High Prairie, has fine facilities and a delightful ecological atmosphere. Far to the south (just west of Barrhead on Highway 18) is another natural and scenic setting—Thunder Lake, one of the few nesting sites of the majestic Blue Heron. Sighting it is a common occurrence.

Camping or trailering is the only viable way to tour the Midnight Twilight area. Here dense forests and tangled wilderness blend well with farmlands. The sun sets late. At 11 o'clock on a summer evening, it is still light enough to sink your final putt . . . to cast your final line . . . to strike your evening camp.

PRACTICAL INFORMATION FOR ALBERTA

HOW TO GET THERE. By car: There is easy east/west access to Alberta via the Trans-Canada, Yellowhead, or number 3 interprovincial. From the south, State highways 88 and 91 (interstate 15) and regional highway 232 connect with Alberta's north/south routes.

By train: *Via Rail* services Medicine Hat, Calgary, and Banff, also Edmonton and Jasper. Full transcontinental passenger service is through Calgary and Banff.

By bus: *Greyhound* is the major carrier to Alberta as well as through and around Alberta. Its head office in Canada is located in Calgary. In the Rockies, *Brewster Bus Lines* provide scheduled service.

By air: Edmonton and Calgary are served by *Air Canada, C.P. Air, Pacific Western, Western Airlines, Wardair* and *United.* Edmonton is also served by *Northwest Orient;* Calgary by *Lufthansa.*

ACCOMMODATIONS in Alberta range from deluxe resorts in the mountain parks and luxury hotels in the cities, to plain highway accommodation in small communities throughout the province. Price categories, for double occupancy, are: *Deluxe,* $75 and up; *Expensive,* $55–75; *Moderate,* $40–55; *Inexpensive,* under $40. There is no provincial tax on accommodations but some hotels and motels charge for local phone calls.

Most places accept the following major credit cards: American Express, MasterCard, and Visa; others may also be honored. Not all establishments accept credit cards, therefore we suggest you call for information.

BANFF. *Deluxe.* **Banff Park Lodge.** Beautifully appointed, modern, in the heart of town. 210 rooms, good restaurants and lounge, pool. Newest full-service hotel in Banff.

Banff Springs Hotel. This famous château-like hotel with 550 rooms is a chain member of the C.P. Hotels and one of Canada's most elegant houses. Beautiful view of the Bow Valley; 18-hole golf course ranks in Canadian top 10.

Tunnel Mountain Chalets. This new operation offers 51 chalets, each with full kitchen, queen-size bed, and extra sleeping loft. Indoor pool, sauna and whirlpool, plus a Bow Valley view add to its popularity. Tops in Banff for families wishing to fix their own meals.

Expensive. **Homestead Inn.** 27 rooms, telephone, color TV, dining room.

Mount Royal Hotel. An older hotel, but a favorite with visitors. Licensed dining room and cocktail lounge, room service, telephones.

The Rimrock Inn. On the Sulphur Mountain. 105 clean, bright rooms feature view of Banff valley townsite. Proximity to upper hot springs and Sulphur Mountain gondola lift is an asset. Tennis, indoor squash/racquetball. Swimming.

The Timberline Hotel. In days past, one of Banff's finest hotels; still clean and gracious. Dining room. Away from town.

Moderate. **Cascade Inn.** In the heart of downtown Banff. Simple, clean rooms. Licensed lounge.

Johnston's Canyon Resort. 26 km. (16 mi.) west of Banff. 41 rustic cabins. Attraction is its location—adjacent to Johnston's Canyon and waterfall.

Red Carpet Inn. 44 units. Central and reasonable.

LAKE LOUISE AREA. *Deluxe.* **Château Lake Louise.** A famous C.P. château hotel, this 380-room showpiece is located on the shore of Lake Louise. A magnificent dining room and lobby; nightclub, pool.

The Lake Louise Inn. 185 rooms, some kitchen apartments, and some hostelry type. Family plan. Licensed dining and swimming pool. Some more moderately priced accommodations available.

Moderate. **Deer Lodge.** Old but good. 69 rooms have a bath; 31 only a washbasin. But magnificent property. Licensed dining.

Moraine Lake Lodge. In valley of the 10 peaks. 14 rustic log cabins; popular. Write for reservations. Box 70, Lake Louise, T0L 1E0.

ICEFIELD PARKWAY. *Expensive.* **Parkway Lodge.** 68 units, service station and groceries. Open all year. Licensed dining. Convenient and well managed.

Moderate. **Num-Ti-Jah Lodge.** For reservations, phone long distance for mobile radio stations at Red Deer. Its location on Bow Lake and a licensed dining lounge make it popular.

BONNYVILLE. *Moderate.* **The Lakelander Motor Hotel.** Air-conditioned, kitchenettes, licensed dining and cocktail lounges; sauna and other amenities. Good choice.

Inexpensive. **Southview Motel.** Kitchenettes, color TV, telephones.

Bonnyville Hotel. Small, older hotel. Some rooms have TV. Good meals. Like most Alberta hotels it has a beer parlor.

BROOKS. *Moderate.* **Heritage Hotel.** Room service, dining room, entertainment, and other amenities.

Inexpensive. **Plains Motel.** A good clean motel with 55 units. TV, telephone, sauna.

Telstar Motor Inn. Cocktail lounge, air conditioning, kitchenettes plus licensed dining make this 51-unit motor hotel a top choice in Brooks.

CAMROSE. *Inexpensive.* **Crystal Springs Motor Hotel.** 68 air-conditioned units, clean, well-equipped; in-house entertainment. Good choice for Battle River zone.

Motel Johnson. A good, clean operation; air conditioning, kitchenette, complimentary coffee.

Norseman Inn. 80 rooms. Telephones. Dining lounge, tavern. Close to shopping.

CANMORE. *Expensive.* **Rocky Mountain Chalets.** 39 units, 1- and 2-bedroom units and lofts. Fireplaces. Kitchenettes supplied.

Moderate. **AKAI Motel.** Wheelchair-equipped units. Complimentary coffee, air-conditioned comfort in neat, clean units.

The A-1 Motel. Kitchenettes and complimentary coffee; pool, playground, laundromat. Pets welcome (if small and quiet).

CARDSTON. *Inexpensive.* **Alice Motel.** 20 units, some wheelchair-equipped; all air-conditioned with kitchenette facilities.

Flamingo Motel. 20 units including five 2-room suites; some wheelchair units; air-conditioned; kitchenettes. Complimentary coffee.

CLARESHOLM. *Inexpensive.* **Golden Pheasant Motor Inn.** 29 units; only some have air conditioning, color TV, and telephones. Several suites.

DRAYTON VALLEY. *Inexpensive.* **West-Wind Motor Inn.** Box 1287, Drayton Valley. The 31 rooms are air-conditioned with dial telephones, color TV. Also has licensed dining room, tavern, and cocktail lounge.
Drayton Valley Hotel. 45 older rooms, TV. Licensed dining, bar, tavern.

DRUMHELLER. *Moderate.* **Rockhound Motor Inn.** Fine dining facilities and lounge add to charm of riverside units.
Drumheller Motor Inn. 36 air-conditioned units, color TV, radio, telephones.
Inexpensive. **Dinosaur Motel.** 15 units, air-conditioned, complimentary coffee. Next to recreation complex.

EDSON. *Moderate.* **Edson Motor Hotel.** 67 rooms with kitchenettes, all amenities. Tavern and licensed dining.
Plainsman Motor Inn. 109 rooms. Largest in town.

ELKWATER. *Inexpensive.* **Green Tree Motel.** 19 units. Some are family units with slight extra charge for kitchens.

FORESTRY TRUNK ROAD. *Moderate.* **Highwood House.** 14 rustic log bungalows with convenience of store and service station. Kitchenettes; restaurant is adjacent.

FORT MACLEOD. *Inexpensive.* **Sunset Motel.** 22 units, some 2-room units, all air-conditioned with kitchenettes; complimentary coffee.
Fort Motel. 15 units with kitchenettes, TV, telephones, air conditioning.

FORT McMURRAY. *Expensive.* **Peter Pond Hotel.** 136 rooms and executive suites, TV, telephones. Licensed dining, cocktail lounge, tavern.
Moderate. **Twin Pine Motor Inn Motel.** Kitchenettes in 42 units, some executive suites, air conditioning, TV, telephones.

GRANDE PRAIRIE. *Moderate.* **Grande Prairie Motor Inn.** 216 rooms, direct-dial phones, air conditioning. Licensed dining and tavern. Swimming pool.
Inexpensive. **Silvercrest Lodge.** 95 units, waterbeds, complimentary coffee.

HINTON. *Expensive.* **Inn West.** 96 rooms. Honeymoon/Executive suites with whirlpool and in-room movies. Wheelchair facilities, swimming pool. Complimentary coffee.
Moderate. **Hinton Greentree Motor Lodge.** 100 units, sauna, all amenities. Swimming pool. Dining and cocktail lounge.
Tara Vista Motel. 28 units, TV, telephones, powder rooms, complimentary coffee.
Twin Pine Motor Inn. 54 rooms, TV, telephones, dining room; complimentary coffee. Swimming pool. Wheelchair facilities.

JASPER. *Deluxe.* **Becker's Roaring River Chalets.** Three miles south of Jasper townsite. Fantastic view. Open fireplaces. Seasonal. Licensed dining.

Chateau Jasper. Downtown. New in 1982. 119 attractive units. Dining room and lounge.

Jasper Park Lodge. The "something else" of the Rockies. 397 units with all amenities. Tennis courts, boating, fishing, stables, pool, golf course, luxurious dining and entertainment. The most expensive. MAP offered.

Jasper Inn Motor Lodge. 124 units with living rooms, fireplaces, balconies, queen-size beds, sauna, kitchens, indoor pools. Attractive to families.

Sawridge. New in 1983. An impressive structure: 154 rooms around a central courtyard. Licensed dining, pool.

Expensive. **Marmot Motor Lodge.** 106 air-conditioned rooms with king- and queen-size beds, amenities, sauna, cabaret, swimming pool. Wheelchair facilities.

Tonquin Motor Inn. 74 units with kitchens, TV. Licensed dining.

Moderate. **Pine Bungalows.** 58 cabins, some with 2 bedrooms; open fireplaces.

Pyramid Lake Bungalows. 10 units on terraced lakeside with boat rentals and fishing. Dining room.

Roche Bonhomme Bungalows. Some of these 21 units have fireplaces; all have kitchens, TV.

Tekarra Resort Lodge. Total of 53 units. Open fireplaces in cabins; licensed dining lounge available. Cabins are more expensive.

JASPER AREA. *Moderate.* **Columbia Icefield Chalet.** Telephone through Red Deer mobile operator. 22 rooms directly overlooking Athabasca Glacier. Restaurant facilities available.

Miette Hot Springs Resort Motel. 38 varied units, chalets and bungalows; all have kitchen facilities. Grocery store, giftshop, playground. Licensed dining.

Pocahontas Bungalows. Located 40 kms. (25 miles) east of Jasper at Miette Hot Springs junction. 48 bungalows. Swimming. Store.

LAC LA BICHE. *Moderate.* **Almac Motor Hotel.** 80 units and a tavern. Kitchens and licensed dining.

Inexpensive. **Parkland Motel.** 22 units, kitchen, radio and TV, telephones, complimentary coffee.

LACOMBE. *Inexpensive.* **Juniper Lodge.** 22 air-conditioned motel units overlooking picturesque lake. Balcony rooms, TV, restaurant, swimming.

LETHBRIDGE. *Moderate.* **Bridge Townhouse Motel.** 37 air-conditioned units. Cable TV, direct-dial telephones, pool. Wheelchair facilities.

El Rancho Motor Hotel. 106 rooms, swimming pool, convention facilities. Licensed dining.

Heidelberg Inn. 67 hotel rooms, sauna, licensed dining, bar, and entertainment. Wheelchair facilities.

Lethbridge Lodge Hotel. 4th Ave. and Scenic Dr. Family rates, in-door pool. Complimentary coffee. A good choice.

Lodge Motel. 94 units with kitchenettes. Swimming pool, sauna; Continental breakfasts and other amenities.

Park Plaza Motor Hotel. 68 air-conditioned rooms, cable TV, telephone. Licensed dining and lounge.

Sandman Inn. 421 Mayor Magrath Dr. 139 rooms, sauna, convention facilities. Licensed dining. Swimming pool. Wheelchair facilities.

LLOYDMINSTER. *Moderate.* **Wayside Inn.** 99 rooms, with families in mind. Tennis, swimming, sauna.

Inexpensive. **Lodge Motel.** 66 units. Comp. breakfast.

Thunderbird Best Western Motel. 36 units, kitchens, TV, radio, telephones. Complimentary coffee.

LONGVIEW. *Inexpensive.* **Twin Cities Hotel.** Misnamed! Longview is not a city or even a hamlet. It's a cowtown and has no twin. Rustic and Western. 12 rooms, but bathtub in only 2 of them. Outside bathrooms when last seen. Beer parlor.

MEDICINE HAT. *Moderate.* **Best Western Flamingo Terrace.** 61 units. Some 2-room family units. Laundromat. On Trans-Canada Highway.

Continental Inn. 65 rooms. All amenities, sauna. Licensed dining, cocktails, and tavern.

Medicine Hat TraveLodge. 92 units, all amenities, swimming pool. Executive suites available.

Westlander Inn. 40 rooms, all amenities. Licensed dining, cocktails, beer parlor, and entertainment (best in the 'Hat).

Inexpensive. **Assiniboia Inn.** 68 clean hotel rooms, air conditioning, dining, color TV, telephones. This is a new hotel and a real price treat.

Bel Aire Motel. 12 units with kitchens, air conditioning, TV, radios, telephones.

Parklane Motor Hotel. 79 units, air-conditioned, cable TV, telephones, swimming pool. Licensed facilities.

OLDS. *Inexpensive.* **Sportsman's Inn..** 44 units. Picnic, play area.

Siesta Motel. 26 units, friendly. Pets allowed. Complimentary coffee.

PEACE RIVER. *Inexpensive.* **Crescent Motel.** 95 units; some with queen-size beds, all with color TV, kitchens and air conditioning. Complimentary coffee.

PINCHER CREEK. *Inexpensive.* **Foothills Motel.** 30 units; kitchens and most amenities. Licensed dining.

Parkway Motel. 41 units including some family units. Complimentary coffee.

PONOKA. *Inexpensive.* **Oasis Motel.** 24 units, color TV, radio, telephones, air conditioning. Complimentary coffee.

Rancher's Inn. 42 units, phones, color TV. Coffeeshop, tavern, dining.

RED DEER. *Moderate.* **The Capri Centre.** 262 rooms, all amenities. Swimming pool and licensed facilities, conference center.

Black Knight Inn. 100 rooms, air conditioning and amenities. Swimming pool, licensed facilities and entertainment.

Quality Inn-Greatwest. 99 rooms, health club, TV, licensed dining.

Red Deer Lodge. 240 rooms. Swimming pool and all amenities, including licensed dining and tavern.

Inexpensive. **Granada Motor Inn.** 56 rooms, radios, color TV, telephones, air-conditioning. Wheelchair units. Licensed facilities.

The Red Deer Inn. 73 rooms, all amenities. Licensed dining and tavern.

ROCKY MOUNTAIN HOUSE. *Inexpensive.* **Mountview Hotel.** 54 rooms. TV, telephones. Licensed tavern and cabaret.

Wilderness Village. Adjacent to Crimson Lake provincial park. 10 bunga-lows—all 1- and 2-bedroom units with kitchens.

ST. PAUL. *Inexpensive.* **Galaxy Motel.** 53 units with kitchens, TV, tele-phones, complimentary coffee.

Lakeland Motel. 22 units, telephones, color TV, complimentary coffee.

SLAVE LAKE. *Moderate.* **Nash's Cabins.** 3 log cabins, 5 kms. (3 miles) north of Slave Lake on a private beach. Phone ahead! Open May to October.

Sawridge Motor Hotel. 120 rooms, some executive suites, dining and tavern. Wheelchair facilities.

Highway Motor Inn. 75 rooms, some suites. No restaurant.

STETTLER. *Inexpensive.* **Crusader Motel.** 33 kitchen units with telephones and TV.

Stettler Hotel. 49 rooms with TV. Dining room.

VALLEYVIEW. *Moderate.* **Plainsman Motor Inn.** 35 air-conditioned units, kitchenettes, TV, telephones, complimentary coffee, swimming pool.

Inexpensive. **The "Y" Motor Hotel.** 60 rooms, telephones, T.V., sauna. Beer parlor and licensed dining.

WAINWRIGHT. *Moderate.* **Buffalo Springs Motor Inn.** 30 units with good dining facilities, telephones, color TV, and tavern.

WATERTON LAKES NATIONAL PARK. *Expensive.* **Bayshore Inn.** On Lake. Private balconies. Cocktails and magical evenings. Seasonal.

Kilmorey Motor Lodge. Lakeside location; 28 rooms and lounges with fire-places; dining room.

Emerald Bay Motel. Overlooking Emerald Bay and dock; 23 units have kitchens; complimentary coffee.

Aspen Ponderosa Windflower Motel. 53 units, TV, sauna, complimentary coffee, and kitchen. Family suites are available in more expensive price range.

Prince of Wales Hotel. Most photographs of Waterton Lake feature this hotel in foreground. 82 rooms. Licensed dining and lounge. American Plan available.

Moderate. **El Cortez.** 34 units.

Inexpensive. **Crandell Lodge.** 11 units including some 3-room family units. All have kitchens; complimentary coffee.

WETASKIWIN. *Moderate.* **Wayside Inn.** New property with a friendly way of accommodating. Most room amenities. Fine dining and cabaret facilities.

WHITECOURT. *Moderate.* **Plainsman Motor Inn.** 112 units; suites. Lic-ensed dining.

Rivers Motor Hotel. 70 rooms, telephones, TV. Beer parlor.

HOSTELS. There are hosteling centers in three cities in Alberta—Calgary, Edmonton, and Medicine Hat. Fourteen more hostels (mainly in the mountain region between Banff and Jasper) bring the total to 17. Overnight fees are $3–9 for members and $7–12 for nonmembers. Full and complete information may be obtained by writing *Alberta Hosteling Association,* 10926 88th Ave., Edmonton, Alberta T6G 0Z1.

TELEPHONES. The area code for all of Alberta is 403.

HOW TO GET AROUND. By car: Alberta has a total of 150,412 kms. (90,247 mi.) of highways and roads. Speed limits vary according to road conditions: from 112 kms.p.h. (70 m.p.h.) to 32 kms.p.h. (20 m.p.h.). In general, the maximum highway speed limit in Alberta is 104 kms.p.h. (65 m.p.h.) by day and 88 kms.p.h. (55 m.p.h.) by night. School and playground zones are usually 32 kms.p.h. (20 m.p.h.). A note of caution: Canada is in the final stage of conversion to the metric system of measurement. Thus, mileages and speed limits are now posted in kilometers.

By train: *Via Rail* runs good dayliner service between Calgary and Edmonton. Via Rail also maintains regular line services on a network throughout the province.

By bus: Full interprovincial bus coverage is provided by *Greyhound, Canadian Coachways, Brewster Transport, Lethbridge, Northern Bus Lines, Cardinal, Diversified (PWT), Grey Goose* and local companies.

By transit and taxi: Calgary's transit fare is 95¢ exact change; Edmonton's is 90¢ exact change. Cabs are relatively expensive. The taxi trip from the airport is very expensive in Edmonton; in Calgary, for 3 or more people, it's more economical than the bus.

By air: The prime provincial carriers are *Time Air, Pacific Western Air Lines* and, to a lesser degree, *Canadian Pacific.*

FACTS AND FIGURES. Alberta, Canada's fourth largest province in land area, entered confederation on September 1, 1905. It was named by the Marquis of Lorne, then Governor General of Canada, in honor of his wife Princess Louise Caroline Alberta, fourth daughter of Queen Victoria. Its crest, issued by royal warrant in 1907, is a pictorial landscape of the province looking from east to west. It shows wheatfields, prairie, foothills, mountains, sky and a St. George's Cross. The flag of Alberta, adopted in 1968, bears the crest centered on a royal ultramarine blue background. Its floral emblem is the wild rose, and its tartan is primarily shades of green with interwoven stripes of blue, yellow and pink.

Bounded on the north by the Northwest Territories, on the west and southwest by British Columbia, on the south by Montana, and on the east by Saskatchewan, Alberta has a population of 2.3 million. Edmonton is its capital. Climate varies with specific areas. Winters see heavy snowfall in the mountains and northern portions, cold conditions in the north and eastern prairies, but moderate winters in the southwestern regions. Summers are warm throughout. Trees leaf in the first and second weeks in May. The heaviest rainfall occurs in June.

TOURIST INFORMATION. Comprehensive literature regarding attractions, accommodations, prices, and maps may be obtained by mailing a request to Travel Alberta, Capital Square 14th Flr., 10065 Jasper Ave., Edmonton, Alberta, Canada T5J 0H4, (403) 427–4321. Travel Alberta will also reply to requests concerning any aspect of tourism: i.e., canoeing, hunting, fishing, skiing, events. This literature can be supplemented by direct requests to tourist organizations in any of the 14 areas of the province. Addresses are:

Chinook Country: Travel and Convention Association of Southern Alberta, 2805 Scenic Dr., Lethbridge T1K 5B7, 329–6777.

The Gateway: South-East Alberta Travel & Convention Association, Box 605, Medicine Hat, T1A 7G5, 527–6422.

Big Country: The Big Country Tourist Association, 170 Centre St., Drumheller, T0J 0Y0, 823–5885.

Land of David Thompson: David Thompson Country Tourist Council, 4811 48th Ave., Red Deer, T4N 3T2.

Battle River: Battle River Tourist Association, Box 1515, 6107 48th Ave., Camrose, T4V 1X4, 672–8555.

Lakeland: The Lakeland Tourist Association, Box 374, St. Paul, T0A 3AO.

Evergreen Area: The Evergreen Tourist Association, Box 2548, Edson, Alberta T0E 0P0, 723–4711.

Land of the Mighty Peace: Land of the Mighty Peace Tourist Association, Box 3210, Peace River, Alberta T0H 2X0, 624–4042.

Jasper: Jasper Park Chamber of Commerce, Box 98, Jasper, T0E 1E0, 852–3858.

The Livin' West: Calgary Tourist and Convention Association Hospitality Centre, 140 6th Ave. S.E., Calgary, T2G OG2.

The Capital: Edmonton Convention and Tourism Authority, #500, 10123 99th St., Edmonton, T5J 3H1, 426–4715.

Banff: Tourist Committee, Banff-Lake Louise Chamber of Commerce, Box 1298, 94 Banff Ave., Banff, T0L 0C0. 762–3777.

Game Country: Game Country Travel Association, Box 1254, Grande Prairie, Alberta T8V 4B6, 539–6024.

Land of the Midnight Twilight: Midnight Twilight Tourist Association, #1 Sturgeon Rd., St. Albert, Alberta, T8H 0E8, 458–5600.

Alberta maintains 17 information centers located at entry points to the province. In addition, Alberta centers are located in St. Mary, Montana and Golden, British Columbia. Supplementing these are another 88 travel information outlets scattered throughout the province.

Travel information on Alberta may also be obtained from Canadian Government Office of Tourism locations in Atlanta, Boston, Buffalo, Chicago, Cleveland, Dallas, Detroit, Los Angeles, Minneapolis, New York City, Philadelphia, San Francisco, Seattle, and Washington, D.C.; Sydney, Australia; London, England; Paris, France; Frankfurt, W. Germany; The Hague, Netherlands; Tokyo, Japan; and Mexico City, Mexico.

TIME ZONE. Alberta is on Mountain Standard or Daylight Saving Time.

SEASONAL EVENTS. January: Height of ski season. The five big areas: *Sunshine Village, Lake Louise,* and *Mount Norquay,* all in Banff National Park, plus *Marmot Basin* in Jasper and *Fortress Mountain* in the Kananaskis Provincial Park, are busy with slope activity and major competitions. Late January, *Banff Lake Louise Winter Festival.*

February: *Ski competitions* on all slopes. *Winter carnivals* at Medicine Hat, Athabasca, Grande Prairie, Airdrie, High River. *Dog Sled Races* at Fox Creek. *North/Am International Snowmobile Races* at Wetaskiwin.

March: *Winter carnivals* at Calgary, Strathmore, Swan Hills. *Figure Skating* at Leduc. The *rodeo* season begins (all indoor this time of year) with events at Calgary, Edmonton, Medicine Hat, and Lethbridge.

April: *Rodeos* at Camrose, Red Deer, Vermillion, Cardston, Lloydminster, Vulcan, and Drumheller. *Figure Skating* at Two Hills and Stony Plain. *Ski Competitions* on all slopes throughout the month.

May: *Calgary International Horse Show. Summer Showcase* at Banff opens, 1st-July 31. Many *rodeos,* including Leduc, Hanna, Fox Creek, Taber, and Hobbema. At High River, the internationally acclaimed *Little Britches Rodeo* is an important event.

June: Two dozen *rodeos* throughout the province. *Horse shows* at Sundre, Claresholm, Edmonton and Red Deer. *Raft Race* at Big Valley. *Fish Derby* at Buck Lake. *International Folk Festival* at Red Deer.

July: July 1st is a national holiday and *Dominion Day* celebrations are held in most communities in Alberta. 20 *rodeos* are scheduled this month; most important are; *Calgary Stampede, Medicine Hat Stampede, Whoop-Up Days* at Lethbridge, and the *Professional* at Red Deer. *Fish Derby* at Buck Lake. In Edmonton *Klondike Days,* a glorification of the trek of '98. *Jet Boat Races* at Grande Cache and Edmonton. *Ukrainian Festival* at Vegreville, *Whitewater Canoe Races* at Sundre, Banff's *Indian Days,* hot-air balloons at Grande Prairie.

August 1st is *Heritage Day* with major ethnic festivals in Edmonton and Calgary. Banff *Festival of the Arts, Fish Derby* at Bonnyville and Lac La Biche. Ten *rodeos* occur and *horse shows* at Lloydminster, Didsbury, and Calgary. Also at Calgary is the *Annual Flower Show. Summerfest* (art, folk music, jazz) in Edmonton.

September: Ft. McMurray, *Annual Blueberry Festival. Rodeos* and *golf tournaments* happening. At Peace River, a major festival occurs during the first two weeks of the month. *Spruce Meadows Masters* equestrian event in Calgary.

October: *Rodeos* at Bassano, Claresholm, Vermillion, Caroline, Three Hills, and Hines Creek. An *Octoberfest* at Hinton, Medicine Hat, Red Deer.

November: The *Canadian Finals Rodeo* will be held in Edmonton, also annual *Farmfair.*

December: *Hockey* in every community. *Annual Christmas Carol Festival* at Foremost. In Calgary, the *Christmas Box Concert,* and the *Singing Christmas Tree. Curling Bonspiels* throughout the winter in many locations.

TOURS. By bus: Many bus tours through the Canadian west (including Alberta) are offered by tour companies whose main booking offices are in Toronto. These bus packages include variations of Alberta highlights; Calgary, Banff, Jasper, Edmonton. A few of the many are *UTL Holiday Tours,* 22 College Street; *SunTours Ltd.,* 1470 Don Mills Road, Don Mills; *Horizon Holidays of Canada,* 44 Victoria Street, all from Toronto. *De West Tours Ltd.,* 1104 510 W. Hastings Street, Vancouver, also offer Canada West packages.

In Alberta, *Brewster Transport,* Box 1140, Banff, offers the most comprehensive Banff and Jasper bus plans. *Greyhound Bus Lines,* 222 1st Ave. S.W., Calgary, is able to get you around and about in Alberta. If you would like to see the cities, *Grayline* can help.

By air: *Time Air* lands at all major Alberta cities. *Air Charter Services* (located primarily at Calgary and Edmonton) are always available to take you into the most remote locations. Alberta Air Facilities maps and supplemental booklets are available from the *Alberta Aviation Council,* 220 Terminal Building, Municipal Airport, Edmonton, T5G 0W6.

By water: You can literally paddle your own canoe in Alberta. The province has charted every major waterway (and many minor ones, too). No other province has developed its waterways so extensively for visitor traffic. Six comprehensive guide books have been prepared, as well as a waterways map. All are available from *Travel Alberta* in Edmonton.

Commercial white water and quiet water raft tours are available in both Banff and Jasper.

By horseback: Once again Alberta has extended its visitor service by assisting in the development of mountain trail riding tour packages. Originating out of Waterton, Banff and Jasper (available on a day or week basis), groups or individuals can enjoy the Rockies on horseback. Information is available from *Travel Alberta,* Edmonton.

By snowmobile: One of the most unusual tours offered anywhere in the world is a 45 minute tour over a live glacier at the Columbia Ice Fields. Located on the Banff/Jasper highway at about the half way point. Travelers should not miss this.

On skis: All major ski resorts in Alberta offer guide service and instruction for cross country skiing, using hundreds of miles of summer hiking trails to see-the-sights. Downhill skiing takes place in numerous locations, with the season extending from November to May at the top five—Fortress, Norquay, Lake Louise, Marmot Basin and Sunshine.

Canadian Rockies Helicopter skiing (with guide) takes you to the tops of slopes, lets you down, and picks you up at the bottom. Day packages are available at Banff and Jasper.

On foot: A number of guided hiking tours are available throughout the mountain parks. *Skyline Hikers,* Box 3514, Postal Station "B," Calgary, is one; and *Travel Alberta,* Edmonton, can give you information on more. Advice for mountain climbers: always seek advice and information, and register in and out with the Park Warden.

 INDUSTRIAL TOURS. Visits to an oil industry drill site or refinery are available. Also, tour possibilities exist in agro-business. Visitors are also welcome at smaller operations: glass blowing, pottery, communications. Contact local tourist information centers for more complete information.

 NATIONAL PARKS. Alberta has five national parks: *Elk Island,* about 27 kms. (17 miles) west of Edmonton; *Waterton,* in the extreme southeast corner of the province; *Banff,* 128 kms. (80 miles) west of Calgary; *Jasper,* 336 kms. (210 miles) west of Edmonton; *Wood Buffalo* in the extreme northeast.

No pass through charge for any motor vehicle. To spend a day or less, a 24-hour stopping pass can be purchased for $1.00. Most convenient is to purchase a $10.00 annual national parks pass, good until March 31st of the year following at any national park in Canada. Annual angling licenses cost $4.00, valid for all national parks.

For safety reasons, visitors must register at a Parks Warden Office before embarking on or completing any climbing, extensive backpacking, hiking, or cross-country skiing expeditions. Use of open campfires is restricted to National Park Campsites specifically designed to accommodate them. Dogs and cats must be on leash. Use of firearms and bow string equipment is forbidden; all such equipment must be sealed at park entry points.

 PROVINCIAL PARKS. There are 60 provincial parks in Alberta varying in size and facilities offered. For an overnight stay the charge is $3.00 to $5.00 a night depending on services provided. Some parks will accept reservations. Contact Travel Alberta for details.

Most of Alberta's provincial parks provide picnicking and cooking facilities (including the wood). No firearms may be used, although they are allowed entry into the park providing they are kept locked securely within your vehicle.

The following provincial parks are among the most outstanding:

Cypress Hills Provincial Park: One of the largest, 64 kms. (40 miles) southeast of Medicine Hat, the hills rise 2,000 feet above surrounding prairie: skiing, tobogganing, ice fishing, curling, skating, golf, swimming, and hiking. Reesor Lake and Elk Water Lake provide excellent water settings.

Chain Lakes Provincial Park: 39 kms. (23 miles) west of Nanton. One of Alberta's most heavily stocked trout lakes, primarily set up to accommodate fishermen. Camping and boating.

Bragg Creek Provincial Park: 32 kms. (20 miles) southwest of Calgary. Primarily a picnicking area; adjacent to the Rocky Mountains Forest Reserve; a scenic site of vast wilderness touring opportunities.

Bow Valley Provincial Park: 64 kms. (40 miles) west of Calgary. Many types of glacial remnants; spectacular mountain terrain.

Crimson Lake Provincial Park: Located in the central foothills region, 14 kms. (9 miles) northwest of Rocky Mountain House; suitable for swimming. Wildlife is abundant in the dense evergreen forest of this region;

Entrance Provincial Park: Located in the foothills 22 kms. (14 miles) northwest of Hinton; surrounds a chain of 5 small lakes; canoeing and hiking. Wildlife is abundant.

Big Knife Provincial Park: 64 kms. (40 miles) northeast of Stettler on site of an Indian battleground. The Battle River weaves through the park, providing a facility for boating.

Aspen Beach Provincial Park: 11 kms. (7 miles) west of Lacombe; features the warm waters of Gull Lake for swimming and water skiing and a wide, sandy beach that is safe for children.

Big Hill Springs Provincial Park: 16 kms. (10 miles) northeast of Cochrane, in the transition area between the Parkland and Foothills terrain. Spectacular bubbling springs provide water for 30 small waterfalls.

Jarvis Bay Provincial Park: On Sylvan Lake 19 kms. (12 miles) west of Red Deer. Dense, unspoiled undergrowth; camping.

Miquelon Lake: 64 kms. (40 miles) southeast of Edmonton; large warm-water lake and a wide, safe beach. Boating, swimming; picnicking and camping facilities are highly rated.

Pigeon Lake Provincial Park: 48 kms. (30 miles) west of Wetaskiwin on the west shore of Pigeon Lake. One of Alberta's more popular lakes for watersports is developed for camping and picnicking. Its foliage of poplar, conifers, and underbrush provide a habitat for many types of birds. Waterfowl and bird-watching.

Saskatoon Island Park: 24 kms. (15 miles) west of Grande Prairie; a bird watching park.

Wabamum Lake Provincial Park: 64 kms. (40 miles) west of Edmonton on highway 16. The natural beauty of the lake and its recreational qualities are the attractions. Angling is good for northern pike, yellow perch and lake whitefish.

Dinosaur Provincial Park: 22,000 acres located 42 kms. (26 miles) northeast of Brooks. Noted for its magnificent badlands, dinosaur quarries and displays, a major portion of this park is restricted and accessible only by means of guided bus tour. Also self-guided nature trails and walks through areas of great historical and geological interest.

Little Fish Provincial Park: 32 kms. (20 miles) southeast of Drumheller is a popular Alberta sailboating lake.

Writing on Stone Provincial Park: 32 kms. (20 miles) east of Milk River on highway number 4. One of the most interesting parks to visit. Contains vast badlands and hoodoos; the Milk River flows through its wooded and grassed picnic area. Indian stories (called pictographs) are inscribed on the rocks.

Lesser Slave Lake Provincial Park: 16 kms. (10 miles) north of the town of Slave Lake. Massive lake and large sandy beaches.

Moonshine Provincial Park: 32 kms. (20 miles) west of Spirit River. This park's current name reflects some of the goings-on in the surrounding forest at an earlier time. Known as Mirage Lake geographically, there is a rich variety of plant and animal life here.

Sir Winston Churchill Provincial Park: Located on an island in Lac La Biche with natural sandy beaches for sun bathing and swimming. The lake offers northern pike, yellow perch, and walleye.

Gregoire Lake Provincial Park: 40 kms. (25 miles) southeast of Fort McMurray. Interesting hiking trails, a scenic shoreline and a good sandy beach with boat launching facilities are highlights. The park is within a boreal forest type of topography. Pike and perch fishing are excellent.

Williamson Provincial Park and *Youngspoint Provincial Park:* Both located on Sturgeon Lake 24 kms. (15 miles) west of Valleyview off Highway 34. Two of northern Alberta's favorite campsites. Sturgeon Lake has all watersports and is noted for pike, walleye, and perch fishing.

Thunder Lake Provincial Park: 24 kms. (15 miles) west of Barrhead on Highway 33. Boating is made interesting by islands in the lakes and many uninhabited coves. Thunder Lake is one of the few nesting sites of the majestic Blue Heron.

 GARDENS. Three you might visit are: the *Sick's Brewery Gardens* in **Lethbridge**, *Reader Rock Gardens* in **Calgary**, and the *Banff Gardens* at the Administration Centre in **Banff**. There are more . . . just ask.

 FARM VACATIONS AND GUEST RANCHES. Rural families and visitors have discovered the two-way benefits of participating in Alberta's *Country Vacation* program. Facilities range from ranch to farm; from modern to rustic; from simple to most comfortable. All accommodations meet provincial health, fire, and municipal safety standards. Three basic types of accommodation are offered: room and board; housekeeping units; and camping areas. Facilities are available to families, children unaccompanied by adults, or adults (couples or singles). The plan is flexible. You can stay in your trailer, or tent, or live in the home with the family. You may arrange your own meals or share with the family. You can simply enjoy the farm atmosphere, or participate in farm chores.

The board and room rates vary slightly with the farm or ranch and the arrangement. In general, they are $18 a day or $125 a week for individuals, and $10 a day for children, 6 and under. Complete information and reservations can be obtained by contacting Travel Alberta, Box 2500, Edmonton, T5J 2Z4.

 CHILDREN'S ACTIVITIES. Most provincial parks have hiking trails, hills to climb, fields to play in, water to splash in, and playgrounds to swing and slide around in. Children can also accompany you on trail riding, fishing trips, and ski trips. All ski instructors are using the short-ski method of teaching the sport. In **Calgary**, *St. George's Island Zoo* and *Calaway Park* are popular. In **Edmonton**, *Valley Zoo* and *Fort Edmonton* are your best bets.

SUMMER SPORTS. Participant sports. Nearly every town of any size has at least one *golf* course, *swimming* pool and *tennis* court. In major centers, you can participate in anything from *squash* to *chess*.

An evolved and highly popular summer pastime is *trail riding* in the Rockies. *Horseback* tours are available all the way from Waterton National Park in southern Alberta to the Willmore Wilderness 350 miles farther north. Rides include horses, food, wrangling, and all camp making or cabin servicing. They can be taken for durations as short as one hour or for weeks in length. Cycle tours, mountain climbing, fly-in fishing and river rafting adventures are available. Details can be had by contacting Travel Alberta.

Spectator sports. The favorite spectator sports in the summer are *baseball, soccer, rodeos, lacrosse . . .* even *hockey* and *figure skating*.

FISHING. Angling is permitted in Alberta 24 hours a day and year-round, subject to closed season on specific waters. A fishing license for Albertans and nonresident Canadians costs $5.00. For a nonresident or non-Canadian, it costs $12.00. A license is issued on an annual basis and is valid until the following March 31. A three-day-limit license is also available to nonresidents and non-Canadians at $5.00. Angling permits are required by all fishermen except children under 16 years of age. A special trophy license ($5.00) is required for some lakes which offer specimens of unusual size. If sturgeon is what you are after, you should know that sturgeon is a protected species in many Alberta waters. A special sturgeon fishing license is required ($5.00). Spear fishermen must possess a $3.00 permit.

A fishing license is required for all national parks in Canada. It costs $4.00 and is good in every national park in Canada, again on an annual basis. Full information, sports fishing guide, and map may be obtained from Department of Energy and Natural Resources, 8th Floor, South Tower, Petroleum Plaza, 9915 108th St., Edmonton, Alberta, T5K 2C9.

HUNTING. Hunting of any sort is not permitted in Alberta's provincial or national parks. Further, revolvers, pistols and fully automatic firearms are prohibited in Canada. Persons entering Canada may possess and bring in rifles, shotguns or fishing tackle but must provide Canadian Customs with a description of such equipment and serial numbers of the guns so that the articles may be readily cleared upon their return. Two hundred rounds of ammunition per person are admitted duty free.

The province is noted for fine goose shooting. Waterfowl and upland game birds such as ducks, pheasants, ptarmigan, grouse and partridge roam abundantly throughout the province. All hawks, owls, falcons and eagles are protected by law. Also, several species of game bird on the "Endangered Species List" nest in Alberta (i.e., Whooping Crane). These birds are protected by law. License fees for bird game are $5.00 for Canadians but nonresidents of Alberta, and $50.00 for non-Canadians. An archery license is available for $3.00.

Big game hunting is still popular in Alberta. You can still hunt grizzly bear, wolf, cougar, and a host of antlered animals. To be sure of the areas that can be hunted and the license fees of specific game animals, prospective hunters must acquire the summary and guide of big game regulations that is revised annually by the Department of Energy, National Resources in Edmonton.

For some idea of costs: a non-Alberta resident (Canadian or otherwise) must purchase a $4 Big Game or Bird Game Certificate. In addition, specific animal licenses cost from $25 to $200, depending on the species. Further, nonresidents must be accompanied by a guide. There are no trophy fees in Alberta and export permits for game are issued free. Information on all hunting situations may be obtained from either Travel Alberta or Department of Energy, National Resources, 8th Floor, South Tower, Petroleum Plaza, 9915 108th St., Edmonton, Alberta T5K 2C9.

CAMPING OUT. On every major roadway, at least every 80 kms. (50 miles), a roadside campsite has been established offering picnic shelters, fireplaces with wood supplied, and drinking water.

The provincial park system also offers more camping opportunities at a very moderate rate. These sites always incorporate recreational possibilities. Many well maintained commercial (e.g., KOA), municipal, and club oriented camping and recreational vehicle parks. Most provide good camping amenities. Travel Alberta publishes an annual accommodations guide listing the specifications and characteristics of every campground within the province. A copy may be obtained by writing to *Travel Alberta,* Capital Square, 14th Floor, 10065 Jasper Ave., Edmonton, Alberta, Canada, T5J 0H4.

TRAILER TIPS. Touring by trailer or motor home is popular. All cities and many major towns provide facilities for service and maintenance of vehicles. While Alberta highways are more than suitable for safe driving, advice should be sought before you attempt to travel the gravel roads of wilderness areas.

In most Alberta provincial parks, overnight camping is allowed. The cost is included in the rate. Electrical hookup in provincial parks is additional per night. Most private trailer parks are able to provide electrical, water, and sewage hookups as well as showers and laundry services. *Travel Alberta*'s accommodation guide lists well over 100 sewage dumping stations distributed conveniently throughout the province. Calgary and Edmonton each have several such stations, while the major centers near Alberta points-of-entry are all able to accommodate these trailering needs.

WINTER SPORTS. The Canadian Rockies in the national parks are among the world's finest **skiing** locales. The slopes of Marmot Basin, Fortress, Norquay, Sunshine, Lake Louise are the major ones, but there are many others—in the heart of Calgary or Edmonton, or at Waterton, Red Deer, Camrose, Cypress Hills, Grande Prairie, Westlock, or Fort McMurray—if not downhill, certainly cross country. Snowmobiling is much the same; however, the machines are not allowed in national parks or many provincial parks although they are allowed in many of the wilderness areas.

HISTORIC SITES. There is evidence of human habitation in Alberta 20,000 years ago. Writing on the **Stone Provincial Park** has sandstone pictographs; and, on a farm near **Viking,** two large rocks are carved and chiselled with lines resembling the ribs of buffalo.

A few miles directly south of **Cluny** in the valley of the Bow River is the site of the signing of Treaty 7 in 1877. The Indians of the southern plains gathered here—representatives of Blackfoot, Blood, Peigans, Sarcee, and Stoneys—who surrendered their rights to their traditional way of life and to their territory to Queen Victoria.

Frank Slide in the **Crowsnest Pass,** between the towns of Blairmore and Bellevue on Highway 3, took the lives of more than 70 persons in 1903 when a gigantic wedge of limestone 2,100 feet high, 3,000 feet wide, and 500 feet thick crashed down from Turtle Mountain wiping out most of the town and taking the lives in approximately 100 seconds.

 MUSEUMS. There are numerous museums in communities throughout the province. Some of the most important are: *The Luxton Museum* in **Banff,** although relatively small, contains one of Alberta's finest collections of Plains and Mountain native Indian paraphernalia.

The *Provincial Museum of Alberta* in **Edmonton** features an excellent display natural and human history.

The *Glenbow Museum* in **Calgary** covers art and Indian and western Canadian history.

The *Reynolds Museum* in **Wetaskiwin** is a power museum, concentrating on aircraft, automobiles, and machinery of the steam era.

 MUSIC. Both Calgary and Edmonton enjoy full philharmonic orchestras. Most cities possess performing groups. There's a *Banff Festival of the Arts* every August.

 SHOPPING. In Alberta, always popular are the Hudson's Bay blankets that have been in use since the days of Indian trade. Furs and fur products are choice items. Native people also produce clothing and tools of a bygone day and a high commercial standard. Artwork, produced by local artisans, includes pottery, ceramics, sculptures, and paintings. You will find at least one shop in the larger communities (*The Calgary Cabin* in Calgary, the *Trading Post* in Banff, *The Bay* in Edmonton) that specializes in Albertan products.

 DRINKING LAWS. Legal age in Alberta is 18 years. Liquor and beer may be purchased only through Alberta Liquor stores. In addition, beer supplies may be obtained from the majority of hotels. Liquor stores are closed Sunday, on major holidays, and days of election. There is no universal standard of opening hours. Some stores stay open until 11:30 P.M., others until 10:00 P.M., and many only until 6:00 P.M.

 DINING OUT. This is cattle country, and Albertans are fiercely proud of the quality of beef that its grazing lands and grain yields. With good reason, too.

Restaurants are listed by price category as follows: *Deluxe,* $28 and over; *Expensive,* $19–28; *Moderate,* $13–19; *Inexpensive,* under $13. Prices include hors d'oeuvres or soup, salad, main course, dessert, and coffee, but not drinks or gratuities. Entertainment (particularly good music in an appealing atmosphere) is the general rule in *Deluxe* and *Expensive* categories.

Two pancake house chains—Smitty's Pancake House and Phil's Pancake House—both *inexpensive,* offer an extensive selection of appealing family foods. Most places accept major credit cards.

BANFF. *Deluxe.* **Banff Springs Hotel.** The Alhambra Dining Room and the Alberta Restaurant have table d'hôte menus, the Rob Roy and the less formal Potpourri have à la carte menus. All are attractive. Worth a visit if only for the view, atmosphere and history.

Le Beaujoulais. Consistent quality in the French tradition. The selection and preparation of ingredients come together well in an attractive setting.

Expensive. **Caboose.** A railroad-theme steakhouse adjoining the train station. Pleasant surroundings.

Drifters. Good salad bar; beef and seafood dominate.

Ticino. Swiss-Italian restaurant specializing in veal dishes, beef, and cheese fondues and steak.

Moderate. **Banff Café.** A local favorite. Informal; broad menu.

CAMROSE. *Expensive.* **Bono's Family Restaurant.** A fine restaurant, specializing in seafood chowder, Alberta beef, and other excellent selections.

The Feedmill. Quiet. Relaxed in atmosphere and service. Good menu.

CLARESHOLM. *Inexpensive.* **The Flying "N."** One of Canada's top 10 restaurants, at a one-time Canadian Air Force Base. Extensive menu; the finest home-cooked food, served buffet-style.

COLEMAN. *Deluxe.* **Crowsnest Guest Ranch.** Western atmosphere in the heart of cattle country. Take steak or their excellent lobster.

Expensive. **Longhorn.** A good menu of wholesome food, prepared well.

DRUMHELLER. *Moderate.* **The Corner Dining Lounge.** Seafood is top of the list with lobsters and shrimp. Also, try the Dinosaur burger (steak sandwich).

Roman's Dining Lounge. Fresh food presented in a Neanderthal style.

EDSON. *Moderate.* **Plainsman Motor Inn.** A good, clean family restaurant.

FORT MACLEOD. *Moderate.* **The Java Shop.** Oven-baked chicken is superb.

Scarlet & Gold Inn. Mounted police atmosphere featuring steak and lobster.

GRANDE PRAIRIE. *Moderate.* **Grande Prairie Motor Inn.** Small, tastefully appointed dining room with a good menu. Excellent specialty is prime rib.

HINTON. *Inexpensive.* **Husky House.** Steak and eggs, plus a fair menu, good food, and a clean operation.

JASPER. *Deluxe.* **Jasper Park Lodge.** A fine steakhouse. The Henry House, and a magnificent main dining room with a spectacular view. Reservations a must.

Expensive. **Tonquin Prime Rib Village.** Good selection of beef and pork. Some seafood. Has become more expensive of late, but a clean, reliable operation.

Chateau Jasper. New. If food lives up to the elegant surroundings, it should be a good find. Broad menu selection. Rather formal.

Tekarra Lodge. Good menu. Lamb is the specialty. Rustic and pleasant.

Moderate. **Diamond.** At Diamond Motel. Good family type meals. Mountain view.

Inexpensive. **L & W.** Best burgers and pizza in town. Relaxed. Popular with locals.

LETHBRIDGE. *Deluxe.* **El Rancho.** Has long been one of the most popular eating establishments in Lethbridge.

Park Plaza Motor Hotel. Southern Alberta elegance with flambés as delicious as they are spectacular. Lobster tails are superb. Menu imaginative.

Sven Ericksen's Family Restaurant. Distinctive dining for the whole family. Informal atmosphere; large and varied menu; good food.

Moderate. **Harvester.** Disco lounge with steak and seafood dining. Echoes of a prairie harvest.

House of Wong. The place for Oriental cuisine in Lethbridge. Portions are large; service is friendly.

Majorette Restaurant. Offers a choice of Western and Chinese cuisine. The menu is large enough to please an entire family.

MEDICINE HAT. *Deluxe.* **Continental Inn.** Gourmet menu. Excellent service in semi-formal atmosphere. Entertainment.

Old Mill Inn. An old flour mill has been converted into a spectacular dining experience. Menu features beef and seafoods.

The Westlander Inn. (Trans-Canada Hwy.) The ultimate in *Medicine Hat.* A first class operation in every aspect, rivaling those of many major cities. Gracious surroundings and service, exquisite food.

Moderate. **Golden Dragon.** Oriental menu is the specialty. Pleasant, quiet atmosphere.

Heidel Haus. Steaks. Old country decor. An upstairs loft offers dancing.

The Ming Tree. Lots of action; friendly faces, good food. Portions are large; specialty is chinese cuisine, but menu covers everything from steak to seafood to barbecued ribs.

PEACE RIVER. *Inexpensive.* **Traveller's.** Daytime smorgasbord. Interesting dining delights in evening with extensive menu.

PINCHER CREEK. *Deluxe.* **Foothills Restaurant.** Pleasing décor, home-cooked meals, and friendly service.

Expensive. **Oasis Restaurant.** Topping the ambitious menu are steak and lobster.

RED DEER. *Deluxe.* **Capri Motor Hotel.** The best in central Alberta. Gourmet cooking; good menu.

Frankonia Gasthaus. Munich specialties and a great variety of European foods. Try Ukrainian cabbage rolls.

Red Deer Lodge. Gracious gourmet dining on an international basis.

Moderate. **Anthony Henday.** English menu and style. Steak-and-kidney pie. Adjacent to London pub.

Ranch House. Excellent steaks at reasonable prices. Good salad bar. Best buy in Red Deer.

ST. ALBERT. *Expensive.* **The Settlement.** A charming, rustic restaurant with a menu featuring French gourmet and international cuisine.

WATERTON LAKES. *Expensive.* **Tourist Cafe.** Pies are the number one attraction, but the steak and the home-cooked meals are good, too.

Prince of Wales. An impressive dining room, friendly staff and a great view.

Bayshore. On the lake. Broad menu selection. Beef is featured.

BRITISH COLUMBIA

Gateway to the Pacific

by
ROCKWELL STENSRUD
and
DAVID WISHART

Rockwell Stensrud, a freelance writer based in New York, is co-author of Whitman's Off Season Guide to Europe *and has written many travel articles. He has been a student of Canadian culture for many years.*

David Wishart is a freelance travel writer based in Vancouver. A former editorial writer and columnist on the morning newspaper there, he has worked as a journalist on four continents.

British Columbia combines all the essentials for the traveler seeking a great outdoor adventure and a comfortable easy-going vacation—or both. For those interested in nature—and wishing to rough it for a while—the province encompasses 948,600 sq. kms. (366,255 square miles) of rugged and beautiful land. Yet cities such as Vancouver and Victoria offer the tourist first-rate amenities, a rich cultural life, and the finest international cuisine.

Canada's gateway to the Pacific and the Orient, British Columbia prides itself on being the dominion's most scenic province—a land of mountain ranges and forests, rivers, streams, and lakes. Tightly bounded by the Pacific on the west, the Rockies on the east, the United States to the south, and the Yukon and Alaska to the north, the province has developed a lifestyle quite different from the rest of the nation—more tuned in to land and sea. With a mild, healthy, though often wet year-round climate, British Columbia is on the upswing economically —a land rich in minerals and wood, with waterways and coastal areas teeming with sea life. For residents and visitors alike, the province generates a great sense of vitality in the northwest stretches of the continent.

A Bit of History

British Columbia was probably first sighted in 1579 by Sir Francis Drake, who was searching for the Northwest Passage. Instead, he saw Vancouver Island—and passed it by. It was another 200 years before anyone was interested in exploring the territory. Juan Pérez of Spain saw its shores in 1774, but it was not until 1778, when Captain James Cook sailed into what is now known as Friendly Cove, at Nootka Sound, Vancouver Island, that a white man stepped on British Columbia land. (Cook was also looking for the Northwest Passage, but settled for fur trading with the Indians instead.) By 1785, many ships were landing in the area in order to get a piece of the highly lucrative fur business.

While the Colonists were waging their War of Independence from Great Britain in the eastern United States, England and Spain were deadlocked over the rights to this vast Pacific territory. Spain assumed ownership and, in 1789, sent a ship commanded by Captain Martinez to seize all British property at Nootka Sound. The British government, by then embarrassed by its loss of the thirteen American colonies, came close to declaring war on Spain. Uneasy about forcing the issue, the Spanish declared the region open to all comers.

England Establishes Its Claim

In 1790, the Nootka Convention between Spain and England ceded the entire northern coast up to Russian Alaska to His Majesty; two years later, the British Admiralty sent Captain George Vancouver to survey and lay claim to the territory.

At about this time, the overland route across Canada was being forged. Alexander Mackenzie reached the Pacific in 1793 in the first crossing of the country anywhere on the continent above Mexico. Mackenzie is a legend, but his journey was a search for wealth, not glory. He made the long trek as a representative of the North West Company, one of the New World trapping and trading alliances—and chief rival of the Hudson's Bay Company. Both were after the profitable fur spoils of the northwest. Mackenzie set up a thriving fur business, and the word spread fast.

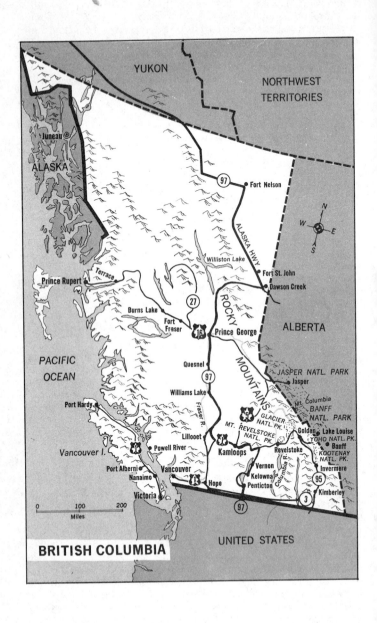

BRITISH COLUMBIA

Rivalry among Trading Companies

Unlike the eastern part of Canada and the United States where national armies clashed, the west never saw real warfare. But there was fierce rivalry of another sort among the great trading companies which represented the competing governments of the day. The early history of British Columbia records bitter struggles on the part of these companies to establish their forts at strategic points around the area's rivers, lakes, and ocean ports.

Beginning in 1805, Simon Fraser entered the area and built several forts for his trading activities—Fort McLeod, Fort St. James, and Fort George. Other pioneers soon arrived and constructed their posts, usually at the confluence of two or more major rivers. In 1821, when the mighty North West Company sold out to the even mightier Hudson's Bay Company, the business battle was over for a time. For the next 30 years, Hudson's Bay controlled the vast territory with only nominal help from London. There were more forts, more people, more fur trapping and trading.

The 49th Parallel

Hudson's Bay Company kept a tight rein on its land, often angering the United States government when Americans were excluded or short-changed by the company. This set the scene for a diplomatic showdown between London and Washington over the uncharted western lands. Both countries wanted title to as much land as possible. Finally in 1846, they settled on the 49th parallel, extending from the Rockies to the Pacific, as the boundary line between the United States and British holdings. Fort Victoria became the seat of government in British Columbia and, in 1849, the Hudson's Bay Company turned over all of Vancouver Island to the British.

The company installed the early governors of the territory. Richard Blanshard only lasted a year; he was succeeded by James Douglas, who ruled alone until a Legislative Assembly was formed in 1856—the first such representative body in the West. There were still less than 800 colonists there at the time.

Those days were not to last long. In 1858, gold was discovered on the Fraser River, and the rush from the south was on. Within the year, close to 30,000 people invaded British Columbia, looking for instant wealth. There were many disappointments, but as one river bed dried up, another "hit" would be found elsewhere. In 1860, the Cariboo region was struck, and thousands more made the trek north. Roads were built; communities sprang up within weeks. The colony was prospering.

At the same time (1858), the colony was officially proclaimed, with Douglas serving as the first governor. In 1866, Vancouver Island and the mainland territory were officially joined; the small colony of New Westminster served as the first capital. Three years later, however, Victoria was designated the capital, which it remains today.

In the east, while British Columbia was undergoing a financial depression, the other Canadian provinces were forming their Confederation. In 1867, the eastern lands joined together. Wanting to make a clean east-west sweep (and also needing British Columbia's outlet to the Pacific), they invited British Columbia to join. At issue was communications! British Columbia said it would unite with her neighbors only if a trans-Canada railroad linked them, shore to shore. The easterners agreed, and British Columbia joined the Canadian Confederation on July 20, 1871.

Linked to the Rest of Canada

A promise to build a railroad over 8,000 kms. (5,000 miles) of difficult terrain and building it were two different things. The federal government, failing at its first attempt, had an incensed group of British Columbians on its hands, some of them shouting for secession. The second attempt, launched by a private company, was successful; by 1885, Vancouver was linked to the rest of Canada by the Canadian Pacific Railroad.

Gold!

British Columbia's new prosperity was suddenly heightened when a large lode of gold was discovered in the Kootenay region in 1887. First came the Hall mines; then the Red Mountain mines were explored three years later. Minerals were found in abundance, bringing more and more prospectors as the word spread throughout the continent. The province was not yet self-sufficient but, as its industries developed, its dependence on the federal government lessened. In the meantime, Vancouver became the primary seaport on the Pacific and, with the opening of the Panama Canal in 1915, the city shot up in size and influence, bringing prosperity to the entire province. Shipbuilding, lumbering, manufacturing, and energy all became major industries. Fishing expanded greatly. Fertile lands were farmed with excellent results. More mineral wealth was discovered. All through the 20th century, British Columbia has continued to be a land of discovery, offering many challenges to man's imagination.

Today, British Columbia remains a vital and prosperous province. Although not as wealthy as the oil and gas-rich Albertans to the east, with their huge timber, mineral, and fishing revenues, British Columbians live a better life than most Canadians. Yet it will always be the great natural beauty of the province (especially the rugged coast and the Canadian Rocky Mountains) that will be the most important drawing card for travelers.

EXPLORING VANCOUVER

Cosmopolitan, prosperous, multiracial, and active, Vancouver is often referred to as Canada's "Gem of the Pacific." A symbol of British

Columbia, it is the largest seaport on the Pacific coast, claiming 160 kms. (100 miles) of water frontage. With mountain ranges to the east and north cutting off the cold Arctic air, and Vancouver Island, to the west, protecting it from rough Pacific winds, Vancouver has such a pleasant mild climate that on a good day in winter or spring, you can play golf in the morning, ski on Grouse Mountain 20 minutes away in the afternoon, and have a swim in the English Bay, warmed by the Japanese Current, before dinner.

But its fine weather is just a start. As Canada's third largest city, with a population of 1.2 million, Vancouver offers excellent hotels and restaurants, a rich cultural life, sports, leisure activities, and interesting sightseeing. Many parts of the city—such as Gastown or Chinatown—are best explored on foot; that is true for the city's many parks, too.

Vancouver is situated on a peninsula between the Burrard Inlet on the north and the Fraser River on the south. Greater Vancouver—including Vancouver, New Westminster (the original settlement), Burnaby, Sea Island (where the airport is located), North Vancouver, and West Vancouver—is connected by a series of bridges. Vancouver City measures 114 sq. kms. (44 square miles), and Metropolitan Vancouver covers 2,067 sq. kms. (798 square miles); therefore, to see many of the sights, a car or a sightseeing bus is a must. Lying 232 kms. (145 miles) from Seattle, Washington, and just 40 kms. (25 miles) from the U.S.–Canadian border, Vancouver is easily accessible by car.

Vancouver's biggest drawing card is its spectacular mountain and sea scenery. Although the city sparkles with new glass-and-steel high-rises and many grand Victorian structures, what sets Vancouver apart from almost any other North American metropolis, with the possible exception of San Francisco, is its beautiful, natural setting.

Stanley Park

For many travelers, the 1,000-acre Stanley Park, just minutes from downtown at the northern tip of the city proper, represents all aspects of Vancouver. The largest natural park in any city on the continent, it is filled with many man-made amusements. You can swim in pools or at two fine beaches on English Bay. You can stroll along the many walking paths through the park or along the sea wall. Most visitors to Stanley Park (named after Lord Stanley, Governor General of Canada in 1889, who also lent his name to professional hockey's prestigious Stanley Cup) will want to see the well-stocked zoo, complete with a miniature railroad. There is also a children's zoo, with baby animals. The aquarium displays aquatic animals from around the world—over 8,300, including several killer whales. Elsewhere in the park, you'll see many totem poles carved, over the centuries, by British Columbia's Coast Indians. The most spectacular stands at Prospect Point, where the famous Lions Gate Bridge—longest in the Commonwealth—crosses the Narrows into residential West Vancouver. Stanley Park's other points of interest are: tennis courts, cricket and rugby fields, the Brockton Point Lighthouse, and the Siwash Rock. Vancouver's Nine O'Clock Gun, which booms each evening to let citizens set their watches, is also located in the park, along with over 100,000 trees.

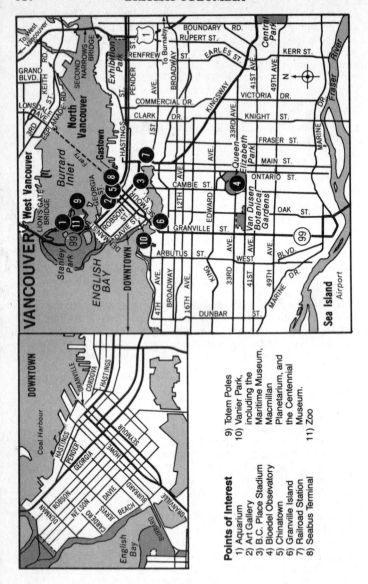

Points of Interest

1) Aquarium
2) Art Gallery
3) B.C. Place Stadium
4) Bloedel Observatory
5) Chinatown
6) Granville Island
7) Railroad Station
8) Seabus Terminal
9) Totem Poles
10) Vanier Park, including the Maritime Museum, Macmillan Planetarium, and the Centennial Museum.
11) Zoo

A short distance away from Stanley Park is Vancouver's busy downtown, where most of the fine hotels and restaurants are located. Broad avenues add to the sense of space and elegance here. The main attractions, for shopping, eating, or strolling, in the heart of Vancouver are the Granville Island market and shops, Gastown, Chinatown, and Robson Street (usually referred to as Robsonstrasse).

Gastown

Gastown is where Vancouver began, back in the 1860's. Many of the city's early stores were established here, as well as a popular hotel run by "Gassy Jack" Deighton, for whom the area was named. The entire section fell on hard times as Vancouver and its suburbs grew—until the 1960's, when urban renewal came on the scene. Gastown is now a lively, historic section, filled with refurbished original structures housing boutiques, restaurants, nightclubs, and antique shops, some of which are open on Sundays. One of the most interesting parts of Vancouver, it should be part of any tour. Hastings Street is the main east-west thoroughfare, but Cordova Street and Water Street offer the most charm and old-time atmosphere. Don't miss the large Gastown Steam Clock on Water Street.

Chinatown

Chinatown in Vancouver is the second largest Chinese section in North America—San Francisco's is number one. Its center is Pender Street, from Shanghai Alley to Gore Street. A thriving community and quite colorful, it is filled with good Chinese restaurants and food markets. Be sure to see what is billed as The World's Thinnest Office Building—a 6-foot-wide structure that still houses offices.

Robsonstrasse

While Granville Street and the Granville Mall for pedestrians are the traditional shopping areas of the city, Robsonstrasse, so named for its European-style shops and restaurants, is one of Vancouver's most chic spots. Buying or just window shopping is a delight on Robsonstrasse (also called Robson St.).

The downtown center is also home of the Queen Elizabeth Theatre and Playhouse, one of Canada's most exciting theaters. Numerous other theaters—the Actors' Workshop and the Arts Club Theatre among them—will also be found near your hotel. For art lovers, the Vancouver Art Gallery is on West Georgia Street in the old Court House. A splendid new Court House now stands on the block behind the old one. Here you will also find the new Robson Square complex, which has a Tourism B.C. office, restaurants, and is a pleasant gathering spot with frequent lunchtime entertainment in the summer months.

Like so many other northern cities, Vancouver has also gone underground to serve shoppers. For convenient strolling and buying, especially if the weather is bad, try the 180-store Pacific Centre Mall under the Four Seasons Hotel on West Georgia near Howe Street; also the Harbour Centre and Royal Centre areas.

After touring Stanley Park and the downtown streets, there's still a great deal more to see. One of the best ways to view Vancouver's beauties is to go by car or bus from downtown, across the Burrard Street Bridge, stopping first at Vanier Park. Here you may visit the Maritime Museum, home of the ship *St. Roch,* the first vessel to sail the hazardous Northwest Passage, east and west. Close by are the Centennial Museum, containing artifacts dating from the rugged pioneer days, and the ultramodern MacMillan Planetarium, which has one of the finest planetarium shows on the continent. Don't miss the new Granville Island development, under the Granville Bridge. It has a superb market, theaters, and restaurants. (It's closed Mondays.)

"Scenic Drive"

Continuing westward on Point Grey Road, you'll see English Bay on the north, and a stunning view of the city behind you. Called the Scenic Drive, its name lives up to its promise. You might want to make a quick stop at the Hastings Mill Store, the first store and post office built in Vancouver and now a museum. Continue on and you'll come to the 100-acre University of British Columbia. Stop by and see the beautiful Nitobe Memorial Japanese Gardens, one of the best re-creations outside the Orient. Also on the campus are the Fine Arts Gallery and the beautiful Museum of Anthropology which features an array of shows from B.C. cultures as well as the totem poles of the Coast Indians.

This coastal drive lets everyone see very quickly why Vancouver is so popular—trees line the shores, and beyond is the large bay, set off against the mountains to the north. Not only is Vancouver clean and fresh and inhabited by friendly citizens, it has such natural attraction that it's easy to want to stay for a long time.

Leaving Marine Drive and circling back eastward at 41st Avenue, continue to Oak Street and go north to the Van Dusen Botanical Gardens. Recently opened to the public, this 55-acre park is filled with native and exotic flowers and plants. Close by is one of the prettiest parks in the city—Queen Elizabeth Park where you'll find the highest elevation in Vancouver city—and a magnificent view. There are walking paths, a Rose Garden, a Sunken Garden, an arboretum, tennis courts, and a restaurant. Aside from the view of the city and the beauty of the park itself, don't miss the Bloedel Conservatory where over 400 varieties of exotic plants and flowers are nurtured.

Artists in a Palace

From Queen Elizabeth Park you can either make the short drive downtown again or continue east to the suburb of Burnaby. There you'll find Heritage Village at Gilpin Street. The village is a fine re-creation of a typical turn-of-the century village in British Columbia. Children will be especially interested. Nearby is the Burnaby Art Gallery, featuring contemporary artists in a grand old palace of a house.

While in Burnaby, head north to the handsome Simon Fraser University campus on top of Burnaby Mountain. Here again, views of the city and the surrounding mountains are superb. The campus is well known because of its modern architectural design. Guided tours are available.

Heading west again, you'll pass Burnaby Mountain and Centennial Park, which is a good spot for a picnic. Next, in Vancouver proper along Hastings Street, you'll pass the 18-acre Pacific National Exhibition Grounds, where the Pacific National Exhibition is held each August. The Grounds also include Vancouver's major sports complex—the Coliseum, home of the National Hockey League Canucks; Empire Stadium, home of the British Columbia Lions football team and the Vancouver Whitecaps Soccer Club; and a fine racetrack, open all summer. British Columbia's Sports Hall of Fame is here, as well as the British Columbia Pavilion, housing a huge three-dimensional relief map of the province.

North Vancouver

Leaving the Vancouver city peninsula at Exhibition Park via the Second Narrows Bridge, you'll cross the Burrard Inlet and find yourself in North Vancouver, a suburb of the city, and site of many lumberyards and shipyards. The land here is probably the most scenic in all of metropolitan Vancouver. North Vancouver is mountainous and green, with the sea at its doorstep. Just over the bridge, off Main Street and Cotton Road, is the Park and Tilford Gardens, a small but lovely series of gardens, open year round. It offers changing displays and is floodlit in summer. As with most of Vancouver's parks, admission is free.

Farther north is the 200-acre Lynn Canyon Park, a natural habitat with fine hiking trails and the Lynn Canyon Ecology Centre. The Centre displays shows, educational films, and other media on the ecology of plants, animals, and man. More exciting is the Suspension Bridge, a 273-foot-high bridge that stretches across Lynn Creek. The hike across can be a bit frightening to those suffering from acrophobia, so the faint hearted should beware. Lynn Canyon Park is one of Vancouver's treasures.

To the east is the huge Mount Seymour Provincial Park, only 16 kms. (10 miles) from downtown Vancouver, yet another world away. Skiing in winter is excellent; during the rest of the year, the natural beauties are enough to hold any visitor's attention. A convenient—and fun—way to visit North Vancouver is to take the SeaBus from the bottom of Granville Street.

Lavish Houses, Lavish Views

But the most popular tourist spots—for Vancouverites and outlanders as well—are situated in North Vancouver but closer to West Vancouver, and are most easily reached by crossing the Lions Gate Bridge if you're coming from downtown. Sightseers interested in opulent manmade communities should head for West Vancouver's British Properties. This is the rich, secluded area featuring lavish houses with even more lavish views of the city and the terrain.

Three magnificent stops are next on your route. Going north on Capilano Road, the first is the spectacular Capilano Suspension Bridge, the world's longest, opened in 1899. You can walk across the 450-foot bridge, which spans the Capilano River and Canyon. Scenes from here are breathtaking. The bridge is safe—but, again, those with some aversion to swaying in the breeze might want to think twice before traversing it. Nearby is the Capilano Salmon Hatchery, an exciting place for anglers and those interested in fish ecology. The Hatchery offers guided tours to help the novice understand the complex world of fish life in the Northwest. Farther north, on your way to Grouse Mountain, is Cleveland Dam, a fine place to hike, rest, or picnic. The dam is known as one of the best places to see the symbol of Vancouver: two mountain peaks known as The Lions.

Grouse Mountain Skyride

Probably the biggest tourist attraction in the city is the Grouse Mountain Skyride, north of Cleveland Dam, yet still only a short ride from town. Grouse Mountain is a favorite in winter for skiing and in summer for hiking and picnicking. The Skyride is an aerial tramway that ascends 3,700 feet above Vancouver, offering the finest view of the city, the surrounding mountains, and the sea. The ride is exciting and safe; when you reach the top, there are restaurants for snacks or gourmet meals. The ride is highly recommended. In winter and spring, you can ski right there at Grouse Mountain—the skiing is quite good—and still be only 15 minutes from downtown.

The last major site of interest, in West Vancouver, and a good spot for a last look at the city, is Lighthouse Park, 8 kms. (5 miles) west of Lions Gate Bridge on Marine Drive. An idyllic park, with long walking paths and some of the area's largest trees, it yields a superb view of the skyline across English Bay.

Vancouver lives in a state of nature. While the city provides excellent entertainment, architecture, and ambiance, its parks, waterways, and mountains make the city as beautiful and refreshing as it is.

PRACTICAL INFORMATION FOR VANCOUVER

HOW TO GET THERE. By air: Vancouver International Airport is a major terminal for domestic and international flights. Numerous carriers serve the city, including *Air Canada, British Airways, CP Air, Cathay Pacific, Japan Air Lines, Lufthansa, United, Western* and *PWA*. The airport is located on Sea Island, just south of the city proper.

By car: Coming from the U.S., in Seattle, Washington, take Hwy. 5 north to the border, where the road turns into Canada Hwy. 99. The drive from Seattle takes about 3 hours. From the east, approach Vancouver on the Trans-Canada Hwy. (Hwy. 1).

By train: the *Canadian Pacific Railroad* and the *Canadian National Railroad* both service Vancouver; many of the overland trains offer glass observation cars.

By bus: *Greyhound* and *Trailways* both have good schedules to the city.

By ferry: Vancouver can be reached from Alaska, Victoria, and other points on Vancouver Island. You can get there from Seattle by changing at Victoria. British Columbia has the most extensive ferry system in the world.

ACCOMMODATIONS. Most of Vancouver's hotels and motels are very comfortable. Those in the deluxe range are all excellent. Price categories are as follows: *Deluxe* $105 and up for doubles; *Expensive,* $70–95; *Moderate,* $50–70; *Inexpensive,* under $50.

Most places accept the following major credit cards: American Express, MasterCard, and Visa; others may also be honored.

Deluxe

Bayshore Inn. West Georgia and Cardero Sts. Modern 20-story tower; on harbor, near downtown; all amenities. Phone 682–3377.

Four Seasons Hotel. 791 W. Georgia St.; in shopping district; very pleasant; fine cuisine. One of the Four Seasons Group, this is one of the finest new hotels anywhere in the world; tastefully decorated, superb service. Phone 689–9333.

Georgian Court. 773 Beatty St. New, near B.C. Place. Run by KLM's Golden Tulip. Phone 682–5555.

Hotel Vancouver. 900 W. Georgia St. Beautiful older hotel in center of downtown; fine traditional décor; excellent eating. Phone 684–3131.

Hyatt Regency Vancouver. 655 Burrard St. In Royal Centre, downtown; 34 stories; luxurious rooms, all amenities. Phone 687–6543.

Vancouver Mandarin. 645 Howe St. New, elegant, luxurious, for the discriminating traveler. Top restaurants. Phone 687–1122.

Expensive

Delta Airport Inn. 10251 St. Edward's Dr. A few minutes from airport; spacious rooms; airport limousine. Phone 278–9611.

Century Plaza TraveLodge. 1015 Burrard St. 30-story, elegant; good-size rooms, nightly entertainment. Phone 687–0575.

Denman Hotel. 1733 Comox St. Fine, 36-story hotel near Stanley Park; excellent rooms; splendid views. Phone 688–7711.

Georgia Hotel. 801 W. Georgia St. Newly renovated; in center of town; fine cuisine and atmosphere. Phone 682–5566.

Holiday Inn—Harbourside. 1133 W. Hastings St.; in downtown, with superb views over the harbor; revolving restaurant on 21st Floor. Phone 689–9211.

International Plaza Hotel. 1999 Marine Dr. Beautifully situated; a luxury resort hotel with fine views; gardens. Very good. Phone 984–0611.

Miramar Hotel. 1160 Davie St. Modern. 24-story. Good-size rooms; pool and restaurant. Phone 685–1311.

Palisades Hotel. 1277 Robson St. Pleasant rooms, pool, convenient. Phone 688–0461.

River Inn. 3500 Cessna Dr. On 10 acres of park land; 11 stories, very nice rooms and restaurant. Phone 278–1411.

Sheraton-Landmark Hotel. 1400 Robson St. 42 stories; revolving restaurant; near shopping, saunas, all amenities. Phone 687–0511.

Sheraton-Plaza 500. 500 W. 12th Ave. Attractive modern hotel; fine bar, restaurant. Phone 873–1811.

Moderate

Park Royal Hotel. 440 Clyde Ave. 10 minutes from center, located on north shore; pleasant rooms and atmosphere. Phone 926–5511.

Sheraton Villa Inn. 4331 Dominion St., Burnaby. Quiet, elegant; nice gardens, nice rooms. Restaurant. Phone 430–2828.

TraveLodge-Downtown. 1304 Howe St. Good, central location. Restaurant. Phone 682–2767.

Inexpensive.

Austin Motor Hotel. 1221 Granville St. Fine, comfortable motel in downtown area. Most amenities. Phone 685–7235.

Blue Boy Motor Hotel. 725 S.E. Marine Dr. Convenient location for all touring. Modern, with most amenities. Phone 321–6611.

Nelson Place Hotel. 1006 Granville St. Well located for shopping. Spacious rooms. Phone 681–6341.

Sylvia Hotel. 1154 Gifford. Lovely old ivy-covered hotel on English Bay. Best value in town. Phone 681–9321.

HOW TO GET AROUND. By bus: All fares are 75 cents. The bus system is quite good. A Visitors Map with all the bus lines is available at the tourist office.

By car. The city is easy to tour, but a car is almost essential.

By taxi. Plentiful but expensive if you're going any distance.

TOURIST INFORMATION. *The Greater Vancouver Convention and Visitors Bureau,* Upper Mall, Royal Centre, Burrard and Georgia Sts. Or write: #1625, 1055 West Georgia St., Vancouver, V6E 4C8. Phone 682–2222. Also write: *Tourism B.C.,* Robson Square. Phone 668–2300.

SEASONAL EVENTS: *Vancouver Sea Festival* is in mid-July, *Pacific National Exhibition* annual fair is held the second half of August.

TOURS. The *Gray Line's* tours of the city are the most extensive. You have your choice of about a dozen well-planned excursions within and outside the city. Your hotel will have complete information.

CITY PARKS. Vancouver is dotted with dozens of beautiful parks and gardens, large and small. Many are discussed in the "Exploring Vancouver" section. Major parks are: *Stanley Park, Foreshore Park, Queen Elizabeth Park,* and *Burnaby Mountain Park.*

GARDENS. Also see the "Parks" section for information. Vancouver is full of exotic, beautiful gardens; most are within parks. Others are the *Nitobe Memorial Japanese Gardens* on the campus of the Univeristy of British Columbia. The *Van Dusen Botanical Display Garden* is worth a special visit. *Queens Park* in New Westminster offers over 10,000 varieties of plants and flowers. *Burnaby Century Gardens,* Burnaby, is a 20 acre delight.

CHILDREN'S ACTIVITIES. Many of the places noted earlier are great for children—especially the zoo and aquarium in *Stanley Park.* Many museums would be of interest but, as with adults, the outdoor excursions in the parks and other areas will probably bring the most delight and attention. In particular, the *Capilano Suspension Bridge* and the *Grouse Mt. Skyride* will interest children. The revolving *Observation Deck* at Harbour Centre is a good spot from which to view the city; they also offer a 25-minute audio-visual show on Vancouver.

SPORTS. Just about any sport can be found in or around Vancouver. For spectator sports, you can watch the British Columbia Lions play **football**, the Canucks play pro **hockey**, or the Whitecaps play **soccer**, as well as several minor league teams that compete on the ice. Exhibition Park also houses a **racetrack**. Superb new domed stadium at B.C. Place.

The more active can **ski** at Grouse Mt. or other nearby slopes (see "Winter Sports" section under *Practical Information for British Columbia*). Then there is **golf**—with close to 20 public and private courses in the area. For **boating**, *contact a yacht club or ask at your hotel how to book any type of craft. City parks offer many* **tennis** courts, as do some hotels. If you're interested in **field sports** such as cricket, rugby, or lacrosse, you'll find several teams in the area.

HISTORIC SITES. *Old Hastings Mill Store Museum*, 1575 Alma St., beside Jericho Beach. Built circa 1865, it housed the first store and post office in early Vancouver and was the only building to survive the great fire of 1886. Open 10 A.M. to 4 P.M. daily, from June 1 to September 15; and 1 to 4 P.M. Saturdays and Sundays only, in the winter. Admission by donation. Telephone: 228–1213. *Heritage Village*, Century Park, Burnaby, re-creates this village as it was at the turn of the century. *Langley National Historic Park*, 48 kms. (30 miles) east of the city on Rt. 1A, re-creates the province's beginning days.

MUSEUMS AND GALLERIES. Museums. *Centennial Museum*, 1100 Chestnut St., Vanier Park, offers artifacts from the province's past. *Maritime Museum*, 1905 Ogden St., Vanier Park, houses the ship *St. Roch* and other vessels. *British Columbia Sports Hall of Fame*, Exhibition Park, honors famous athletes. *Museum of Anthropology*, University of British Columbia, is a relatively new building showing extraordinary B.C. Coast Indian artifacts; also from the Americas, Pacific Islands, Asia and Africa. It is a highly recommended stop—and children love it.

Galleries: *Vancouver Art Gallery*, 800 West Georgia St., shows the works of Emily Carr and numerous contemporary exhibitons. *Burnaby Art Gallery*, 6344 Gilpin St., is beautiful in itself, and offers a wide variety of shows.

Downtown Vancouver offers a number of good art galleries; it's best to check the daily newspapers or *Vancouver Guideline Magazine* to see what shows are in town.

STAGE AND REVUES. Vancouver has an active theater life. Best known are the *Arts Club Theatres*, as well as the *Playhouse Company*, and the *Queen Elizabeth Theater* stage performances. Then there's *City Stage*, *Waterfront Theatre*, the *Vancouver East Cultural Centre*, and *Studio 58*. Across the bridge there's the *North Vancouver Centennial Theatre*, the *Community Arts Council Playhouse*, and *Presentation House*. Vancouver also has a distinguished *Bach Choir*. Check local publications for performances.

SHOPPING. *Robsonstrasse,* the *Pacific Centre Mall, Granville Island* and *Gastown* are the best and most convenient places in the city for shopping. Vancouver is well stocked, but often expensive for all kinds of goods. The U.S. resident will find prices higher on most clothing. Some items from the Orient are less expensive, though one could do just as well in San Francisco. Vancouver does have some fine antique stores, especially good if you're hunting for British Columbia Indian goods. If you're interested in English bone china and Irish Belleek, try the Canyon House at 3590 Capilano Rd. in N. Vancouver.

DINING OUT. Vancouver's cosmopolitan nature is reflected in its many restaurants. You'll probably be able to find just about any cuisine somewhere in the city. While beef and fish are the ready staples, you will also find excellent Chinese, Japanese, or Vietnamese food, as well as East Indian, Greek, German, Spanish, and so on. Restaurants are classed as: *Deluxe,* $20 and up; *Expensive,* $15–$20; *Moderate,* $10–$15; *Inexpensive,* below $10, for complete dinners without wine or drinks. The better hotels usually have fine cuisine. Most restaurants are closed on Sundays.

Most places accept the following major credit cards: American Express, MasterCard, and Visa; others may also be honored. Not all establishments accept credit cards, therefore we suggest you call for information.

Deluxe

The Beach House. In Stanley Park on Beach Dr. A beautiful setting and view; Continental cuisine. Quite fine in all ways.

The Cannery Seafood Restaurant. 2205 Commissioner St. Fine seafood. Hard to do better. One of the finest restaurants in Canada. All fish is fresh daily; superb chefs, fine service.

Cristal. In Vancouver Mandarin Hotel. French restaurant with superb cuisine, setting, and service.

Harbour House. On top of Harbour Centre at Hastings and Seymour Sts. Revolving restaurant with grand view of city. Fine cuisine.

Panorama Roof. Top of the Hotel Vancouver. Nouvelle cuisine, yet traditional with dance band. First-rate.

Le Pavillion. In the Four Seasons Hotel. Excellent French cuisine and ambiance. Expensive and worth it.

Trader Vic's. In the Bayshore Inn. One of the chain, but quite good Polynesian food and drink.

Umberto's. 1380 Hornby. Bubbly Italian restaurant, does super rack of lamb.

William Tell. 773 Beatty. Superb old restaurant in new hotel.

Expensive

La Palette. 774 Denman. Elegant nouvelle cuisine.

Café de Paris. 751 Denman near Stanley Park and the Bayshore Hotel. Superb bistro atmosphere. Best value in town.

Château Madrid. 1277 Howe St. Fine Spanish food and surroundings.

Guppy's Original Seafood Restaurant. In North Vancouver at 148 East 2nd. Fun place to eat good seafood. Near SeaBus terminal, so sail over and have a night out.

Maiko Garden. 1077 Richards. Japanese cuisine, fine atmosphere.

Salmon House on the Hill. In West Vancouver, off 21st St. Exit. New and gracious, British Columbian Indian décor. Superb seafood menu, and salmon is king. Excellent.

Seven Seas. At Lonsdale in North Vancouver. Another fine seafood place. People come from all over for this menu. Hard to beat. Can be very expensive.

Moderate

Las Tapas. 760 Cambie. Whitewashed walls, tiled floors and Latin music give good atmosphere.

The Noodle Makers. 122 Powell St. Chinese restaurant; excellent meals.

Orestes. 3116 West Broadway. Greek. Excellent authentic Greek cuisine, good ambience and service.

Pepitas. 1170 Robson St. Mexican all the way. Very good.

Puccini's. 730 Main St. Italian, big portions and fine. One of the most popular places in Vancouver for Italian food.

Vina Vietnamese Cuisine. 2508 Marine Dr., West Vancouver. Very good Vietnamese food.

Schnitzel House. 1060 Robson St. German menu; quite good.

Yang's. 4186 Main St.Spicey Chinese food; great Peking duck, chili prawns.

Inexpensive

Brodie's. 225 Smithe St. Near the stadium at B.C. Place. Superb, tasty, spicey Mediterranean food.

Old Spachetti Factory. 53 Water St., Gastown. Serves simple dishes with family appeal.

P.J. Burger's. 2966 W. 4th St., Kitsilano. Does good hamburgers and special milk shakes.

White Spot restaurants, *Keg 'N Cleaver* restaurants, and *Denny's* restaurants. All inexpensive. Can be found in different locations throughout town. Good.

 NIGHTCLUBS AND BARS. Many of the most popular nightspots are located in the better hotels in town. Other places of interest for the night crowd are: *Richard's,* 1036 Richards, Stylish but loud rock and roll. *Champers,* in Denman Hotel, upmarket nightspot. *Confetti!,* 1255 W. Pender, for young ravers. *Elephant and Castle,* Pacific Centre Mall, an English-style pub. *The Town Pump,* 66 Water St., Gastown, for rock 'n' roll. *Annabelle's,* in the Four Seasons Hotel, an elegant place to drink and dance. *English Bay Café,* 1795 Beach Ave., a fetching San Francisco-style bar with good ocean views. Also the bar at the *Sylvia Hotel,* just across the road, *Hot Jazz Society,* 2120 Main St., dancing, bar, best value in town. *Pelican Bay* at Granville Island Hotel is a delightful bar at water's edge with small dance floor.

EXPLORING VANCOUVER ISLAND AND VICTORIA

West of the city of Vancouver, across the Strait of Georgia, are Vancouver Island and British Columbia's capital, *Victoria.* In between are the beautiful and almost empty Gulf Islands, most of which are accessible from the mainland or from Vancouver Island, by ferry.

Vancouver Island, which juts below the 49th Parallel and seems to invade the United States, is 456 kms. (285 miles) long and about 152 kms. (75 miles) across at its widest point. The east coast is built up and offers a large variety of accommodations, sightseeing, and sporting activities, but the rugged west coast has no roads and is still quite wild. Highway 4 leads from Parksville across the island to Long Beach and the haunting Pacific Rim Park that stretches for miles along the rocky coast. If you want to see the west coast, this is the place to come.

The scenery all over Vancouver Island is majestic: mountainous, forested, and filled with lakes and running streams. It's almost impossible to overemphasize the beauty of this country. The drive up or down the island's east coast, with the mountainous mainland in the distance, reminds one of Norway's fjords. You'll find very good camping sites and hiking trails here, and even the less active will enjoy the sightseeing. While the primary city of interest for many people is Victoria, the island itself yields a vast array of fascinating sights and simple entertainment.

Ferries ply the waters between Vancouver and Departure Bay, at Nanaimo, the island's second largest town. Sidney can be reached from Anacortes in Washington State year round; Victoria is accessible from Seattle in the summer, and from Vancouver year round via the Swartz Bay ferries (20 minutes north of Victoria). The Victoria–Vancouver ferry ride is one hour, 40 minutes; it docks at Tsawwassen, on the mainland, about 20 minutes from downtown Vancouver. Powell River, on the mainland, has a ferry service to Comox, near the *center* of the island.

If you start your journey in Nanaimo, you have your choice of going north to the resort areas and the wilderness, or south some 112 kms. (70 miles) to Victoria. We'll take the north route first.

Petroglyphs and Pioneers

Nanaimo itself had its beginnings as a Hudson's Bay Company post. It has pleasant parks, the best being the Petroglyph Park featuring prehistoric rock carvings and drawings. The Bastion Museum, which is part of the old Hudson's Bay fort, houses some fine old pioneer relics. Nanaimo has achieved real fame, however, for providing one of the most entertaining races in the world: the annual mid-July Nanaimo Bathtub Race which runs from Nanaimo across the Strait of Georgia to Vancouver. The idea is to get across the Strait, in a bathtub! They can be modified and motorized—but many don't make it all the way. It is always a festive, and usually hilarious, day.

Going north from Nanaimo on Highway 19, you'll get to Parksville, 40 kms. (25 miles) away. This popular resort town offers fine beaches and excellent trout and salmon fishing. Two provincial parks are nearby: Englishman River Falls and Little Qualicum Falls. By going west on Highway 4, you'll find Port Alberni, another resort center year-round. Fresh- and saltwater fishing in this area is excellent. So are rafting, waterskiing, tennis, and so on. This is resort and relaxation territory, but for the sports minded, there's everything you could want. Continuing on this road will lead you to the Pacific Rim National Park—a detour that should not be missed.

Back in Parksville, again heading north, is Qualicum Beach, a resort with fine fishing opportunities. The journey through Buckley Bay and

Royston brings you to Courtenay and the Comox Valley—perfect vacation land. Just to the west is the 500,000-acre Strathcona Park, the largest on the island, where you'll see Mount Golden Hind, 7,220 feet high, and the haunting Forbidden Plateau. The scenery here is some of the finest in all of British Columbia.

About 160 kms. (100 miles) from Nanaimo is the Campbell River, famous worldwide for its fishing. Hollywood personalities have fished here for decades, and it has become a sort of mecca for serious trout and salmon fishers. This is great country for sportsmen, and people flock here for hunting and particularly for salmon fishing.

The end of the road is Port Hardy, 235 kms. (146 miles) north, and clearly in the wilds. This is where you catch the ferry to Prince Rupert (a full day and night journey), to the north on the mainland. From there you can connect with other ferries for Alaska. Above Port Hardy, there are no public roads.

Returning to Nanaimo, head south on Highway 19, to Duncan and its interesting Forest Museum, where hundreds of tree-felling and wood-cutting implements are gathered. Before reaching Victoria, you'll ride along the Malahat Drive, which offers one of the island's most spectacular views of the city and the U.S. beyond.

To the west of Victoria, on Highway 14, is Sooke, where fishing for trout and salmon is excellent, and numerous other outdoor activities are available.

The Capital

Victoria is a city of paradoxes: it's the most westerly of Canadian cities; yet, more than any other, it will remind you of a faraway English town. The provincial capital of British Columbia, it appears more like Brighton Beach than London. Victoria is the terminus point of the 8,000-km. (5,000-mile) long Trans-Canada Highway, yet one must take a ferry boat to reach it.

With London double-decker buses (in summer) framed by mountain views, English tea at the famous Empress Hotel, and a wax museum, Victoria is a charming city that delights in putting on airs as long as tourists keep coming. Hanging baskets of bright blossoms bedeck the downtown lampposts, and Victoria is world-famous for its flowers. The city has many interesting features including attractive shops stocking English china and English and Scottish woolens and upmarket clothing, as well as others selling antiques, old maps and prints, and souvenirs, too. And it *is* a beautiful city—clean and fresh, and a drive around the harbor area, or Beacon Hill Park, or through Oak Bay and along the Scenic Drive, will convince anyone that Victoria is a city to be looked at carefully and appreciated.

The city's main area is the Inner Harbor where you'll see the Victorian-style British Columbia Legislative Building (1898), the Empress Hotel, the British Columbia Provincial Museum, and the curious and appealing Thunderbird Park, filled with Indian totem poles. This part of town contains the best of the past, and should be seen on foot.

For a city of gardens, the most famous is the Butchart Gardens, a 35-acre area of the most beautiful flowers from all over the world. It

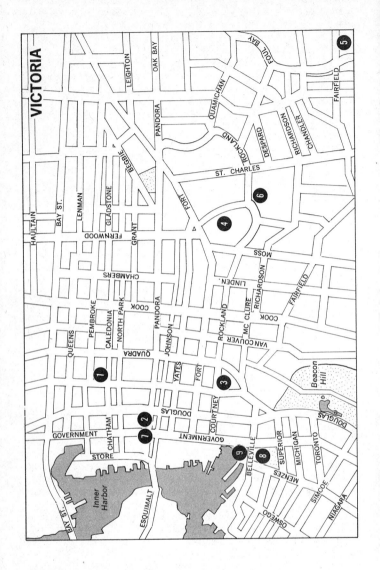

Victoria—Points of Interest

1) Arena
2) City Hall
3) Court House
4) Craigdarroch Castle
5) Gonzales Observatory
6) Government House
7) McPherson Playhouse (Centennial Square)
8) Parliament Buildings
9) Port Angeles Ferry

was started over 75 years ago by a wealthy industrialist, and maintained and improved over the years. A must for flower lovers, this is just 19 kms. (12 miles) from town.

Other places of interest in Victoria? The Seasons of the Pacific at Oak Bay Marina where you descend beneath the sea, behind glass, to see the active marine life; also see the fine Pacific Undersea Gardens; the Royal London Wax Museum, opposite the Parliament Buildings; a copy of Shakespeare's birthplace plus Anne Hathaway's cottage in Stratford-on-Avon; the museum-archive complex of Heritage Court; Craigflower Manor, an authentic 1856 home; Fable Cottage Estate, a little fantasy world of houses and animated scenes; and a Classic Car Museum.

The Bastion Square section is a favorite for most visitors. Shopping is good, restaurants plentiful, and the Olde Towne area is full of history. It was the site of the Hudson's Bay Company's building and the first courthouse—now the fine Maritime Museum. Shopping is also good on Yates Street, Government Street, and Market Square. The city features several wonderful old castles; the best are the Craigdarroch Castle, built in 1888, and Helmecken House, 1853. To get away from man-made structures, head for the 140 acre Beacon Hill Park in the middle of town. Here you can stroll or picnic, and gaze at more totem poles.

To return to the mainland you have several routes: from Victoria directly, from Nanaimo, or you can ferry around, and stop off on, the Gulf Islands. These are rustic and wild, and not many people choose to live here; several have at least one good road. The best to visit are Saltspring, Galiano, Valdes, and Gabriola, the last of which figures in *October Ferry to Gabriola,* by famed British author Malcolm Lowry.

EXPLORING BRITISH COLUMBIA

If you take a look at a roadmap for British Columbia, you'll notice that the major roads are all in the south, with the exception of the Yellowhead Highway and the northerly Alaska Highway. Since most of British Columbia is mountainous, this is understandable. You'll also notice that above Powell River, some 104 kms. (65 miles) north of Vancouver, there are no roads along the rugged Pacific coast for the same reason: vast mountain ranges make highway construction prohibitively expensive.

Therefore, the most numerous vacation and exploring areas are east of Vancouver, in the south. But before heading that way, you might want to take a short 72-km. (45-mile) jaunt north of Vancouver, up Highway 99, to Squamish, an old lumber town and gateway to the 480,000-acre Garibaldi Provincial Park (which connects with Golden Ears Provincial Park, to the south). Farther up Highway 99 is famous Whistler Mountain, one of the finest for winter and spring skiing in all North America. This is excellent ski territory in season and, in warm weather, good for camping and hiking. The terrain is, of course, mountainous—and glorious to see. As you drive along the coastal road, you see Vancouver Island and the beautiful Gulf Islands sparkling in the sea. On a clear sunny day, the scene of mountains and sea is magnificent. After leaving Squamish, heading south now, you can ferry from Horseshoe Bay over to Gibsons, and then proceed up Highway 101 to Powell River, a pulp mill town offering numerous sports, primarily great fishing. If you haven't gone to Vancouver Island, you can ferry across to Comox; or you can head back to Vancouver city, and on to the east.

There are three distinct touring areas in the south of British Columbia. First is the Hope—north to Cache Creek, east to Kamloops, and south to Princeton circle. Second is the summer playground in the Okanagan Valley around Penticton and Kelowna. Third is around the Alberta-British Columbia border, around Kimberley, and north to the Kootenay National Park.

The Hope–Princeton Circle

Leaving Vancouver for Hope, you'll pass Port Moody (where Captain George Vancouver first stepped ashore in 1792) and Chilliwack, on the Fraser River. The area around Hope is built up with resorts which, again, offer very good facilities for hunting, fishing, and relaxing. Turning north on the Trans-Canada Highway (Highway 1—the longest highway in the world), you'll pass through Yale (an old trading town) and then reach the popular Hell's Gate Airtram. The scenery around these parts is breathtaking, and the Airtram's descent into Fraser Canyon is one you'll never forget. The Fraser River is pounding and turbulent here, with more than 200 million gallons of water per minute beating between the shores.

At Lytton, the Fraser and Thompson Rivers meet; this was busy territory a century ago when the Gold Rush was on; the original Cariboo Wagon Trail started just to the north. Today, you may search for jade in the river beds at Lytton.

You can veer to the west here for Lillooet, another old mining town, or continue north on Highway 1 to Cache Creek, and then east for Kamloops.

Kamloops, a thriving, modern town, is at the confluence of the North and South Thompson Rivers. There are hundreds of good swimming and fishing lakes in the district, and trout is the famous specialty. This is also Cariboo Country, which means gold and fur. There's a good Gold Rush Museum in town. In July, Kamloops features an Indian Days Festival and, in April, a giant indoors rodeo. But these events pale next to the splendor of the landscape. It's difficult to imagine a place so clean and sparkling.

If you were to head north from Kamloops on Highway 5, you would reach the wild Wells Gray Provincial Park for excellent camping in the wilderness, as well as good fishing. Trail rides into Wells Gray can be arranged in Clearwater, 43 kms. (27 miles) south of the park's southern entrance.

Heading south from Kamloops on 5, you'll reach Merritt, the heart of cattle country. Just a half hour from town is the Douglas Lake Ranch—over 600,000 acres and nearly 15,000 head of cattle make it one of the largest ranches in the world. Another attraction is the number of good rodeos here each year.

From there, travel on into Princeton, where Tulameen and Similkameen Rivers converge in the Cascade Mountains. This is still summer rodeo territory, and winter ski country.

Okanagan Valley

Continuing southeast on Highway 3, you'll arrive in Osoyoos, on the Washington State border. Here, in Indian land, is the International Viewpoint at 4,000 feet; you can see a long distance into the U.S. to the south and, to the north, far into the fertile fruit-producing Okanagan Valley.

This region is one of Canada's most popular summer resort areas. Temperatures are hot, swimming in lakes is excellent, and vineyards and fruit trees instead of glaciers become part of the landscape.

Penticton is the center of the region, at the south end of the Okanagan Lake. Nicknamed "Peach City," Penticton hosts an elaborate Blossom Time Festival each May, a Peach Festival in August, and a giant Square Dance Jamboree in August. The town also offers some fine diversions aside from watersports: a huge game farm, the Pioneer Museum, and, not far from town, Copper Mountain Ghost Town.

Following Highway 97 up the west side of narrow Okanagan Lake, you'll come to Summerland, another good resort area, and Kelowna, another major center in the valley, offering a good Museum of Natural History, a zoo, and a tour of fruit-packing plants if you're interested. Kelowna's big events of the summer are the International Regatta in August and the Grape Festival each September. In winter, skiing is good and trails plentiful.

Vernon, on Kalamalka Lake, is the next town north, well known for its good boating and swimming. Winter Carnival in February is the big event each year. Near Armstrong is the gracious Silver Star Provincial Park. To the north is Revelstoke, where the Monashee Mountains meet the Selkirks.

The National Parks

Revelstoke serves as the gateway to British Columbia's four National Parks, each of which has a particular splendor and excitement. Stop in Revelstoke before proceeding east. The town, located on the Columbia River, once served as a base town for lumberjacks, miners, and fur traders. This is superb ski country as well as a summer headquarters for hunting, fishing, and sightseeing. If you're driving through these parks in winter or spring, watch the weather closely. Roads will be closed by the Royal Canadian Mounted Police if snow conditions warrant.

Mount Revelstoke Park

The first of the national parks to visit is Mount Revelstoke Park, just out of town. Though not very large, its scenery is some of the most splendid in all of Canada—massive peaks, running streams, glaciers, and trees. Many people contend that the Canadian Rocky Mountains are more spectacular than those farther south. It may be a debatable point, but in any case, all of these parks are glorious to see. By the time you reach the summit, you'll be over 8,000 feet above sea level. The views can hold a person for hours.

Glacier National Park

Heading east on the Trans-Canada Highway, you'll come next to Glacier National Park, not to be confused with the park of the same name in the United States. Its name is apt: there are mountains in excess of 11,500 feet, glaciers, and rugged peaks. With its fine network of trails and picnic spots, you can spend an hour—or several days—in this 1,347-sq.-km. (520-square-mile) wonderland. If you travel by car (trains will take you here, too), you'll head up to Rogers Pass, perhaps the most breathtaking spectacle in all of British Columbia. This experience should not be missed! Descending the mountains, you'll come to Golden, where the Trans-Canada Highway and Highway 95 meet.

Yoho National Park

Golden is the split-off point for the other two National Parks. To the north is the beautiful Yoho National Park. Yoho, an Indian word meaning "how beautiful," truly describes the park. There are good camping grounds and a great deal to see in its 1,295 sq. km. (500 square mile) territory. Drive along the Kicking Horse Trail and view the glaciers, waterfalls, Ice River Valley, and the Hoodoo Valley. Yoho Park borders on Alberta's Banff National Park, so if you're on your way east, continue through Yoho Park to Calgary.

Kootenay National Park

If not, take Highway 1 south to Highway 93 and tour the last park, the famous Kootenay National Park, 96 kms. (60 miles) long, also on the border to Banff. The main attraction here is the fabulous Vermillion Pass from which you'll see an assortment of canyons, lakes, and falls. The drive is a beauty! At the southern end of the park is Radium Hot Springs, where you can stop for a relaxing mineral bath, year round.

Completing the swing through the south, you can head down Highway 93 through Kimberley, the highest city in the nation. This is great ski territory and is also known for its fine lake and stream fishing. Next is Cranbrook, a good-size town with more resorts and scenery. Sixteen kms. (10 miles) northeast is Fort Steele, built in 1887, and now restored. It's fun for everyone, and you'll be able to visualize what an old western fort was really like. An excellent place for children, too.

From Cranbrook, you can travel south into Montana or Idaho, east to Alberta, or west back through Trail and Nelson, both interesting towns, to Vancouver.

The North

The center and north of British Columbia are for adventurers who don't mind great wilderness areas between towns. It's wild, magnificent country; the Yellowhead and Alaska Highways are the only east-west routes, and Highway 97 is the main north-south road. The north offers space, forests, camping, fabulous fishing, hunting—and the isolation that some travelers crave.

The center of the province is Prince George, where the Yellowhead and #97 meet. It's a thriving town, mainly because of its huge lumber business. It's also modern and prosperous-looking. Again, lake and stream fishing in the area is excellent. You'll find numerous hunting and fishing resort camps in the north, many of which are accessible only by small private planes. If you're looking for a really secluded vacation, check into these resort camps; they are listed in the free *Tourist Accommodation* book offered by the British Columbia Government *(Tourism B.C.)* travel offices. There's a museum at Old Fort George that's of interest, too. But this is primarily outdoor country, and best in summer and early autumn. In August, the four-day Prince George Exhibition is like a summer festival.

South of Prince George are three towns worth your attention if you come or go via Highway 97. One is Quesnel on the Fraser and Quesnel Rivers, a former gold-rush boom town, with a good period museum. East of Quesnel is Barkerville, once a rival to San Francisco in size during its heyday in the Gold Rush of the 1860's. It's now a restored ghost town, one of the best of its kind, and a great place for children. The third town on Highway 97, farther south, is Williams Lake, where a four-day Stampede in late June is one of the wildest events anywhere. Here you'll also find museums and resorts.

North of Prince George, on Highway 97, is lonely land. Mackenzie, named after Sir Alexander Mackenzie who made the first trans-Canada journey in the 1790's, grew up from the original fort that Mackenzie founded. Pass on through Chetwynd and on to Dawson Creek on the Alberta border. Dawson Creek is famous mainly because it is Mile Zero of the 2,442-km. (1,526-mile) long Alaska Highway through the Yukon and into Fairbanks, Alaska. Dawson Creek is new and clean; it cannot be called charming, but it has all the amenities. Farther north is Fort St. John, in the midst of hunting territory.

Now back to Prince George, heading west on the Yellowhead. On the almost 800 km. (500 mile) leg from there to Prince Rupert, British Columbia's northern port on the Pacific, you'll pass through Vanderhoof. Here, you can detour north for 66 kms. (41 miles) to Fort St. James, an 1806 Hudson's Bay Company fort that now serves as a base for area resorts. Then south and west again, and you're in the heart of the Fraser Lake region, renowned for fine fishing and hunting. Burns Lake and Smithers are next. New Hazelton is the Ksan Indian Village, with dozens of beautifully carved totem poles. This is fine trout fishing territory as well. Pass through Terrace, and on into Prince Rupert.

Prince Rupert is our final stop. This is a thriving commercial city, proud of its title of "Halibut Capital of the World," and British Columbia's second most important port. Prince Rupert hosts the Museum of Northern British Columbia, filled with pioneer and Tsimpsian and Haida Indian artifacts. You'll also see numerous totem poles in the city's parks.

Prince Rupert is the end point for the Canadian Pacific Railroad's northern line. But not for you. From Prince Rupert, you have the option of ferrying up to Haines, Alaska, driving back on the Yellowhead or, more interesting by far, taking a coastal ferry south to Vancouver. The 24 hour sea voyage is fabulous—calling at the Queen Charlotte Islands, then south through the Queen Charlotte Sound and Strait, the Strait of Georgia, and into Vancouver. It's a relaxing, yet exciting way to end the circular route of British Columbia.

PRACTICAL INFORMATION FOR BRITISH COLUMBIA

HOW TO GET THERE. By air: Major Canadian airlines—*CP Air, Air Canada, Pacific Western Airlines, Air B.C.,* and others fly to Vancouver, which has the province's main air terminal. Flying within British Columbia is also easy—there are dozens of small and large fields in towns outside of Vancouver and out in the wilds.

By train: *Via Rail* serves both Kamloops and Vancouver. *B.C. Railway* travels between Horseshoe Bay and Prince George, with many stops.

By car: There are many routes into B.C. from the United States. In Canada, the Trans-Canada and Yellowhead Hwys. are cross-country and excellent.

By bus: *Trailways* and *Greyhound* have regular service to Vancouver and numerous other towns; check with them for information about bus travel.

By ferry: Vancouver, Vancouver Island, and Prince Rupert are all served by an extensive ferry service. Schedules change seasonally, so check on times when you're there. All ferry services are first-rate, and surprisingly inexpensive.

ACCOMMODATIONS. British Columbia offers a number of resort hotels that cater to hunters and fishermen; some of the best are listed below. Elegance fades for the most part outside of Vancouver and Victoria, but all hotels and motels have basic amenities. Some of the resort complexes, however, are close to luxurious. For the traveler spending a great deal of time in the province and touring some of the back roads, it would be helpful to get a copy of a booklet issued by *Tourism* B.C. titled *British Columbia Accommodation Guide,* which lists just about every hotel or motel in the province. Free. The price categories in this section, for double-occupancy, will average: *Deluxe,* $80 and up; *Expensive,* $50–80; *Moderate,* $30–50; *Inexpensive,* under $30.

Most places accept the following major credit cards: American Express, MasterCard, and Visa; others may also be honored. Not all establishments accept credit cards, therefore we suggest you call for information.

VANCOUVER ISLAND

CAMPBELL RIVER. *Expensive.* **April Point Lodge.** Box 1, Quathiaski Cove. On Quadra Island. Excellent salmon and trout fishing; yacht club nearby; fine amenities, dining. Phone 285–3329.

Delta's Discovery Inn. 975 Tyee Plaza. First-class resort hotel; beside harbor; nice rooms, dining. Phone 287–7155.

The Dolphin's Resort. 4125 Discovery Dr. On the ocean. Resort hotel with fine fishing, spacious rooms. Open April–Oct. Phone 287–3066.

Painter's Lodge and Resort. Famous fishing resort made known to the world by Bob Hope and Bing Crosby; beautiful views; fine rooms. Phone 286–1102.

Moderate: **Austrian Chalet,** 462 South Island Hwy. Attractive motel overlooking Discovery Passage; indoor pool. Phone 923–4231.

Vista Del Mar Motel. 920 South Island Hwy. Housekeeping units, next to store, boat launch. Phone 923–4271.

Inexpensive: **Rod and Reel Resort.** R.R. 2. Housekeeping cottages, boat and bait rentals. Phone 923–5250.

DUNCAN. *Expensive:* **The Village Green Inn.** On the Trans-Canada Hwy. Pleasant Spanish-styled rooms; fine *Steak House Restaurant.* Phone 746–5126.

Moderate: **Duncan Motel.** 2552 Alexander Rd. Near shopping, fishing, and golf. Phone 746–4944.

NANAIMO. *Expensive:* **Highlander Motor Inn.** 96 North Terminal Ave. Convenient for ferry; sauna and restaurant. Phone 754–6355. **Malaspina Hotel.**

Tally Ho Travelodge. 1 Terminal Ave. Comfortable rooms; heated pool. Phone 753–2241.

PARKSVILLE. *Expensive:* **Island Hall Hotel.** 181 W. Island Hwy. Resort hotel on 10 acres; good beach, tennis, fishing, dining. Phone 248–3225.

Tigh-Na-Mara. On R.R.1. Log cabins with fireplaces. Lovely setting. Open all year. Phone 248–3672.

Moderate. **Englishman's River Motel.** Comfortable motel on river, park. Good facilities. Phone 248–6532.

PORT ALBERNI. *Moderate.* **Hospitality Inn.** 3835 Redford St. A fine motor hotel with all amenities. Phone 723–8111.

Timberlodge. Port Alberni Hwy. All amenities; close to skiing at Mt. Arrowsmith. Housekeeping units available. Phone 723–9415.

Tyee Village Motel. 4151 Redford St. First class motel with cozy rooms. Phone 723–8133.

QUALICUM BEACH. *Expensive:* **College Inn.** Overlooking ocean with access to beach. Dining room, indoor pool. Meeting rooms. Phone 752–9262.

Sand Pebbles Inn. On the beach; rooms and dining area have fine ocean views. Sports nearby. Phone 752–6974.

VICTORIA. *Deluxe:* **Château Victoria.** 740 Burdett Ave. Well-located, very pleasant hotel. Good dining; all amenities. Phone 382–4221.

Empress Hotel. 721 Government St. An institution in B.C. Elegant old hotel with European flavor; view of the inner harbor; excellent dining. Like a fine old

European hotel. Take tea every afternoon in the main hall. Atmosphere and service among the best in Victoria. Phone 384–8111.

Executive House Hotel. 777 Douglas St. A 20-story hotel in downtown; pleasant rooms; good restaurants. Phone 388–5111.

Harbour Towers Hotel. 345 Québec St. Modern, excellent hotel, also on the inner harbor; large rooms; pool; dining. Phone 385–2405.

Laurel Point Inn. On Tuner Harbor. Location can't be beat. Phone 386–8721.

Oak Bay Beach Hotel. 1175 Beach Dr. Sea resort in garden setting for views; excellent rooms; English-style pub. Across from golf course. Phone 598–4556.

Victoria Regent. 1234 Wharf St. Overlooking Inner Harbor. Big two-bath condo suites with kitchens. Phone 386–2211.

Expensive: **Colony Motor Inn.** 2852 Douglas St. Tudor-style motel; pleasant rooms; pool. Phone 385–2441.

Olde England Inn. 429 Lampson St. Old Tudor mansion, 17th century decor; on 4 acres near town; atmospheric rooms; very nice. Phone 388–4353.

Moderate: **Century Inn.** 603 Pandora Ave., at Centennial Sq. Modern, pleasant rooms. *Persian Room* dining. Good location. Phone 383–1151.

Strathcona Hotel. 919 Douglas St. Central location. Dining and entertainment, including dancing and disco. Phone 383–7137.

Inexpensive: **Casa Linda Motel.** 364 Coldstream Ave. Some units with kitchens. Phone 474–2141.

Cheltenham Court Motel. 994 Gorge Rd. W. Good value cottages, coffee shop. Phone 385–9559.

Ingraham Hotel. 2915 Douglas St. The restaurant here is inexpensive and open daily.

THE MAINLAND

ALTA LAKE-WHISTLER MOUNTAIN. *Deluxe.* **Delta Mountain Inn.** Superb resort hotel near ski lifts. Pool, whirlpools. Reduced summer rates. Phone 932–1982.

Expensive. **Tantalus Lodge.** Two-bedroom, two-bath units with kitchens. Pool. Phone 932–4146.

ASHCROFT. *Deluxe.* **Sundance Guest Ranch.** Excellent dude ranch resort with fishing, riding, tennis, fine rooms, and grand scenery. Private air strip. Phone 453–2422.

CACHE CREEK. *Moderate:* **Sandman Inn.** On Hwy. 1. Nice, comfortable motel. Phone 457–6284.

CHILLIWACK. *Moderate:* **Parkwood Motor Hotel.** 8600 Young St. Comfortable rooms, all amenities. Phone 795–9155.

Country Inns Motel. First-class; dining. Phone 792–0661.

CLINTON-70 MILE HOUSE. *Deluxe:* **Flying U Guest Ranch, 70 Mile House.** Dude ranch open all year. Beautiful setting, horses, log cabins, winter and summer sports. Very fine experience. Phone 456–7717.

CRANBROOK. *Expensive:* **Towne & Country Motor Inn.** 600 Cranbrook St. First-class motel; pool; restaurant; all amenities. Phone 426–6683.

Moderate: **Mount Baker Hotel.** 1017 Baker St. Air conditioned, satellite TV, whirlpool, room service. Phone 426-5277.

Sandman Inn. 405 Cranbrook St. Central, big beds, indoor pool. Phone 426–4236.

Inexpensive: **Nomad Motel.** 910 Cranbrook St. Sleeping and housekeeping units. Pool, playground. Phone 426–6266.

DAWSON CREEK. *Moderate:* **TraveLodge.** Near "Mile Zero" marker for Alaska Hwy. Comfortable. Phone 782–4837.

FAIRMONT HOT SPRINGS. *Deluxe:* **Fairmont Hot Springs Resort.** In Kootenay region; resort open year-round; cabins and ski lodge; 18 hole golf course; skiing, riding. Phone 345–6311.

FORT NELSON. *Moderate:* **Provincial Motel.** At Mile 300 of the Alaska Hwy. Good rooms, full amenities and dining facilities. Phone 774–6901.

FORT ST. JAMES. *Expensive:* **Nakalat Lodge.** Secluded fishing and hunting resort; nice cabins; rustic; in the wilds. Radio Phone N688602.

FORT ST. JOHN. *Moderate:* **Fort St John Travelodge.** 9810–100th St. Central, kitchenettes, air-conditioning, family rates. Phone 785–6647.

GABRIOLA ISLAND (A GULF ISLAND). *Expensive:* **Surf Lodge.** Open year-round. On water. Dining rooms, sports, comfortable rooms. Phone 247–9231.

GALIANO ISLAND (A GULF ISLAND). *Moderate.* **Galiano Lodge.** Motel with view; on Sturdies Bay; many sports, all amenities, quiet and beautiful. Phone 539–2233.

HARRISON HOT SPRINGS. *Deluxe:* **Harrison Hotel.** Year-round resort hotel in mountains on lake; 2 hot spring pools; fine cuisine, all sports. Phone 796–2244.

Moderate: **Harrison Lakeshore Motel.** Esplande Ave. Large units facing lakefront, heated pool. Phone 796–2441.

Harrison Village Motel. Overlooking Harrison Lake. Very comfortable; sports available. Phone 796–2616.

Inexpensive: **Glencoe Motel.** Box 181. Sleeping and housekeeping units, opposite mineral pool. Phone 796–2574.

HOPE. *Moderate:* **Imperial Motel.** On the Hope-Princeton Hwy. Indoor pool; all rooms with full facilities. Very comfortable. Phone 869–9951.

KAMLOOPS REGION. *Expensive:* **Coast Canadian Inn.** 339 St. Paul St., in Kamloops. Heated pool, well-done rooms. Dining rooms. Phone 372–5201.

Expensive: **David Thompson Motor Inn.** 650 Victoria St. Fine downtown motel with complete hotel facilities. Phone 372–5282.

Dome Motor Hotel. In Kamloops on Columbia St. First class, pleasant rooms; dining; pool. Phone 374–0358.

Stockmen's Hotel. Centrally located in town; nice rooms; all amenities. Phone 372–2281.

Moderate: **Four Seasons Motel.** On Hwy. 1 in East Kamloops. Fine motel, some units with kitchens; picnic area, pool. Phone 372–2313.

Lac Le Jeune Resort. On Lac Le Jeune; resort lodge; near Tod Mt. for skiing, other sports and dining available. Phone 372–2722.

Sandman Inn. 550 Columbia St. at 6th. Sleeping and kitchenette units, handy to town. Phone: 374–1218.

Village Hotel. 377 Tranquille Rd. On 3-acres between two arms of the Thompson River. Coffee shop and dining room. Phone 376–8811.

Inexpensive: **Thrift Inn.** 2459 Trans Canada Hwy. 1 E., Kamloops. Air-conditioned, satellite TV, seasonal pool, handy for shopping. Phone 374–2488.

KELOWNA. *Expensive:* **Canamara Beach Motel.** On Lakeshore Rd. On beach; all amenities; golf, boating, etc. Pleasant. Phone 763–4717.

Capri Hotel. On Harvey Ave. Modern hotel; good dining; pool. Phone 860–6060.

County Inn. On Harvey Ave. Near golf course; tennis; private patios, heated pool. Phone 860–1212.

Eldorado Arms Resort Hotel. Summer resort in mountains with gardens; nice rooms and cottages, all sports. May to Sept. Phone 764–4126.

Moderate-Deluxe: **Beacon Beach Resort Motel.** 3766 Lakeshore Rd. A year-round resort with small or large units; private beach; boating; other sports. Phone 762-4225.

Moderate. **Stetson Village Motel.** 1455 Harvey Ave. Near airport. All amenities, indoor pool. Some kitchenettes. Phone 860–2490.

Willow Inn Hotel. 235 Queensway. Downtown, close to park and lake. Phone 762–2122.

Kelowna TraveLodge. 1780 Glenmore St. Opposite shopping center with restaurants and entertainment. Some kitchenettes. Phone 762–3221.

Western Budget Motel. 2679 Hwy 97N. Big picnic area, pets welcome. Phone 860–4990.

NELSON. *Moderate:* **Peebles Motor Inn.** 153 Baker St. downtown. Full facilities, some suites, bar and restaurant. Phone 352–3525.

"108." *Deluxe:* **108 Ranch Resort.** On Hwy. 97 and "108." Huge, well-planned resort hotel offering golf, tennis, winter skiing, cattle drives, fishing, etc. All amenities, very nice. Phone: 791–5211.

PENTICTON. *Expensive:* **Delta Lakeside.** On Okanagan Lake. Luxurious resort with indoor pool and tennis courts. Phone 493–8221.

Bowmont Motel. 80 Riverside Dr. Rooms and suites; full amenities. Near lakes and beaches. Phone 492–0112.

Penticton Motel. On Lakeshore Dr. First-class motel on lake; pool, sauna. Phone 492–2922.

Penticton TraveLodge. On Westminster Ave. Some rooms with kitchens; full facilities; dining room and coffee shop; pools and sauna. Phone 492–0225.

Pilgrim House Motor Hotel. On Eckhardt Ave. Near lake and sports; fine first-class hotel. Phone 492–8926.

Moderate: **Log Cabin Motel:** 3287 Skaha Lake Rd. Log cabin housekeeping units. Phone 492–3155.

Stardust Motor Inn. 1048 Westminster Ave. Near lake and airport, some kitchenettes, heated pool. Restaurant. Phone 492-7015.

POWELL RIVER. *Expensive:* **Beach Gardens Resort Hotel.** Open year-round; overlooking marina; pleasant rooms. Phone 485–6267.

PRINCE GEORGE. *Expensive:* **Inn of the North.** On Brunswick St. Modern, nice rooms; dining facilities; indoor pool. Phone 563–0121.

Moderate: **Connaught Motor Inn.** 1550 Victoria St. Modern, comfortable motel with all necessities; indoor pool; dining room. Phone 562–4441.

Sandman Inn. 1650 Central St. Near airport. Full restaurant facilities, some kitchenettes, pool. Phone 563–8131.

Inexpensive: **Roblyn Motel.** 3755 John Hart Hwy. Family atmosphere, housekeeping units. Phone 962–7081.

PRINCE RUPERT. *Expensive:* **Crest Motor Hotel.** On 1st Ave. W. overlooking harbor; all rooms good size; dining. Phone 624–6771.

Prince Rupert Hotel. At 2nd Ave. and 6th St. Downtown location, with view of harbor. Full service; dining rooms. Phone 624–6711.

Totem Lodge Motel. 1335 Park Ave. Near ferry terminals for Alaska or Kelsey Bay. Full amenities. Pleasant. Phone 624–9161.

Moderate: **Parkside Resort Motel.** 11th Ave. and McBride St. Close to city center, car storage. Phone 624–9131.

PRINCETON. *Moderate:* **Evergreen Motel.** A quarter mile E. of city center. Color TV, heated pool. Sports nearby. Pretty setting. Phone 295–7733.

Sandman Inn. On Hwy 3. Modern, pleasant; dining. Phone 295–6923.

RADIUM HOT SPRINGS. *Expensive:* **Radium Hot Springs Lodge.** First-class, beautiful views; all sports, heliocopter skiing available. Phone 347–9622.

Big Horn Motel. Comfortable units, color TV, restaurant nearby. Near Bugaboo ski area. Phone 347–9522.

REVELSTOKE. *Expensive:* **Revelstoke TraveLodge.** 601 1st St. W. Pleasant motel with full facilities and heated pool. Phone 837–2181.

Moderate: **Columbia Slumber Lodge.** 1601 Second St. W. Housekeeping units, heated pool. Restaurant adjacent. Phone 837–2191.

McGregor Motor Inn. Downtown; very comfortable. Phone 837–2121.

Inexpensive: **King Edward Motor Hotel.** Central location. Dining room, lounge, pub. Phone 837–2104.

Mountain View Motel. 1017 First St. W. Some waterbeds. Phone 837–2057.

ROGERS PASS. *Moderate:* **Best Western Glacier Park Lodge.** 45 miles east of Revelstoke. Pool, sports, views. Phone 837–2126.

SALMON ARM. *Expensive:* **Totem Pole Resort and Marina.** Located at Tappen, 17 mi. off Hwy. 1. Chalets and nice cottages, open year round. Fireplace, huge beach. Sports available, boat rentals. Quite nice. Phone 835–4567.

SMITHERS. *Moderate:* **Sandman Inn.** On Hwy 16. Comfortable, amenities. Phone 847–2637.

Tyee Motor Hotel. Pleasant units, all amenities, full dining room. Very nice. Phone 847–2201.

Florence Motel Ltd. Hwy. 16 West. Full facilities, very comfortable. Phone 847–2678.

TRAIL. *Moderate:* **Terra Nova Motor Inn.** On Rossland Ave. near downtown. First-class; pool, dining. Phone 368–3355.

Inexpensive **Glenwood Motel.** 2769 Glenwood Dr. 2 miles east of Trail. Fine rooms and suites, all amenities, swimming pool. Phone: 368–5522.

VALEMOUNT. *Expensive:* **Mount Robson Ranch.** P.O. Box 301, Valemount. A true horse ranch with numerous riding plans. Cabins are rustic. Phone 566–4370.

VERNON. *Expensive-Deluxe:* **The Village Green Inn.** Located at junction of Hwy. 97 and Silver Star Rd. Lovely modern hotel; fine dining, sports available. Spacious grounds. Phone 542–3321.

HOW TO GET AROUND. By air: Private and public airplanes are a way of life within B.C. *CP Air* has the most extensive flight pattern in the province; *Pacific Western* will take you to Kamloops, Penticton, Prince George, Prince Rupert, and many other towns. Renting planes is not difficult; check at any airport. Also check on *Air Canada, Air B.C., Gulf Air Aviation, Island Airlines,* and *North Coast Air Services, Ltd.*

By car: Traveling by car is easy, but your choice of roads is somewhat limited by the terrain. For sightseeing, a car is the best way to travel.

By bus: The *Gray Line* offers many itineraries for sightseeing. *Greyhound* has a good network of stops throughout the province. *Coachways* serves the north. *Vancouver Island Coach Lines* makes numerous stops on the island. *Pacific Stage Lines* serves the southern portion of B.C.

By ferry: Major routes are outlined in the "Exploring" sections of this chapter; the line is *British Columbia Ferries.* Most extensive routes are between Vancouver Island and the mainland, whether it be to Prince Rupert in the north, Vancouver, or ports of call in Washington State. Summer schedules mean more boats and more routes; in winter, service is normally cut back. Detailed information on exact times and prices of these various ferry routes can be obtained within B.C. at most tourist information centers.

TOURIST INFORMATION. *Tourism B.C.,* Parliament Buildings, Victoria, B.C., V8W 2Z2 and 800 Robson St., Vancouver, B.C. You can also write to *Tourism B.C.,* 1117 Wharf St., V8W 2Z2, Victoria, B.C. For Vancouver, see *Practical Information* section for the city. Other city tourist offices are located in Prince George, Vernon, Victoria, and Penticton.

TIME ZONE. British Columbia is on Pacific Time.

TELEPHONES. The area code for all of British Columbia is 604. Pay phones take quarters.

BUSINESS HOURS AND HOLIDAY CLOSINGS. Most stores are open from 9:30 A.M. to 5:30 P.M. Monday to Saturday, with late shopping until 9 P.M. on Thursdays and Fridays. Banks generally open at 10 A.M. and close at 4 P.M., some stay open until 6 P.M., Thursdays and Fridays, and a few open Saturday mornings.

Statutory holidays are New Year's Day, Good Friday, Easter Sunday, Victoria Day (May 19), Dominion Day (July 1), B.C. Day (August 4), Labor Day

(September 1), Thanksgiving Day (October 13), Remembrance Day (November 11), Christmas Day, and Boxing Day.

TOURS. The *Gray Lines* offers many tours around B.C. Most of them originate in Vancouver.

The adventurous might want to try a raft trip in the white waters of the Thompson and Fraser rivers. It helps to be a swimmer, but life jackets are provided. Most tours originate in Lytton and start at $50 for a one-day outing. Contact *West-Can Treks-Adventure Travel,* 3415 West Broadway, Vancouver. Phone 734–1066.

Westours, 100 W. Harrison Plaza, Seattle, Washington 98119, provides several tours of B.C. Some are two weeks long, others shorter. You'll be able to find many other tours to and within B.C. by checking with a travel agent.

If you're on Vancouver Island, take a trip on the M.V. *Lady Rose,* a mail, passenger, and cargo ship that leaves at 8 A.M. from Port Alberni and sails up the beautiful West Coast. Rugged country, plus you'll see the Pacific Rim Park. The trip takes all day.

Another great West Coast cruise is on the Gold River-based M.V. *Uchuck,* which makes day trips to the logging communities of Tahsis and Zeballos and historic Nookta Island, where Captain Cook first landed in Canada.

PARKS. There are four National Parks in B.C.—*Glacier, Kootenay, Yoho,* and *Revelstoke* and more than 125 provincial parks, many of them in excess of 500,000 acres. The tourist offices have good information on location, rules, camping and hiking.

CHILDREN'S ACTIVITIES. Many suggestions have been included in the "Exploring" sections. Sites of most interest for children are the old forts or gold rush boom towns that have been restored—**Barkerville, Fort Steele,** and others.

In **Victoria,** at the Empress Hotel, is *Miniature World,* a unique and splendid show of miniature scenes. Near Victoria is *Fable Cottage Estate* with thatched cottages and animated characters. Farther north on the island is the *Forest Museum* around Duncan.

Near **Revelstoke** is the re-creation of *Frontier Museum Town* that children love. *Vancouver Pacific National Exhibition* has Playland open daily in July and August; open weekends only April to May and September to mid-October. Phone 253–2311 for details.

By and large, B.C. is family territory; often the adults and the children end up enjoying the same things and seeing the same sights.

SUMMER SPORTS. British Columbia offers every kind of sport. The real attractions are **fishing** and **camping** and **hunting.** Possibilities for camping and **hiking** are infinite, but the best places are in the provincial or national parks where trails have been marked. For *camping,* there are public and private sites scattered throughout the province; some are accessible by boat only (in the Gulf Islands). For detailed camping information, see or write the *Government Travel Bureau.*

Fishing licenses for nonresidents cost about $15. Hunting licenses are $25 for all game and birds.

You'll find over 110 **golf** courses in B.C. and countless **tennis** courts. **Watersports** are very popular and offered by most resorts. You can also swim at public or secluded beaches.

Mountain climbers will find parks the best place for climbing.

Yacht clubs in Victoria, on the Gulf Islands, and in Vancouver, and at many lakes can provide you with a boat for rent. **Canoeing** is also popular; canoes can be rented at resorts and at some inland hotels. Again, Tourism B.C. has up-to-date, detailed information on most sporting opportunities. It's best to check thoroughly on regulations, dates, and fees.

WINTER SPORTS. It is hard to find better **skiing** elsewhere in North America. In fact, British Columbia has some of the most difficult and enjoyable runs anywhere in the world. Some areas are limited to the experts, while there are resorts that cater to every level of skier. Near Vancouver you have Grouse Mt., Mt. Seymour, Hemlock Valley, and Cypress Bowl. Whistler Mt., an excellent ski spot, is just 2 hours north of Vancouver, as is Blackcomb Mountain. All have fine lift systems, good for beginners and experts. For the ultimate—**helicopter glacier skiing**—there is the famous Bugaboos in the east, in the Canadian Rockies. Other well-known ski resorts include Forbidden Plateau on Vancouver Island; Tod Mt.; Mt. Baldy; and Big White in the Okanagan Valley; Snow Valley and Red Mt. in Kootenay region; and the incomparable Cariboo and Bugaboo skiing. For more information, contact Tourism B.C. Don't forget that you can golf year-round in Victoria, and often in Vancouver.

MUSEUMS AND GALLERIES. **Barkerville:** the whole town is restored and a museum in itself. **Campbell River:** *Indian Museum.* **Courtenay:** *Lumberjack Museum.* **Dawson Creek:** *Regional Pioneer Museum.* **Duncan:** *Cowichan Valley Forest Museum* (logging artifacts). **Fort Langley:** renovated Hudson's Bay Company post. **Fort Steele:** North West Mounted Police post and re-created village. **Kamloops:** another Hudson's Bay fort. **Vernon:** *O'Keefe Ranch;* re-created old ranch. **Victoria:** many museums are listed in the "Exploring" section.

DRINKING LAWS. The drinking age is 19. Liquor, beer, and wine can be served in licensed dining rooms and pubs or bars. Taverns are open till 1 A.M.; bars and cabarets till 2 A.M.

DINING OUT. Seafood's the thing in coastal areas, with salmon topping the list, and halibut, black cod, king crabs, oysters and shrimps crowding in for second place. The Okanagan Valley is noted for its fruit and fruit wines. Restaurants in cattle ranching areas usually feature prime beef. Dinner in an *expensive* restaurant will run upwards of $15; in a *moderate* restaurant from $10 to $15; in an *inexpensive* one, under $10, drinks and wine excluded.

Most places accept the following major credit cards: American Express, MasterCard, and Visa; others may also be honored. Not all establishments accept credit cards, therefore we suggest you call for information.

GOLDEN. *Expensive:* **Selkirk Inn.** Excellent cuisine. Bar.

KAMLOOPS. *Expensive:* **David Thompson Dining Room.** 650 Victoria St. Steak, lobster, prime ribs. Children's portions.

Moderate: **China Village Restaurant.** 165 Victoria St. Chinese and North American food. Serves liquor.

Oriental Gardens. 545 Victoria St. Chinese and Japanese.

Inexpensive: **Highlander Restaurant.** 444 Victoria St. Seafood, steaks, trout. Dancing. Serves liquor.

NANAIMO. *Moderate:* **Villa Hotel Harbourside Restaurant.** 70 Church St. Downtown. Free parking. Cabaret.

PARKSVILLE. *Moderate:* **Island Hall Hotel Dining Room.** 181 Island Hwy. Outdoor garden overlooking the sea.

PENTICTON. *Moderate:* **Pilgrim House Motor Hotel Restaurant.** 1056 Eckhardt Ave. Specializing in prime beef.

PRINCE GEORGE. *Moderate:* **Outrigger Restaurant.** 1208 6th Ave. South Sea décor. Polynesian and Continental food.

Vienna Schnitzel Restaurant. 6th Ave. and Brunswick St. European cuisine in an Old World atmosphere. Entertainment.

PRINCE RUPERT. *Moderate:* **Crest Motor Hotel Restaurant.** 222 W. 1st Ave. Continental cuisine in a dining room that overlooks the harbor.

VERNON. *Moderate:* **Vernon Lodge Hotel Restaurant.** 3914 32nd St. Good selection, especially seafood. Entertainment.

VICTORIA. *Deluxe:* **Parrot House Rooftop Restaurant.** A top Château Victoria Hotel. Scenic views; very good menu of mostly Continental items. Well worth it.

Raven's. In Harbor Towers Hotel. Award-winning international cuisine.

Expensive: **Captain's Palace.** 309 Belleville St., on the inner harbor. A beautiful 1897 Victorian house now reopened with a wonderful luncheon menu. House filled with antiques. Charming, and good food.

Chauncey's. 614 Humboldt St., near inner harbor. Excellent seafood.

Empress Dining Room. 721 Government St. Continental cuisine, elaborate décor. Entertainment. This is *the* gem of elegant dining in the West. The room is Victorian style; the food absolutely first rate. Same for the service. *Bengal Room* does a very good curry lunch.

Chez Ernest. 4496 W. Sannich, on route to Butchart Gardens. Good food in pretty chalet.

Jack Lee's Chinese Village Restaurant. 755 Finlayson. Probably the best Chinese food on Vancouver Island.

La Petite Colombe. 604 Broughton. Good French food.

Marina Dining Lounge. 1327 Beach Dr., Oak Bay. Seafood a specialty at this waterfront restaurant.

Moderate: **Princess Mary Restaurant.** Extensive seafood menu. 344 Harbour Rd. On a land-locked ship. Good for family dinners; children's portions.

Sherwood Room. 123 Gorge Rd. Robin Hood artifacts from England will please the children. Also children's portions. Entertainment, dancing.

Inexpensive: **London Fish and Chips.** 723 Pandora. Best fish and chips on this British outpost.

NORTHERN CANADA

NORTHWEST TERRITORIES

Canada's Frontier

by
RAY PRICE

Born in Surrey, England, Ray Price was a soldier, teacher, award-winning actor, and a professional cricket player. He canoed down the Peace and Mackenzie Rivers and served as a mining claims inspector for the Territorial government. He wrote three books, Yellowknife, The Howling Arctic, *and* Trapper George. *Ray Price died in 1983.*

> **Editor's Note:** Because of the unique character of the Northwest Territories, we have departed from our usual format in this chapter. You will find Practical Information for each section listed within the text and under a separate heading for each region, for greater ease in planning a trip into these wilderness areas.

The Northwest Territories is vast—over a million and a third square miles. On the east its shores are washed by the cold, gray waters of the Atlantic, and on the west only the Yukon Territory separates it from the borders of Alaska. Five provinces share its southern border, and its Arctic islands reach to within 200 miles of the North Pole.

The capital of the Northwest Territories is Yellowknife, a city of 10,000 which represents almost 25 percent of the total population of the entire Northwest Territories. A population that divides itself into roughly three equal parts: one-third Indian, one-third Inuit, and one-third "Other."

Only in the last thirty years has advancing civilization reached its tentacles into this exciting land of Eskimo and Indian, of fur trader and explorer, and of missionary and trapper. Primitive people are being wrenched into the world of aluminum and chrome, aircraft and schools, politics and plastics, precooked food, and deodorants.

These people have not taken kindly to some of the changes and are resisting the complete takeover of their land and lives by the forces of civilization that feed on oil, demand minerals, and threaten to lay waste the land of their fathers and home of their hopes.

The Northwest Territories are divided into regions, each one immense and each one offering to the visitor exciting and novel experiences—the Districts of Franklin, Keewatin, and Mackenzie.

District of Franklin

In the east is the District of Franklin, a mass of water and land that embraces Baffin Island, all the High Arctic Islands, and is the biggest of the three. Frobisher Bay is the largest community in this district. Situated on the shores of an inlet that plunges between the low rock hills of Southern Baffin Island, it is named after the white discoverer of the land, Martin Frobisher, who landed there in 1576. He believed he had found fabulous deposits of gold, collected a considerable cargo, met and fought with the Natives, was ignominiously shot in the backside by a flint-tipped arrow, and then returned to England. Once back in the homeland he learned that the glorious gold was valueless iron pyrite.

Frobisher's voyages marked the beginning of great interest in the lands north and west of the British Isles. Slowly the whalers and the fur traders followed the paths of the explorers. The Davis Straits became known, and the cloud-haunted, ice-clad mountains of Baffin Island soon were familiar landmarks for those who sought wealth from the ocean.

Scattered across the white face of the District of Franklin are tiny Eskimo communities. Few have populations numbering more than several hundred, and only where mining or the search for oil has become extensive is there any industrialization. Resolute Bay on the north shore of Lancaster Sound has become a center of activity and so has Nanisivik on the northwestern shore of Baffin Island.

Many oil companies are using Resolute Bay as a supply/distribution center. Here, there is an all-weather airstrip, and flights from Montreal and Vancouver terminate. Nordair has regular flights from the east, and Pacific Western Airlines, from the west. These flights usually call at the largest cities and towns en route.

At Nanisivik there is a mining development. Barely a decade ago an enormous mountain of high-grade iron ore was found, and it was deemed feasible to start mining operations. As a result, the tiny Eskimo settlement that clings under towering cliffs to the shore of the Arctic Sea has become a center for wage earning activity. This is not welcomed by some of the free and easy Eskimos whose prime love is the hunt and the never-ending battle for survival in a hostile environment.

Until the end of the Second World War there was minimal interest in what happened in the vast reaches of the District of Franklin. One of Canada's postwar prime ministers is quoted as saying, "We have governed Canada's North with a great absence of mind." Policed by a handful of Mounties, served by an occasional traveling doctor, ministered to by a few Anglican and Roman Catholic priests, and invaded by the Hudson's Bay Company for fur, both the land and the people remained beyond the ken of the average Canadian and far out of the reach of an embryonic tourist industry. During the last few years, however, more and more visitors have stepped tentatively into this vast land. Well to the fore have been archaeologists, geologists, and anthropologists, all of whom have made major contributions to our expanding knowledge of the Canadian Arctic. Numerous exciting discoveries have been made. Natural gas in abundance has been found and archaeological sites of considerable importance have been uncovered on Axel Heiberg, Bathwest, Coburg, Devon, Ellesmere, and Cornwallis islands. Aircraft, politics, radio, and economics have knifed aside the curtain of silence drawn across Canada's North, and she now lies open for us all to visit, to see, to enjoy, to begin to understand.

The District of Keewatin

Lying alongside the Province of Québec and nestling under the far reaching arm of the District of Franklin is the District of Keewatin. This mass of land and water embraces the whole of the Hudson and James bays and most of the barren lands of the Central Northern Plain. Its principal communities lie along the coast of the Hudson Bay and the Arctic Ocean.

The Hudson Bay was named after Henry Hudson, who sailed into it in 1611 and never returned. What happened to him is a matter for speculation and has become one of the mysteries that stays locked in the bosom of that fog-shrouded, ghost-inhabited inland sea. All that can be conjectured comes from stories handed down from generation to generation by the Eskimos who have made their homes on the shores of the Bay.

After Henry Hudson, his son, and several faithful members of his crew were cast adrift by the mutinous crew, they disappeared from the page of factual, recorded history, but reappear in wraithlike fashion in the Eskimos' stories. The stories agree in a few particulars. A boatload of white men was discovered with all persons on board dead save the youngest—Henry Hudson's son. This boy was taken by the Eskimos and tethered among the dogs. They were terrified by this strange apparition, a white-faced animal that looked like a human but could be a god. These new people they called *Kabloona,* which means "bushy eyebrowed." One of Henry Hudson's most obvious characteristics was his heavy, bushy eyebrows.

The largest community in the Keewatin is Baker Lake, which lies inland from the west coast of Hudson Bay. Rankin Inlet is the administrative center of the Keewatin.

Eskimos are the only indigenous inhabitants of the Keewatin and until this century roamed over the vast inland plain in pursuit of the caribou or sallied onto the Bay's unfriendly waters for walrus, seal, and whale.

The Natives of the far Northern Region of Keewatin, who live on the shores of the Arctic Ocean, were those who saw the Franklin Party trek hopelessly to their death. These Eskimos live in the most inaccessible part of Canada's inhabited North. Scarcely half a century has elapsed since missionaries first moved among them, and rare indeed were explorers who encountered them. In 1771 Samuel Hearne plunged north and west from Fort Churchill and reached the mouth of the Coppermine River; no one followed him until half a century or more later, and even then neither the trading companies nor the church reached those elusive, isolated, fascinating people. Today we can reach them by aircraft. The very adventurous tourist can visit their small communities and see an occasional relic of their culture.

Few now live in snowhouses at any time of the year. Occasionally they still build them when overnighting on the trail. Rather large, fully serviced houses have been supplied by the government, schools built, telephones installed, and television made available through Anik, the Canadian communications satellite. Girls wear pantyhose, boys play guitars, and liquor and cigarettes are readily available. In the space of very few years these people have traveled from the use of primitive tools of bone, sinew, and flint to the use of high-powered rifles, aircraft, and electric generators. No more are these people nomadic; no more are whole tribes on the move; no more are teepees being erected or snowhouses built. What they once were is only to be found in their carefully crafted carvings, prints, and garments; occasional relics; and the clear memories of their patriarchs.

The Mackenzie Region

West of the Keewatin is the District of Mackenzie, the best known area of Canada's Northwest Territories. In 1789, the year of the French Revolution, Alexander Mackenzie—one of Canada's great explorers, fur traders, and adventurers—traveled the length of the mighty river that now bears his name. In his wake came traders, Roman Catholic priests, Anglicans, and prospectors. One of the richest fur-bearing areas of Canada was now readied for exploitation.

After the fierce conflict of the Hudson's Bay Company and the Northwesters was resolved, Mackenzie Region became the sole province of the Hudson's Bay Company trader. Apart from a few explorers, individual adventurers, and (after 1850) hardworking missionaries, that vast repository of renewable resources was ignored. The Hudson's Bay Company enjoyed their unchallenged monopoly.

In 1870 the Hudson's Bay Company sold their right to the sole trading privileges in the Northwest Territories, and free traders began to move in. Then the discovery of gold in the Yukon shattered the silence forever. The introduction of steamboats made the Delta accessible, and more and more people invaded that vast land.

In 1919 oil was discovered at Norman Wells, and a decade later Gilbert Labine landed at Great Bear Lake and discovered radium. Things now moved fast. Aircraft were flying mail as far north as Aklavik; prospectors were looking for gold, base metals, and oil; white trappers were spreading into every nook and cranny of the magnificent mountains to the west and the vast expanses of tundra north of the tree line.

Gold was discovered in Yellowknife Bay in the early thirties, and another rush for riches was precipitated. From the prairie dust bowl, the hopefuls came. They came from newly established homesteads in the Peace River region and from every province of Canada and most of the states in America. Yellowknife was born and today is the capital of one and one third of a million square miles.

The Second World War slowed the pace of development in the Mackenzie District until the Japanese threatened the underbelly of Alaska and the need for a source of oil in the north became urgent. With frantic desperation a pipeline was built from Norman Wells to Whitehorse in the Yukon. The war ended as the line was completed, and oil was never pumped through it.

Near the end of the war, more gold was discovered in Yellowknife and a new rush followed the coming of peace. The population of Yellowknife swelled to several thousand, a new town was planned and built, and the foundations laid for the moment in 1967 when it was declared the capital.

As Yellowknife developed, so did other settlements in the Mackenzie River District: Fort Smith (once the capital), Hay River, Fort Simpson, Aklavik, Fort Macpherson, and then the brand-new town of Inuvik in 1960.

In the last few years the pressing need of the world for oil and gas has brought the Mackenzie region into sharp focus. Indians are seeking a land claims settlement, oil companies are seeking more concessions, and the government is seeking solutions to the innumerable problems all these developments are causing.

EXPLORING THE DISTRICT OF FRANKLIN

If you love the out-of-doors, enjoy hiking, mountaineering, fishing, and photography; and are prepared to rough it, then go to Baffin Island. Few of its settlements have hotels, and those, while adequate, are not luxurious. However, there are many opportunities for memorable holidays.

To be sure of a reasonable measure of comfort while visiting the most remote parts of North America, the wisest plan is to join one of the several Arctic tours that start in Montréal. These tours are varied in both route and price. There are as many as nine different trips to choose from, ranging in price from approximately $1,000 to $3,000.

These tours give you a chance to see the very beautiful scenery of Baffin Island, visit several of its Eskimo communities, and catch sight of some of the wildlife to be found on land and in the surrounding waters. Most travel is by air, although some side trips by boat are offered. Details of these tours may be obtained from Montréal-based travel agencies.   from Travel Arctic in Yellowknife.

For the most part, Baffin Island is not ready for an intensive and extensive tourist business. It is still a country for specialists: anthropologists, sociologists, photographers, geologists, writers, mountaineers, and the like. Visitors most likely to enjoy themselves are those who like roughing it, love fishing, are lured by the mountains, have the curiosity of a naturalist and the appreciation of a painter.

Pangnirtung

Pangnirtung, the gateway to the Auyuittuq National Park, is one of Baffin Island's most beautiful places, and has been called the "Switzerland of the Arctic." Ringed by mountains and washed by the waters of Cumberland Sound, it is a place that once visited is never forgotten. For many years whalers sailed into the Sound, and they were the first to bring some of the benefits of civilization to the Inuit People. Now it is fully civilized with an airstrip, Peyton Lodge, accommodating fifty persons, and a regular mail service. The latest television programs of the Canadian Broadcasting Corporation can also be viewed through facilities supplied by the communications satellite Anik.

Plunging north and east into the mountains is the Pangnirtung Fiord, one of the two main sledge routes through the Baffin mountains. The fiord also marks the entrance to the National Park.

Auyuittuq National Park

This park has special treats for those seeking an exciting Arctic experience. Lying 1,500 miles northeast of Montréal, Canada's northernmost park covers 21,470 sq. kms. (8,290 square miles) of the island.

The Penny Highlands dominate the park, rising 7,000 feet above sea level, and carry on their peaks the Penny Ice Cap, 2,200 square miles of solid ice—a remnant of the last Ice Age. Glaciers, spawned by the ice cap, flow majestically into the surrounding valleys. The park can be reached by flying direct to Pangnirtung.

Here you will find wonderful camping spots and first-class opportunities to climb, fish, hike, read rocks, study nature, and take pictures. The Auyuittuq National Park can be explored year after year and still surprise, excite, and fill with wonder.

Holiday by Charter Aircraft

If funds are no problem, an exciting way to move comfortably around Baffin Island is by charter aircraft. Although some of the places can be reached on a scheduled run, a flight over Baffin Island's wild terrain and its formidable environs in a small aircraft can be an exciting, fascinating experience. Rarely visited places like Lake Harbour and Clyde River and Port Burwell on the south side of the Hudson Straits become reachable. It is usually possible to overnight in such places, although it is essential to make inquiries from the government offices in Yellowknife or the settlement manager. Letters can be addressed to the "Settlement Manager" in each of the above mentioned places. If writing to the settlements, please enclose a self-addressed return envelope to ensure a speedy, accurately directed answer.

The pilots of charter air companies know all the settlements and places of interest and will gladly share their expertise with you. Not only will charter air companies get you quickly and safely to less frequently visited places, they also can take you and your party to the finest spots for fishing, the greatest places for camping, and the best places to see the local fauna whether on land or sea.

A short flight (80 miles) from Frobisher will take you to Lake Harbour, a small Eskimo community that is still comparatively unaffected by the onrush of 20th-century technology. From there a longer hop will put you in Cape Dorset, the home of some of Canada's finest Eskimo carvers, painters, and printmakers.

To complete a very exciting tour, fly on to Igloolik and see an island that has yielded some of the most interesting artifacts of early Eskimo culture. The Hudson Bay has slowly receded during the centuries following the Ice Age, and as the shoreline has moved, the Eskimo population has followed it. As archaeologists move toward the highest part of the island, tools and implements from more and more ancient peoples are uncovered.

The Eskimo are proud of their heritage and will be glad to talk of their way of life and show you their carvings, paintings, prints, and beautiful fur garments. The latter are often for sale, although in recent years carvings, paintings, and garments have become expensive. Carvings frequently sell for well over $1,000.

Complete your trip by flying back via the far northern settlements of Arctic Bay and Pond Inlet, places ideal for the photographer and offering good chances to see whale, narwhal, and polar bear.

If you plan a trip like this, do not expect luxurious accommodations in the settlements. But in most places it is possible to obtain a good night's rest and reasonable food. The Eskimo are cheerful, reasonable, and pleasant hosts.

Such a trip will give you ample opportunity for talking with Eskimos —all of the younger generation read and speak English well—photographing their communities and their country and the Eskimo themselves. Be courteous in your use of a camera; remember you are a guest in their homeland. They are hospitable, but do not like being treated as curiosities.

Should you travel in wintertime—during which there is often the best flying weather, although daylight hours are very short—side trips by dogteam or skidoo can be arranged. It is not easy to make such arrangements in advance. Eskimos are not time or schedule conscious like the more regimented peoples in Western civilizations.

Keeping the above in mind, it is essential when planning such a once-in-a-lifetime trip to allow some room for possible, and indeed probable, delays. Weather in the eastern Arctic is frequently uncertain, and almost every year there are several days when radio communication becomes impossible. For example, this writer was stranded in Pangnirtung Fiord for nine days in 1972. The aircraft was damaged on landing and radio communication ruled out by sunspot activity. Eventually escape from the rapidly melting fiord had to be made by placing the aircraft's wheels onto toboggans and using them as skis when taking off.

It is unlikely that you will experience anything that unusual and frightening; however, anything can happen when touring Baffin Island and the surrounding land masses by small, chartered aircraft.

Charter Airline Service: Kenn Borek Aviation, Twin Otter Unit Service to Grise Fiord, and Pond Inlet. DC3 and Twin Otter Charter Service throughout the Northwest Territories Base at Resolute Bay and Inuvik. Telephone: Resolute Bay (819) 252–3848. Telephone: Inuvik (403) 979–3937. Bradley Air Service, Box 477, Frobisher Bay N.W.T. XOA OHO. Telephone: (819) 979–5810; Telex (Carp, Ontario) 063–15533.

Pond Inlet

Like Pangnirtung, it is set in spectacular scenery. Although it is on the far northern shore of Baffin Island, it is not a land of interminable snow and ice. Go there in the summer and see for yourself.

Take a boat trip to Bylot Island, 25 miles from the settlement. Here you will find a land of mountains and rivers, icebergs and sandstone, glaciers and snowfields, thousands of birds, and a sea alive with fish and mammals.

Pond Inlet can be reached from either the east of Canada or the west. Nordair flies from Montréal to Resolute, and Pacific Western Airlines flies from Edmonton or Calgary to Resolute, then from Resolute there is a feeder line operated by Kenn Borek Aviation to Pond Inlet.

A few years ago, Pond Inlet was especially honored by the Canadian government when a postage stamp was printed showing the spectacular view across the Inlet to the iceberg that for many years has been the source of the community's fresh water.

Write directly to Toonoonik-Sahoonik Cooperative, Pond Inlet, for up-to-date information concerning costs and the availability of accommodations. If Pond Inlet is your destination, then be sure to make your booking months in advance; accommodation is seriously limited.

Fishing

Arctic char, the salmon of the North, can be caught in the high tide waters of Cumberland Sound and the waters around Pond Inlet. This delicious fish, one of the most prized by sportsmen, frequently weighs in excess of 10 pounds. Boats are available from local people in Pangnirtung and Pond Inlet. Fish can also be caught in the unusually beautiful Summit Lake, high on the pass between the mountains.

Photography

There is magnificent unspoiled scenery to be photographed by the light of the midnight sun, under the fleeting, multicolored brilliance of the Aurora Borealis, or as the sun sweeps morning mists from river and sea.

For the wildlife photographer, there are subjects on both land and sea. Though sparse on land, some mammals can be seen by the alert photographer. Watch for the polar bear, lemming, fox, and very rarely, the barren ground caribou. Contrasted with this rather sparse land-bound fauna, there is an abundance of life in the surrounding waters. Not infrequently, beluga, various species of seals, bowhead whales, and narwhals can all be spotted. The narwhal is of particular interest. It is a strange species of whale that grows one long tusk, a tooth that has been used for all sorts of things, including aphrodisiacs.

Hiking

The majority of visitors to the Auyuittuq National Park come for the firsthand experience of the country that hiking affords. Difficult terrain and changeable weather demand considerable outdoor experience, careful selection of equipment, and adequate planning. The best time for hiking is from late June to early August, when the valleys are clear of snow.

Pangnirtung Pass has all the ingredients for a great hiking challenge: gravel flats, boulder-strewn moraines, glacial tongues, and icy streams to ford. A hiker will do well to travel at two miles per hour under these conditions. Overlord campground is located on the Weasal River Delta, some 20 miles from Pangnirtung very close to the boundary of the park. From here it is possible to walk to Summit Lake. Seven shelters are placed at strategic locations in Pangnirtung Pass. Each shelter holds a first-aid kit, and three of them have radiotelephones. Northwest Territorial publications emphasize the need for caution to all would-be travelers in the park. Winds can reach 100 miles per hour; freezing temperatures can occur during any month of the year; and avalanches and rockfalls are not uncommon.

Minimum equipment for a hiking trip into Auyuittuq National Park should include lightweight camping gear, warm windproof clothing, stout hiking boots, a camp stove, matches, maps, compass, and first-aid kit. A walking stick doubles as a probe to locate shallow points when fording streams. A lightweight rain suit should also be taken.

Climbing

Climbers from Europe, Japan, and North America have been drawn to peaks such as Mount Asgard, Mount Odin, and Tete Blanche. These peaks range from 5,000 to 6,000 feet above sea level (1,500–2,000 m.). The best climbing months are June and July, although snow conditions in April and May are usually good. Travel to and from the best climbing areas is difficult. Location of supply bases and the drop-off of supplies require careful organization. Until the end of May or early June, access is possible by ski-equipped aeroplane or snowmobile. During the best climbing period the only way to reach the mountains requires hard foot slogging over many miles or a helicopter.

Winter Sports

Snowmobiling, snowshoeing, and skiing: get away from mundane things in the spring of the year and enjoy fun in the snow at Pangnirtung and in the nearby National Park. Temperatures are moderate in April, May, and June, and the surrounding country can be explored by skidoo, ski, or snowshoe. Equipment can be rented from Eskimos at Pangnirtung, and guides are also available.

Note: There is a special information bureau in Auyuittuq National Park. Information can be obtained at the park's office in Pangnirtung. Address your letters to: The Superintendent, Auyuittuq National Park, Pangnirtung, N.W.T. X0A 0R0. For their own safety, all park visitors are requested to register at the park's office in Pangnirtung or Broughton Island.

General Information

The following services are available in Pangnirtung: nursing station; Royal Canadian Mounted Police; post office; Anglican Church; hotel with dining facilities; Hudson's Bay Store; Eskimo Cooperative Weaving Shop; regular airline service via Nordair.

PRACTICAL INFORMATION FOR THE DISTRICT OF FRANKLIN

TRANSPORTATION SERVICES. Bus Service and Vehicle Rental: *Arctic Resources Ltd.,* Frobisher Bay; tel. 819–979–6465.

Airlines. Scheduled Services: *Austin Airways,* Box 1160, Timmins, Ontario P4N 7H9. Scheduled service to Cape Dorset from Arctic Québec subject to traffic demand. *Nordair Limited,* Box 4000, Montréal International Airport, Dorval, Québec H4Y 1B8. Bases: Frobisher Bay, N.W.T. X0A 0H0; Resolute, N.W.T. X0A 0V0; Nanisivik/Arctic Bay, N.W.T. X0A 0A0; Hall Beach, N.W.T. X0A 0K0.

Nordair: Daily jet service Toronto–Ottawa–Montréal–Frobisher Bay (except Sunday). Twice weekly service to Hall Beach, Resolute Bay, and Nanisivik/Arctic Bay. Connecting flights from Frobisher to several Baffin Island communities. Fare and schedules available from your travel agent. Aircraft: DC-3 Twin Otter, Boeing 737.

Kenn Borek Aviation (scheduled and charter services): Box 1159, Inuvik, N.W.T., X0E 0V0. B.C. Twin Otter Unit Toll Service to Arctic Bay, Igloolik, Grise Fiord, and Pond Inlet. DC-3 and Twin Otter Charter service throughout N.W.T. Base at Resolute Bay, tel. 819–252–3849.

First-Air Ltd.: Box 477, Frobisher Bay, N.W.T. X0A 0H0. DC-3 and Twin Otter Service to Greenland and throughout Baffin Island. Telephone (819) 979–5810.

VEHICLE RENTALS. Cars and trucks are available in Frobisher Bay at: *Arctic Resources Ltd.* Telephone (819) 979–6465. *Baffin Leasing,* Box 699. Telephone (819) 979–6949.

ACCOMMODATIONS. Due to limited accommodation available in most Northwest Territories communities, please make reservations as early as possible. This is especially necessary for travel in the summer months. All hotels and motels listed in this section are open year-round unless noted otherwise. (At the time of publication, there are no bellhop services in most Northwest Territories hotels.)

Most places accept major credit cards; however, not all establishments accept credit cards, therefore we suggest you call for information.

CAMBRIDGE BAY. Ikaluktutiak Eskimo Hotel. 18-room motel can accommodate 40 persons, shared bathrooms. Dining room for guests only. TV in each room. Rates $80 single; $70 double per person without meals. $120 single; $110 per person double with meals. Major credit cards accepted. Write: Manager, Box 38, Cambridge Bay, N.W.T. X0E 0C0. Telephone (403) 983–2215.

CAPE DORSET. Kingnait Inn. Accommodation for 25. Rates $120 per night single, including meals. Proprietor: Sandy Reynolds. Telephone (819) 897–8863 or 897–8847.

FROBISHER BAY. Frobisher Inn. Located in a complex on Astro Hill. Open year-round. Accommodates 100 in 50 rooms, all with bath, TV, and phones. Licensed dining room, cocktail lounge, barber shop. Convention facilities available. Fish freezing. Rates $97 single; $110 double. Write: Box 610, Frobisher Bay, N.W.T. X0A 0H0. Telephone (819) 979–5241. MasterCard, VISA accepted.

PANGNIRTUNG. Peyton Lodge. Accommodates 40 in a 20-room motel. Central bath and shower facilities. Dining room and lounge. Side trips to spectacular Clearwater Fiord by boat for char fishing, sealing, and sightseeing. Rates $127 per day including meals; $75 per day without meals (shared occupancy). For reservations October 1 through March 31 contact John Faber, General Manager, Peyton Enerprises, Lynden Park Mall, Brantford, Ontario N3R 6B8.

POND INLET. Toonoonik-Sahoonik Hotel. Open all year, accommodating 42 guests with TV, bath and shower, dining room for 40 people; lounge. Rates $115 per day with meals. Discounts for conferences booking entire hotel. Write: Manager, Toonoonik Sahoonik Hotel, Pond Inlet, N.W.T. X0E 0S0. Telephone (819) 899–9928.

FISHING OUTFITTERS AND LODGES. Alivuktuk Outfitting. Transportation to and from Auyuittuq National Park to points of interest around Cumberland Sound. Trips from ½ day to 1 week long from July 1 to September 1. Rates vary. Write: Joavee Alivuktuk, Pangnirtung, NWT X0A 0R0.

Aurora Marketing Ltd. Excellent fishing for trout, grayling, pickerel and pike. Trips for three from $15 to $850. Motors, guides by the hour, day, or longer. Write: Aurora Marketing Ltd., Fort Providence, NWT X0E 0L0. Tel. 403–699–4321.

Arctic Char Lodge. 84 km. (52 miles) northeast of Cambridge Bay on Victoria Island. Open July and August. Accommodates 24 in heated framed tents, plus modern main lodge. Arctic char and lake trout. Guides, boats and motors. Floatplane at camp. Write: U.S. Headquarters (Box) 15406, Pheonix, AZ, 85060 –5406. Tel: 602–275–8634.

Creswell Bay Enterprises. Package fishing trips to outpost camp. Write: Timothy Idlout, Resolute Bay, NWT X0A 0V0.

Ikaluktutiak Co-op Outfitting Service. Fly from Cambridge Bay to spectacular fishing for Arctic char and trout. All camping equipment and fishing tackle supplied. Write: Manager, Ikaluktutiak Hotel, Cambridge Bay, NWT X0E 0C0. Tel. 403–983–2215.

Kuluktoo Bay Camp. Located 70 air miles (112 km.) southwest of Pond Inlet on Robertson River. Open August 8 to September 15. Accommodates 16 in tent frames. Excellent Arctic char fishing. Nearby attractions include ancient Eskimo campsites and narwhal calving grounds. Handicrafts and tackle available. Write: Joe Enook, Toonoonik-Sahoonik Co-op, Pond Inlet, N.W.T. X0E 0S0. Telephone (819) 899–9928.

Lake Hazen Lodge. Accommodates 15. World's northernmost fishing camp —656 kms. (410 miles) north of Grise Fiord. Excellent Arctic char fishing. Rates $160 per day, including guides and meals. Write: Bezal Jesudason, Box 200, Resolute Bay, N.W.T. X0A 0V0. Telephone (819) 252–3875.

EXPLORING THE DISTRICT OF KEEWATIN

To see the great spreading tundra that sweeps across Canada's northland, visit the Keewatin. Treeless, forbidding, almost uninhabited, it offers a new experience to those whose life is spent on concrete highways and admist the shining glass of a thousand highrises.

Although many refer to the tundra as "the Barrens," it is anything but barren. It is a land of rock, low willows, a million streams, thousands of lakes thick with fish, vast herds of caribou, small groups of muskox, waterfowl by the millions, and crystal-clear skies flickering with Northern Lights or flashing with sunset colors that finger the entire horizon.

For an exciting and different trip that is of minimum cost, drive as far as Thompson City in Northern Manitoba; the road is good all the way and well maintained. Then board a Canadian National train for Fort Churchill. Churchill is on the edge of the tundra and marks the border between the Northwest Territories and the province. Here you can see historic Fort Prince of Wales before moving deep into the territories.

From Churchill catch a plane to any of the small settlements along the coast of the Hudson Bay—Pacific Western Airlines has a scheduled service to most of them. These communities—Whale Cove, Eskimo Point, Rankin Inlet, Coral Harbour, Chesterfield Inlet, and Repulse Bay—are all Eskimo villages. In each of them you will be able to visit the local Hudson Bay store or Eskimo Cooperative, examine local works of art, talk with the native people, and travel into the surrounding area with rented equipment. The largest community, and the one with the best facilities for visitors, is Rankin Inlet. This settlement is a vibrant synthesis of the past and present.

What to Do at Rankin Inlet

Spend a few hours strolling through the town and browsing in the shops examining the Eskimo craft and talking with the people. Wander to the lake or the shore of Hudson Bay. Photograph the disused head-frame of the old nickel mine—catch it silouetted against the low-slung midnight sun.

Explore

Thirty miles from Rankin Inlet, set in the mist-hung waters of the Hudson Bay, is Marble Island—an island of ghosts. Two centuries ago, 83-year-old James Knight, searching for the Northwest Passage, per-ished on this island together with all the crews of the ships with him. For more than a year those lonely, marooned British stayed alive, but slowly famine, scurvy, and accident destroyed each one until only the blacksmith remained. His body was discovered unburied, not far from the anvil on which he had worked. Legend has grown around the fate of these men, and for the Eskimos it is a haunted, cursed land, not to be visited casually. Anyone visiting the island must crawl up the beach on hands and knees or else risk serious misfortune in the coming year.

Boats and guides can be rented in Rankin Inlet.

Fish

Go in almost any direction and there will be rivers, lakes, or the sea to fish. Arctic char, a most delectable fish ranging in size from four to twenty pounds, and the fighting lake trout, as big as fifty pounds, can both be caught. Even if you are not a keen fisherman, you will enjoy being in this unspoiled country where there need be no noise other than the dip of a paddle and the swish of the canoe moving steadily forward.

Visit the Eskimo

Charter either a Peterhead boat or a small aircraft and head for Daly Bay. Quite likely you will see the Eskimo out after seal, and perhaps you'll see a walrus.

Here taste life that is similar to the Eskimo age-old ways—fishing for food, sleeping in tents, and watching keenly for the appearance of seal and walrus.

Clothing

Whatever type of holiday you plan to spend in the Keewatin region of the Territories, it is essential that you have warm clothing, rubber boots, and sunglasses.

The Arctic Coast

In the far north of the District of Keewatin there are three interesting communities, each of which has hotel accommodations: Pelly Bay, Spence Bay, and Gjoa Haven.

PRACTICAL INFORMATION FOR THE DISTRICT OF KEEWATIN

HOW TO GET THERE. Scheduled air service is provided to each of these locations by *Northwest Territorial Airways Ltd.* Usually these schedules provide for two flights per week. To connect with these services, it is necessary to catch a *Pacific Western Airlines* flight out of one of the major western cities to Yellowknife. Northwest Territorial Airways will take you from there or you can fly all the way with Territorial Airways from Winnipeg.

ACCOMMODATIONS. Due to limited accommodation available in most Northwest Territories communities, please make reservations as early as possible. This is especially necessary for travel in the summer months. All hotels and motels listed in this section are open year-round unless noted otherwise. (At the time of publication, there are no bellhop services in most Northwest Territories hotels.)

Most places accept the following major credit cards: American Express, MasterCard and Visa; others may also be honored. Not all establishments accept credit cards, therefore we suggest you call for information.

BAKER LAKE. Iglu Hotel. Accommodates 50, double-occupancy. Conference facilities. Lounge, dining room seats 44. Rates $70 single. Write: Manager, Baker Lake, N.W.T. Telephone 819–793–2801; Telex 034–4214.

CORAL HARBOUR. Esungarq Motel. Situated in Coral Harbour on Southampton Island, this 4-room motel will accommodate 14 guests and features a dining room. The motel is owned by the Eskimo people of Coral Harbour. Rates $85 per night single, including all meals. Write: Katudgevik Cooperative Association. Coral Harbour, N.W.T. X0C 0C0. (Seasonal operation.) Telephone (819)925–9926.

ESKIMO POINT. Ootakevik Motel. In Eskimo Point the cooperative has a new 4-room motel to accommodate 12 guests. Meals are provided. Rates $50 per night without meals; $90 per night with meals. Padlei Cooperative will also supply fishermen with boats, motors, tents, and guides and take them to the Maguse River. Write: Padlei Cooperative Ltd., Eskimo Point, N.W.T. X0C 0E0. Telephone (819) 857–2933.

PELLY BAY. Pelly Bay Hotel. Opened in 1982. Accommodates 18 people in 6 rooms. Rates $70 single. Write: Koomiut Cooperative Association Ltd., Pelly Bay, N.W.T. X0E 1K0. Telephone (403) 769–6231.

RANKIN INLET. Rankin Inlet Lodge. Located on west shore of Hudson Bay. Open year-round. Accommodates 58 in double rooms. All rooms with bath and wall-to-wall carpet, excellent dining room and lounge. Trophy Arctic char, lake trout, whitefish, and grayling. Rates $95 per day, including meals; side trips extra. Write: Rankin Inlet, N.W.T. X0C 0G0. Telephone (819) 645-2807.

SANIKILUAQ. Amaulik Motel. Run by the Eskimo of the Mitiq Cooperative Association in Sanikiluaq in the Belcher Islands. Accommodates 16 in a new 4-room motel with dining room. Rates $95 per day, including meals. The Belcher Island people are famous for their soapstone carvings, done in their own particular style right in the settlement. Sanikiluaq is now serviced by Lamb Air. Write: The Manager, Mitiq Cooperative Association, Sanikiluaq, Belcher Islands, N.W.T. Telephone (819) 266-8860.

FISHING OUTFITTERS AND LODGES. Canoe Arctic Inc. Fly-in canoe trips in remote areas of taiga and tundra including Thelon and Coppermine Rivers. Photograph caribou, white wolves, muskox; rich in birdlife and fine fishing. All parties (six persons maximum) guided exclusively by Alex Hall, wildlife biologist. Eight years' experience in Arctic canoeing. Both sexes and all ages welcome. Previous canoeing experience not essential. Route selected for compatibility with clients' interests and capabilities. Two-way radio. Bookings, June 1-September 15. Twelve days from $1,200 per person; 18 days from $2,500, all-inclusive, from Fort Smith. References available. For brochure contact: Canoe Arctic Inc., Box 130, Fort Smith, N.W.T. X0E 0P0. Telephone (403) 872-2308.

Chantrey Inlet Camp. At the mouth of the Back River, open July 8-August 8. All-inclusive seven-day trip from Fort Francis, Ontario, US $1,595 for the week. Eskimo guides, boats, etc. Arctic char, trophy lake trout, grayling. Two-way radio. Write: Northern Wilderness Outfitters Ltd., Box 637. Fort Francis, Ontario P9A 3M1. Telephone (807) 274-3666.

Dubawnt Outpost Camp. Located at Outlet Bay, Dubawnt Lake. Accommodates 4-6 in heated, carpeted tent-framed dwellings. All-inclusive package with air charter from Winnipeg and return. Two guests to a tent. Daily maid service, comfortable beds, sleeping bags, meals, guides, boats, gas and motor. Separate dining tent with picture window. Radio at camp. Open July 10-August 30. Trophy lake trout and grayling. Write: Keewatin Arctic Camp Co. Ltd., 155, St. James Post Office, Winnipeg, R3J 0P7. Telephone (204) 885-5217. Telex May-September at Lynn Lake, Manitoba 0766313. Major credit cards.

Kasba Lake Lodge. Located 265 miles (426 km.) northwest of Lynn Lake, Manitoba. Accommodates 37 in cabins. Meals served in main dining room. Lake trout, Arctic grayling, and northern pike. Fish filleting, freezing, and packaging available. Rates US $1,650 per week, all inclusive, from Winnipeg. Write: D.E. Hill, Box 96, Parksville, B.C. V0R 2S0. Telephone (604) 248-3572.

Keewatin Arctic Lodge. On South Henik Lane, 250 miles (402 km.) northeast of Churchill, Manitoba, and 850 miles (1,368 km.) north of Winnipeg. Open July to September. Accommodates 8 to 12 with meals, guides, boats, motors. Lake trout, grayling, and whitefish. Electricity and fish freezing. Private 4,000-foot (1,219 m.) airstrip. Gas available. Write: 2639 Portage Ave., Winnipeg, Manitoba R3J 0P7. Telephone 204-889-8347.

Lynx Tundra Camp. On the northeast shore of Lynx Lake, at the headwaters of the famed Thelon River in the Barrenlands. Main cabin with cooking and dining facilities, and three tent frames to accommodate 8. Aluminum boats, motors, etc. Rates around $1,500 per person per week from Yellowknife, including meals, guides, and return fare from Yellowknife. Write: Henry J. Faess, Box 733, Red Lake Ontario P0V 1M0. Telephone 403-874-6897.

Neultin Narrows Sub Arctic Camp. Just below the tree line, in Keewatin area north of Manitoba on Neultin Lake. Can accommodate 8. Lake trout, grayling, and pike. Guests can view the old native camping structures on the nearby island. Rates $1,200 per week, all inclusive, from Lynn Lake. Write: B. Bennett, Box 935, Campbellford, Ontario K0L 1L0. Telephone (705) 653–3280.

Obre Lake Lodge. In a sheltered bay on the shore of Obre Lake, north of the Saskatchewan-Manitoba border. Cabins set in a forested area, up from a sandy beach. Accommodates 14 people for $1,200 per week. Dining room. Airstrip. Write: Stan Geddes, Box 568, Lynn Lake, Manitoba. R0B 0W0. Telephone (204) 356–2621.

Snowbird Lake Lodge. Located on Snowbird Lake 439 km. (273 miles) north of Lynn Lake, Manitoba. Accommodation for 20. Good cabins. Guides, boats, motors. Lake trout, Arctic grayling, and northern pike. Rates US $1,350 per week, all inclusive, from Winnipeg. Write Snowbird Enterprises Ltd., Box 70184, St. Paul, Minnesota, U.S.A. 55107. Telephone (612) 228–9320.

Windy River Camp. On north end of Nueltin Lake. Fastwater fishing for trout and grayling. Accommodates 10. Guests do own cooking. Rates $1,100 per week from Lynn Lake. Open July 1 to September 15. Write: Box 935, Campbellford, Ontario K0L 1L0. Telephone (705) 653–3280.

TRANSPORTATION SERVICES. Airlines. Scheduled service: *Calm Air International Ltd.* (Scheduled and charter services.) Base Rankin Inlet. Telephone (819) 645–2846. Serves Keewatin communities on the west coast of Hudson Bay. *Keewatin Air Ltd.,* 1129 Sanford St., Winnipeg, Manitoba R3E 3A1. Telephone 204–772–7968. Aircraft: Cessna 185, Single Otter. Base at Rankin Inlet. *Pacific Western Airlines.* (Scheduled and charter services.) This airline serves most of the Keewatin and Mackenzie Districts. Offices at: Edmonton Inn Tower, 9th Floor, 119th St. and Kingsway Ave., Edmonton, Alberta T5G 0X5; Winnipeg International Airport, Winnipeg, Manitoba R3J 0H7. Telephone 204–632–2811.

WHAT TO SEE. These far northern communities will be of special interest to those who enjoy the remote. They offer the chance to see people who, until the middle of this century, knew little about the rest of the world. At **Pelly Bay** there is an aboveground graveyard; a beautiful stone church built with loving care by Father Henry, who first went there in the early thirties; and rugged scenery that seems right for this windswept, icy corner of Canada. Each of these three northern settlements is the home of excellent carvers. Ivory carving is a specialty in Pelly Bay. These carvings can be examined and purchased and you can watch the carvers as they pursue their craft.

WHAT TO DO. Depending on weather conditions, it is possible to travel in the surrounding countryside on foot, rented skidoo, or in a rented boat. Fishing and hunting can be arranged from this community.

EXPLORING THE MACKENZIE REGION

The proposed Mackenzie Pipeline focused world attention on this area, and most of the settlements were mentioned by name on national and international radio and television. It is the most developed region of the Northwest Territories and the location of several of the Territories' largest communities, Yellowknife being both the biggest and the only city in a million-and-a-third square miles. It is the territorial capital.

How to Get There

Nearly all the communities can be reached by scheduled airline, and those that cannot are within easy reach of small chartered aircraft. The southern terminus for airline trips to the Mackenzie region is Edmonton. Pacific Western operates a fleet of jet aircraft that ensures fast, efficient service to Fort Smith, Hay River, Yellowknife, Fort Simpson, Norman Wells, and Inuvik. Feeder lines from these centers offer scheduled service to almost every other community in the Mackenzie, and where there is no such service, settlements can be reached by using small chartered aircraft.

Not only is the Mackenzie region easily accessible by air, but it is also feasible to drive to this part of the Northwest Territories. The road from Edmonton passes through such fascinating places as Whitecourt, Fox Creek, Peace River, High Level, and Indian Cabins on its way to the southern border of the Northwest Territories. Once in the territories, the Mackenzie Highway branches into an enticing system of roads, generally in such good condition as to surprise travelers. They reach the Slave River, the Northern Peace, cross the Hay and the Yellowknife, and provide free ferry service over the Liard and mammoth Mackenzie.

Enjoy a Driving Camping Tour

In this part of the Territories, you can take with you all those things that you might like to have along. Trailers, motor homes, boats, canoes —the many extras that make camping comfortable and more acceptable—need not be left behind. You do not have to be an expert outdoorsman to enjoy an exciting, fun-filled trip on the Mackenzie's roads, rivers, and lakes.

Before setting out on these northern gravel roads, be sure your vehicle is in good condition. It is the practice of seasoned travelers on these roads to carry extra gasoline and an extra spare tire, to cover the headlights with plastic, ensure the windshield (flying gravel from passing trucks not infrequently cracks them), protect the gas tank with a thick rubber sheath (ideal for this is a length of old conveyor belt), and take along a shovel, an axe, matches, a sleeping bag, and some food. These latter items are especially important if you are planning a winter trip when temperatures could drop very suddenly to minus forty degrees Fahrenheit *or* Celsius.

Note: If you have a trailer and a boat or put a canoe on top of your car, you will find endless opportunities to paddle or run your outboard in placid lakes and smooth, flowing rivers.

When driving north to Yellowknife, you drive through some of the world's finest fishing country. Should you never have fished in your life, now you have a chance—toss in a line and lure and watch northern pike, pickerel, and grayling fight for the hook.

The Mackenzie Highway

The Mackenzie Highway stretches one thousand miles from Edmonton to Yellowknife. Its hundreds of miles of wilderness, lakes, rivers, waterfalls, frontier settlements, and campgrounds provide challenge and interest all the way. (For those who do not like tents, trailers, or motor homes, there are motels and hotels reasonably spaced along the length of the highway.)

Once inside the Territories a variety of choice is open to you. You can drive the network of roads that links Fort Smith, Hay River, Pine Point, Enterprise, Fort Simpson, and Yellowknife, or you can hurry north to the mammoth Mackenzie and the Ingraham Trail that pushes out of Yellowknife to nowhere through what one writer called "a fish-laden Precambrian delight."

At Fort Smith you can visit the Wood Buffalo National Park, home for herds of northern bison and the almost extinct whooping crane; at Pine Point view the open pit mine of the biggest lead-zinc producer in North America; in Hay River watch the Northern Transportation riverboats preparing for their journey to the Arctic Ocean and all the while enjoy the forest. Watch for wildlife. Many animals can be seen by the alert observer—bear, wolf, lynx, and coyote to mention but a few. And be sure to train your glasses on the eagles that can be frequently seen soaring watchfully over the Great Slave Lake.

From Hay River drive to Fort Providence. Here you can buy beautifully worked pictures of dyed moose hair and garments of fur and skin, then move on to Fort Rae, home of the Dogrib Indians (the largest Indian community in the north).

From there it is but seventy miles to Yellowknife, Canada's newest capital. Here is a modern city with high-rise buildings, hotels, restaurants, a museum, an old and new town, two gold mines, and a busy dock.

While in Yellowknife it would be a good idea to replenish your supplies. The city offers the best choice of stores in the north and, as a rule, the most competitive prices.

In Yellowknife

Guided bus tours of the city are available. These usually take about an hour-and-a-half and will give you a quick introduction to its exotic history. Tour information is available from the Yellowknife Chamber of Commerce, Box 906, Yellowknife, N.W.T.

Boat trips on the Great Slave Lake. Four commercial companies offer a variety of cruises. East Arm Freighting, Box 2547, Yellowknife, N.W.T. X0E 1H0, telephone (403) 873–2018; Yellowknife Traders, 2 Lessard Drive, Yellowknife, NWT X1A 2G5, telephone (403) 873–3746; and Snowcraft Cruises, Box 2006, Yellowknife, N.W.T. X0E 1H0, telephone (403) 920–4024 or 873–8858.

Mine Tours. At the discretion of the local gold mines, tours of the aboveground workings and underground are available for a limited number of visitors each week.

If you are lucky, you may even witness a gold pour. Giant Mines usually pour gold twice each week. The other gold mine owned and operated by Cominco celebrated the pouring of its 5,000th gold brick on September 23, 1976. Since the first brick was poured at the Cominco mine, the oldest mine in the Northwest Territories has produced close to 3,000,000 troy ounces of gold. Arrangements to visit a mine can be made through the local tourist office.

At least seven charter air companies have immediately available aircraft to fly you to a lake or river of your choice, 10 miles away or 1,000 miles away. If you have time, a visit to one of the many beautiful, uninhabited lakes should be a priority.

When you leave Yellowknife and start the long drive south, plan to stay at all those places missed on the way north. With careful planning, and that's the secret of a successful trip into the Mackenzie region, you should not miss many of the interesting things there are to see and do when driving and camping along its highways.

Note: Camping permits are required for use of N.W.T. territorial park campgrounds. At a cost of $5 a night. They should be purchased daily from a supervisor at the park.

Adventure by Boat or Canoe

The Mackenzie River, one of the mightiest rivers in the world, can be traveled by canoe, kayak, speedboat, cabin cruiser, and even raft. More than a few northerners have used crude but serviceable craft to reach the far-off communities of Inuvik, Aklavik, and Fort Macpherson. Boats can be easily launched at Fort Providence or Fort Simpson and returned from the Arctic aboard one of the many Northern Transportation barges. Throughout the summer, tugs ply the river carrying a year's supplies to settlements and oil companies. Barges being brought up river are empty, so it is easy to have boats loaded and returned south. On the way down river, stops can be made at every settlement and supplies replenished. Food you have purchased can be supplemented with fish.

At the mouths of most of the creeks and rivers, grayling and pickerel can be caught, and should they not grab for your hook, you can be sure the ubiquitous northern pike will be there to swallow it.

Keep your eyes open wide for birds and beasts. Bear, moose, and larger game animals are only occasionally seen, but there are birds by the thousand: sandpipers, falcons, eagles, many kinds of geese, and more than twenty-five species of ducks. If you plan to travel the Mackenzie, you should allow two or three weeks for the trip.

Placid rivers, wide lakes, and torrential mountain streams all beckon to the boating and canoeing enthusiasts. In the Territories there is something for everyone who loves the water: tiny forest-ringed lakes within easy reach of every community; wide, windswept bodies of water closely akin to inland seas that demand seaworthy boats, navigational charts, and skillful seamanship; placid rivers that the most amateur of canoeists can enjoy safely; and rushing torrential mountain streams that challenge the experts, demanding the utmost in skill and determination. U-paddle canoes and kayaks are available in the Territories, as are small boats equipped with outboard motors. Canoes can be rented from the Hudson's Bay Company in much the same way as cars can in the south. A canoe may be picked up at one store and delivered to another. This makes a trip downriver possible without the arduous task of paddling back upstream. Arrangements for this type of rental should be made well in advance thorugh Hudson's Bay Company, Northern Stores Department, 800 Baker Centre, 10025 106 Street, Edmonton, Alberta. Matters would be made especially simple if you have a Hudson's Bay Company credit card.

Should you want one of the greatest canoe experiences offered in Canada, then travel the South Nahanni River. This river has been made famous through books, legends, and films. It is an awesome river, tearing through rapids, plunging over the spectacular Virginia Falls (321 feet), twisting through canyons under 2,000-foot cliffs, wandering over spreading mud flats, and slipping by hot springs that may one day become a mecca for tourists. Excellent maps can be obtained from the government of Northwest Territories as well as interesting, essential descriptions of the river's hazards.

For less expert canoeists, why not follow the steps of Sir John Franklin and travel up the Yellowknife River, or paddle the shores of the innumerable lakes. The options are almost unlimited. In the old days, many trappers and hunters used to move from the Great Slave Lake to Great Bear Lake. This is a long trip, but one that can be made by determined persons who can read maps and like hard work. There are no serious hazards on the way. Distance makes careful preparation essential.

Should you prefer to be a passenger, a variety of choices is open to you. There are boat cruises on Great Slave Lake. These can be arranged for a few hours, a few days, or several weeks. Airboat trips up to South Nahanni starting from Fort Simpson.

Hunting and Fishing

Presidents and royalty have come to the Northwest Territories to hunt and fish. Trout of such size that fishermen don't have to exaggerate are waiting to be lured from the depths of Great Slave Lake and the ice-cold waters of Great Bear Lake. Grayling, pickerel and northern pike will fight for your hook. If it is fish you are after, the Northwest Territories is the place to come. There are more than fifty fishing lodges and outfitters operating in the Territories, most of them in the Mackenzie region. Licenses are available in all communities. For the hunter, there is an impressive list of animals to be sought: black bear, grizzly, moose, Dall sheep, mountain goat, polar bear, bison, and woodland caribou.

Because regulations for hunting are subject to change at short notice, it is advisable to contact the government office in Yellowknife for up-to-date information. Write to TravelArctic, Yellowknife, N.W.T. X0E IH0. All nonresident hunters are required to use a licensed outfitter. Throughout the Mackenzie Region at all the strategic locations there are well-equipped outfitters who engage excellent guides. From these outfitters you may purchase the necessary game license. For information write to: Government of N.W.T., Fish and Wildlife Service, Yellowknife, N.W.T.

PRACTICAL INFORMATION FOR THE MACKENZIE REGION

TRANSPORTATION SERVICES. Bus Service: For those wishing to enjoy the Mackenzie Highway and who would prefer to leave the driving to someone else, there is a regularly scheduled, modern bus service operating over the highway except to Yellowknife and Rae during a 6-week period in the late fall and early spring, when freeze-up and breakup of the Mackenzie River occur.

Canadian Coachways System, 10202 102 Street, Edmonton, Alberta. Daily services between Edmonton and Hay River via Peace River. Connections for Fort Providence, Rae, Edzo, and Yellowknife at Enterprise three times weekly, via N.W.T. Coachlines. Fares and schedules through any Greyhound Lines office or agency. 403–421–4211.

Flying Dutchman Bus Lines, Box 900, Fort Smith, N.W.T. 403–872–2727.

N.W.T. Coachlines Limited, Box 1480, Hay River, N.W.T. X0E # 0R0. Three trips per week Yellowknife, Rae, Edzo, Fort Providence, Enterprise, Hay River. Daily trips between Hay River, Pine Point, and Fort Smith. Twice weekly between Hay River, Pine Point, and Fort Resolution. 403–874–2216.

Frame and Perkins Bus Lines, Box 400, Yellowknife, N.W.T. X0E IH0. City scheduled service and charters. 403–873–4437.

Airlines. Scheduled Service: Air Providence Ltd. Connecting Ft. Providence with Yellowknife, Ft. Simpson, Hay River, Pine Point and Fort Smith. Fort Providence X0E 0L0. Telephone 3551.

Northwest Territorial Airways Ltd., Box 9000, Yellowknife, N.W.T. X0E IH0. Regular service from Winnipeg to Yellowknife and twice-weekly service to Rankin Inlet and Frobisher Bay. DC–3 service to all Central Arctic communities. Fares and schedules available from the airline.

Pacific Western Airlines, Ninth Floor, Edmonton Inn Tower, 119 St., Kingsway Ave., Edmonton, Alberta T5G 0X5. Service: Scheduled Boeing 737 and 727 jet from Edmonton to Yellowknife, 18 flights weekly; and Edmonton to Inuvik, 6 flights weekly. Hay River and Norman Wells are served daily except Sunday. Fort Smith is served daily except Saturday and Sunday. Fort Simpson is served thrice weekly. Cambridge Bay twice weekly. Boeing 727 serves Resolute twice weekly. Fares and schedules are available from your travel agent. Connecting flights to other communities in the western Arctic.

Ptarmigan Airways Ltd., Box 66, Yellowknife, N.W.T. X0E IH0. Service: Regular service to Snowdrift, Pine Point, Lac La Martre, and Rae Lakes.

Other Scheduled Airlines: Air Canada serves the northern gateway airports of Edmonton, Winnipeg, and Montréal. *CP Air* serves Whitehorse as well as these 3 cities. A number of United States and other foreign airlines serve Canadian international airports, enabling travelers to easily reach their Northwest Territories destinations in comfort via modern airliners. Your travel agent can recommend the easiest route to the North.

CHARTER SERVICE. Charter aircraft, to take you into isolated settlements and historically famous Arctic adventure areas, are also conveniently available on reasonable advance notice. Charter aircraft rates are scaled according to the size of the aircraft used. Whether yours is a two-person or a busload, the most economically suitable aircraft can easily be chartered.

Adlair Aviation Ltd., Rene Laserich, Box 2946, Yellowknife, N.W.T. Telephone (403) 873–2828.

Air Providence, Fort Providence, N.W.T. X0E 0L0. Aircraft: wheels, skis; floats, charter service for fishing and hunting trips. Piper Cherokee Cessna 180B. Telephone (403) 699–3551.

Aklavik Flying Service, Box 1158, Inuvik, N.W.T. X0E 0T0. Aircraft: Cessna 185, Cessna 337, Twin Otter. Telephone (403) 979–3190.

Buffalo Airways, Box 168, Fort Smith, N.W.T. X0E 0P0. Bases: Fort Simpson, N.W.T. X0E 0N0. Aircraft: fixed-wing and helicopters. Telephone (403) 872–2216.

Carter Air Service, Box 510, Hay River, N.W.T. X0E 0R0. Telephone (403) 874–2281.

Fort Smith Air Service, Box 415, Fort Smith, N.W.T. X0E 0P0. Aircraft: Cessna 337, 206, 185; Norseman—floats, skis, wheels. Telephone (403) 872–2312.

Inuvik Central Airways Ltd., Box 2629, Inuvik, N.W.T. X0E 0T0. Telephone (403) 979–3372.

Kenting Helicopters, #3 Hangar, McCall Field, Calgary, Alberta. Bases: Resolute Bay, N.W.T.

LaRonge Aviation Ltd. (Mackenzie Air Ltd.), Box 2489, Yellowknife, N.W.T. X0E IH0. Aircraft: Twin Otter, Single Otter, Twin Dornier, F–27, and Lear Jet on request. Bases: In Hay River, N.W.T. X0E 0R0. Edmonton, Hangar #3, Industrial Airport, Edmonton, Alberta.

Latham Island Airways, Box 791, Yellowknife, N.W.T. X0E IH0. Telephone (403) 873–2891.

Nahanni Air Services, Box 123, Norman Wells, N.W.T. X0E 0V0. Aircraft: Cessna 185, Cessna 337, Helio Courier. Telephone (403) 587–2288.

Okanagan Helicopters, Box 1492, Inuvik, N.W.T. X0E 0T0. Bases: Box 24, Norman Wells, N.W.T. X0E 0V0. Telephone (403) 979–2875.

Ptarmigan Airways Ltd., Box 66, Yellowknife, N.W.T. X0E IH0. Aircraft: Turbo Beaver, Cessna 185, Piper Aztec, Navajo and Twin Otter. Telephone (403) 873–4461.

Ram Air, Box 1530, Inuvik, N.W.T. X0E 0T0. Aircraft: single- and multi-engine; wheels, skis, floats. Cessna 185, 206, Beech E-185, Twin Bonanza, Aztec, and Helio Courier. Telephone (403) 979–3341.

Simpson Air Ltd., Box 90, Fort Simpson, N.W.T. X0E 0N0. Aircraft: Turbo Beaver, Baron, Cessna 185, Islander and Trilander. Telephone (403) 695–2505.

Twin Air Ltd., Box 880, Yellowknife, N.W.T. X0E 1H0. Telephone (403) 873–5877.

Wolverine Air Ltd., Box 316, Fort Simpson, N.W.T. X0E 0N0. Aircraft: Cessna 180, Cessna 185, Cessna 336 Islander. Telephone (403) 695–2263.

ACCOMMODATIONS. Due to limited accommodation available in most Northwest Territories communities, please make reservations as early as possible. This is especially necessary for travel in the summer months. All hotels and motels in this section are open year-round unless noted otherwise. (At the time of publication, there are no bellhop services in most Northwest Territories hotels.)

Most places accept the following major credit cards: American Express, MasterCard and Visa; others may also be honored. Not all establishments accept credit cards, therefore we suggest you call for information.

AKLAVIK. Mcleod's Hotel. Accommodates 6. Shared bathrooms. Dining facilities. Rates $60 per night. Write: McLeod Hotel, Box 36, Aklavik, N.W.T. X0E 0A0. 403–978–2218.

COLVILLE LAKE. Colville Lake Lodge. Main building in village accommodates 12. Also fishing for lake trout, pike. Rates $600 per week. Open year-round. Airstrip. Write: B.W. Brown, Colville Lake, N.W.T.

COPPERMINE. Igloo Inn. Open all year. Accommodates 31 in 5 housekeeping cabins, plus 9 in a motel unit with central bath, shower, and kitchen. Rates $85 per night double or single. Boats, motors, and guides available. Char fishing in late July and August. River trips to Bloody Falls. Write Igloo Inn, Coppermine, N.W.T. X0E 0E0. Telephone (403) 982–3333. Telex. 034–4370.

ENTERPRISE. Motel El Camino. Sam's Place at junction of Hwys. 1 and 2. Open all year. Near scenic spots, Louise Falls, Alexandra Falls, McNally Creek, Hart Lake, Tower and Lady Evelyn falls on Kakisa River. Arctic grayling, northern pike, and pickerel. Motel, cocktail lounge, and restaurant. Texaco service station, general store, ice, and propane. Motel accommodates 43 people in 14 units. Cots and cribs available. Rates $27 single; $45 double with private bath and shower facilities. Write: Box 277, Hay River, N.W.T. X0E 0R0. Hosts Sam and Louise Petersen. Telephone (403) 984–3361.

FORT NORMAN. Bear Lodge. Accommodates 15, with central baths, dining room. Overlooking Mackenzie River, Northwest Territories' oldest church nearby. Rates $60 without meals; $95 with meals. Write Bear Lodge, Fort Norman, N.W.T. X0E 0K0. Telephone (403) 588–4311.

FORT PROVIDENCE. Big River Motel. On Hwy. 3 near Fort Providence. Open all year. Accommodates 18 in 5 units with bath. Service station, restaurant, and cocktail lounge nearby. Rates $30 single; $40 double. Write Z. Demir, Big River Service Centre, Fort Providence, N.W.T. X0E 0L0. Telephone (403) 699–4301.

Snowshoe Inn. Modern facilities overlooking the mighty Mackenzie River. Year-round accommodation for 63 people in 35 units, full bath, room phones, individual thermostats, kitchenettes. Rates $49 single, $62 double. Café, licensed dining and cocktail lounge, banquet and convention facilities. General store. Finest Indian and Eskimo handicraft selection, coin laundry, and showers. Fishing trips arranged, car and truck rental. Write Snowshoe Inn, Fort Providence, N.W.T. X0E 0L0. Telephone (403) 699–3511.

FORT SIMPSON. Fort Simpson Hotel. Located at the confluence of the Mackenzie and Liard Rivers. Open all year. All rooms complete with tub and shower, 4 suites with cooking facilities. Room phones, restaurant, licensed dining room, cocktail lounge. Scheduled and charter air service available. All-weather road to all points south. Rates $62–68 singles; $72–78 doubles. Write Box 248, Fort Simpson, N.W.T. X0E 0N0. Telephone (403) 695–2201.

FORT SMITH. Pelican Rapids Inn. In downtown Fort Smith. Modern motel with all conveniences. Accommodates 60 in 30 large, comfortable rooms. Room phones, radios, TV's, plug-ins, hot water heating, full baths in all rooms, carpeting. Rates $48 single, $54 double. 13 kitchenettes available. Restaurant across the street. Write Box 248, Fort Smith, N.W.T. X0E 0P0. Telephone (403) 872–2789.

Pinecrest Hotel. Open all year. Accommodates 60 in 30 rooms—18 with bath, 12 with basin and toilet. Two public showers. Cocktail lounge, licensed dining room, telephone. Road runs through Wood Buffalo National Park. Rates $29 single, $35 double. Write Fort Smith, N.W.T. X0E 0P0. Telephone (403) 872–2104.

HAY RIVER. Caribou Motor Inn. In the new town of Hay River. Open all year. Accomodates 64 in 29 large, comfortable rooms. Room radios, phones, TV's, plug-ins, hot-water heating, full baths in all rooms. Licensed cocktail lounge and restaurant. Rates $40 single, $45 double, kitchenettes: $42 single, $52 double. Write Box 1114, Hay River, N.W.T. X0E 0R0. Telephone (403) 874–6706.

Migrator Motel Ltd. Located in new town. Open all year. Eighteen rooms with 2 double-beds, 4 rooms with kitchen facilities, 2 suites. All rooms with bath and shower. TV, phone, and winter plug-in. Rates $42 single, $52 double, $48 twin, $70 4 persons, $60 family, kitchenettes: $48 single, $58 double. Write Box 1847, Hay River, N.W.T. X0E 0R0. Telephone (403) 874–6792.

Ptarmigan Inn. Fully licensed hotel at Hay River in the center of new town. Open all year. Accomodates 106 in 44 rooms, all with TV, ice, radio, telephone. Cocktail lounge, bar, coffeeshop, dining room, two banquet rooms. Rates from $59 single, $74 double. Write Box 1000, Hay River, N.W.T. X0E 0R0. Telephone (403) 874–6781.

INUVIK. Eskimo Inn. Open year-round. Accomodates 158 in 79 rooms, all with bath, wall-to-wall carpet, telephones, color TV in all rooms. Two cocktail lounges, licensed dining room, coffeeshop, convention and banquet facilities seating up to 150 people. Gift and fur shop next door. This hotel is regarded by most travelers as the best one in Inuvik. Rates $66 single, $70 double. Write Box 1740, Inuvik, N.W.T. X0E 0T0, or contact your travel agent. Telephone (403) 979–2801 or telex 034–44519.

Finto Motel. New 23-room motel accommodates 52. Doubles have full kitchenette facilities and baths. Singles have showers only. Rates $60 single, $65 single with kitchenette, $70 double. Write Box 1925, Inuvik, N.W.T. X0E 0T0. Telephone (403) 979–2647.

Mackenzie Hotel. Open all year. Accommodates 74 in 38 rooms, 28 with private bath. Bar, licensed dining room, cocktail lounge, coffeeshop, telephone, color TV in 28 rooms, black-and-white in 12. Rates $70 single, $80 double, $70 triple. Write Box 1618, Inuvik, N.W.T. X0E 0T0. Telephone (403) 979–2861.

NORMAN WELLS. Mackenzie Valley Hotel. Open year-round. Accommodates 50 in 24 fully modern single and double rooms. All with bath and shower or shower only. Also new 5-room motel. Showers and baths in all rooms. Dining lounge, coffeeshop. Cocktail lounge; gift shop, supplying native handicrafts, magazines, and books. Phones in all rooms; color TV available to rent. The best in hospitality and meals is always available. Rates $60 single, $100 double. Write Box 125, Norman Wells, N.W.T. X0E 0V0. Telephone (403) 587–2511.

Norwel Inn. 10-room hotel. Accomodates 20, TV, bath and shower. Restaurant. Rates $75 single, $90 double. Write: Box 37, Norman Wells, N.W.T. X0E 0V0. Telephone (403) 587–2345.

PINE POINT. Pine Point Hotel. 53 miles (85 km.) east of Hay River, Hwy. 5, open year-round. Accommodates 60 in 23 rooms with baths and 8 suites. TV in all rooms. Cocktail lounge, licensed dining room, ice, telephone. Banquet facilities, accomodates up to 55 persons. Nearby attractions include tours of the lead-zinc mines. Rates $51 single, $57 double. Write Box 148, Pine Point, N.W.T. X0E 0W0. Telephone (403) 393–2851.

TUKTOYAKTUK. Beaufort Motel. Twelve double rooms, 6 housekeeping units. Telephones and TV. Rates $55 single, $65 double. Write Box 60, Tuktoyaktuk, N.W.T. X0E 1C0. Telephone (403) 977–2381.

Tuktoyaktuk Lodge. Located on the shores of the Arctic Ocean. Modern accommodation for 14 in 7 rooms. Summer season only. Hot and cold running water, baths, etc. Sightseeing and fishing trips can be arranged. Write Manager, Tuktoyaktuk Lodge, Tuktoyaktuk, N.W.T. X0E 1C0. 403–977–2538.

YELLOWKNIFE. Explorer Hotel. 120-room hotel in downtown area. Five convention and banquet rooms accommodate 10 to 500 persons. Cafeteria, dining room, lounges, game room. All rooms with phone, color TV, bath, and shower. Rates $85 single, $95 double. Write Box 7000, Yellowknife, N.W.T. X0E 1H0. Telephone (403) 873–3531.

Gold Range Hotel. Located in downtown Yellowknife. Open year-round. Accommodates 75 in 52 rooms, 18 with private bath, all with telephones. Cocktail lounge, licensed dining room, newsstand, barbershop. Banquet facilities accommodates up to 40 persons. Rates $30 single, $35 double. Write Box 698, Yellowknife, N.W.T. X0E 1H0. Telephone (403) 873–4441.

Twin Pine Motor Inn. 44-room motel. Some rooms have cooking facilities. Rates $65 single, $68 double. Two conference rooms. Write: Box 596, Yellowknife, N.W.T. X0E 1H0 Telephone (403) 873–8511.

Yellowknife Inn. In center of town. Open all year. 162 rooms accommodating over 200. Two large suites also available. All with bath or shower, telephone, radio, room service, ice, soft-drink dispensers on second and third floors, two cocktail lounges, dining lounge, cafeteria, two banquet rooms, newsstand, souvenirs, B/W TV in most rooms (additional $1 charge for color TV). Rates $54 single, $59 double. Write: Box 490, Yellowknife, N.W.T. X0E 1H0. Telephone 403–873–2601.

YWCA. Accommodates 119 in 43 rooms; 30 private kitchenette apartments. Rates $30 per night; 10 shared units, $20 per night; 3 overnight shared units—no cooking facilities, $12 per night. Located at the corner of Franklin Ave. and 54 St., 403–920–2777.

FISHING OUTFITTERS AND LODGES. Namushka and Watta Lodges, operated by Adventure North Ltd.; June to September. Fly-in fishing rates, $900 per week or $155 per day, include flight to and from lodges, boats, motors, fuel, guides, food, trolling equipment, cleaning and freezing fish, radio telephones. Namushka Lodge is located on Harding Lake, 32 air miles (51 km.) east of Yellowknife, equipped with resident cook, licensed lounge, baths, and showers. Watta Lodge is 42 air miles (68 kms.) east of Yellowknife. Also side trips to Buckham Lake. Fishing for lake trout, northern pike, Arctic grayling, walleye, and whitefish. Write Site 484, Box 6, R.R. 4, Sherwood Park, Alberta T8A 3K4. Telephone (403) 467-4857.

Arctic Circle Lodge. On Great Bear Lake, only 14 miles (22.4 kms.) from the Arctic Circle. Under all new management. Fishing for trophy lake trout, grayling, side trips for Arctic char. All new boats and motors, excellent cuisine. Accommodates 34. Rates, $1,795 per week, include accommodations, boat and guide, all meals, round trip flight from Edmonton, Alberta. Write: Box 503, Edmonton, Alberta T5J 2K1. Telephone (403) 458-3383.

Blackford Lake Lodge. Located on Blackford Lake 96 kms. (60 miles) east of Yellowknife. Accommodates 10 in comfortable log cabins. Sauna and ice house. Excellent fishing: trout, walleye, northern pike, and whitefish. Season: June 2-Sept. 30. Rates $65 per day, include use of boat and motors. Food, fishing gear and sleeping bags must be brought by guests. Special family and group rates available on request. Write: Box 1538, Yellowknife, N.W.T. X1A 2P5. Telephone (403) 873-2074.

Brabant Lodge. On an island in the Mackenzie River 32 miles (51 kms.) by air from Hay River. Will accommodate up to 36 guests in comfortable cabins with modern plumbing or in lodge containing twin bedrooms. Boats, motors, fuel, cold storage, meals, and lodging provided. Cocktail lounge, telephone, guide service, and angling equipment available. Fishing excellent. Arctic grayling, pickerel, northern pike, whitefish. Side trips arranged. Hunting duck and goose in September. Open June 15 to September 30. Rates—4 nights $1,100, 5 nights $1,320—include return charter flight from Hay River. Group rates available on request. Write: Brabant Lodge, 1095 Hay River, N.W.T. X0E 0R0. Telephone Linda Proctor 403-874-2600.

Branson's Lodge. East side of Great Bear Lake, 5 miles (8 kms.) from Port Radium, scenic protected waters. Open July and August. Accommodation for 40. Carpet throughout; modern plumbing and heating. Licensed lounge. Side trips for Arctic char, grayling, trout, Eskimo villages. Visit abandoned mine, other local historic attractions. Licenses available. Convention facilities. Box 1538, Yellowknife, N.W.T. X1A 2P2, 403-873-2074.

Colville Lake Lodge. Located on south end of Colville Lake, 36 miles (58 kms.) above the Arctic Circle. Main lodge, situated in Hareskin Indian Village, accommodates 6. Dining room. Four twin-engined boats. Outpost camp 25 miles (40 kms.) farther north has 2 cabins, boats, motors. Twenty-four hour fishing for trout and Arctic grayling. Canoeing and camping equipment available. Rate US $600 per week. Telecommunications. Write Mr. Bern Will Brown, Colville Lake, N.W.T. (via Fort Good Hope) X0E 0H0 or contact your travel agent.

Drum Lake Lodge. Located on Wrigley Lake. Open June 15 to October 15. Accommodates 6. Lake trout, Arctic grayling, and Dolly Varden. Fishing tackle available. Hunting trips arranged for N.W.T. residents. Private 1,000-foot (305 m.) airstrip. Write Mr. Paul Wright, Fort Norman, N.W.T. X0E 0K0. Telephone (403) 588-3161.

Frontier Fishing Lodge. (Jerry Bricker's). At Snowdrift on the east arm of Great Slave Lake, 115 miles (185 km.) from Yellowknife; 2,300-foot airstrip. Open mid-June to mid-September. Accommodates 24 in lodge and cabins. Dining room, licensed facilities, sauna. Lake trout, Arctic grayling, northern pike, and whitefish. Walk-in fish freezing facilities. Fish packed for return trip. One week (Saturday to Saturday) $1,640. Rates include air travel from Yellowknife and return, guides, motors, boats, gas, oil, food, and lodging. Indian village nearby. Write: Jerry Bricker, Box 4495, Edmonton, Alberta T6E 4T7. Telephone (403) 433–4914.

Great Bear Lake Lodge. (Plummer's). On Dease Arm. Open July and August. Accommodates 54 in 16 cabins with showers, flush toilets. Rates 8-day package $1,975 include charter flight and return from Winnipeg, boats, motors, fuel, guides, angling equipment, and cold storage. Dining room, telephone. Lake trout and Arctic grayling. Plane at lodge for side trips to Tree River on Arctic Coast for char; 5,000-foot (1,524 m.) airstrip. Write: Great Bear Lake Lodge, 1110 Sanford St., Winnipeg, Manitoba R3H 0B7. Telephone (204) 774–5775.

Great Bear Lodge. On Sawmill Bay. Open July and August. Accommodates 54 at main lodge, outpost camp, and Neiland Bay Camp; Rates $1,895 per week include charter flight from Edmonton and return, boat, motors, guides, food, and lodging. Modern facilities, forced air heat, bar and rec room, native handicrafts, microwave telephone, 7,000-foot (2,134-m.) sand airstrip, Arctic grayling, lake trout. Side trips available for char, Eskimo village. Write: 2701 W. 7th St. Sioux Falls, South Dakota 57105, U.S.A. Telephone (605) 336–2008.

Great Bear Trophy Lodge. On Ford Bay on Smith Arm, west side of Great Bear Lake at Arctic Circle. Open July and August. Accommodates 40 in 20 rooms with bath, twin beds, electricity, wall-to-wall carpets. Rates US $1,995 per week, are all-inclusive, Edmonton return. Dining room, bar, lounge, commissary, telecommunications, boats, motors, and guides; 4,800-foot (1,463 m.) airstrip. Lake trout, Arctic grayling, northern pike. Native villages and wild animals nearby. Charters arranged. Write Box 9000, Ponoka, Alberta, Telephone (403) 783–4994, or contact your travel agent.

Great Slave Lake Lodge. At Taltheilei Narrows, 900 miles (145 kms.) east of Yellowknife. Open June 15 to August 30. Accommodates 44. From Winipeg $1,075 five-day trip, or $1,675 eight-day trip, includes 2,200 miles (3,540 km.) transportation. Charter propjet from and to Winnipeg. Private 5,200-foot (1,-585-m.) airstrip. Meals, guides, boats, motors, gas, and care of fish. Modern plumbing, two-way radio, ice, bar, dining room. Lake trout, Arctic grayling, northern pike, flyout for walleye. Write 1110 Sanford St., Winnipeg, Manitoba R3E 2Z9. Telephone (204) 772–8833.

Hanging Ice Fishing Lodge. New lodge northeast of Fort Smith, N.W.T. Lake trout, pickerel, northern pike, Opportunity to visit Fort Smith's *Northern Life Museum.* Lodge open May to October. Rates $70 per day (does not include $80 round-trip flight from Ft. Smith; take your own food). Write: Hanging Ice Fishing Lodge, Box 148, Pine Point. Telephone (403) 393–2851.

Indian Mountain Lodge. Thompson Landing, East Arm, Great Slave Lake. Open July and August. Accommodates 10 persons in 5 cabins. Float base. Dining room, fish freezing, tackle store, boats, motors, guides, fuel. Superb trout and Arctic grayling. Radio phone. Write Box 2793, Yellowknife, N.W.T. X0E 1H0, or contact your travel agent. Telephone 306–731–3551.

Lady Grey Lake Outfitters. Lodge located 70 miles (112 kms.) northeast of Fort Smith. Open June 1 to September 15 for lake trout and northern pike. Guides, cabins, boats, motors. Guests supply own food. Accommodates 6. Winter season January 1 to March 15 for ice fishing, dogteam trips along a working trapline. Rates $70 per day. Write: Lady Grey Lake Outfitters, Box 364, Fort Smith, N.W.T. X0E 0P0. Telephone (403) 872–2095.

Nonacho Lake Camp. On Nonacho Lake 200 miles (322 kms.) east of Hay River. Lake trout and northern pike. Cabin accommodation. Boats, motors, gas, sleeping bags, and housekeeping facilities (everything except food and fish tackle) supplied. Side trips can be arranged. Rates $720 per week include round trip from Hay River. Write: Merlyn Carter, Carter Air Service Ltd., Box 510, Hay River, N.W.T. X0E IG0. 403–874–2281.

Pilot Lake Cabins. Fly-in cabins on Pilot Lake just 35 miles from Fort Smith. Boats, motors, and guide service available. Accommodates 8 in housekeeping cabins. The fishing is great, and it's an interesting place for rockhounds. Rates $60 per day. Guests must supply their own fishing tackle and food. Write: Pilot Lake Cabins, Box 1053, Fort Smith, N.W.T. In winter write: 4206 62 St., Camrose, Alberta. Telephone 403–853–2704.

Prelude Lodge. On Prelude Lake, 20 road miles (32 kms.) east of Yellowknife. Open May 15–September 30. Accommodates 12 guests. Two- and 3-bed housekeeping cabins. Rates for housekeeping cabins $30–40. Boats and rafts may be rented at hourly rate which includes gas and safety equipment. Restaurant, ice, tackle store, licensed dining lounge. Falls on Cameron River nearby. Write: Prelude Lodge, Box 2548, Yellowknife, N.W.T. X0E 1H0.

Rutledge Lake Lodge. Located 170 miles (274 kms.) east of Hay River. Fishing for lake trout and northern pike. Modern fully equipped housekeeping cabins. Rates include Zodiac boat, motors, gas, life jackets, sleeping bags. All you need is fishing tackle and food. Write: Rutledge Lake Lodge, Box 342, Hay River, N.W.T. X0E 0R0. Telephone 403–874–2571.

Snowshoe General Store. Outfitters on the "mighty Mackenzie River." Easily accessible by road, air, and water. Excellent fishing for trout, Arctic grayling, pickerel, and great northern pike. Boats, motors, guides by the hour, day, or trip. Their aircraft will take you for trout. They carry a complete stock of angling supplies, groceries, meats, produce, clothing, gas and oil, propane, ice and fish freezing facilities. Write Snowshoe General Store, Fort Providence. N.W.T. X0E 0L0. Telephone 403–699–3511.

Sitidgi Lake Fishing Lodge. 31 miles (51 kms.) from Inuvik. Accommodates 6 persons in 2 tents. Open June 15–Sept. 15; $150 per day, rates include meals and use of boats and motors. Main lodge building includes a dining room. Excellent fishing very close by. Write: A. McInnes, Box 1332, Inuvik, X0E 0T0. Telephone 403–979–3349.

Trophy Lodge. At Fort Reliance on Great Slave Lake. 160 miles (257 kms.) east of Yellowknife. Open June 25 to September 15. Accommodation in housekeeping cabins with showers and fully equipped kitchens. Boats, motors, gas, fish freezing, tackle store. Can arrange charter flights to camp. Lake trout, Arctic grayling; nearby attractions include Captain Back's Chimneys and Parry Falls. Rates $80 per day. Write Reliance Sport Fishing Ltd., Box 670 Yellowknife, N.W.T. X1A 2N5. Telephone 403–873–5420.

Trout Lake Indian Lodge. Owned and operated by the Slavey Indians, this camp is a naturalist's paradise. It offers sandy beaches and pine forests, a variety of plants and wildlife, good northern fishing, a rare opportunity to observe the traditional ways of the Slavey people, and quiet seclusion at the only camp on the lake. Comfortable accommodation is provided in log housekeeping cabins. Boats, motors, guides, available. Rates $150 per day for 4, $175 for 6. Family and group rates available. For information, write Area Economic Development Officer. Government N.W.T. Ft. Simpson, N.W.T. X0E 0N0. Telephone (403) 695–2248.

Watta Lake Lodge. Located 68 kms. (42 miles) east of Yellowknife. Great fishing. Accommodates 12, plus 5 in tent camp. Open June 1–September 30. Rates $950 per week or $150 per day. Minimum stay 4 days. Rates include round-trip air charter from Yellowknife, boats, motors, meals, guides and some fishing equipment. Write: Site 484, Box 12 Sherwood Park, Alberta T8A 3K4. Telephone (403) 467–4857.

VEHICLE RENTALS. Many visitors prefer to fly to communities, then arrange ground transportation locally to see the area. The following is a list of car rental agencies in major centers.

Fort Simpson: Telephone (403) 695–2675. Telex 034–4376. *Tilden Rent-A-Car Service.* Telephone (403) 873–2911.

Fort Smith. *Avis Rent-A-Car,* Fort Smith Auto Services, N.W.T. Telephone 403–872–2211.

Hay River. *Hertz Rent-A-Car,* John's Cartage and Rental Service, Box 1398, Hay River, N.W.T. X0E 0R0. *Tilden Rent-A-Car Service* (also trucks), Box 1668. Telephone (403) 874–6668. Telex 034–4224. *Avis Rent-A-Car.* N.W.T. Rentals Box 5, Hay River, N.W.T. X0E 0R0. Telephone (403) 874–2571. Telex 034–4333.

Inuvik: *Tilden Rent-A-Car,* Box 2118. Inuvik. N.W.T. X0E 0T0. Telephone (403) 979–3383.

Norman Wells: *Norman Wells Transportation Ltd.* Box 125, Norman Wells. N.W.T. X0E 0V0. Telephone (403) 873–4437.

Yellowknife: *Avis Rent-A-Car,* Frame & Perkins Ltd., Box 400., Yellowknife, N.W.T. X0E 1H0. *Tilden Rent-A-Car,* The Sportsman, Box 162, Yellowknife, N.W.T. X0E 1H0. *Hertz Rent-A-Car.* Air Northwest Ltd., Northwest Hangar, Yellowknife Airport, Box 9000, Yellowknife, N.W.T. X0E 1H0. *Budget Rent-A-Car,* Box 2464, Yellowknife, N.W.T.

WATER TRANSPORTATION. Cargo. Persons wishing to ship freight, cargo, or personal effects of any size will find that shipment by barge water transport in the Northwest Territories is economical and readily available in the summer.

Acnav Marine Ltd., Hay River, telephone (403) 874–2477; Inuvik, telephone (403) 979–3517.

Arctic Navigation & Transportation, 1900 425 1st St. S.W., Calgary, Alta. Telephone (403) 234–7524.

MacTugs, Fort Simpson, N.W.T., (Mackenzie Valley Service). Administrator MOT Marine Services, Transport Canada Building, Place de Ville Ottawa, Ontario, Eastern and High Arctic Service.

Norlan Rentals, Box 1760, Inuvik, N.W.T. X0E 0T0.

Northern Transportation Co. Ltd., 9945 108 St., Edmonton, Alberta T5K 2G9. Mackenzie Valley and Hudson Bay Service, Hay River, Norman Wells, Inuvik, and Tuktoyaktuk.

R.A.M. Enterprises Ltd., Box 342, Hay River, R.W.T. X0E 0R0.

Snowshoe General Store, Fort Providence, N.W.T. X0E 0L0.

Streeper Bros. Marine Transport, Box 213, Fort Simpson, N.W.T. Mackenzie and Liard Valley Service.

The Sportsman. Box 162, Yellowknife, N.W.T. X0E IH0.

Yellowknife River Boat Rentals. 16-foot canoes, 17-foot freighters, motorboats. Rates include life jackets, paddles, gas for motors. Contact: Box 1343, Yellowknife, N.W.T. X0E IH0.

CANOES AND BOATS. Boats and motors can be rented on the spot in some communities; or large boats, complete with guides can be arranged to transport you on fishing or sightseeing jaunts. River trips in the Mackenzie district are an exciting reality this year with the offerings varying from wilderness boat camping to a luxury cruise.

Hudson's Bay Company. Northern Stores Department, 77 Main St., Winnipeg, Manitoba R3C 2R1. Telephone (304) 943–0881. Canoes may be rented from the Hudson's Bay Company with advance reservations made through their above address. Arrangements can be made to pick canoes up at one point and leave them at another where there is a Bay Post.

 SPECIAL EVENTS. Fort Smith: *Wood Buffalo Frolics.* Usually held in mid-March to celebrate the coming of spring. The Frolics feature snowmobile racing, muskrat skinning, log chopping, hockey tournament, cross-country skiing, variety night, and Wood Chopper's Ball. For more information, write President, Fort Smith Lion's Club, Fort Smith, N.W.T. X0E 0P0.

Frobisher Bay: *Toonik Tyme:* The arrival of spring in Frobisher Bay is marked by a carnival called Toonik Tyme. The week-long fiesta is filled with events: contests in seal skinning, igloo building, ice sculpturing, and the toughest power toboggan race of the world. The highlight is the choosing of a Mr. Toonik and a Queen held in late April. Write: Secretary Manager, Halmet Office, Frobisher Bay, N.W.T. X0E 0H0.

Hay River: *Ookpik Carnival:* Three-day carnival, March 18–21, events include Ice Carnival, snowshoe and snowmobile races, log sawing, tea making, adult and teen dances, carnival queen contest, games of chance. For further information, write: Chairman, Recreation Board, Town Hall, Hay River, N.W.T. X0E 0R0.

Pine Point: *Karnival Kapers:* Enjoy a weekend after the long winter competing and being involved in the annual winter carnival. Highlight of the weekend is a two-day, 50-mile dogteam race with prizes totaling $2,000. Nail pounding, log sawing, snowmobile races, skating races, tea boiling, and many other novelty events. For further information, write: Karnival Kapers, Pine Point, N.W.T. X0E 0W0.

Sachs Harbour: *White Fox Jamboree:* Spring comes late in the High Arctic, so everyone is really ready for a celebration, dogteam and snowmobile races, shooting contests; munch on caribou burgers in the White Fox Capital of the World. Held in mid-April.

Tuktoyaktuk: *Beluga Jamboree:* Third week of April, with Eskimo skill contests such as harpoon throwing, ice-hole digging, dogteam races, traditional games of physical skill.

Yellowknife: *Caribou Carnival:* Winters are long and dark in Canada's north, but Yellowknife residents forget this aspect and accentuate the positive during the Caribou Carnival. It is a fun-filled three days, with the excitement and color of a local parade to start the action. Competitions are held in everything from ice sculpturing to tea making. Feature attraction is the *Dog Derby Race* open to all dog mushers in North America. To join the festivities, visit Yellowknife the last weekend in March and judge the celebration for yourself. For further information write Caribou Carnival Committee, Box 2005, Yellowknife, N.W.T.

Annual Midnight Sun Golf Tournament: Gaining popularity as golfers from far and wide participate in this rollicking social event which tees off at midnight, June 21. Contact the President, Yellowknife Golf Club for details and entry forms.

OTHER EVENTS. *Annual Northern Games:* Dates and locations to be announced early in year. A festival of traditional Inuit and Indian sports, dances, drumming, competitions, displays, crafts, and the "Good Woman" contest. Join the celebrations as northern people again gather from the N.W.T., Yukon, and

Alaska. Write: Western Arctic Northern Games Association, Box 2656, Inuvik, N.W.T. X0E 0T0.

PRACTICAL INFORMATION FOR NORTHWEST TERRITORIES

PACKAGE TOURS. There are many established package tours into the Northwest Territories. Each year new ones are being added.

Arctic Adventure Tour. Fully escorted 14-day holiday by ship, air, and private motorcoach. Visits Yellowknife, Inuvik, Tuktoyaktuk, Dawson City, Whitehorse, and Skagway, plus cruise of inside passage aboard CP's *Island Princess.* Tours depart June, July, and August from Vancouver and Toronto. Write: Horizon Holidays of Canada Ltd., 37 Maitland St., Toronto, Ontario M4Y 2R9. Telephone (416) 585–9911; Telex 06–22957.

De West Tours Ltd. This company offers a tour to the North Pole with various ports-of-call. Departures from Edmonton in April and May. Rates $6,973 per person, all inclusive. Three other High Arctic Adventure tours are offered; rates range from $2,461 to $3,367 per person. Full information from: De West Tours Ltd., 1104–510 W. Hastings St., Vancouver, B.C. V6B 1L8. Telephone: (604) 684–5155.

North-West Expeditions Ltd. Raft trips on South Nahanni River. Spectacular scenery. Visits to hot springs. Operates from July to September. Write North-West Expeditions Ltd., 1511 Anderson St., Vancouver, B.C. B6H 3R5. Telephone: 604–669–1100.

Pacific Western Airlines. PWA invites you to take part in wilderness river expeditions, fishing trips, or specialized naturalists' trips. They offer five package tours: South Nahanni River Expedition; fishing tours to Arctic Star Lodge on the north shore of Great Slave Lake, Frontier Fishing Lodge near Snowdrift, and Brabant Lodge, where the Mackenzie flows from the Great Slave Lake; and a special for naturalists at the Bathust Inlet Naturalists Lodge. For full information write: PWA Package Tours, Vancouver International Airport, B.C., and for a copy of *Great Canadian Adventures* write: PWA, 310–1177, Hastings St., Vancouver, B.C. V6E 2G5.

Pioneer Cruise Tour. An 11-day tour from Vancouver, cruising northbound on the Rhapsody to Juneau, air/coach to Whitehorse and motorcoach via Dawson City and the Dempster Highway to Inuvik. Also included is a day excursion from Inuvik to Tuktoyaktuk. Write: Atlas Tours, Box 4340, Whitehorse, Yukon Y1A 3T5. Telephone: 403–668–3161.

Project High Arctic and Northwest Passage. 11 full days; depart day 3 from Edmonton to Resolute Bay, north of the Arctic Circle. Travel in comfortable sleds pulled by snowmobiles. Also visit Beechey Island and Lake Hazen Base-camp. Write: Special Odysseys, Special InteresTours, Box 37, Medina, Washington, 98039. Telephone: 206–455–1960.

Special InteresTours, Inc. This company offers an interesting package of exciting, exotic tours to the High Arctic. Visit Ellesmere Island, stand at the North Pole, play midnight golf in Yellowknife and travel the sea-ice at Grise Fiord. Write: Special InteresTours, Inc., Box 37, Medina, WA 98039. Telephone (206) 455–1960 TWX 910–443–2366 BELSECBVUE.

RAILWAYS. There is no passenger rail service in the Northwest Territories. The *Great Slave Lake Railway* provides a freight service (car lots only) as far as Hay River, N.W.T.

THE YUKON

The Call of the Wild

by
RAY PRICE

Yukon, the name of the river and the Territory, is an Indian word meaning "greatest." Indeed, superlatives are needed to describe the natural beauties of this land of jagged mountains, boundless waterways, infinite varieties of wildlife, and sharply contrasting seasons—a land that still maintains a frontier flavor despite a tumultuous era of exploitation that could have destroyed it forever.

Situated in the far northwest of Canada and extending northward beyond the Arctic Circle to the Beaufort Sea, the Yukon lies between Alaska on the west, the Northwest Territories on the east, and British Columbia on the south. More than twice the size of the British isles, the Yukon has vast mineral wealth within its 1,389,079 sq. kms. (536,-324 square miles). Yet despite the fact that mining is, today, the Yukon's major industry, most of its resources remain unearthed because of its Arctic climate and rugged terrain. Perhaps these are also reasons why the Yukon was among the last areas of North America to attract the European explorer. Still sparsely settled, its population is around 23,000, mostly concentrated in Whitehorse, its capital city. Fifteen percent are Native Indians; the rest are of European descent or mixed European and Indian stock.

One of the coldest regions in the world, it is a land of long, dark winters, harsh blizzards, and almost impenetrable mountains, rivaling in naked grandeur those in any part of the world. Yet summers are brilliant, shimmering with heat that drives the grizzly and the moose, the lynx and the coyote, the sheep, the mink, the wolf and the wolverine to cool themselves in the ubiquitous streams, pools, and rivers that define the territory.

A River of Gold

The land was shaped by the Yukon River which finds its source a scant 15 miles from the ocean into which it empties after wandering inland for more than 2,000 miles. Beginning high in the Elias Mountains, carving its way through the interior of the Territory, and slashing across the heart of Alaska, it finally cascades into Norton Sound through a sprawling delta of muskeg, sand, gravel, and mud. Into this river tumble the sparkling waters of its tributaries—the streams that carried the dust particles and nuggets of gold that were to make the Yukon world famous and thrust it, unprepared, into the industrial age. For gold was everywhere—on the sandbars and shoals scattered along the length of the Yukon; beneath the mud and silt of creeks and rivers whose waters found new channels; and caught in crevices and rocks that lay in the path of the tumbling mountain streams.

Furs Before Gold

Before gold became the magnet in the late 19th century, the Yukon was already being exploited for its furs. Russian traders, coming west from their ports on the Alaskan Coast, moved steadily inland and the goods they traded moved faster and farther east. Evidence of Russian products could be found in the Mackenzie Delta and along the Peel and Porcupine Rivers long before the magic word "gold" had been uttered. As deliberately as the Russians moved eastward, so the British owned Hudson's Bay Company moved westward establishing Fort Yukon in 1847 in what is now Alaska. This far northwestern hold of the Hudson's Bay Company had to be relinquished when the Chilkat Indians attacked and destroyed the fort in 1852. As a result, like a snail encountering salt, the Hudson's Bay Company withdrew and entrenched itself more firmly to the east of the Mackenzie and Richardson Mountains.

During the first half of the 19th century as the fur trade flourished in the North, occasional rumors of gold were heard. The Hudson's Bay clerk at Fort Yukon spoke of it, and the Reverend Archdeacon Robert MacDonald, a "country-born" Anglican minister who later married an Indian, was reported to have dug it up by the spoonful; but for neither was gold important. The Company wanted furs and the Reverend was concerned with souls.

It was inevitable that rumors would spread south and that men would push north toward the rumors' source. Moving through the vastness of the Rockies, they trickled steadily into the Yukon.

Strike!

But it was not until 1896 that the first great strike was made by George Carmack, Skookum Jim, and Targish Charlie who found gold by the fistful in Rabbit Creek, which flows into the Thronduike (hammer water) not far from where it joins the Yukon River. To the prospector, Thronduike became "Klondike" and Rabbit Creek "Bonanza Creek," names that are now synonymous with the world's last great gold rush.

No sooner was the news out than men flocked toward the North from almost every country in the world and by every known route and means of transport. There were three main routes to the Yukon. The most feasible was through Skagway and over the Chilkoot Pass; the second, possible though difficult, was an overland route that went up the crumpled hide of British Columbia; most improbable of all was an inland water route down the Peace, Slave and Mackenzie and up the Peel or Rat, Liard, and Gravel Rivers into the northeastern part of the Yukon.

Dawson City, Boom Town

Gold is an hypnotic word. It lured thousands into incredibly hazardous journeys, all too frequently resulting in accident, starvation, murder, financial ruin, the breakup of partnerships, and the end of dreams. Only a few—a very few—of those who prospected in the Klondike became rich and were able to live in comfort on the return from their frantic race to the lodestone of the Yukon.

Yet, for a short while, excitement ran high. Dawson City, the most famous gold rush city in the world, became a boom town that was as flamboyant as women, liquor, gambling, and the search for gold could make it. To the newly mobilized Royal Northwest Mounted Police, the stampede provided one of the stiffest challenges it was ever to face. The possibility of fast wealth brought not only professional prospectors who preferred prospecting to discovery; greenhorns who willingly tossed aside their petty businesses; and monied investors looking for another world to conquer; but gangsters, card sharps, pimps, prostitutes, outlaws, fugitives from justice—an ugly spectrum of those whose aim was to mine the miners not the ground. Hotels burgeoned, gamblers thrived, whores grew rich, and swindlers grew fat. Dawson had come alive but the adrenalin of gold did not last. Colors faded in the pans and fewer and fewer prospectors hit paydirt. In only five years, the rush was almost over.

Thousands who had set out never reached the city of gold; and thousands who did returned empty handed. But the Yukon was never the same again. Many who came to make a quick stake and get out fast stayed on, captured by what the famed Yukon poet and balladeer Robert Service called the Spell of the Yukon: "Black mountains heaved to heaven,/Which the blinding sunsets blazon,/Black canyons where the rapids rip and roar."

Service was a prolific writer (he lived to be 84); his verse, his best selling novel *The Trail of Ninety-Eight*, and his ballads are a living chronicle of the period. Carl F. Klincke's biography of this colorful adventurer, published late in 1976, would be a fascinating resource for the Yukon traveler.

Whitehorse

Most who stayed behind gathered in Whitehorse, a community which came to prominence during the gold rush as a staging and distribution center; today it is the administrative center for the entire Yukon. A busy city, situated at the foot of Miles Canyon, with wide streets, good restaurants, several hotels and government offices, it was a natural place for boats to converge. At one time, there were more than 250 riverboats on the Yukon's rivers and, for a short while, Whitehorse became a river port—the rival of any on the Mississippi.

As Whitehorse grew, Dawson shrank, but it refused to die. Through the glittering days when its population was 40,000 to the dormant years, when scarcely 200 could be found, men and women have continued to make Dawson City their home.

The Beginnings of Change

Still virtually uninhabited except for its capital city, the Yukon has remained a territory since 1898, administered by a Commissioner appointed by the federal government and an elected Advisory Council with some legislative functions. Yet there is no question but that this land of Carmack, Skookum Jim, and Robert Service, the Chilkat Indians, Russian traders, and the Hudson's Bay Company is beginning to experience change. A network of publicly operated radio stations reaches into every town and hamlet, and the television antenna is now part of the landscape.

The steady expansion of the highway network has also served to make much more of the Yukon accessible for the visitor and somewhat less formidable for its inhabitants. It is now possible to drive amid some of the Yukon's most spectacular scenery.

The Alaska Highway built during World War II by the American Army and Canadian engineers is the only land route into the Yukon from Southern Canada. It is a scenic adventure route that is maintained throughout the year. This highway started a new era in the Yukon, revitalizing historic communities and spawning new ones. At Watson Lake the highway meets the Robert Campbell Highway, which traverses the southeastern region of the Territory and joins the Klondike Highway at Carmacks.

The Klondike Highway follows the trail of '98 to Dawson City and the heart of the Yukon. In recent years the highway has been extended south via Carcross to Skagway, Alaska. At Carcross on the shores of Bennett Lake clusters of log cabins dating back to the gold rush can still be seen.

Another highway into Alaska is the Haines Road, which runs along the eastern edge of the Elsa Mountains and connects Haines, Alaska, with Haines Junction, Yukon. Haines is a picture postcard fishing port nestling against the mountains. Ferry boats and cruise ships stop here and many travelers began their exploration of the Yukon by driving north through lush forests, then alongside the Chilkat River to northwestern B.C. and eventually Haines Junction, Yukon.

The newest and, in some ways, the most adventurous route that is now open for the motor tourist is the Dempster Highway. It links Dawson City to Inuvik in arctic Northwest Territories. This road is for the motorists who like rugged travel through uninhabited mountainous terrain. The highway snakes across the Richardson Mountains and slides into the sprawling delta of the Mackenzie River. Before setting out check road conditions; in wet weather it becomes very slippery and occasionally is closed. There are two ferry crossings on the way. Garage and restaurant services are very sparse; make sure you are well equipped. There is only one garage between Dawson City and the N.W.T. border.

From Dawson it is also possible to travel one of the Yukon's most spectacular routes, "The Top of the World Highway." The correct name for this road is "the Dawson-boundary Road" but its nickname is much more apposite. This route has to be one of the Yukon's most memorable—for lovers of tangled wilderness, tumbled mountains, and twisting rivers, this is a must.

There are yet other roads to travel—roads that now seem to lead to nowhere but give the camper, the canoeist, the fisherman, and the simple lover of the outdoors more opportunities to see the expansive wilderness of Canada's great northwest. There are roads whose names alone whet the appetite for adventure, Tagish Road, Canol Road, Nahanni Range Road to mention but three.

Motorists, check your maps, check your vehicles, check the time you have available and then plunge into the Yukon, wandering where you will.

Herschel Island

North of mainland Yukon lies another spectacular reminder of Canada's winter days. Herschel Island, named by Sir John Franklin, English rear admiral and Arctic explorer, is the northernmost part of the Yukon. For one decade at the turn of the century, according to Hudson Stuck, Anglican missionary, explorer, and writer, it was the edge of the world where drunkenness and lawless living had never been rivaled. Here whalers, who had ranged far from home ports, chased the elusive bowhead around the Alaskan coastline, as far as the Beaufort Sea. As their ships could not make the return trip during the same season, they were forced to wait out the winter at Herschel Island. There, Pauline Cove provided a natural harborage and whaling ships, sometimes more than a dozen at a time, would freeze in and wait for breakup in the spring. One ship, the *Mary D. Hume,* remained for six years before returning to San Francisco.

The End of an Era

The invention of spring steel ended the profitable whaling industry. No longer were whalebone corsets, whalebone whips, or whalebone umbrellas manufactured, and windswept Herschel Island retreated into the Arctic mists to become a refuge for a few Eskimos, a stopping-off-place for random traders, and the location of an Anglican mission and a Royal Canadian Mounted Police (R.C.M.P.) station and custom-house.

Now, only a cemetery and a few derelict buildings mark the passage of the wild days of whaling and the more sober pursuit of the shipboard trader. In the cemetery, frost action has uncovered a number of coffins, and the skeletons of long-dead sailors may be seen through the cracks in the rudely fashioned boxes. Only one grave is tended—that of a young R.C.M.P. constable who died of typhoid in the second decade of this century. Gone are the gallows where two Eskimos were hanged for murder in 1923. Gone, too, are the wrecks of whaling vessels, the rough sod houses of whalers and their Eskimo wives, and the old trading posts. Now, all but deserted, the island remains a tantalizing invitation to the wanderer, the naturalist, the adventurer—all those, perhaps, who rejoice when nature triumphs over man.

EXPLORING WHITEHORSE

Whitehorse, capital of the Yukon since 1952, covers an area of 420 sq. kms. (162 square miles), has a population of about 15,000, and offers all the facilities you'd expect in a modern city anywhere in North America. The city began as a stopping point on the route to the Klondike—the first place goldseekers could beach their boats after coming down the Miles Canyon and shooting the Whitehorse Rapids.

In 1900 the White Pass Railway was completed, thereby ensuring a future for the small community. It became an all important stop for travelers to and from the goldfields, linking the Yukon to Vancouver, Seattle and San Francisco. Riverboats sailed from its piers to Dawson City and the many other mining centers that flourished at the turn of the century.

Still in existence are old steam engines, Yukon-style coaches, the old telegraph office, and the McBride Museum, with its fine collection of Yukon relics. The Anglican Parish Church (1900), the first church built in the city, is now the old log museum. It was for a church concert here, in 1904, that one of its parishioners, the poet Robert Service, composed "The Ballad of Dangerous Dan McGrew."

Those who enjoy local customs might visit Whitehorse during its annual winter event, "The SourDough Rendezvous," a free-wheeling week of fun and relaxation, usually held during the last full week of February. Dog races, trials of strength, Native games, and evening entertainments in the bars and cabarets are all part of this winter festival.

EXPLORING DAWSON CITY

Dawson City, incorporated in 1906, is located 240 kms. (150 miles) from the Arctic Circle where the Klondike flows into the Yukon River. In 1898, it was a thriving metropolis of 30,000–40,000 people; today 750 keep it alive. One-third of this population is Kutchin or part Kutchin Indian whose ancestors hunted here a thousand or more years before men came north for its gold. Today the city subsists on jobs provided by Territorial and Federal government agencies, tourism, goldmines, and an asbestos mine operating some sixty miles west.

While in Dawson City, visit its museum; spot the Klondike and Yukon Rivers and surrounding goldfields from the Midnight Dome Viewpoint; see the old Bonanza Creek, and try your hand at goldpanning on Poverty Bar or at Claim #6 which is always open.

PRACTICAL INFORMATION FOR THE YUKON

HOW TO GET THERE. As thousands of Klondikers discovered in the 1890's, the Yukon was almost inaccessible. Now it can be reached in a variety of ways. **By air:** *C.P. Air* jet flights operate regularly between Vancouver, Edmonton, and Whitehorse for those who prefer comfort, speed, and convenience. Reservations can be made at any recognized travel agency.

By car: The Alaskan Hwy., one of North America's greatest, was built during the Second World War to provide land access to Alaska. A fascinating trail that winds its way from Dawson Creek (not to be confused with Dawson City) in Northern British Columbia to Fairbanks, Alaska, the highway is a well-maintained gravel road as far as the Alaskan border. *Note:* Those who drive over its extensive gravel roads to the Yukon should take special precautions: Make sure your car is in good mechanical condition; take two spare tires; and cover the gas tank with heavy rubber to avoid holes caused by flying gravel. Drive with lights on and protect headlights with plastic covers. Also protect radiator and paint with a wire-mesh screen placed across front of vehicle. Listen to radio reports of road condition given daily over the Yukon Radio System. When trucks pass, pull over to side of road but do not stop; avoid soft shoulders. Between the months of October and April when temperatures as low as −21° C. (−70°F.) have been recorded in the Yukon, emergency survival gear should be on board at all times—an axe, matches, sleeping bag, paper, kindling, sensible outdoor clothing, and food. The car should be properly winterized with light oil in the engine and transmission, a block heater, anti-freeze, and chains.

By bus: *Greyhound* travels the Alaska Hwy. Connections may be made at Dawson Creek, British Columbia, through Edmonton or Vancouver. The bus takes 31 hours from Edmonton to Whitehorse and 40 hours to Dawson City. Overnight stops on the road may be made at no extra cost; hotel reservations should be secured in advance.

By boat and rail: One of the most interesting approaches to the Yukon follows the route hewed out in the 1890's by men from San Francisco, Seattle, and Vancouver. A steamer trip up the inland coast of British Columbia to Skagway is followed by a 110-mile ride on the narrow-gauge, privately owned White Pass Railroad.

By charter boat or charter aircraft: To reach Herschel Island from Inuvik, Northwest Territories.

ACCOMMODATIONS. In view of the very heavy tourist flow through the Yukon Territory during the summer, you will be well advised to make hotel and motel reservations early in the year. Price ranges for double occupancy are: Expensive, $55 and up; Moderate, $40–$55; Inexpensive, under $40. Price will also be lower if room does not have private bath.

Most places accept the following major credit cards: American Express, MasterCard and Visa; others may also be honored. Not all establishments accept credit cards, therefore we suggest you call for information.

CARMACKS. *Expensive:* **Carmacks Hotel.** Box 16. Carmacks. Telephone (403) 863–5221. Café, lounge. Retail liquor sales. Laundromat. Open all year.
Moderate. **Sunset Motel.** General Delivery, Carmacks. Telephone (403) 863–5266. Housekeeping units available. Open all year.

DAWSON CITY. *Expensive:* **Eldorado Hotel.** 3rd and Princess, Box 338, Dawson City. Telephone (403) 993–5451. Restaurant, lounge. Retail liquor sales. Major credit cards.
Sheffield Dawson City. Box 420, Dawson City. Telephone (403) 993–5542. Dining room, lounge. Retail liquor sales. City shop. Open May 1-September 30.
Gold Nugget Hotel. Box 86, Dawson City. Telephone (403) 993–5445. Open June 1-September.
Klondike River Lodge. 25 mi. S of Dawson at the Dempster Hwy. Cutoff. Telephone (403) 993–6892. Restaurant, garage, liquor. Cedar-log motel units.
Triple "J" Motel. Box 359, Dawson City. Telephone (403) 993–5323.

DESTRUCTION BAY. *Moderate:* **Burwash Lodge.** Mile 1093, Alaska Hwy. N., Burwash Landing. Telephone (403) 841–4441. Licensed dining room. Retail liquor sales. Small store. Open May–September.
Talbot Arm Motel Ltd. General Delivery, Destruction Bay. Telephone (403) 841–4461. Licensed dining room. Retail liquor sales. Service station. Open all year.

FARO. *Expensive:* **The Faro Hotel.** Box 238, Faro. Telephone (403) 994–2610. Dining room, lounge. Retail liquor sales.
Little Salmon Lodge. Located 54.7 kms. (34 miles) west of Faro, Box 129, Faro. Dining room, café, licensed. Garage. Open all year. Radio phone 2M4570 (Salmon channel).

HAINES JUNCTION. *Moderate–Expensive:* **Gateway Motel.** Telephone (403) 634–2371. Open all year.
Moderate: **Kluane Park Inn.** Telephone (403) 634–2261. Lounge. Retail liquor sales. Open all year.

Inexpensive: **Mackintosh Lodge.** Haines Junction, Yukon. Telephone (403) 634–2301. Licensed dining room. Retail liquor sales. Laundromat. Open all year.

MAYO-KENO. *Moderate:* **Chateau Mayo.** Box 66, Mayo. Telephone (403) 996–2366. Lounge. Retail liquor sales. This hotel is a fun place to visit.

Inexpensive: **Keno City Motel.** Keno. Telphone (403) 995–2312. Lounge. Retail liquor sales. Open all year.

North Star Motel. Box 34, Mayo. Telephone (403) 996–2231. Housekeeping facilities. Open all year.

WHITEHORSE. *Expensive:* **Klondike Inn.** 2288 2nd Ave. Telephone (403) 668–4747. 98 rooms. Dining room, lounge, cabaret.

Sheffield House–Whitehorse. Box 4250, Whitehorse. Telephone (403) 668–4700. 190 units. Licensed dining room, lounge. Travel agency. Barbershop. Banquet facilities.

T & M Hotel. 401 Main St. Telephone (403) 668–7644. 30 units. Licensed dining room, lounge. Retail liquor sales.

Taku Hotel. 4109 4th Ave. Mailing address: Box 4308. Telephone (403) 668–4545. 53 units. Licensed café open 24 hours. This hotel is one of the oldest established places in Whiteshore. It has a bar with "atmosphere."

Yukon Inn. 4220 4th Ave. Telephone (403) 667–2527. 47 units. Licensed dining room, café. Retail liquor sales.

Moderate: **Ben Elle Motel.** 411 Main St. Telephone (403) 668–4500. Licensed dining room. Retail liquor sales. Housekeeping units; refrigerators all units.

Chilkoot Trail Inn. 4190 4th Ave. Telephone (403) 668–4910. 37 units, across from shopping mall and theater. Recently renovated.

New North Motor Inn. 2141 2nd Ave. Telephone (403) 668–4646. 31 units (18 housekeeping). Licensed café, cabaret, and quiet lounge.

Regina Hotel. 102 Wood St. 51 units. Licensed dining room. Retail liquor sales. Heated parking.

Whitehorse Centre Motor Inn. 206 Jarvis St. Telephone (403) 668–4567. 30 units; housekeeping units available. Lounge. This hotel used to be the Shannon. It is centrally located. Free winter plug-ins available and off-street parking.

TOURIST INFORMATION. For **Whitehorse,** write Whitehorse Chamber of Commerce, Box 4367, Whitehorse, Yukon, Canada. For **Dawson City,** write Box 23, Dawson City, Yukon, Canada. Excellent information can also be obtained from: Tourism Yukon, Box 2703, Whitehorse, Yukon Territory Y1A 2C6.

PACKAGE TOURS. To see the Yukon in comfort and at reasonable cost, try one of the many well-paced organized tours. Some include Alaska and the western part of the Northwest Territories as well as the centrally located Yukon.

Anderson Tours. 153 Conneant Lake Rd., Greenville, Pennsylvania 16125. Detailed brochures available on request. *Princess Tours,* P.O. Box 21185, 727 Washington Building, Seattle, Washington 98111. Detailed brochures available on request.

Gold Rush River Tours, a company based in Whitehorse, offers seven-day river cruises from Whitehorse to Dawson City. Two specially constructed riverboats, *Goldrush I* and *Goldrush II,* are used. Full information from Gold Rush River Tours, P.O. Box 4835, Whitehorse, Y.T.

Majestic Tours Ltd. Air, bus, and cruise tours of Yukon and Alaska. #102 Riverside Towers, 8620 Jasper Ave., Edmonton, Alberta, T5H 3S6. Telephone 403–429–0352.

Questers Tours. 257 Park Ave. So., New York, N.Y. 10010. Telephone 212–673–3120.

U.T.L. with its central office at 22 College St., Toronto, Ontario M5G 1Y6, Telephone (416) 967–3355, invites you "to pack your sense of adventure and discover the real north." Their tours start in Toronto (you may join them in Edmonton) and take you to Yellowknife, Inuvik, Tuktoyaktuk, Dawson City, Tok Junction, then along the "top-of-the-world highway" to Haines, Skagway, back to Whitehorse by rail on the narrow gauge White Pass Railroad, south to Vancouver, and finally to Toronto on a Canadian Pacific Jet. These tours are fully escorted.

Universal Fun Finders Tours. 102 5809 Macleod Trail So., Calgary, Alberta T2H 0V9. Telephone (403) 259–5522 or toll-free 1–800–661–1063.

SPECIAL INTEREST TOURS. Norline coaches has regular service to and from Whitehorse to (Dawson City), and offers daily transportation to points in Alaska. For leisurely river travel, join a 2-day raft excursion to the Forty Mile townsite. From there, journey by power up the Forty Mile River to Clinton Creek and then back to Dawson City over the "top-of-the-world highway" (Alaska Hwy.). Fourteen-day raft trips from Whitehorse to Dawson City and a 5-day trip on the Stuart River are also available: all expeditions are fully outfitted and have experienced boatmen using Zodiac inflatable rafts.

For more information write Box 23, Dawson City, Yukon, Canada.

WILDERNESS TOURS. *Brooklands Wilderness Camp,* General Delivery, Carcross, Yukon Y0B 1B0, telephone (604) 651–7679.

Ecosummer Canada, Box 5095, Whitehorse, Yukon Y1A 4Z2. Telephone (403) 667–2202. *Kluane Adventures,* Box 5466, Haines Junction, Yukon Y0B 1L0, radio phone 2M5020 Haines Jct. Channel.

Yukon Expeditions, 2 Kluhini Crescent, Whitehorse, Yukon Y1A 3P3, telephone (403) 667–7960.

PHOTOGRAPHY. What an opportunity for the photographer—professional as well as amateur! At the height of summer, the midnight sun creates unique light conditions as do the flashing colors of the aurora borealis to be seen on many nights in the fall, winter, and spring. Be sure to use an ultra-filter (ultra-violet filter) as the air is very clean and clear and photographic contrast is high. The filter will cut down the amount of blue in your pictures and, at the same time, protect your lens. Also, as you are likely to encounter considerable dust, protect your camera and other gear with plastic bags.

Wilderness Yukon Photography Tour. Box 577, Faro, Yukon Y0B 1K0, radio phone 2M4583.

FISHING. The fish are there! Only a fishing license is necessary—the cost is $5 for Canadian residents for the season; $5 for nonresidents for 1 day, $10 for 5 days, and $20 for the season. Special National Park Fishing License is $4 for season.

The most abundant species are lake trout, northern pike, and Arctic grayling. Catch limits on these fish are generous and are outlined to the fisherman when the license is purchased. In recent years, the limit has been twenty pike per day, ten Arctic grayling, and five lake trout. Less common are the Dolly Varden, rainbow trout, steelhead, and the king and coho salmon and the catch limit is less generous, too. Grayling and all trout less than eight inches long have to be returned to waters. Fishing lodges can be reached readily by road. For those in pursuit of a very special fishing experience, there are also fly-in camps, listed later in this section.

The Department of Tourism and Information, Whitehorse, Yukon, publishes a booklet, *Hospitality Yukon,* which contains an up-to-date list of fishing lodges and a description of the lakes and rivers where various fish may be found. All locations listed are close to the Yukon's network of highways. For example, at Mile 275 on the Mayo-Dawson road is Minto Lake where lake trout, northern pike, and cisco can be caught. For grayling, try Fox Lake at Mile 35 or Lake la Barge at Mile 26. Similar fishing can be found close to the Watson Lake–Carmacks road in the Carcross Area, by the Alaskan Hwy. and along the Haines Rd.

Fishing Guides: *Grizzly Creek Lodge,* Watson Lake; 701–772–5475. *Johnnie John's Fishing Trips,* Carcross; 403–821–3116. *Peacock's Yukon Camps,* Whitehorse; 403–667–2846. *Toobally Lakes Fishing Camps,* Fort Nelson, B.C.; 604–774–2876. *Wolf Lake Wilderness Camp,* Teslin, Yukon; Radio: SQ 707. *Yukon Fishing Safaris Ltd.,* Whitehorse; 403–668–2287.

Fly-in Fishing Camps: *Air-In Fishing Lodge,* Box 158, Watson Lake, Yukon. *Kluane Wilderness Lodge,* General Delivery, Whitehorse, Yukon. *Northern Wilderness Fishing Lodge,* Box 264, Watson Lake, Yukon.

HUNTING. The hunter is in his element in the Yukon. Among the mountains and river valleys are Dall sheep, the Stone and Fannin sheep, mountain goats, moose, barrenground and woodland caribou, black and brown bears, and the mighty grizzly. All **big game hunting** by nonresidents must be done in the company of a licensed guide. Hunting is only allowed during prescribed seasons. Any game or trophies to be taken home require export permits (free) from the Director of Game or any Government Agent. Open season on the black and grizzly bear is usually from mid-April to mid-June. Open season on moose (male only), caribou, and mountain goat (either sex) is from August 1 to November 30, mountain sheep (male only), August 1 to November 10. Dates are subject to change. Up-to-date regulations, fees, seasons, and limits may be obtained from Director of Game, Box 2703, Whitehorse, Yukon, Canada.

Bird hunting is permitted in the fall. Waterfowl as well as ruffed, willow, blue, and sharp-tailed grouse may be hunted from September 1 until November 30. Spruce (Franklin) grouse and ptarmigan seasons are September 1 to January 31 following. Licensed outfitters are controlled by the Yukon Territorial Government through the Game Branch. The Yukon is divided into Guiding Areas with one outfitter in each having exclusive rights.

Big Game Outfitters (usually prefer to conduct hunts for 14 days): *Stan ︙nolds,* Box 108, Dawson City, Yukon Y0B 1G0. *Doug Low,* Tagish, Yukon

Y1A 3K4, telephone (403) 667–2030. *Rick Furniss,* Box 5364, Whitehorse, Yukon Y1A 4Z2, telephone (403) 667–2721. *Don Marino,* General Delivery, Carmacks, Yukon Y0B 1C0, radio phone 2M2572 Carmacks. *Werner Koser,* General Delivery, Ross River, Yukon, Y0B 1S0, telephone (403) 667–2030. *John L. Otashek,* General Delivery, Destruction Bay, Yukon Y0B 1C0, radio phone 2M3974. *Gordon Toole,* Box 368, Watson Lake, Yukon Y0A 1C0, telephone (403) 536–7346.

This is only a representative listing. All the above are licensed outfitters for certain areas of the Territory. Complete information can be obtained by writing to the Yukon Visitors Association of Tourism, Yukon, Whitehorse.

CANOEING. The Yukon's waterways are an open invitation to the canoeist. Each river has its own challenge—some with rapids to be run and others to be circumnavigated. Before launching a canoe in the Yukon, obtain the best maps available at the Government Office in Whitehorse, and inform the Royal Canadian Mounted Police of your proposed route and estimated time of return. No law requires these precautions but police encourage all wilderness wanderers to adhere to them.

Experts favor the sturdy aluminum canoes although a few traditionalists still prefer those made of wood and canvas. Be sure to carry adequate emergency supplies and canoe repair outfits and know how to signal for help in the event of any emergency. Recommended reading for all wilderness travelers is the Canadian Government publication *Down But Not Out,* also available at the Government Office in Whitehorse.

Canoe Rentals: *Arctic Edge Canoe Expedition Outfitting,* Whitehorse. Telephone 403–633–2443. *Karpes & Pugh Co.,* Whitehorse. Telephone 403–668–4899. *Norseman Adventures Ltd.,* Atlin, B.C. Telephone 604–651–7535. *Tutshi Boat Rentals,* Carcross, Yukon. Telephone 403–821–4461.

TRAILER CAMPING. Trailer camps and tenting facilities are available on the growing network of roads. Excellent pertinent information can be found in *Come on into Canada's Yukon,* a free publication of Yukon Tourism, Whitehorse. Some camps have laundry facilities and electrical hook-ups, for example, Klondike Gold Kamp in Dawson City.

HIKING AND CLIMBING. From the St. Elias Range, which has many peaks of more than 10,000 ft., and Mt. Logan, the highest point in Canada (19,850 ft.), to low rounded hills and flat river banks—there is something for everyone on foot. Maps should always be constant companions. For those who like to ramble through country that does not demand the skills of a mountaineer there are 155 miles of hiking trails in Kluane National Park. For more information write to Dept. Tourism, Govt. of Yukon, Whitehorse, and ask for leaflet *Hiking in Kluane National Park,* or for more general information that includes hiking trails outside the park, request the booklet *Yukon, Canada's Great Frontier.*

Outfitted Pack Trips: *Atlas Outdoor Yukon,* Whitehorse; 403–668–3161. *Ecosummer Yukon,* Whitehorse; 403–667–4363.

MUSEUMS AND HISTORIC SITES. In **Keno,** a mining town of less than one hundred and one of the prettiest communities in the Yukon, there is the *Keno Mining Museum,* open 1 P.M.–5 P.M. June 1–Sept. 30.

Dawson City is home for a museum that boasts a collection of over 25,000 artifacts from the days of the gold rush. It also provides the visitor with a view of history right on its streets—the *Redfeather* and the *Monte Carlo,* two derelict saloons, still stand as mute reminders of the swinging nineties. Then, down by the river, sternwheel forever stilled, is the *Keno,* last of the riverboats to travel the Whitehorse–Dawson City route.

The well-known *MacBride Museum* is in **Whitehorse.** This museum contains an excellent display of Yukon animals. Historic places of interest worth visiting in the Yukon's largest community are the "Old Log Church," the S.S. *Klondike,* now a National Historic site, and the much-talked-about log "skyscrapers."

ENTERTAINMENT. In **Dawson City** during the summer season (early June until roughly September 10), the *Gaslight Follies* in the Palace Grand Theatre is a vaudeville show, nightly except Tuesdays, at 8 P.M. Advance tickets available between 4 and 6 P.M. *Diamond Tooth Gertie's Gambling Hall* is open nightly, except Sunday from 8 P.M. to 2 P.M. Gambling tables, bingo, bar, and three floor shows (9 and 11 P.M. and 1 A.M.). *Robert Service's cabin* opens daily at 4 P.M. and 10 A.M. when the "ghost" of the famed Yukon poet returns to recite his ballads (free). *Jack London's cabin* offers readings at 1 P.M. daily (also free). Free slide show of historic Dawson, 1:15 P.M. daily in the *Palace Grand.* Films of the Klondike Gold Rush shown daily at 9 A.M. and 4:45 P.M. in *St. Paul's Church* (silver collection toward restoration of church).

DINING OUT. Your best bet for dining out in the Yukon Territory is to stick to the dining facilities in your hotel. There are about five restaurants in Dawson City that are open throughout the summer months. The following listing are suggestions for dining out in Whitehorse. Prices for a meal generally run under $10.

Most places accept the following major credit cards: American Express, MasterCard and Visa; others may also be honored. Not all establishments accept credit cards, therefore we suggest you call for information.

WHITEHORSE. Christie's Place. 208 Main St. Telephone (403) 667–7671. Open Monday–Thursday, 11 A.M.–1 A.M.; Friday and Saturday, 11 A.M.–3 A.M.; Sunday, 6 P.M.–midnight. Licensed. Italian food. Takeout available.

Dairy Queen. 2nd Ave. and Eliot St. Telephone (403) 667–2272. All the usual products of the Dairy Queen chain. Specializes in ice milk sundaes, soft ice cream, and hamburgers. A great place for children.

Golden Garter. 212 Main St. Telephone (403) 667–2626. Open Monday–Saturday, 6 P.M.–10 P.M. Closed in January. Licensed. Specializes in French cuisine and seafood.

Hannigan's. Km. 1477.5 Alaska Hwy. Telephone (403) 668–4740. Open 7 days a week, 7:30 A.M.–9 P.M. Chicken, hamburgers, soft ice cream. Eat-in or takeout.

Monte Carlo. 404 Wood St. Telephone (403) 667–2116. Open 7 days a week, 5:30 P.M., May–September; open 6 days a week at 6 P.M. the rest of the year. Licensed. King crab, fresh salmon. French cuisine.

Mr. Mike's. 4114 4th Ave. Telephone (403) 667–2242. Usual opening hour 11:30 A.M. Hours of business vary according to the season. Food is primarily steaks, hamburgers, served in a cafeteria, fast-food style. Seafood and salad bar available. Licensed.

Oriental Restaurant. 210 Ogilvie St. Telephone (403) 668–6565. Open 4:30 P.M.–midnight, 7 days a week. Licensed. Chinese and Western foods.

SUPPLEMENTS

LANGUAGE/30

For the Business or Vacationing International Traveler

In 25 languages! A basic language course on 2 cassettes and a phrase book . . . Only $14.95 ea. + shipping

Nothing flatters people more than to hear visitors try to speak their language and LANGUAGE/30, used by thousands of satisfied travelers, gets you speaking the basics quickly and easily. Each LANGUAGE/30 course offers:

- approximately 1½ hours of guided practice in greetings, asking questions and general conversation
- special section on social customs and etiquette

Order yours today. Languages available: (New) POLISH

ARABIC	GREEK	JAPANESE	RUSSIAN
CHINESE	HEBREW	KOREAN	SERBO-CROATIAN
DANISH	HINDI	NORWEGIAN	SPANISH
DUTCH	INDONESIAN	PERSIAN	SWAHILI
FRENCH	ITALIAN	PORTUGUESE	SWEDISH
GERMAN	TURKISH	VIETNAMESE	TAGALOG

To order send $14.95 per course + shipping $2.00 1st course, $1 ea. add. course. In Canada $3 1st course, $2.00 ea. add. course. NY and CA residents add state sales tax. Outside USA and Canada $14.95 (U.S.) + air mail shipping: $8 for 1st course, $5 ea. add. course. MasterCard, VISA and Am. Express card users give brand, account number (all digits), expiration date and signature.
SEND TO: FODOR'S, Dept. LC 760, 2 Park Ave., NY 10016-5677, USA.

FRENCH–ENGLISH TOURIST VOCABULARY

DAILY EXPRESSIONS

Can anyone here speak English?	Y a-t-il quelqu'un qui parle anglais?
Do you speak English?	Parlez-vous anglais?
Do you understand?	Comprenez-vous?
Don't mention it	Pas de quoi
I beg your pardon	Pardon! (pahrr'dong)
Good morning . . . day . . . afternoon	Bonjour
Good evening . . . night	Bonsoir
Goodbye	Au revoir
How are you?	Comment allez-vous?
How much . . . many?	Combien?
I don't know	Je ne sais pas
I don't understand	Je ne comprends pas
Yes	Oui
No	Non
Please speak more slowly	Parlez plus lentement, s'il vous plaît
Stop	Arrêtez
Go ahead	Continuez
Hurry	Dépêchez-vous
Wait here	Attendez ici
Come in!	Entrez! (ahn'tray)
Sit down	Asseyez-vous
Thank you very much	Merci bien
There is, there are	Il y a
Very good . . . well	Très bien
What is this?	Qu'est-ce que c'est? (kes-kuh-say)
What do you want?	Que voulez-vous?
Please	S'il vous plaît (seevooplay)
I'm sorry	Je regrette
You're welcome	Je vous en prie
What time is it?	Quelle heure est-il?
What is your name?	Comment vous appelez-vous?
With pleasure	Avec plaisir
You are very kind	Vous êtes bien aimable

DAYS OF THE WEEK

Sunday	Dimanche
Monday	Lundi
Tuesday	Mardi
Wednesday	Mercredi
Thursday	Jeudi
Friday	Vendredi
Saturday	Samedi

COMMON QUESTIONS

Is there . . .	Y a-t-il . . .
—a bus for . . . ?	—un autobus pour . . . ?
—a dining car?	—un wagon-restaurant . . . ?
—an English interpreter?	—un interprète anglais?
—a guide?	—un guide?
—a good hotel at . . . ?	—un bon hôtel à . . . ?
—a good restaurant here?	—un bon restaurant ici?
—a sleeper?	—une place dans le wagon-lit?
—time to get out?	—le temps de descendre?
—a train for . . . ?	—un train pour . . . ?
Where is . . .	Où est . . .
—the airport?	—l'aéroport?
—a bank?	—une banque?

—the bar?	—le bar?
—the barber's shop	—le coiffeur?
—the bathroom?	—la salle de bain?
—the ticket (booking) office?	—le guichet?
a chemist's shop (drugstore)?	—une pharmacie?
—the movies (cinema)?	—le cinéma?
—the cloakroom?	—le vestiaire?
—the British (American) Consulate?	—le consulat d'Angleterre (d'Amérique)?
—the Customs office?	—la douane?
—a garage?	—un garage?
—a hairdresser? (barber)	—un coiffeur?
—the lavatory?	—le lavabo?
—the luggage?	—les bagages?
—the museum?	—le musée?
—the police station?	—le gendarmerie?
—the post office?	—le bureau de poste?
—the railway station?	—le gare?
—the theater?	—le théâtre?
—a tobacconist?	—un débit de tabac?
When . . .	Quand . . .
—is lunch?	—le déjeuner est-il servi?
—is dinner?	—le diner est-il servi?
—is the first (last) bus?	—le premier (dernier) autobus part-il?
—is the first (last) train?	—le premier (dernier) train part-il?
—does the theater open?	—ouvre-t-on le théâtre?
—will it be ready?	—sera-t-il (elle) prêt(e)?
—does the performance begin (end)?	—le séance commence-t-elle (finit-elle)?
—will you be back?	—rentrerez-vous?
—can you return them?	—pouvez-vous me las rendre?
—can I have a bath?	—pourrais-je prendre un bain?
Which is . . .	Quel est . . .
—the way to . . . street?	—Par où va-t-on à la rue . . . ?
—the best hotel at . . . ?	—le meilleur hôtel de . . . ?
—the train (bus) for . . . ?	—le train (autobus) pour . . . ?
What is . . .	Quel est . . .
—the fare to . . . ?	—le prix du billet á . . . ?
the single fare?	le prix d'aller?
—the round trip (return) fare?	le prix d'aller et retour?
—the fare (taxi)?	—Je vous dois combien?
—the price?	—le prix?
—the price per day? per week?	—le prix par jour? par semaine?
—the price per kilo? (2.2 pounds)	Combien le kilo?
—the price per meter? (39½ inches)	Combien le mètre?
—the matter?	Ou'est-ce qu'il y a?
—the French for . . . ?	—Comment dit-on . . . en français?
Have you . . .	Avez-vous . . .
—any American (English) cigarettes?	—des cigarettes américaines (anglaises)?
—a timetable?	—un indicateur?
—a room to let?	une chambre à louer?
—anything ready? (Food)	—quelque chose de prêt?
How often?	Combien de fois?
How long?	Combien de temps?

DAILY NEEDS

I want . . .	Je désire . . . Je voudrais . . .
—my bill	—l'addition (la note)
—to buy	—d'acheter
—cigars, cigarettes	—des cigares, cigarettes
—a dentist	—consulter un dentiste
—a dictionary	—un dictionnaire
—a doctor	—consulter un médicin
—something to drink	—prendre quelque chose à boire
—something to eat	—manger quelque chose
—some American (English)	—des journaux américains

papers
—a haircut
—a shave
—to go to
—a porter
—to see . . .
—to send a telegram
—some stamps
—a taxi
—to telephone
—the waiter
—some beer
—change for . . .
—water
—my key
—razor blades
—a road map
—soap

(anglais)
—me faire couper les cheveux
—me faire raser
—aller à (au) . . .
—un porteur
—voir . . .
—envoyer un tétégramme
—des timbres
—un taxi
—téléphone
—parler avec le garçon
—de la bière
—la monnaie de . . .
—de l'eau
—ma clé
—des lames de rasoir
—une carte routière
—due savon

MENU TRANSLATOR

Meats (Viandes)

Agneau	Lamb	Jambon	Ham
Bifteck	Steak	Lapin	Rabbit
Boeuf	Beef	Lard	Bacon
Charcuterie	Pork cold cuts	Mouton	Mutton
Châteaubriand	Rump steak	Porc	Pork
Côte	Chop	Rosbif	Roast beef
Entrecôte	Rib steak	Saucisse	Sausage
Gigot d'agneau	Leg of Lamb	Veau	Veal
Gibier	Wild game		

Poultry (Volaille)

Canard	Duck	Oie	Goose
Caneton	Duckling	Pintade	Guinea hen
Coq	Young cock	Poulet	Chicken
Faisan	Pheasant		

Offal (Abats)

Cervelles	Brains	Langue	Tongue
Foie	Liver	Rognon	Kidney

Fish (Poisson)

Anguille	Eel	Perche	Bass
Maquereau	Mackerel	Saumon	Salmon
Morue	Cod	Truite	Trout

Shellfish (Coquillages, Crustaces)

Crevettes	Shrimp	Homard	Lobster
Ecrevisses	Crawfish	Huîtres	Oysters
Escargots	Snails	Langouste	Spiny rock lobster
Fruits de mer	Mixed shellfish	Moules	Mussels
Grenouilles	Frogs' legs	Palourdes	Clams

Vegetables (Légumes)

Aubergine	Eggplant	Epinards	Spinach
Chou	Cabbage	Haricots	Beans
Cresson	Watercress	Haricots verts	Green beans

Desserts (Desserts)

Beignets	Fritters	Glace	Ice cream
Gáteau	Cake	Tarte	Pie

MAP OF
CANADA

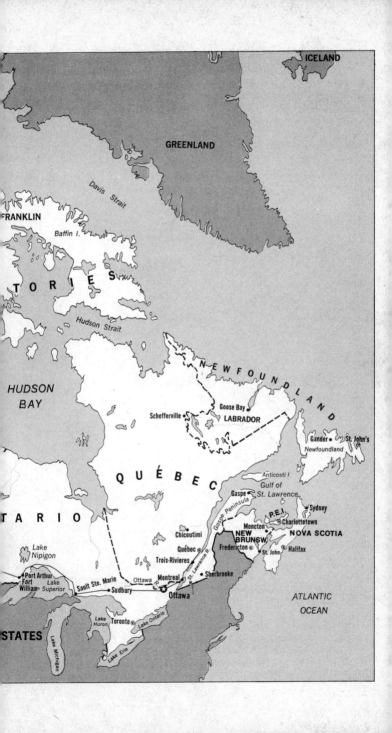

INDEX

The letters H and R indicate hotels and restaurant listings.

GENERAL
(See also Practical Information sections in the chapter for each province)

**NORTHWEST TERRITORIES
PRACTICAL INFORMATION**

GEOGRAPHICAL

ONTARIO
PRACTICAL INFORMATION

GEOGRAPHICAL

SASKATCHEWAN
PRACTICAL INFORMATION